Mechanics of Materials Labs with SolidWorks Simulation 2014

Huei-Huang Lee
Department of Engineering Science
National Cheng Kung University, Taiwan

SDC
Publications

SDC Publications
P.O. Box 1334
Mission, KS 66222
913-262-2664
www.SDCpublications.com
Publisher: Stephen Schroff

ISBN-13: 978-1-58503-895-4
ISBN-10: 1-58503-895-4

Printed and bound in the United States of America.

Contents

Preface

A New Way of Thinking in Engineering Mechanics Curricula

Figure 1. illustrates how engineering mechanics curricula are implemented nowadays. Engineering students learn physics and mathematics in their high school years and their first college year. Based on this foundation, the students go further into studying engineering mechanics courses such as Statics, Dynamics, Mechanics of Materials, Heat Transfer, Fluid Mechanics, etc. This paradigm has been practiced for as long as any university professor can remember. I've grown up with this paradigm too. More than 30 years has passed since I graduated from my college, and even the contents of the textbooks remain essentially identical. The only "improvement" is that we have CAD and CAE courses now, as shown in the figure. So, what are the problems of this conventional paradigm of engineering mechanics curricula?

First, conventional curricula relies too much on mathematics to teach the concepts of engineering mechanics. Many students are good at engineering thinking but not good at mathematical thinking. For these students, especially in their junior years, mathematics is an inefficient tool (a nightmare, some would say). As a matter of fact, very few students enjoy mathematics as a tool of learning engineering ideas and concepts. Nowadays, CAE software has matured to a point that it can be used as a tool to learn engineering ideas, concepts, and even formulas. We'll show this through each section of this book. Often, mathematics is not the only way to show engineering concepts, or to explain formulas. Using graphics-based CAE tools is often a better way. It is possible to reduce the dependency on mathematics by a substantial extent.

Second, as shown in the figure, the CAD course is usually taught as a stand-alone subject in a sense that it doesn't serve as part of foundation for engineering mechanics courses. The 3D modeling techniques learned in the CAD course can be a powerful tool. For example, modern CAD software usually allows you to build a mechanism and study the motion of parts. However, our engineering mechanics textbooks haven't illuminated these advantages yet.

Third, the CAE course is usually taught in the senior or graduate years, because the CAE textbook requires some background knowledge of engineering mechanics. It is my long-term observation that the CAE course should be taught as early as junior years, for the following reasons: (a) If a student begins to learn CAE in his junior years, he will have many years to become proficient at this important engineering skill. (b) After knowing what and how CAE can help him solving problems, a student will be more knowledgeable and confident about what direction he should concentrate on when learning engineering mechanics courses. (c) As mentioned earlier, CAE can be used as a learning tool, just like mathematics, for the ensuing subjects. It'll largely facilitate the learning of engineering mechanics courses.

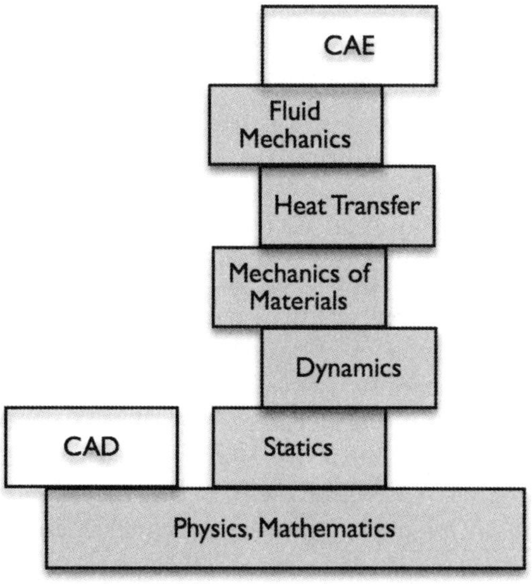

Figure 1. Conventional Paradigm of Engineering Mechanics Curricula

Figure 2. shows an idea that I'd like to propose for engineering mechanics curricula; this book is developed based on this idea. Engineering students usually learn CAD tools in their junior years. For example, among many CAD tools, **SolidWorks** has been popularized in many colleges. Naturally **SolidWorks** might serve as a "virtual laboratory" for the ensuing engineering mechanics courses, such as Statics, Dynamics, Mechanics of Materials, Heat Transfer, Fluid Mechanics, etc. The idea is simple, the benefits should be appreciated, but the implementation needs much more elaboration.

First, a series of well-designed lab exercise books are the key to the success of this idea. These software-based lab books must map their contents to contemporary textbooks.

Second, a CAE software platform must be chosen to serve as the virtual laboratory. We (Mr. Stephen Schroff of SDC Publications and I) have chosen **SolidWorks Simulation** as the platform for this book, for the following reasons: (a) As mentioned, **SolidWorks** has been popularized in many colleges. Many students are familiar with this software. (b) The **Simulation** is an integrated part of **SolidWorks** and a natural extension of **SolidWorks**. (c) The licensing of the **Simulation** is included with a **SolidWorks** license. (d) Compared with other CAE software I've investigated, the **Simulation** is very friendly for college juniors. (e) Finally, after a thorough investigation, I've concluded that **SolidWorks Simulation** has capabilities to implement all of the ideas I want to cover.

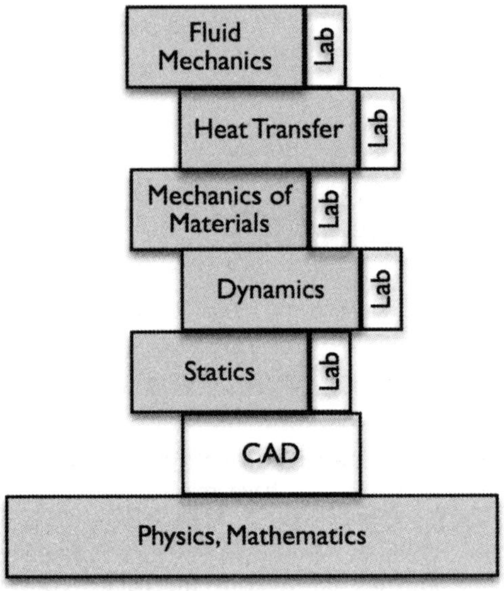

Figure 2. Proposed Paradigm of Engineering Mechanics Curricula

Use of This Book

This book is designed as a software-based lab book to complement a standard textbook in a Mechanics of Material course, which is usually taught in junior undergraduate years. As a secondary function, this book also can be used as an auxiliary workbook in a CAE or Finite Element Analysis course for undergraduate students.

There are 14 chapters in this book. Each chapter is designed as one week's workload, consisting of 2 to 3 sections. Each section is designed for a student to follow the exact steps in that section and learn a concept or topic of Mechanics of Materials. Typically, each section takes 15-40 minutes to complete the exercises.

How I Use This Book in My Classroom

This is how I proceed in my classroom. Each week, I assign a chapter to my students, without offering any lecture about the chapter. I also set up a discussion forum on an e-learning system maintained by the university. After completing the exercises of the chapter, the students are required to discuss them in the forum. In the discussion forum, the students may post their questions, help or answer other students' questions, or share their comments. In addition to taking part in the discussion, I rate each posted article with 1-5 stars. The sum of the ratings becomes the grade of a student's performance for that week.

Most of the students were willing to spend time working on these step-by-step exercises, because these exercises are tangible, rather than abstract. Students of this generation are usually better at picking up knowledge through tangible software exercises rather than abstract lecturing. Furthermore, the students not only feel comfortable to post questions in the forum but also enjoy helping other students or sharing their comments with others. Due to students' enthusiastic responses, I'm optimistic about the paradigm shown in Figure 2.

I'm eager to share my teaching experiences here because I think this might be a good course model for a workbook like this one.

Companion Webpage

A webpage is maintained for this book:

http://myweb.ncku.edu.tw/~hhlee/Myweb_at_NCKU/SWM2014.html

The webpage contains links to following resources: (a) videos that demonstrate the steps of each section in the book, (b) finished **SolidWorks** files of each section, (c) an 121-page PDF tutorial, *Part and Assembly Modeling with SolidWorks 2014*.

The videos, hosted by YouTube, have a maximum resolution of 1280x720 (half HD).

As for the finished **SolidWorks** files, if everything works smoothly, you may not need them at all. Every model can be built from scratch by following the steps described in the book. I provide these files just in cases you need them. For example, when you run into trouble and you don't want to redo it from the beginning, you may find these files useful. Or you may happen to have trouble following the steps in the book, you can then look up the details in the files. In fact, the main reason I provide these finished files is as follows. It is strongly suggested that, in the beginning of a section when previously saved **SolidWorks** files are needed, you use my files rather than your own files so that you are able to obtain results that have minimum deviations in numerical values from those in the book. To reduce file sizes, these finished files don't include the result files (i.e., **CWR** files) generated by the finite element solver. Therefore, before viewing results, make sure **SolidWorks Simulation** is loaded and issue a **Run** command to generate the results.

I provide the 121-page PDF tutorial (*Part and Assembly Modeling with SolidWorks 2014*), for those students who have no experience in **SolidWorks** and want to acquire some, to feel more comfortable working on the exercises in this book. Please note that this book (*Mechanics of Materials Labs with SolidWorks Simulation 2014*) is self-contained and requires no pre-existing experience in geometric modeling with **SolidWorks**.

Companion DVD

For each hardcopy of the book, we also provide a DVD containing some of the resources in the webpage to save your time of downloading the files, including (a) the finished **SolidWorks** files of each section, including the result files (**CWR** files) to save your time of regenerating the results; and (b) the 121-page PDF tutorial, *Part and Assembly Modeling with SolidWorks 2014*.

Notations

Chapters and sections are numbered in a traditional way. Each section is further divided into subsections. For example, the first subsection of the second section of Chapter 3 is denoted as "3.2-1." Text boxes in a subsection are ordered with numbers, each of which is enclosed by a pair of square brackets (e.g., [4]). We refer to that text box as "3.2-1[4]." When referring to a text box from the same subsection, we drop the subsection identifier. For example, we simply write "[4]." Equations are numbered in a similar way, except that the equation number is enclosed by a pair of round brackets rather than square brackets. For example, "3.2-1(2)" refers to the 2nd equation in the subsection 3.2-1. Notations used in this book are summarized as follows (see page 9 for more details):

3.2-1	Numbers after a hyphen are subsection numbers.
[1], [2], ...	Numbers with square brackets are text box numbers.
(1), (2), ...	Numbers with round brackets are equation numbers.
SolidWorks	**SolidWorks** terms are boldfaced to facilitate the readability of text
Round-cornered text boxes	A round-cornered text box indicates that mouse or keyboard actions are needed.
Sharp-cornered text boxes	A sharp-cornered box is used for commentary only; i.e., mouse or keyboard actions are not needed in that step.
#	A symbol # is used to indicate the last text box of a subsection.

Acknowledgement

The contents of this book have been used in my classroom for three years before the publication. I've received much feedback from my students, so that the book could be improved accordingly. Many of my graduate students helped to proofread the book and produce the videos. I want to express my gratitude to these students. I would also like to thank Professor Sheng-Jye Hwang, of the ME Department, NCKU, and Professor Durn-Yuan Huang, of Chung Hwa University of Medical Technology. They are my long-term research partners. Together, we have accomplished many projects, and, in carrying out these projects, I've learned much from them.

My publisher, Mr. Stephen Schroff, provided many valuable suggestions during the writing of this book. I owe him a gratitude. Thanks to Danny Usher, a Canadian, a friend, and my English tutor, who patiently helps me enhance my English. Lastly, thanks to my wife, my son, and our three pet dogs, for their patience and sharing of excitement with me.

Huei-Huang Lee

Associate Professor
Department of Engineering Science
National Cheng Kung University, Tainan, Taiwan
e-mail: hhlee@mail.ncku.edu.tw
webpage: myweb.ncku.edu.tw/~hhlee

Chapter 1

Stresses

Stresses are quantities to describe the intensity of force in a body (either solid or fluid). Its unit is force per unit area (i.e., N/m^2 in SI). It is a position-dependent quantity.

Imagine that your arms are pulled by your friends with two forces of the same magnitude but opposite directions. What are the stresses in your arms? Assuming the magnitude of the forces is 100 N and the cross-sectional area of your arms is 100 cm^2, then you may answer, "the stresses are 1 N/cm^2. everywhere in my arms." This case is simple and the answer is good enough. For a one-dimensional case like this, the stress σ may be easily defined as

$$\sigma = \frac{P}{A}$$

where P is the applied force and A is the cross sectional area.

In general 3D cases, things are much more complicated. Now, imagine that you are buried in the soil by your friends, and your head is 100 meters deep below the ground surface. How do you describe the force intensity (i.e., stress) on your head?

If the soil is replaced by still water, then the answer would be much simpler. The magnitude of the pressure (stress) on the top of your head would be the same as the pressure on your cheeks, and the direction of the pressure would always be perpendicular to the surface where the pressure applies. You've learned these concepts in your high school. And you've learned that the magnitude of the pressure is $\sigma = \rho gh$, where ρ is the mass density of the water, g is the gravitational acceleration, and h is the depth (100 meters in this case). In general, to describe the force intensity at a certain position in water, we place an infinitesimally small body at that position, and measure the force per unit surface area on that body.

In the soil (which is a solid material rather than water), the behavior is quite different First, the magnitude of the pressure on the top of your head may not be the same as that on your cheeks. Second, the direction of pressure is not necessarily perpendicular to the surface where the pressure applies. However, the above definition of stresses for water still holds. Let me restate as follows:

> *The stress at a certain position in a solid material is defined as the force per unit surface area on an infinitesimally small body placed at that position.*

Note that the infinitesimally small body could be any shapes. However, if we know the stresses on a certain shape of small body, we can infer the stresses on other shapes. We usually take a small cube to describe the stresses.

This chapter will guide you to learn the concepts of stresses.

Section 1.1

Stress Components

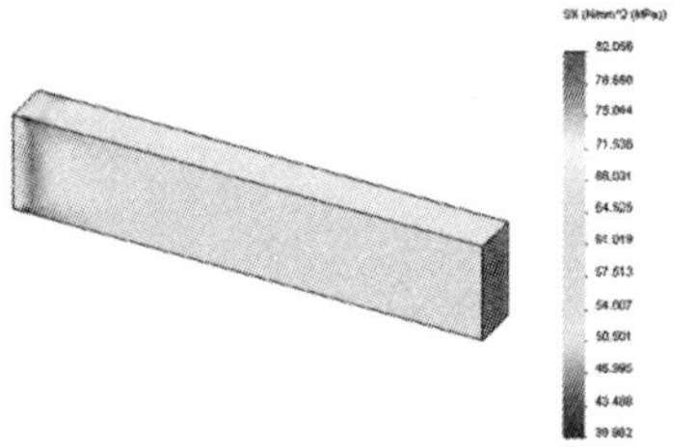

1.1-1 Introduction

[1] Consider a cantilever beam made of an alloy steel and of dimension 10 mm x 20 mm x 100 mm [2], which is fixed at one end [3] and subjected to a force on the other end [4]. The force is in positive X-direction and has a magnitude of 10,000 N. Note that we've used a reference coordinate system as shown in [5].

In theory, the stress is uniform over the body; i.e., every point in the beam has the same stress. How do we describe this stress? Can we simply say, the stress is 50 MPa, which is calculated by

$$\frac{10{,}000 \text{ N}}{10 \text{ mm} \times 20 \text{ mm}} = 50 \text{ MPa?}$$

For a simple case like this, that may be adequate. In order to apply to more general cases, we need to say something more, specifically, what is the direction of the stress? What is the surface on which the stress acts?

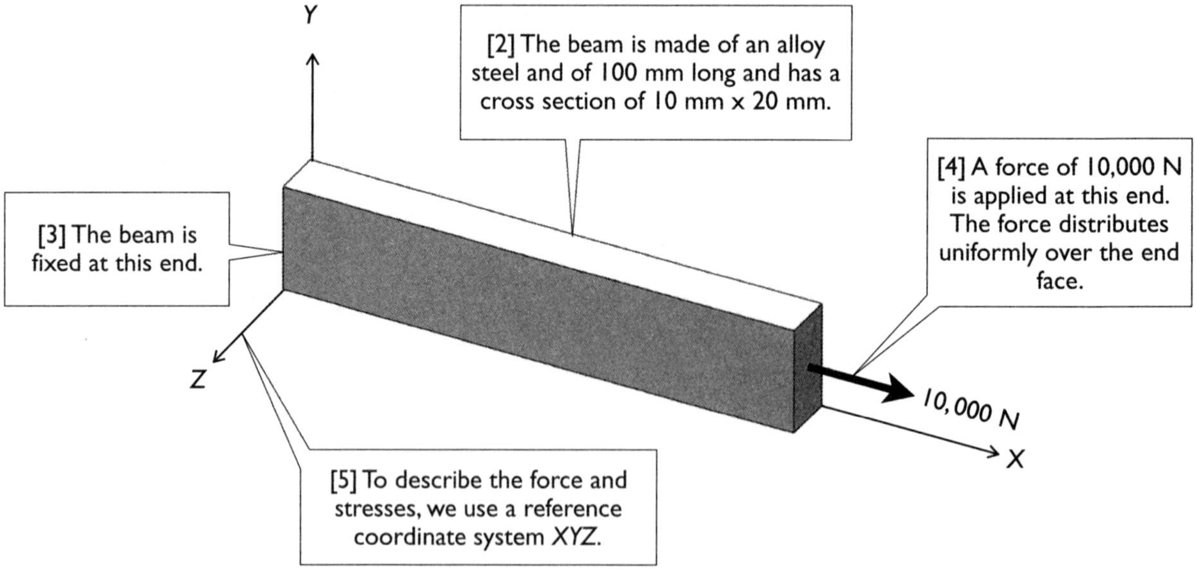

[6] Definition of Stress

The stress at a certain point can be defined as *the force per unit area acting on the boundary surfaces of an infinitesimally small body centered at that point* [7]. The stress values may be different at different locations of the boundary surfaces. The small body can be any shape. However, for the purpose of describing the stress, we usually use a small cube [8] of which each edge is parallel to a coordinate axis. If we can find the stresses on a small cube, we then can calculate the stresses on any other shapes of small body (see [18]).

[9] X-Face, Y-Face, and Z-Face

Each of the six faces of the cube can be assigned an identifier as X-face, Y-face, Z-face, negative-X-face, negative-Y-face, and negative-Z-face, respectively [10-13].

[14] Stress Components

Let $\vec{p}_X$ be the force per unit area acting on the X-face. In general, $\vec{p}_X$ may not be normal or parallel to the X-face. We may decompose $\vec{p}_X$ into X-, Y-, and Z-component, and denote σ_{XX}, τ_{XY}, and τ_{XZ} respectively [15]. The first subscript (*X*) is used to indicate the **face** on which the stress components act, while the second subscript (*X*, *Y*, *or Z*) is used to indicate the **direction** of the stress components. Note that σ_{XX} is normal to the face, while τ_{XY}, and τ_{XZ} are parallel to the face. Therefore, σ_{XX} is called a **normal stress**, while τ_{XY}, and τ_{XZ} are called **shear stresses**. In Mechanics of Materials, we usually use the symbol σ for a normal stress and τ for a shear stress.

Similarly, let $\vec{p}_Y$ be the force per unit area acting on the Y-face and we may decompose $\vec{p}_Y$ into a normal component (σ_{YY}) and two shear components (τ_{YX} and τ_{YZ}) [16]. Also, let $\vec{p}_Z$ be the force per unit area acting on the Z-face and we may decompose $\vec{p}_Z$ into a normal component (σ_{ZZ}) and two shear components (τ_{ZX} and τ_{ZY}) [17]. Organized in a matrix form, these stress components may be written as

$$\{\sigma\} = \begin{pmatrix} \sigma_{XX} & \tau_{XY} & \tau_{XZ} \\ \tau_{YX} & \sigma_{YY} & \tau_{YZ} \\ \tau_{ZX} & \tau_{ZY} & \sigma_{ZZ} \end{pmatrix} \qquad (1)$$

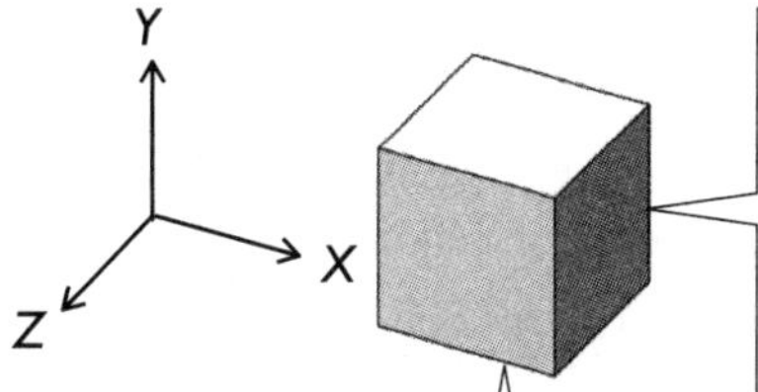

[7] The stress at a certain point can be defined as the force per unit area on the boundary surfaces of an infinitesimally small body centered at that point.

[8] We usually use a small cube for the purpose of describing the stress.

[13] Negative-X-face (opposite of the X-face).

[11] Y-face.

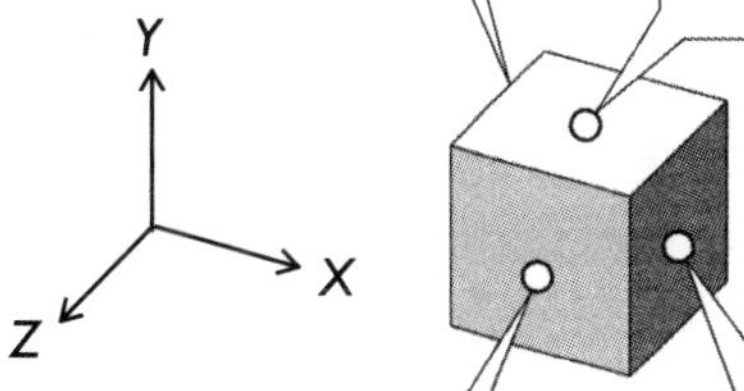

[10] X-face.

[12] Z-face.

[16] The $\vec{p}_Y$ (force per unit area on Y-face) can be decomposed into σ_{YY}, τ_{YX}, and τ_{YZ}.

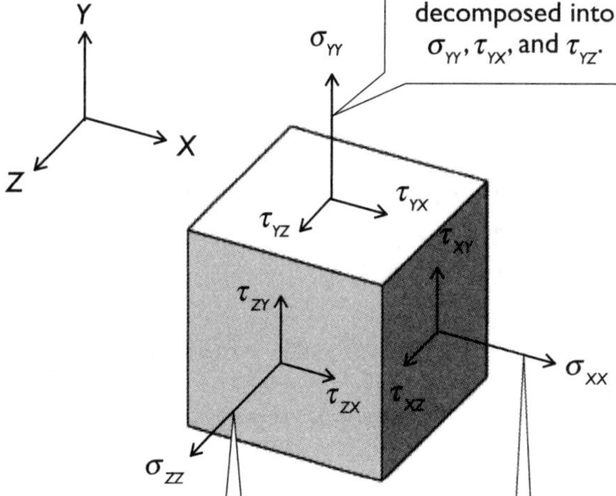

[17] The $\vec{p}_Z$ (force per unit area on Z-face) can be decomposed into σ_{ZZ}, τ_{ZX}, and τ_{ZY}.

[15] The $\vec{p}_X$ (force per unit area on X-face) can be decomposed into σ_{XX}, τ_{XY}, and τ_{XZ}.

[18] Stress Components on Other Faces

It can be proven that the stress components on the negative-X-face, negative-Y-face, and negative-Z-face can be derived from the 9 stress components in Eq. (1). For example, on the negative-X-face, the stress components have exactly the same stress values as those on the X-face but with opposite directions [19]. Similarly, the stress components on the negative-Y-face have the same stress values as those on the Y-face but with opposite directions [20], and the stress components on the negative-Z-face have the same stress values as those on the Y-face but with opposite directions [21].

The proof can be done by taking the cube as free body and applying the force equilibria in X, Y, and Z directions respectively.

On an arbitrary face (which may not be parallel or perpendicular to an axis), the stress components also can be calculated from the 9 stress components in Eq. (1). We'll show that this can be done using Mohr's circles (Section 10.1).

[19] The stress components acting on the negative-X-face have exactly the same stress values as those on the X-face but with opposite directions.

[21] The stress components acting on the negative-Z-face have exactly the same stress values as those on the Z-face but with opposite directions.

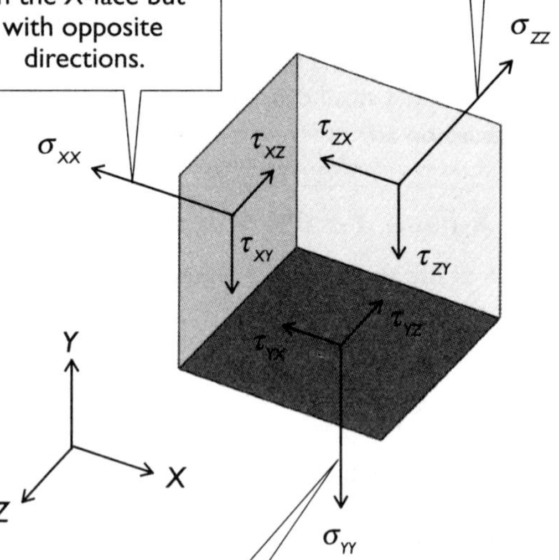

[20] The stress components acting on the negative-Y-face have exactly the same stress values as those on the Y-face but with opposite directions.

[22] Symmetry of Shear Stresses

It also can be proven that the shear stresses are symmetric, i.e.,

$$\tau_{XY} = \tau_{YX},\ \ \tau_{YZ} = \tau_{ZY},\ \ \tau_{ZX} = \tau_{XZ} \qquad (2)$$

The proof can be done by taking the cube as free body and applying the moment equilibria in X, Y, and Z directions respectively.

[23] **Stress State**

We now conclude that 3 normal stress components and 3 shear stress components are needed to describe the **stress state** at a certain point, which may be written in a vector form

$$\{\sigma\} = \{\ \sigma_X \ \ \sigma_Y \ \ \sigma_Z \ \ \tau_{XY} \ \ \tau_{YZ} \ \ \tau_{ZX}\ \} \qquad (3)$$

Note that, for more concise, we use σ_X in place of σ_{XX}, σ_Y in place of σ_{YY}, and σ_Z in place of σ_{ZZ}.

The purpose of this section is to guide the students familiarize the 6 stress components in Eq. (3). The stress field in this section is uniform over the entire body. In the next section, we'll explore a nonuniform stress field.

Another purpose of this section is to familiarize the **SolidWorks Simulation** user interface. #

1.1-2 Launch **SolidWorks** and Create New Part

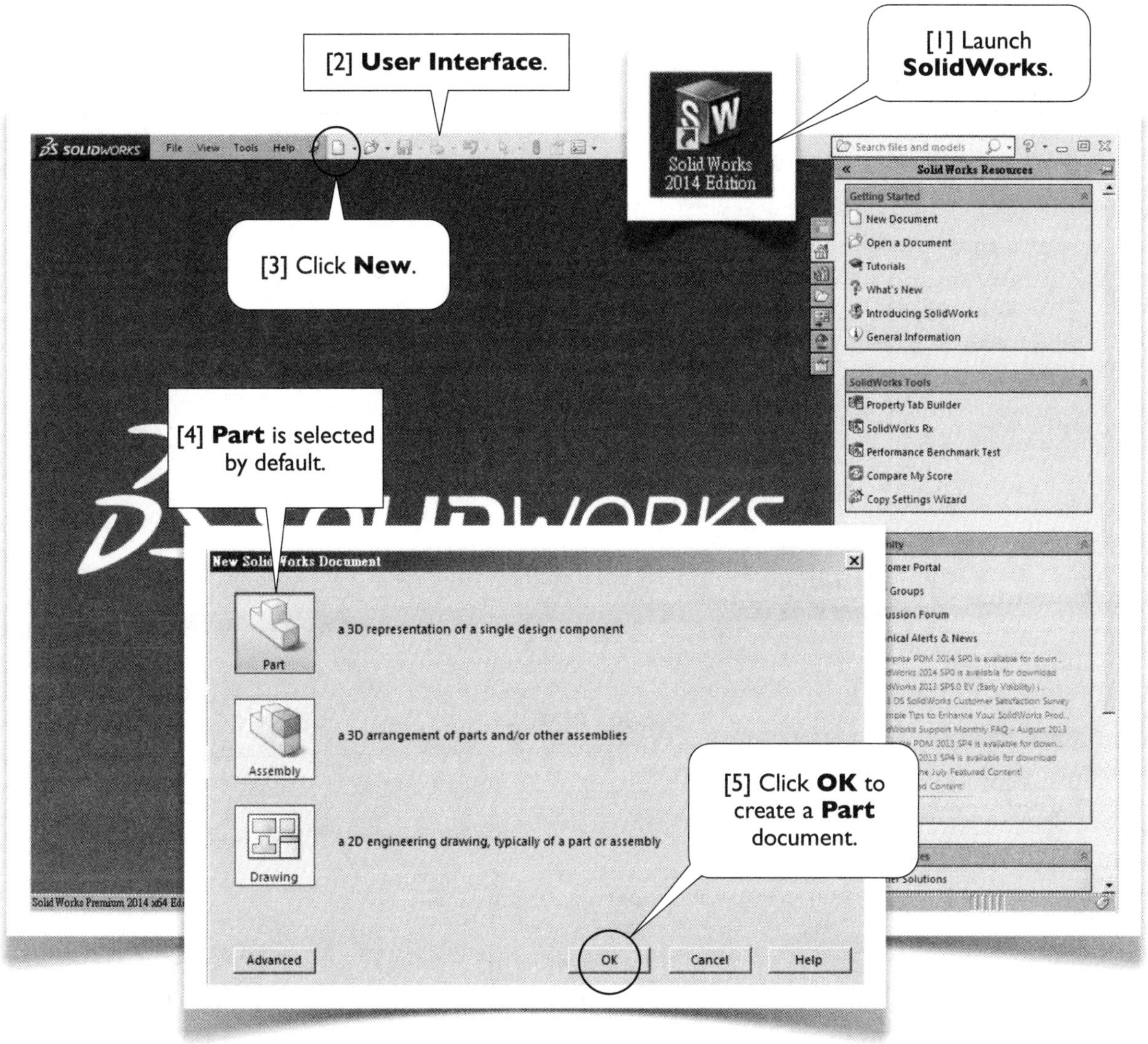

About the Text Boxes

1. Within each subsection (e.g., 1.1-2), text boxes are ordered with numbers, each of which is enclosed by a pair of square brackets (e.g., [1]). When you read the contents of a subsection, please follow the order of the text boxes.
2. The text box numbers are also used as reference numbers. In the same subsection, we simply refer to a text box by its number (e.g., [1]). From other subsections, we refer to a text box by its subsection identifier and the text box number (e.g., 1.1-2[1]).
3. A text box is either round-cornered (e.g., [1, 3, 5]) or sharp-cornered (e.g., [2, 4]). A round-cornered box indicates that **mouse or keyboard actions** are needed in that step. A sharp-cornered box is used for commentary only; i.e., mouse or keyboard actions are not needed in that step.
4. A symbol # is used to indicate the last text box of a subsection, so that you don't leave out any text boxes.

SolidWorks Terms

In this book, terms used in the **SolidWorks** are boldfaced (e.g., **Part** in [4, 5]) to facilitate the readability. #

1.1-3 Set Up Unit System

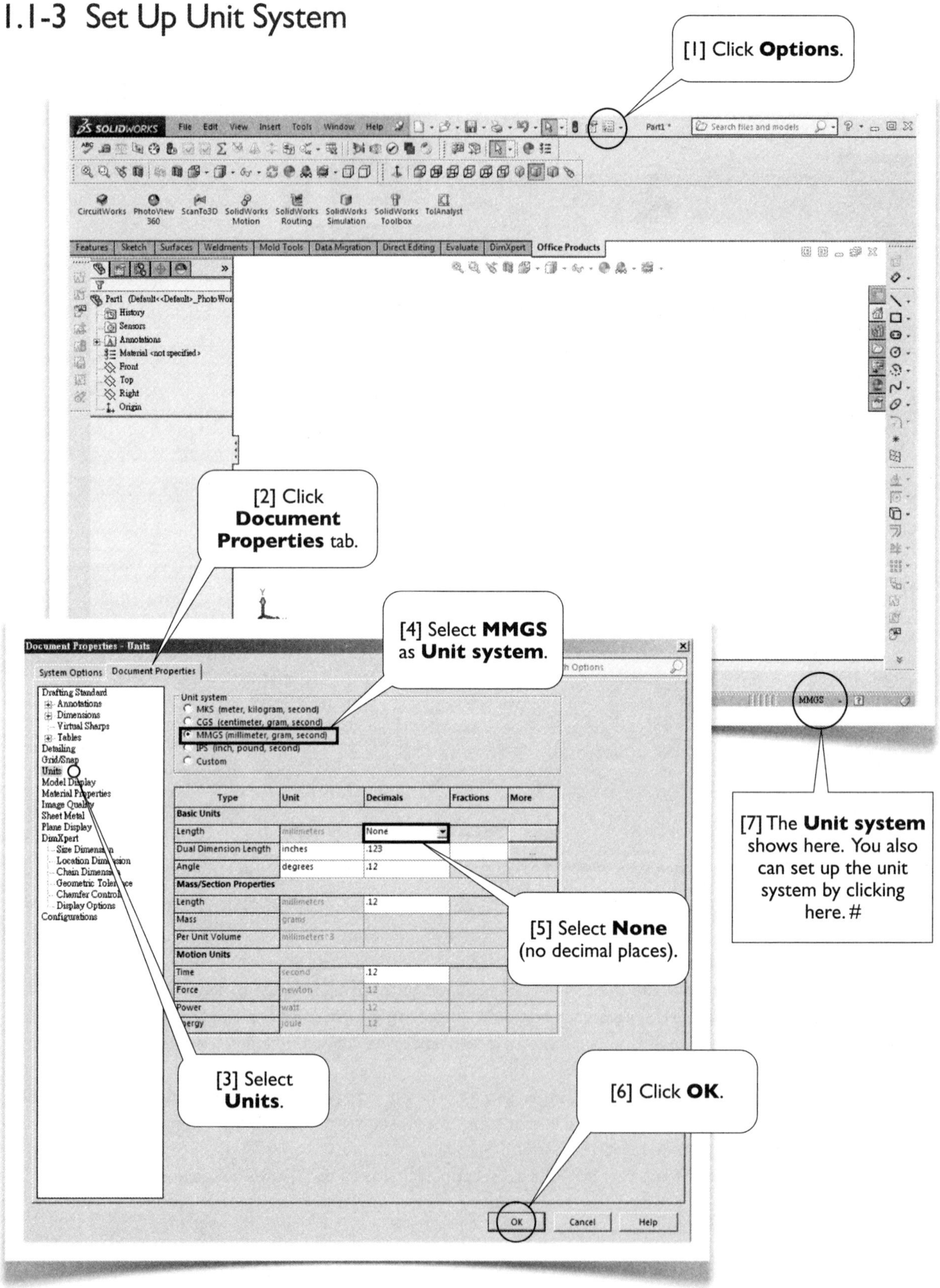

1.1-4 Create Geometric Model

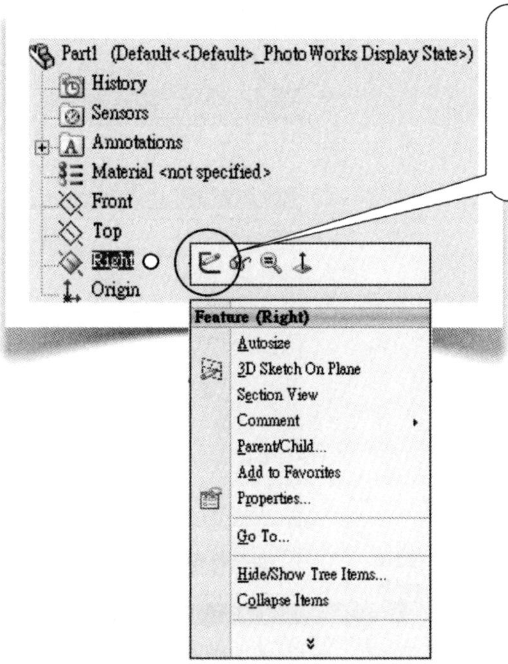

[1] In the **Features Tree** (also called **Part Tree** in this book, on the left of the user interface), right-click **Right** plane and select **Sketch** from the **Context Menu**.

[2] In the **Sketch Toolbar**, select **Center Rectangle**.

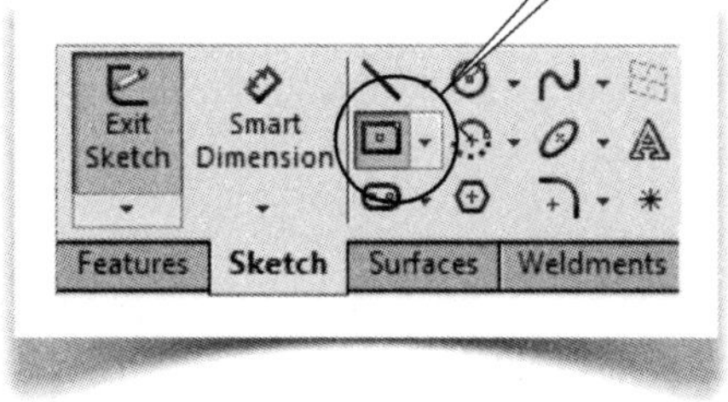

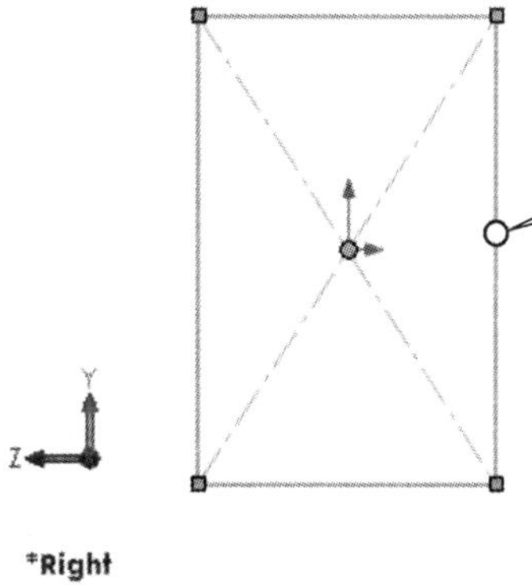

[3] Draw a rectangle centered at the origin (the sizes are arbitrary for now).

[4] In the **Sketch Toolbar**, click **Smart Dimension**.

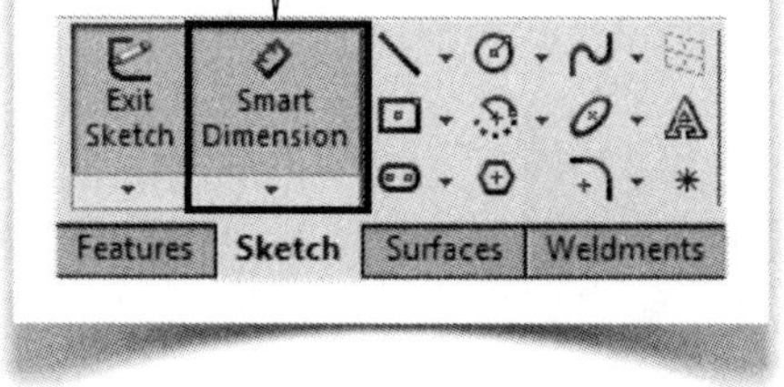

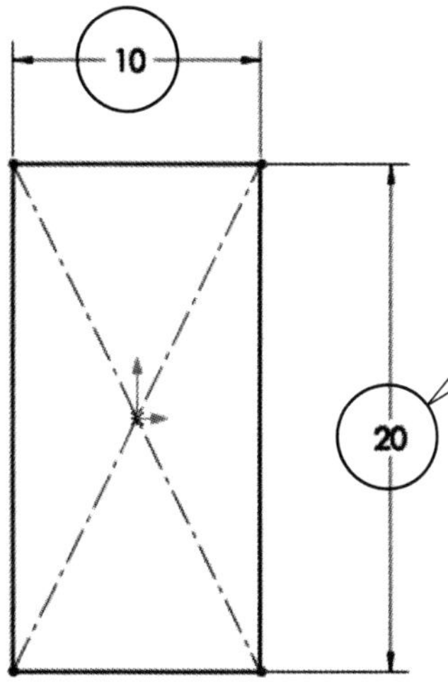

[5] Specify dimensions (10 mm and 20 mm) like this.

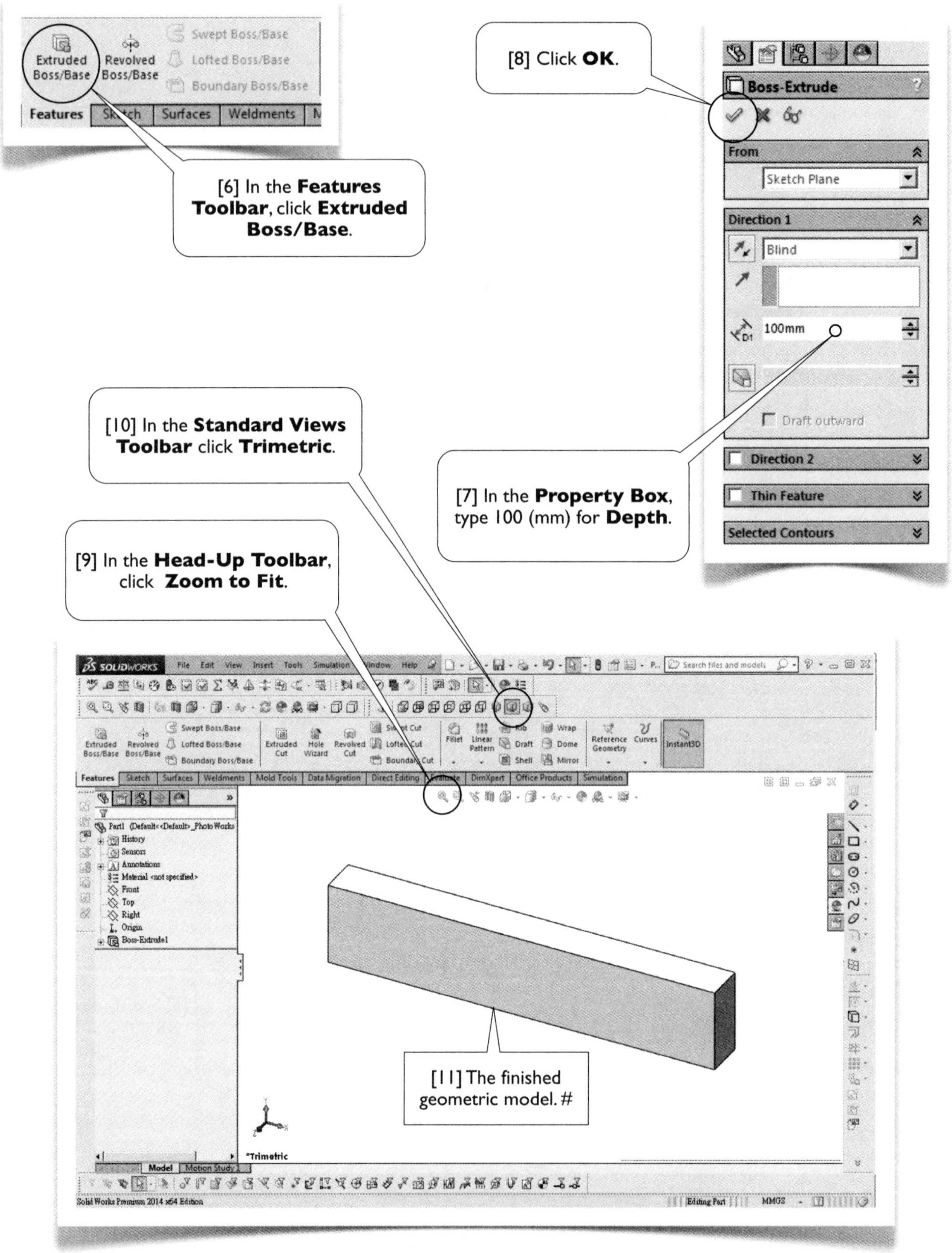
[6] In the **Features Toolbar**, click **Extruded Boss/Base**.
[8] Click **OK**.
[7] In the **Property Box**, type 100 (mm) for **Depth**.
[10] In the **Standard Views Toolbar** click **Trimetric**.
[9] In the **Head-Up Toolbar**, click **Zoom to Fit**.
[11] The finished geometric model. #
Boss-Extrude
From
Sketch Plane
Direction 1
Blind
100mm
Draft outward
Direction 2
Thin Feature
Selected Contours
*Trimetric

1.1-5 Load **SolidWorks Simulation**

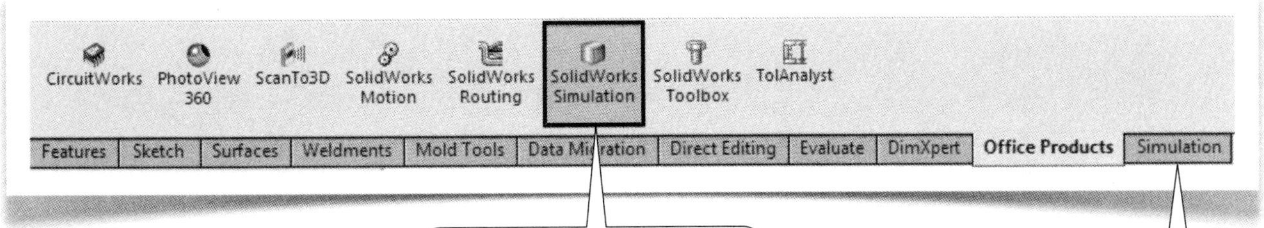

[1] If a **Simulation** tab is already present, which means the **SolidWorks Simulation** is already loaded, you may jump to 1.1-6 (next page) otherwise continue on step [2].

[2] In the **Office Products Toolbar**, click to load **SolidWorks Simulation**.

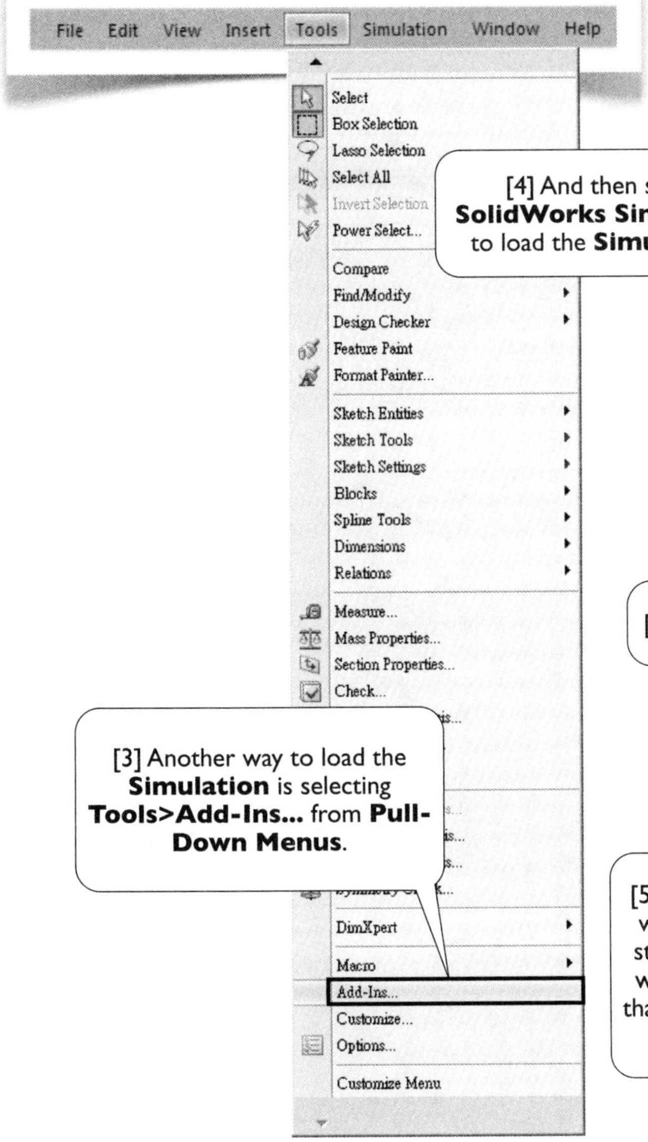

[3] Another way to load the **Simulation** is selecting **Tools>Add-Ins...** from **Pull-Down Menus**.

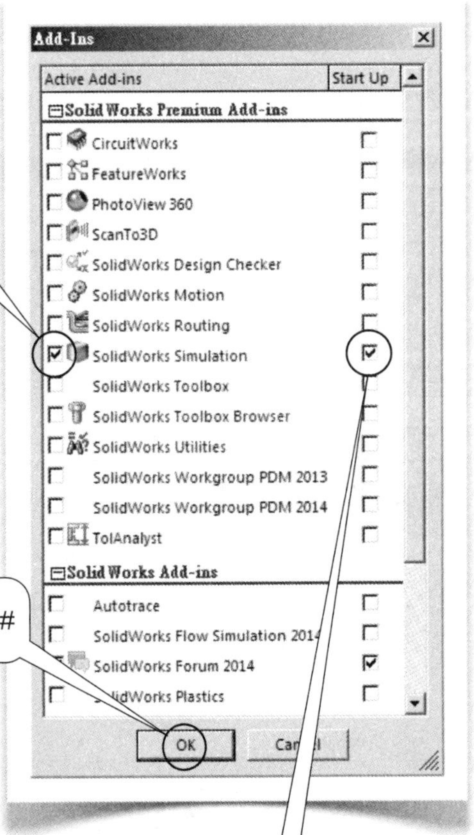

[4] And then select **SolidWorks Simulation** to load the **Simulation**.

[5] Also click here so that the **Simulation** will be loaded automatically each time you start up **SolidWorks**. Through this book, we assume that you've checked this box so that the **Simulation** is loaded automatically each time you start up **SolidWorks**.

[6] Click **OK**. #

1.1-6 Create a Static Structural Study

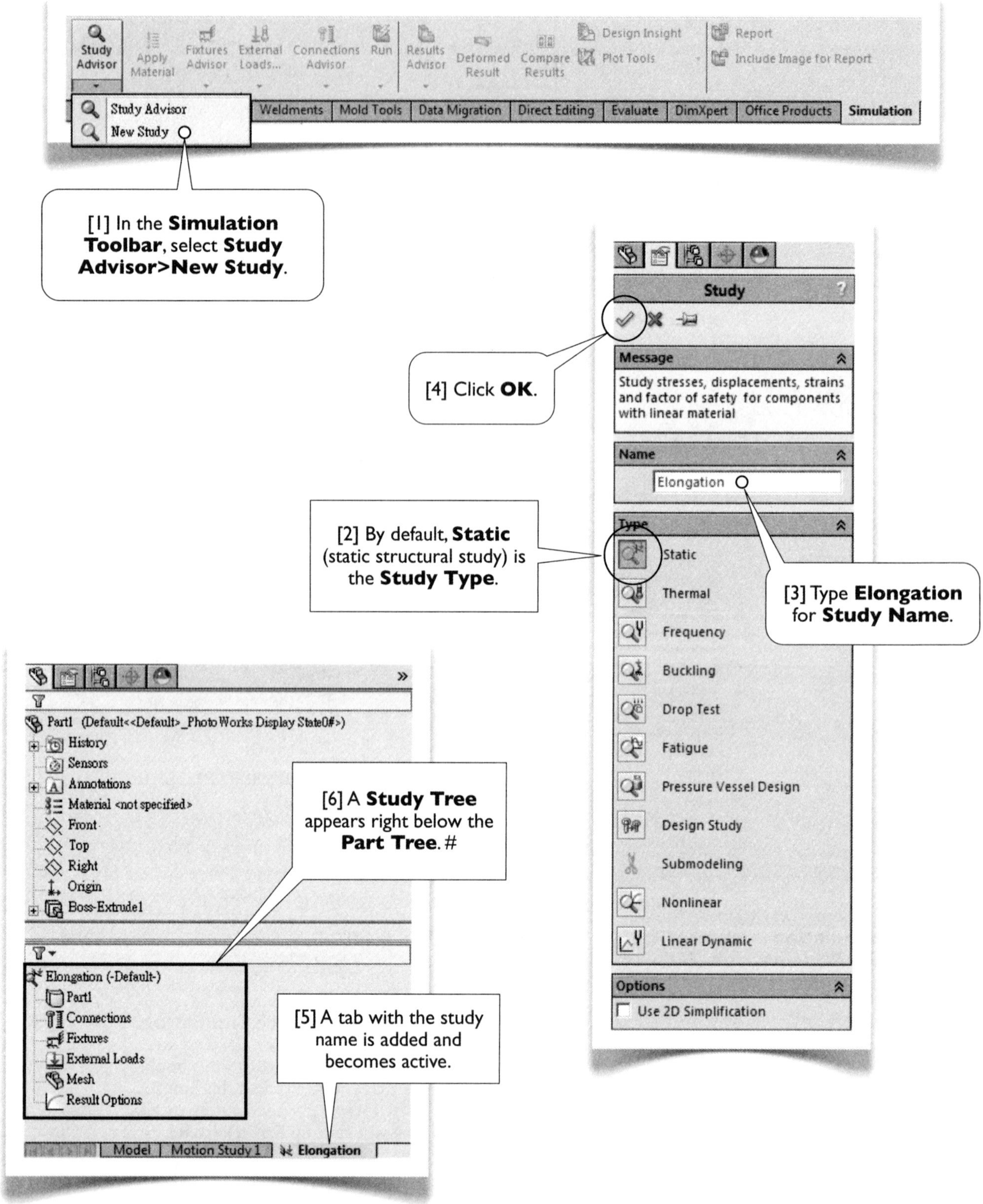

1.1-7 Set Up **Options** for **SolidWorks Simulation**

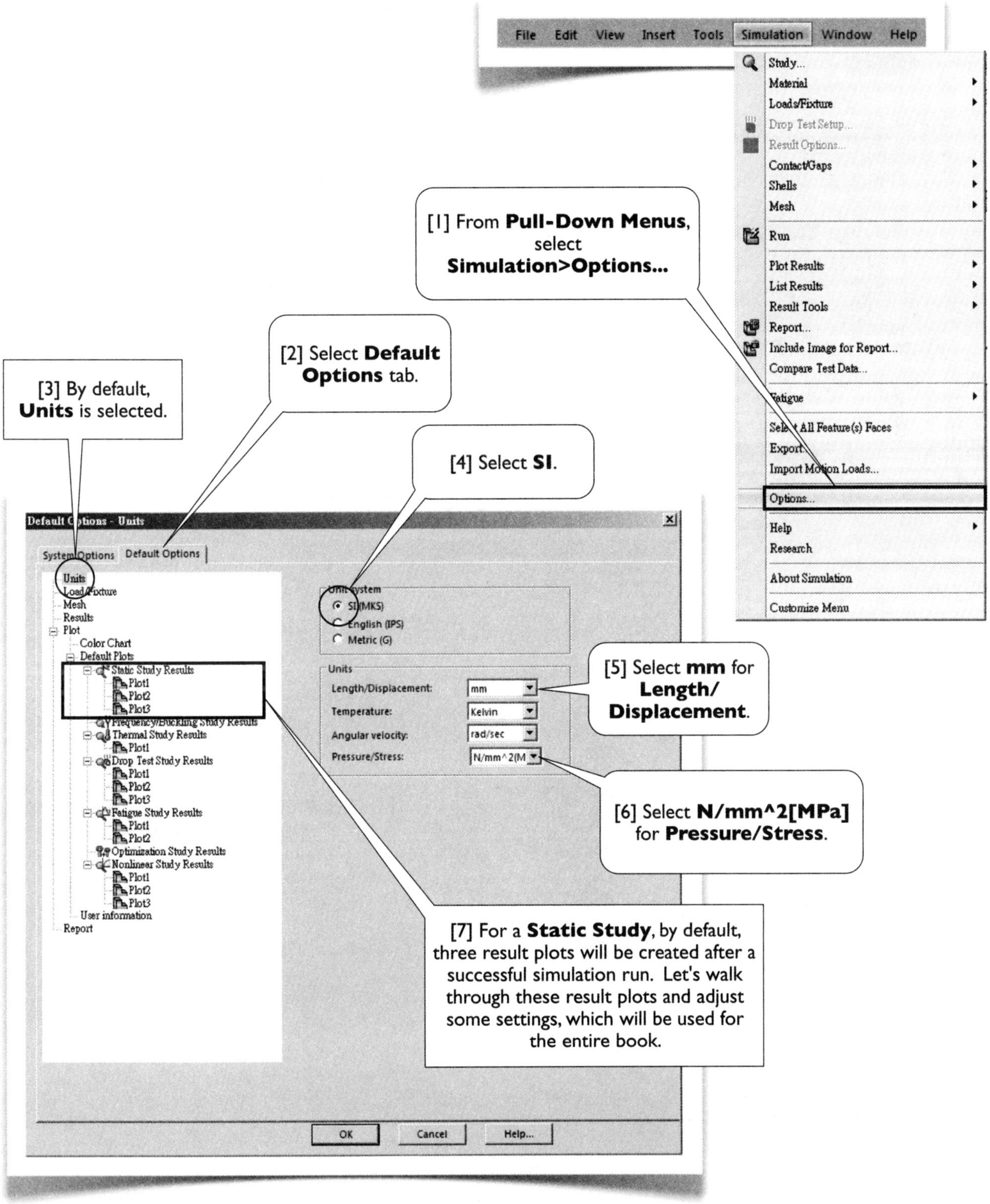

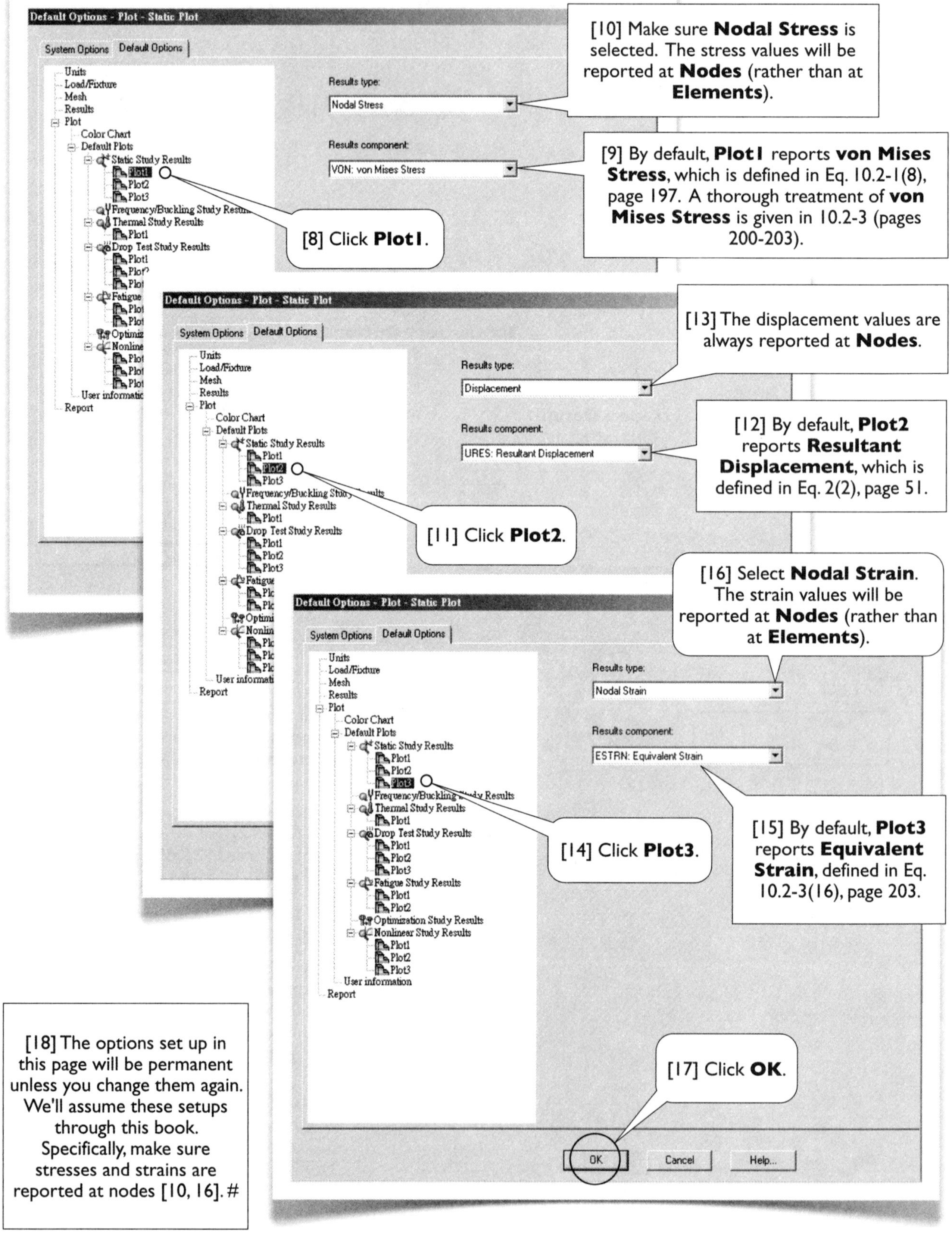

[18] The options set up in this page will be permanent unless you change them again. We'll assume these setups through this book. Specifically, make sure stresses and strains are reported at nodes [10, 16]. #

1.1-8 Apply Material

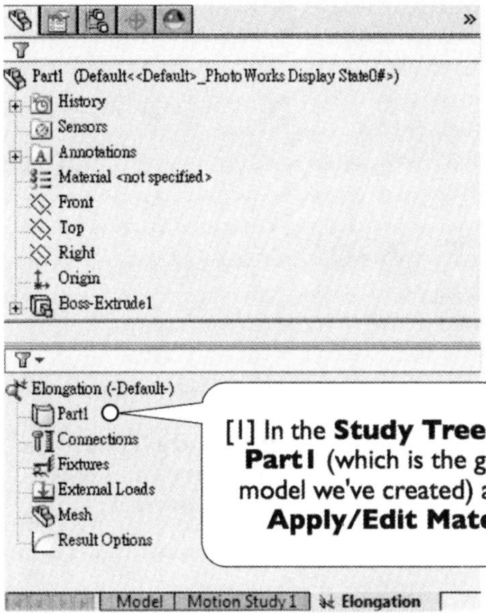

[1] In the **Study Tree**, right-click **Part1** (which is the geometric model we've created) and select **Apply/Edit Material...**

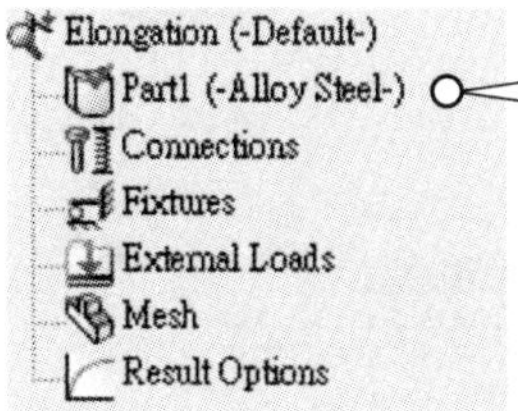

[6] **Alloy Steel** is assigned to the model. #

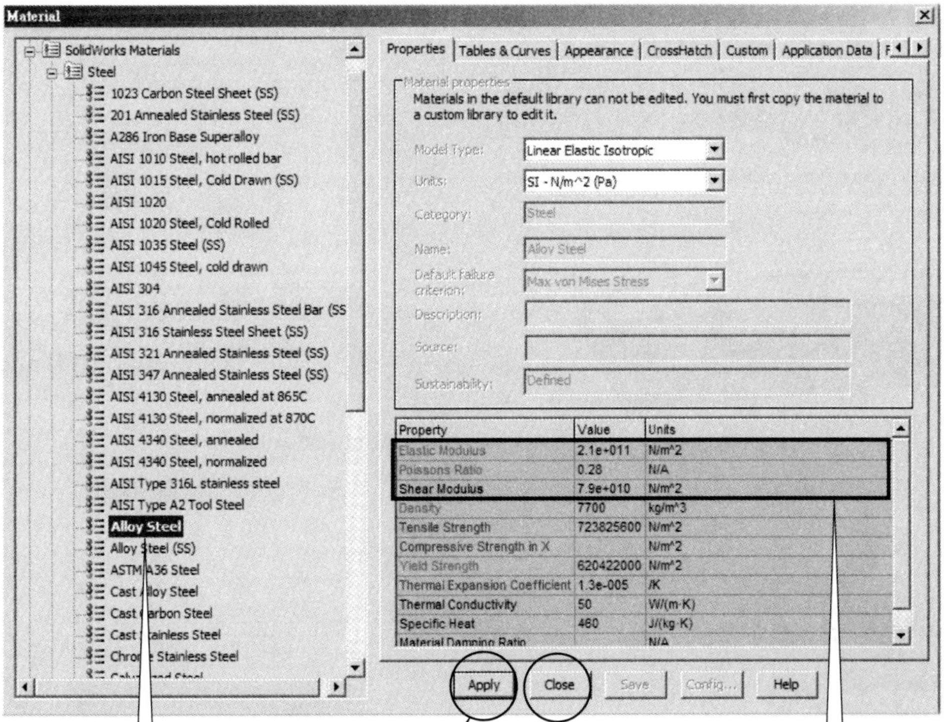

[2] By default, **Alloy Steel** is selected.

[4] Click **Apply**.

[5] Click **Close**.

[3] **Elastic Modulus**, **Poisson's Ratio**, and **Shear Modulus** are the three most important material properties in the course of Mechanics of Materials. They are defined in Sections 4.1 and 4.2.

1.1-9 Apply Support

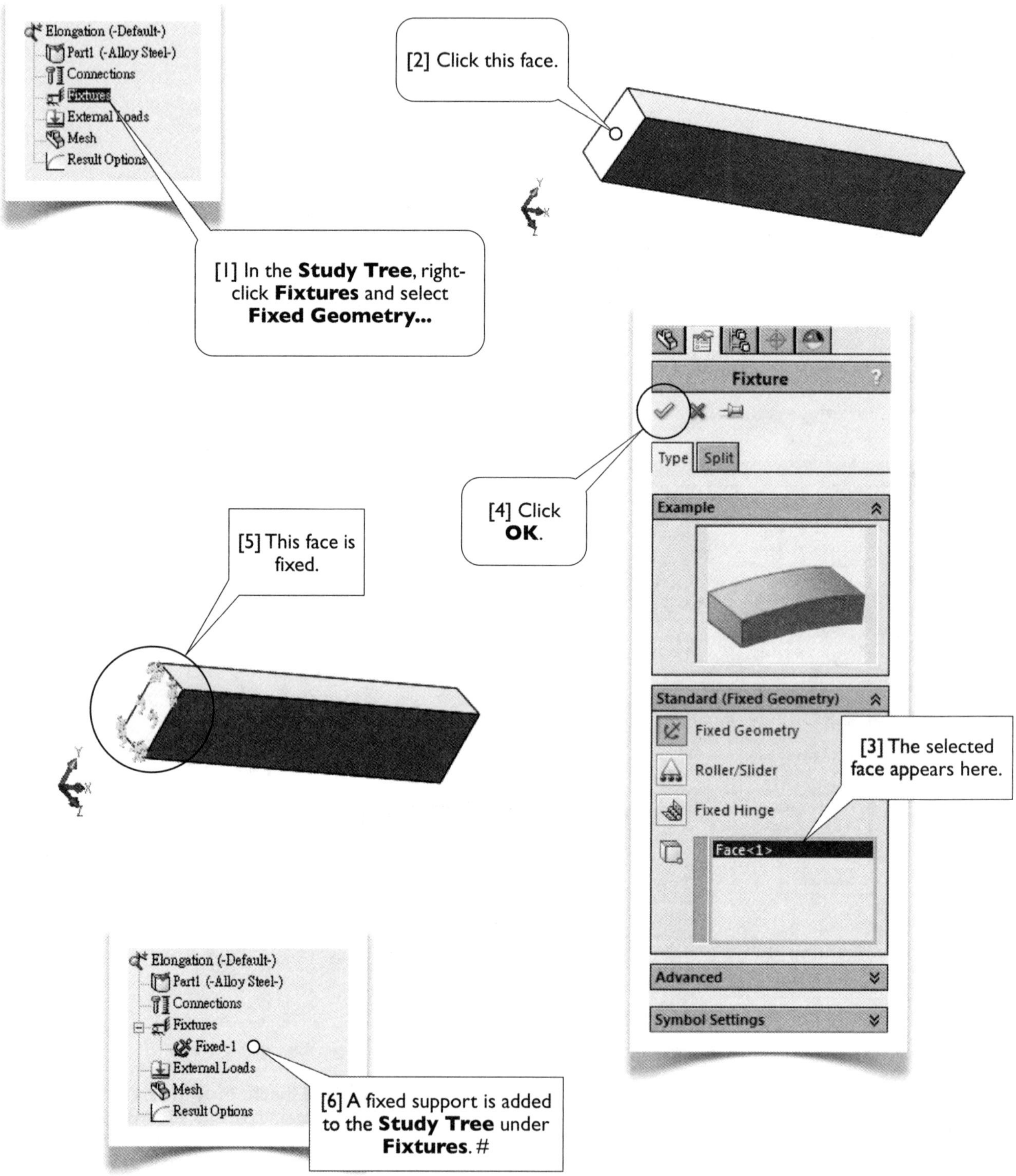

1.1-10 Apply Load

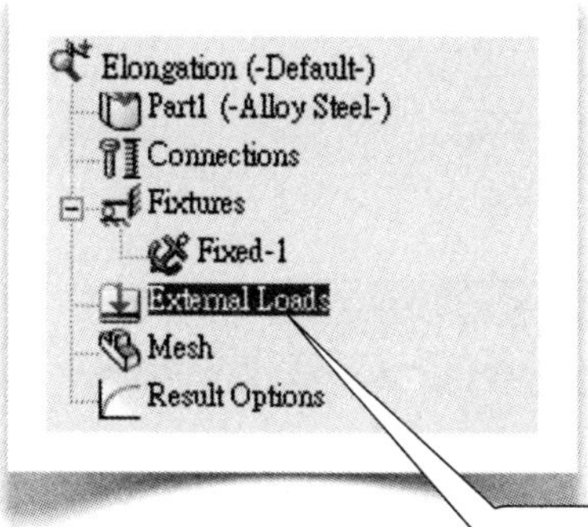

[1] In the **Study Tree**, right-click **External Loads** and select **Force...**

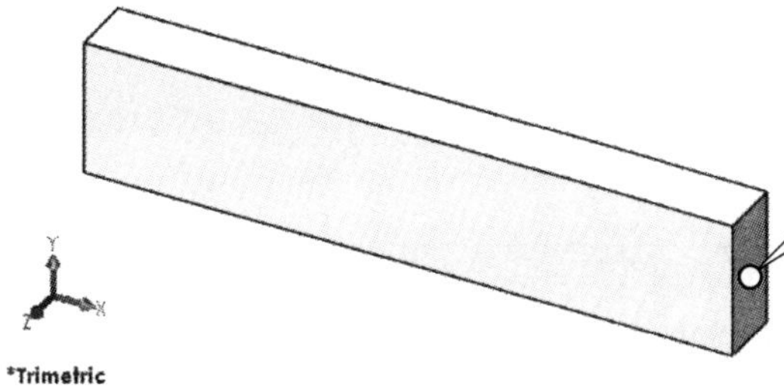

[2] Click this face.

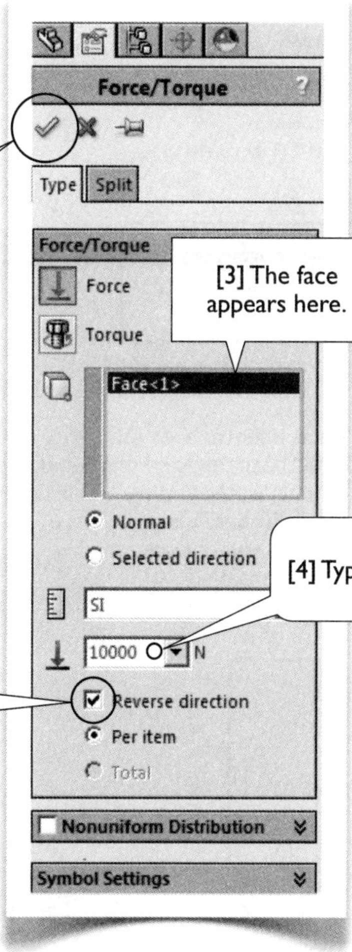

[3] The face appears here.

[4] Type 10000 (N).

[5] Check **Reverse direction**.

[6] Click **OK**.

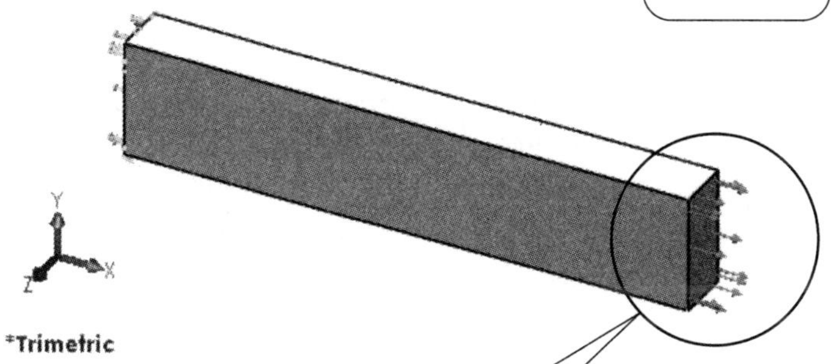

[7] A force of 10,000 N is applied uniformly on this face.

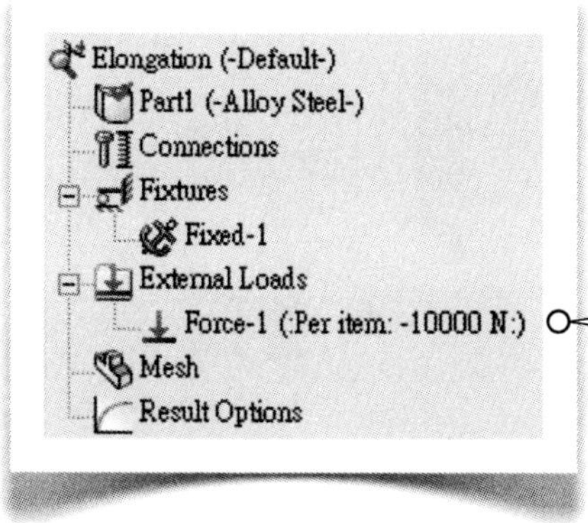

[8] A **Force** is added to the **Study Tree** under **External Loads**. #

1.1-11 Solve the Model

[1] In the **Simulation Toolbar**, click **Run**. It takes only a few seconds to solve the model.

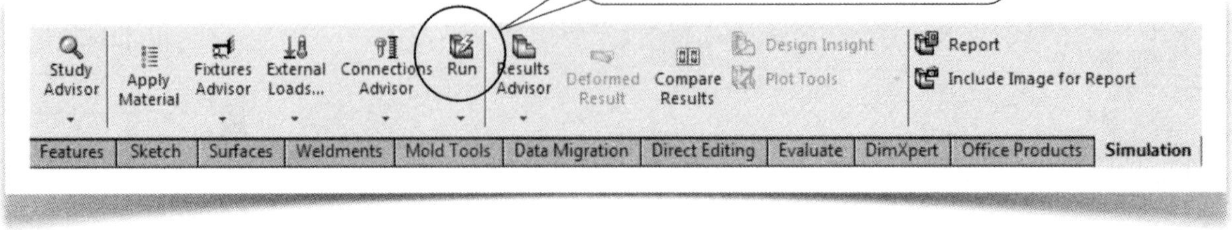

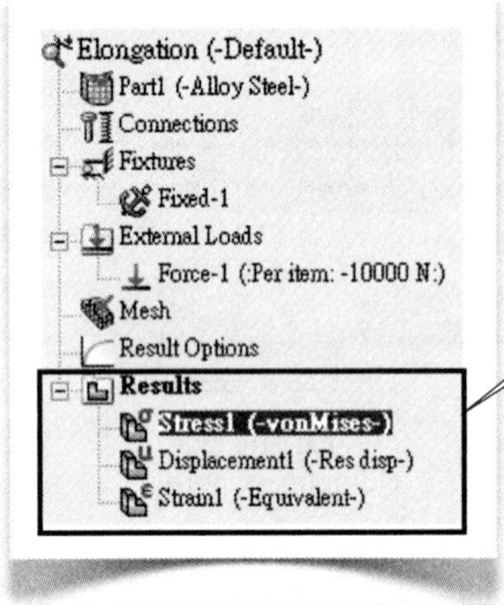

[2] As mentioned earlier (1.1-7[7], page 15), by default, results for **Von Mises Stress, Resultant Displacement**, and **Equivalent Strain** are created. Note that **Stress1** is highlighted, meaning it is active and displayed in the **Graphics Area**.

[4] Even you follow the exactly steps in this book, your results may deviate from the results in this book. It is normal, as long as the deviation is not too large.

[3] By default, **Von Mises Stress** is displayed. We'll change to display σ_x later.

[5] The stress is uniform over the entire body except the area near the fixed end, where the stresses are complicated and we'll explain this phenomenon in 5.2-3[16, 17], page 102. Let's neglect these stress values here for now.

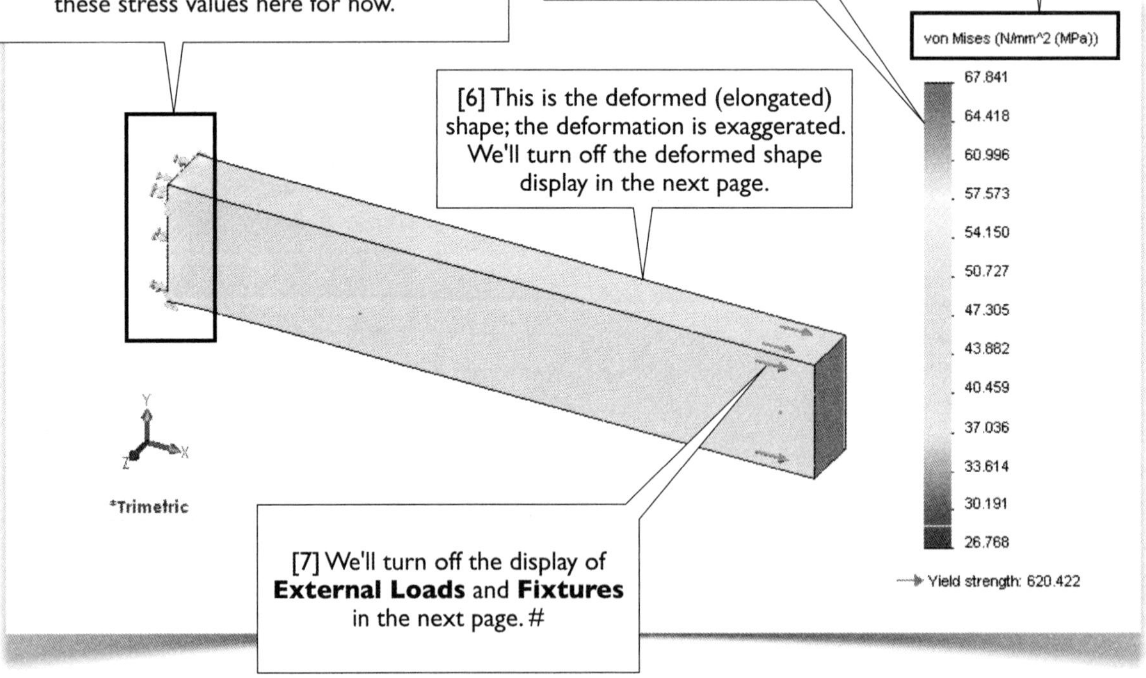

[6] This is the deformed (elongated) shape; the deformation is exaggerated. We'll turn off the deformed shape display in the next page.

[7] We'll turn off the display of **External Loads** and **Fixtures** in the next page. #

1.1-12 View the Normal Stress σ_x

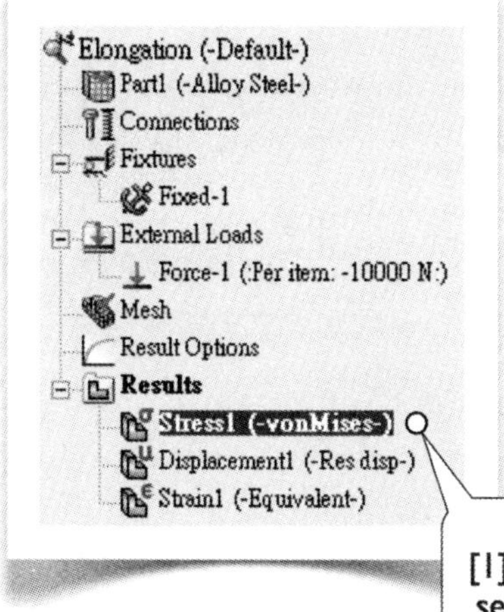

[1] Right-click **Stress1** and select **Edit Definition...** (or simply double-click it).

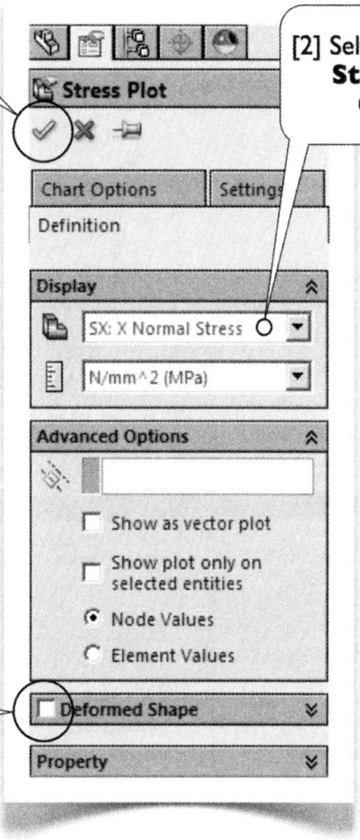

[2] Select **SX: X Normal Stress** (i.e., σ_x) for **Component**.

[3] Uncheck **Deformed Shape**. The undeformed shape will be displayed.

[4] Click **OK**.

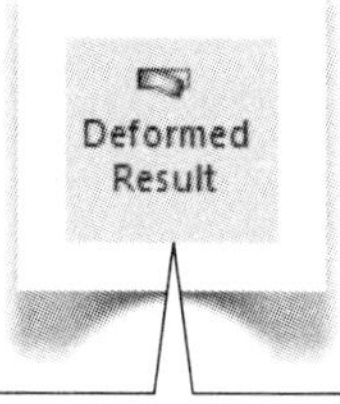

[5] **Deformed Shape** can be toggled on/off by clicking this button in the **Simulation Toolbar**.

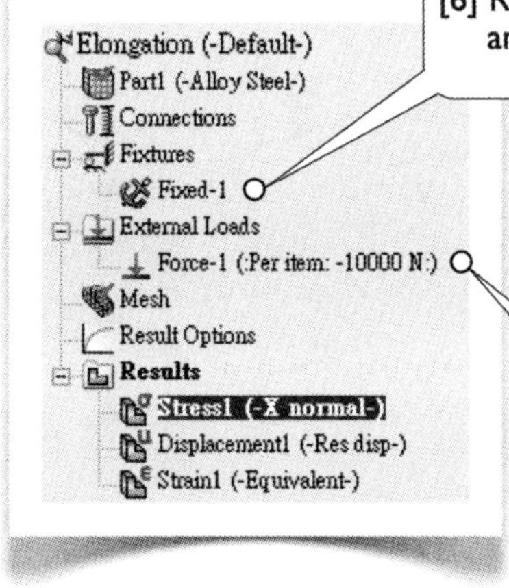

[6] Right-click **Fixed-1** and select **Hide**.

[7] Right-click **Force-1** and select **Hide**.

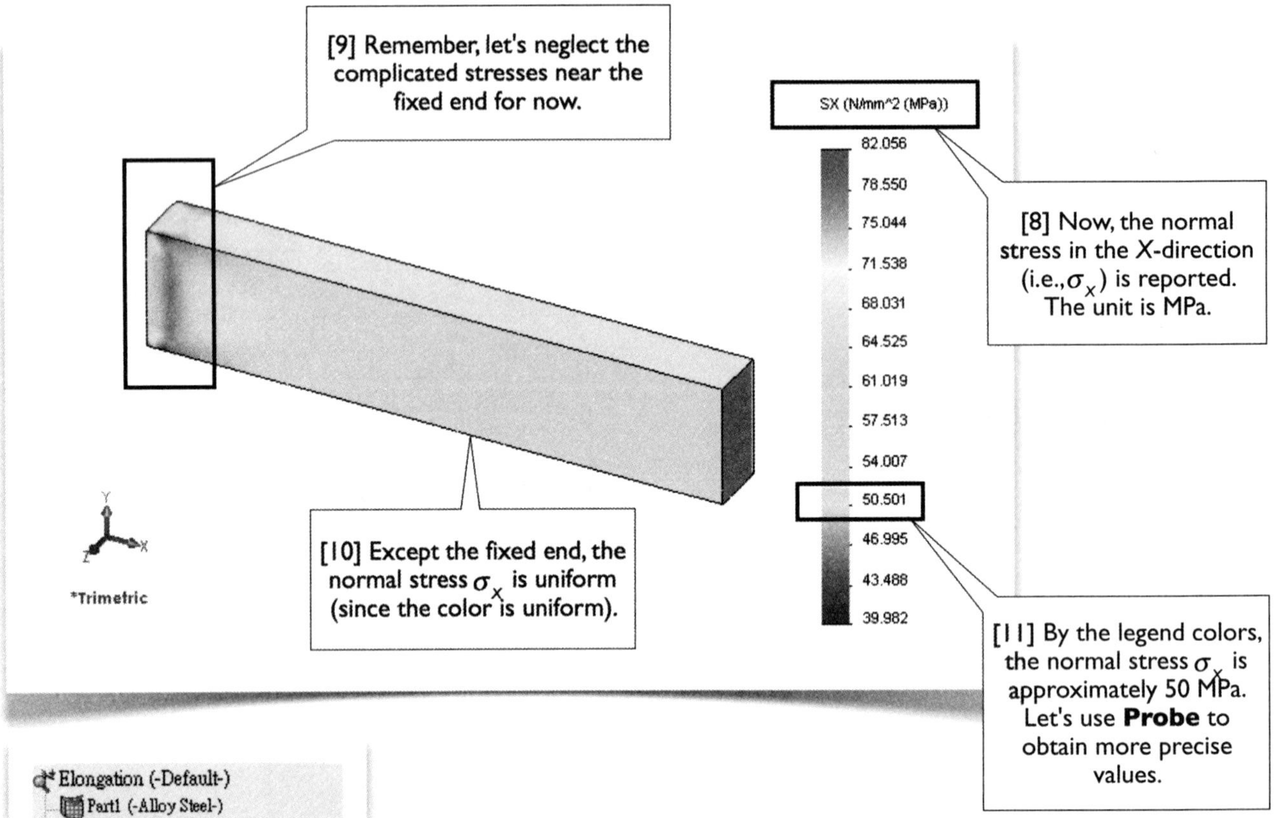
[9] Remember, let's neglect the complicated stresses near the fixed end for now.
SX (N/mm^2 (MPa))
82.056
78.550
75.044
71.538
68.031
64.525
61.019
57.513
54.007
50.501
46.995
43.488
39.982
[8] Now, the normal stress in the X-direction (i.e., σ_x) is reported. The unit is MPa.
[10] Except the fixed end, the normal stress σ_x is uniform (since the color is uniform).
*Trimetric
[11] By the legend colors, the normal stress σ_x is approximately 50 MPa. Let's use **Probe** to obtain more precise values.

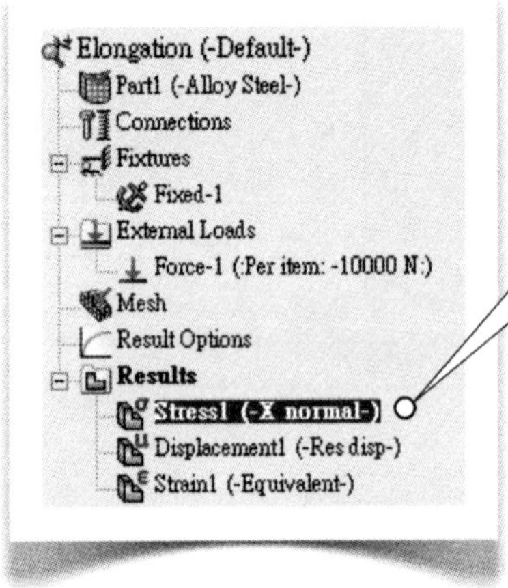
Elongation (-Default-)
Part1 (-Alloy Steel-)
Connections
Fixtures
Fixed-1
External Loads
Force-1 (:Per item: -10000 N:)
Mesh
Result Options
Results
Stress1 (-X normal-)
Displacement1 (-Res disp-)
Strain1 (-Equivalent-)
[12] Right-click **Stress1** and select **Probe**.

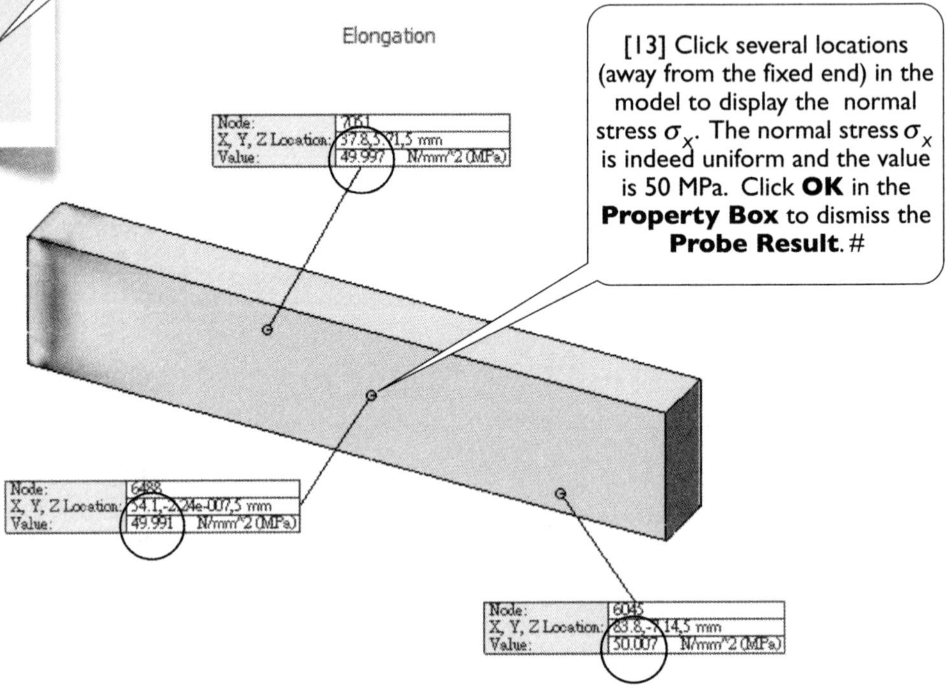
Elongation
[13] Click several locations (away from the fixed end) in the model to display the normal stress σ_x. The normal stress σ_x is indeed uniform and the value is 50 MPa. Click **OK** in the **Property Box** to dismiss the **Probe Result**. #
Node: 7061
X, Y, Z Location: 37.8,3.71,5 mm
Value: 49.997 N/mm^2 (MPa)
Node: 6488
X, Y, Z Location: 54.1,-2.24e-007,5 mm
Value: 49.991 N/mm^2 (MPa)
Node: 6045
X, Y, Z Location: 83.8,-7.14,5 mm
Value: 50.007 N/mm^2 (MPa)

1.1-13 View Other Stress Components

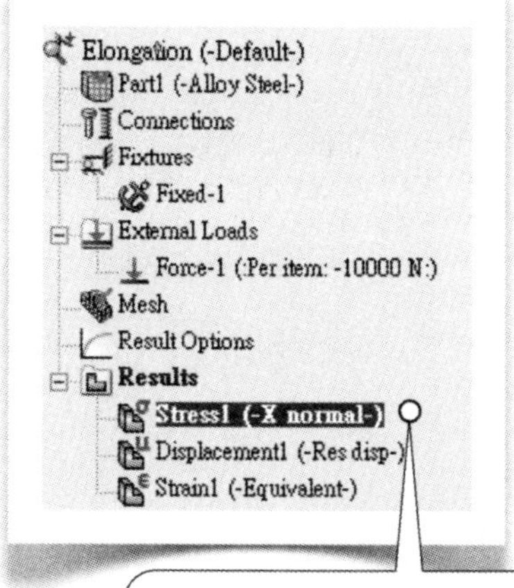

[1] Right-click **Stress1** and select **Edit Definition...** (or double-click it).

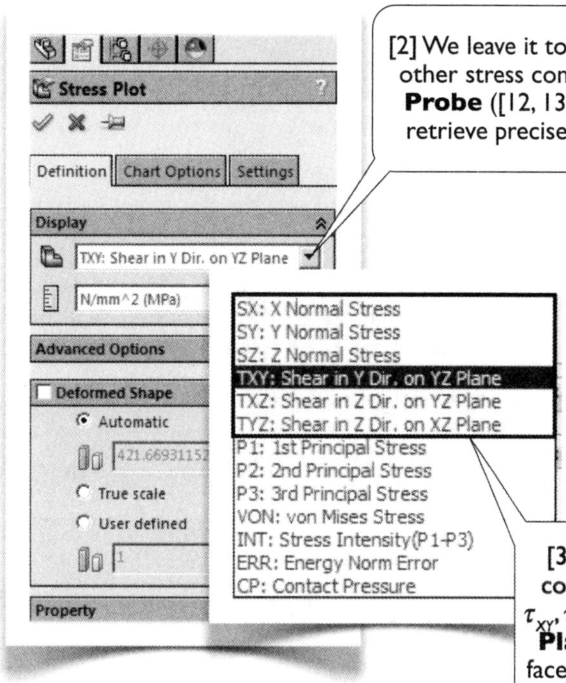

[2] We leave it to you to explore other stress components. Use **Probe** ([12, 13], last page) to retrieve precise stress values.

[3] These are six stress components ($\sigma_X, \sigma_Y, \sigma_Z, \tau_{XY}, \tau_{XZ}, \tau_{YZ}$). Note that **YZ Plane** is the same as *X*-face, and **XZ Plane** is the same as *Y*-face.

Stress Component	Stress Value
σ_X	50 Mpa
σ_Y	0
σ_Z	0
τ_{XY}	0
τ_{XZ}	0
τ_{YZ}	0

[4] Write down each stress component value. The results should be like this. In this example, all stress components are essentially zeros, except σ_X (which is 50 MPa).

[5] The stress state of any point in this cantilever beam can be represented like this. In the next exercise, we'll explore a case in which a shear stress component is non-zero and the stress states are non-uniform. #

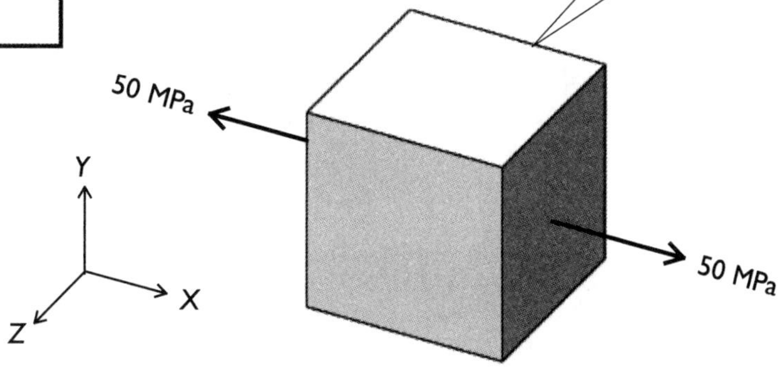

1.1-14 Save the Document and Exit **SolidWorks**

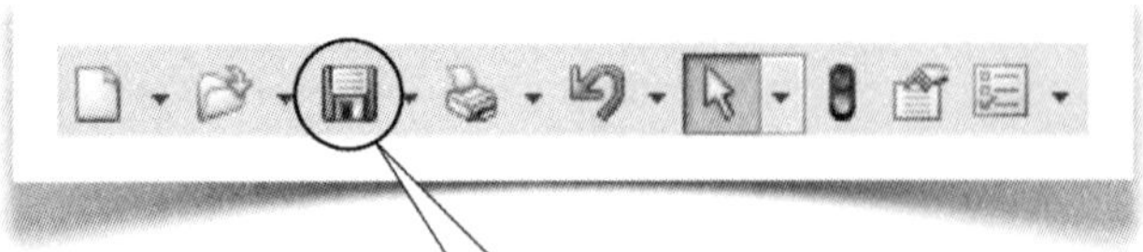

[1] Click **Save** and save the document with the name **Cantilever**. Two files are created in your working folder: **Cantilever.SLDPRT** and **Cantilever-Elongation.CWR**; the former is the main project file, while the later stores the result data generated by a finite element solver. Other files, if any, are not relevant; they can be deleted.

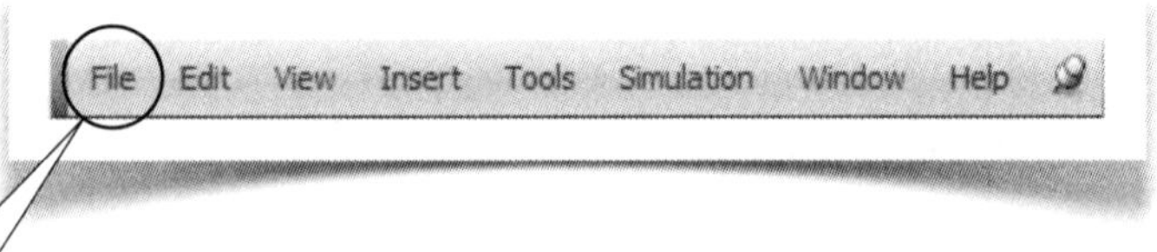

[2] From the **Pull-Down Menus**, select **File>Exit** to exit **SolidWorks**. #

Section 1.2

More on Stress Components

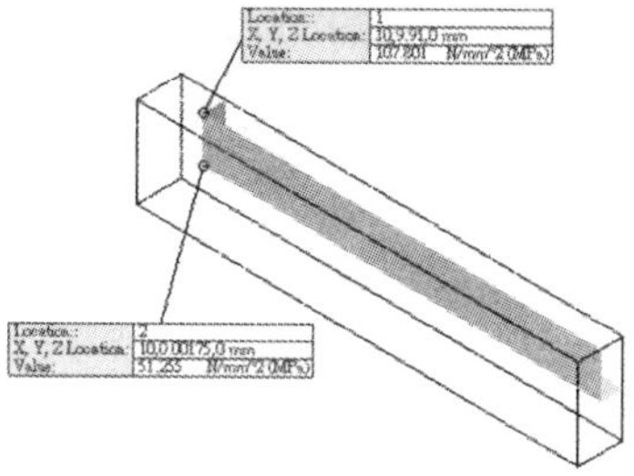

1.2-1 Introduction

[1] In the last section, the stress field is uniform over the body and the only non-zero stress component is σ_x. In this section, we'll use the same model in the last section [2-5] but add a uniformly distributed transversal pressure of 1.0 MPa on the upper face of the beam [6]. In this case, the resulting stress will not be uniform, and non-zero shear stress components exist in the beam.

This section also demonstrates a way to retrieve results at specific locations in a body, namely the **Section Clipping** method.

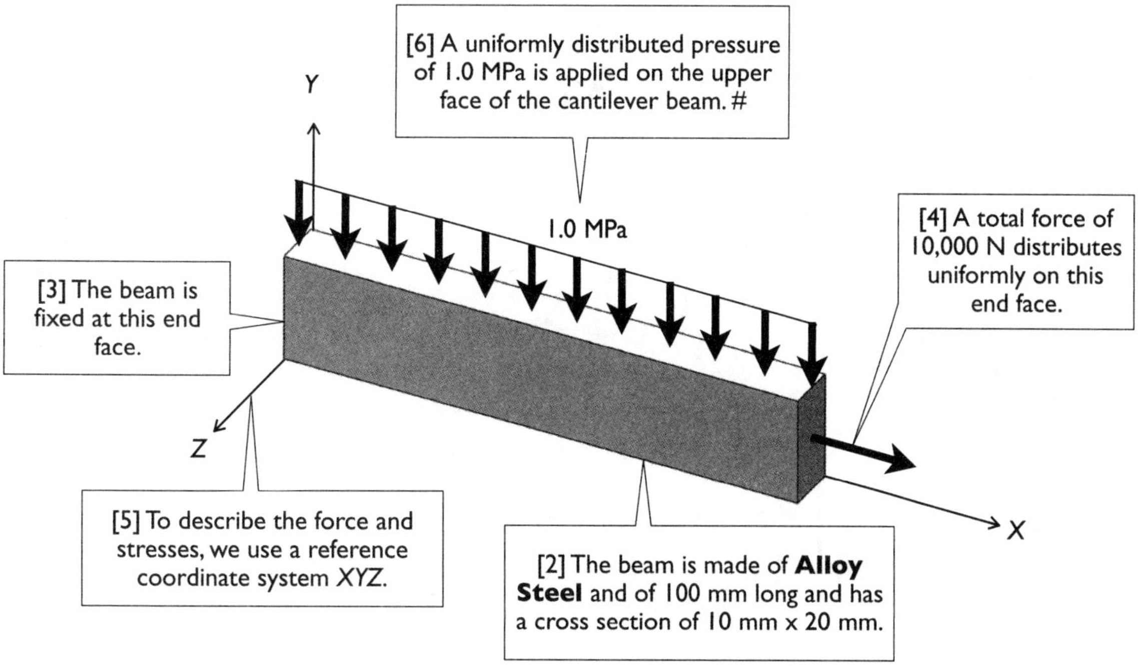

1.2-2 Start Up

[1] Launch **SolidWorks** and open the file **Cantilever** which was saved in Section 1.1. Make sure **SolidWorks Simulation** is loaded (1.1-5, page 13).

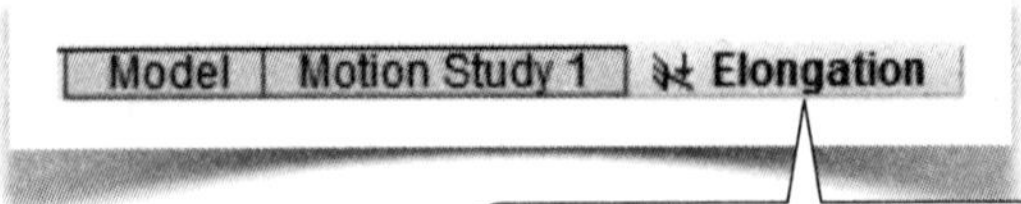

[2] Right-click **Elongation** tab and select **Duplicate** from the **Context Menu**.

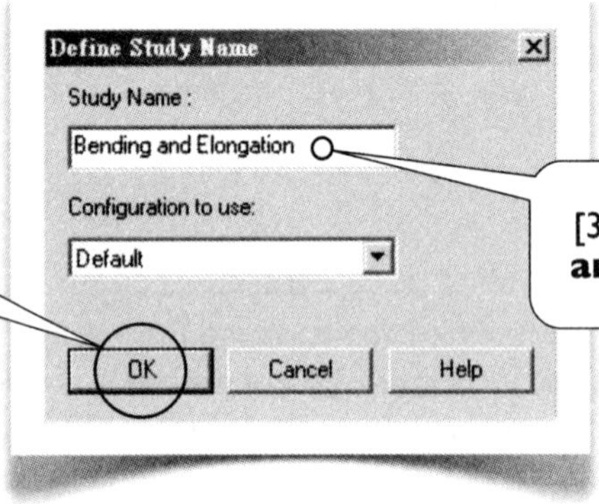

[3] Type **Bending and Elongation**.

[4] Click **OK**.

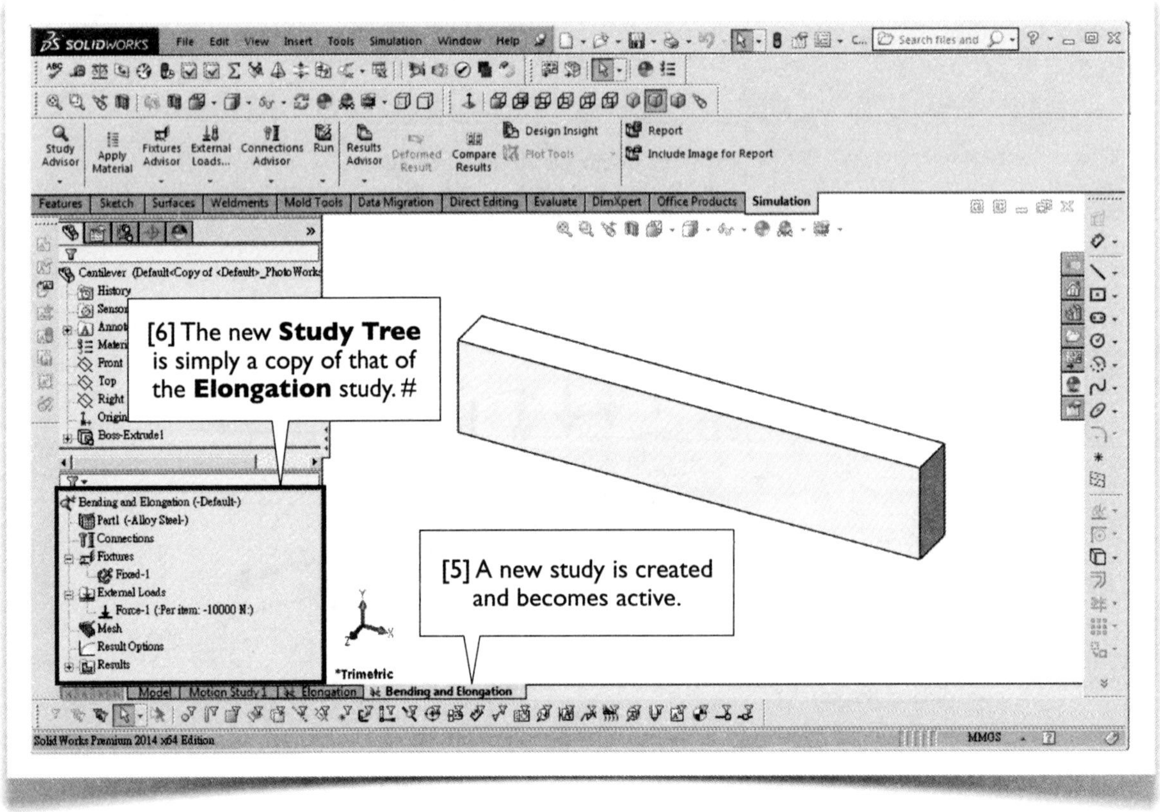

[5] A new study is created and becomes active.

[6] The new **Study Tree** is simply a copy of that of the **Elongation** study. #

1.2-3 Add Transversal Load

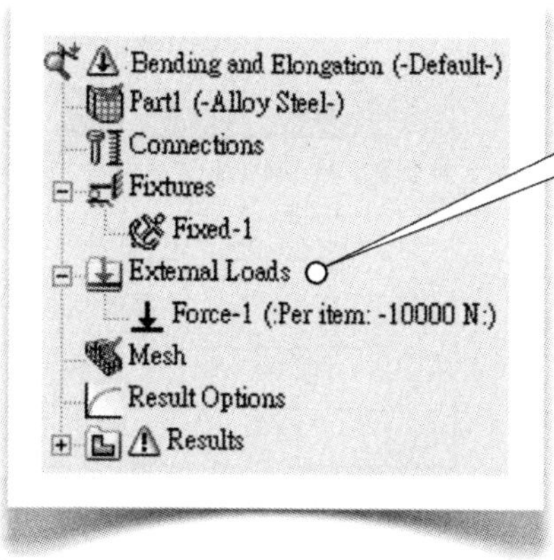

[2] Right-click **External Loads** and select **Pressure...**

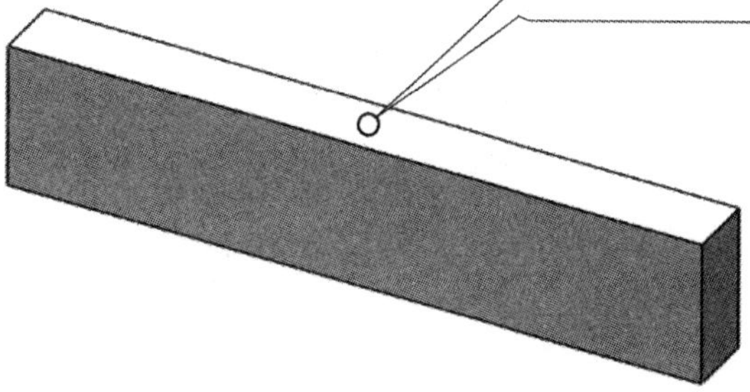

[1] Select the upper face of the cantilever beam.

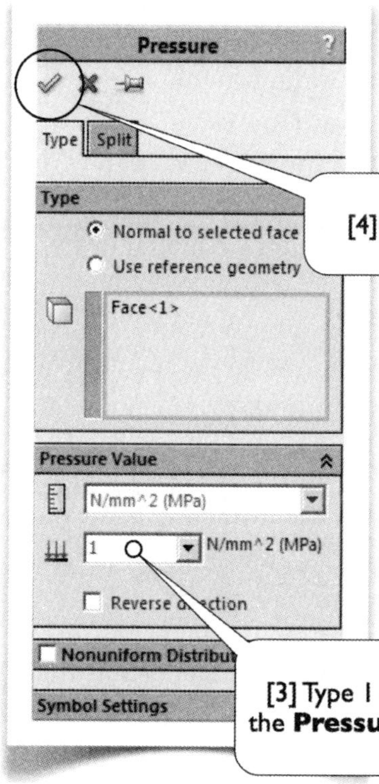

[4] Click **OK**.

[3] Type 1 (MPa) for the **Pressure Value**.

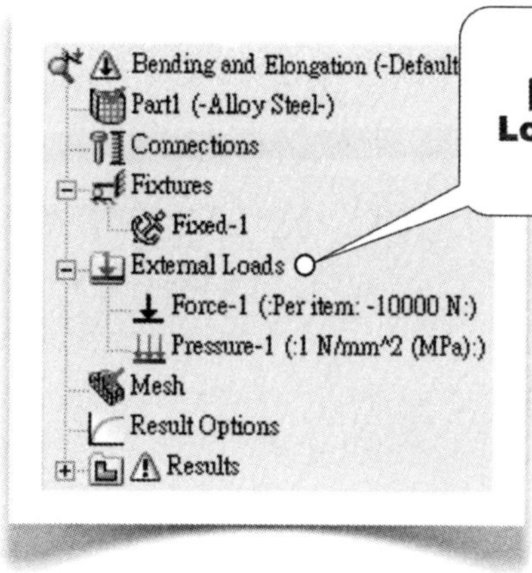

[5] Right-click **External Loads** and select **Hide All**.

[6] In the **Simulation Toolbar**, click **Run**.

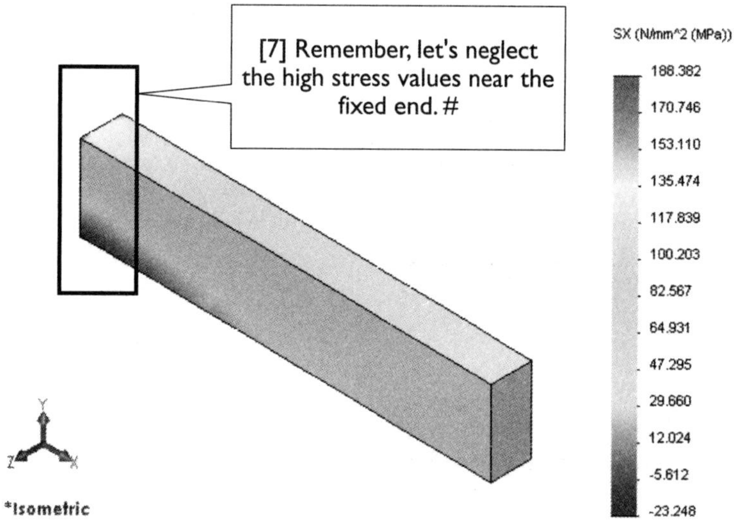

[7] Remember, let's neglect the high stress values near the fixed end. #

1.2-4 Animate the Deformation

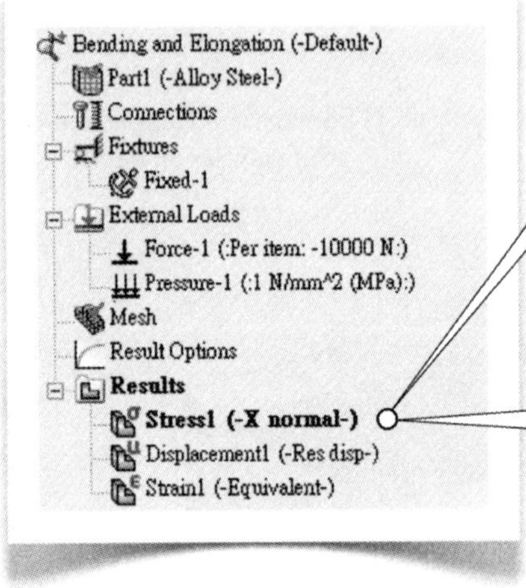

[1] Double-click **Stress1** to edit the definition.

[4] Right-click **Stress1** and select **Animate...**

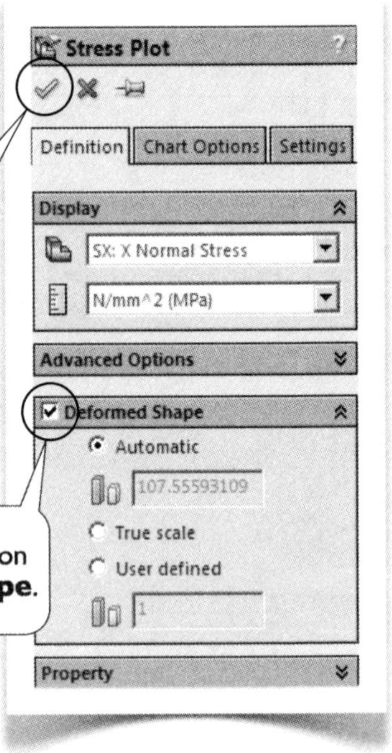

[3] Click **OK**.

[2] Click to turn on **Deformed Shape**.

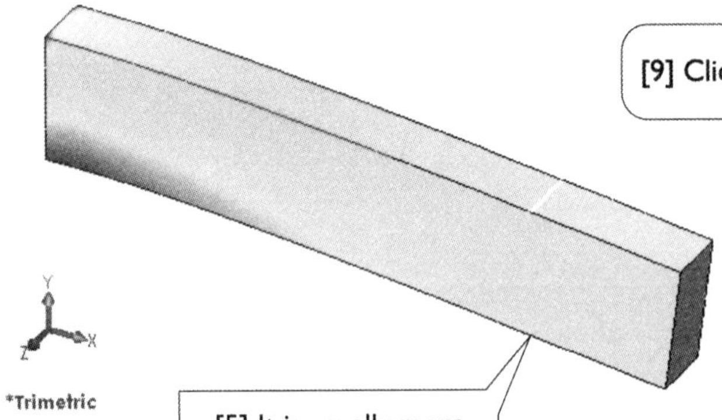

[5] It is usually more informative with an animation.

[9] Click **OK**.

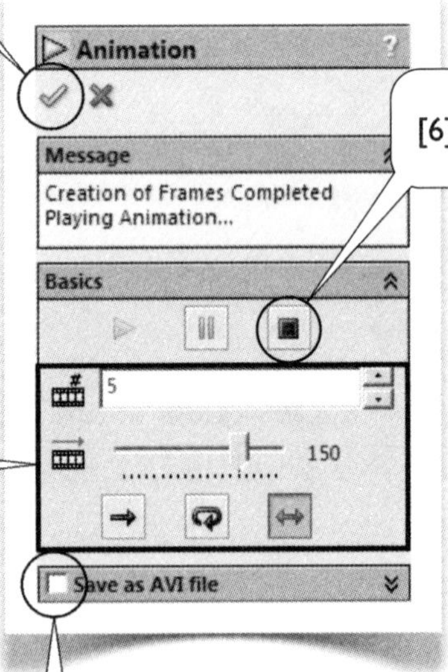

[6] Click **Stop**.

[7] You may adjust these animation parameters to satisfy your needs.

[8] You may save the animation as an **AVI** file.

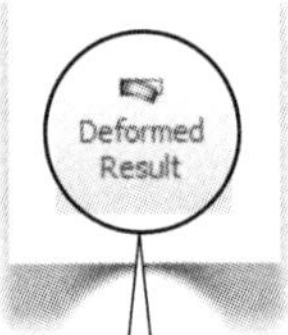

[10] **Deformed Shape** can also be turned on/off by clicking this button in **Simulation Toolbar**. Now, click to turn it off. #

1.2-5 Create Section View

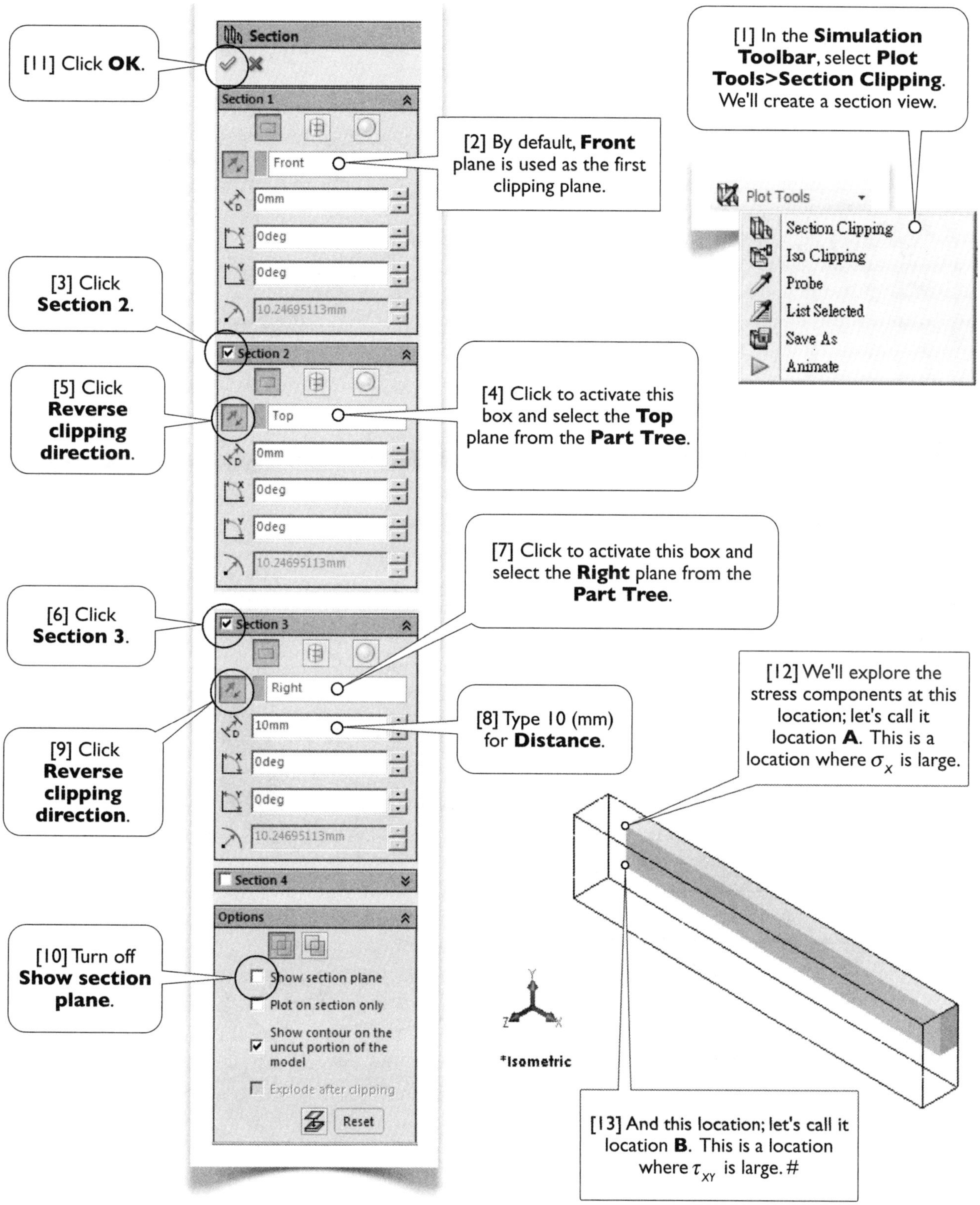

1.2-6 Stress Components at the Locations **A** and **B**

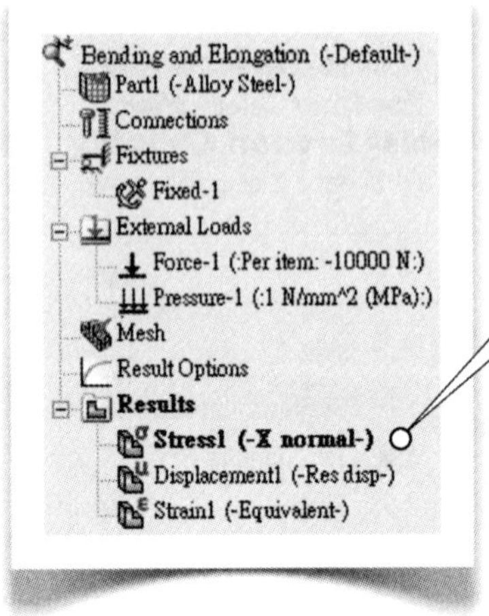

[1] Right-click **Stress1** and select **Probe**.

[2] Click location **A** to display the stress σ_X. You may enlarge the model to locate the corner more accurately.

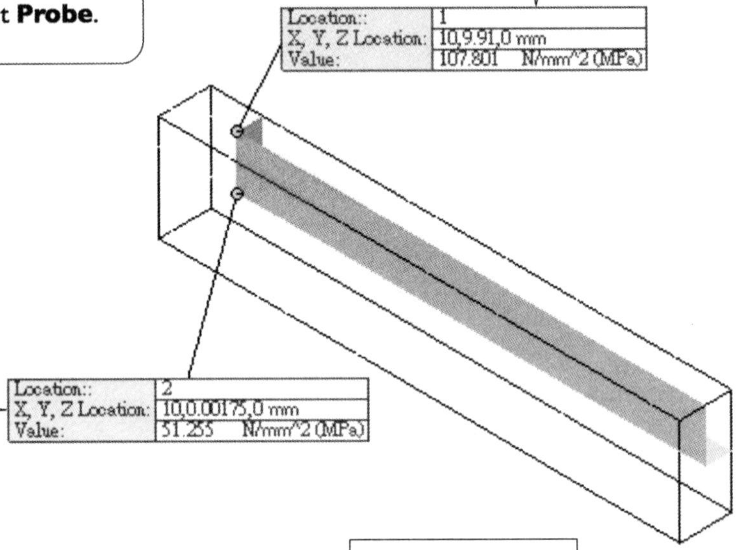

[3] Click location **B** to display the stress σ_X.

Stress Component	Location **A**	Location **B**
σ_X	107.801 Mpa	51.255 Mpa
σ_Y	0	0
σ_Z	0	0
τ_{XY}	0	-6.833 MPa
τ_{XZ}	0	0
τ_{YZ}	0	0

[4] Use **Probe** to explore other stress components and tabulate the data like this. Your stress values may not be exactly the same as here. Note that the shear stress τ_{XY} at location **B** is negative.

[5] The stress state at location **A**.

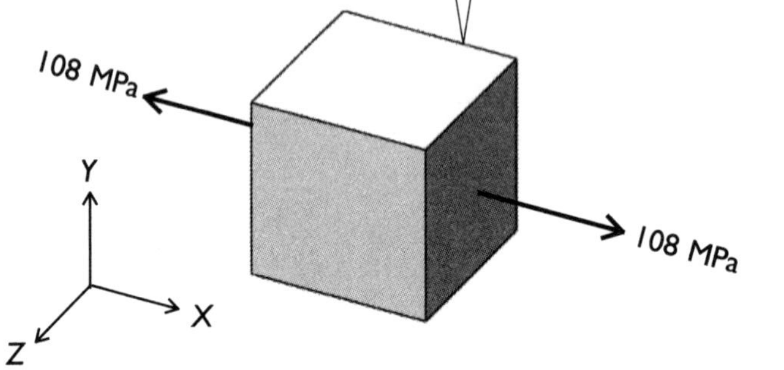

[6] The stress state at location **B**. Note that the shear stresses point to negative directions. #

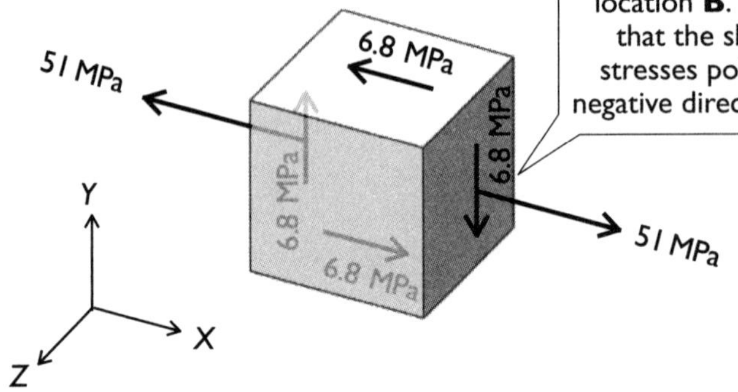

1.2-7 Distribution of σ_x Along Horizontal and Vertical Edges

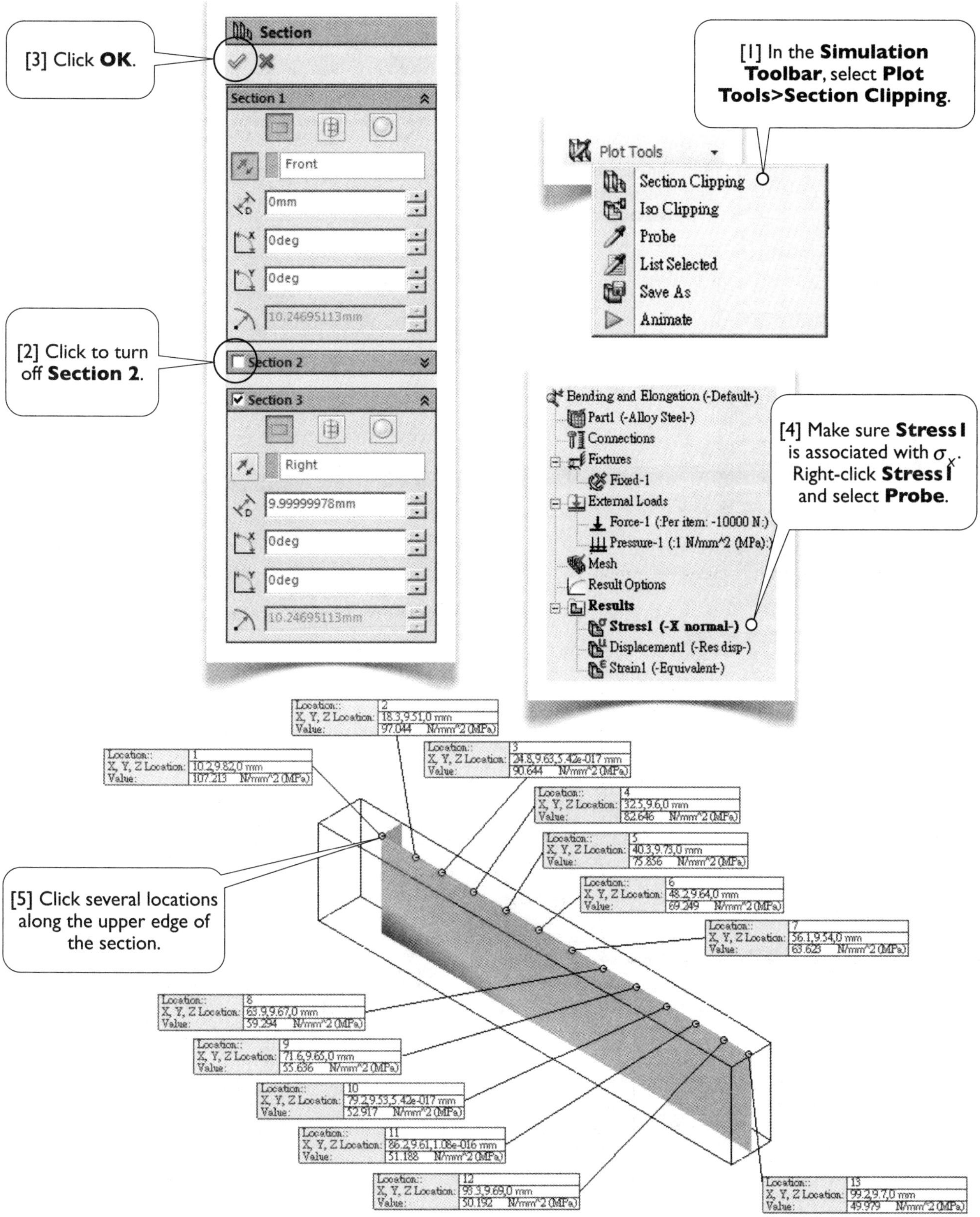

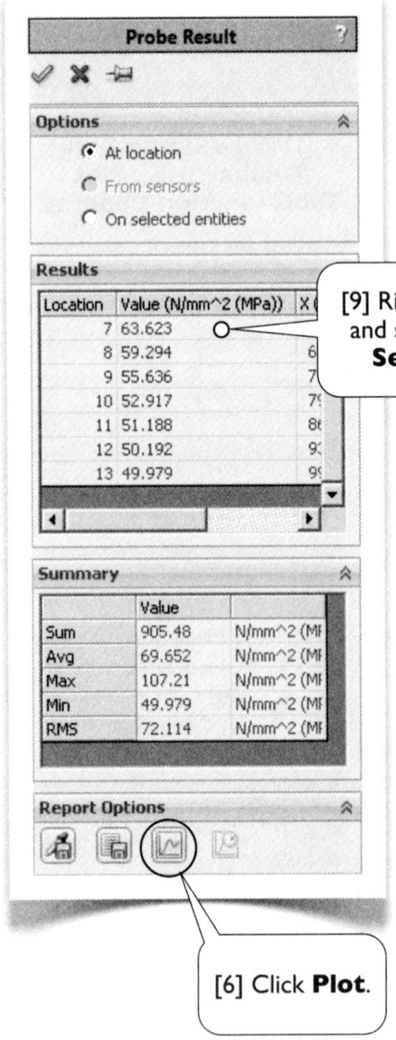
Probe Result
Options
At location
From sensors
On selected entities
Results
Location | Value (N/mm^2 (MPa))
7 63.623
8 59.294
9 55.636
10 52.917
11 51.188
12 50.192
13 49.979
Summary
Value
Sum 905.48 N/mm^2 (MPa)
Avg 69.652 N/mm^2 (MPa)
Max 107.21 N/mm^2 (MPa)
Min 49.979 N/mm^2 (MPa)
RMS 72.114 N/mm^2 (MPa)
Report Options
[9] Right-click here and select **Clear Selections**.
[6] Click **Plot**.

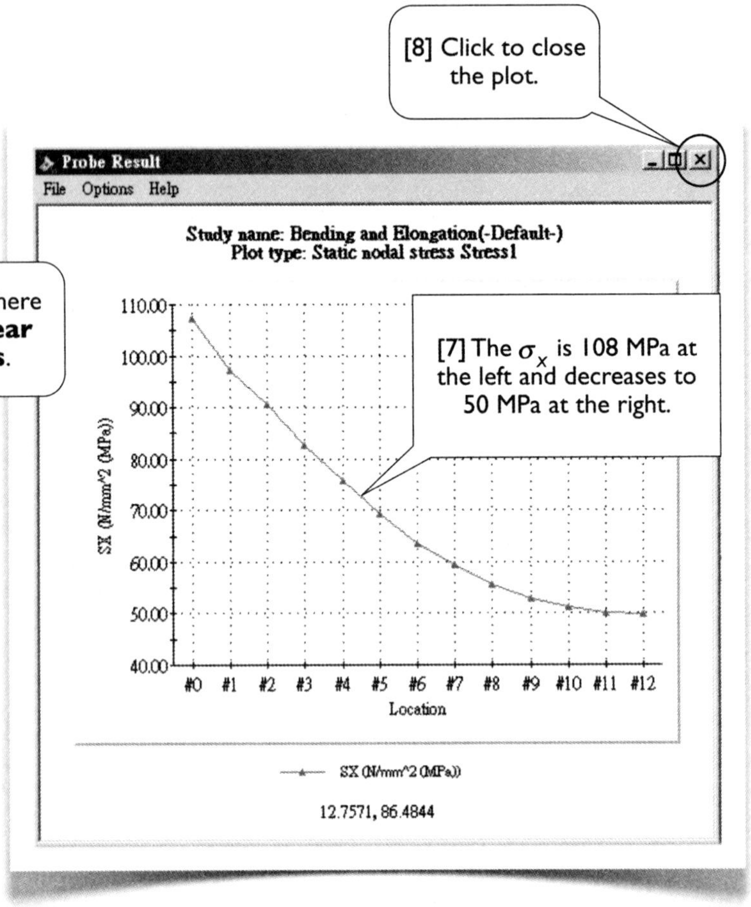
[8] Click to close the plot.
Probe Result
File Options Help
Study name: Bending and Elongation(-Default-)
Plot type: Static nodal stress Stress1
[7] The σ_x is 108 MPa at the left and decreases to 50 MPa at the right.
SX (N/mm^2 (MPa))
Location
SX (N/mm^2 (MPa))
12.7571, 86.4844

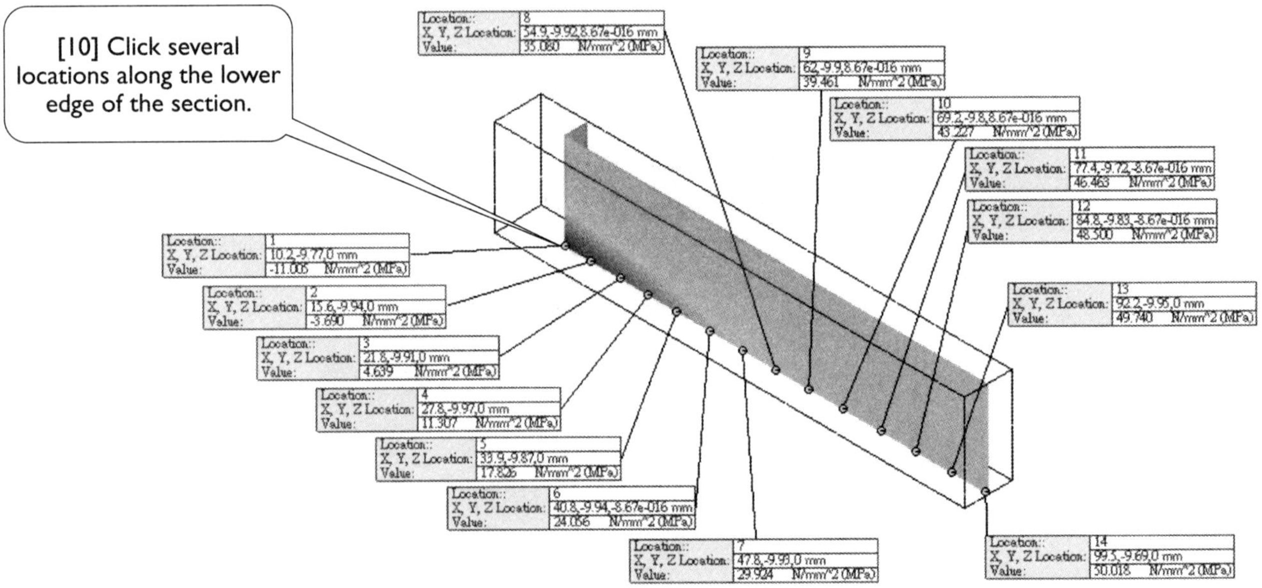
[10] Click several locations along the lower edge of the section.
Location: 1 X, Y, Z Location: 10.2,-9.77,0 mm Value: -11.005 N/mm^2 (MPa)
Location: 2 X, Y, Z Location: 15.6,-9.94,0 mm Value: -3.690 N/mm^2 (MPa)
Location: 3 X, Y, Z Location: 21.8,-9.91,0 mm Value: 4.639 N/mm^2 (MPa)
Location: 4 X, Y, Z Location: 27.8,-9.97,0 mm Value: 11.307 N/mm^2 (MPa)
Location: 5 X, Y, Z Location: 33.9,-9.87,0 mm Value: 17.826 N/mm^2 (MPa)
Location: 6 X, Y, Z Location: 40.8,-9.94,-8.67e-016 mm Value: 24.056 N/mm^2 (MPa)
Location: 7 X, Y, Z Location: 47.8,-9.93,0 mm Value: 29.924 N/mm^2 (MPa)
Location: 8 X, Y, Z Location: 54.9,-9.92,8.67e-016 mm Value: 35.080 N/mm^2 (MPa)
Location: 9 X, Y, Z Location: 62,-9.9,8.67e-016 mm Value: 39.461 N/mm^2 (MPa)
Location: 10 X, Y, Z Location: 69.2,-9.8,8.67e-016 mm Value: 43.227 N/mm^2 (MPa)
Location: 11 X, Y, Z Location: 77.4,-9.72,-8.67e-016 mm Value: 46.463 N/mm^2 (MPa)
Location: 12 X, Y, Z Location: 84.8,-9.83,-8.67e-016 mm Value: 48.500 N/mm^2 (MPa)
Location: 13 X, Y, Z Location: 92.2,-9.95,0 mm Value: 49.740 N/mm^2 (MPa)
Location: 14 X, Y, Z Location: 99.5,-9.69,0 mm Value: 50.018 N/mm^2 (MPa)

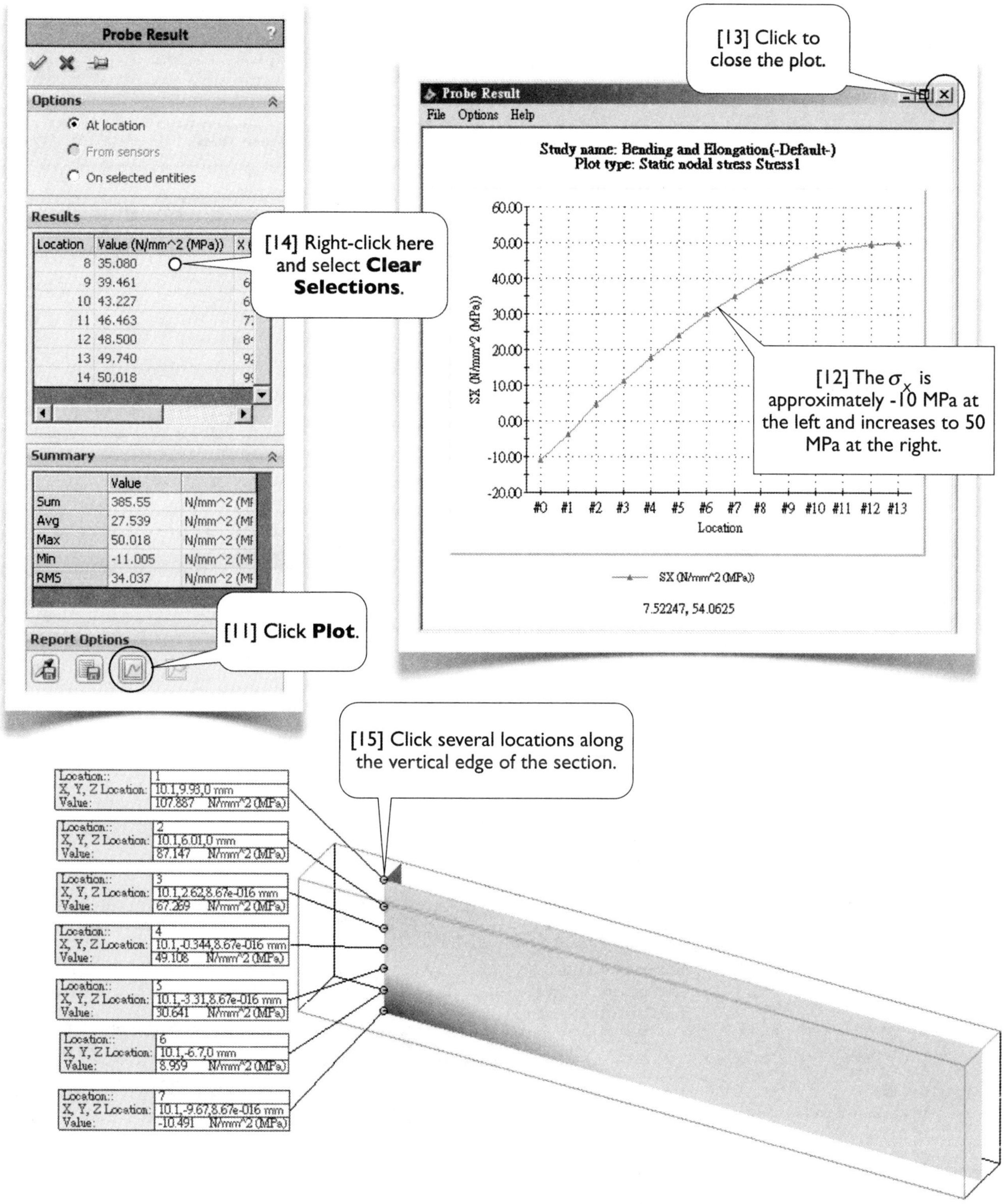
Probe Result
Options
At location
From sensors
On selected entities
Results
Location Value (N/mm^2 (MPa))
8 35.080
9 39.461
10 43.227
11 46.463
12 48.500
13 49.740
14 50.018
Summary
Value
Sum 385.55 N/mm^2
Avg 27.539 N/mm^2
Max 50.018 N/mm^2
Min -11.005 N/mm^2
RMS 34.037 N/mm^2
Report Options
[14] Right-click here and select **Clear Selections**.
[11] Click **Plot**.
[13] Click to close the plot.
Probe Result
File Options Help
Study name: Bending and Elongation(-Default-)
Plot type: Static nodal stress Stress1
SX (N/mm^2 (MPa))
Location
SX (N/mm^2 (MPa))
7.52247, 54.0625
[12] The σ_x is approximately -10 MPa at the left and increases to 50 MPa at the right.
[15] Click several locations along the vertical edge of the section.
Location:: 1
X, Y, Z Location: 10.1,9.93,0 mm
Value: 107.887 N/mm^2 (MPa)
Location:: 2
X, Y, Z Location: 10.1,6.01,0 mm
Value: 87.147 N/mm^2 (MPa)
Location:: 3
X, Y, Z Location: 10.1,2.62,8.67e-016 mm
Value: 67.269 N/mm^2 (MPa)
Location:: 4
X, Y, Z Location: 10.1,-0.344,8.67e-016 mm
Value: 49.108 N/mm^2 (MPa)
Location:: 5
X, Y, Z Location: 10.1,-3.31,8.67e-016 mm
Value: 30.641 N/mm^2 (MPa)
Location:: 6
X, Y, Z Location: 10.1,-6.7,0 mm
Value: 8.959 N/mm^2 (MPa)
Location:: 7
X, Y, Z Location: 10.1,-9.67,8.67e-016 mm
Value: -10.491 N/mm^2 (MPa)

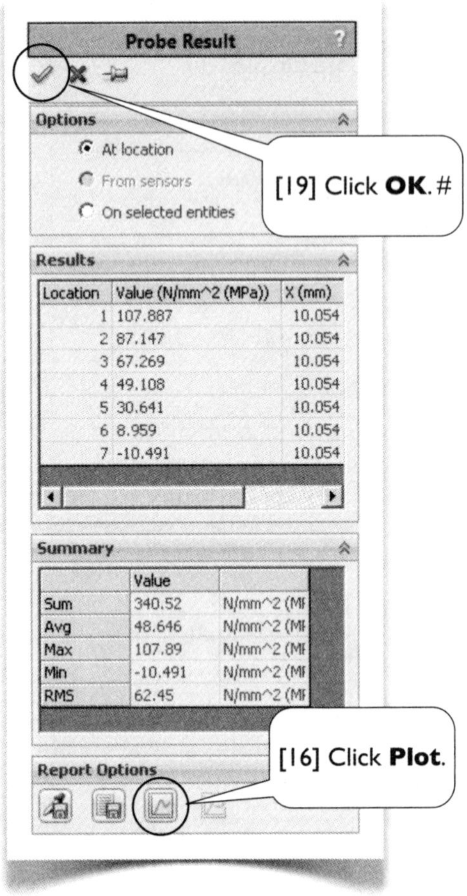

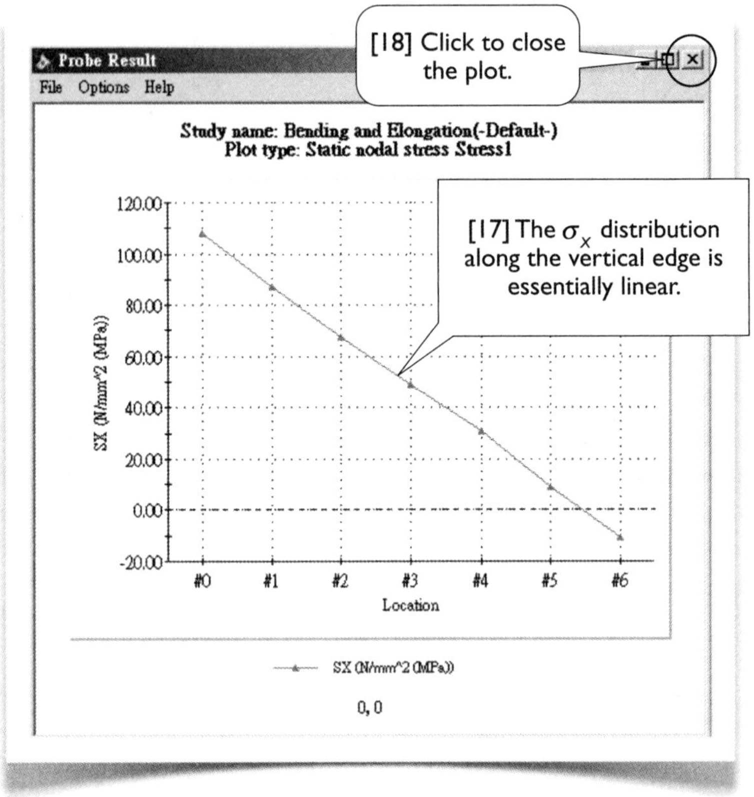

1.2-8 Distribution of τ_{XY} Along a Vertical Edge

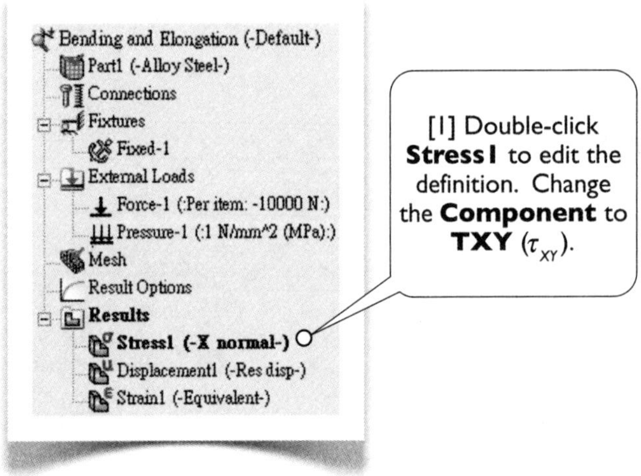

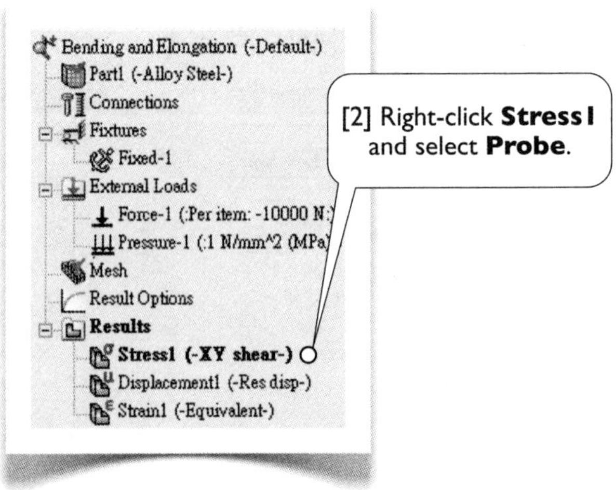

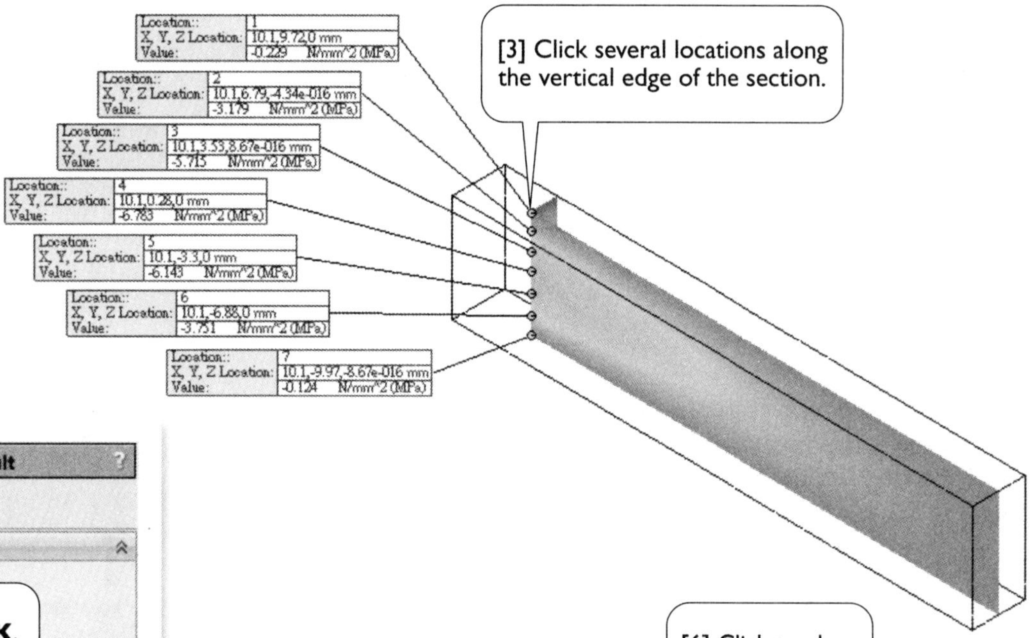
[3] Click several locations along the vertical edge of the section.
Location:: 1
X, Y, Z Location: 10.1,9.72,0 mm
Value: -0.229 N/mm^2 (MPa)
Location:: 2
X, Y, Z Location: 10.1,6.79,-4.34e-016 mm
Value: -3.179 N/mm^2 (MPa)
Location:: 3
X, Y, Z Location: 10.1,3.53,8.67e-016 mm
Value: -5.715 N/mm^2 (MPa)
Location:: 4
X, Y, Z Location: 10.1,0.28,0 mm
Value: -6.783 N/mm^2 (MPa)
Location:: 5
X, Y, Z Location: 10.1,-3.3,0 mm
Value: -6.143 N/mm^2 (MPa)
Location:: 6
X, Y, Z Location: 10.1,-6.88,0 mm
Value: -3.751 N/mm^2 (MPa)
Location:: 7
X, Y, Z Location: 10.1,-9.97,-8.67e-016 mm
Value: -0.124 N/mm^2 (MPa)

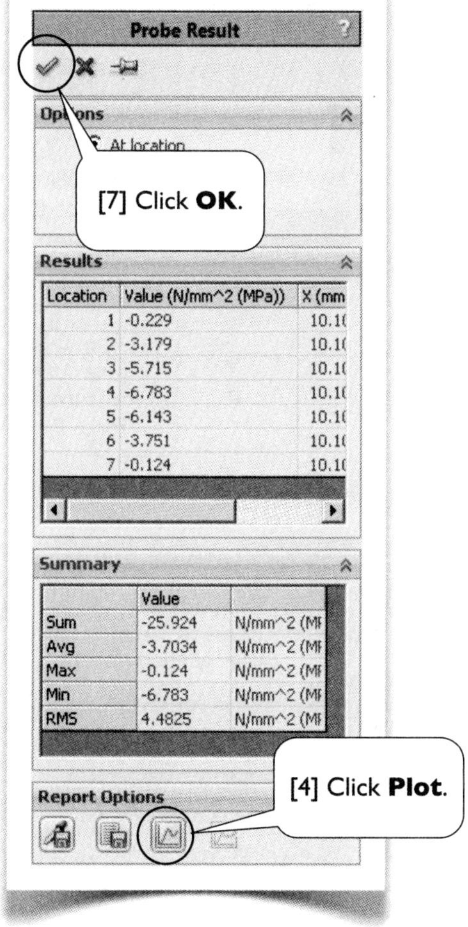
Probe Result
Options
At location
[7] Click **OK**.
Results
Location | Value (N/mm^2 (MPa)) | X (mm
1 -0.229 10.1
2 -3.179 10.1
3 -5.715 10.1
4 -6.783 10.1
5 -6.143 10.1
6 -3.751 10.1
7 -0.124 10.1
Summary
Value
Sum -25.924 N/mm^2 (MP
Avg -3.7034 N/mm^2 (MP
Max -0.124 N/mm^2 (MP
Min -6.783 N/mm^2 (MP
RMS 4.4825 N/mm^2 (MP
Report Options
[4] Click **Plot**.

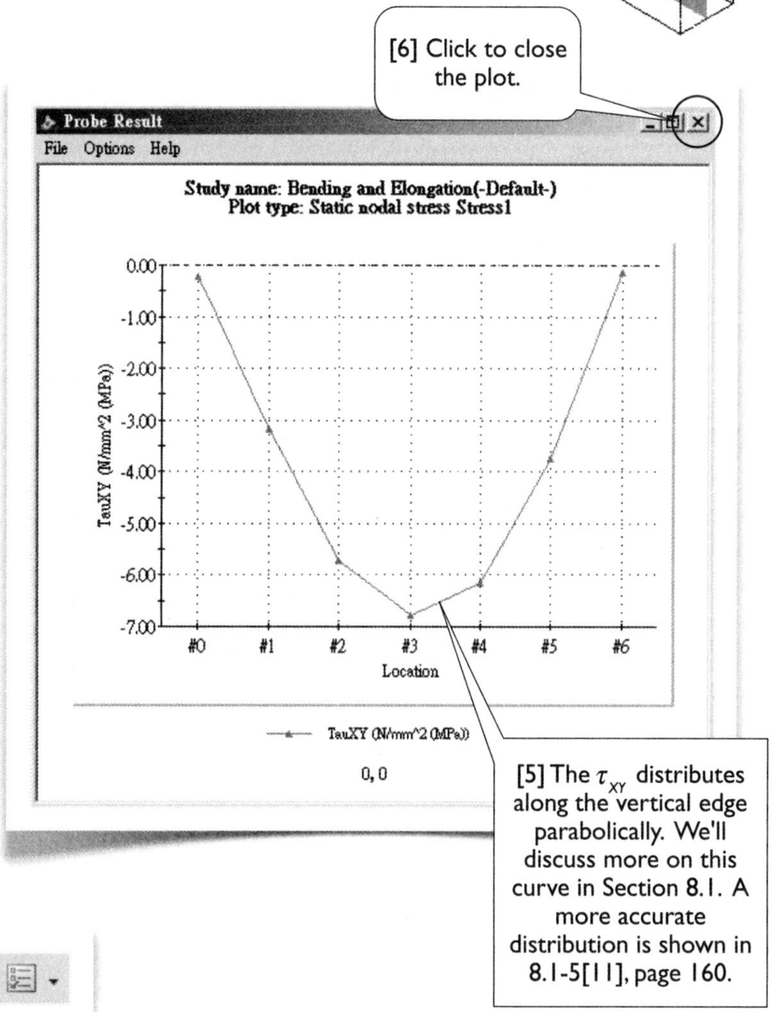
[6] Click to close the plot.
Probe Result
File Options Help
Study name: Bending and Elongation(-Default-)
Plot type: Static nodal stress Stress1
0.00
-1.00
-2.00
-3.00
-4.00
-5.00
-6.00
-7.00
TauXY (N/mm^2 (MPa))
#0 #1 #2 #3 #4 #5 #6
Location
TauXY (N/mm^2 (MPa))
0, 0
[5] The τ_{XY} distributes along the vertical edge parabolically. We'll discuss more on this curve in Section 8.1. A more accurate distribution is shown in 8.1-5[11], page 160.

[8] Save the document and exit **SolidWorks**. #

Section 1.3

Stresses in a C-Bar

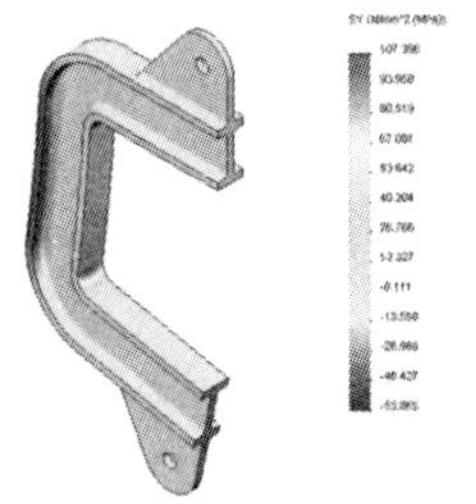

1.3-1 Introduction

[1] The C-shaped bar is made of an alloy steel and used as a dynamometer, a device to measure the magnitude of a force *P* [2]. A strain gauge is usually attached to the surface of a location as shown [3], and the measured strain is used to calculate the force *P*.

In this exercise, we will create a 3D solid model for the C-bar [4-6] and perform a static structural analysis under a force P = 2000 N. We'll examine the stress states at two locations, **A** [7, 8] and **B** [9, 10]. We examine location **A** since it is where the strain gauge situated and its normal stress σ_Y is high. Location **B** is arbitrarily chosen for its non-zero shear stress τ_{XY}.

This section also demonstrates a way to obtain stress results at specific location, namely using **Sensors**.

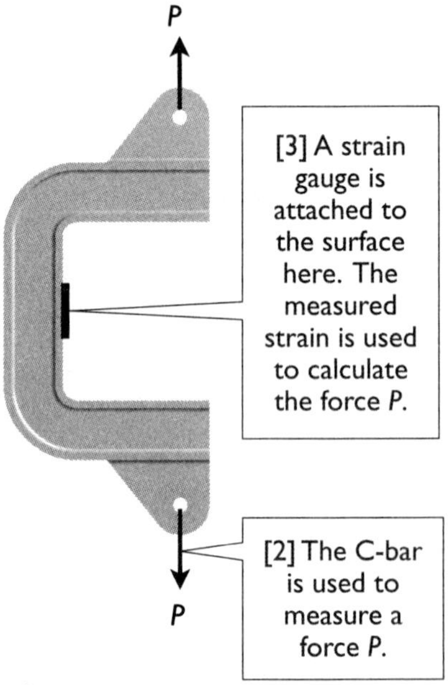

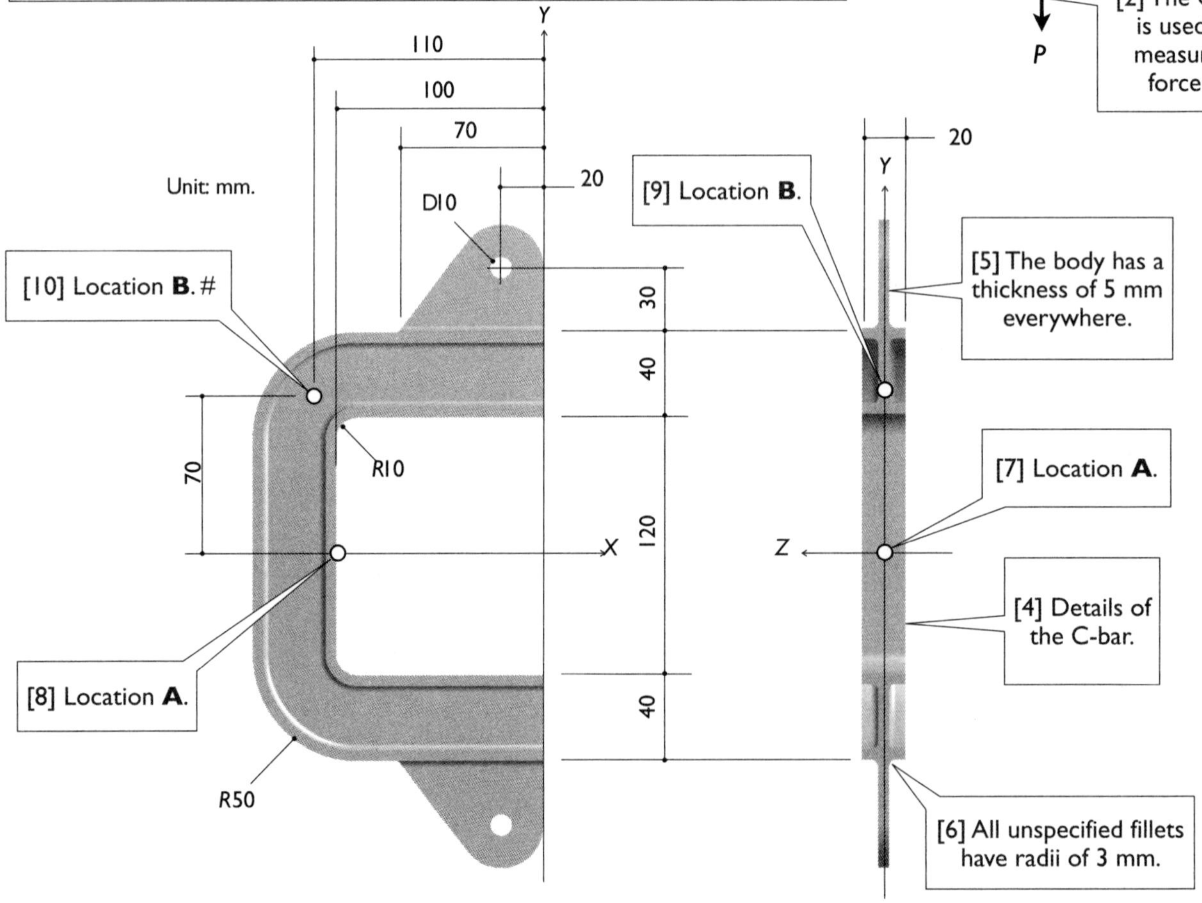

1.3-2 Start Up

[1] Launch **SolidWorks** and create a new part. Set up **MMGS** unit system with zero decimal places for the length unit. #

1.3-3 Create a Sketch for the Sweeping Path

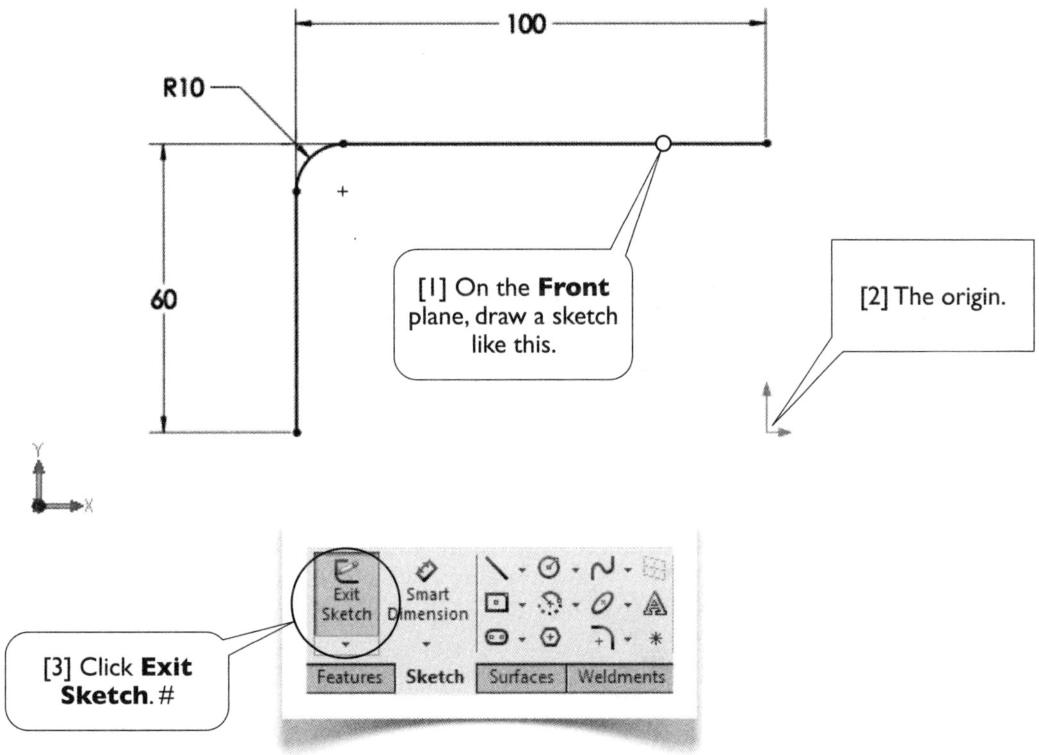

1.3-4 Create a New Plane

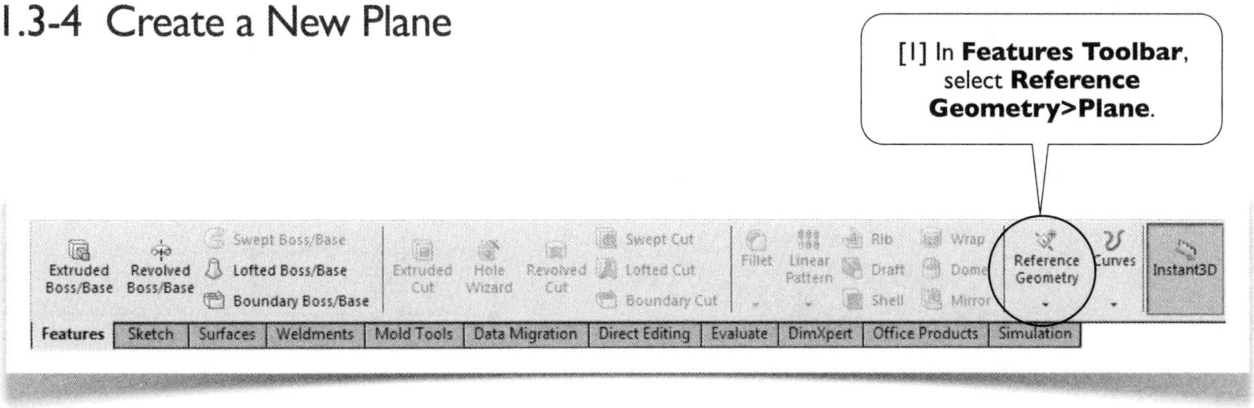

[6] Click **OK**. #

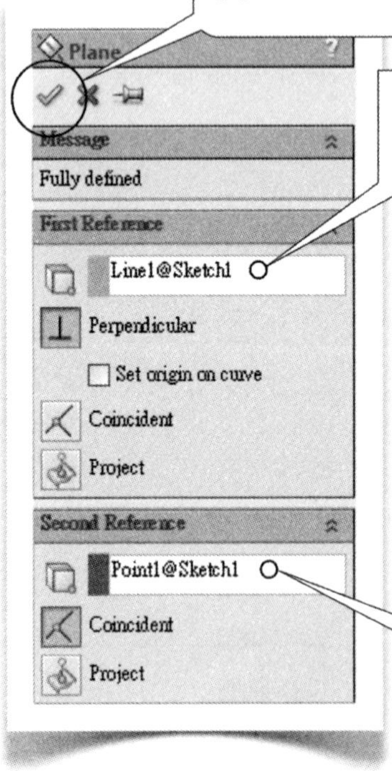

[3] The line is used as **First Reference**.

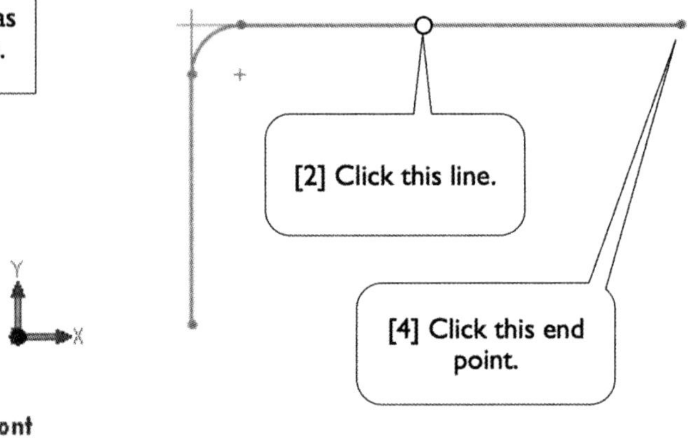

[2] Click this line.

[4] Click this end point.

[5] The point is used as **Second Reference**. A plane normal to the **First Reference** and passing through the **Second Reference** will be created.

1.3-5 Create a Sketch for the Profile

[1] While the new plane (**Plane1**) is highlighted in the **Part Tree**, click **Sketch**.

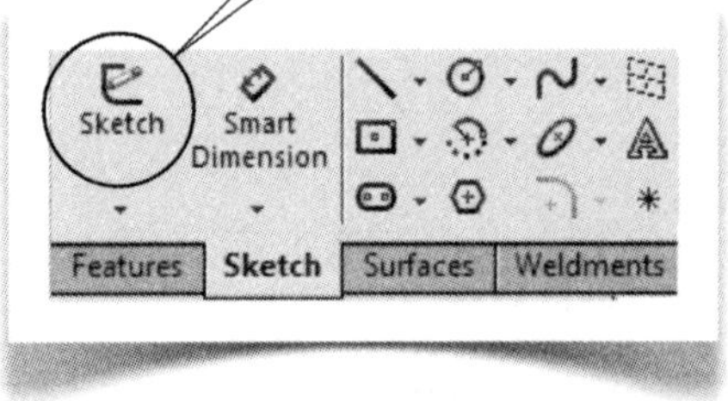

[2] In the **Standard Views Toolbar,** Click **Normal To**.

[3] Draw a sketch like this.

[4] This is the line of symmetry. #

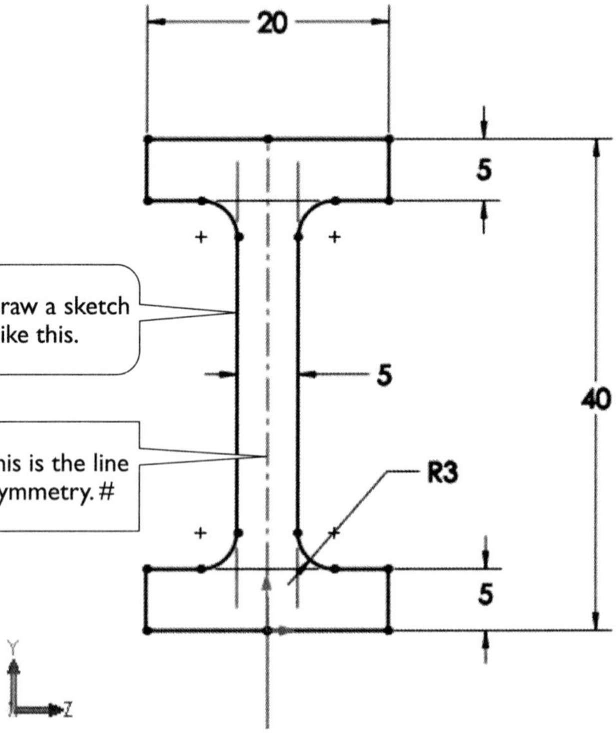

1.3-6 Create a Solid Body Using **Sweep**

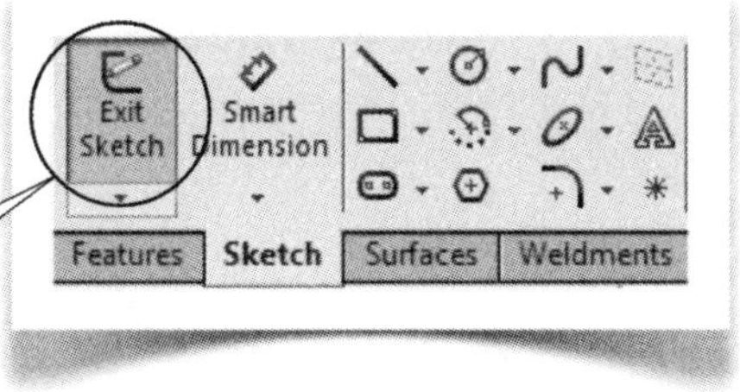

[1] Click **Exit Sketch**.

[2] In **Features Toolbar**, click **Swept Boss/Base**.

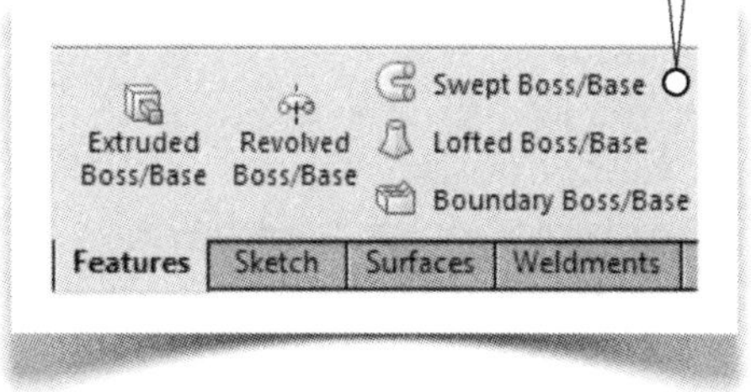

[5] Click **OK**.

[3] The profile sketch (**Sketch2**) should be pre-selected. If not, select it from the **Part Tree**.

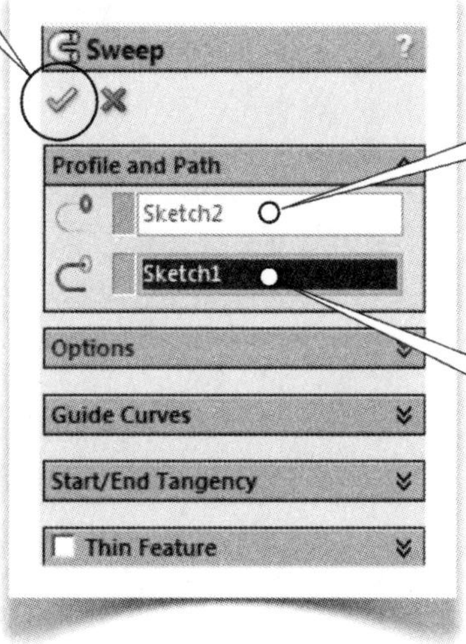

[4] Select the path sketch (**Sketch1**) from the **Part Tree**.

[7] A solid body is created. #

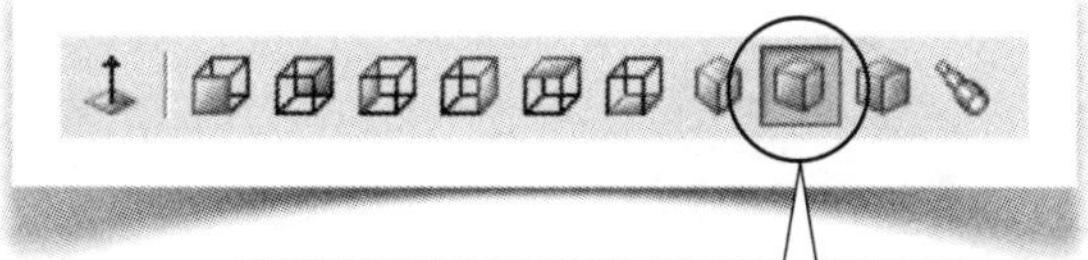

[6] In the **Standard Views Toolbar,** Click **Trimetric**. Also, in the **Head-Up Toolbar**, turn-off **View Planes**.

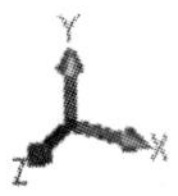

*Trimetric

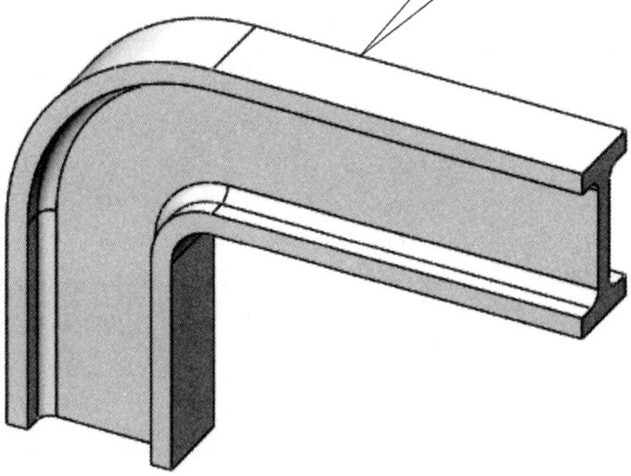

1.3-7 Create an Ear

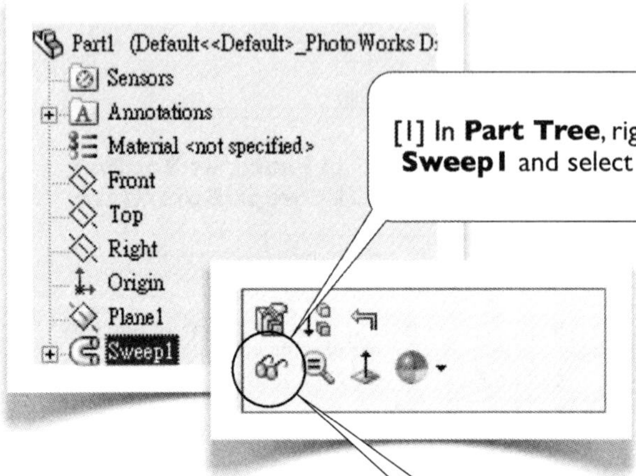

[1] In **Part Tree**, right-click **Sweep1** and select **Hide**.

[2] In the **Front** plane, draw a sketch like this. Click **Exit Sketch**.

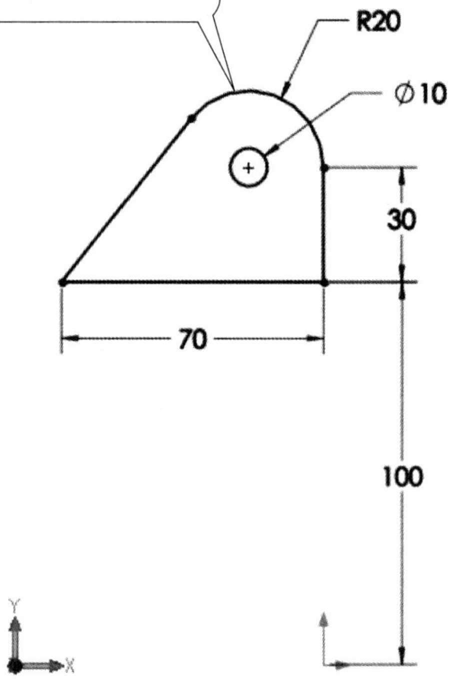

[3] Right-click **Sweep1** and select **Show**.

[4] In the **Part Tree**, click to highlight the newly created sketch (**Sketch3**) and, In **Features Toolbar**, click **Extruded Boss/Base**.

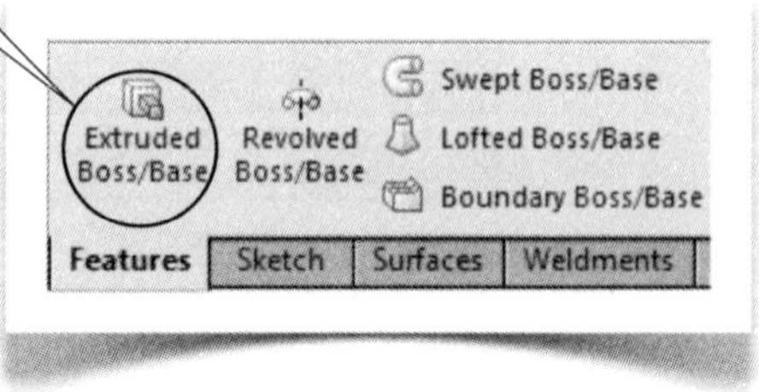

[5] Select **Mid Plane**.

[6] Type 5 (mm).

[7] Make sure **Merge result** is enabled.

[8] Click **OK**. #

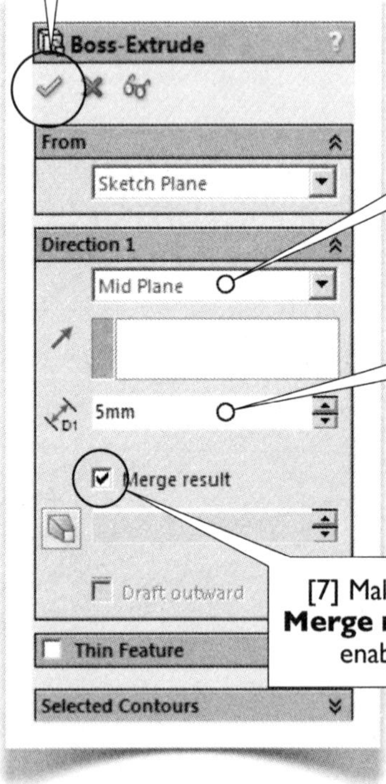

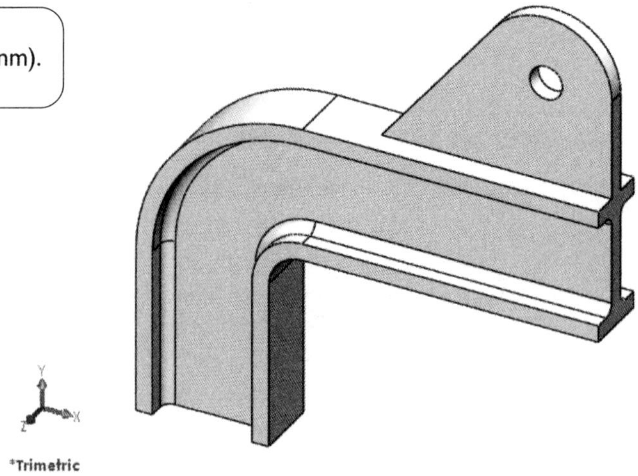

1.3-8 Create Fillets

[1] In **Features Toolbar**, click **Fillet**.

[2] Create fillets of 3 mm on both sides. #

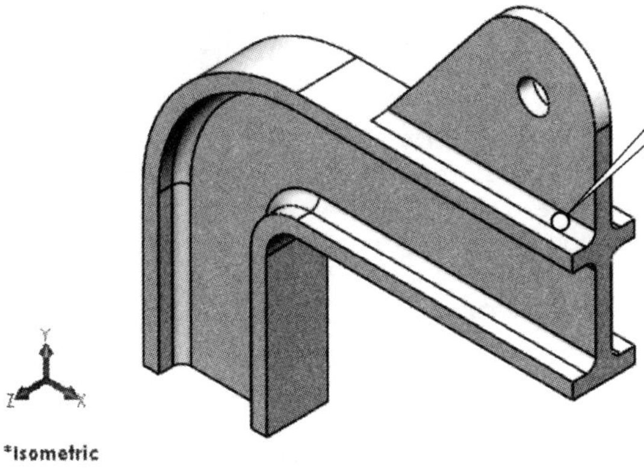

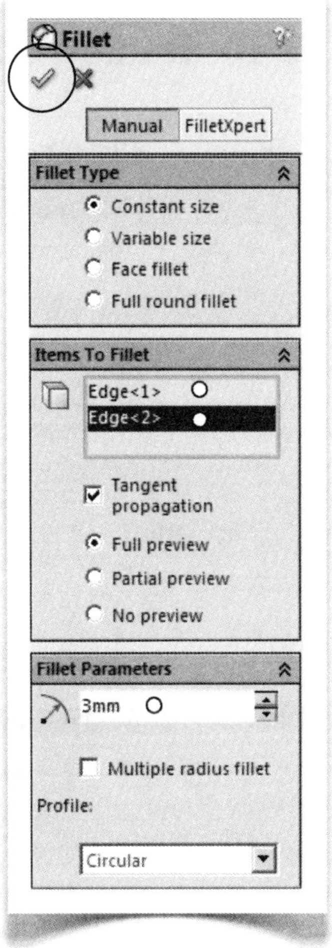

1.3-9 Mirror the Body

[1] In **Features Toolbar**, click **Mirror**.

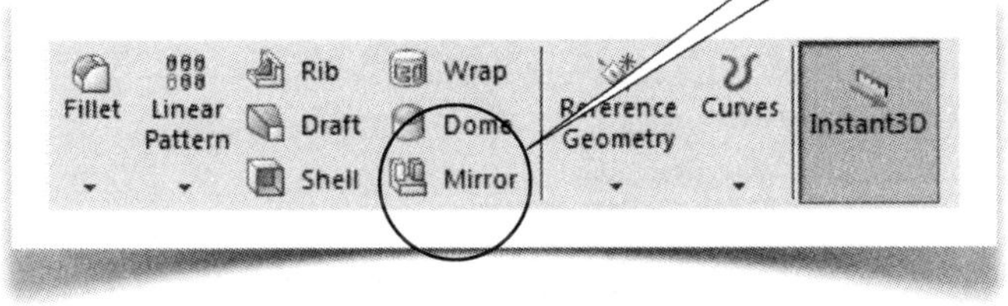

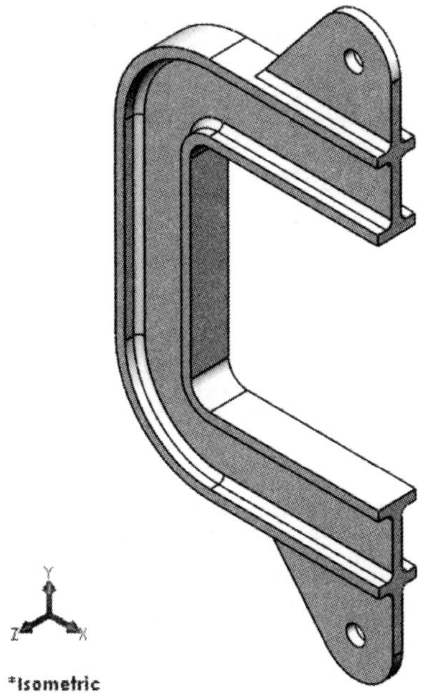

[2] From **Part Tree**, select **Top** plane.

[3] Click **Bodies to Mirror**.

[4] In the **Graphics Area**, select the body.

[5] Click **OK**. #

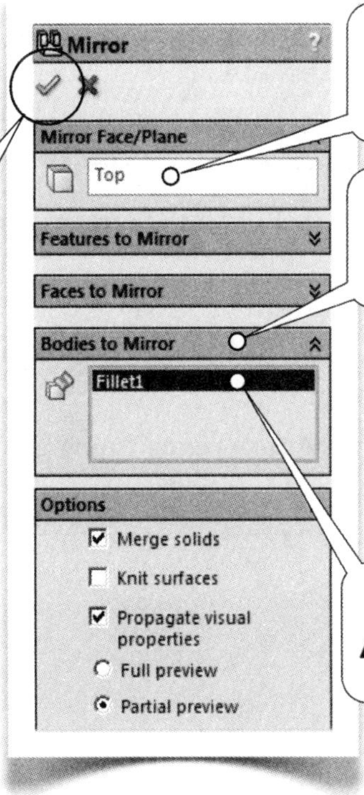

1.3-10 Create **Sensor** at Location **A**

[1] In **Features Toolbar**, select **Reference Geometry>Point**.

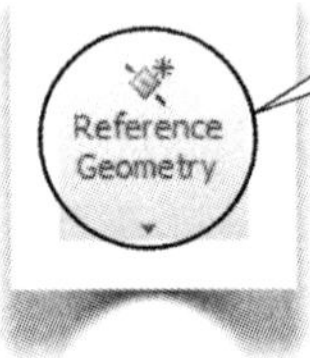

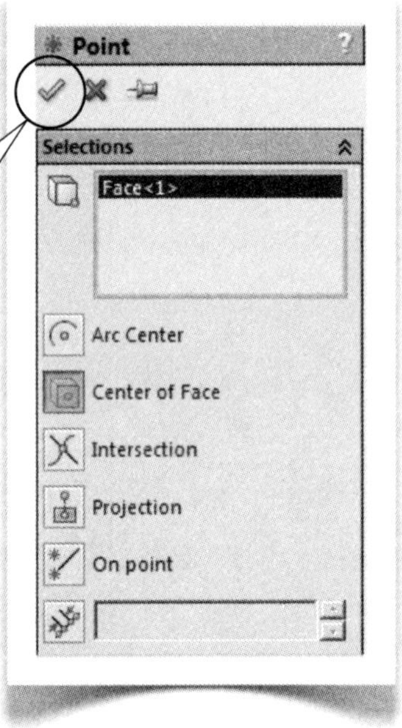

[3] Click **OK**.

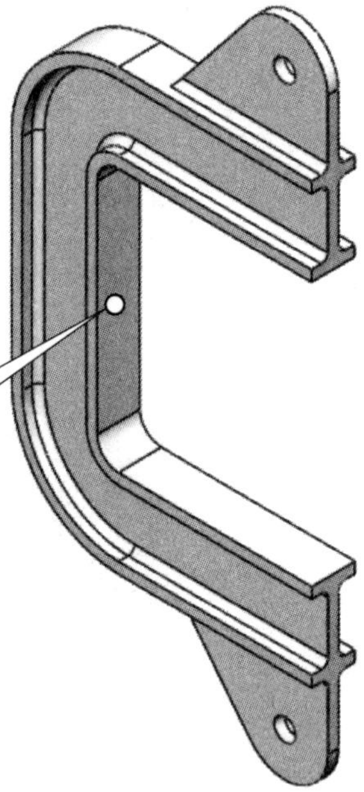

[2] Click this face. A **Reference Point** is created at the center of the face. This is the location **A**, where we want to set up a **Sensor**.

[9] Click **OK**. #

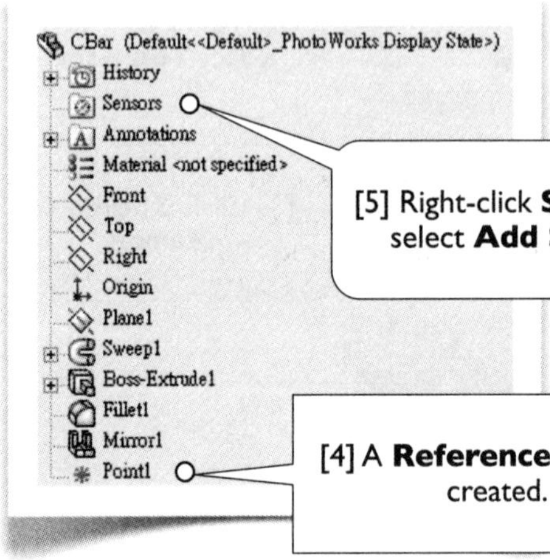

[5] Right-click **Sensors** and select **Add Sensor...**

[4] A **Reference Point** is created.

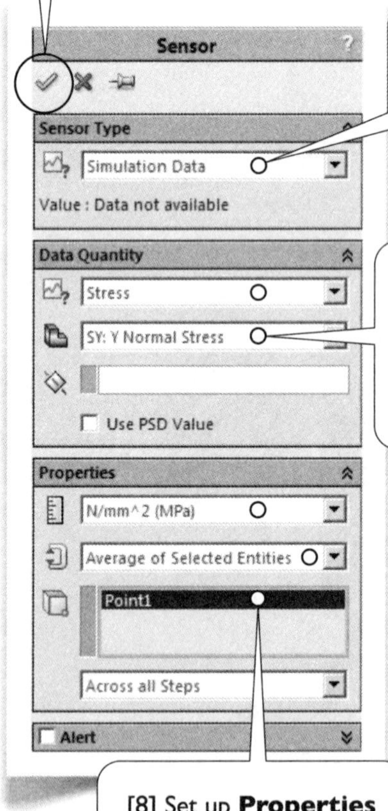

[6] Select **Simulation Data**.

[7] Select **SY**. The **Sensor** is initially set up to be associated with σ_Y. It can be changed later.

[8] Set up **Properties** like this and select **Point1** from **Part Tree**.

1.3-11 Create **Sensor** at Location **B**

[1] On the **Front** plane, draw a **Sketching Point** (see [2]) like this. Specify the location of the point. Click **Exit Sketch**.

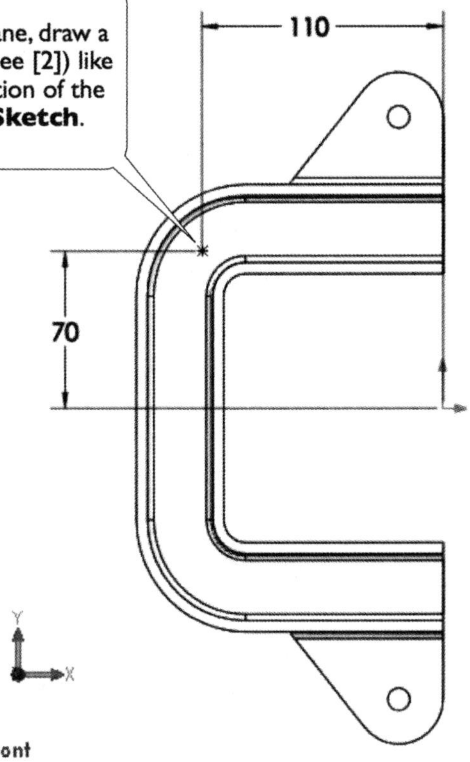

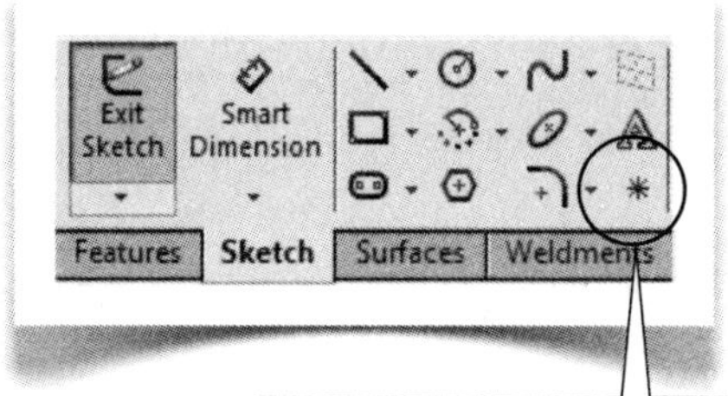

[2] **Sketching Point**.

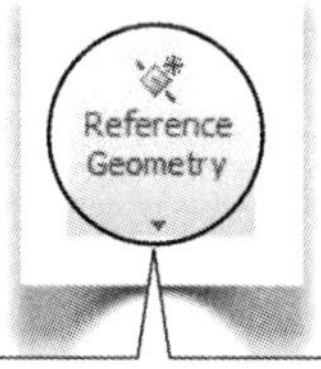

[3] In **Features Toolbar**, select **Reference Geometry>Point**.

[6] Click **OK**.

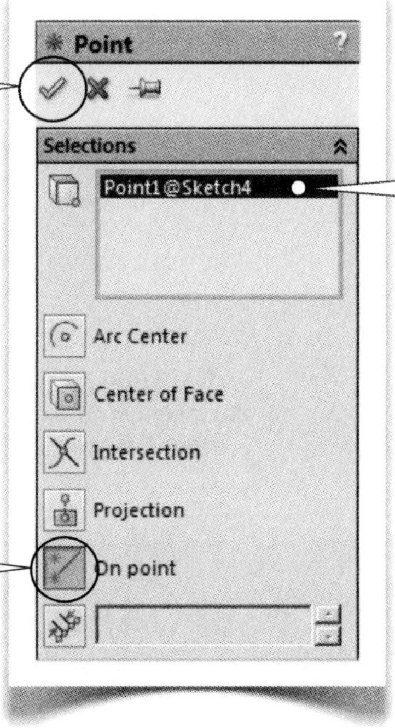

[5] In the **Graphics Area**, select the **Sketching Point**. A **Reference Point** is created at the location of the **Sketching Point**.

[4] Click **On Point**.

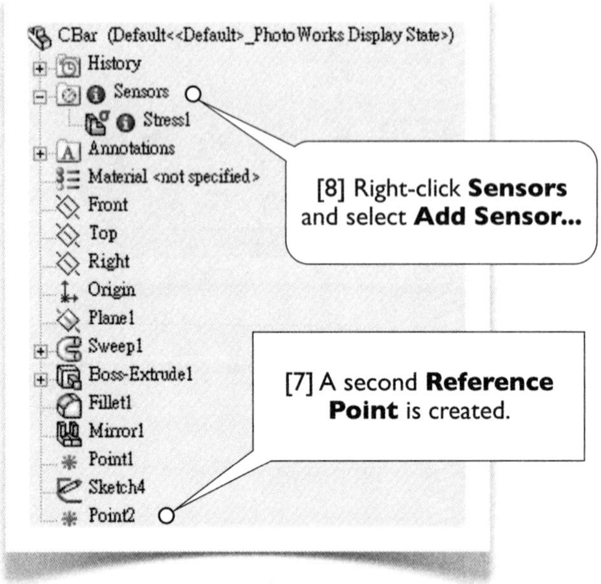
CBar (Default<<Default>_PhotoWorks Display State>)
History
Sensors
Stress1
Annotations
Material <not specified>
Front
Top
Right
Origin
Plane1
Sweep1
Boss-Extrude1
Fillet1
Mirror1
Point1
Sketch4
Point2
[7] A second **Reference Point** is created.
[8] Right-click **Sensors** and select **Add Sensor...**

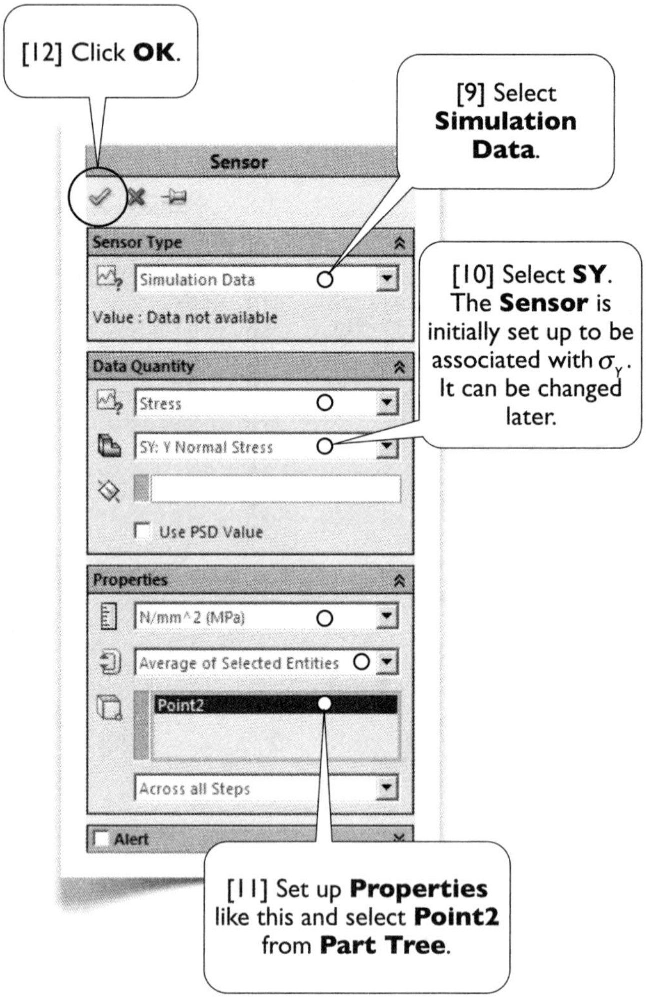
Sensor
Sensor Type
Simulation Data
Value : Data not available
Data Quantity
Stress
SY: Y Normal Stress
Use PSD Value
Properties
N/mm^2 (MPa)
Average of Selected Entities
Point2
Across all Steps
Alert
[9] Select **Simulation Data**.
[10] Select **SY**. The **Sensor** is initially set up to be associated with σ_Y. It can be changed later.
[11] Set up **Properties** like this and select **Point2** from **Part Tree**.
[12] Click **OK**.

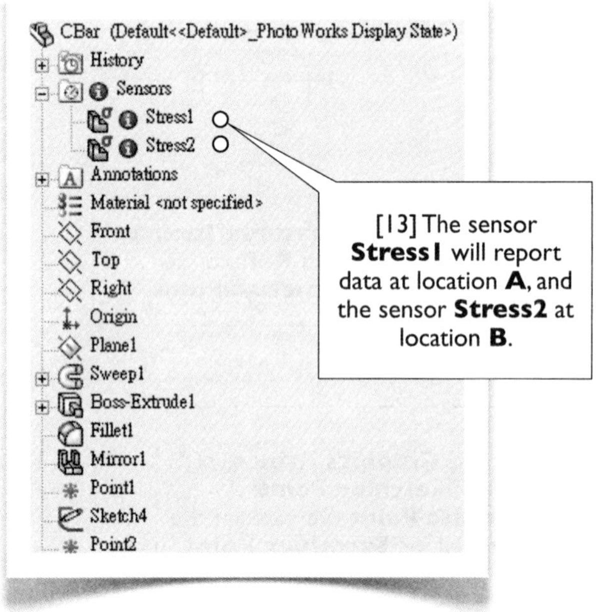
CBar (Default<<Default>_PhotoWorks Display State>)
History
Sensors
Stress1
Stress2
Annotations
Material <not specified>
Front
Top
Right
Origin
Plane1
Sweep1
Boss-Extrude1
Fillet1
Mirror1
Point1
Sketch4
Point2
[13] The sensor **Stress1** will report data at location **A**, and the sensor **Stress2** at location **B**.

[14] Save the document with the name **CBar**. #

1.3-12 Create a Static Structural Study and Set Up Unit System

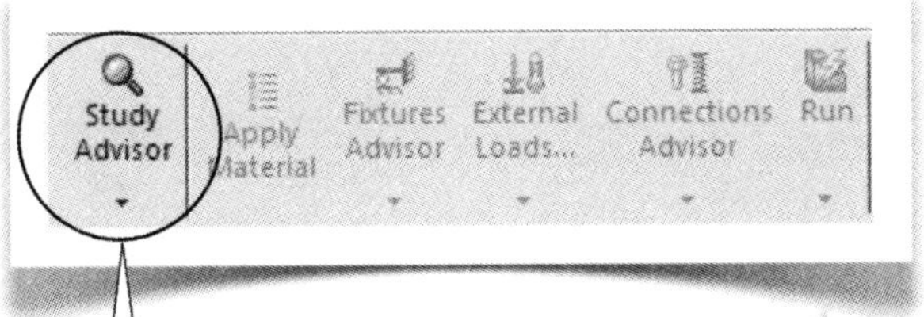

[1] Make sure **SolidWorks Simulation** is loaded (1.1-5, page 13). In the **Simulation Toolbar**, select **Study Advisor>New Study**. Type **Static Force 2000 N** for **Name**. Leave **Static** as default **Study Type**.

[3] The **Study Tree**.

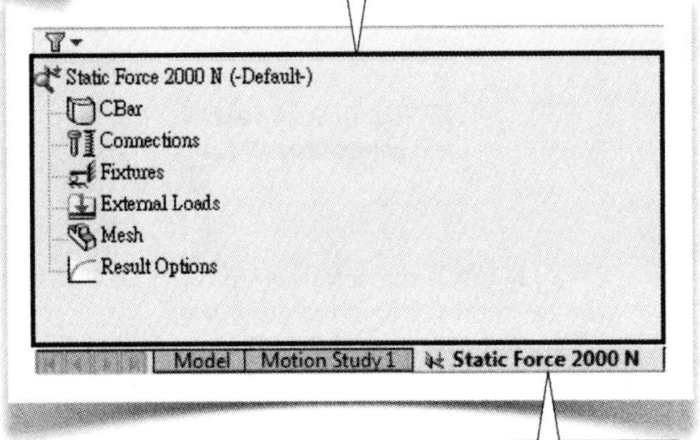

[2] A tab is added and becomes active.

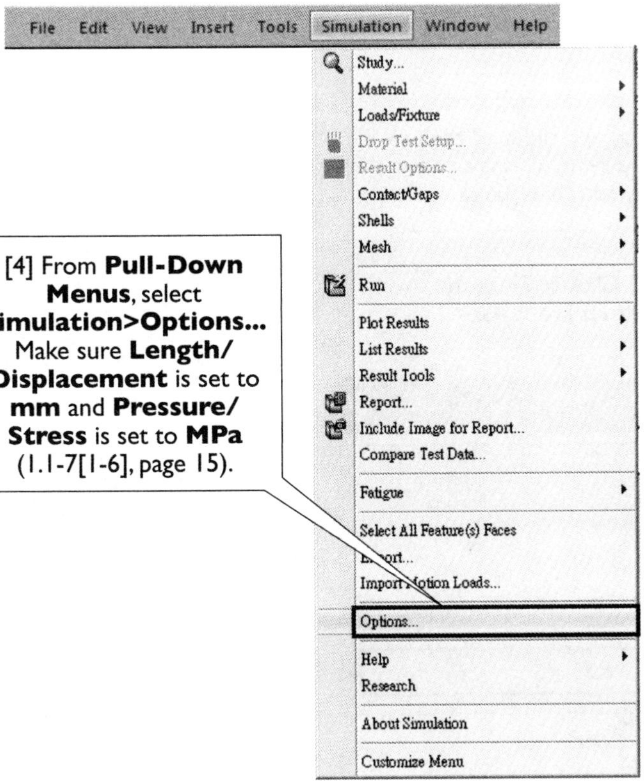

[4] From **Pull-Down Menus**, select **Simulation>Options...** Make sure **Length/ Displacement** is set to **mm** and **Pressure/ Stress** is set to **MPa** (1.1-7[1-6], page 15).

[5] In the **Study Tree**, right-click **CBar** and select **Apply/Edit Material...** and apply **Alloy Steel** for the model (1.1-8, page 17). #

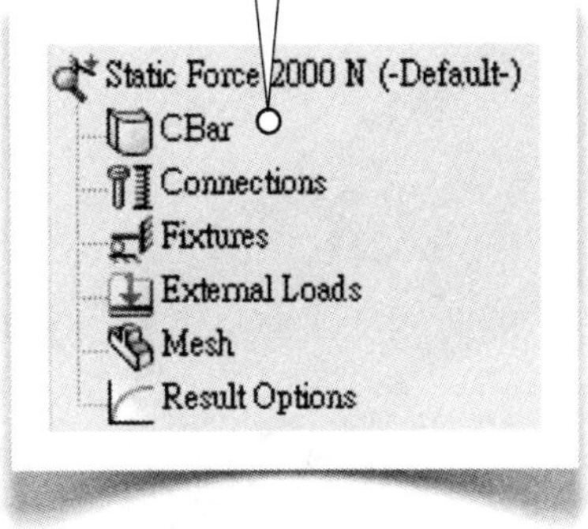

1.3-13 Create Mesh

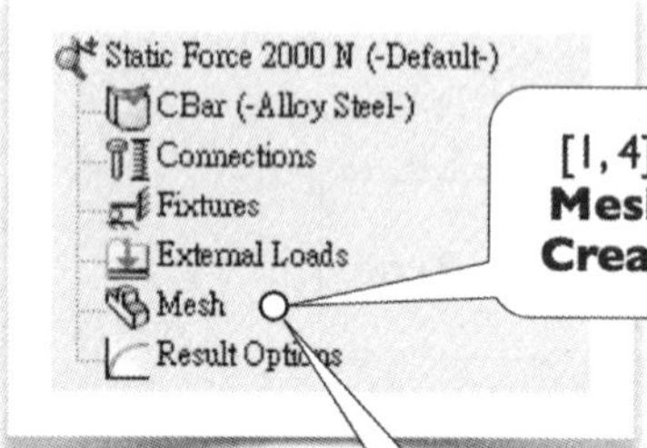

[1, 4] Right-click **Mesh** and select **Create mesh...**

[2] Click **OK** to accept the default settings.

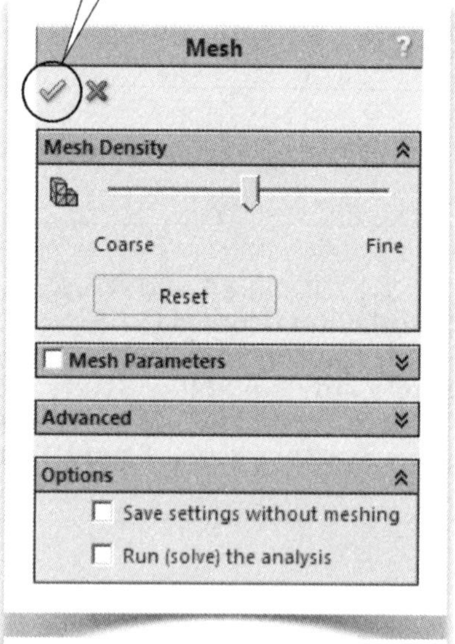

[8] Right-click **Mesh** and select **Details...**

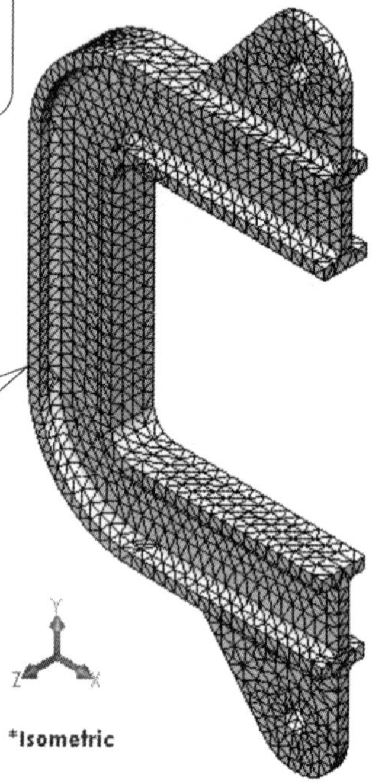

[3] This is the default mesh. In general, the finer the mesh, the more accurate the solutions. Let's make the mesh finer.

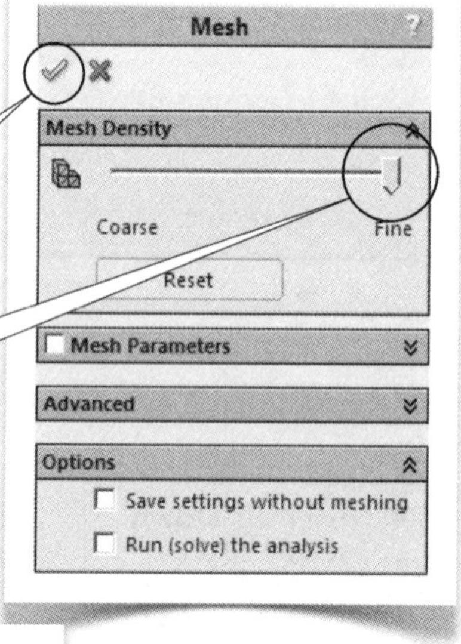

[6] Click **OK**.

[5] Drag the slider all the way to the right. This is an easy way to refine the mesh.

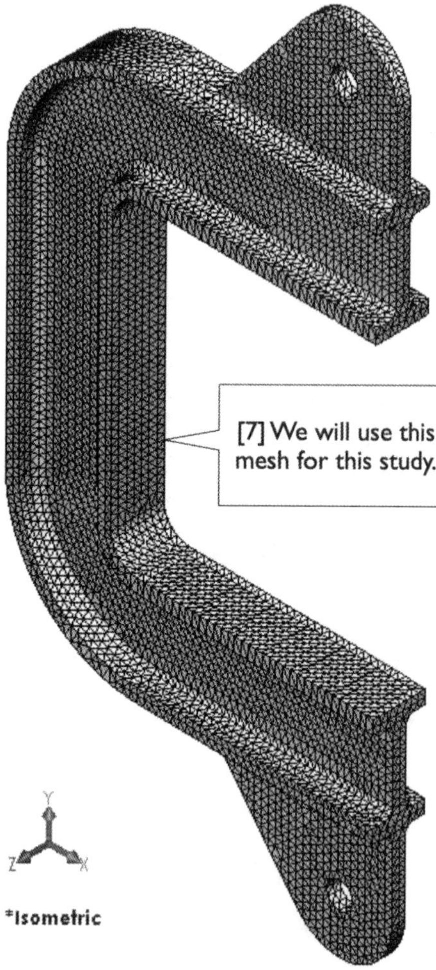

[7] We will use this mesh for this study.

[10] Click to close the **Mesh Details**. #

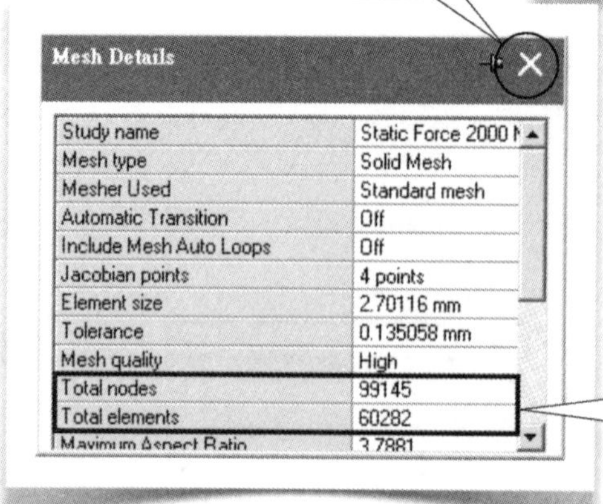

Mesh Details

Study name	Static Force 2000 N
Mesh type	Solid Mesh
Mesher Used	Standard mesh
Automatic Transition	Off
Include Mesh Auto Loops	Off
Jacobian points	4 points
Element size	2.70116 mm
Tolerance	0.135058 mm
Mesh quality	High
Total nodes	99145
Total elements	60282
Maximum Aspect Ratio	3.7881

[9] The **Mesh Details** shows that the mesh consists of 99,145 nodes and 60,282 elements. Your numbers may not be exactly the same as here. If you don't create a mesh, the program will automatically create a default mesh right before solving the model.

1.3-14 Set Up Boundary Conditions and Run the Model

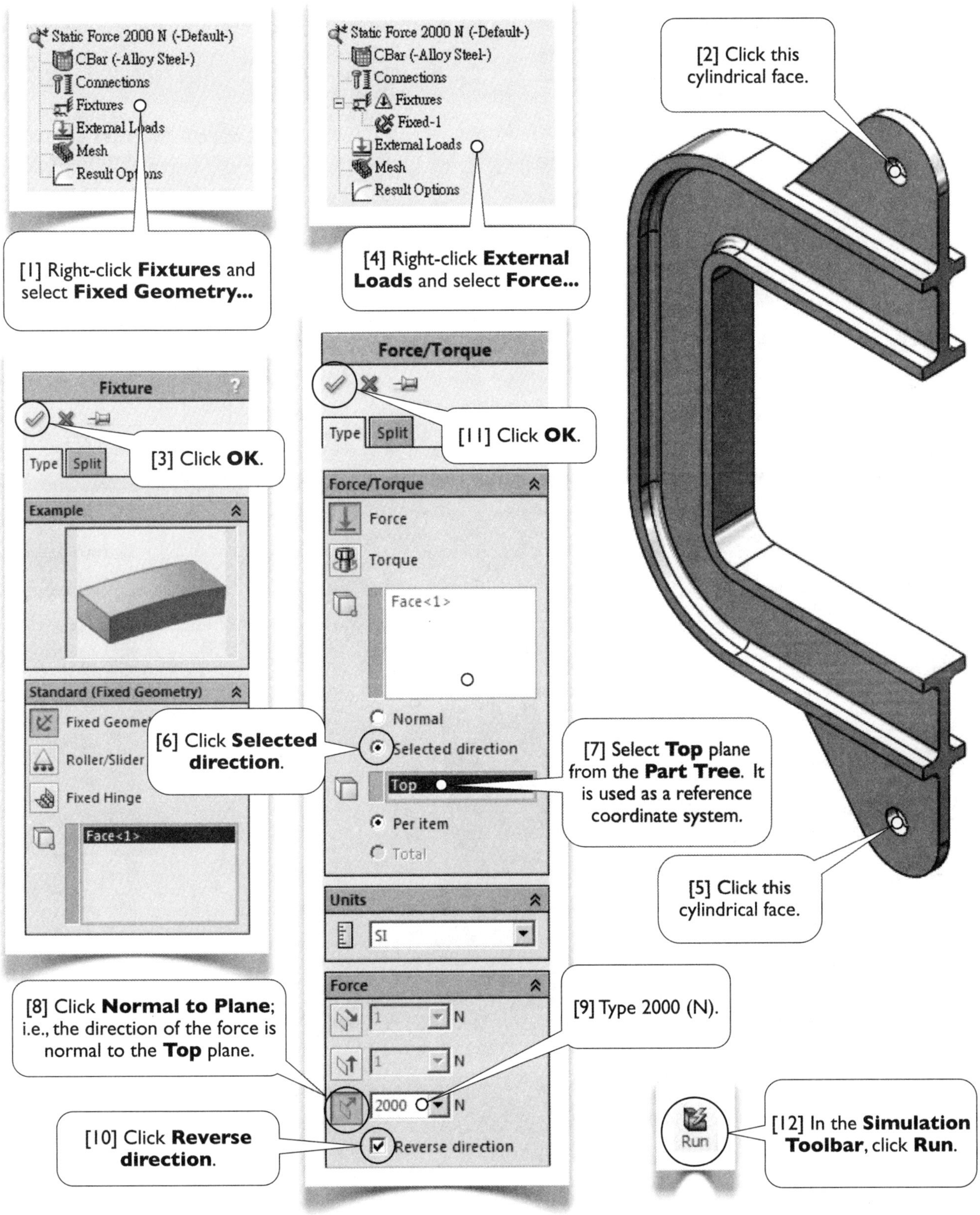

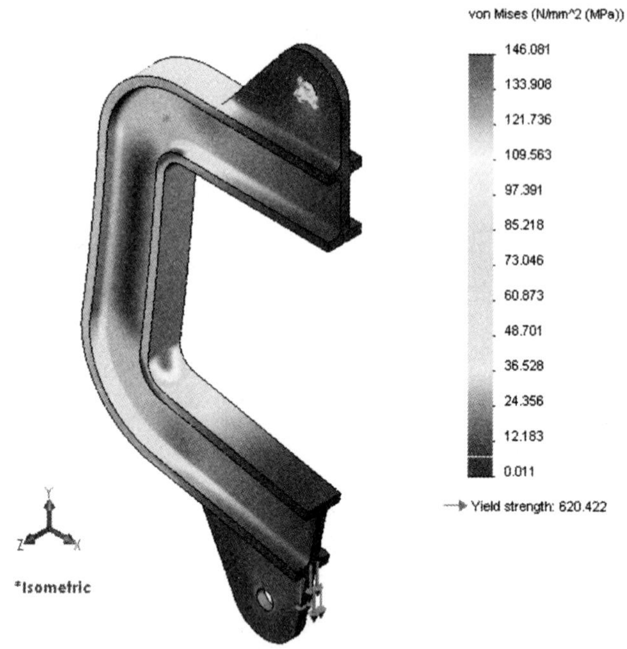

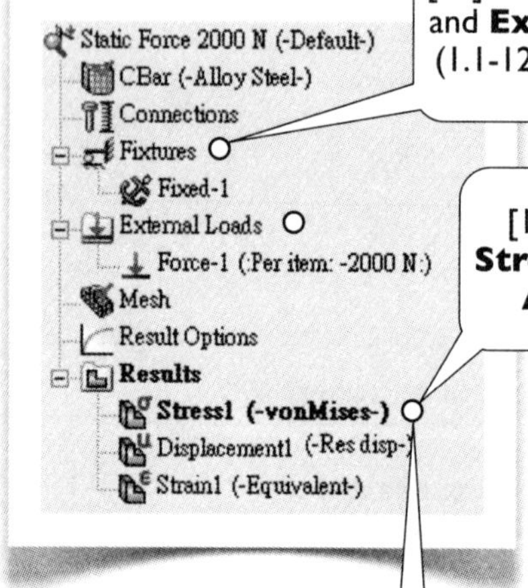

[14] Hide all **Fixtures** and **External Loads** (1.1-12[6, 7], page 21).

[15] Right-click **Stress1** and select **Animate...**

[13] Change to display **SY** (σ_Y) (1.1-12[1, 2, 4], page 21).

[16] Click **OK** after viewing the animation.

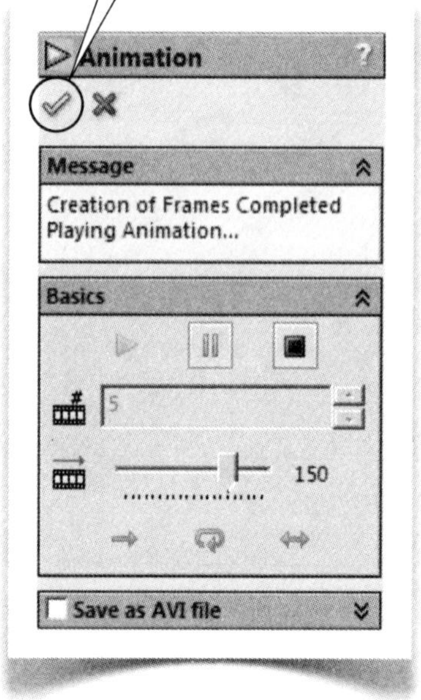

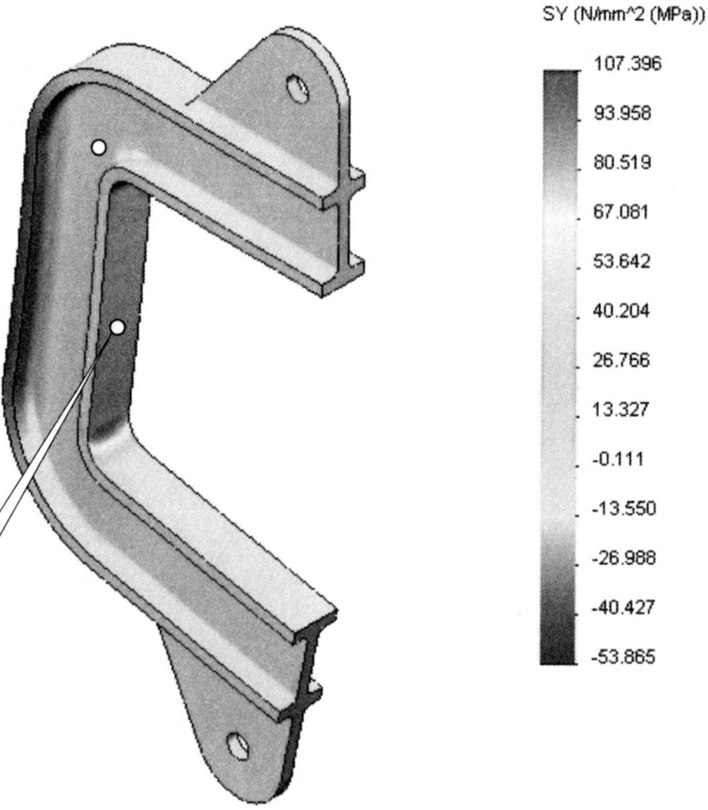

[17] Next, we'll explore the stresses at locations **A** and **B**. #

1.3-15 The Stresses at Location **A**

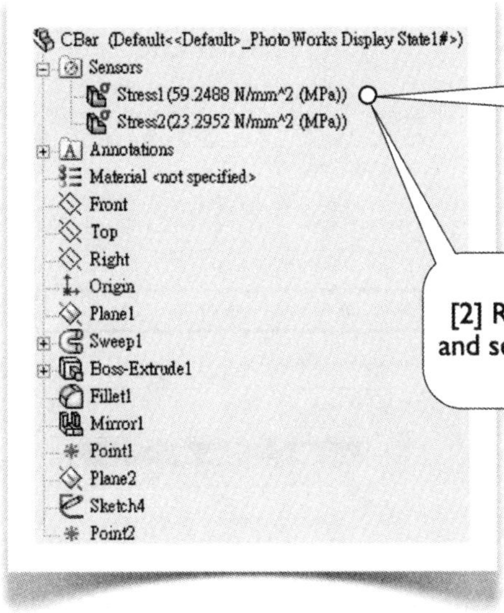

[1] Recall that the sensor **Stress1** is initially set up to be associated with σ_Y. Write down this stress value (59.2488 MPa) [5].

[2] Right-click **Stress1** and select **Edit Sensor**.

[6] Click **OK**.

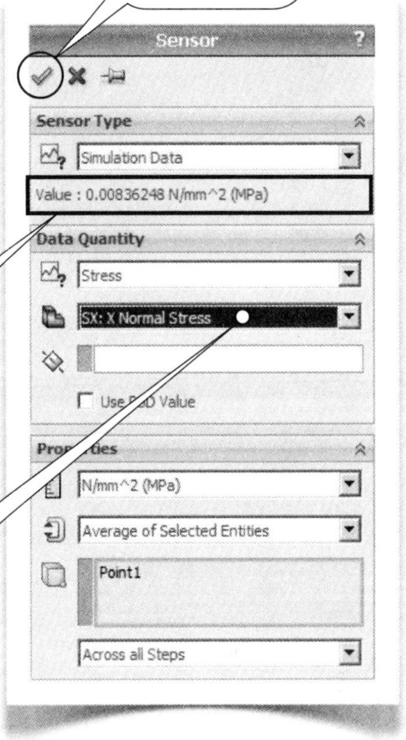

[4] The sensor **Stress1** reports σ_X value here. The σ_X is essentially zero.

[3] Change to **SX** (σ_X).

Stress Component	Stress Value
σ_X	0
σ_Y	59.2488 MPa
σ_Z	0
τ_{XY}	0
τ_{YZ}	0
τ_{ZX}	0

[5] Repeat steps [3, 4] to obtain other stress components. All other stress components than σ_Y are essentially zeros.

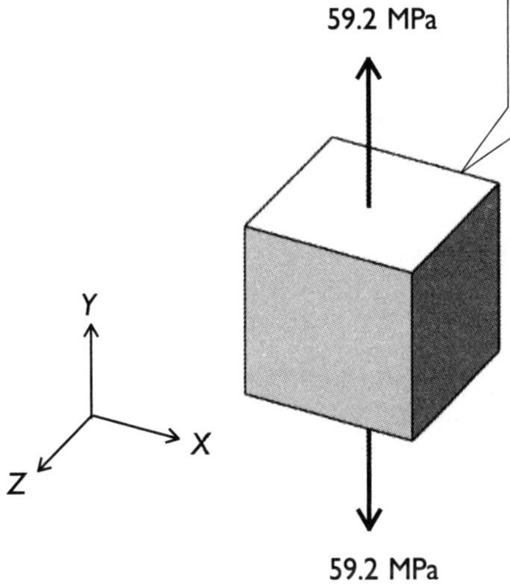

[7] The stress state at location **A**. #

1.3-16 The Stresses at Location **B**

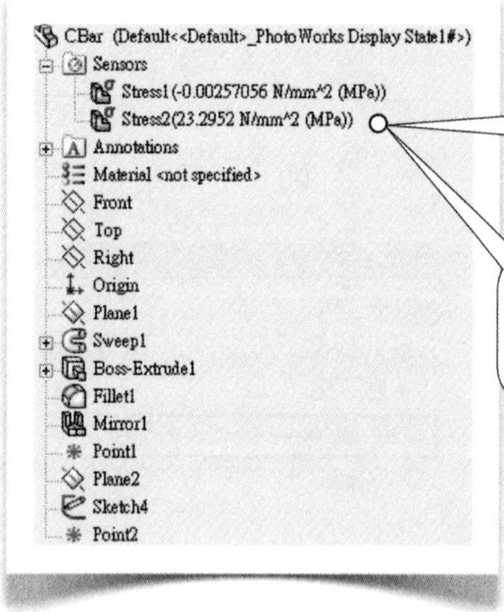

[1] The sensor **Stress2** is initially set up to be associated with σ_Y. Write down this stress value (23.2952 MPa) [5].

[2] Right-click **Stress2** and select **Edit Sensor**.

[6] Click **OK**.

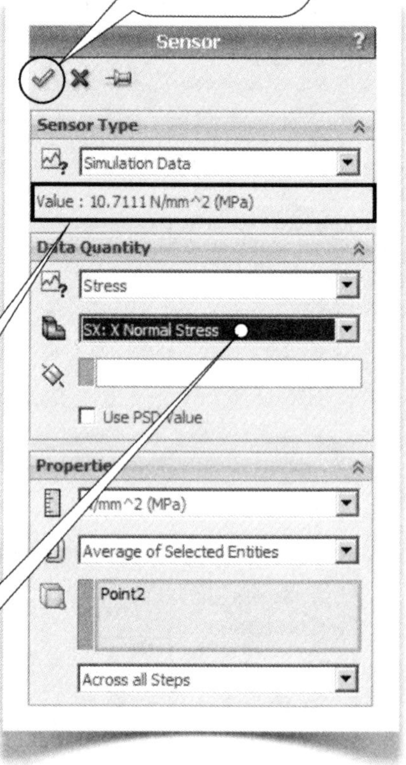

[4] The sensor **Stress2** reports σ_X value here (10.7111 MPa).

[3] Change to **SX** (σ_X).

Stress Component	Stress Value
σ_X	10.7111 Mpa
σ_Y	23.2952 MPa
σ_Z	0
τ_{XY}	-20.2619 MPa
τ_{YZ}	0
τ_{ZX}	0

[5] Repeat steps [3, 4] to obtain other stress components. Your results may not be exactly the same as here. Note that the Z-components (σ_Z, τ_{YZ}, τ_{ZX}) are all zeros; it is called a **plane stress state** (Section 12.1). The stress states discussed in this chapter are all plane stress states.

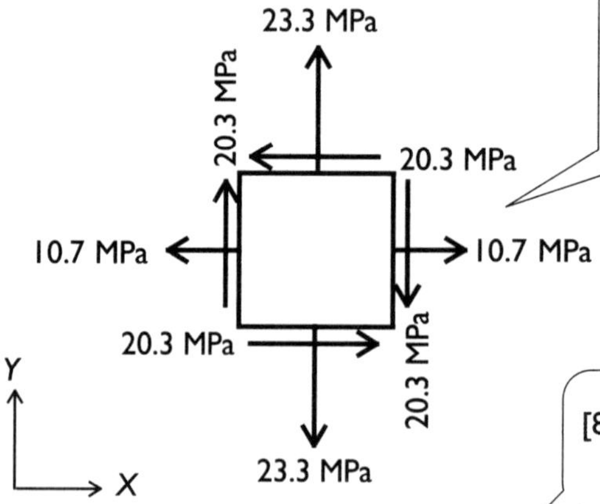

[7] The stress state at location **B**. Note that the shear stresses point to the negative directions.

[8] Save the document and exit **SolidWorks**. #

Chapter 2

Displacements

Concepts of displacements are much easier to understand than that of stresses. This is because the displacement can be defined using the notion of vectors, and you've learned vectors since high school.

The displacement of a particle in a body is defined as the vector formed by connecting from its location before deformation to its location after deformation. A displacement $\vec{u}$, which is a vector quantity, can be decomposed into three **displacement components** u_X, u_Y, u_Z in the 3D space; i.e.,

$$\vec{u} = \begin{pmatrix} u_X & u_Y & u_Z \end{pmatrix} \tag{1}$$

Each particle in a body has its own displacement quantity. That is, like stresses, displacements are functions of position. The **resultant displacement** u is the magnitude of the vector $\vec{u}$, i.e.,

$$u = \sqrt{u_X^2 + u_Y^2 + u_Z^2} \tag{2}$$

The purpose of this chapter is to familiarize the concepts of displacements.

Section 2.1

Displacements in the Cantilever Beam

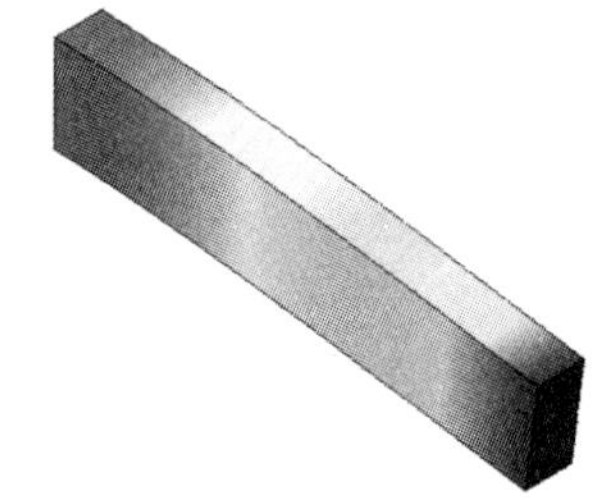

2.1-1 Start Up

[1] Launch **SolidWorks** and open the file **Cantilever** which was saved in Section 1.2.#

2.1-2 View the Displacements for the **Elongation** Case

[1] Click **Elongation** tab.

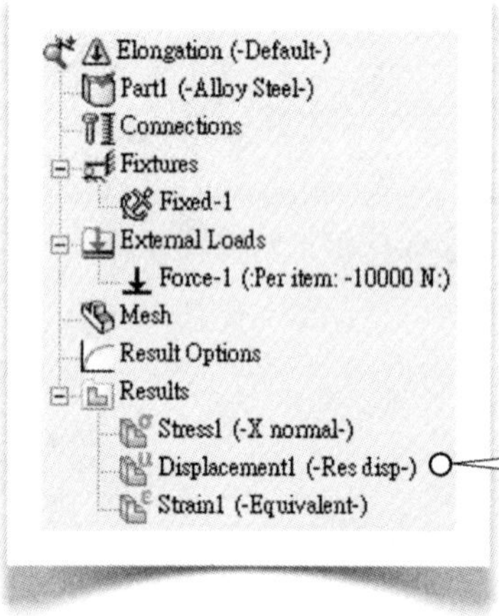

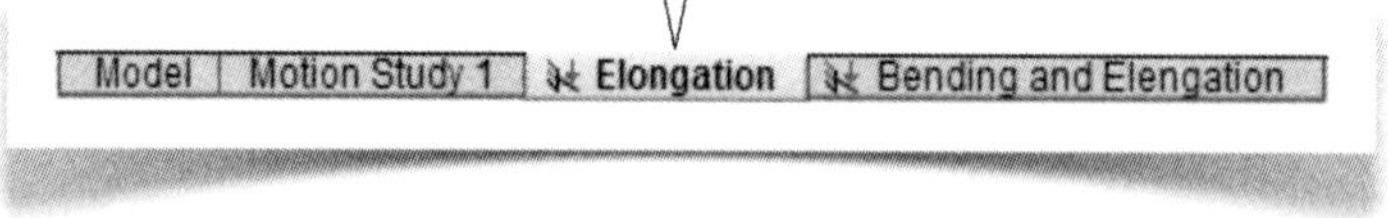

[2] Double-click **Displacement1** to activate it.

[3] Here shows the resultant displacement (u). Since this case is a pure elongation in X direction, the resultant displacement u is the same as u_x.

[4] The maximum displacement (0.02373 mm) is at the free end.

[5] The minimum displacement (which is essentially zero) is at the fixed end.

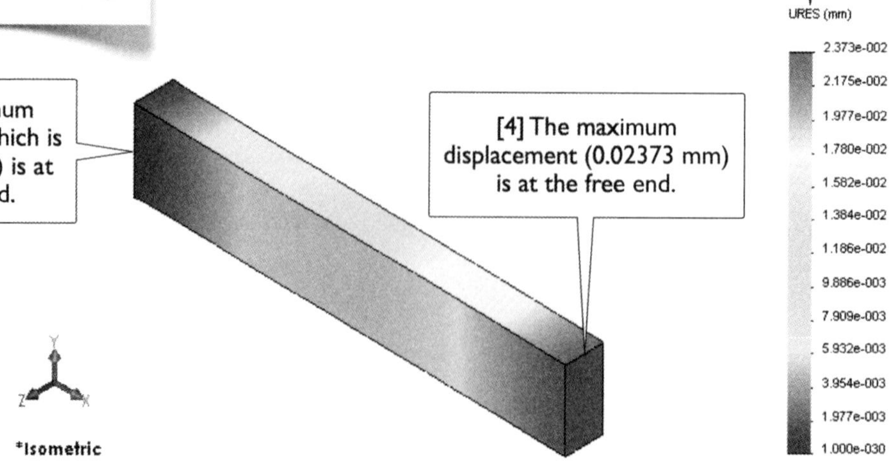

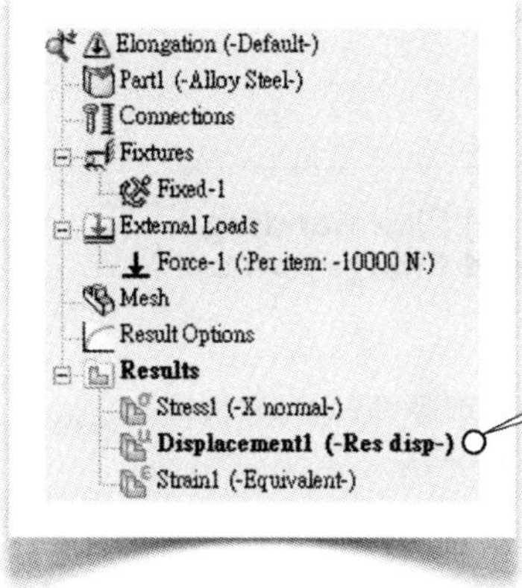

[14] Click **OK**. #

[7] Click **On selected entities**.

[6] Right-click **Displacement1** and select **Probe**.

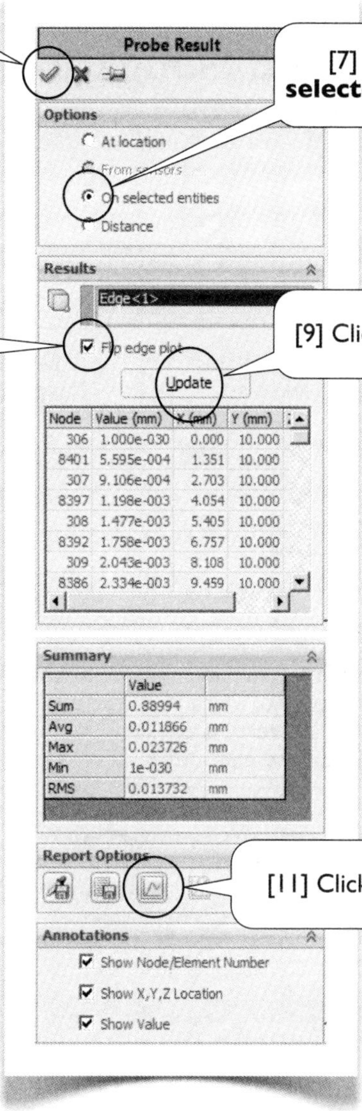

[10] Click **Flip edge plot**.

[9] Click **Update**.

[8] Select any edge parallel to the X-direction.

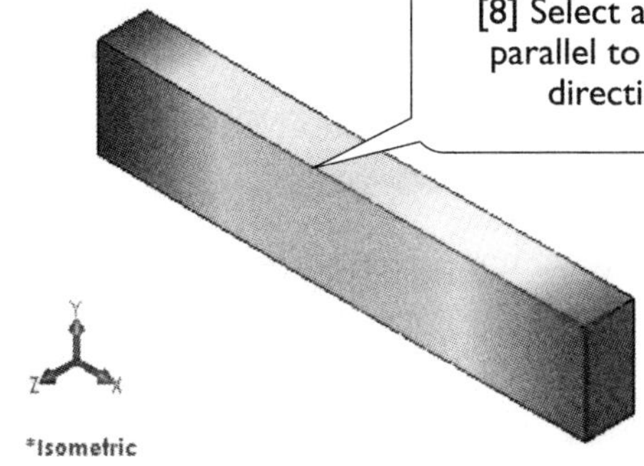

[13] Click **Close**.

[11] Click **Plot**.

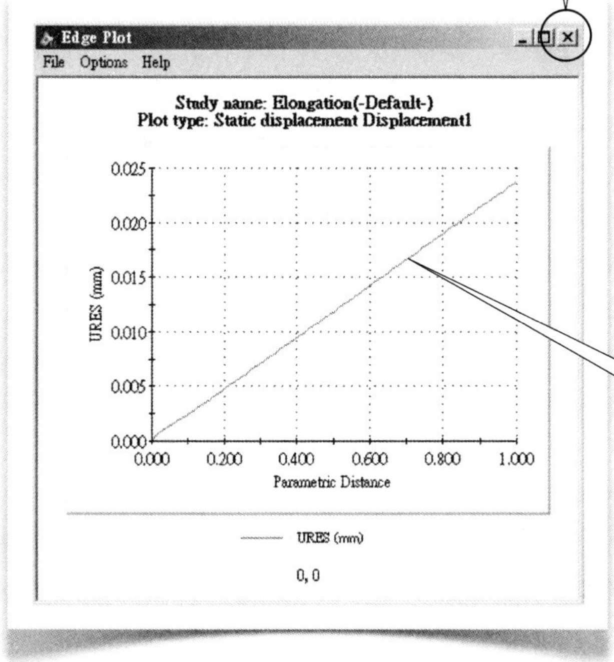

[12] The displacement changes linearly from the fixed end (0 mm) to the free end (0.02373 mm). Selecting any of four edges parallel to the X-direction [8] should have the same results.

2.1-3 View the Resultant Displacements of the **Bending and Elongation** Case

[1] Click **Bending and Elongation** tab.

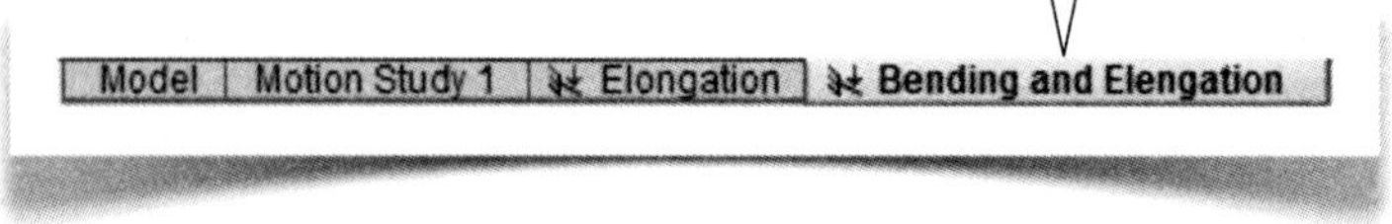

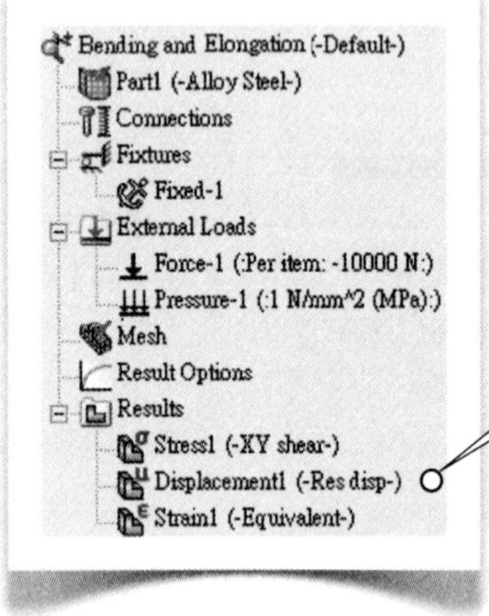

[2] Double-click **Displacement1** to activate it.

[3] The maximum resultant displacement (0.09958 mm) is at the free end. It is a combination of u_X, u_Y, and u_Z.

[4] The minimum displacement (which is essentially zero) is at the fixed end.

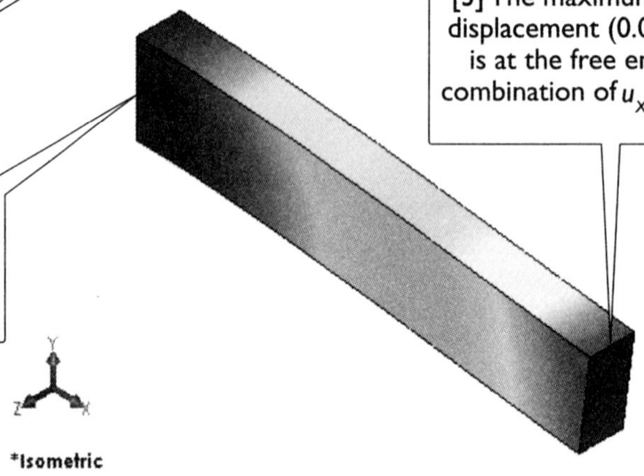

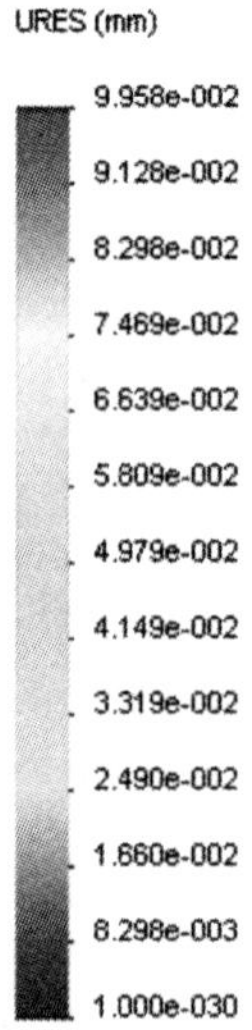

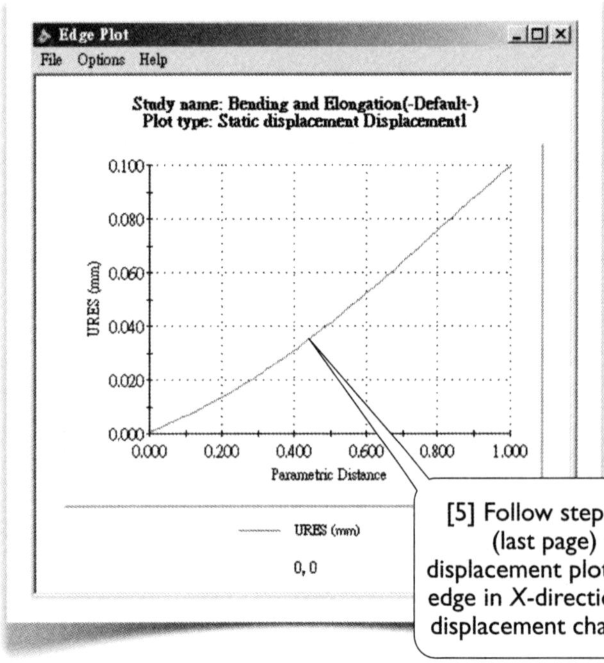

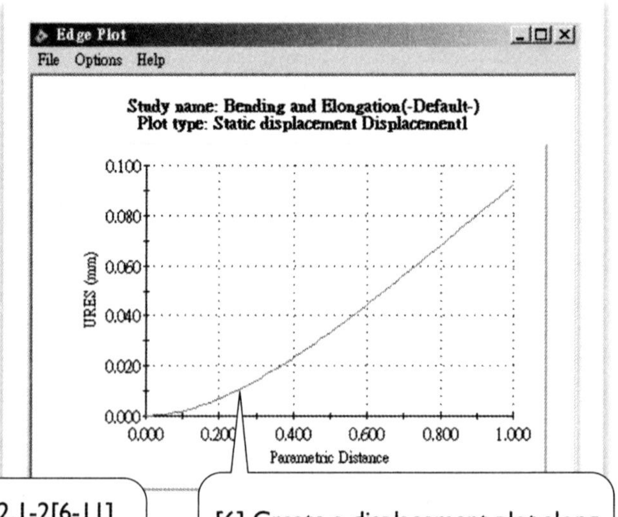

[5] Follow steps in 2.1-2[6-11] (last page) to create a displacement plot along an UPPER edge in X-direction. The resultant displacement changes nonlinearly.

[6] Create a displacement plot along a LOWER edge in X-direction. It is slightly different from the upper edge. Dismiss **Probe Result**. #

2.1-4 View u_X of the **Bending and Elongation** Case

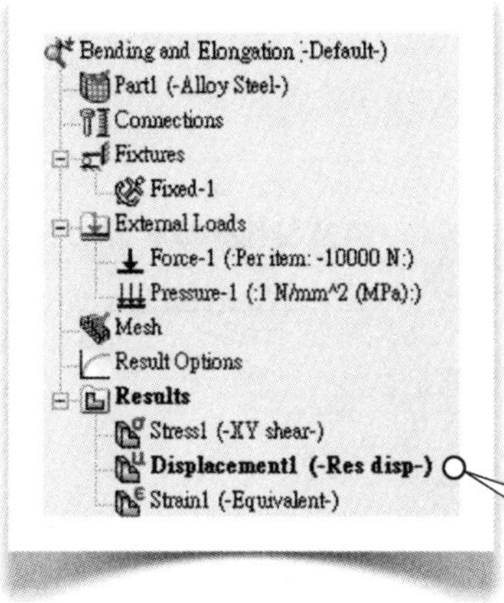

[1] Double-click **Displacement1** to edit the definition.

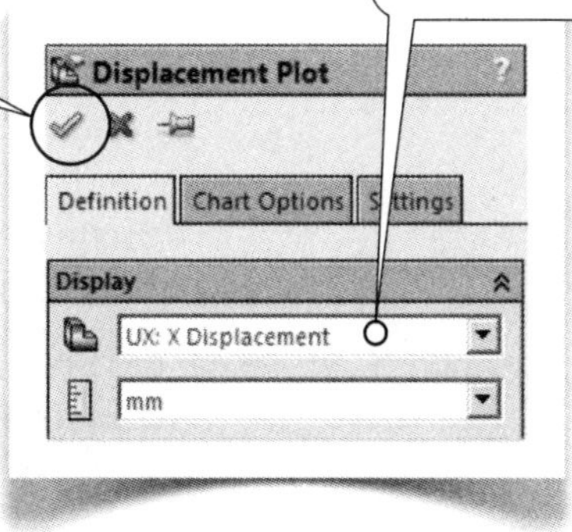

[2] Select **UX** (u_X).

[3] Click **OK**.

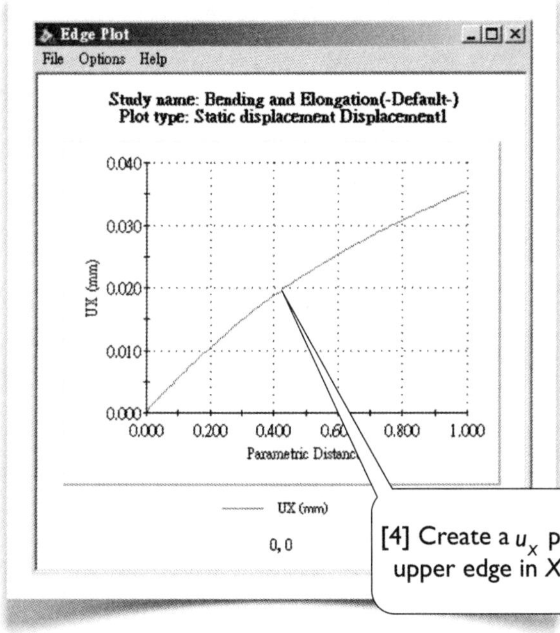

[4] Create a u_X plot along an upper edge in X-direction.

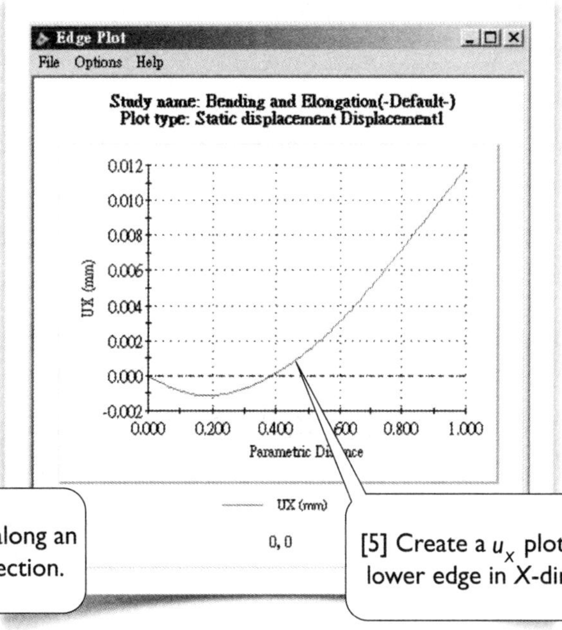

[5] Create a u_X plot along a lower edge in X-direction.

[6] Questions

The difference between plots [4, 5] and plot 2.1-2[12] (page 53) is that plots [4, 5] have a transversal load applied on the cantilever beam. How does the transversal load make the difference? #

2.1-5 View u_Y of the **Bending and Elongation** Case

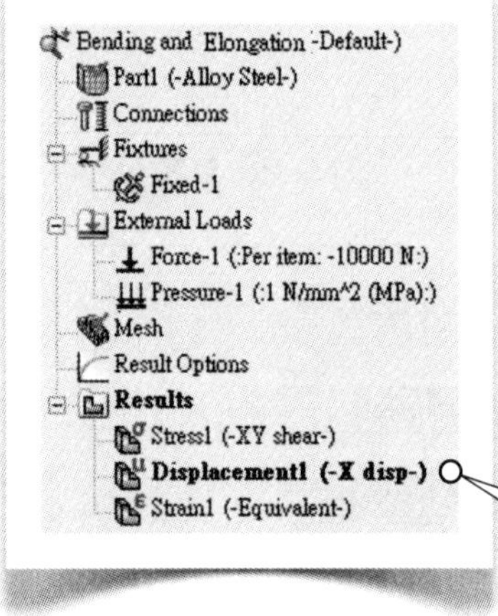

[1] Double-click **Displacement1** to edit the definition.

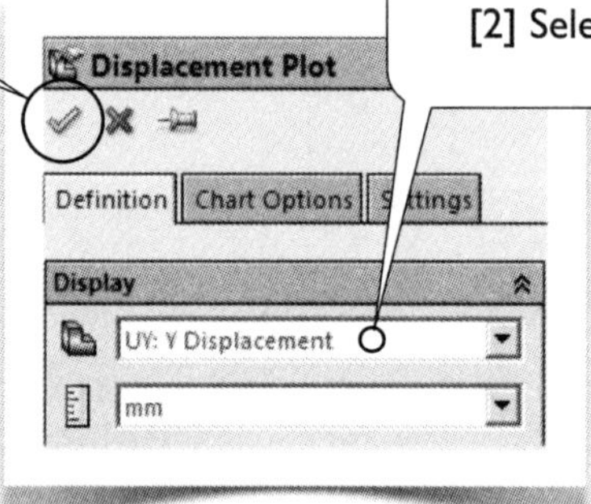

[2] Select **UY** (u_Y).

[3] Click **OK**.

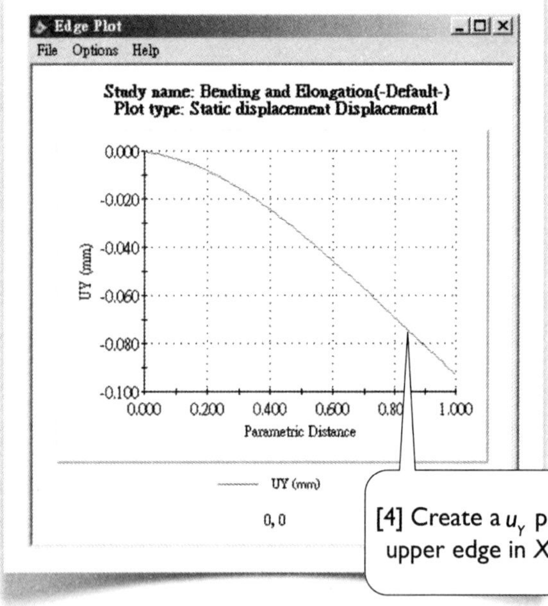

[4] Create a u_Y plot along an upper edge in X-direction.

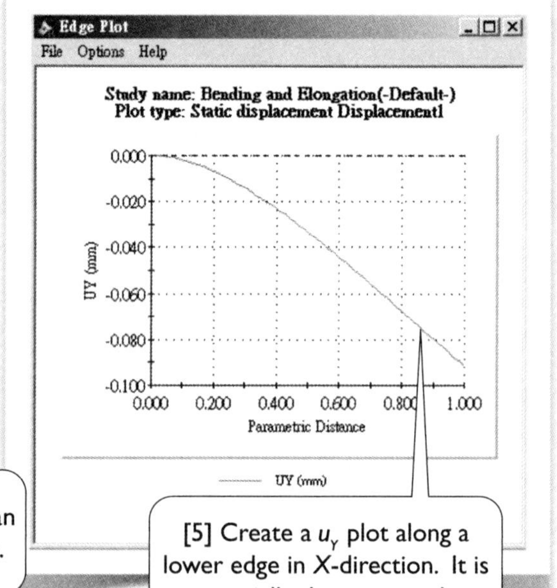

[5] Create a u_Y plot along a lower edge in X-direction. It is essentially the same as the upper edge.

[6] Save the document and exit **SolidWorks**. #

Section 2.2

Displacements in the C-Bar

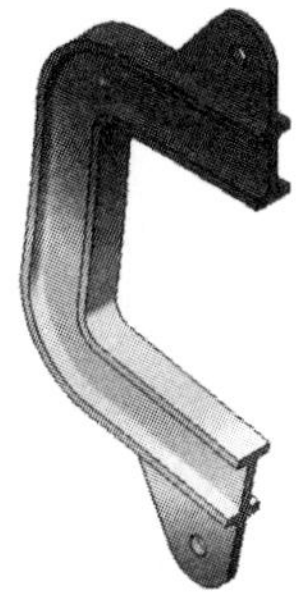

2.2-1 Start Up

[1] Launch **SolidWorks** and open the file **CBar** which was saved in Section 1.3. #

2.2-2 View the Deformed Shape

[1] Click **Static Force 2000 N** tab.

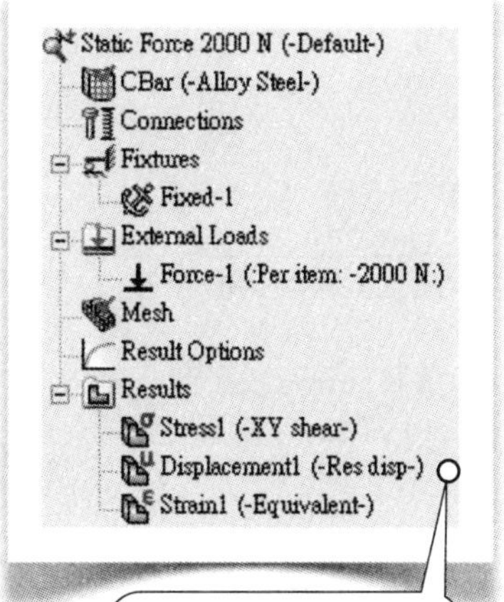

[2] Double-click **Displacement1** to activate it.

[3] This is a resultant displacement (u) plot.

[4] The minimum displacement (which is essentially zero) is at the fixed support.

[5] The maximum displacement (0.6201 mm) is at the lower end.

[6] We'll explore the displacements at location **A** in 2.2-3. #

[7] We'll explore the displacements at location **B** in 2.2-4.

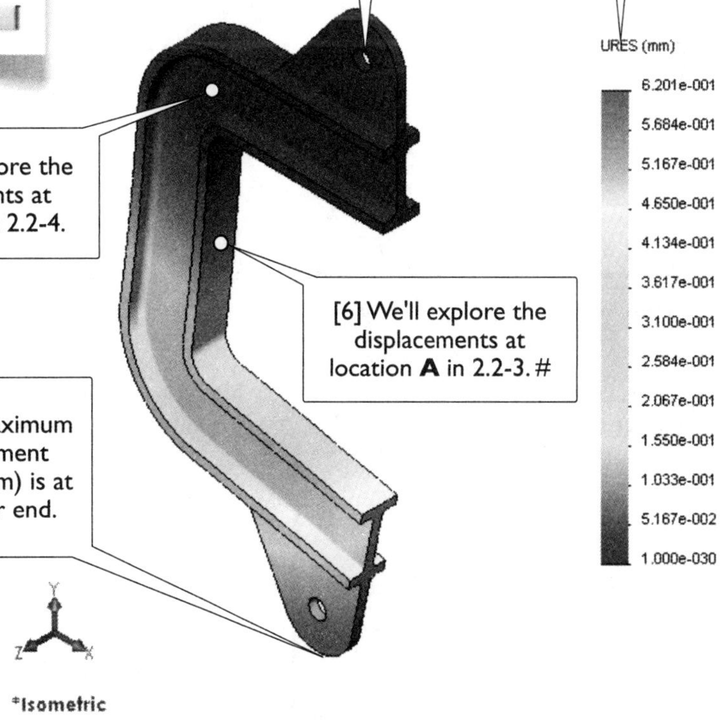

2.2-3 Displacements at Location **A**

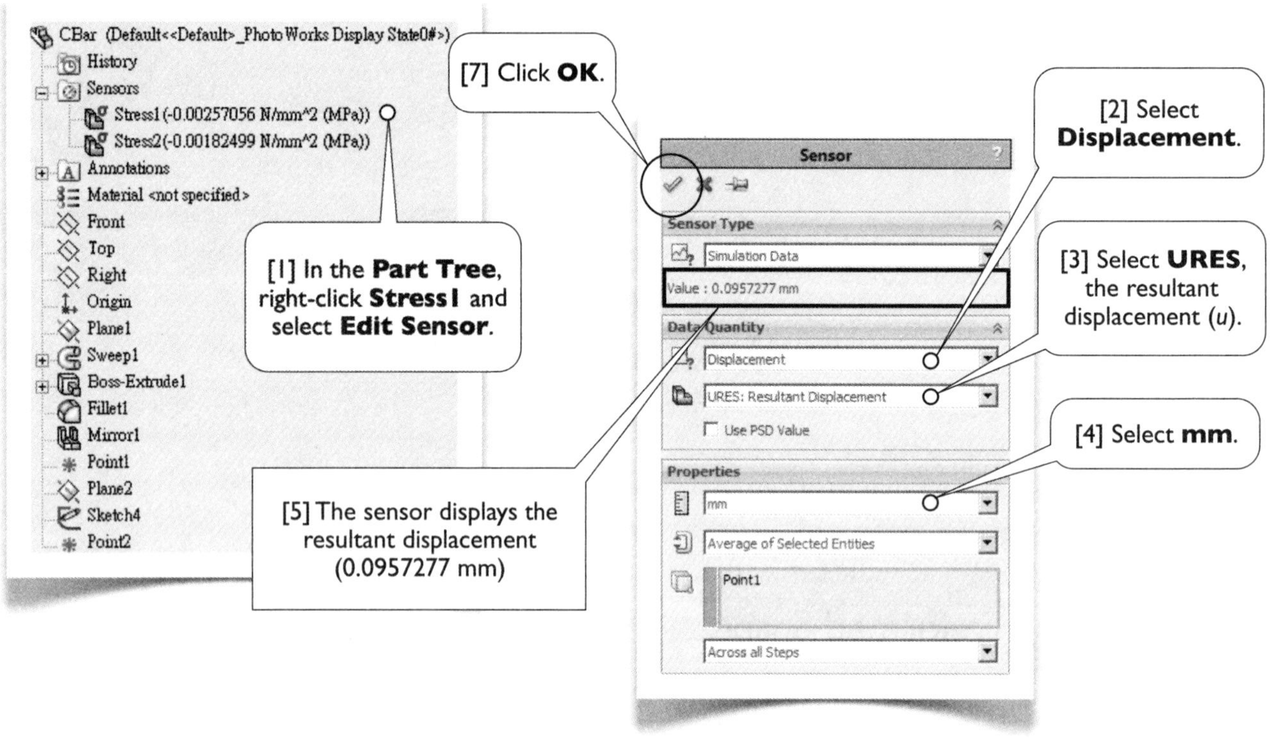

[6] Repeat steps [3, 5] to obtain three displacement components. Tabulate the results like this. Your results may not be exactly the same as here.

Displacement Component	Displacement Value
Resultant Displacement (u)	0.0957277 mm
u_X	-0.094486 mm
u_Y	-0.0153686 mm
u_Z	0

[8] Discussion

The relationship between the resultant displacement (u) and the three components (u_X, u_Y, u_Z) is simply (Eq. 2(2), page 51)

$$u = \sqrt{u_X^2 + u_Y^2 + u_Z^2}$$

It is easy to verify, from the results in [6], that

$$0.0957277 \approx \sqrt{(-0.094486)^2 + (-0.0153686)^2 + 0^2}$$

Note that, while the resultant displacement (u) is always positive, the displacement components (u_X, u_Y, u_Z) are signed values.

[9] Question

Explain that, in location **A**, u_X and u_Y are negative, while u_Z is zero. #

2.2-4 Displacements at Location **B**

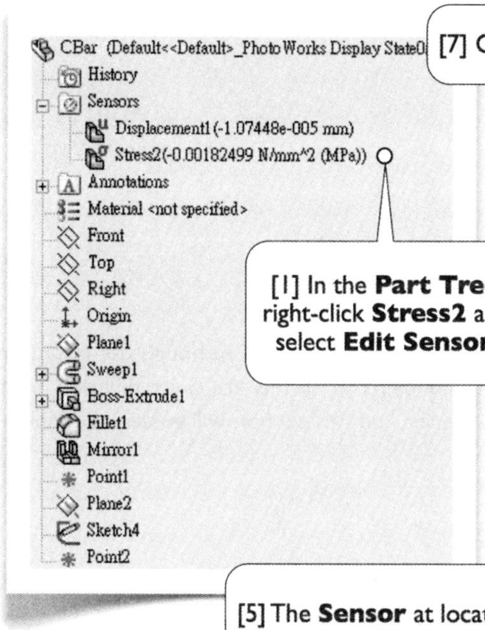

[1] In the **Part Tree**, right-click **Stress2** and select **Edit Sensor**.

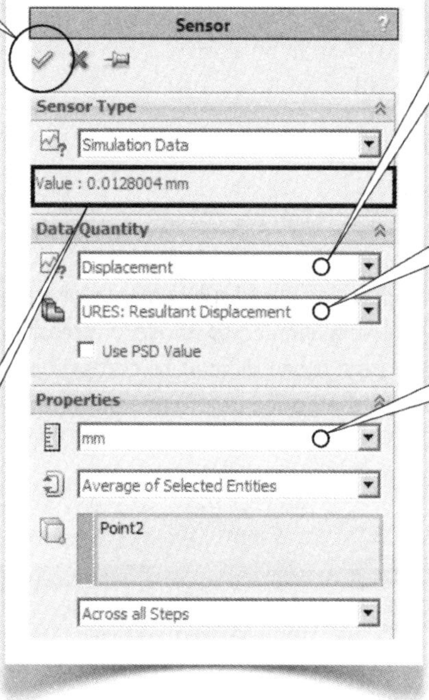

[2] Select **Displacement**.

[3] Select **URES**, the resultant displacement (u).

[4] Select **mm**.

[5] The **Sensor** at location **B** displays the resultant displacement (0.0128004 mm)

[6] Repeat step [3] to obtain three displacement components. Tabulate the results like this. Your results may not be exactly the same as here.

Displacement Component	Displacement Value
Resultant Displacement (u)	0.0128004 mm
u_X	-0.00590032 mm
u_Y	0.0113594 mm
u_Z	0

[7] Click **OK**.

[8] Discussion

It is easy to verify, from the results in [6], that

$$0.0128004 \approx \sqrt{(-0.00590032)^2 + (0.0113594)^2 + 0^2}$$

[9] Question

Explain that, in location **B**, u_X is negative, u_Y is positive, while u_Z is zero.

[10] Save the document and exit **SolidWorks**. #

Chapter 3

Strains

Strains are quantities to describe the displacements of a point relative to its neighboring points. Although the notations of strain components are very similar to those of stress components, the concepts of strains are quite different from those of stresses and are even more difficult to comprehend. Pay a little patience, and this section will guide you step-by-step to get acquainted with the concepts of strains.

Section 3.1

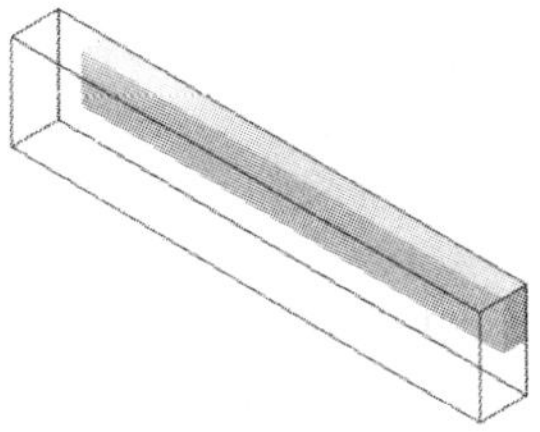

Strains in the Cantilever Beam

3.1-1 Introduction

[1] Strains are quantities to describe how the material in a body is stretched and distorted. Or, more specifically, strains are displacements of a point relative to its neighboring points. Let's consider 2D cases first. The concepts can be easily extended to 3D cases.

Let's consider a point A and its neighboring points B and C, which are respectively along X-axis and Y-axis [2]. Suppose that, after deformation, ABC displaces to a new configuration $A'B'C'$ [3]. Keep in mind that, in the following illustration, we assume the deformation is infinitesimally small. Under the **small deformation** assumption, the **normal strains** in X-axis and Y-axis can be defined respectively as

$$\varepsilon_X = \frac{A'B' - AB}{AB} \text{ (dimensionless)} \quad (1)$$

$$\varepsilon_Y = \frac{A'C' - AC}{AC} \text{ (dimensionless)} \quad (2)$$

The strains defined in (1) and (2) represent the stretch at the point A in X-direction and Y-direction respectively. Stretch are not the only deformation modes; there are other deformation modes: changes of angles; e.g., from $\angle CAB$ to $\angle C'A'B'$, which is defined as the **shear strain** in XY-plane,

$$\gamma_{XY} = \angle CAB - \angle C'A'B' \text{ (rad)} \quad (3)$$

Note that the normal strains (1, 2) are dimensionless, while the shear strain (3) has a unit of radian, which is also regarded as dimensionless.

In the above illustration, we consider only 2D cases. In general, the stretching may also occurs in Z-direction and the shearing may also occurs in YZ-plane and ZX-plane. Therefore, we need six **strain components** to completely describe the stretching and shearing of the material at a point:

$$\{\varepsilon\} = \{\ \varepsilon_X \quad \varepsilon_Y \quad \varepsilon_Z \quad \gamma_{XY} \quad \gamma_{YZ} \quad \gamma_{ZX}\ \} \quad (4)$$

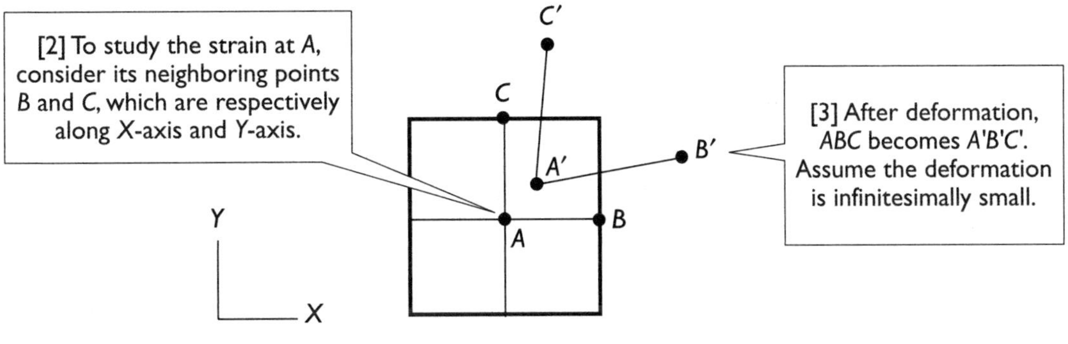

[4] The definitions of (1), (2), and (3) do not explain why they are called normal strains and shear strain respectively. To clarify this, let's redefine normal and shear strains using a different but equivalent way.

First, we translate and rotate $A'B'C'$ such that A' coincides with A and $A'C'$ aligns with AC [5]. Now the vector BB' represents the displacement of a neighboring point B which is on X-axis [6]. This displacement BB' can be decomposed into two components: BD and DB', the former is called the **normal component**, while the latter is called the **shear component**. They are so named because BD is normal to the X-face and DB' is parallel to the X-face. The normal strain and shear strain on X-face are then defined respectively by dividing the components with the original length,

$$\varepsilon_X = \frac{BD}{AB} \text{ (dimensionless)} \tag{5}$$

$$\gamma_{XY} = \frac{DB'}{AB} \text{ (rad)} \tag{6}$$

Note that, under the assumption of small deformation, the definition of (5) is the same as (1), while the definition of (6) is the same as (3). Also note that there are two subscripts in the shear strain γ_{XY}. The first subscript X is the face where the shearing occurs, while the second subscript Y is the direction of the shearing.

Similarly, we may translate and rotate $A'B'C'$ such that A' coincides with A and $A'B'$ aligns with AB [7]. Now the vector CC' represents the displacement of a neighboring point C which is on Y-axis [8]. This displacement CC' can be decomposed into two components: CE and EC', the former is the normal component, while the latter is the shear component. The normal strain and shear strain on Y-face is then defined by

$$\varepsilon_Y = \frac{CE}{AC} \text{ (dimensionless)} \tag{7}$$

$$\gamma_{YX} = \frac{EC'}{AC} \text{ (rad)} \tag{8}$$

Note that, under the assumption of small deformation, the definition of (7) is the same as (2), while the definition of (8) is the same as (3). We may in turn conclude

$$\gamma_{XY} = \gamma_{YX} = \text{change of a right angle in } XY\text{-plane (rad)} \tag{9}$$

This section will guide the students to familiarize the strain components defined in (1-9).

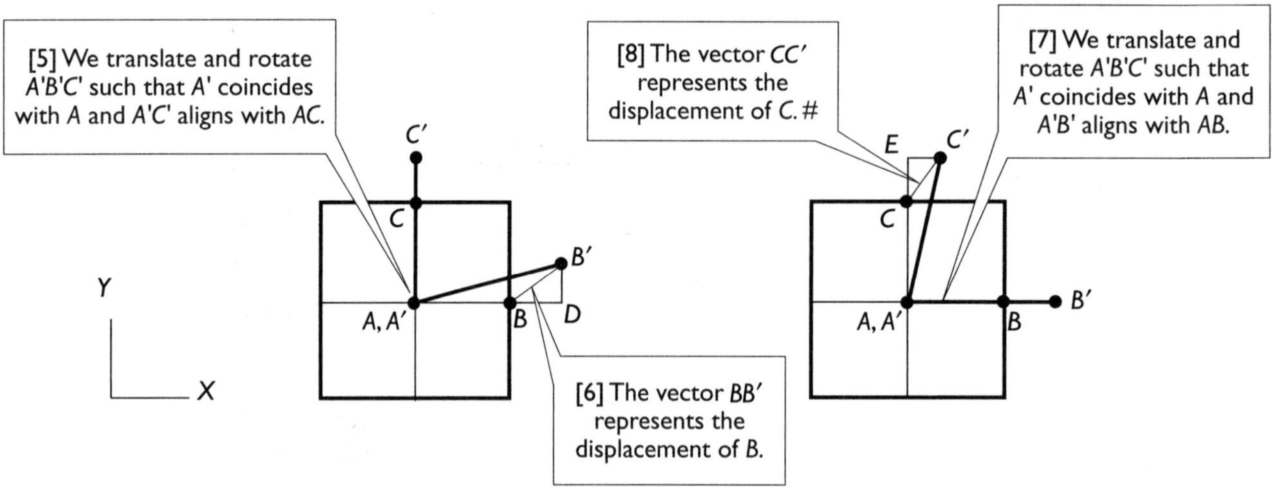

3.1-2 Start Up

[1] Launch **SolidWorks** and open the file **Cantilever** which was saved in Section 2.1.#

3.1-3 Strains of the **Elongation** Case

[1] Click **Elongation** tab.

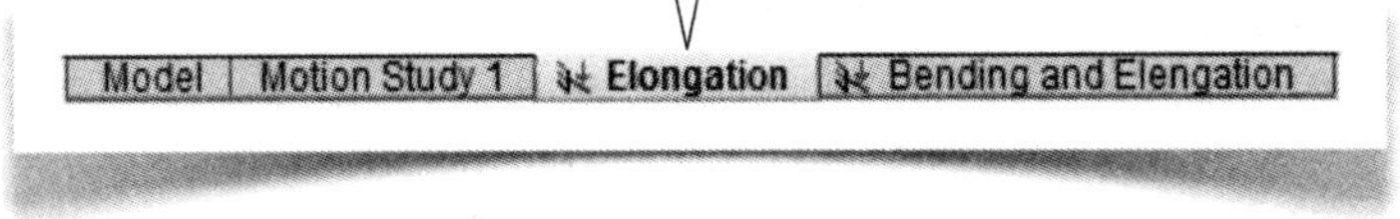

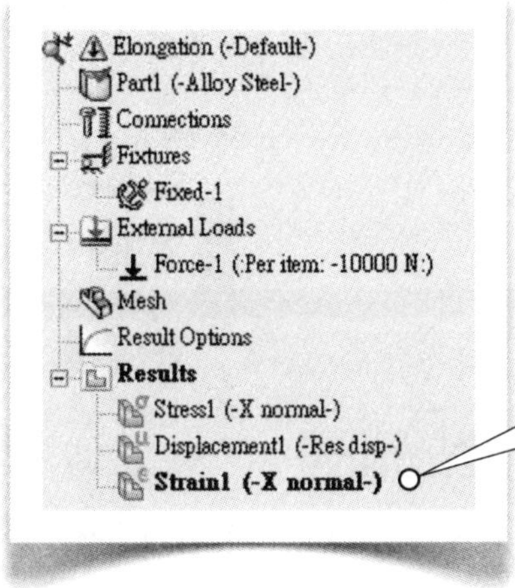

[2] Double-click **Strain1** to activate it. Double-click **Strain1** again to edit the definition. Select **EPSX** (ε_x) for **Component**.

[3] The strain component ε_x is the only non-zero component in this pure elongation case.

[4] The strain is uniform over the entire body except around the fixed end, for the same reason we'll explain in 5.2-3[16, 17], page 102.

[5] Use **Probe** to obtain the strain value (0.0002381) anywhere away from the fixed end. We'll demonstrate how this strain value is calculated from Eq. 3.1-1(1) in steps [6-8], next page.

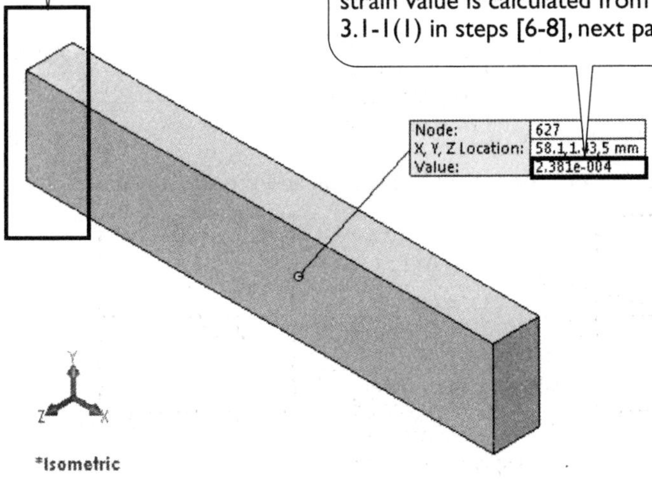

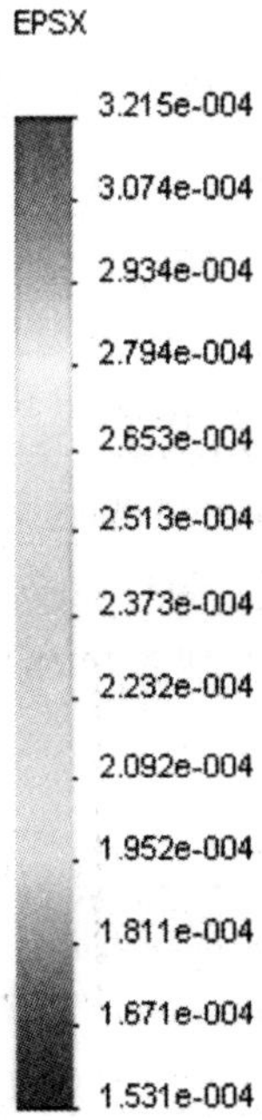

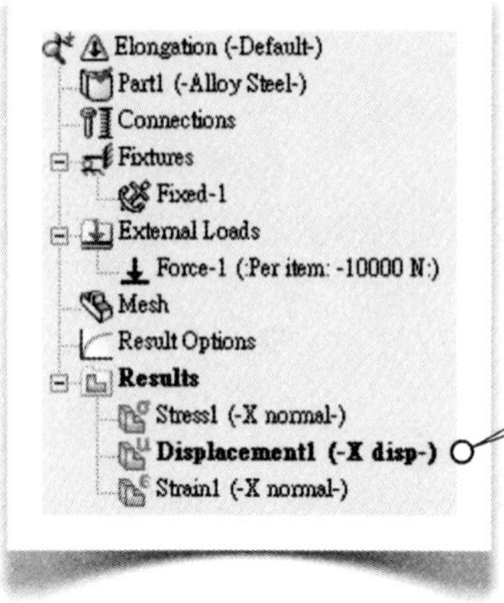

[6] Double-click **Displacement1** to activate it. Double-click **Displacement1** again to edit the definition. Select **UX** (u_X) for Component.

[7] Use **Probe** to obtain displacement values at any two locations aligned in X-direction. Here, the coordinates of the two locations are (47.3, 10, 5) and (54.1, 10, 5) and their displacements are 0.01117 mm and 0.01278 mm respectively. Your values may not be the same as here.

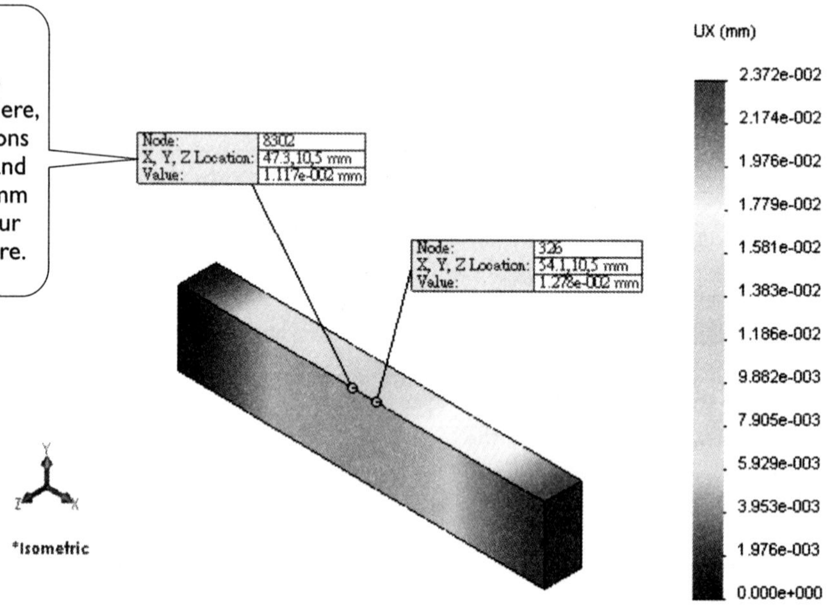

[8] Calculation of strains from displacements

Knowing the displacements at two neighboring locations along X-direction and the coordinates of the two locations, the strain can be calculated using Eq. 3.1-1(1),

$$\varepsilon_X = \frac{\Delta u_X}{\Delta X} = \frac{0.01278 - 0.01117}{54.1 - 47.3} = 0.0002368$$

which is consistent with the value in [5] with negligible numerical deviation.

Note that, for this pure elongation case, the strain is uniform over the entire body. Therefore, selecting any two locations will have the same strain value, as long as they are (a) away from the fixed end, and (b) aligned in X-direction. #

3.1-4 Strains for the **Bending and Elongation** Case

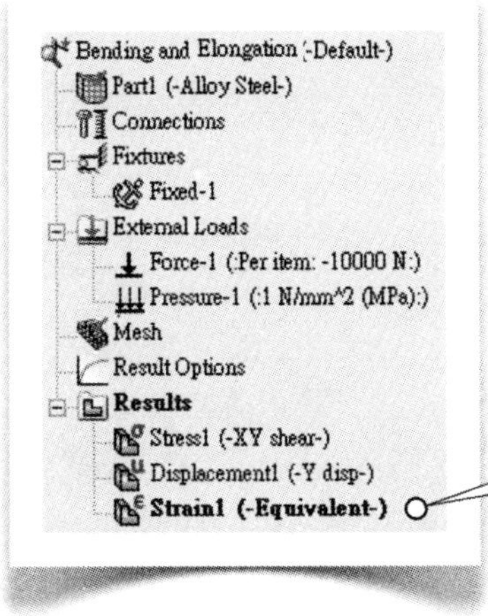

[1] Click **Bending and Elongation** tab.

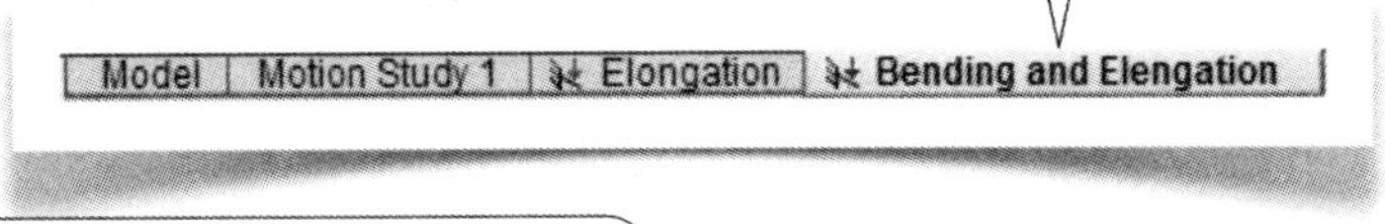

[2] Double-click **Strain1** to activate it. Double-click it again to edit the definition. Select **EPSX** (ε_X) for **Component**. Turn off **Deformed Shape** (1.1-12[3, 5], page 21).

[4] This is location **A**.

[3] Follow the steps in 1.2-5 (page 29) to create this section view.

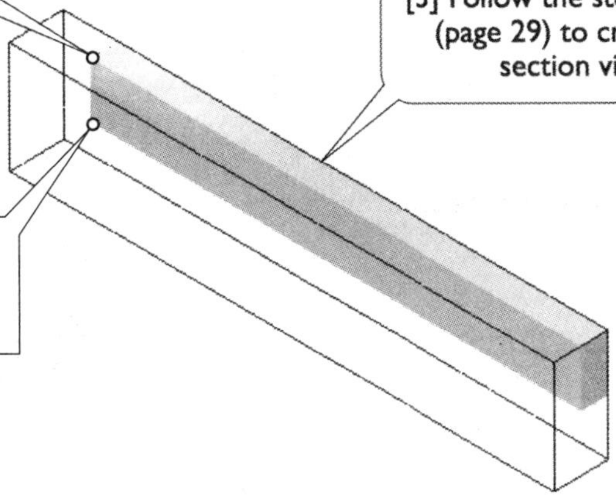

[5] This is location **B**.

[6] Use **Probe** to obtain the strain components at the two locations.

Strain Component	Location **A**	Location **B**
ε_X	0.0005176	0.0002441
ε_Y	-0.0001481	-0.00006664
ε_Z	-0.0001463	-0.00007014
γ_{XY}	0	-0.00008331
γ_{YZ}	0	0
γ_{ZX}	0	0

[7] Questions

1. A positive normal strain means the material is stretched, while a negative normal strain means the material is compressed. Explain that, in both locations **A** and **B**, ε_X is positive while ε_Y and ε_Z are negative. We'll see, in Section 4.1, this is called the **Poisson's effect**.

2. A positive shear strain means an originally $\pi/2$ angle become less than $\pi/2$, while a negative shear strain means an originally $\pi/2$ angle become larger than $\pi/2$. Explain that, at location **B**, γ_{XY} is negative.

[8] Let's use location **B** as an example to explore how the strain components are calculated using the definitions in 3.1-1 (pages 61, 62). #

3.1-5 Calculation of Strains from Displacements

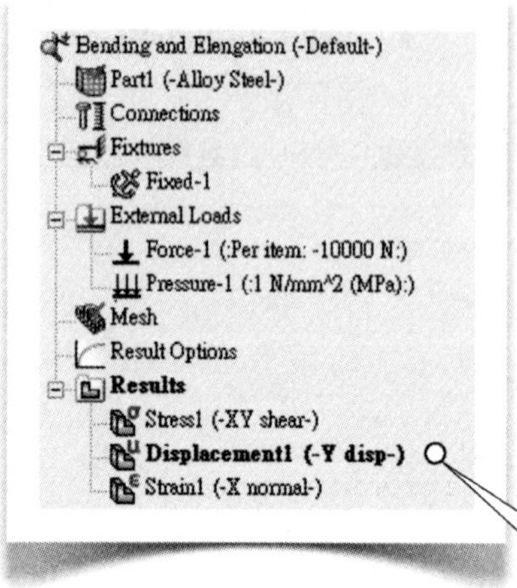

[1] Double-click **Displacement1** to activate it.

[2] Follow the steps in 1.2-5[1-10] (page 29) to create a section view. In addition, add two more section planes like this. This creates a 1x1x5 mm small cuboid [3]. Click **OK**.

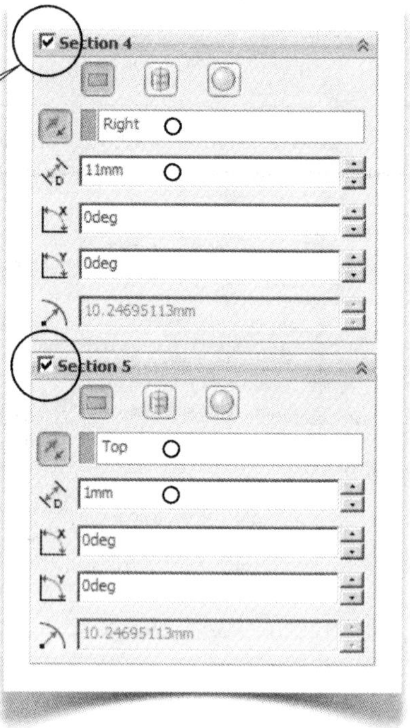

[6] Let's call it location **D**, which represents a neighboring point in *Y*-direction.

[4] This is location **B**.

[3] The result is a 1x1x5 mm small cuboid.

[5] Let's call this location **C**, which represents a neighboring point in *X*-direction.

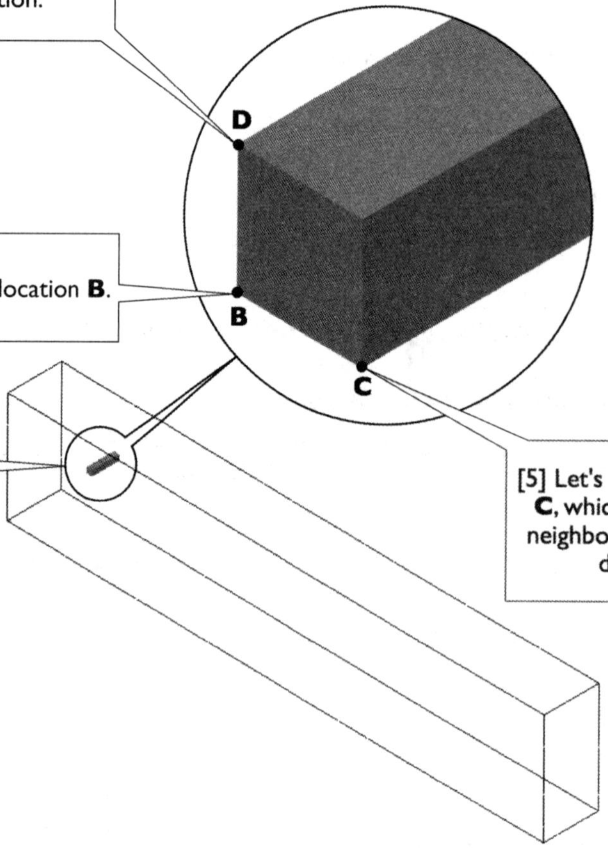

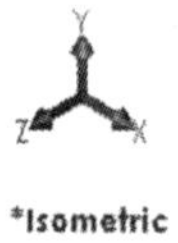

Displacement Component	Location **B**	Location **C**	Location **D**
u_X	0.002254 mm	0.002495 mm	0.002552 mm
u_Y	-0.002168 mm	-0.002563 mm	-0.002244 mm

[7] Use **Probe** to obtain the displacement components at locations **B**, **C**, and **D**.

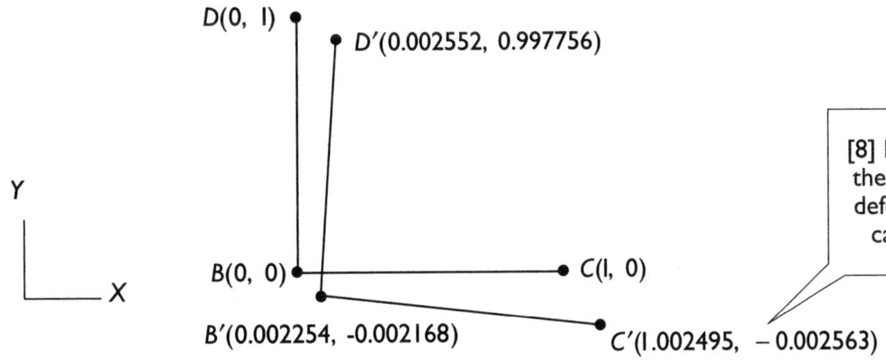

[8] From the table [7], the coordinates after deformation ($B'C'D'$) can be calculated.

[9] Calculation of strains from displacements

The normal strains can be calculated using definitions 3.1-1(1) (page 61),

$$B'C' \approx 1.002495 - 0.002254 = 1.000241, \quad \varepsilon_X \approx \frac{1.000241 - 1}{1} = 0.000241$$

$$B'D' \approx 0.997756 + 0.002168 = 0.999924, \quad \varepsilon_Y \approx \frac{0.999924 - 1}{1} = -0.000076$$

which are close to the values in 3.1-4[6] (page 65).

The length $D'C'$ is

$$D'C' \approx \sqrt{(1.002495 - 0.002552)^2 + (-0.002563 - 0.997756)^2} = 1.414399$$

The angle $\angle D'B'C'$ can be calculated using the Law of Cosine,

$$\angle D'B'C' = \cos^{-1} \frac{1.000241^2 + 0.999924^2 - 1.414399^2}{2 \times 1.000241 \times 0.999924} = 1.570881 \text{ (rad)}$$

$$\gamma_{XY} = \frac{\pi}{2} - \angle D'B'C' = 1.570796 - 1.570881 = -0.000085$$

which is close to the value in 3.1-4[6] (page 65).

[10] Save the document and exit **SolidWorks**. #

Section 3.2

Strains in the C-Bar

Strain Component	Location **B**
ε_X	0.00001996
ε_Y	0.00009667
ε_Z	-0.00004541
γ_{XY}	-0.0002470
γ_{YZ}	0
γ_{ZX}	0

3.2-1 Start Up

[1] Launch **SolidWorks** and open the file **CBar** which was saved in Section 2.2. #

3.2-2 View the Resultant Displacements

[1] Click **Static Force 2000 N** tab.

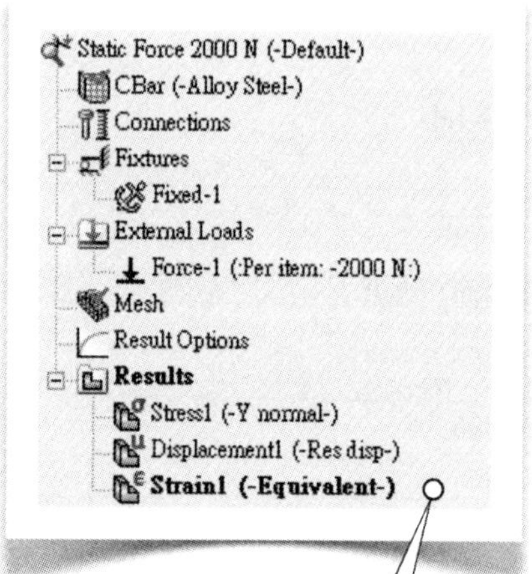

[2] Double-click **Strain1** to activate it.

[3] By default, **Equivalent Strain** (Eq. 10.2-3[16], page 203) is reported.

[5] We'll explore the strains at location **B** in Section 3.2-4. #

[4] We'll explore the strains at location **A** in Section 3.2-3.

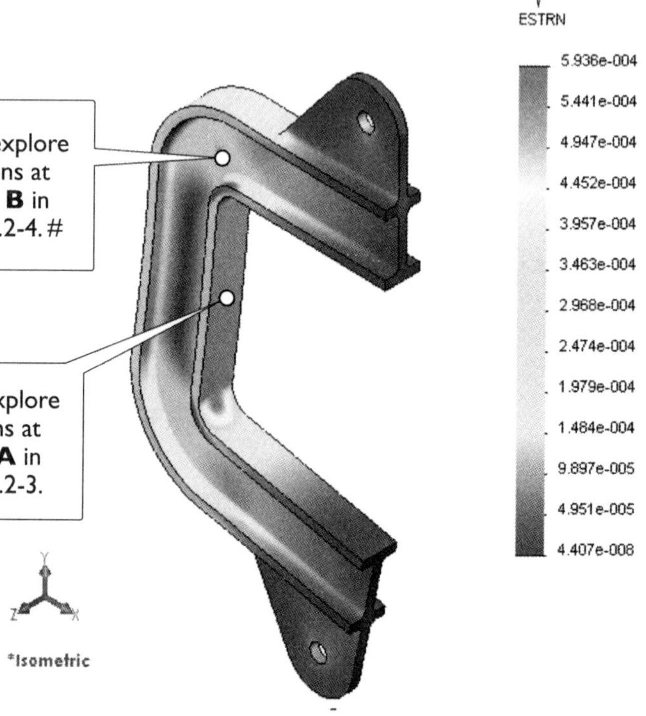

3.2-3 Strains at Location **A**

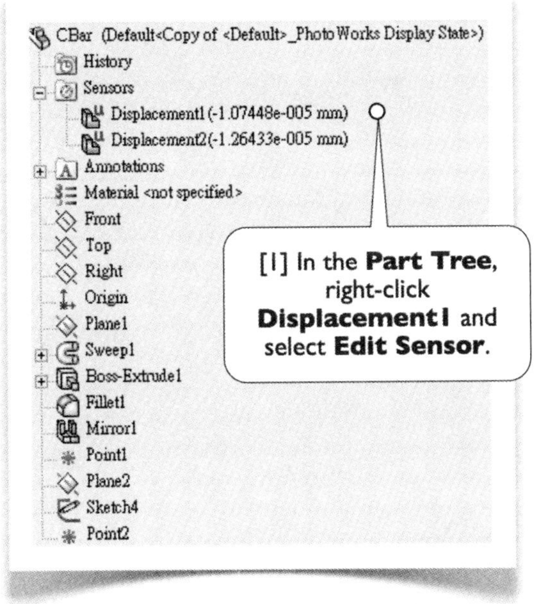

[1] In the **Part Tree**, right-click **Displacement1** and select **Edit Sensor**.

[2] Select **Workflow Sensitive**. This is a workflow sensitive sensor, meaning the **Data Quantity** will be determined in the upcoming workflow. We use this method because strain components are not available with the usual way as described in 2.2-3 and 2-2-4 (pages 58-59).

[3] Click **OK**.

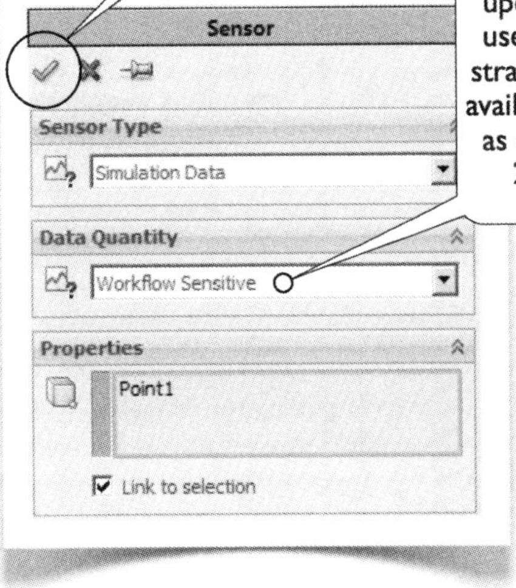

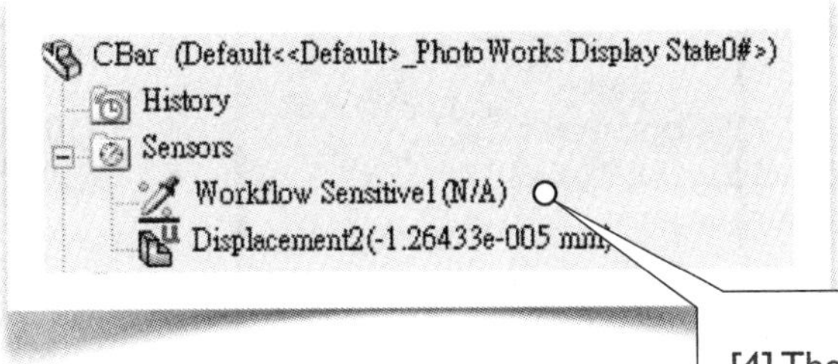

[4] The sensor's name changes to **Workflow Sensitive1**.

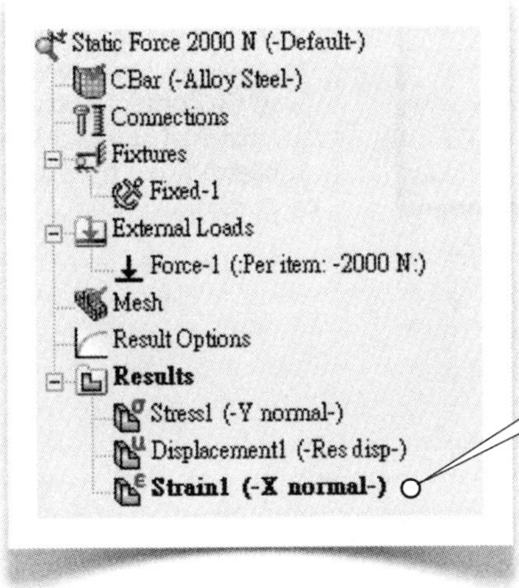

[5] In the **Study Tree**, double-click **Strain1** to edit the definition and select **EPSX** (ε_x) for **Component**. Right-click **Strain1** and select **Probe**.

[9] Click **OK**.

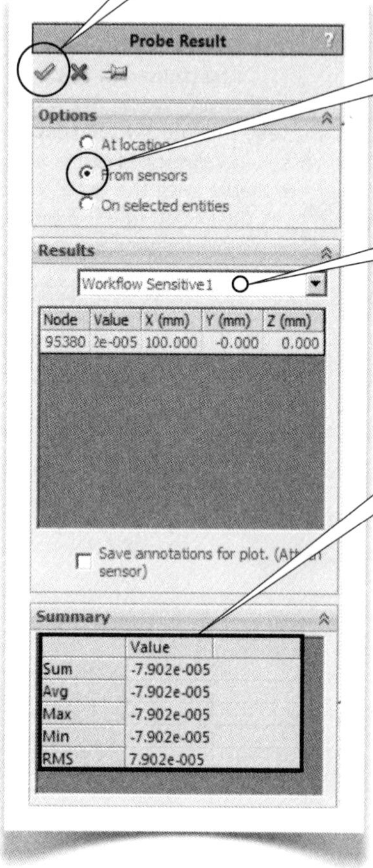

[6] Select **From sensor**.

[7] Select **Workflow Sensitive1**.

[8] The strain value is 0.00007902 (dimensionless).

Strain Component	Location **A**
ε_X	-0.00007902
ε_Y	0.0002821
ε_Z	-0.00007881
γ_{XY}	0
γ_{YZ}	0
γ_{ZX}	0

[10] Repeat the procedure similar to steps [5-9] to obtain other strain components.

[11] The results show that, at location **A**, there are no shear strain components; i.e., the material at location **A** is subjected to a pure stretching/compression without distortion.

[12] **Question**

A positive normal strain means the material is stretched, while a negative normal strain means the material is compressed. Explain that ε_Y is positive while ε_X and ε_Z are negative. We'll see, in Section 4.1, this is called the **Poisson's effect**. (Also see the questions in 3.1-4[7], page 65.) #

3.2-4 Strains at Location B

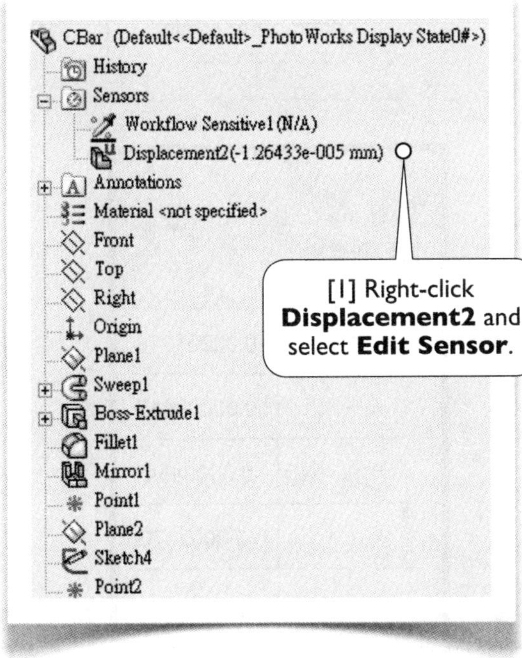

[1] Right-click **Displacement2** and select **Edit Sensor**.

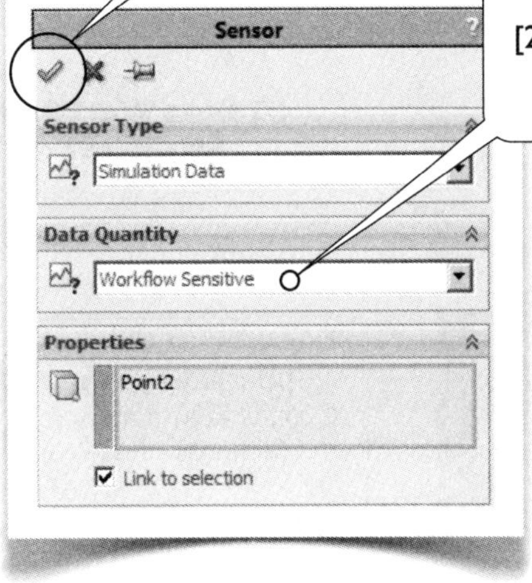

[2] Select **Workflow Sensitive**.

[3] Click **OK**.

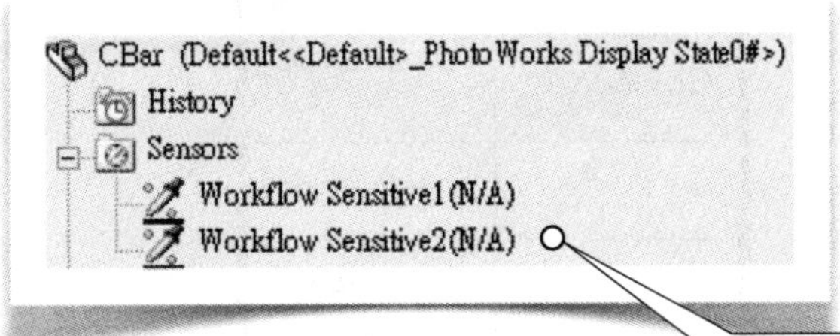

[4] The sensor's name changes to **Workflow Sensitive2**.

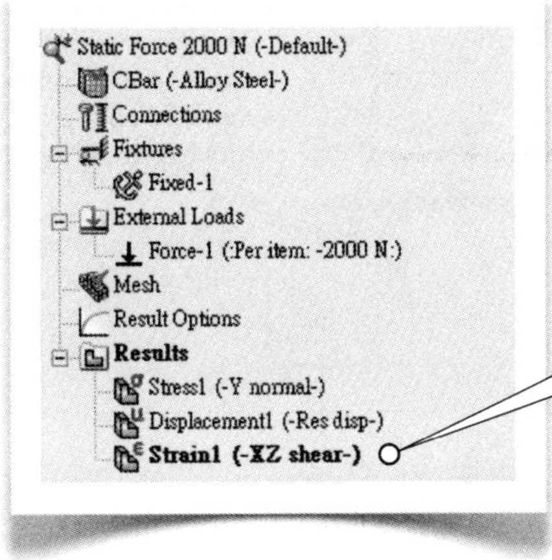

[5] Double-click **Strain1** to edit the definition and select **EPSX** (ε_x) for **Component**. Right-click **Strain1** and select **Probe**.

[9] Click **OK**.

[6] Select **From sensor**.

[7] Select **Workflow Sensitive2**.

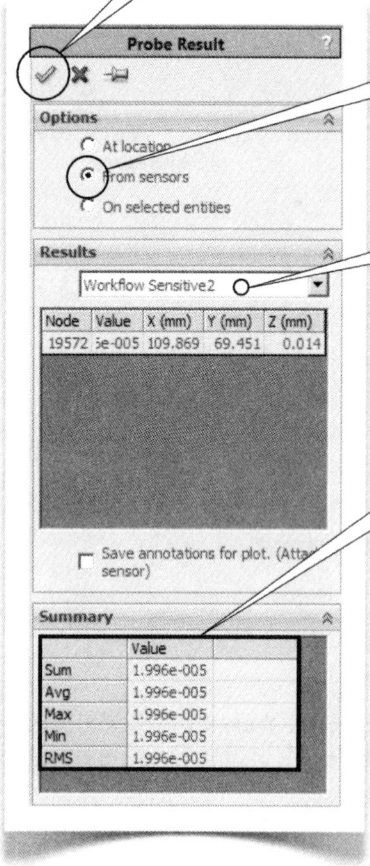

[8] The strain value is 0.00001996 (dimensionless).

[10] Repeat the procedure similar to steps [5-9] to obtain other strain components.

Strain Component	Location **B**
ε_X	0.00001996
ε_Y	0.00009667
ε_Z	-0.00004541
γ_{XY}	-0.0002470
γ_{YZ}	0
γ_{ZX}	0

[11] Save the document and exit **SolidWorks**. #

Chapter 4

Stress-Strain Relations

In linear elasticity (4.2-3[12], page 82), the relations between stresses and strains are related by

$$\varepsilon_X = \frac{\sigma_X}{E} - \nu\frac{\sigma_Y}{E} - \nu\frac{\sigma_Z}{E}$$
$$\varepsilon_Y = \frac{\sigma_Y}{E} - \nu\frac{\sigma_Z}{E} - \nu\frac{\sigma_X}{E} \qquad \text{Copy of 4.3-1(1)}$$
$$\varepsilon_Z = \frac{\sigma_Z}{E} - \nu\frac{\sigma_X}{E} - \nu\frac{\sigma_Y}{E}$$

$$\gamma_{XY} = \frac{\tau_{XY}}{G},\ \gamma_{YZ} = \frac{\tau_{YZ}}{G},\ \gamma_{ZX} = \frac{\tau_{ZX}}{G} \qquad \text{Copy of 4.3-1(2)}$$

where three material parameters are involved: the **Young's Modulus** *E*, the **Poisson's Ratio** ν, and the **Shear Modulus** *G*. These three material parameters are not independent, they are related by Eq. 4.2-1(1), page 80. These three parameters are the most important material parameters in the study of Mechanics of Materials; therefore, it is very important to fully understand the physical meaning of these parameters. Note that, in **SolidWorks Simulation**, the **Young's Modulus** is also called the **Elastic Modulus**.

Section 4.1

Poisson's Effects

4.1-1 Introduction

When a body is stretched, the body's lateral dimensions usually contract; when the body is compressed, the lateral dimensions expand. This phenomenon is called the **Poisson's Effect**. The ratio between a lateral contracting strain and the longitudinal stretching strain is called the **Poisson's ratio** ν, which is typically between 0 and 0.5 (although a negative Poisson's ratio is possible). For a steel, $\nu \approx 0.3$, while for a rubber, $\nu \approx 0.5$. **Poisson's ratios** are important characteristics of engineering materials. The purpose of this section is to guide the students to fully understand the **Poisson's effect** and **Poisson's ratio** of a material.

4.1-2 Start Up

[1] Launch **SolidWorks** and create a new part. Set up **MMGS** unit system with zero decimal places for the length unit. #

4.1-3 Create a 10 x10 x10 mm^3 Cube

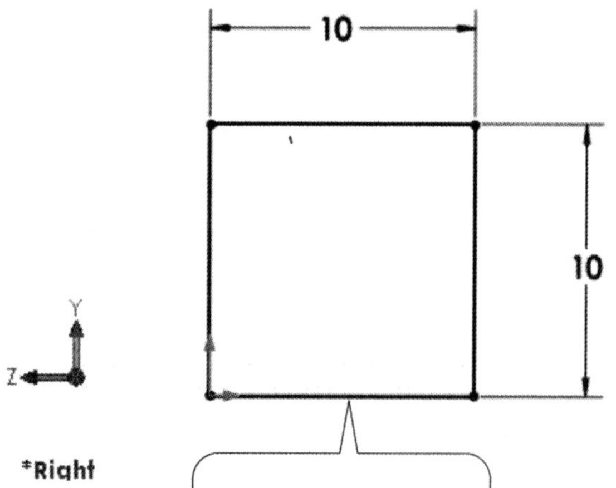

[1] On the **Right** plane, draw a square like this.

[2] **Extrude** 10 mm to create a 10x10x10 mm^3 cube.

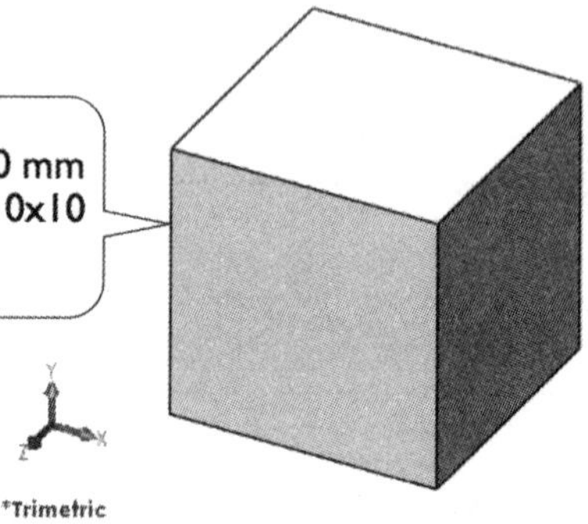

[3] Save the document with the name **Cube**. #

4.1-4 Create a Static Study and Assign Material

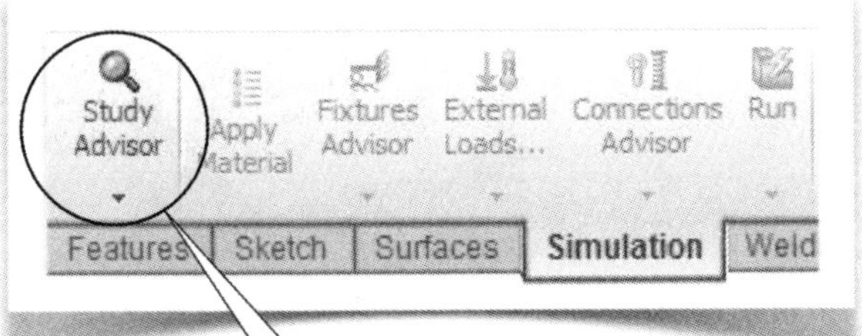

[1] In the **Simulation Toolbar**, select **Study Advisor>New Study**. Name the new study **Poisson Effect**. Leave **Static** as default **Study Type**.

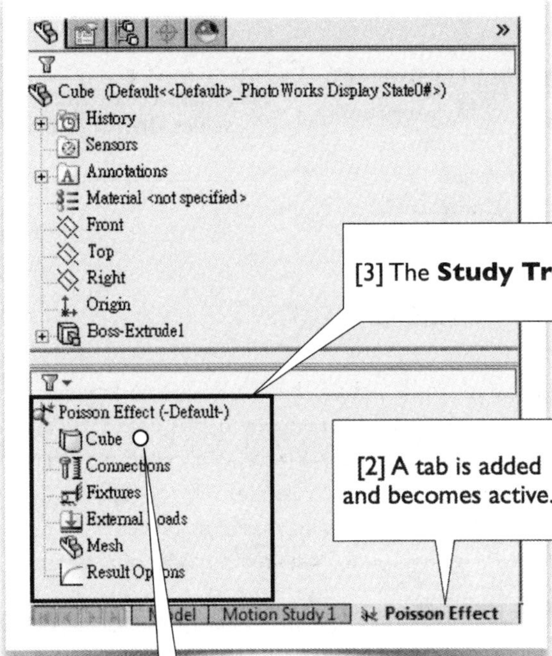

[3] The **Study Tree**.

[2] A tab is added and becomes active.

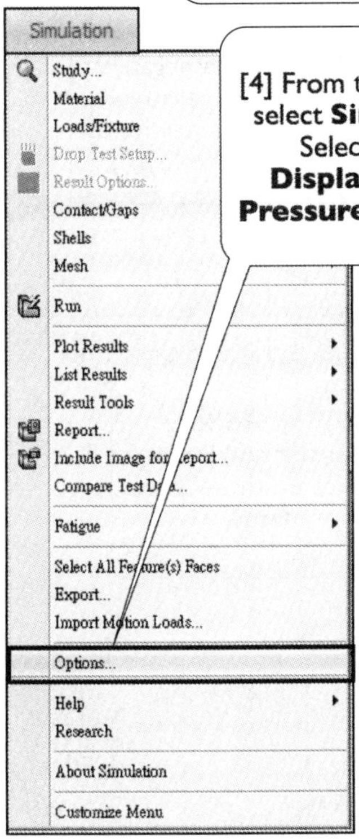

[4] From the **Pull-Down Menus**, select **Simulation>Options...** Select **mm** for **Length/ Displacement** and **MPa** for **Pressure/Stress** (1.1-7, page 15).

[5] Right-click **Cube** and select **Apply/ Edit Material...** and apply **Alloy Steel** for the model (see [6-10]).

[8] For an explanation of the **Linear Elastic Isotropic** material model, see 4.2-3[12], page 82.

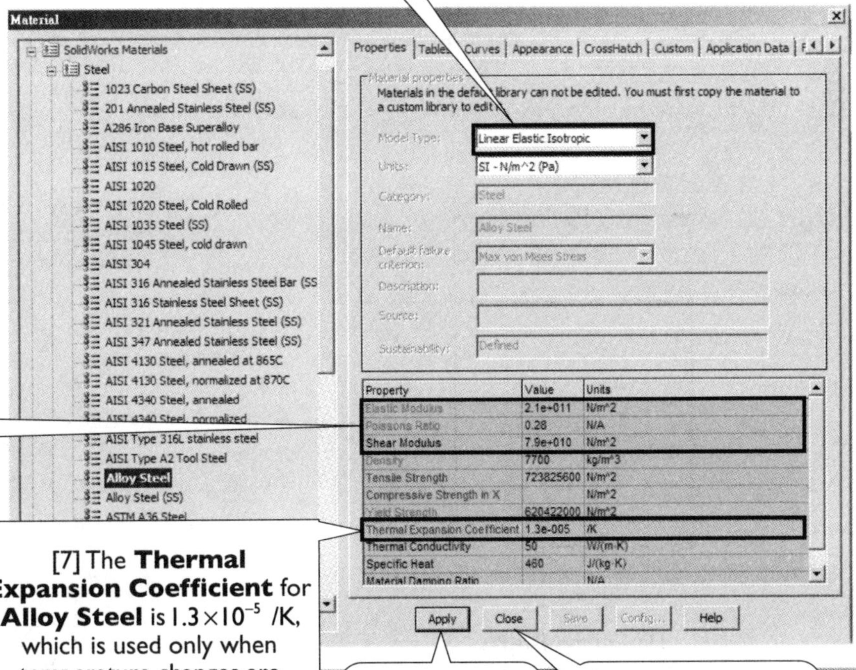

[6] The **Poisson's Ratio** for **Alloy Steel** is 0.28. We'll verify this value in 4.1-7[2], page 79. Also note that the **Elastic Modulus** (another name for the **Young's Modulus**) is 210 GPa and the **Shear Modulus** is 79 GPa. We'll discuss these two moduli in Section 4.2.

[7] The **Thermal Expansion Coefficient** for **Alloy Steel** is 1.3×10^{-5} /K, which is used only when temperature changes are involved (see Section 5.3).

[9] Click **Apply**.

[10] Click **Close**. #

4.1-5 Set Up Boundary Conditions and Run the Model

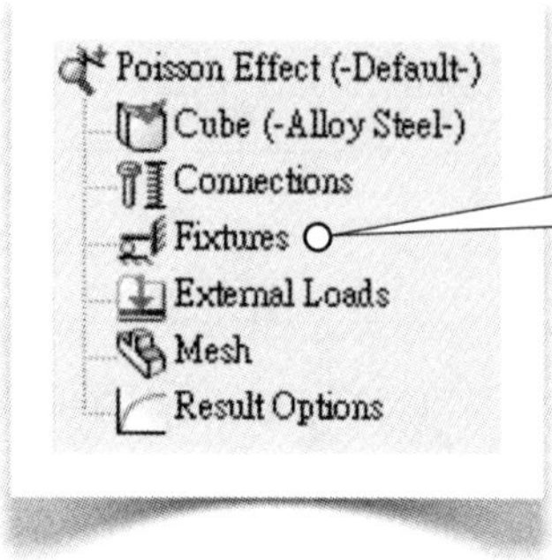

[1] Right-click **Fixtures** and select **Roller/Slider...**

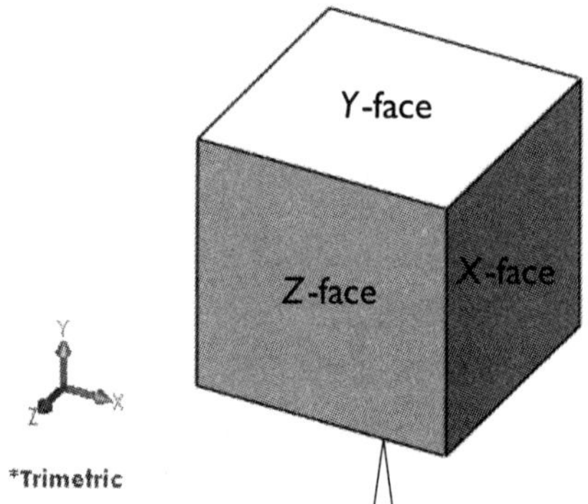

[4] The **Roller/ Slider** condition will apply on the negative-X-face, the negative-Y-face, and the neative-Z-face. (see [5]).

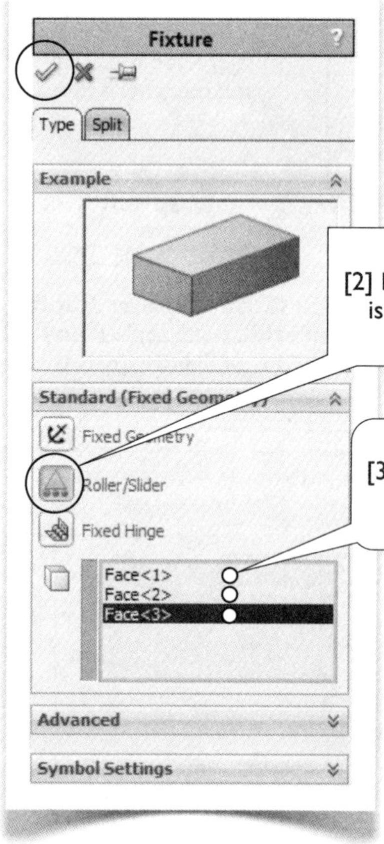

[2] **Roller/Slider** is pre-selected.

[3] Select three faces shown in [4, 5].

[5] The **Roller/ Slider** condition applies on these three faces.

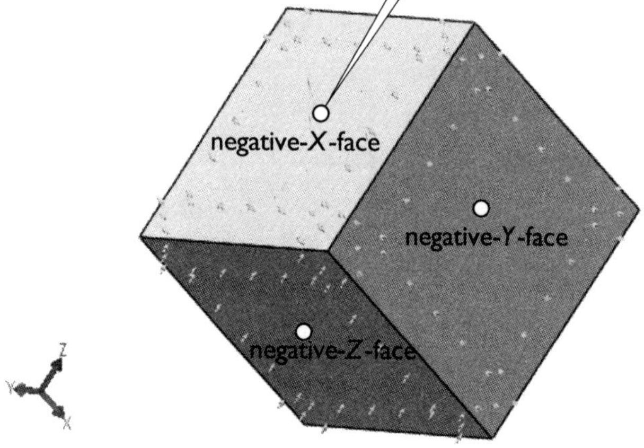

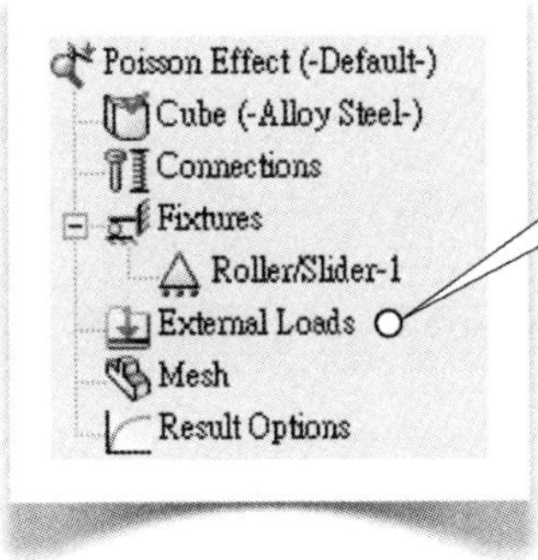

[6] Right-click **External Loads** and select **Force...**

[9] Click **OK**.

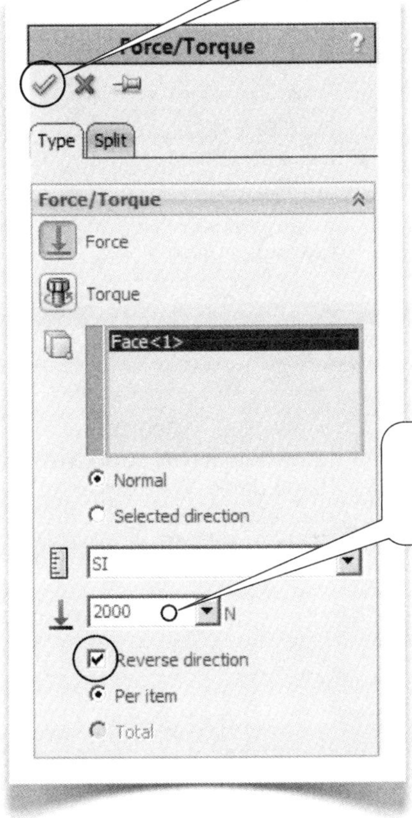

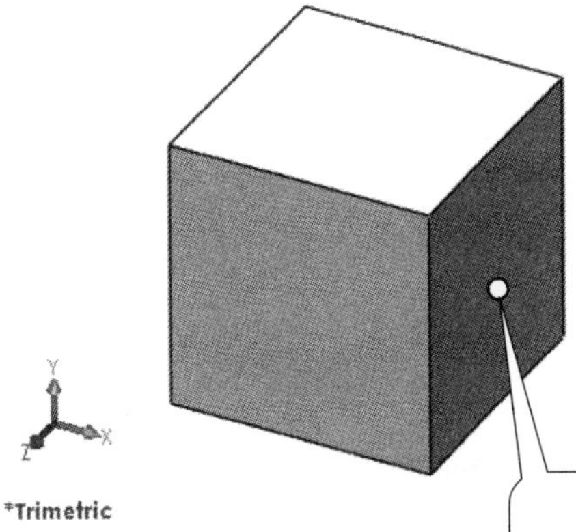

[7] Select this face.

[8] Type 2000 (N) and click **Reverse direction**.

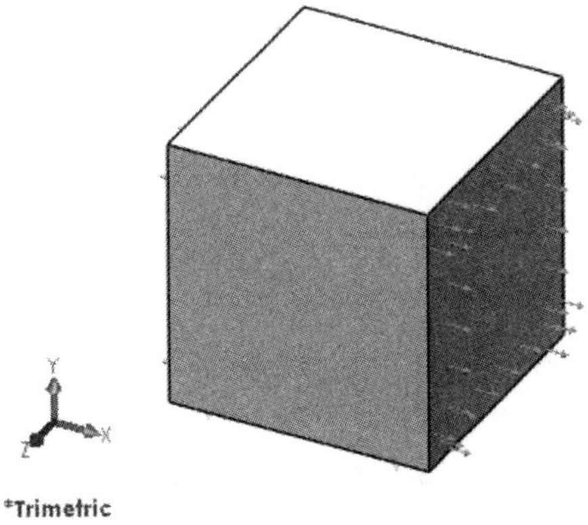

[10] In the **Simulation Toolbar**, click **Run**. #

4.1-6 Animate the Deformation

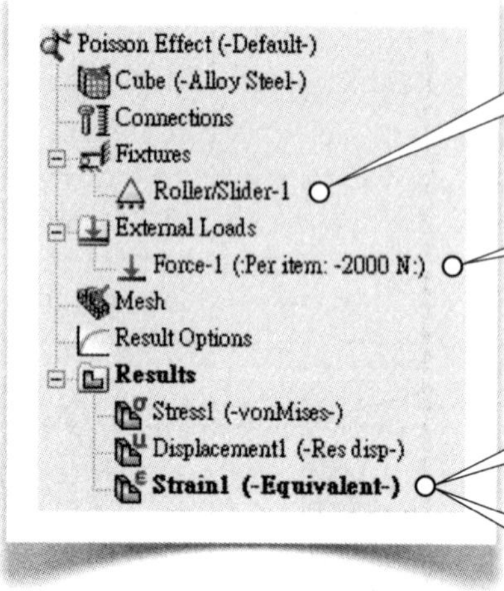

[1] Hide **Roller/Slider-1**

[2] Hide **Force-1**.

[3] Double-click **Strain1** to activate it.

[4] Double-click **Strain1** again to edit the definition.

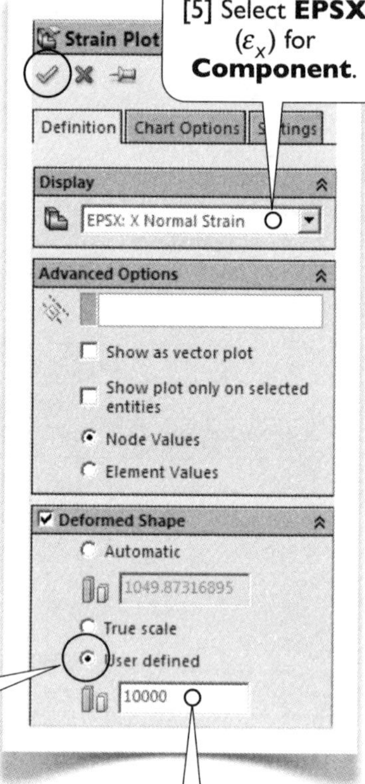

[5] Select **EPSX** (ε_x) for **Component**.

[6] Click **User defined**.

[7] Type 10000. The deformation will be scaled 10000 times. We exaggerate the deformation so that the **Poisson's effect** will be observed more easily.

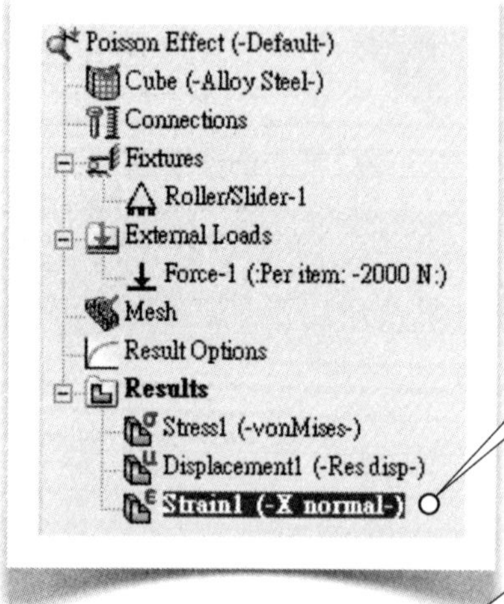

[8] Right-click-select **Animate...**

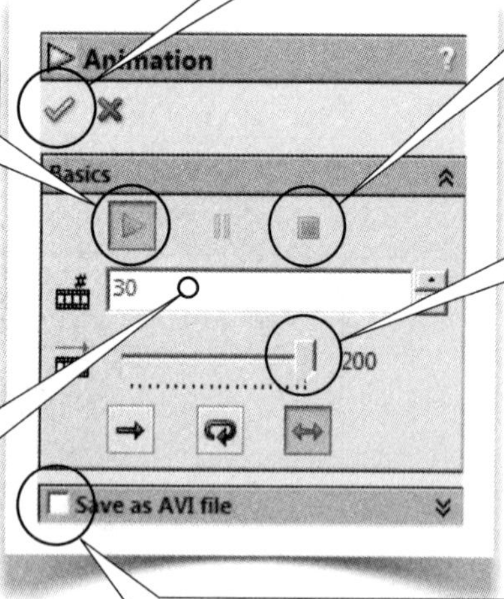

[9] Click **Stop**.

[10] Type 30 for **Frames**.

[11] Drag the slider all the way to the right to set the max **Speed**.

[12] You may save the animation as an **AVI** file.

[13] Click **Play**.

[14] As the cube is stretched along *X*-direction, the cube contracts in both *Y*- and *Z*-directions. This phenomenon is called the **Poisson's Effect**. #

[15] Click **OK**.

4.1-7 Calculate **Poisson's Ratio**

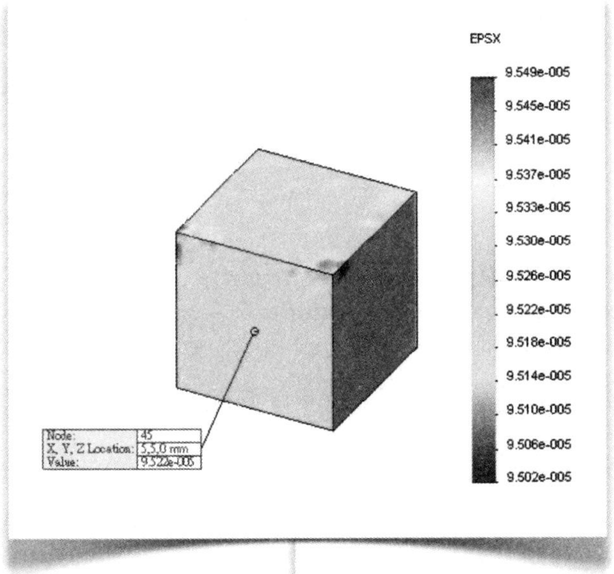

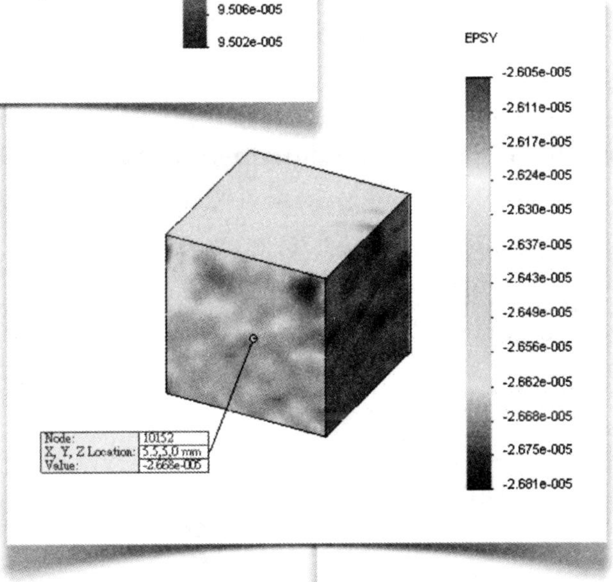

Strain Component	Anywhere in the body
ε_X	0.00009522
ε_Y	-0.00002668
ε_Z	-0.00002666
γ_{XY}	0
γ_{XZ}	0
γ_{YZ}	0

[1] Use **Probe** to obtain strain components. Note that the strain is essentially uniform over the entire body.

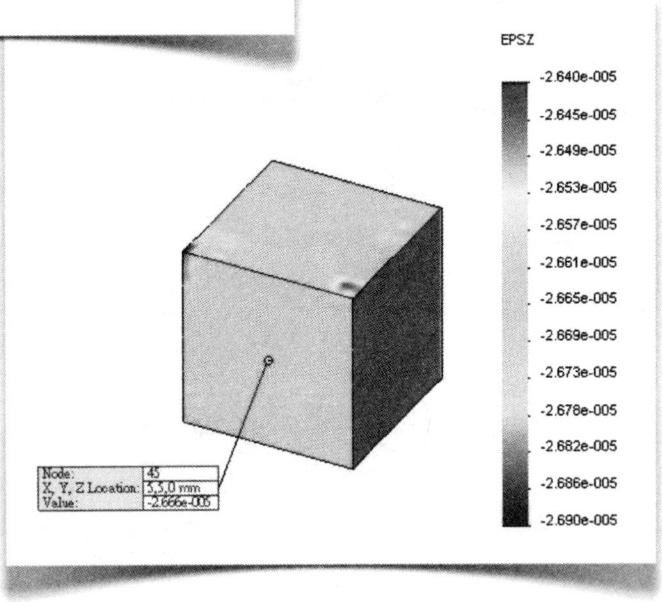

[2] Poisson's Ratio

By definition, **Poisson's ratio** is the ratio between the lateral contracting strain and the longitudinal stretching strain, i.e., in this case

$$\nu = -\frac{\varepsilon_Y}{\varepsilon_X} = -\frac{\varepsilon_Z}{\varepsilon_X} = \frac{0.00002668}{0.00009522} = 0.28$$

which is consistent with the value in 4.1-4[6], page 75.

[3] Save the document and exit **SolidWorks**. #

Section 4.2

Young's Modulus and Shear Modulus

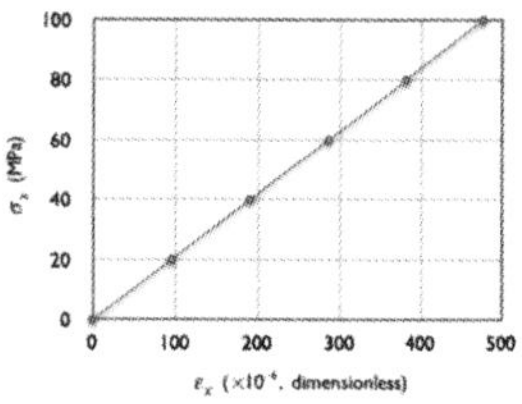

4.2-1 Introduction

In this section, we'll conduct a tensile test and a shear test on the 10x10x10 mm^3 steel cube, created in Section 4.1. The purpose is to introduce two material parameters, **Young's modulus** E and **shear modulus** G. Together with the **Poisson's ratio** ν, these three parameters are the most fundamental properties of an engineering material. These three parameters are not independent one another; there exists a relationship among them:

$$G = \frac{E}{2(1+\nu)} \quad (1)$$

SolidWorks Simulation allows you to input a **Young's modulus** and a **Poisson's ratio** for a material, and the **shear modulus** will be calculated according to Eq. (1). In the case of **Alloy Steel** (4.1-4[6], page 75), the **Poisson's ratio** is 0.28, **Young's modulus** is 210 GPa, therefore, the **shear modulus** is

$$G = \frac{E}{2(1+\nu)} = \frac{210}{2(1+0.28)} = 82 \text{ GPa} \quad (2)$$

Note that, in 4.1-4[6] (page 75), the **shear modulus** is input as 79 GPa, however, **SolidWorks Simulation** internally uses the value 82 GPa, calculated in Eq. (2), instead.

4.2-2 Start Up

[1] Launch **SolidWorks** and open the file **Cube** which was saved in Section 4.1.

[2] Right-click **Poisson Effect** tab and select **Duplicate**.

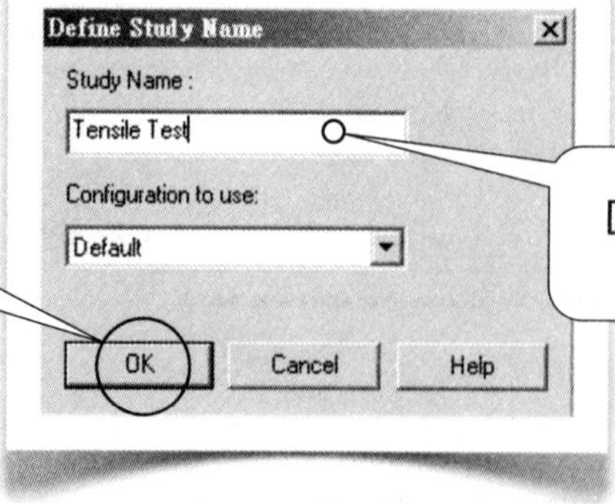

[3] Type **Tensile Test**.

[4] Click **OK**. #

4.2-3 Young's Modulus

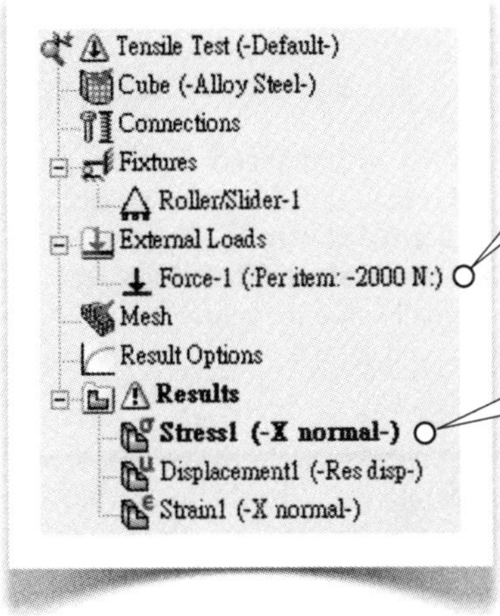

[1] Remember that the applied tensile force is 2,000 N.

[2] Redefine **Stress1** so that it displays σ_x.

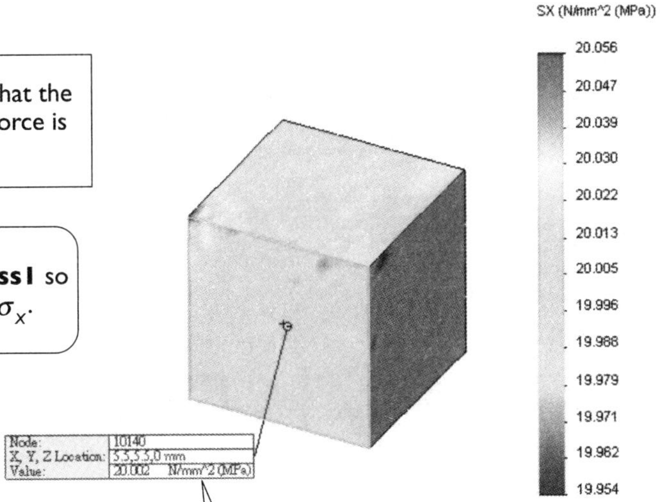

[3] Use **Probe** to obtain the stress σ_x (20 MPa).

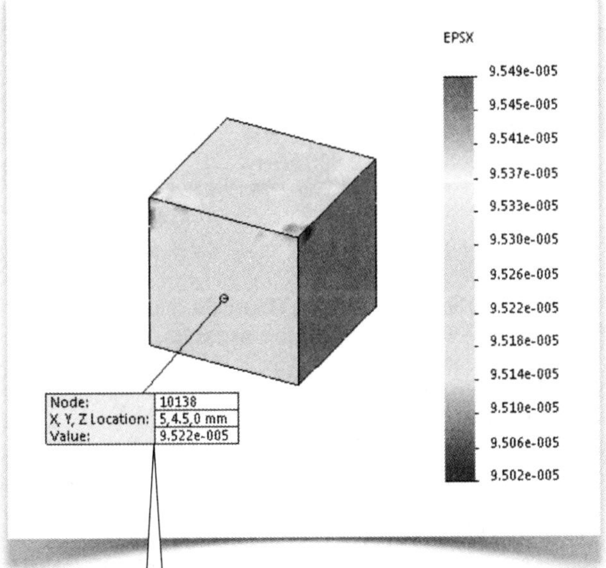

[4] Use **Probe** to obtain the strain ε_x (0.00009522).

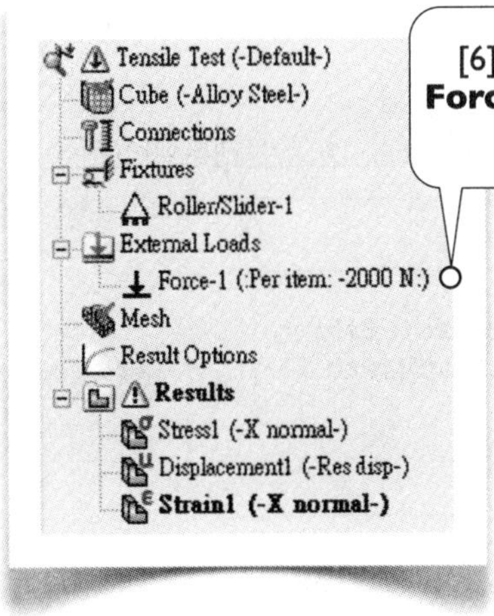

[6] Double-click **Force-1** to edit the definition.

[5] Tabulate the results like this.

Applied force (N)	Stress (MPa)	Strain (Dimensionless)
2,000	20	0.00009522

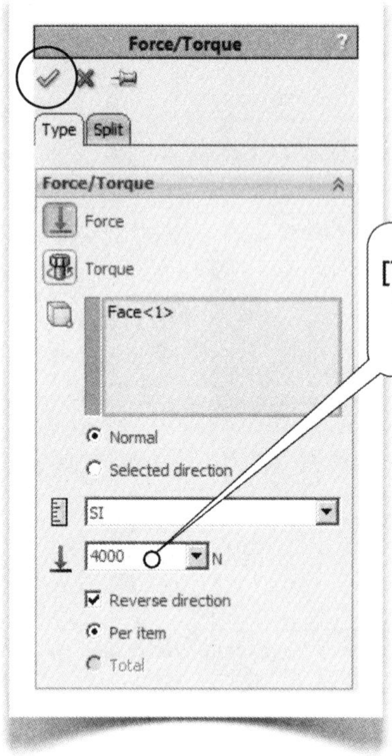

[8] Click **Run**. Use **Probe** to obtain σ_x and ε_x. Record the results.

[7] Change the **Force Value** to 4,000 (N). Click **OK**.

[9] Repeat steps [6, 7, 8] with different **Force Values** and tabulate the results (stress and strain) like this. Note that the **Simulation** does not allow you to input a zero **Force Value**. Therefore, we input a very small value instead.

Applied Force (N)	Stress (MPa)	Strain (Dimensionless)	Stress/Strain (MPa)
0.001	0	0	n.a.
2000	20	0.00009522	210040
4000	40	0.0001904	210084
6000	60	0.0002856	210084
8000	80	0.0003809	210029
10000	100	0.0004761	210040

[10] Plot a stress-versus-strain graph (using a spreadsheet program such as **Microsoft Excel**), it should be like this.

[11] The slope of this straight line is called the **Young's modulus** (in 4.1-4[6] (page 75), it is also called the **Elastic modulus**) of the material. In this case, the slope is 210 GPa (see the last column of [9]), which is consistent with the value in 4.1-4[6] (page 75).

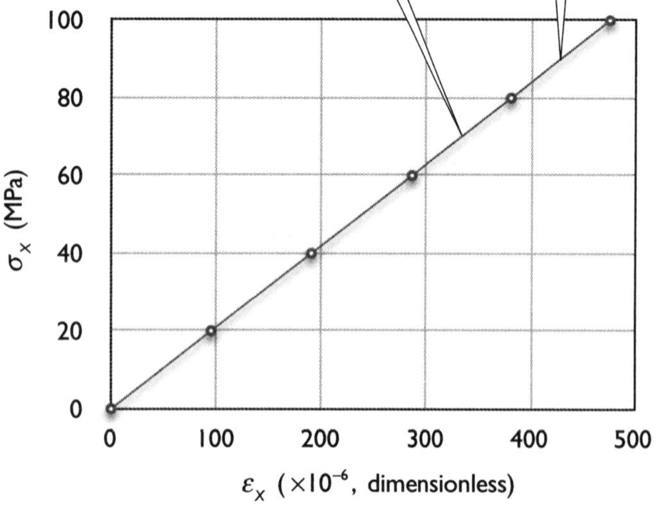

[12] Linear Elastic Isotropic Model

Note that when we scale the applied forces, the responses (displacements, strains, and stresses) are also proportionally scaled. This behavior is called the **linear elasticity**, which can be characterized with a **Young's modulus** and a **Poisson's ratio**. When the material properties (**Young's modulus** and **Poisson's ratio**) are independent of directions, the material is called an **Isotropic** material. In this book, we discuss only **Linear Elastic Isotropic** material model (see 4.1-4[8], page 75) almost exclusively except in Section 7.2, where a **Plasticity** material model is used. #

4.2-4 Shear Modulus

[1] Right-click **Tensile Test** tab and select **Duplicate**.

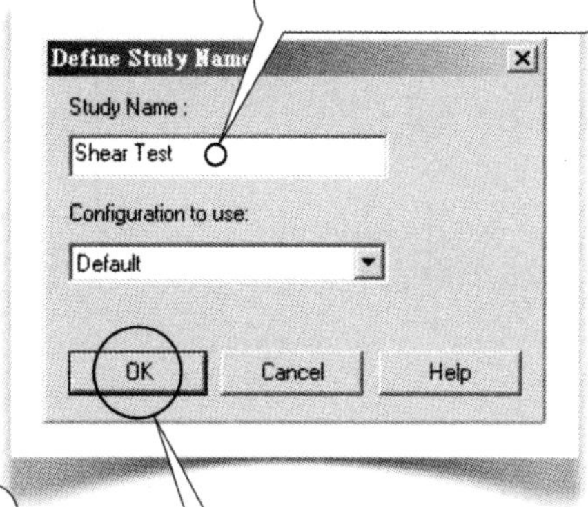

[2] Type **Shear Test**.

[3] Click **OK**.

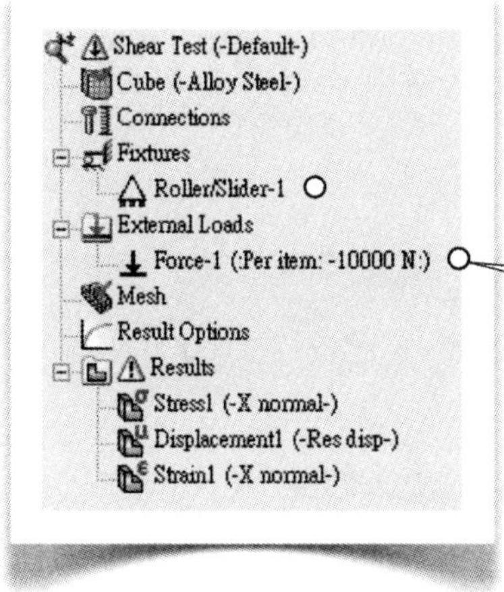

[4] In the **Shear Test**, right-click **Force-1** and select **Delete**. Also right-click **Roller/Slider-1** and select **Delete**.

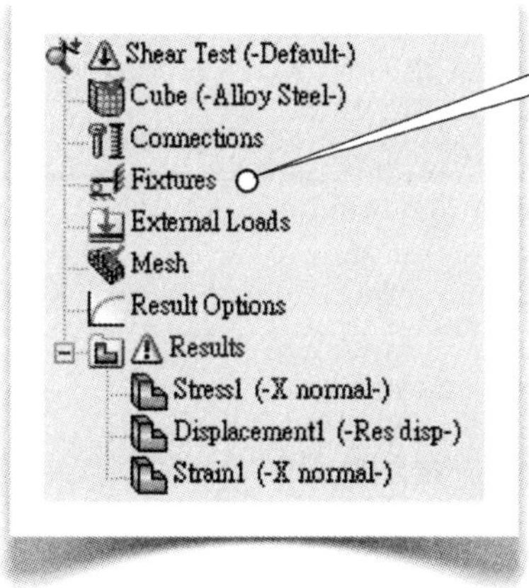

[5] Right-click **Fixtures** and select **Roller/Slider...**

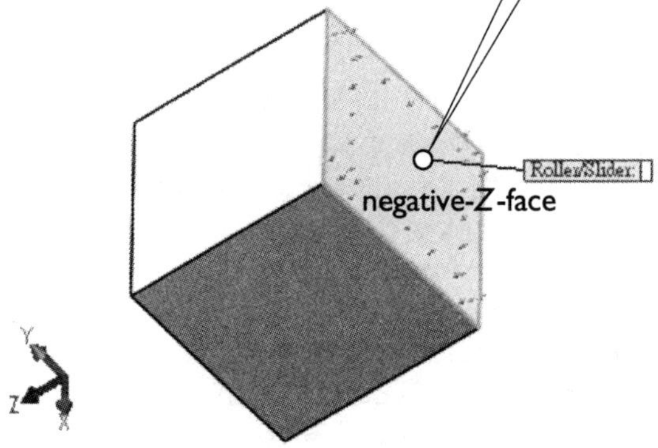

[6] Apply **Roller/ Slider** condition on the negative-Z-face.

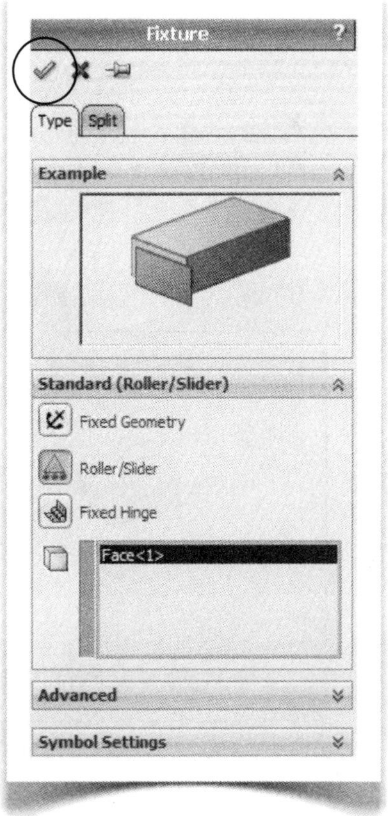

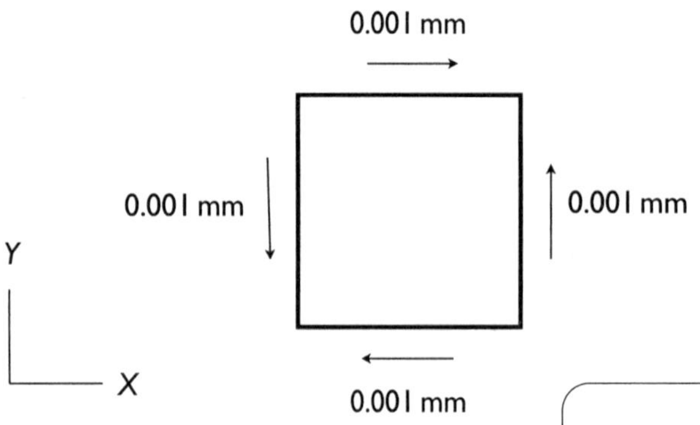

[7] Next, we will apply displacements of 0.001 mm on *X*-face, *Y*-face, negative-*X*-face, and negative-*Y*-face like this.

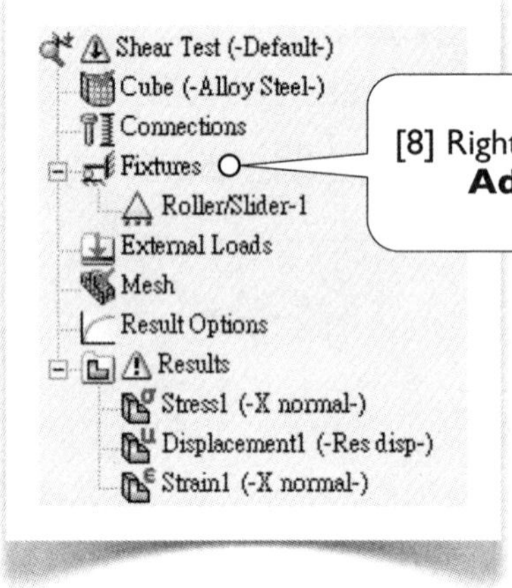

[8] Right-click **Fixtures** and select **Advanced Fixtures...**

[9] Select **On Flat Faces**.

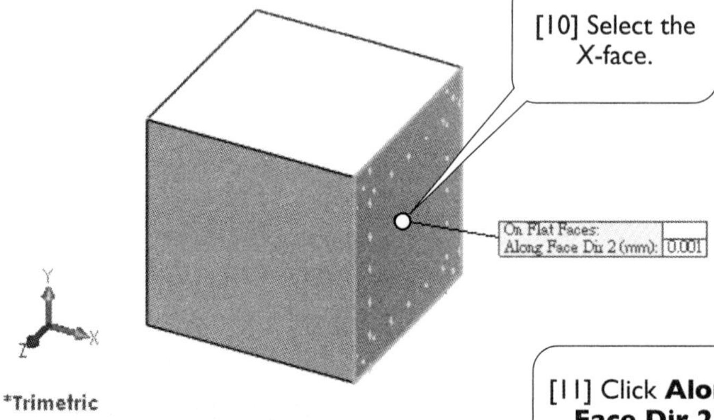

[10] Select the *X*-face.

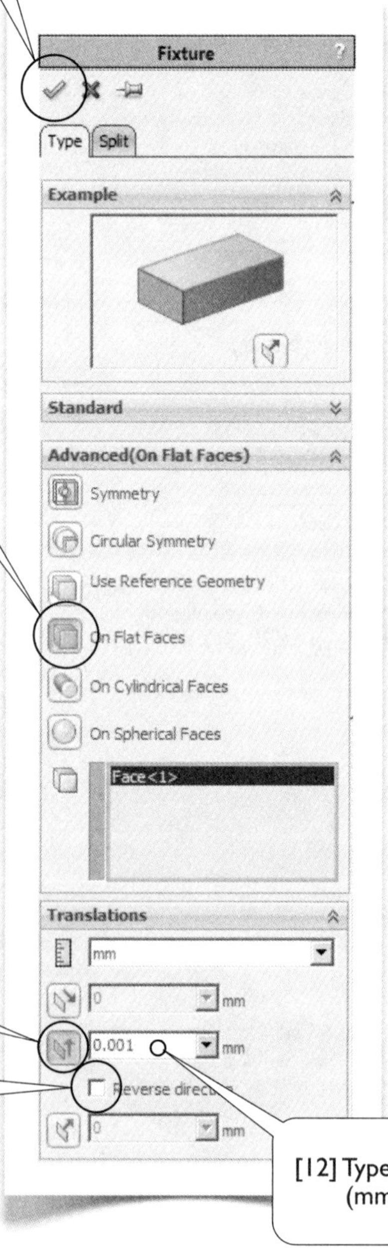

[11] Click **Along Face Dir 2**.

[12] Type 0.001 (mm).

[13] If the arrows point to the negative-*Y*-direction, then click **Reverse direction** so that the arrows point to the positive-*Y*-direction

[14] Click **OK**.

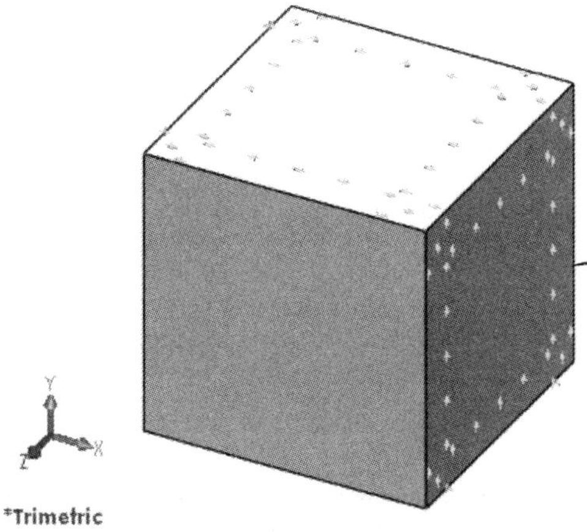

[15] Repeat the procedure similar to steps [8-14] to define the displacements shown in [7], which is a state of **pure shearing** on *XY*-plane; i.e., the only non-zero stress/strain components are τ_{XY} and γ_{XY}.

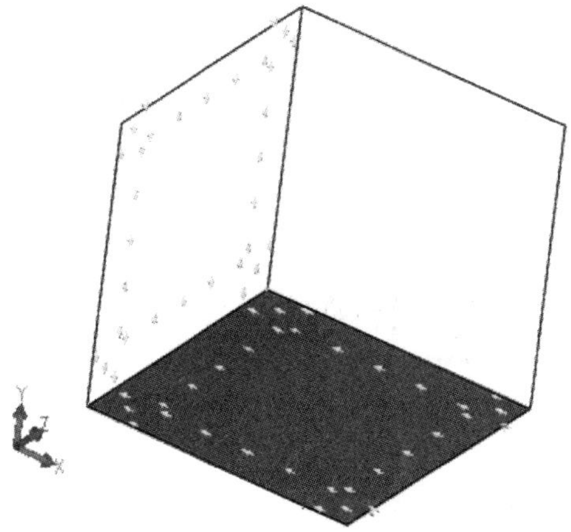

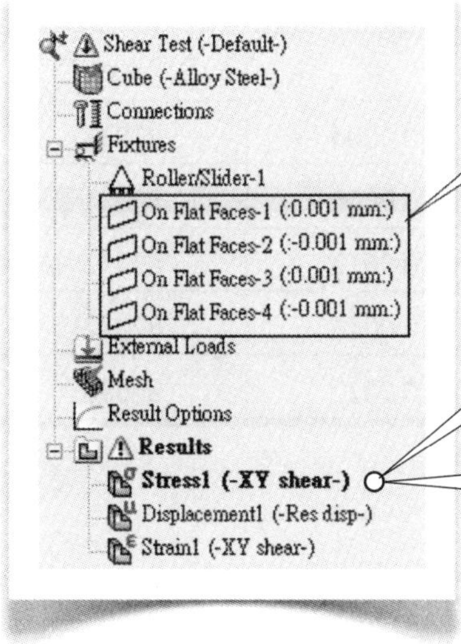

[16] The four displacement conditions.

[18] Activate **Stress1** and make sure the **Component** is τ_{XY}.

[17] Click **Run**. Obtain τ_{XY} (32.813 MPa) and γ_{XY} (0.0004) and tabulate the results (see [23], next page).

[20] Right-click-select **Animate...**

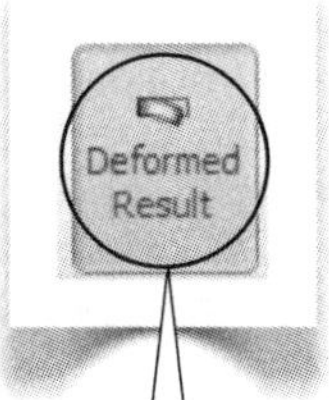

[19] On **Simulation Toolbar**, turn on **Deformed Results**.

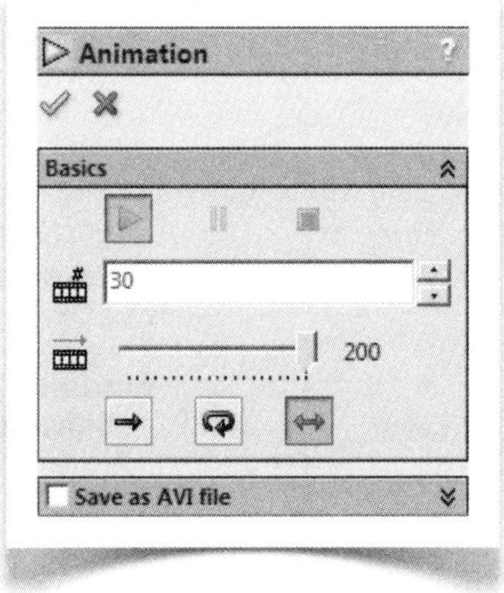

[21] Observe this pure shearing deformation. Note that we've turned off the **Fixrures**.

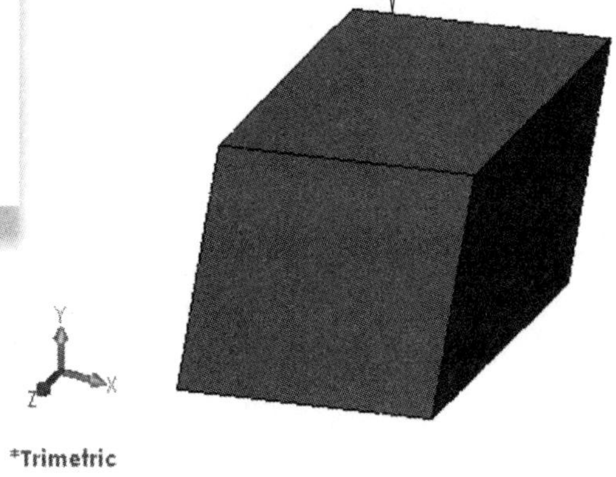

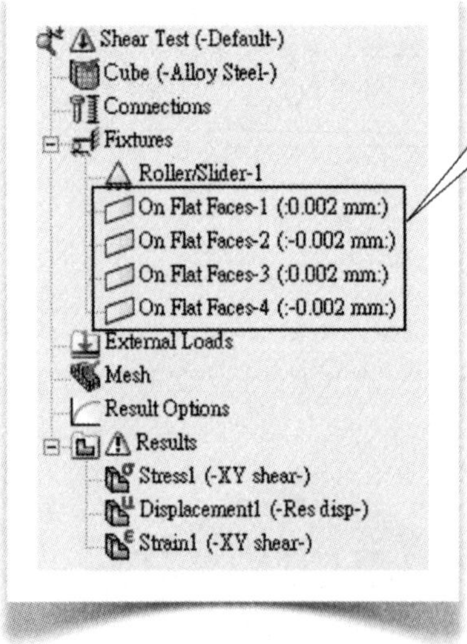

[22] Change the displacement values to 0.002 (mm), click **Run**, and obtain τ_{XY} and γ_{XY} [23].

[23] Repeat step [22] with different displacement values and tabulate the results like this. Note that the **Simulation** does not allow you to input all-zero displacement values. Therefore, we input a very small value instead.

Applied Displacements (mm)	Shear Stress (MPa)	Shear Strain (Dimensionless)	Shear Stress / Shear Strain (MPa)
0.000001	0	0	n.a.
0.001	32.813	0.0004	82033
0.002	65.625	0.0008	82031
0.003	98.438	0.0012	82032
0.004	131.250	0.0016	82031
0.005	164.062	0.0020	82031

[24] Plot a stress-versus-strain graph (using a spreadsheet program such as **Microsoft Excel**), it should be like this.

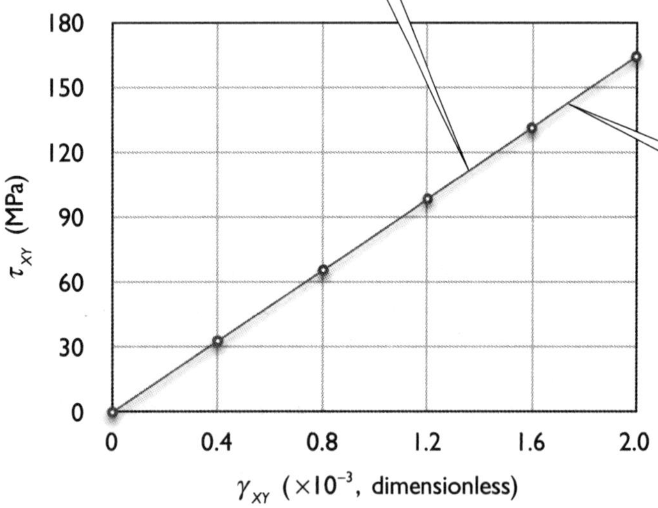

[25] The slope of this straight line is called the **shear modulus**. In this case, the slope is 82 GPa (see the last column of [23]). Note that, in 4.1-4[6] (page 75), the **shear modulus** is input as 79 MPa. However, the **Simulation** internally uses the value calculated in Eq. 4.2-1(2) (page 80); i.e., 82 GPa instead.

[26] Save the document and exit **SolidWorks**. #

Section 4.3

Hooke's Law

$$\varepsilon_X = \frac{\sigma_X}{E} - \nu\frac{\sigma_Y}{E} - \nu\frac{\sigma_Z}{E} \qquad \gamma_{XY} = \frac{\tau_{XY}}{G}$$
$$\varepsilon_Y = \frac{\sigma_Y}{E} - \nu\frac{\sigma_Z}{E} - \nu\frac{\sigma_X}{E} \qquad \gamma_{YZ} = \frac{\tau_{YZ}}{G}$$
$$\varepsilon_Z = \frac{\sigma_Z}{E} - \nu\frac{\sigma_X}{E} - \nu\frac{\sigma_Y}{E} \qquad \gamma_{ZX} = \frac{\tau_{ZX}}{G}$$

4.3-1 Introduction

Exercises in Sections 4.1 and 4.2 show that, if we apply a **uniaxial** force along X-direction, the only nonzero stress component is σ_X. However, the nonzero strain components are

$$\varepsilon_X = \frac{\sigma_X}{E} \text{ and } \varepsilon_Y = \varepsilon_Z = -\nu\varepsilon_X = -\nu\frac{\sigma_X}{E}$$

where E is the **Young's modulus** and ν is the **Poisson's ratio** of the material. For **Alloy Steel**, E = 210 GPa and ν = 0.28 (4.1-4[6], page 75). Similarly, if we apply a uniaxial force along Y-direction, the only nonzero stress component is σ_Y and the nonzero strain components are

$$\varepsilon_Y = \frac{\sigma_Y}{E} \text{ and } \varepsilon_Z = \varepsilon_X = -\nu\varepsilon_Y = -\nu\frac{\sigma_Y}{E}$$

And if we apply a uniaxial force along Z-direction, the only nonzero stress component is σ_Z and the nonzero strain components are

$$\varepsilon_Z = \frac{\sigma_Z}{E} \text{ and } \varepsilon_X = \varepsilon_Y = -\nu\varepsilon_Z = -\nu\frac{\sigma_Z}{E}$$

Now, consider that we apply a general force which has nonzero components in X-, Y-, and Z-directions. The three normal stresses ($\sigma_X, \sigma_Y, \sigma_Z$) are now nonzero and the three normal strains ($\varepsilon_X, \varepsilon_Y, \varepsilon_Z$) can be obtained by combining the above three sets of equations,

$$\begin{aligned}\varepsilon_X &= \frac{\sigma_X}{E} - \nu\frac{\sigma_Y}{E} - \nu\frac{\sigma_Z}{E}\\ \varepsilon_Y &= \frac{\sigma_Y}{E} - \nu\frac{\sigma_Z}{E} - \nu\frac{\sigma_X}{E}\\ \varepsilon_Z &= \frac{\sigma_Z}{E} - \nu\frac{\sigma_X}{E} - \nu\frac{\sigma_Y}{E}\end{aligned} \qquad (1)$$

The first equation states that the normal strain ε_X is a combination of three contributors: σ_X, σ_Y, and σ_Z. Without loss of generality, we assume that all three stress components are tensile, then the contribution of σ_X is to elongate a strain of σ_X/E, the contribution of σ_Y is to contract a strain of $\nu\sigma_Y/E$, and, the contribution of σ_Z is to contract a strain of $\nu\sigma_Z/E$. The second and third equations can be interpreted in a similar way.

Shearing doesn't involve **Poisson's effects**. As demonstrated in 4.2-4 (pages 83-84), shear stresses and the shear strains have a simple linear relationship,

$$\gamma_{XY} = \frac{\tau_{XY}}{G},\ \gamma_{YZ} = \frac{\tau_{YZ}}{G},\ \gamma_{ZX} = \frac{\tau_{ZX}}{G} \qquad (2)$$

where G is the **shear modulus**.

Eqs. (1-2) are called the **Hooke's law** for an **linear elastic isotropic material** (see 4.2-3[12], page 82). In this section, we will verify the **Hooke's law** using results of simulations conducted in some of previous sections.

4.3-2 Verification of Hooke's Law (Cantilever Beam)

Stress Component	Location **A**	Location **B**
σ_X	107.801 Mpa	51.255 Mpa
σ_Y	0	0
σ_Z	0	0
τ_{XY}	0	-6.833 MPa
τ_{XZ}	0	0
τ_{YZ}	0	0

[1] This table of stress components is duplicated from 1.2-6[4], page 30. Locations **A** and **B** are shown again in [2, 3].

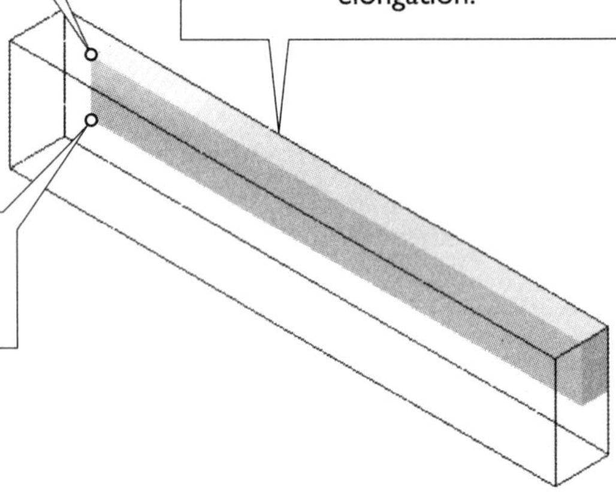

Strain Component	Location **A**	Location **B**
ε_X	0.0005176	0.0002441
ε_Y	-0.0001481	-0.00006664
ε_Z	-0.0001463	-0.00007014
γ_{XY}	0	-0.00008331
γ_{XZ}	0	0
γ_{YZ}	0	0

[5] This table of strain components is duplicated from 3.1-4[6], page 65.

[6] Verification of Hooke's Law

At location **A**,

$$\varepsilon_X = \frac{\sigma_X}{E} = \frac{107.801}{210000} = 0.0005133$$

$$\varepsilon_Y = \varepsilon_Z = -\nu\frac{\sigma_X}{E} = 0.28\frac{107.801}{210000} = -0.0001437$$

which are consistent with the values in [5].

At location **B**,

$$\varepsilon_X = \frac{\sigma_X}{E} = \frac{51.255}{210000} = 0.0002441$$

$$\varepsilon_Y = \varepsilon_Z = -\nu\frac{\sigma_X}{E} = -0.28\frac{51.255}{210000} = 0.00006834$$

$$\gamma_{XY} = \frac{\tau_{XY}}{G} = \frac{-6.833}{82000} = -0.00008333$$

which are consistent with the values in [5]. #

4.3-3 Verification of Hooke's Law (C-Bar)

Stress Component	Location **A**	Location **B**
σ_X	0	10.7111 Mpa
σ_Y	59.2488 MPa	23.2952 MPa
σ_Z	0	0
τ_{XY}	0	-20.2619 MPa
τ_{XZ}	0	0
τ_{YZ}	0	0

[1] This table of stress components is duplicated from 1.3-15[5] (page 49) and 1.3-16[5] (page 50). Locations **A** and **B** are shown again in [2, 3].

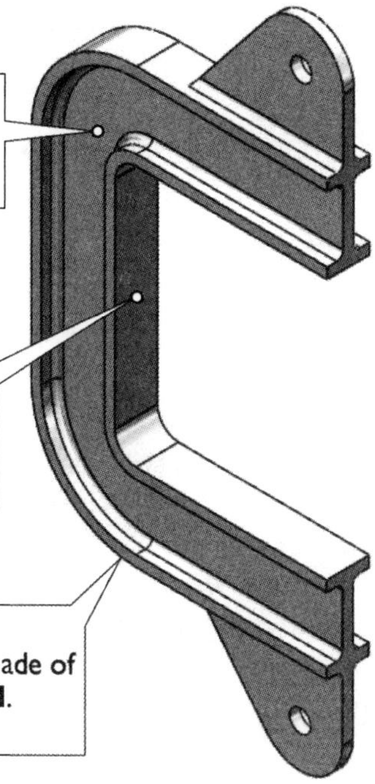

Strain Component	Location **A**	Location **B**
ε_X	-0.00007902	0.00001996
ε_Y	0.0002821	0.00009667
ε_Z	-0.00007881	-0.00004541
γ_{XY}	0	-0.0002470
γ_{XZ}	0	0
γ_{YZ}	0	0

[5] This table of strain components is duplicated from 3.2-3[10] (page 70) and 3.2-4[10] (page 72).

[6] Verification of Hooke's Law

At location **A**,

$$\varepsilon_Y = \frac{\sigma_Y}{E} = \frac{59.2488}{210000} = 0.00028214$$

$$\varepsilon_X = \varepsilon_Z = -\nu\frac{\sigma_Y}{E} = 0.28\frac{59.2488}{210000} = -0.000078998$$

which are consistent with the values in [5].

At location **B**,

$$\varepsilon_X = \frac{\sigma_X}{E} - \nu\frac{\sigma_Y}{E} = \frac{10.7111}{210000} - 0.28\frac{23.2952}{210000} = 0.00001995$$

$$\varepsilon_Y = \frac{\sigma_Y}{E} - \nu\frac{\sigma_X}{E} = \frac{23.2952}{210000} - 0.28\frac{10.7111}{210000} = 0.00009665$$

$$\varepsilon_Z = -\nu\frac{\sigma_X}{E} - \nu\frac{\sigma_Y}{E} = -0.28\frac{10.7111}{210000} - 0.28\frac{23.2952}{210000} = -0.00004534$$

$$\gamma_{XY} = \frac{\tau_{XY}}{G} = \frac{-20.2619}{82000} = -0.0002471$$

which are consistent with the values in [5]. #

Chapter 5

Axial Loading

Using simple axial deformation mode, this chapter explains some important concepts or phenomena, namely, stress concentration, Saint-Venant's principle, and temperature effects.

Stress concentrations occurs everywhere, and these high stress values often govern the design requirements. Thus, an engineer has to be aware of the existence of stress concentrations. When conducting mechanical analyses of materials, we often simplify our models to some degree. For example, replacing distributed loads with concentrated loads, replacing round-corners with sharp-corners, or idealizing supports. The question is: How do these simplifications or idealizations affect the results? The **Saint-Venant's principle** will answer this question. The third topic, **temperature effects**, gives some fundamental concepts about thermal stresses.

Section 5.1

Stress Concentration

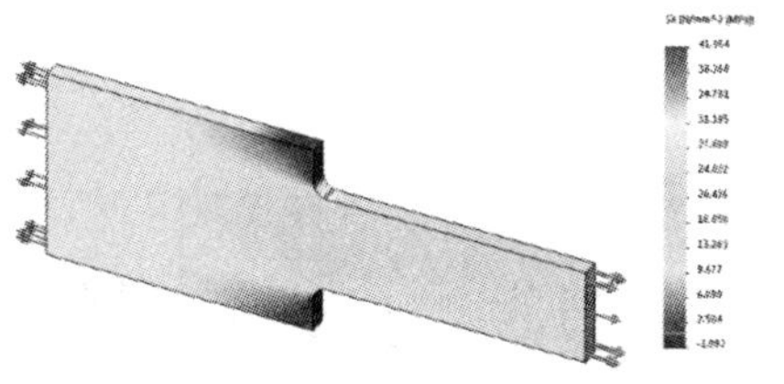

5.1-1 Introduction

[1] Stress concentration occurs most commonly on concave corners. In this section, we'll use a filleted plate [2-4] to show that the degree of stress concentration depends on the radius of the fillets. The smaller the radius, the larger the degree of stress concentration. The stress concentration factor *K*, which will be defined in 5.1-7[7] (page 96), is commonly used to describe the degree of stress concentration. We'll complete a chart (5.1-9[2], page 98) that shows how the stress concentration factor decreases as the radius of the fillets increases.

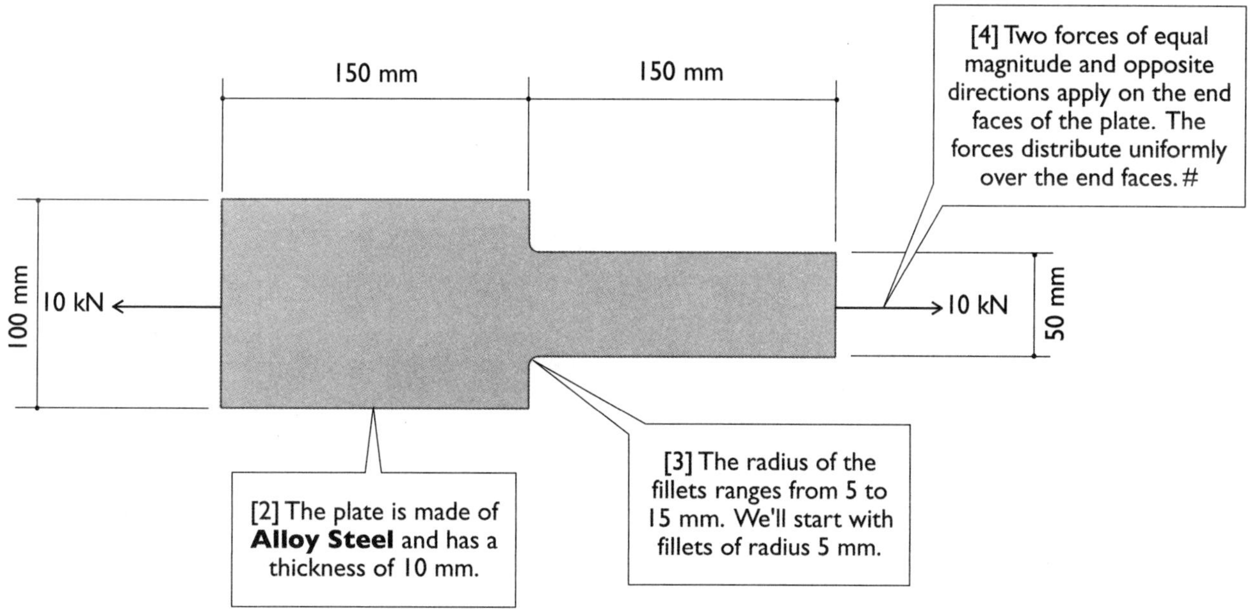

5.1-2 Start Up

[1] Launch **SolidWorks** and create a new part. Set up **MMGS** unit system with zero decimal places for the length unit. #

5.1-3 Create the Geometry Model

[1] On the **Front** plane, draw a sketch like this.

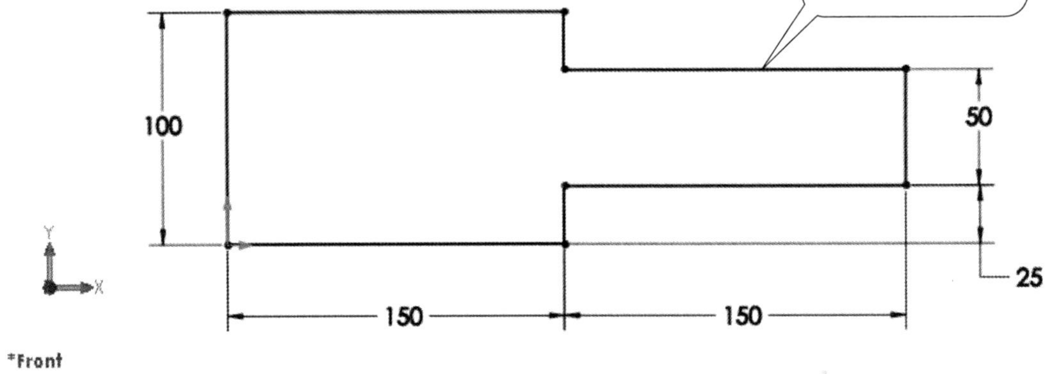

[2] **Extrude** 10 mm.

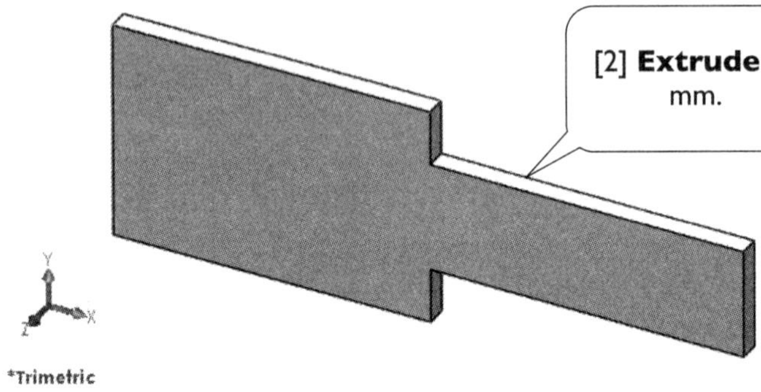

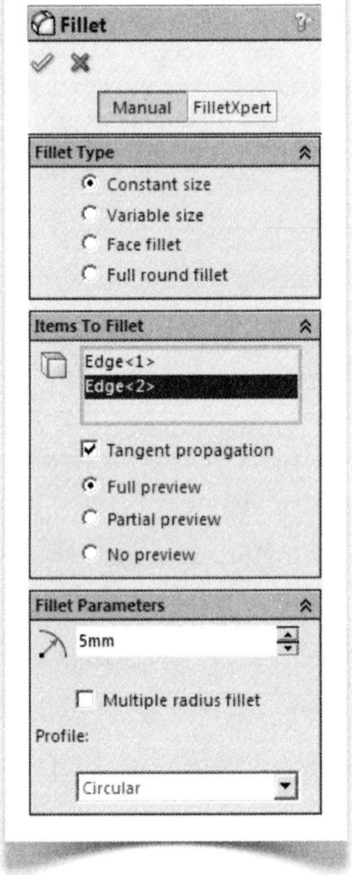

[3] Add **Fillet** of radius 5 mm at this corner...

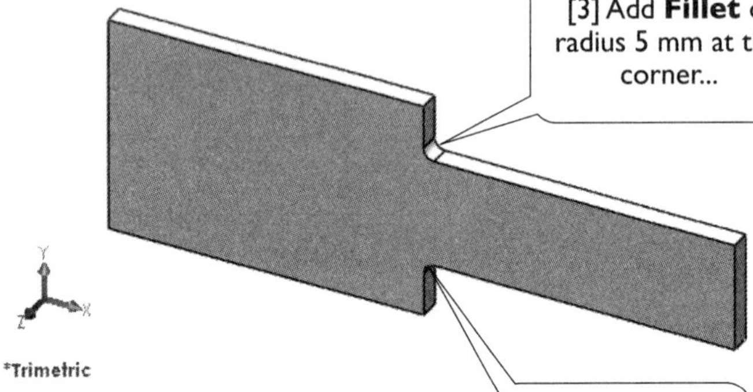

[4] And this corner.

[5] Save the document with the name **Plate**. #

5.1-4 Create a Static Structural Study and Apply Material

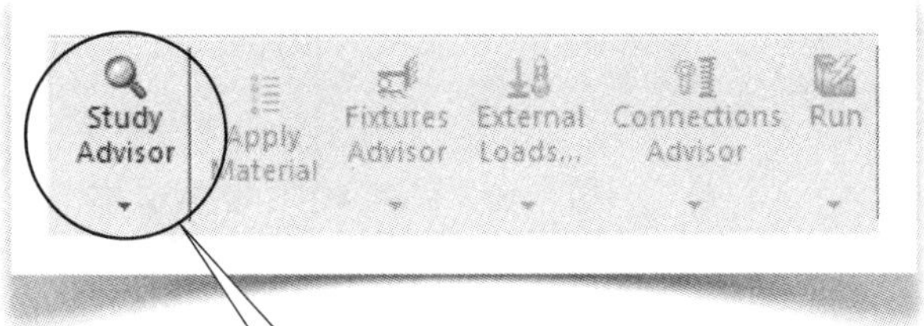

[1] In the **Simulation Toolbar**, select **Study Advisor>New Study**. Name the new study **Stress Concentration**. Leave **Static** as default **Study Type**.

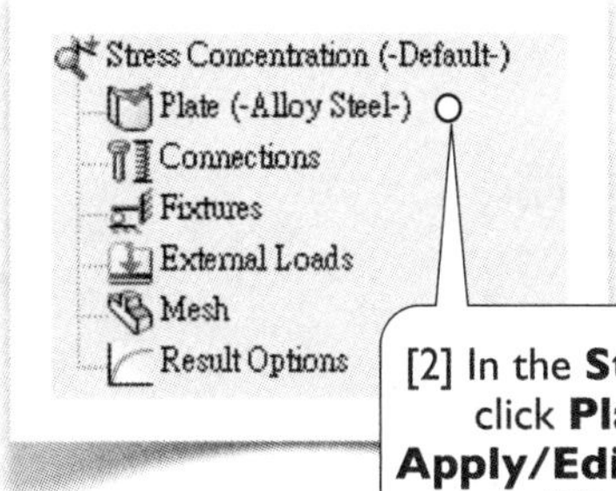

[2] In the **Study Tree**, right-click **Plate** and select **Apply/Edit Material...** and apply **Alloy Steel** for the model. #

5.1-5 Set Up Boundary Conditions

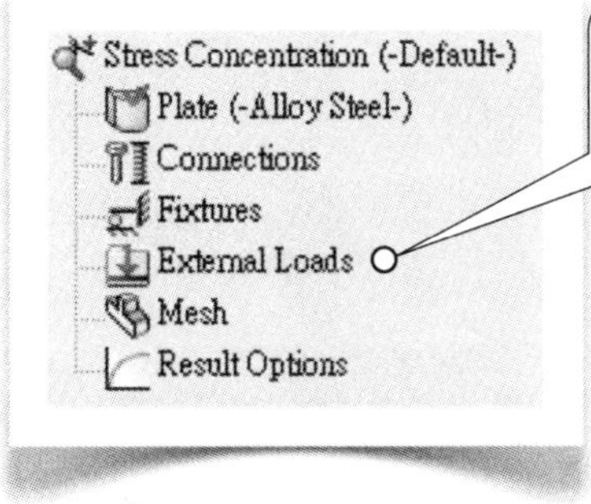

[1] Right-click **External Loads** and select **Force...**

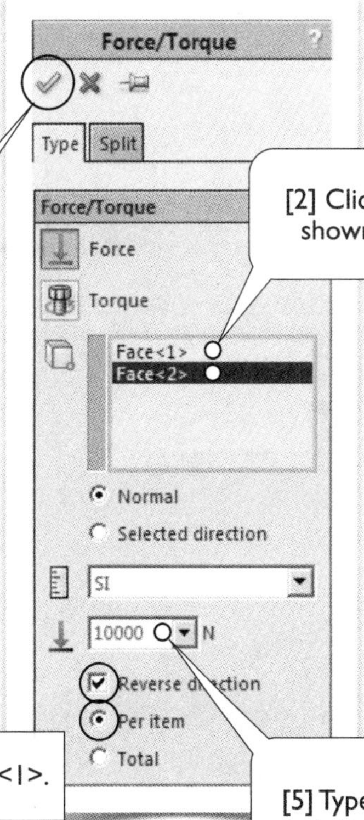

[6] Click **OK**.

[2] Click the faces shown in [3, 4].

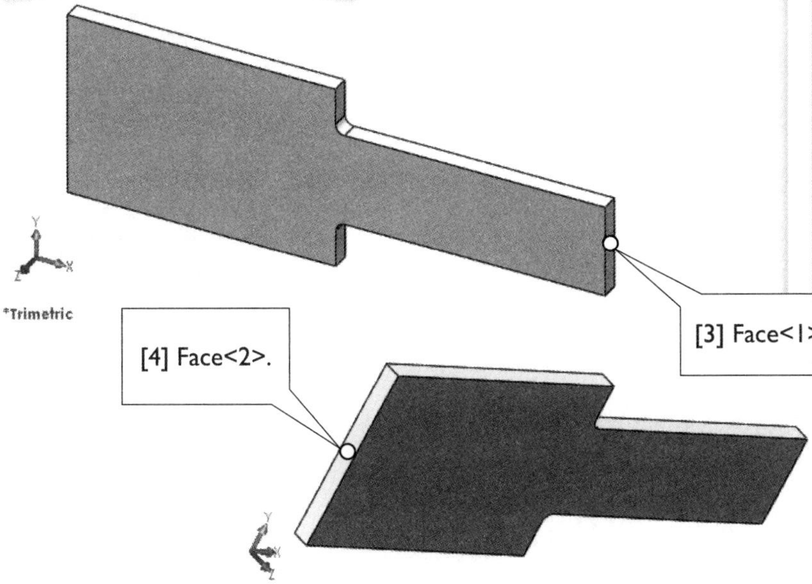

[3] Face<1>.

[4] Face<2>.

[5] Type 10000 (N) and click **Reverse direction**. Also make sure **Per item** is checked.

[7] Right-click **Stress Concentration** and select **Properties...**

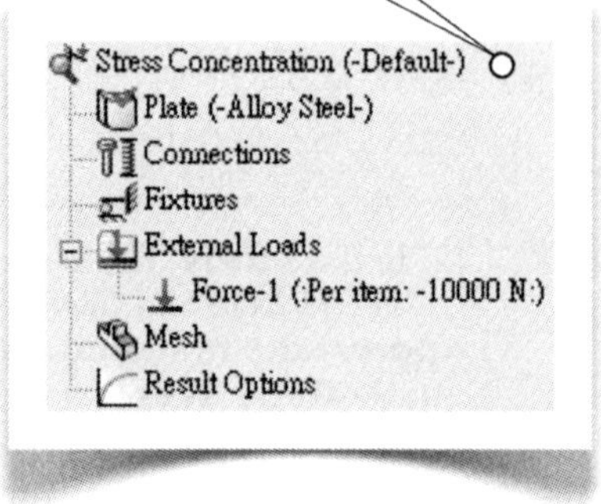

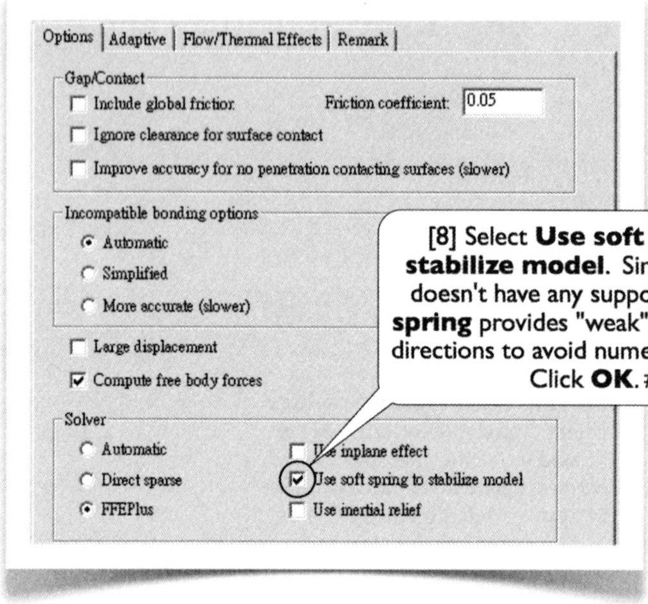

[8] Select **Use soft spring to stabilize model**. Since the model doesn't have any supports, the **soft spring** provides "weak" supports in all directions to avoid numerical problems. Click **OK**. #

5.1-6 Create Mesh

[2] Click **OK**.

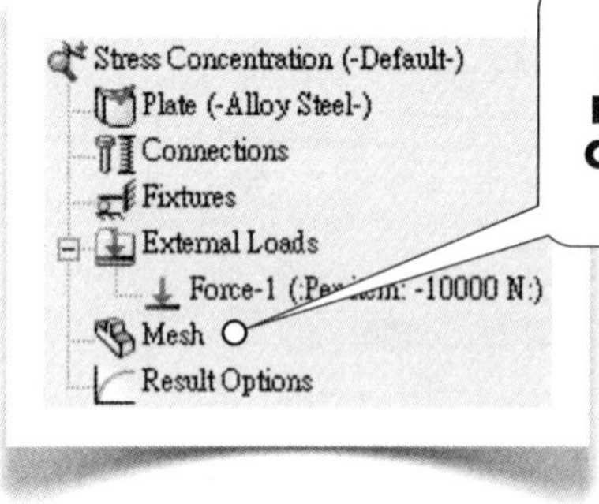

[1, 4] Right-click **Mesh** and select **Create mesh...**

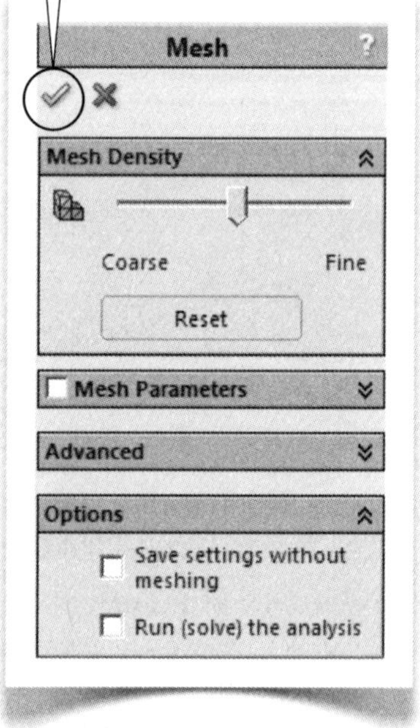

[3] This is the default mesh. We need finer mesh around the fillets. In general, we need finer mesh in areas where the stress gradient is large; i.e., the stress changes sharply.

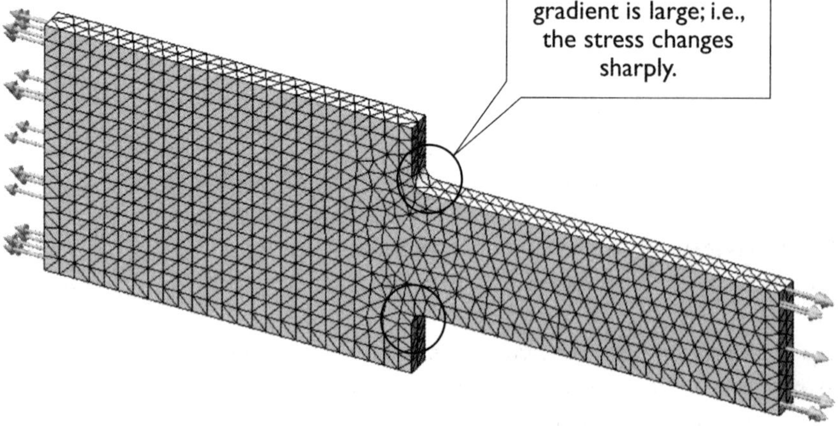

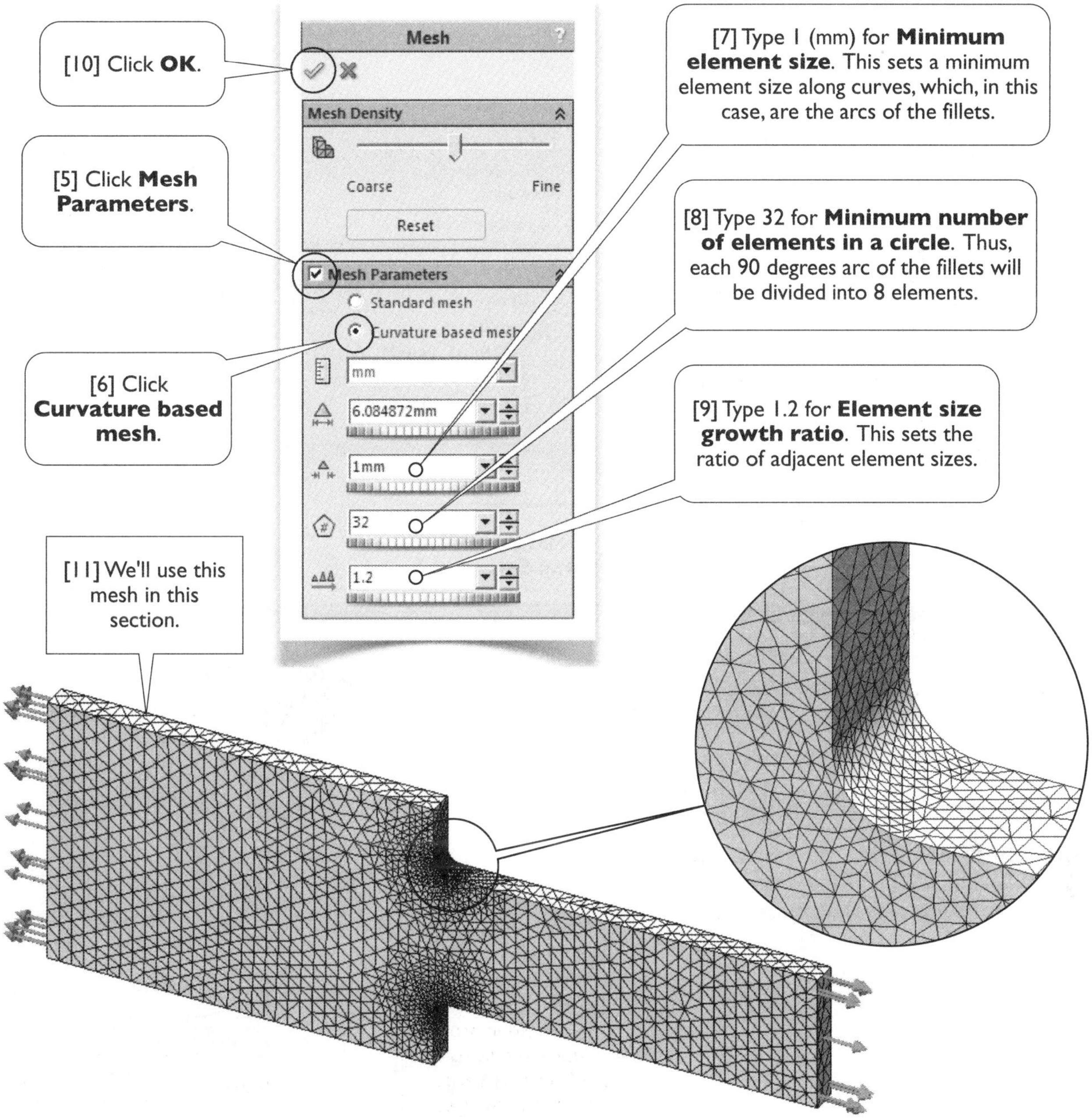

[12] Mesh: A Group of Elements Connected by Nodes

SolidWorks Simulation uses **finite element methods** to solve a model. A basic idea of finite element methods is to divide the entire body into many small and geometrically simple bodies, called **elements**, so that equations of individual element can be written down, and all the equations of the elements are then solved simultaneously. The elements used in the **Simulation** have shapes of **tetrahedra**. Elements are connected at four corner points and four mid-edge points; these connecting points are called **nodes**. A group of elements connected by the nodes is called a **mesh**.

In general, as the number of elements increases, the computing time increases, and the solution accuracy also improved. To be efficient, we usually use fine mesh around the regions where the stress gradients are large and use coarse mesh around the regions where the stress gradients are small. #

5.1-7 Obtain the Stress and Calculate the Stress Concentration Factor

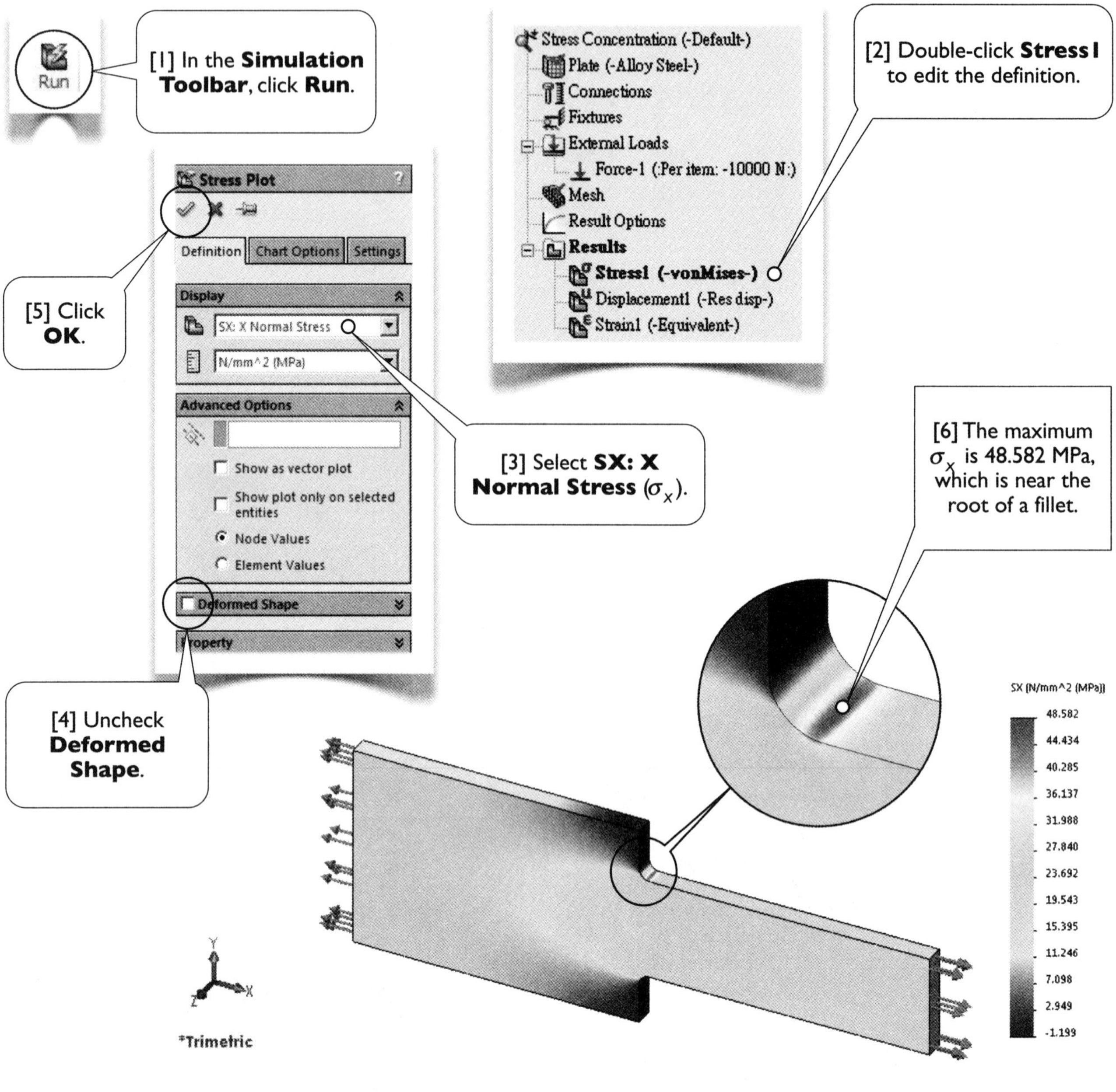

[7] Stress Concentration Factor

The stress concentration factor K is defined as the ratio between the maximum stress (σ_{max}) and the average stress (σ_{ave}). In this case, $\sigma_{ave} = (10000\text{ N})/(10\text{ mm} \times 50\text{ mm}) = 20\text{ MPa}$. Therefore,

$$K = \frac{\sigma_{max}}{\sigma_{ave}} = \frac{48.6\text{ MPa}}{20\text{ MPa}} = 2.43 \qquad \#$$

5.1-8 Change the Radius of the Fillets and Re-Run the Model

[1] Click **Model** tab.

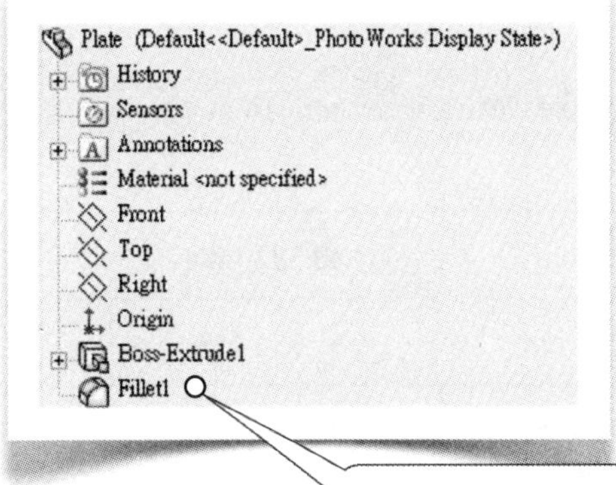

[2] In the **Part Tree**, right-click **Fillet1** and select **Edit Feature...**

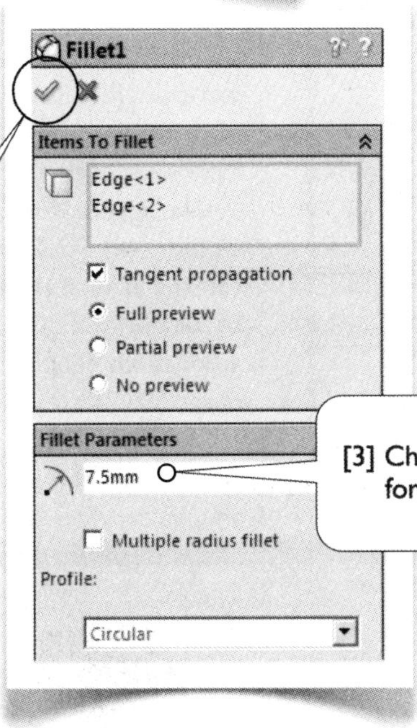

[3] Change to 7.5 (mm) for the **Radius**.

[4] Click **OK**.

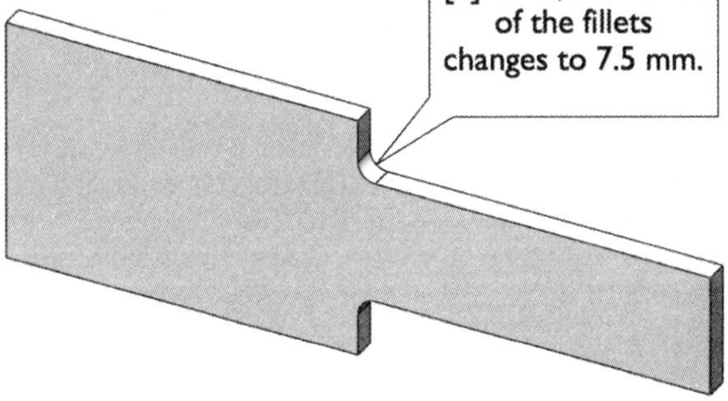

[5] Now, the radius of the fillets changes to 7.5 mm.

[6] Click **Stress Concentration** tab. The radius of the fillets is also updated.

[7] Click **Run**.

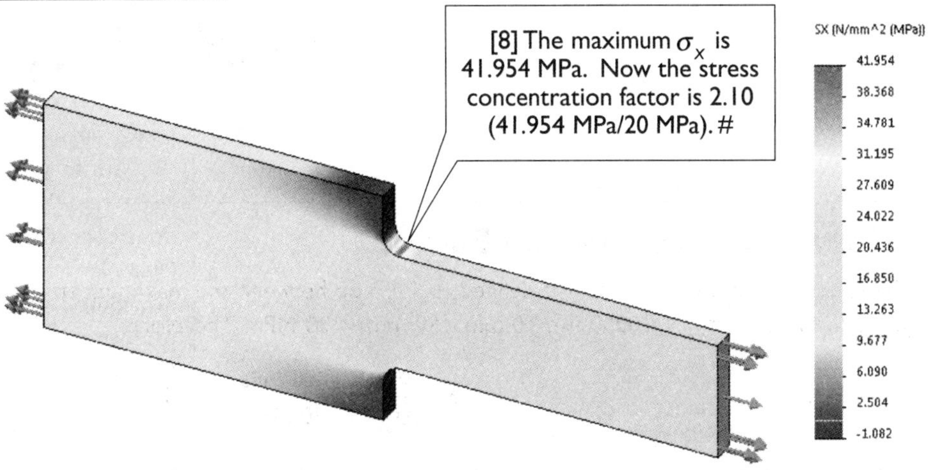

[8] The maximum σ_x is 41.954 MPa. Now the stress concentration factor is 2.10 (41.954 MPa/20 MPa). #

5.1-9 Repeat for Additional Radii

Radius of Fillets	Maximum Stress	Stress Concentration Factor K
5 mm	48.582 MPa	2.43
7.5 mm	41.954 MPa	2.10
10 mm	38.452 MPa	1.92
12.5 mm	36.106 MPa	1.80
15 mm	34.243 MPa	1.71

[1] Repeat steps in 5.1-8 (last page) for additional radii (10 mm, 12.5 mm, and 15 mm) and tabulate the stress concentration factors *K*.

[2] This is a radius-versus-*K* plot. (This plot is produced by a spread sheet program.) It shows that, as the radius increases, the *K* value decreases.

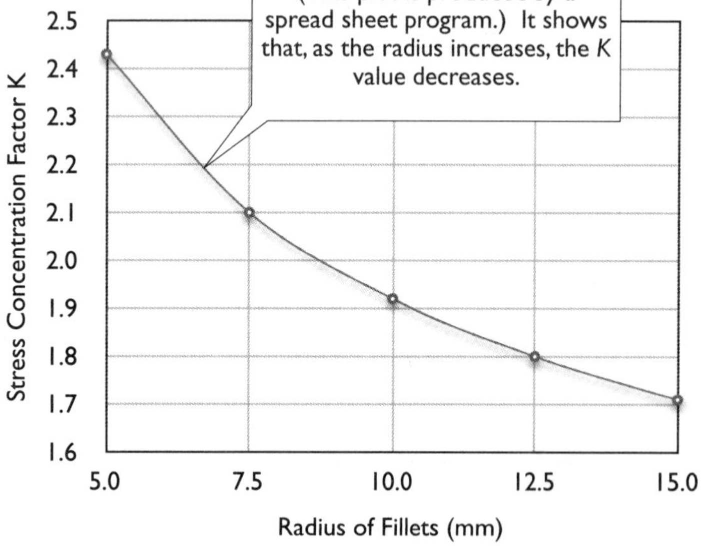

[4] Save the document and exit **SolidWorks**.#

[3] Singular Stresses

The foregoing study shows that as the radius of the fillets decreases, the maximum stress increases [2]. It naturally raises a question: How large would be the maximum stress, if the radius of the fillets approaches zero?

In elasticity theory, the maximum stress would approach infinity! A stress of infinity is called a **singular stress**. Singular stresses occur not only at zero-radius fillets, but also at locations subject to point loads (see 5.2.4, pages 104-105).

In numerical simulation, a singular stress is always reported as a finite value (rather than an infinity). This is because the mesh is not fine enough. As the mesh gets finer, the singular stress value would become larger. An infinitely fine mesh would give an infinitely large value for a singular stress.

In the real world, singular stresses never happen, for the following reasons: (a) There is no such thing as a point load, which implies the load is applied on a zero-area point. (b) Zero-radius fillets are not common. (c) A material always has a limiting stress value. When reaching this value, the material either **fractures** or enters a **plastic state**, and the stresses re-distribute to other regions.

In simulation, we often simplify a model by replacing a fillet with a zero-radius corner or replacing a distributed load with a point load (see Section 5.2). In these cases, you'll often encounter singular stresses and you shouldn't take a singular stress as a real stress.

You simply neglect a singular stress, if the real stress there does not concern you. (If it does concern you, then you need to model a fillet with an accurate radius or apply a distributed load rather than point loads.) The problem is: How does the simplification affect the overall solution accuracy?

That is the subject of the next section: **Saint-Venant's Principle**.

Section 5.2

Saint-Venant's Principle

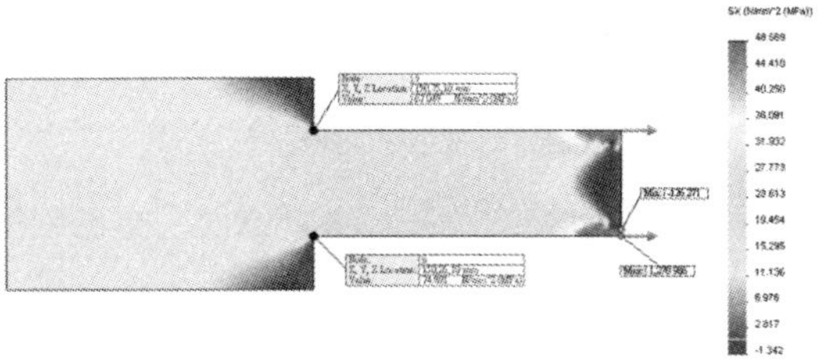

5.2-1 Introduction

[1] In Section 5.1, we've studied a model which pretty much describes real-world situations [2, 3]: a filleted plate is applied with two forces of equal magnitude and opposite directions; both of the forces distribute uniformly over the faces on which they apply. In engineering simulation, we often made some simplification or idealization for the model [4]. For example: replacing one of the uniform load with statically equivalent point loads [5], replacing the other uniform load with a fixed support [6], or even replacing the fillets with sharp corner [7]. The question is: Does any of these simplifications influence the solutions? If so, how? The answer is: It does influence the solutions. However, the influence is usually local to the neighborhood of the simplification: *the farther away from the location of the simplification, the influence becomes less*. This phenomenon is called the **Saint-Venant's Principle**. This section is designed to guide the students fully appreciate the Saint-Venant's Principle.

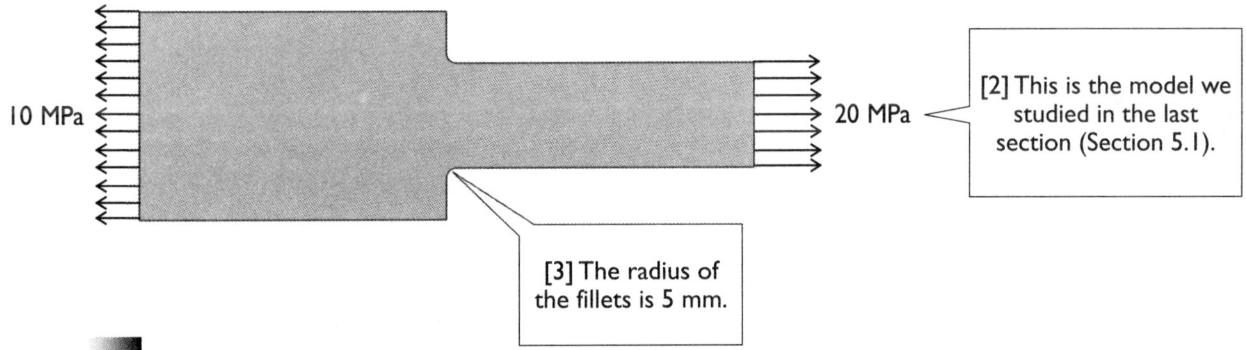

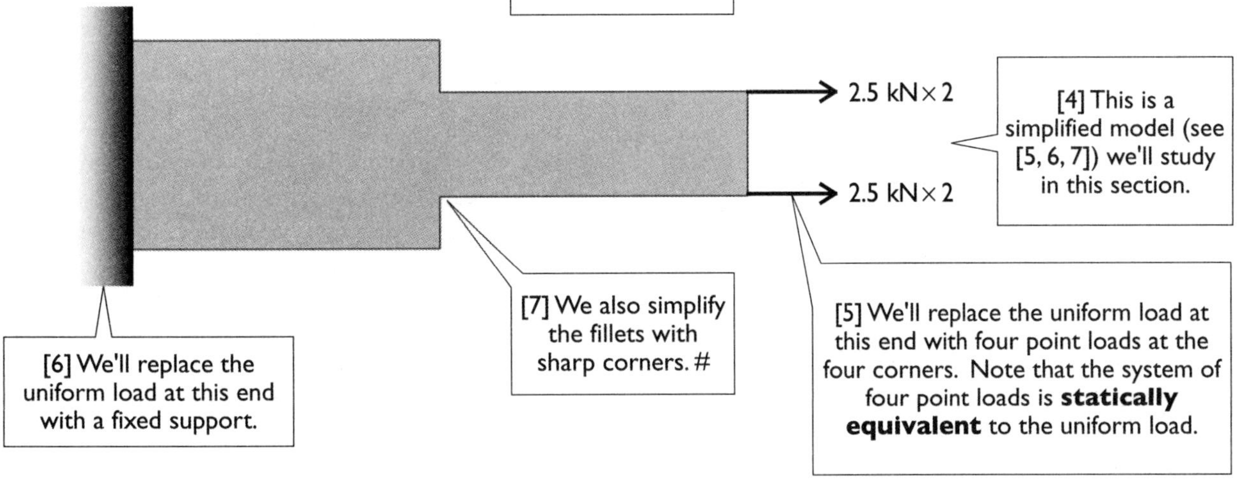

5.2-2 Start Up

[1] Launch **SolidWorks** and open the file **Plate**, which was saved in Section 5.1.

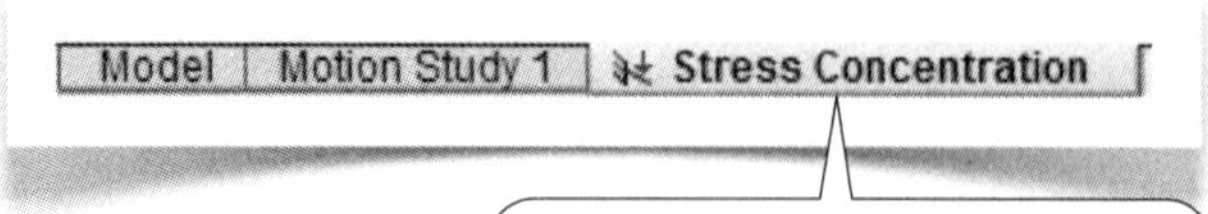

[2] Right-click **Stress Concentration** tab and select **Duplicate**.

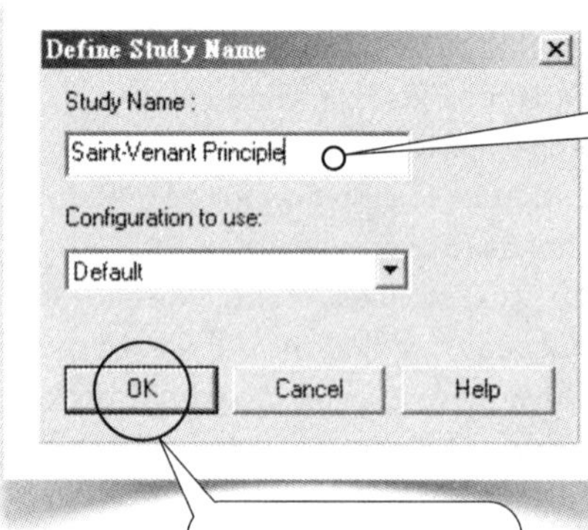

[3] Type **Saint-Venant Principle**.

[4] Click **OK**.

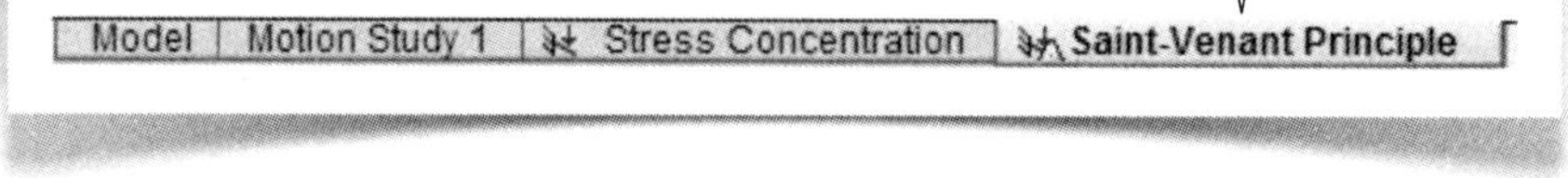

[5] A new study is created and becomes active. #

5.2-3 Use Fixed Support

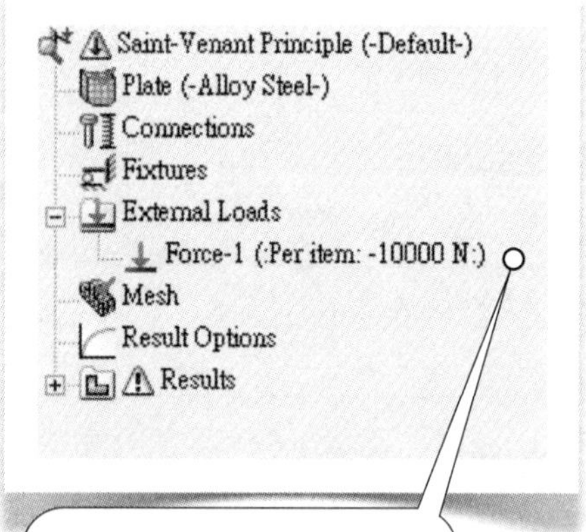

[1] Double-click **Force-1** to edit the definition.

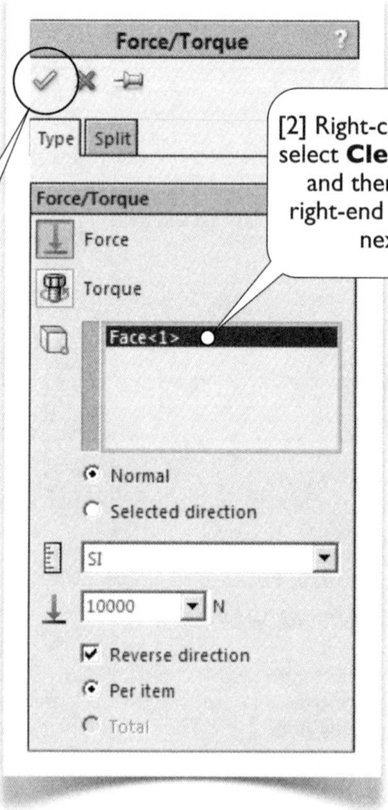

[2] Right-click this box and select **Clear Selections** and then reselect the right-end face (see [4, 5], next page).

[3] Click **OK**.

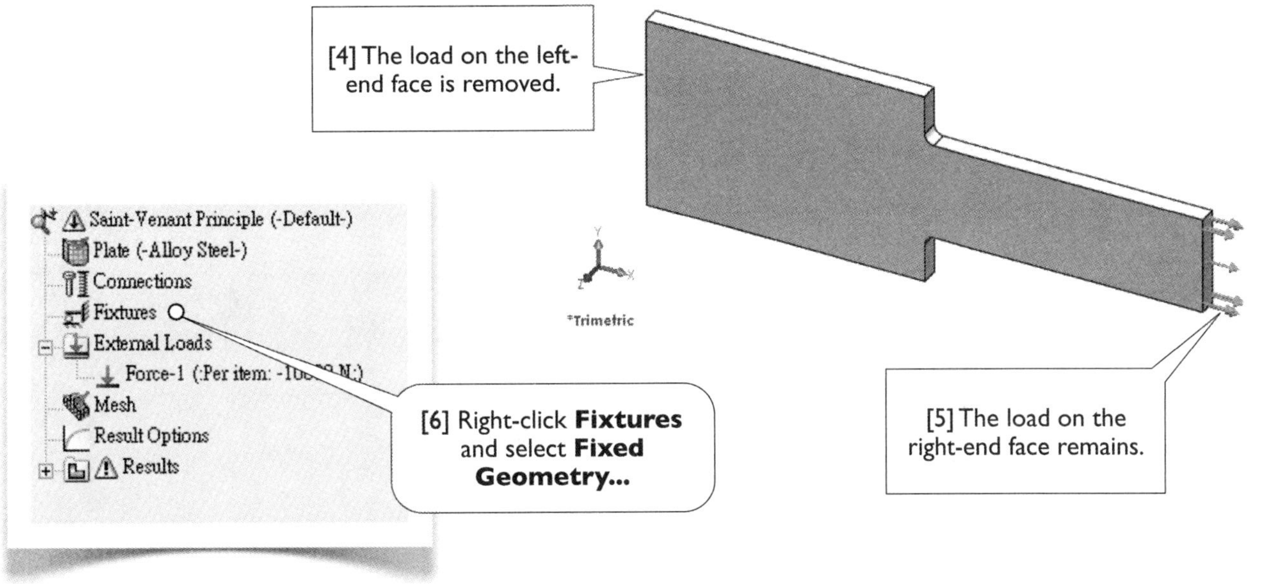
[4] The load on the left-end face is removed.
Saint-Venant Principle (-Default-)
Plate (-Alloy Steel-)
Connections
Fixtures
External Loads
Force-1 (:Per item:
Mesh
Result Options
Results
*Trimetric
[6] Right-click **Fixtures** and select **Fixed Geometry...**
[5] The load on the right-end face remains.

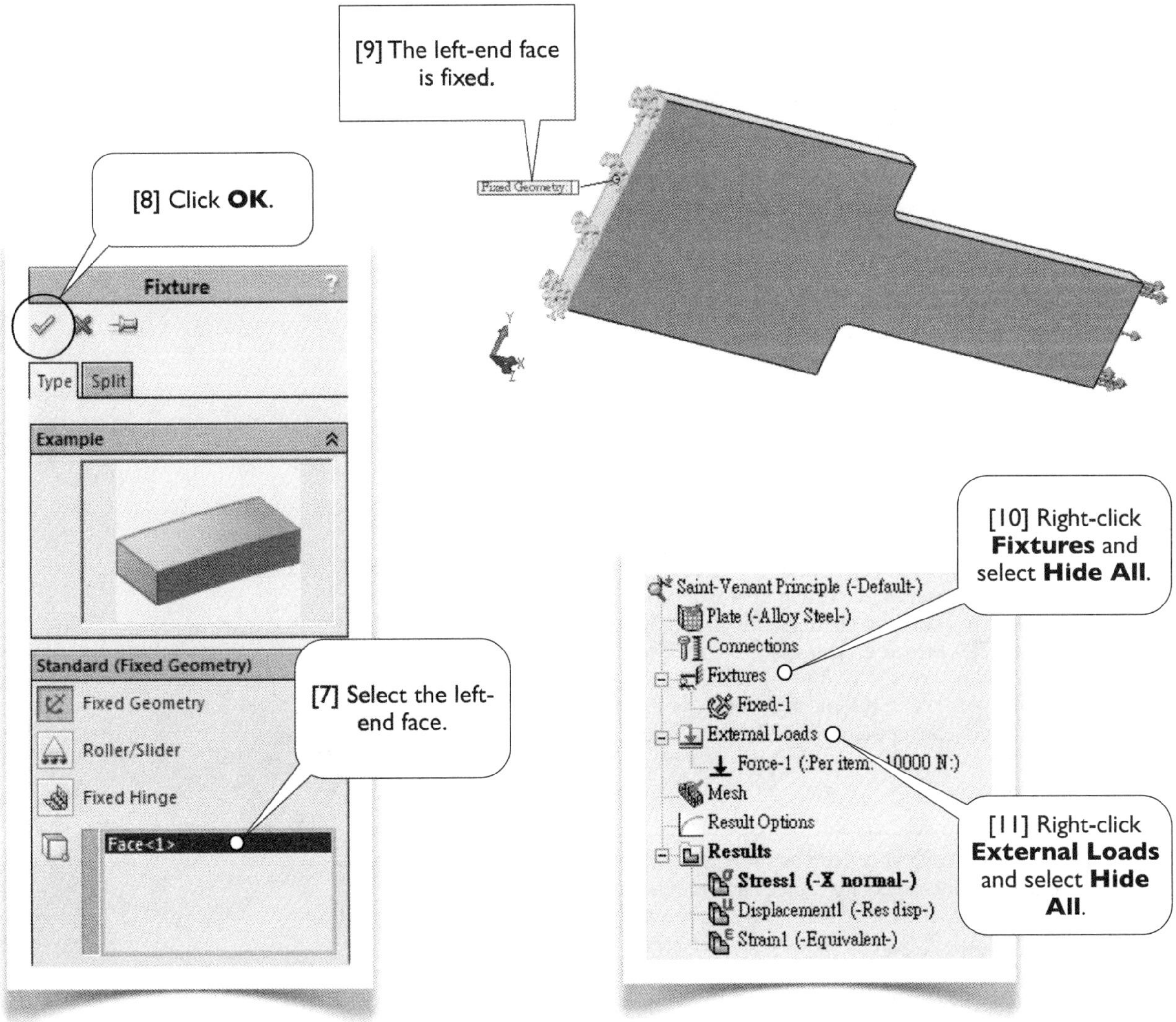
[9] The left-end face is fixed.
Fixed Geometry:
[8] Click **OK**.
Fixture
Type
Split
Example
Standard (Fixed Geometry)
Fixed Geometry
Roller/Slider
Fixed Hinge
Face<1>
[7] Select the left-end face.
[10] Right-click **Fixtures** and select **Hide All**.
Saint-Venant Principle (-Default-)
Plate (-Alloy Steel-)
Connections
Fixtures
Fixed-1
External Loads
Force-1 (:Per item: 10000 N:)
Mesh
Result Options
Results
Stress1 (-X normal-)
Displacement1 (-Res disp-)
Strain1 (-Equivalent-)
[11] Right-click **External Loads** and select **Hide All**.

[12] Click **Run**. See 5.1-6[11] (page 95) for the mesh used.

[14] Except that the stresses near the fixed end are dramatically different (see [15]) from the results in 5.1-7, where σ_x = 10 MPa uniformly over the end face (please verify this yourself).

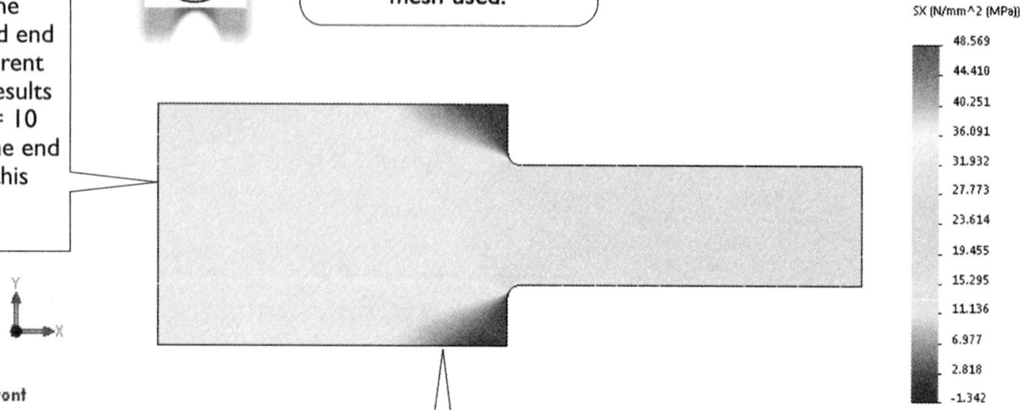

[13] The results are almost identical to the results in 5.1-7 (page 96).

[15] Use **Probe** to retrieve stresses at several locations on the fixed end.

[16] The stress values at the edges of the left-end face are actually singular. Because, when setting up a fixed support, you in effect create sharp concave corners along the edges of the end face (see[17]). However, you don't see infinite values (here, the maximum stress is 17.8 MPa) because the mesh is not fine enough. Let's refine the mesh around the fixed end to confirm this concept (see [18-23], next page).

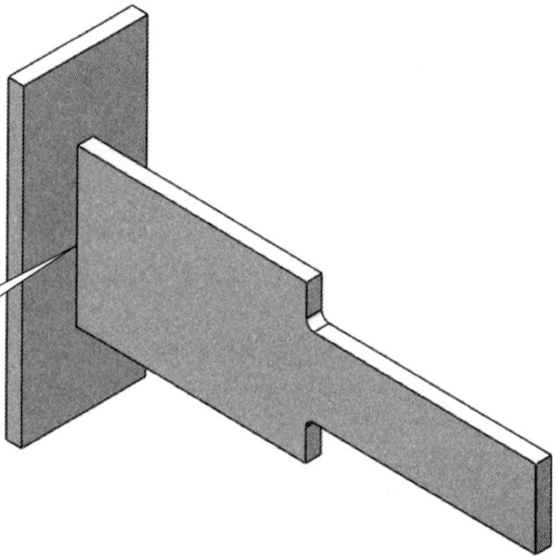

[17] When setting up a fixed support, you in effect create sharp concave corners (i.e., zero-radius fillets,) along the edges of the end face, in which the stresses are singular (5.1-9[3], page 98). Note that zero-radius fillets seldom exist in the real-world; for example, welds are usually used in this case.

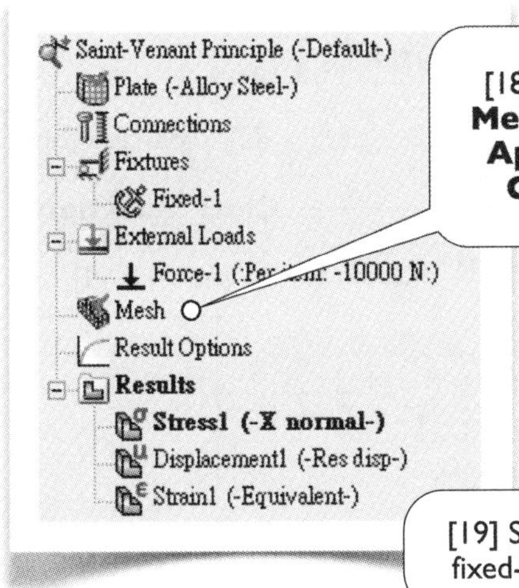

[18] Right-click **Mesh** and select **Apply Mesh Control...**

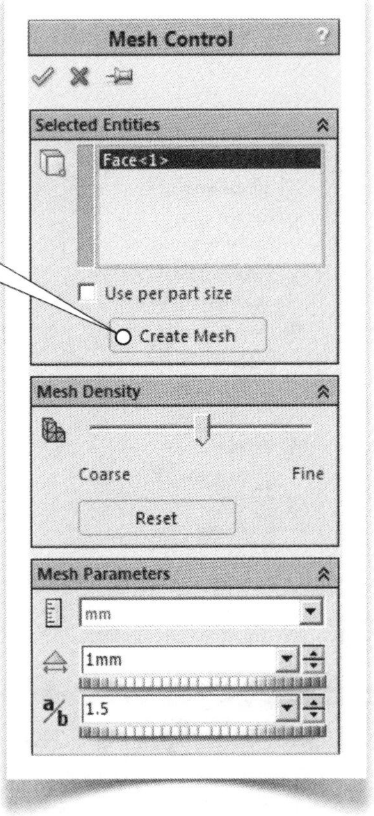

[21] Click **Create Mesh**. Click **Yes** for a warning message.

[19] Select the fixed-end face

[20] Type 1 (mm) here for **Element Size**.

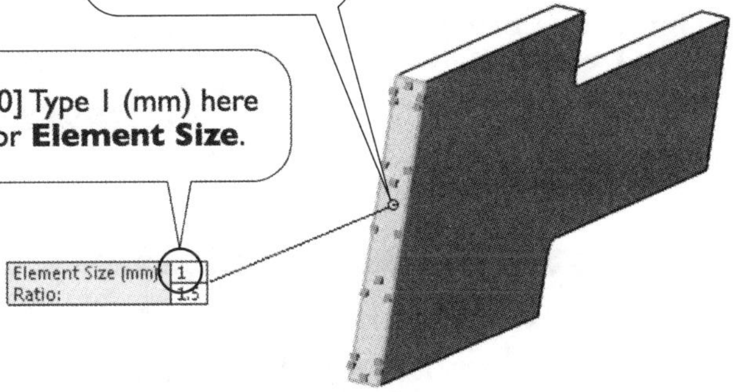

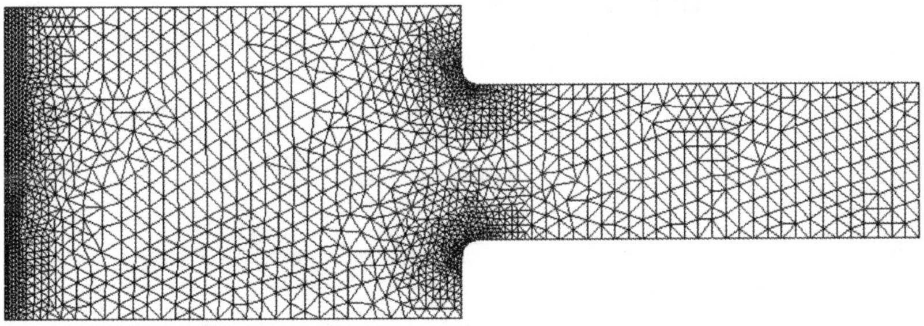

[22] Click **Run**.

[23] Now, the maximum stress increased to 34.8 MPa. If you refine the mesh further, the stress would increase further. This is a characteristics of singular stresses: the finer the mesh, the larger the stress. Remember, in the real-world, singular stresses never exist; you shouldn't take any singular stresses as critical stress when designing your engineering project. #

5.2-4 Use Point Loads

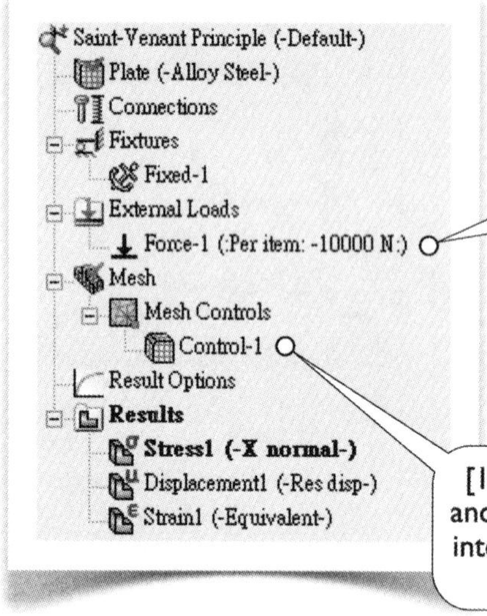

[1] Double-click **Force1** to edit the definition.

[2] Right-click this box and select **Clear Selections**. Select four vertices shown in [3].

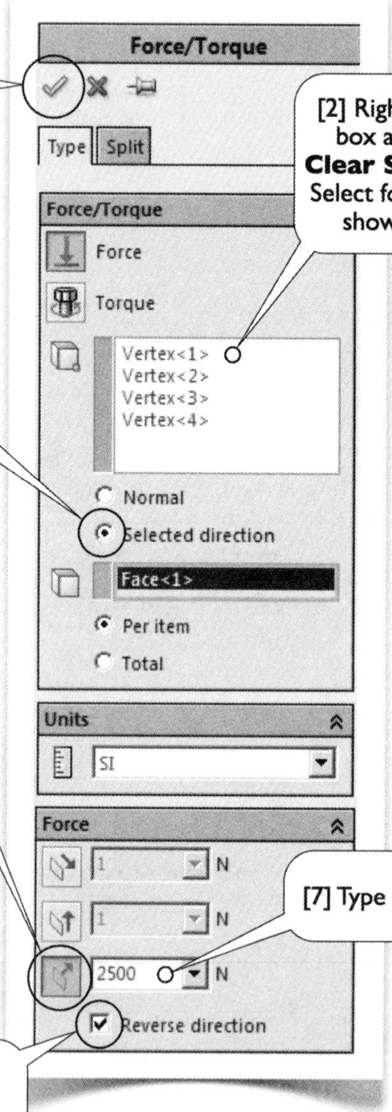

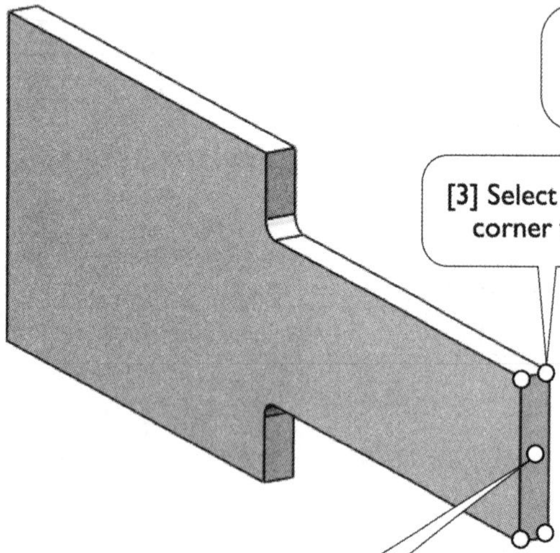

[3] Select these four corner vertices.

[4] Click **Selected direction**.

[5] Select the end face to define the direction.

[6] Click **Normal to Plane**.

[7] Type 2500 (N).

[8] Click **Reverse direction**.

[9] Click **OK**.

[10] Right-click **Control-1** and select **Delete**. We're not interested in the stresses near the fixed end.

[11] Click **Run**.

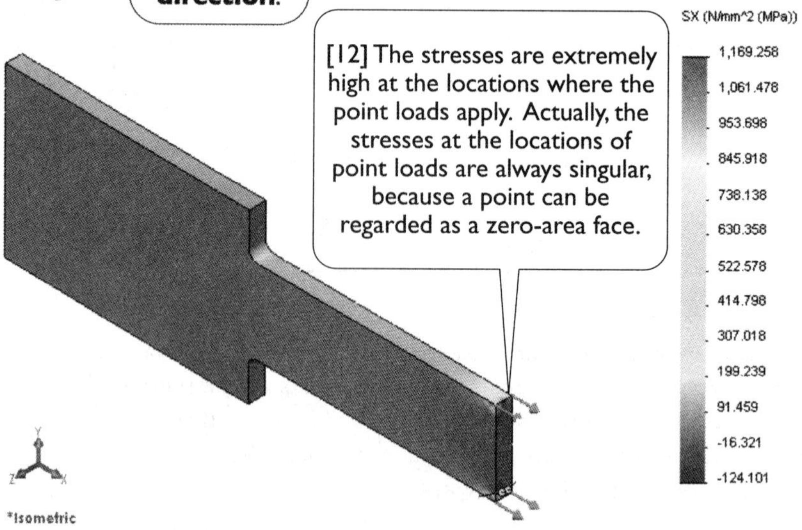

[12] The stresses are extremely high at the locations where the point loads apply. Actually, the stresses at the locations of point loads are always singular, because a point can be regarded as a zero-area face.

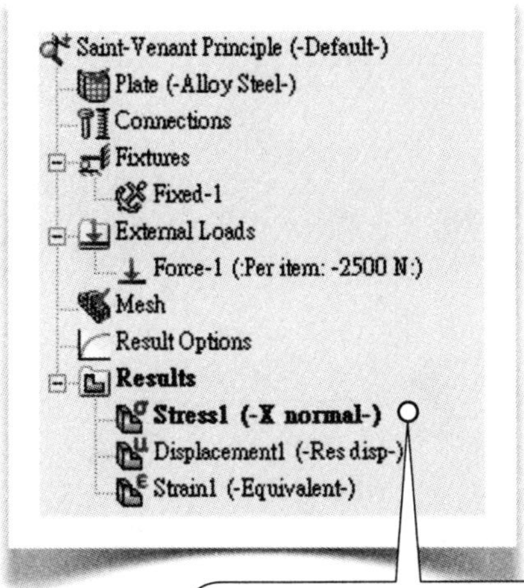

[13] In order to compare the stresses with those in 5.2-3[13] (page 102). Let's modify the legend. Right-click **Stress1** and select **Chart Options...**

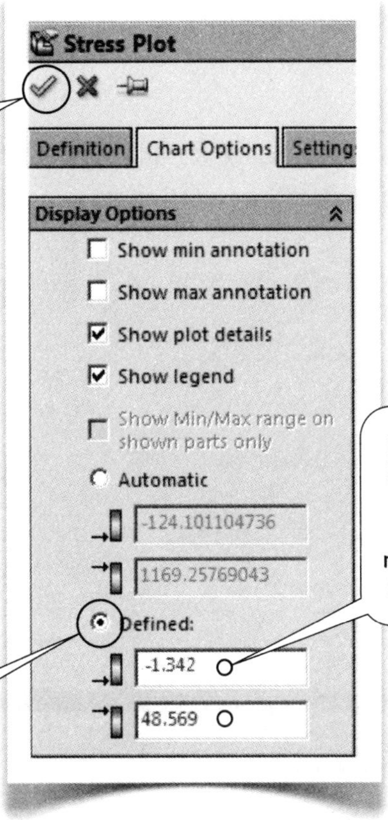

[14] Click **Defined**.

[15] Type -1.342 for **Min** and 48.569 for **Max**; these are minimum and maximum stresses in 5.2-3[13], page 103.

[16] Click **OK**.

[16] The plot are similar to the results in 5.2-3[13] (page 103), except the extremely large stresses near the point loads.

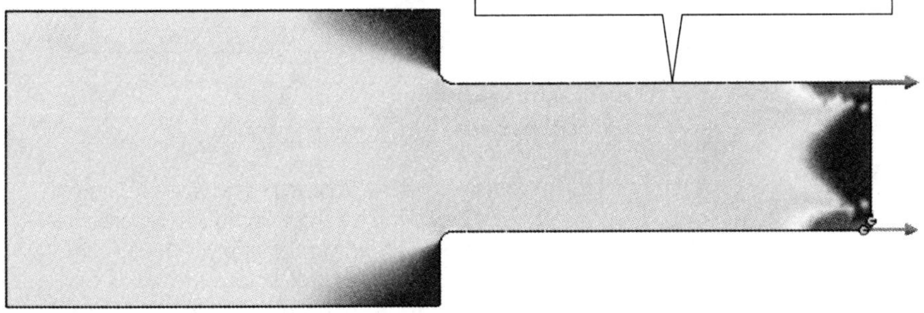

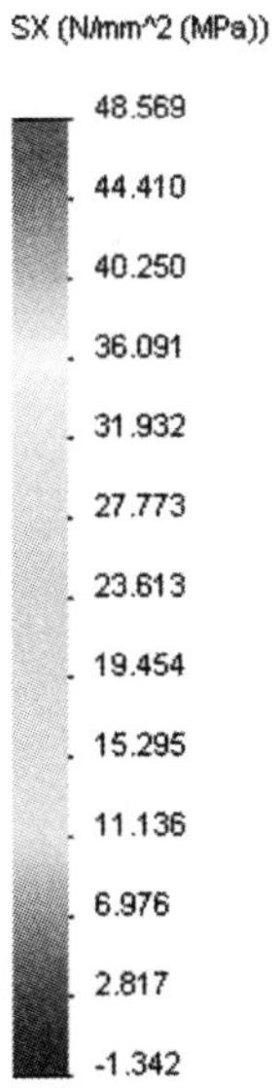

[17] Summary

Here, we replace the uniform load on the right-end face with a set of statically equivalent point loads. The results almost remain the same, except the stresses near the point loads. In other words, the influence of the simplification is local to the neighborhood of the simplification. #

5.2-5 Use Sharp Corners

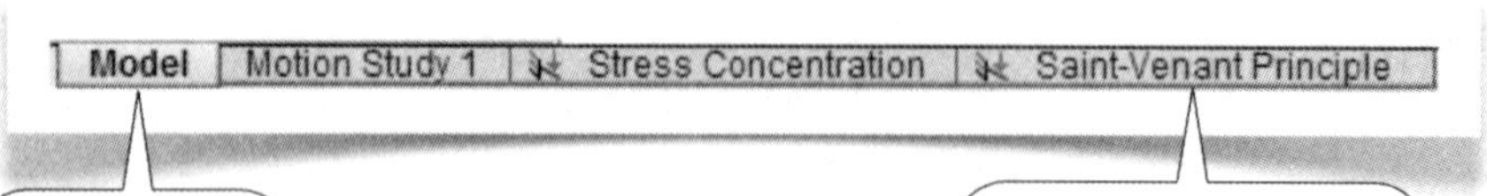

[1] Click **Model**.

[3] Click **Saint-Venant Principle**.

[4] Now, the fillets become sharp corners.

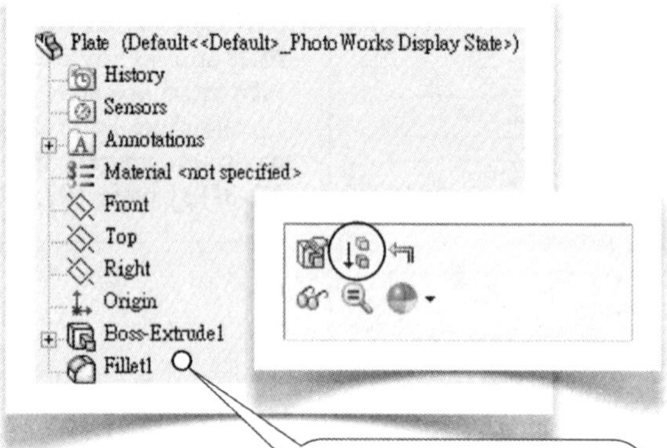

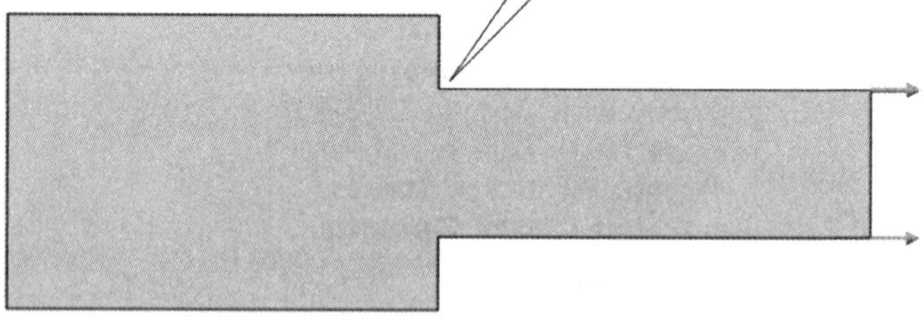

[5] Click **Run**.

[2] In the **Part Tree**, right-click **Fillet1** and select **Suppress**.

[6] Use **Probe** to retrieve stresses at the sharp corners.

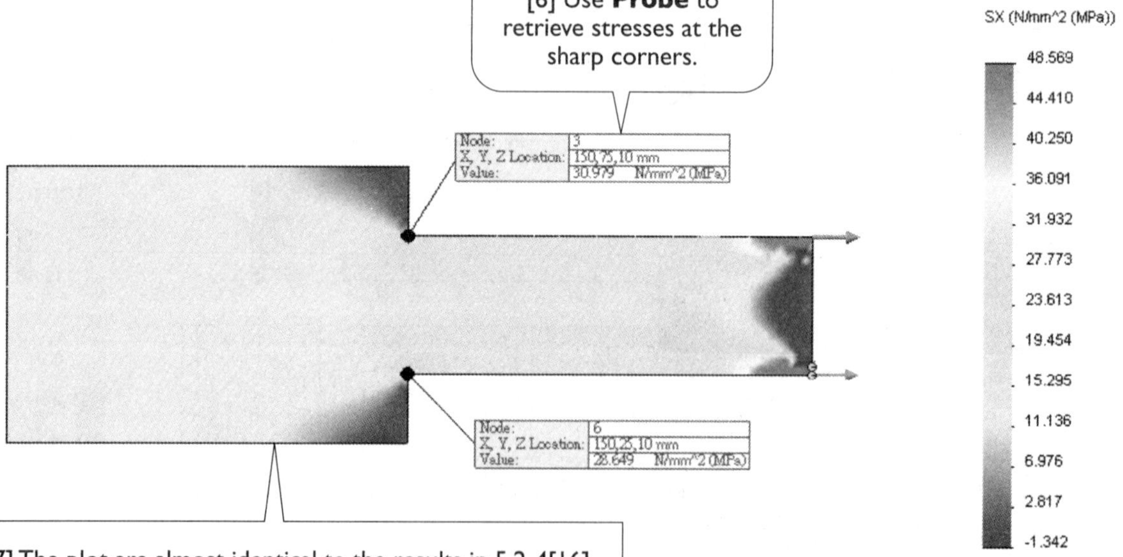

[7] The plot are almost identical to the results in 5.2-4[16] (last page). The stresses at the sharp corners should be large, because they are singular stresses; however, you don't see large stresses at the sharp corners. This is because the mesh is not fine enough. Let's refine the mesh at the sharp corners.

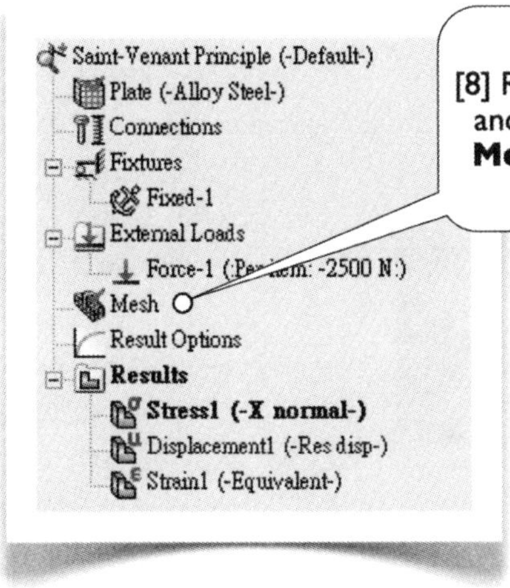

[8] Right-click **Mesh** and select **Apply Mesh Control**...

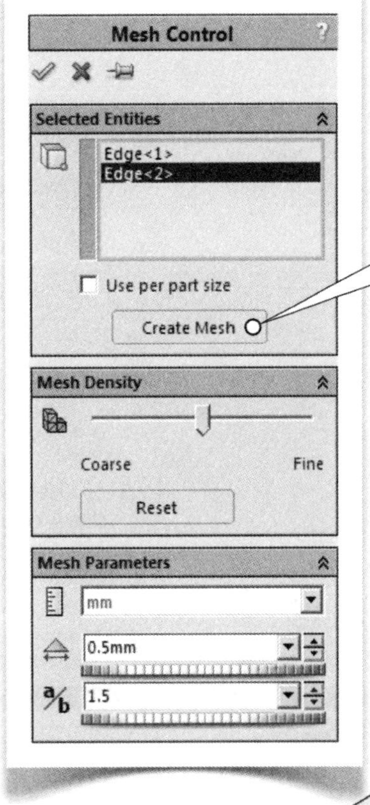

[12] Click **Create Mesh.** Click **Yes** for a warning message.

[9] Select the edge of the upper sharp corner...

[11] Type 0.5 (mm) here for **Element Size**.

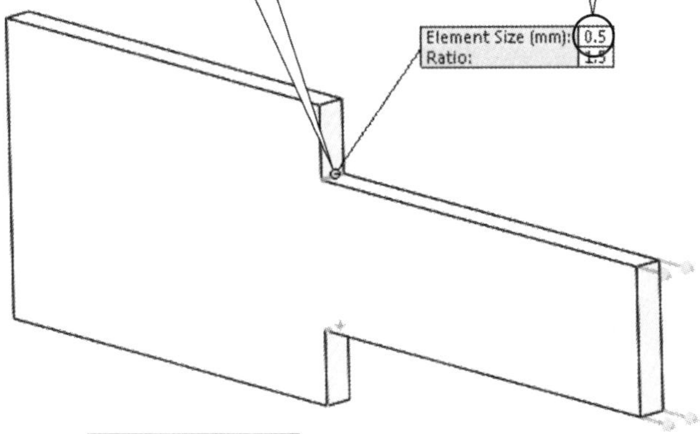

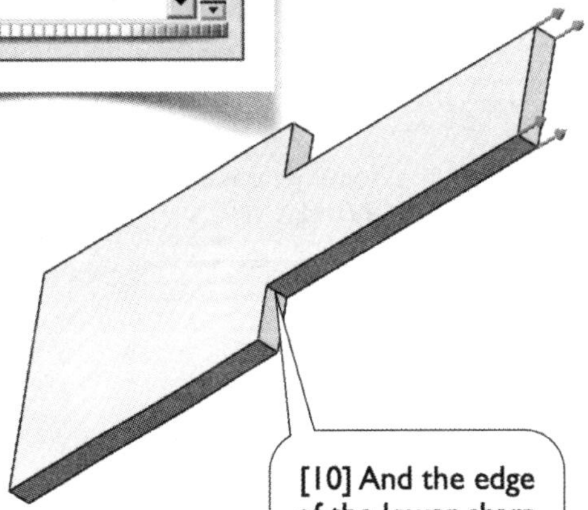

[10] And the edge of the lower sharp corner.

[13] The mesh.

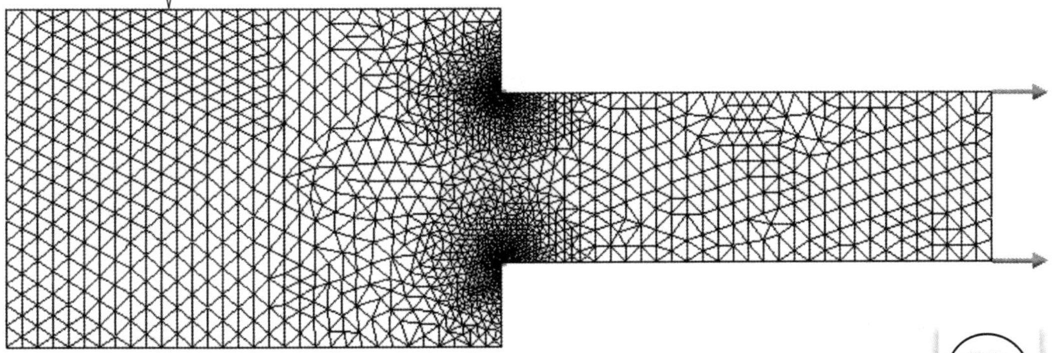

[14] Click **Run**.

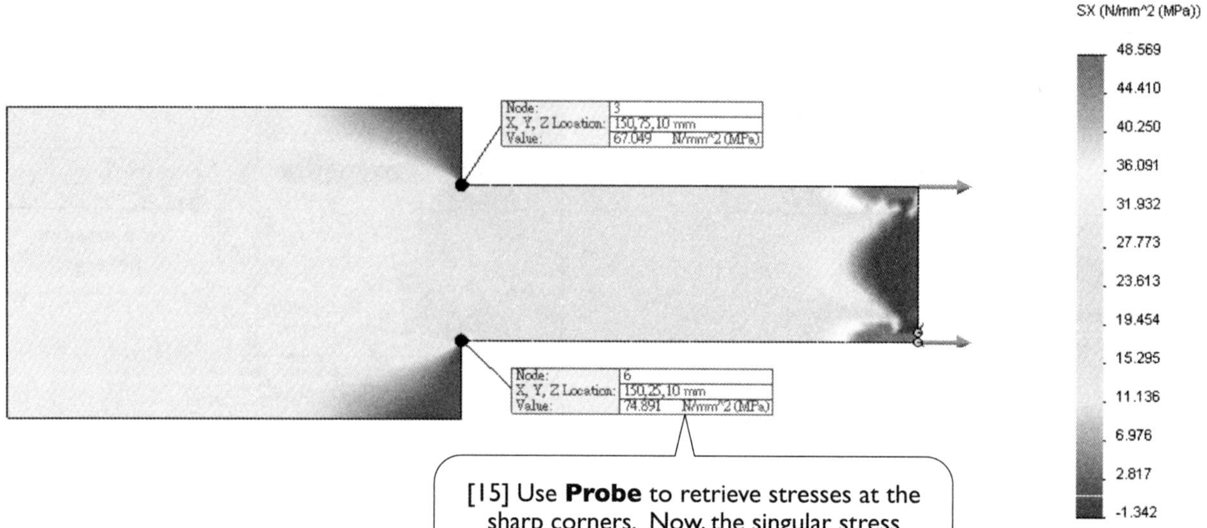

[15] Use **Probe** to retrieve stresses at the sharp corners. Now, the singular stress increases dramatically. Remember, theoretically a singular stress has a value of infinity. In finite element simulations, the finer the mesh, the larger the singular stress. Singular stresses do not exist in the real-world; you should simply neglect singular stresses in a simulation model.

[16] Save the document and exit **SolidWorks**. #

Section 5.3

Temperature Effects

	Elastic Normal Strain	Thermal Normal Strain	Total Normal Strain	Maximum Displacement	Normal Stress
X-Direction	+0.000975	-0.000975	0	0	+204.75 MPa
Y-Direction	-0.000273	-0.000975	-0.001248	-0.01248 mm	0
Z-Direction	-0.000273	-0.000975	-0.001248	-0.01248 mm	0

5.3-1 Introduction

Temperature change causes a body to deform, which in turn induces strains and stresses. Temperature change should be treated as loads to the body. When temperature change is involved, the **total normal strains** must include the thermal strains; i.e.,

$$\varepsilon_X^{total} = \varepsilon_X + \varepsilon_T,\quad \varepsilon_Y^{total} = \varepsilon_Y + \varepsilon_T,\quad \varepsilon_Z^{total} = \varepsilon_Z + \varepsilon_T \qquad (1)$$

Where the **elastic normal strains** (ε_X, ε_Y, and ε_Z) are defined in Eq. 4.3-1(1) (page 87), and the **thermal strain** ε_T is the strain due to the temperature change ΔT,

$$\varepsilon_T = \alpha \Delta T \qquad (2)$$

The **coefficient of thermal expansion** (CTE) α has an SI unit of $1/\text{K}$ (equivalent to $1/{}^\circ\text{C}$). For **Alloy Steel**, $\alpha = 1.3 \times 10^{-5}$ /K (see 4.1-4[7], page 75).

In this section, we'll use the cube in Section 4.2 to illustrate some basic concepts about temperature effects: (a) No stresses occur in a direction of free expansion or contraction, although the strains are not zeros. (b) Compressive stresses develop in a direction that is constrained, when the temperature raises. (c) Tensile stresses develop in a direction that is constrained, when the temperature decreased.

This section also helps the students to clarify the meaning of Eqs. (1, 2).

5.3-2 Start Up

[1] Launch **SolidWorks** and open the file **Cube** which was saved in Section 4.2.

[2] Right-click **Tensile Test** tab and select **Duplicate**.

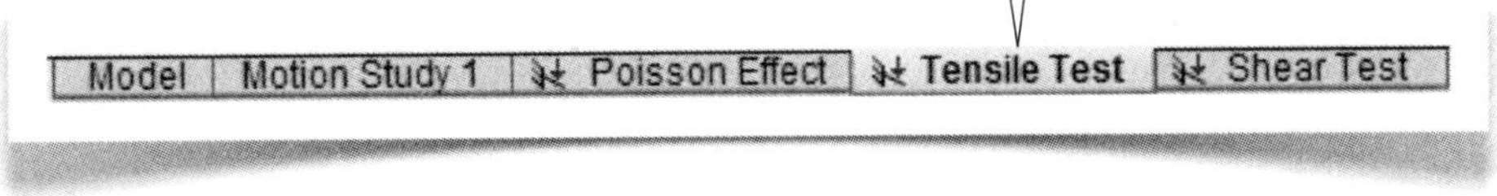

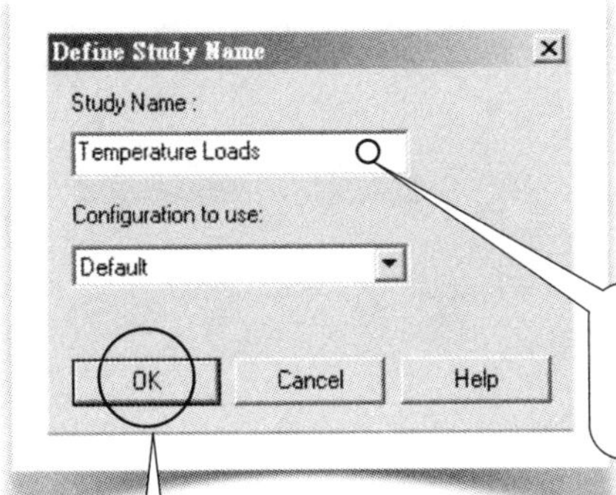

[3] Type **Temperature Loads**.

[4] Click **OK**.

[5] Right-click **Temperature Loads** and select **Properties...**

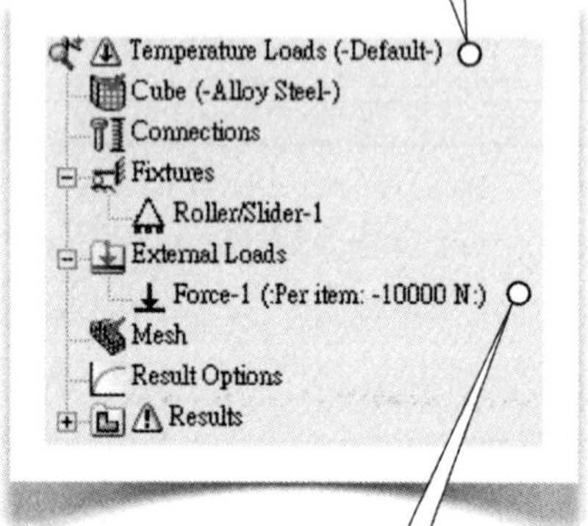

[8] Right-click **Force-1** and select **Delete...** #

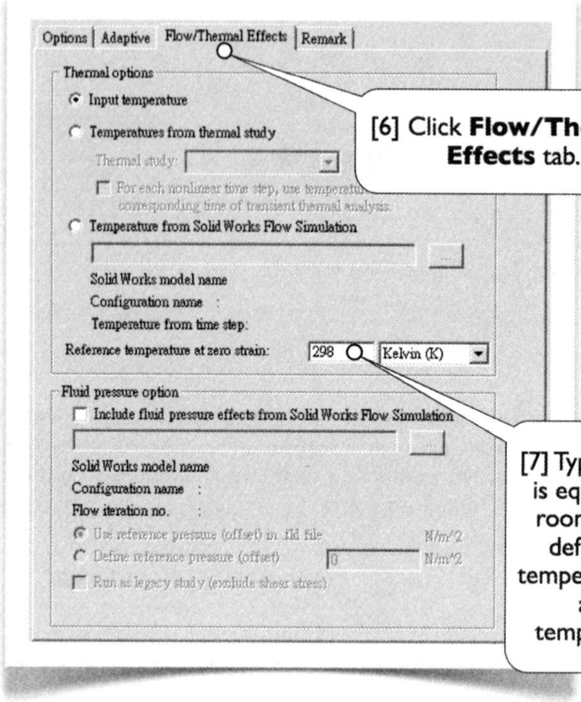

[6] Click **Flow/Thermal Effects** tab.

[7] Type 298 (Kelvin), which is equivalent to 25°C, the room temperature. This defines the strain-free temperature; i.e., the strains are zeros at this temperature. Click **OK**.

5.3-3 Free Expansion

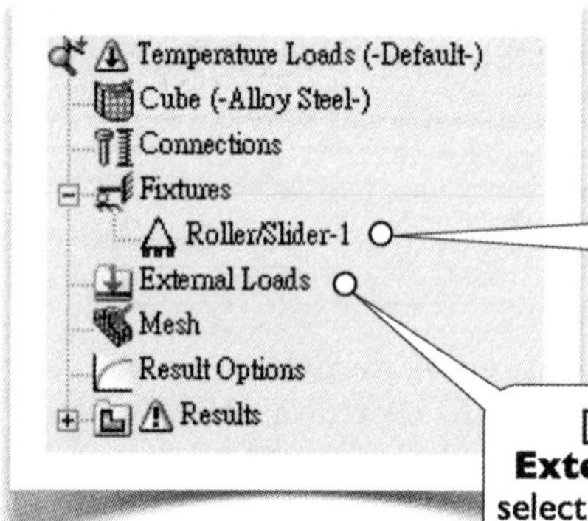

[1] Remember that the **Roller/Slider** conditions apply on negative-X-face, negative-Y-face, and negative-Z-face (see 4.1-5[4, 5], page 76). The other three faces are free to expand or contract under temperature changes.

[2] Right-click **External Loads** and select **Temperature...**

[3] Click **Filter Solid Bodies** and select the cube in the **Graphics Area**. If the **Selection Filter** doesn't show at the bottom, then from **Pull-Down Menus**, select **View>Toolbars>Selection Filter**.

[4] Type 373 (Kelvin), which is equivalent to 100°C. The temperature is raised from 25°C to 100°C. The total temperature change is 75°C.

[5] Click **OK**.

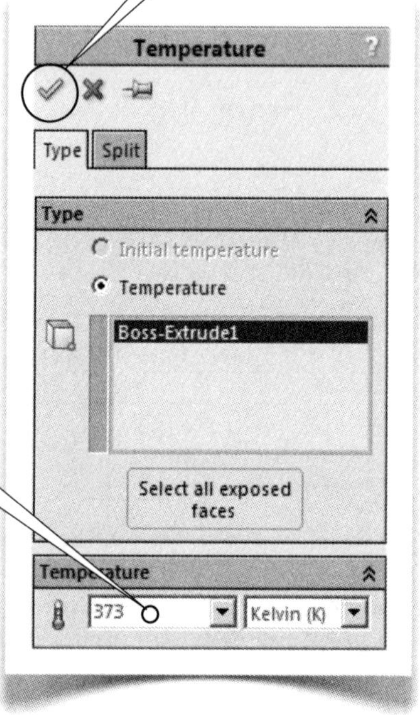

[6] Click **Run**.

[7] It leaves for you to retrieve the normal strains. It is important to note that, in a linear analysis, the strain reported by the **Simulation** are actually elastic strains. See 5.3-1 (page 109) for a definition of elastic strains.

[8] It also leaves for you to retrieve the maximum displacements.

[9] It also leaves for you to retrieve the normal stresses. Because the cube is free to expand in all three directions, there are no stresses in the body.

	Elastic Normal Strain	Thermal Normal Strain	Total Normal Strain	Maximum Displacement	Normal Stress
X-Direction	0	+0.000975	+0.000975	+0.00975 mm	0
Y-Direction	0	+0.000975	+0.000975	+0.00975 mm	0
Z-Direction	0	+0.000975	+0.000975	+0.00975 mm	0

[10] For **Alloy Steel,** $\alpha = 1.3\times10^{-5}$ /K (see 4.1-4[7], page 75). The thermal strain (Eq. 5.3-1(2), page 109) $\varepsilon_T = \alpha\Delta T = 1.3\times10^{-5}/\text{K}\times 75\ \text{K} = 0.000975$.

[11] The total strains are the sum of the elastic strains and the thermal strains.

[12] The maximum displacements are the length (10 mm) multiplies the total strains.

[13] To see how these stresses are calculated from the elastic strains, see [14].

[14] Calculate Stresses from Strains

Eq. 4.3-1(1) (page 87) can be inverted and rewritten as

$$\sigma_X = \frac{E}{(1+\nu)(1-2\nu)}\left[(1-\nu)\varepsilon_X + \nu\varepsilon_Y + \nu\varepsilon_Z\right]$$
$$\sigma_Y = \frac{E}{(1+\nu)(1-2\nu)}\left[(1-\nu)\varepsilon_Y + \nu\varepsilon_Z + \nu\varepsilon_X\right] \qquad (1)$$
$$\sigma_Z = \frac{E}{(1+\nu)(1-2\nu)}\left[(1-\nu)\varepsilon_Z + \nu\varepsilon_X + \nu\varepsilon_Y\right]$$

For a proof of Eq. (1), please see Appendix at the end of Section 12.2 (page 245). If the elastic strains $(\varepsilon_X, \varepsilon_Y, \varepsilon_Z)$ are zeros, then the stresses are also zeros [13]. #

5.3-4 Constrain the Body in X-Direction

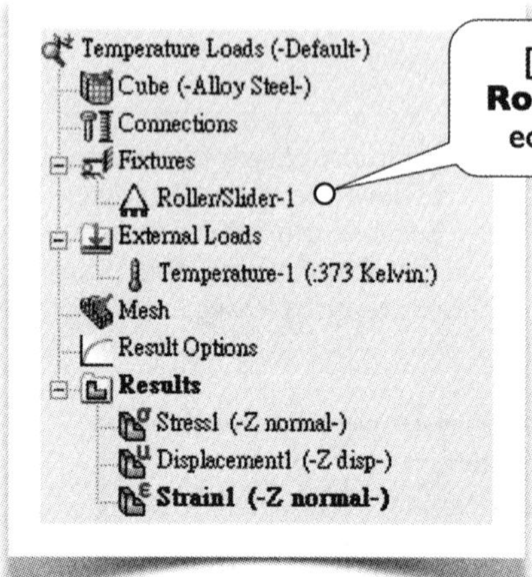

[1] Double-click **Roller/Slider-1** to edit the definition.

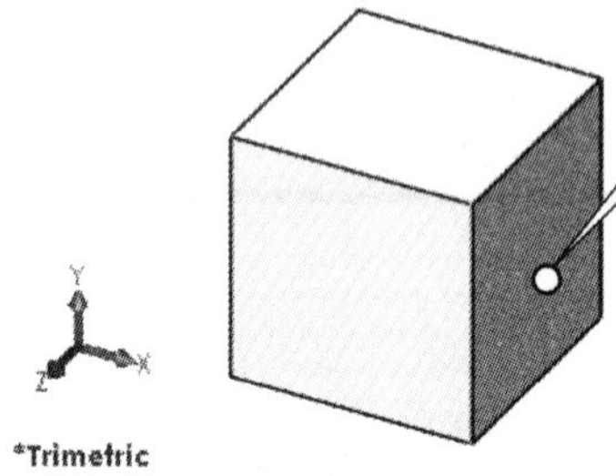

[2] Click this face.

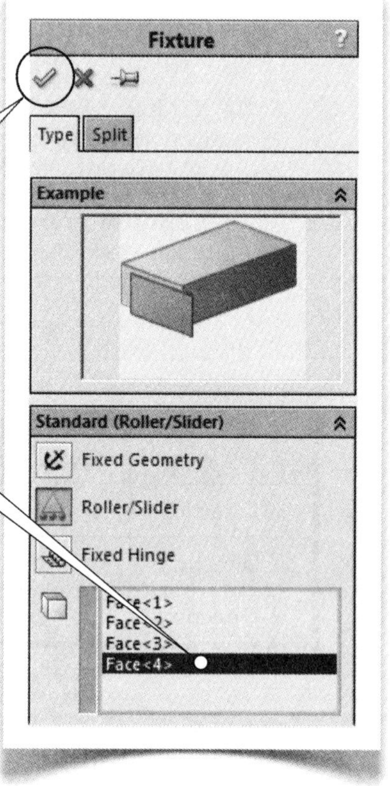

[3] The *X*-face is also constrained. Now only the *Y*-face and the *Z*-face are free to expand (or contract).

[4] Click **OK**.

[5] Click **Run**.

[6] These normal strains are what you retrieve from the results.

[7] These displacements are what you retrieve from the results.

[8] These normal stresses are what you retrieve from the results.

	Elastic Normal Strain	Thermal Normal Strain	Total Normal Strain	Maximum Displacement	Normal Stress
X-Direction	-0.000975	+0.000975	0	0	-204.75 MPa
Y-Direction	+0.000273	+0.000975	+0.001248	+0.01248 mm	0
Z-Direction	+0.000273	+0.000975	+0.001248	+0.01248 mm	0

[9] The ratio between ε_Y (or ε_Z) and ε_X is 0.28, which is the **Poisson's ratio** of the material.

[10] Calculation of the thermal strains is the same as in 5.3-3[10], last page.

[11] The total strains are the sum of the elastic strains and the thermal strains.

[12] The maximum displacements are the length (10 mm) multiplies the total strains.

[13] The body has a compressive stress of 204.75 MPa in the *X*-direction. It leaves for you to calculate these three stresses using Eq. (1) in 5.3-3[14], last page. #

5.3-5 Lower the Temperature

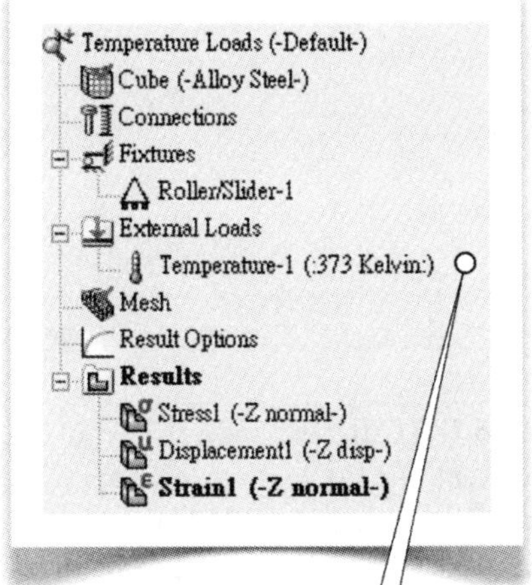

[1] Double-click **Temperature-1** to edit the definition.

[2] Type 223 (Kelvin), which is equivalent to –50°C. The temperature is decreased from 25°C to –50°C. The total temperature change is –75°C.

[3] Click **OK**.

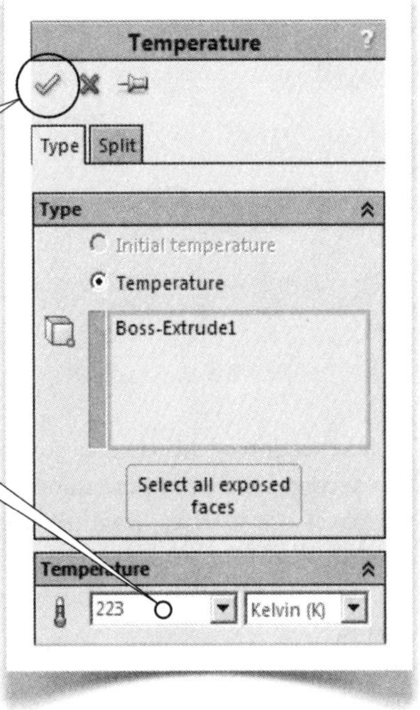

[4] Click **Run**.

[5] These normal strains are what you retrieve from the results.

[6] These displacements are what you retrieve from the results.

[7] These normal stresses are what you retrieve from the results.

	Elastic Normal Strain	Thermal Normal Strain	Total Normal Strain	Maximum Displacement	Normal Stress
X-Direction	+0.000975	-0.000975	0	0	+204.75 MPa
Y-Direction	-0.000273	-0.000975	-0.001248	-0.01248 mm	0
Z-Direction	-0.000273	-0.000975	-0.001248	-0.01248 mm	0

[8] The ratio between ε_Y (or ε_Z) and ε_X is 0.28, which is the **Poisson's ratio** of the material.

[9] Calculation of the thermal strains is the same as in 5.3-3[10] (page 111) but in reverse direction.

[10] The total strains are the sum of the elastic strains and the thermal strains.

[11] The maximum displacements are the length (10 mm) multiplies the total strains.

[12] The body has a tension of 204.75 MPa in the X-direction. It leaves for you to calculate these three stresses using Eq. (1) in 5.3-3[14], page 111.

[13] Save the document and exit **SolidWorks**. #

Chapter 6

Torsion

The first section of this chapter guides the students to learn the torsion formula, Eqs. 6.1-1(1, 2), next page.

The second section lets the students familiarize stresses in cylindrical coordinate system. As we've done in Chapter 1, to describe the stresses, we often use a cube in which all the edges are parallel to the coordinate axes. When a cylindrical coordinate system is used, this "cube" becomes twisted and somewhat peculiar (see picture in 6.2-1[5], page 123). Section 6.2 offers an opportunity for the students to get accustomed to the notions of cylindrical coordinate systems.

Section 6.3 solves a statically indeterminate problem. With hand-calculation, a statically indeterminate problem is quite different from a statically determinate problem, in terms of the efforts to solve the problem. However, modern software such as **SolidWorks Simulation** solves both types of problems with the same methods, namely the Finite Element Methods.

Section 6.1

Torsion in a Circular Shaft

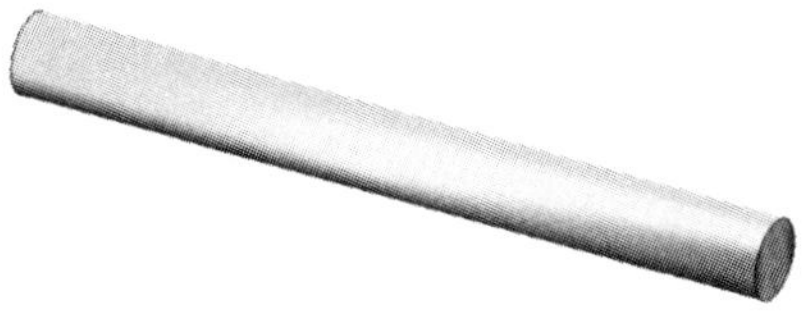

6.1-1 Introduction

[1] In this section, we'll study the torsional behavior of a circular shaft. The shaft is made of **Alloy Steel** with shear modulus G = 82 GPa (see Eq. 4.2-1(2), page 80), has a length L = 1000 mm and a radius r = 50 mm [2]. The shaft is fixed at one end [3], and a torque T = 10,000 N-m is applied at the other end [4]. The circular cross section has a polar moment of inertia $J = \pi r^4/2 = \pi 0.05^4/2 = 9.8175 \times 10^{-6}\ \text{m}^4$. The maximum shear stress occurs at the outer edge of the cross section, which is

$$\tau_{\text{max}} = \frac{Tr}{J} = \frac{(10{,}000)(0.05)}{9.8175 \times 10^{-6}} = 50.9 \times 10^6\ \text{Pa} = 50.9\ \text{MPa} \qquad (1)$$

The twist angle is

$$\phi = \frac{TL}{JG} = \frac{(10{,}000)(1)}{(9.8175 \times 10^{-6})(82 \times 10^9)} = 0.0124\ \text{(rad)} \qquad (2)$$

The purpose of this section is to help students fully understand the torsion formula (1) and (2).

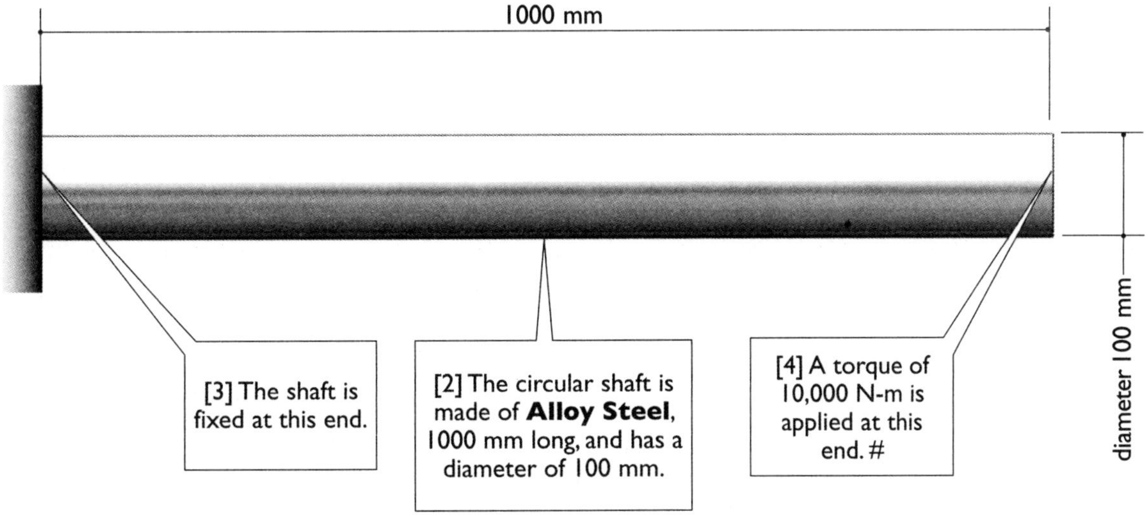

6.1-2 Start Up

[1] Launch **SolidWorks** and create a new part. Set up **MMGS** unit system with zero decimal places for the length unit. #

6.1-3 Create Geometric Model

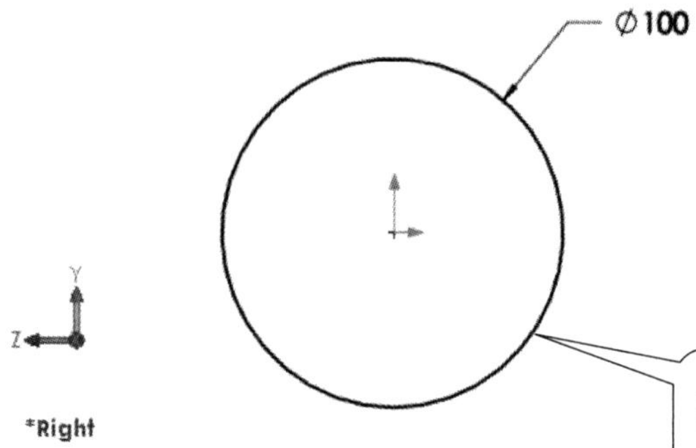

[1] On the **Right** plane, draw a sketch like this.

[2] **Extrude** 1000 mm.

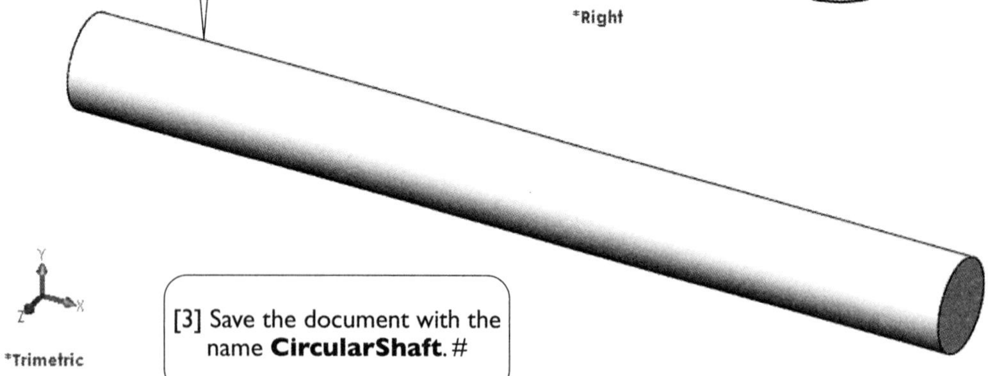

[3] Save the document with the name **CircularShaft**. #

6.1-4 Create a Study and Apply Material

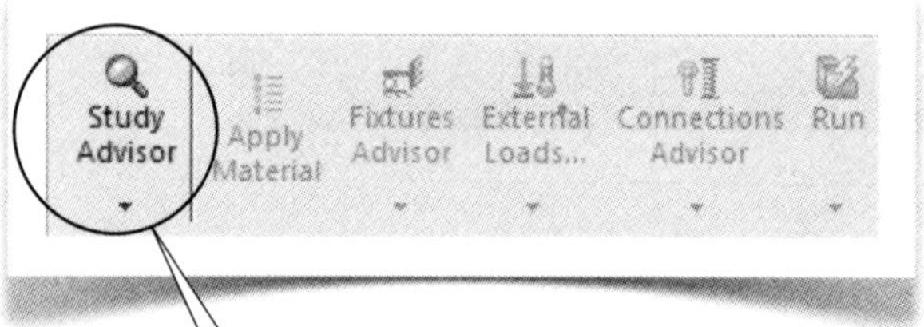

[1] In the **Simulation Toolbar**, select **Study Advisor>New Study**. Name the new study **Torsion**. Leave **Static** as default **Study Type**.

[2] Right-click **CircularShaft** and select **Apply/Edit Material...** and apply **Alloy Steel** for the model. #

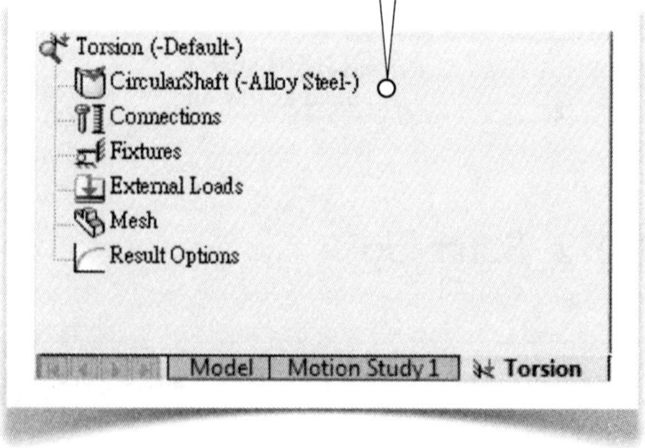

6.1-5 Set Up Loads and Supports

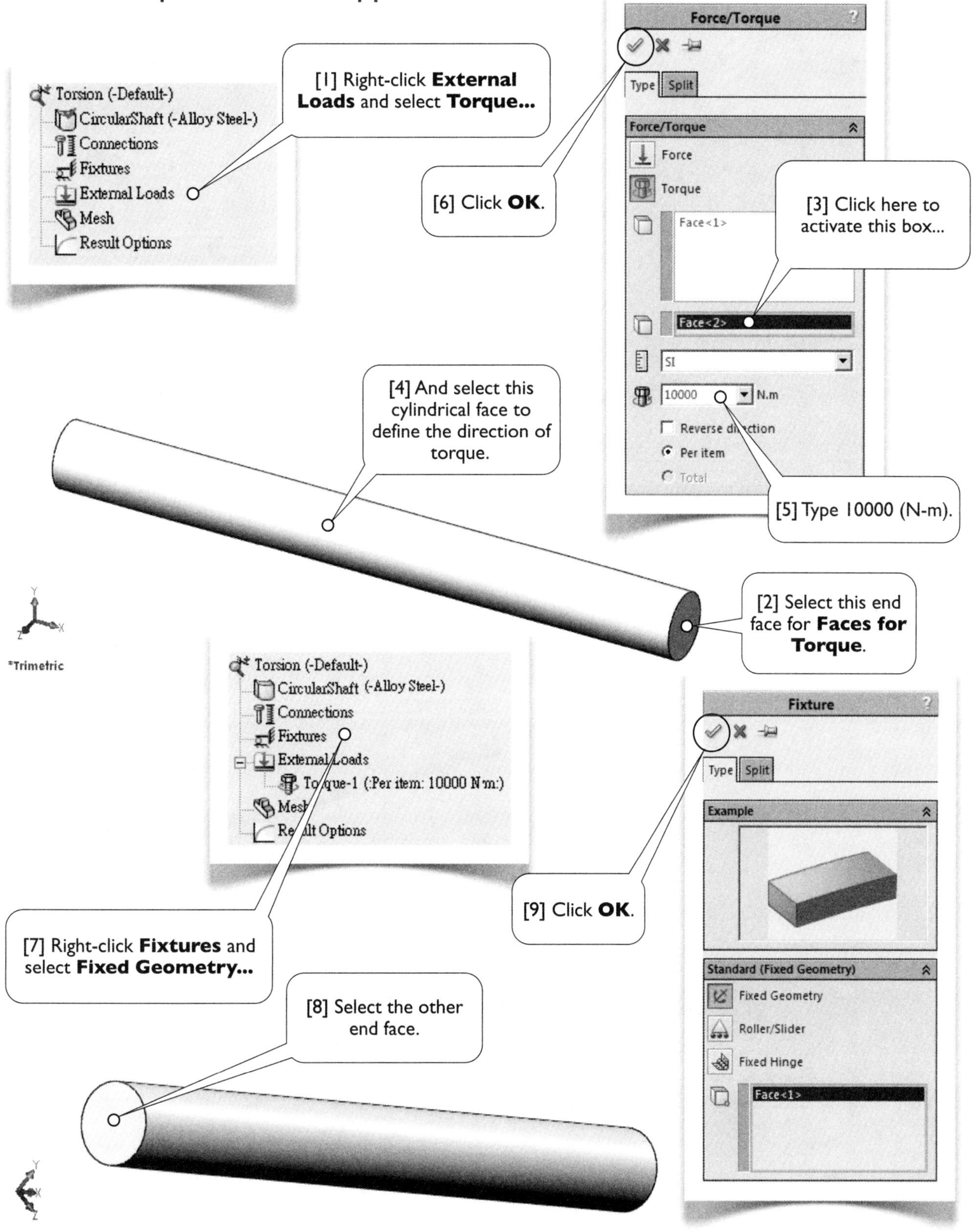

[10] Right-click **Fixtures** and select **Roller/Slider...**

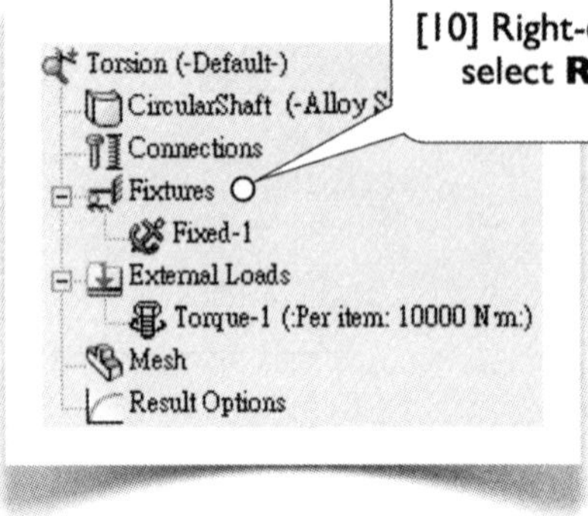

[11] Select this cylindrical face.

[12] Click **OK**.

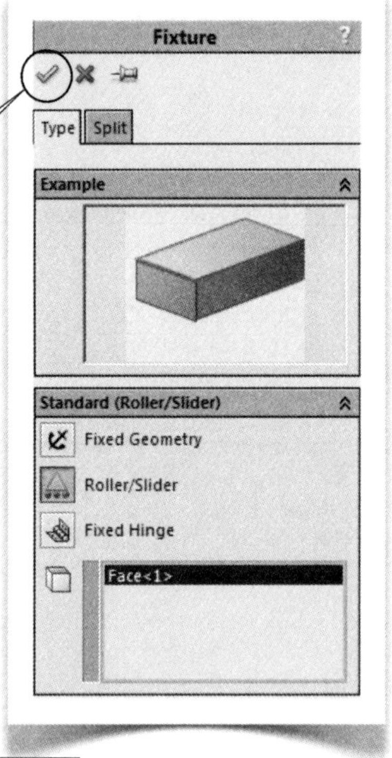

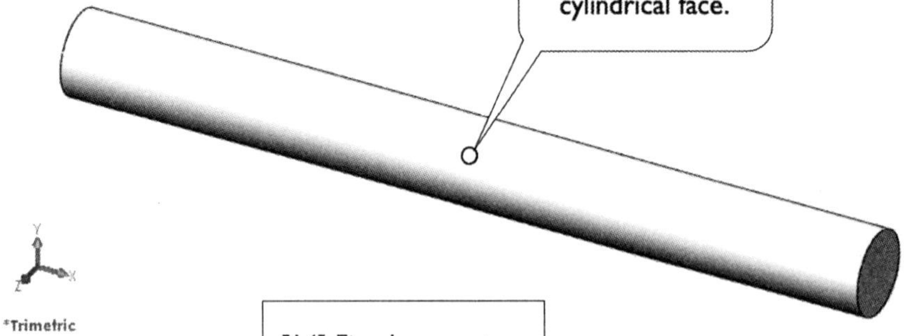

[14] Fixed support on this end face.

[15] Roller support on the cylindrical face. This boundary condition is not really necessary. However, we include it to avoid deviation from theoretical solutions.

[13] The applied torque (10,000 N-m) on this end face.

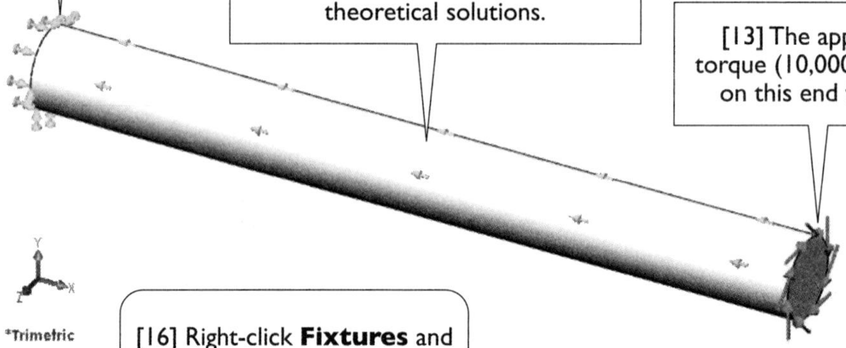

[16] Right-click **Fixtures** and select **Hide All**.

[17] Right-click **External Loads** and select **Hide All**. #

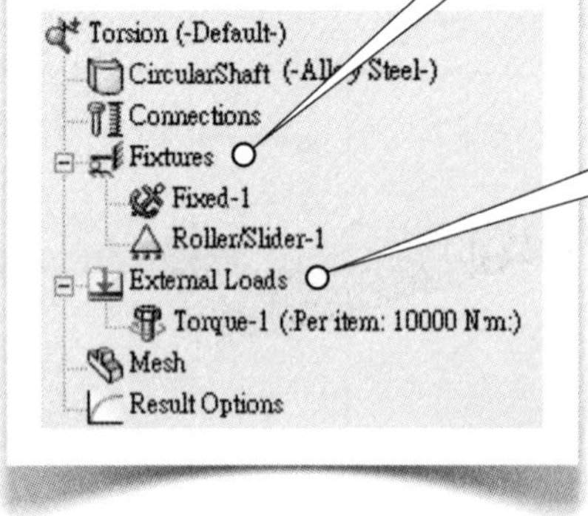

6.1-6 Obtain the Solution

[1] Click **Run**.

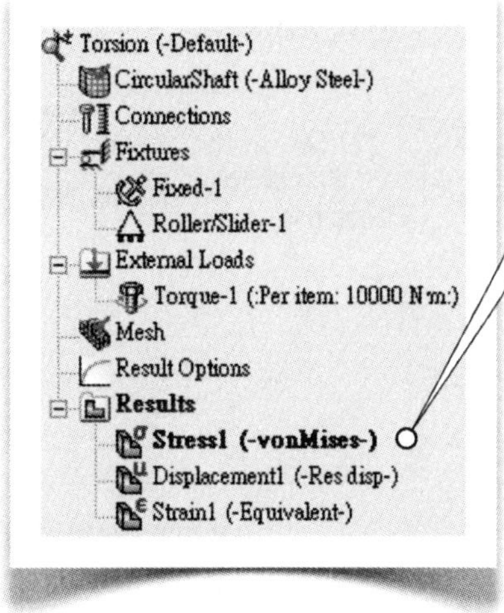

[2] Double-click **Stress1** to edit the definition.

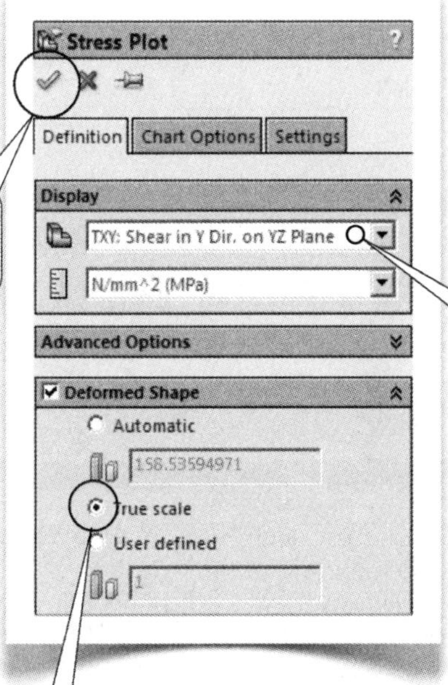

[3] Select **TXY: Shear in Y Dir. on YZ Plane** (τ_{XY}).

[4] Select **True scale**.

[5] Click **OK**.

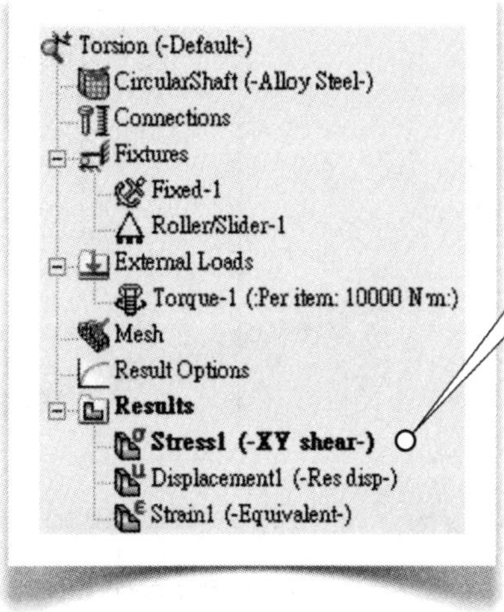

[7] Right-click **Stress1** and select **Chart Options...** and turn off **Max** and **Min** annotations. #

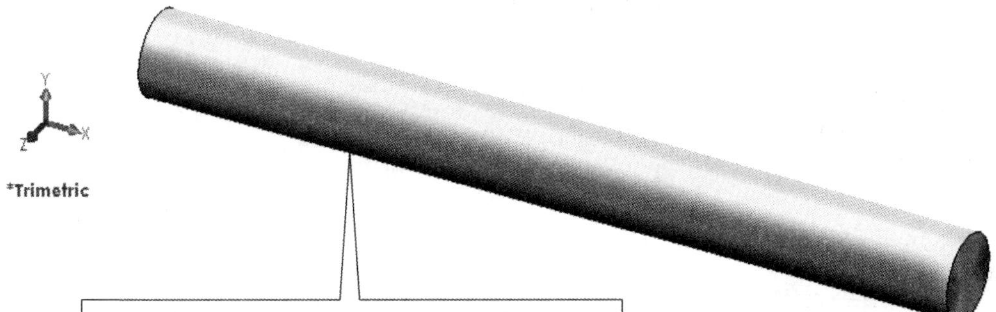

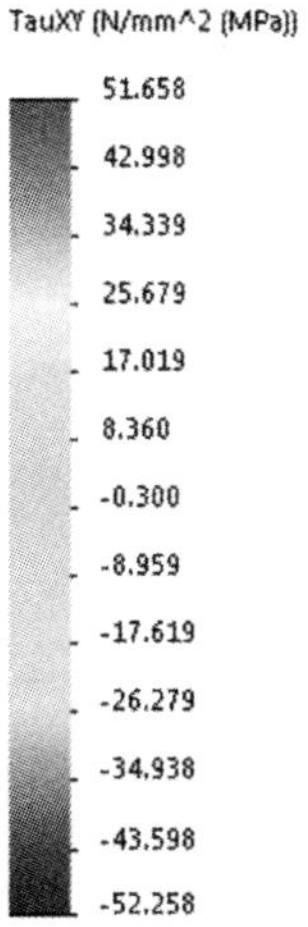

[6] The maximum shear stress is close to the value in Eq. 6.1-1(1), page 115. Let's look into the shear stresses across a diameter.

6.1-7 Obtain Shear Stresses Across Diameter

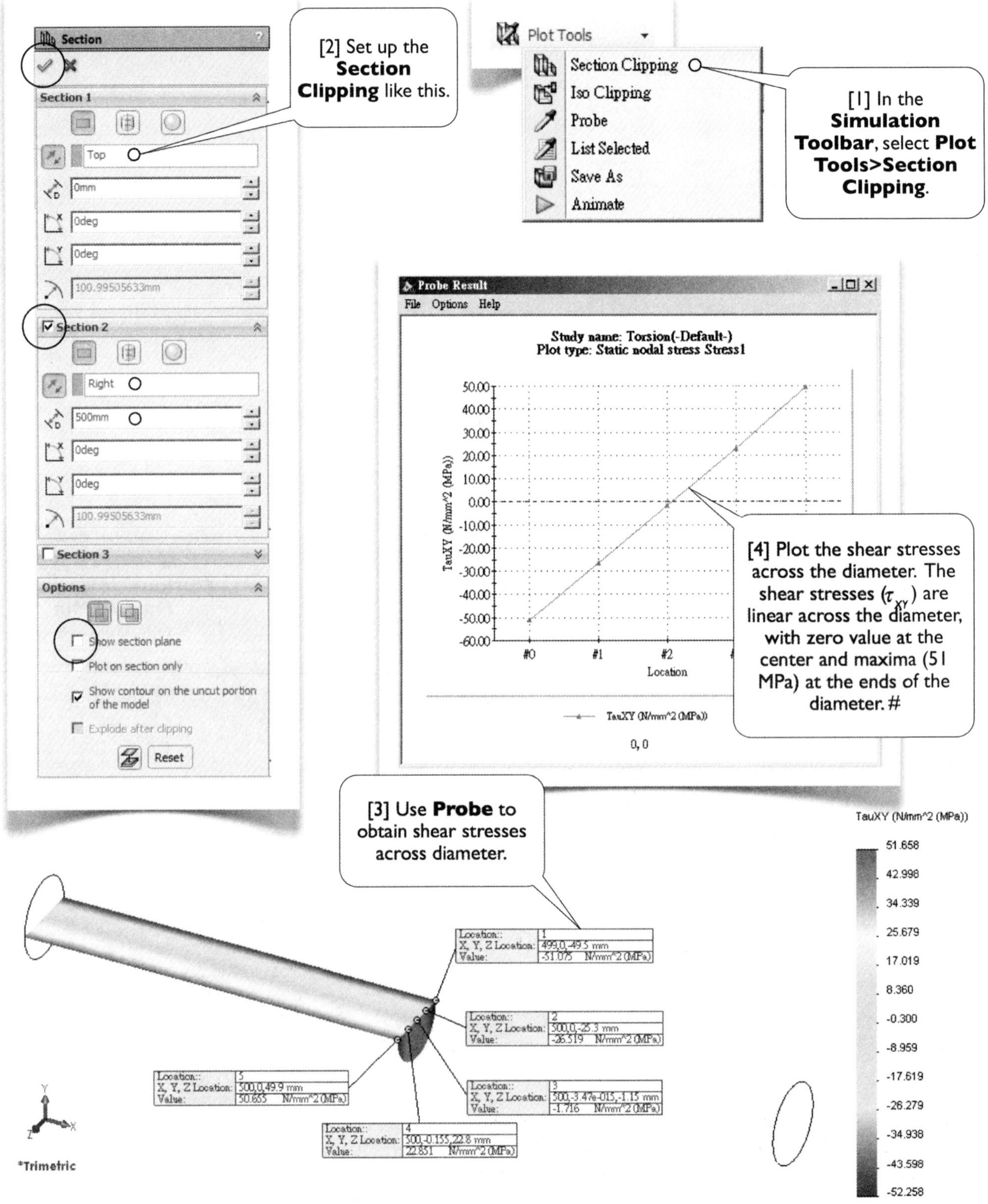

6.1-8 Stress States at Locations of Cylindrical Surface

Stress Component	Location **A**	Location **B**
σ_X	0	0
σ_Y	0	0
σ_Z	0	0
τ_{XY}	-51 MPa	51 MPa
τ_{XZ}	0	0
τ_{YZ}	0	0

[1] You may verify that, at locations **A** and **B** (the two locations are defined in [2, 3]), other components than τ_{XY} have zero values.

[2] The stress state at location **A**.

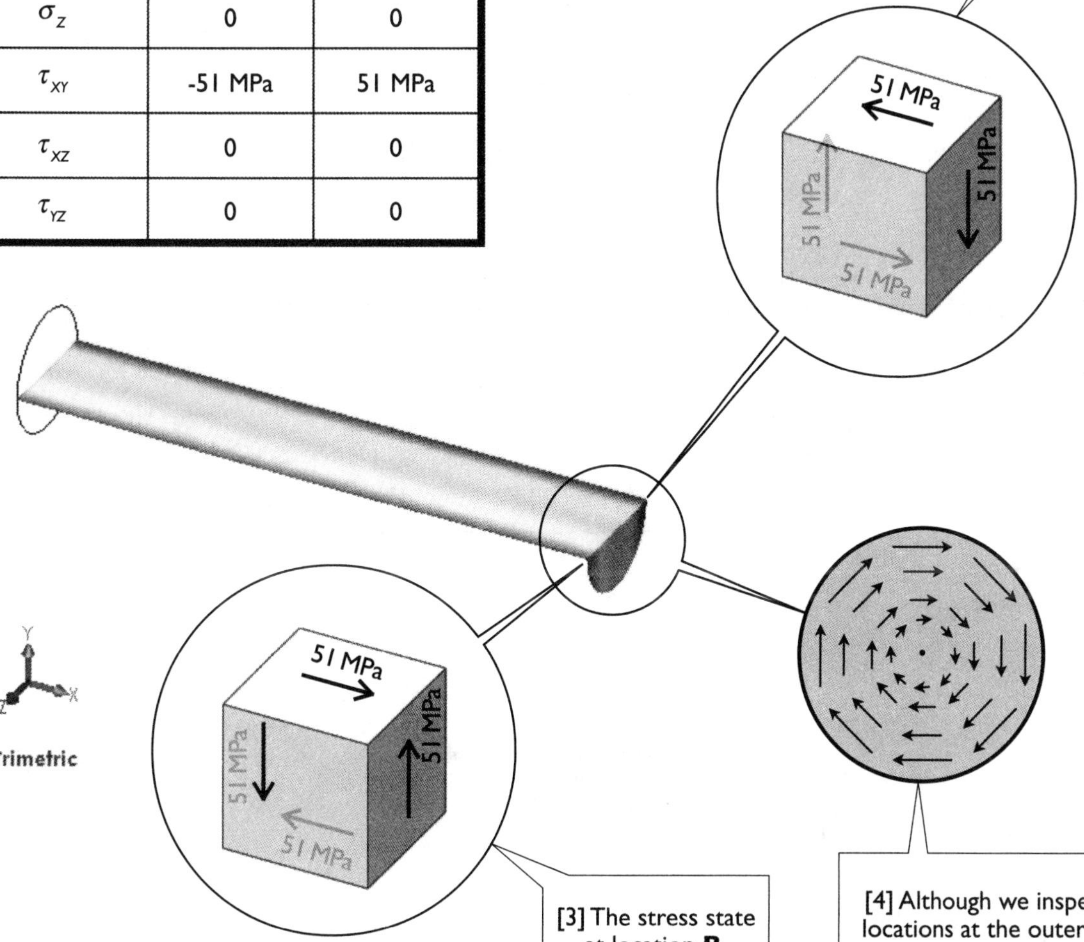

[3] The stress state at location **B**.

[4] Although we inspect only two locations at the outer edge of the cross section, it turns out that every point on the outer edge has similar stress state. It is easy to figure out that the shear stresses distribute over a cross section like this.

[5] For a case like this, a cylindrical coordinate system would be much more convenient. In the next section, we'll show you how a cylindrical coordinate system facilitates the visualization of the results. #

6.1-9 Obtain the Twist Angle

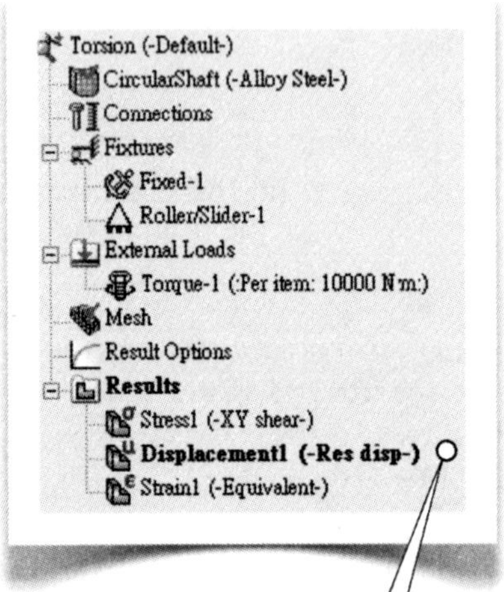

[1] Double-click **Displacement1** to activate it. Double-click **Displacement1** again to edit the definition.

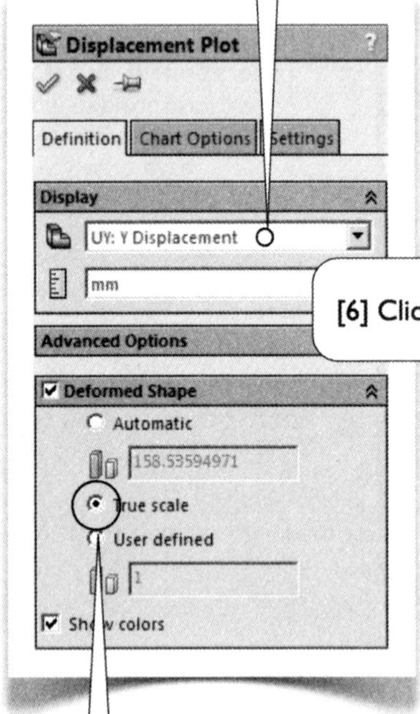

[2] Select **UY: Y Displacement**.

[3] Select **True scale**.

[4] Click **Chart Options**.

[5] Turn on **Show min annotation** and **Show max annotation**.

[6] Click **OK**.

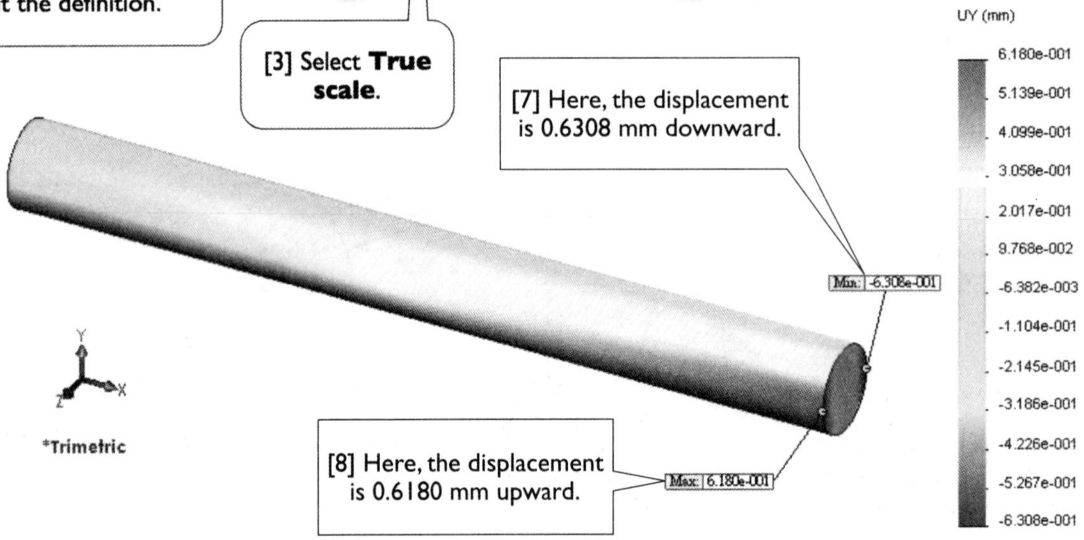

[7] Here, the displacement is 0.6308 mm downward.

[8] Here, the displacement is 0.6180 mm upward.

[9] Calculation of the Twist Angle

From [7, 8], we may calculate the twist angle as follows:

$$\phi = \frac{0.6308 + 0.6180}{100} = 0.01249 \text{ (rad)}$$

which is consistent with the value in Eq. 6.1-1(2), page 115. This is the twist angle at the free end of the shaft. At the fixed end, the twist angle is zero. Between the two ends, the twist angle changes linearly.

[10] Save the document and exit **SolidWorks**. #

Section 6.2

Stresses in Cylindrical Coordinate Systems

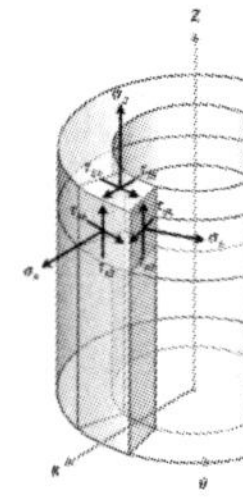

6.2-1 Introduction

[1] When a model is geometrically axisymmetric, a cylindrical coordinate system is often much more convenient than a cartesian coordinate system. The three directions in a cylindrical coordinate system are denoted by R, θ, and Z [2, 3, 4]. The **Simulation**, however, retains the use of notations X, Y, and Z for a cylindrical coordinate system. Therefore, X should read R, and Y should read θ. For example, τ_{XY} should be interpreted as $\tau_{R\theta}$. The six stress components are σ_R, σ_θ, σ_Z, $\tau_{R\theta}$, $\tau_{\theta Z}$, and τ_{ZR} ($\tau_{\theta R} = \tau_{R\theta}$, $\tau_{Z\theta} = \tau_{\theta Z}$, and $\tau_{RZ} = \tau_{ZR}$) [5, 6]. Similarly, the six strain components are ε_R, ε_θ, ε_Z, $\gamma_{R\theta}$, $\gamma_{\theta Z}$, and γ_{ZR} ($\gamma_{\theta R} = \gamma_{R\theta}$, $\gamma_{Z\theta} = \gamma_{\theta Z}$, and $\gamma_{RZ} = \gamma_{ZR}$). The three displacement components are u_R, u_θ, and u_Z.

In the **Simulation**, a coordinate system must be used for referring the directions of stresses, strains, displacements, external loads, or support conditions, therefore, the three directions of the axes are the only information we need to know (the origin is not relevant). You may chose an axis as the Z-axis. This axis alone completely defines the three directions of a cylindrical coordinate system [2].

Using the example in Section 6.1, this section helps the students get accustomed to cylindrical coordinate systems.

[6] These are the stress components expressed in a cylindrical coordinate system. Note that we purposely show the "positive" faces of the cube and all stresses here are in positive directions. #

[5] When using a cylindrical coordinate system, we take a small cube like this. Note that each edge is parallel to a direction of the cylindrical coordinate system.

[3] R is the **radial direction**; the positive direction is outward (away from the Z-axis). The exact orientation of the R-axis is not relevant, as long as it is perpendicular to the Z-axis.

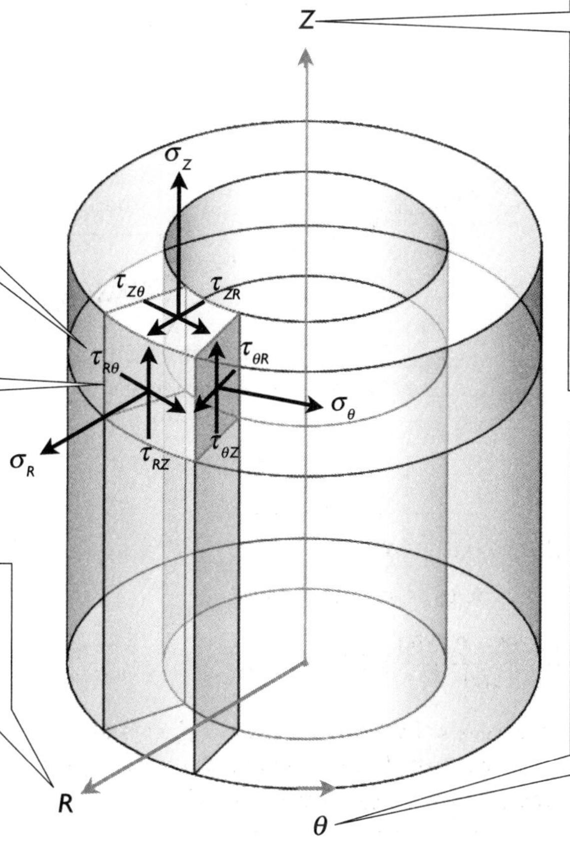

[2] In the **Simulation**, you may chose an axis as the Z-axis. This axis alone completely defines the three directions of a cylindrical coordinate system. The location of the origin is not relevant. Z-direction is also called the **axial direction**.

[4] θ is the **tangential direction** (or **hoop direction**); the positive is counterclockwise when viewed above from Z-axis. The location where $\theta = 0$ is not relevant.

6.2-2 Start Up

[1] Launch **SolidWorks** and open the file **CircularShaft**, which was saved in Section 6.1.

[2] Make sure **Model** tab is active. #

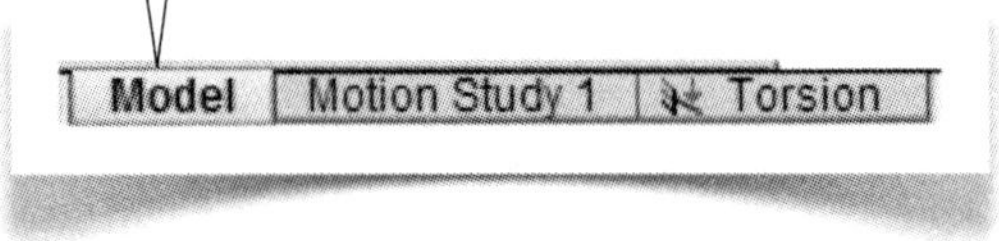

6.2-3 Create an Axis

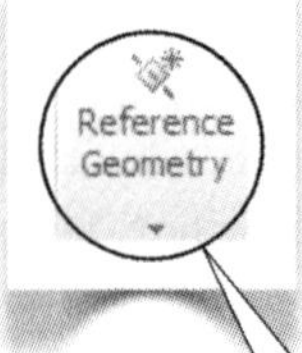

[1] in the **Features Toolbar**, select **Reference Geometry>Axis**.

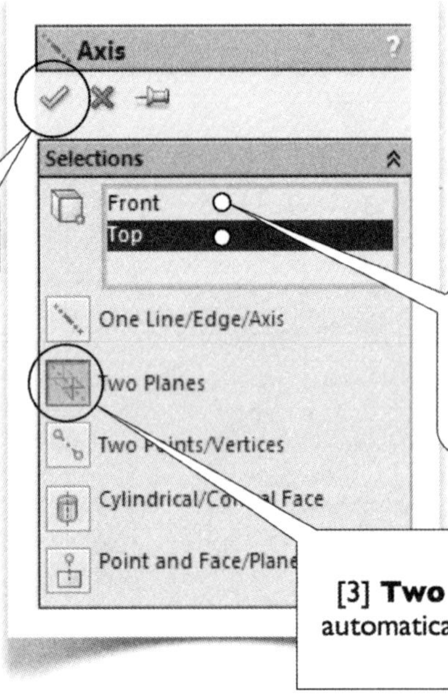

[2] Select **Front** and **Top** planes from the **Part Tree**. An axis is created using the intersection of these two planes.

[3] **Two Planes** is automatically selected.

[4] Click **OK**.

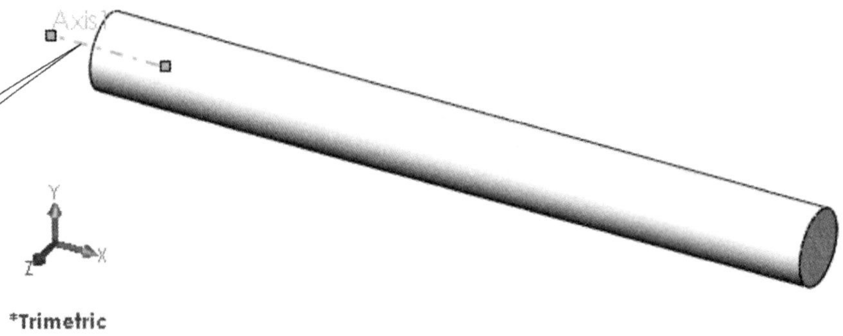

[5] An axis is created and highlighted. Click anywhere in the **Graphics Area** to deselect it. #

6.2-4 Obtain Shear Stresses

[1] Click **Torsion** to activate it.

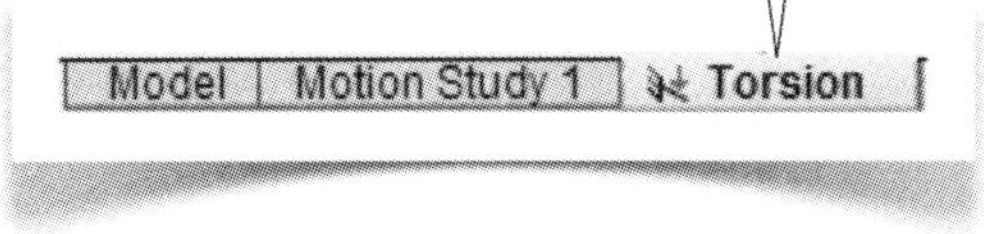

[2] Double-click **Stress1** to activate it.

[3] Double-click **Stress1** again to edit the definition.

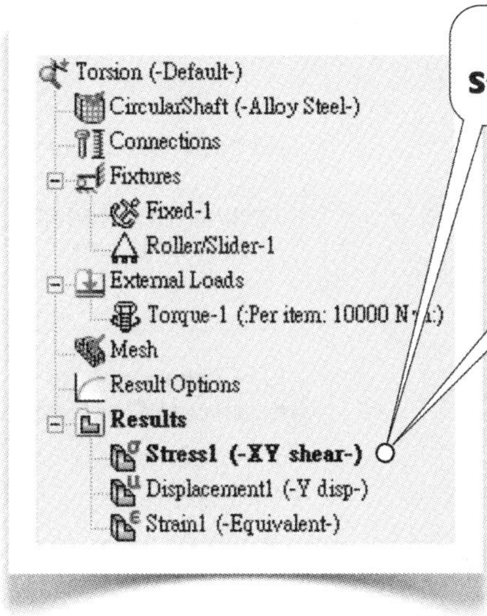

[4] Click to expand **Advanced Options**.

[5] In the **Part Tree**, select **Axis1**. This is used as the *Z*-axis to define a cylindrical coordinate system, which'll be referred by the stress $\tau_{Z\theta}$.

[6] Select **TYZ**, which should read $\tau_{\theta Z}$ (or $\tau_{Z\theta}$).

[7] Click **OK**.

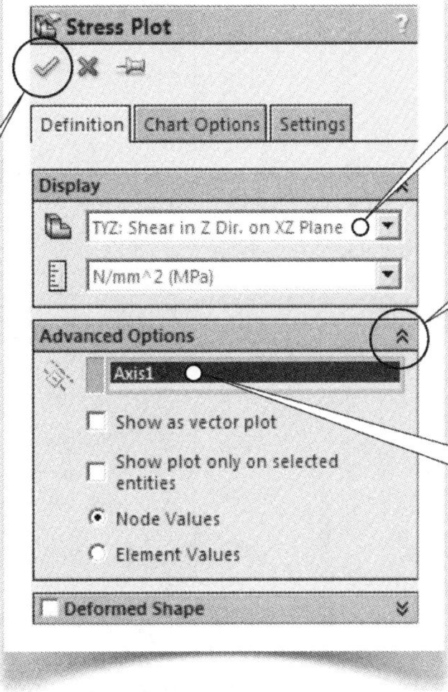

[8] A triad of cylindrical system displays at the lower-right corner, showing directions of *R*, θ, and *Z*.

[9] This is the global coordinate system, which is not referred by the stresses now.

[10] The shear stresses $\tau_{Z\theta}$ (or $\tau_{\theta Z}$) are displayed.

[11] The colors reveal that the shear stresses distribute axisymmetrically, with zero value (red) at the center and maximum (blue) at the edge of the cross section, which is consistent with the value calculated in 6.1-1(1), page 115. Note that the negative value of the shear stress indicates that the direction is clockwise when viewed from the free end of the shaft.

[12] It leaves for you to show that, except $\tau_{Z\theta}$ ($\tau_{\theta Z}$), all other stress components have zero values over the entire shaft. #

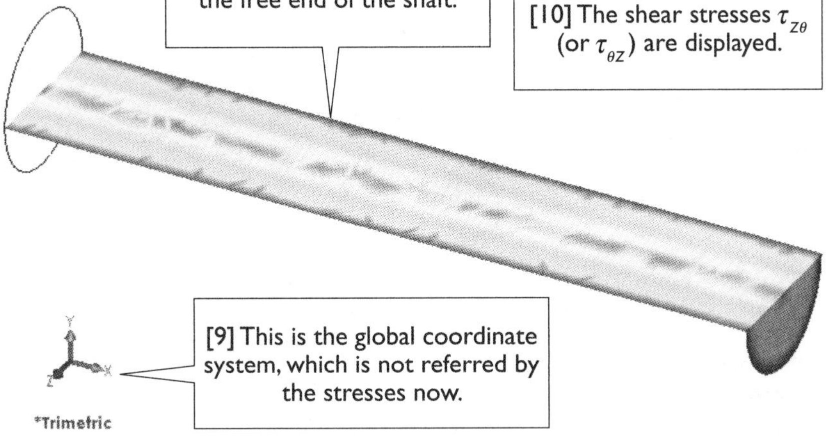

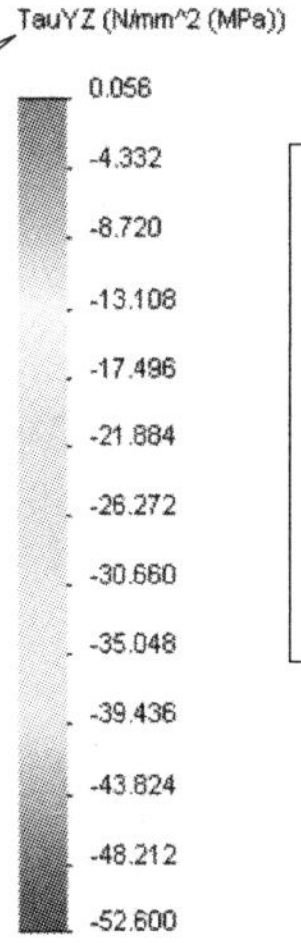

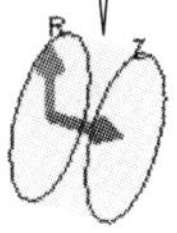

6.2-5 Obtain Tangential Displacement

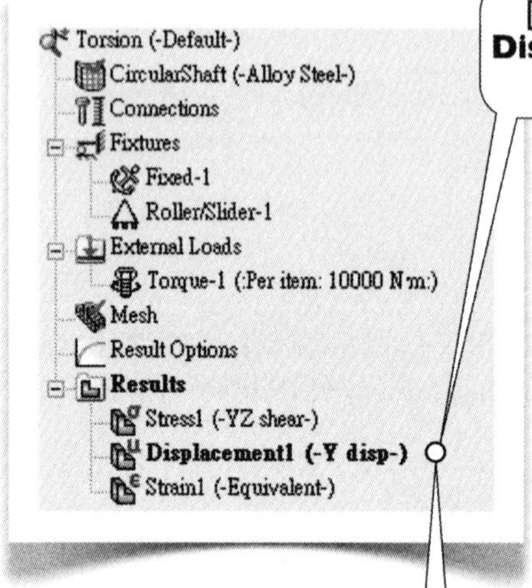

[1] Double-click **Displacement1** to activate it.

[2] Double-click **Displacement1** to edit the definition.

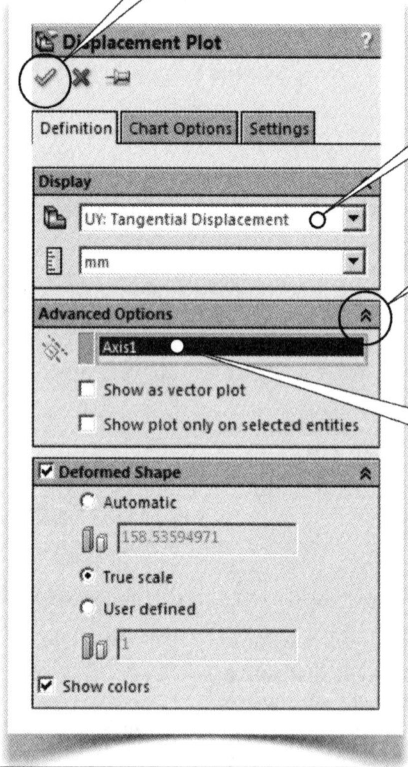

[3] Click to expand **Advanced Options**.

[4] In the **Part Tree**, select **Axis1**.

[5] Now **UY** should read u_θ, which is the tangential displacement, the unit is mm.

[6] Click **OK**.

[7] The tangential displacement u_θ.

[8] The colors reveal that the tangential displacements distribute axisymmetrically, with zero value at the center (red) and maximum (blue) at the edge of the cross section of the free end (-0.6308 mm), which is the same as that in 6.1-9[7], page 122. Note that the negative value indicates that the displacement is clockwise when viewed from the free end of the shaft.

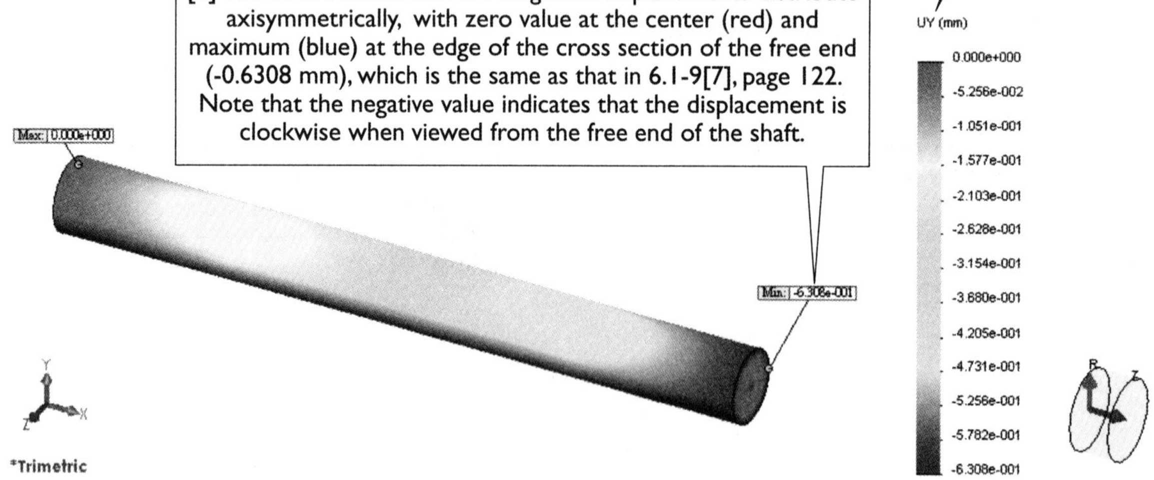

[9] Save the document and exit **SolidWorks**. #

Section 6.3

Statically Indeterminate Shaft

6.3-1 Introduction

[1] Two solid steel shafts are connected by a disk [2] and the two other ends of the shafts are fixed on rigid walls [3]. A torque of 500 N-m is applied to the disk [4], and we want to investigate the stresses and the twist angles of the shafts. The steel has a **Young's modulus** of 200 GPa and a **Poisson's ratio** of 0.3. The **shear modulus** can be calculated using Eq. 4.2-1(1) (page 80), $G = E/2(1+\nu) = 200/2(1+0.3) = 76.9$ GPa.

This is a statically indeterminate problem, meaning that both equilibrium of forces and compatibility of deformation must be considered to solved the problem. The equilibrium of forces gives $T_A + T_B = 500$ N-m, where T_A and T_B are respectively the torques in the two shafts [5, 6]. The compatibility of deformation gives $\phi_A = \phi_B$, where ϕ_A and ϕ_B are respectively the twist angles in the two shafts. In terms of torques, the twist angles can be written down as follows

$$\phi_A = \frac{T_A L_A}{G J_A}, \text{ where } L_A = 0.6 \text{ m}, J_A = \frac{\pi 0.015^4}{2} = 79.522 \times 10^{-9} \text{ m}^4$$

$$\phi_B = \frac{T_B L_B}{G J_B}, \text{ where } L_B = 0.9 \text{ m}, J_B = \frac{\pi 0.018^4}{2} = 164.896 \times 10^{-9} \text{ m}^4$$

Substituting these into the equilibrium equation and the compatibility equation, we can solve for the torques and the twist angles

$$T_A = 209.87 \text{ N-m}, T_B = 290.13 \text{ N-m}, \phi_A = \phi_B = 0.020592 \text{ (rad)}$$

The maximum stresses are then calculated as follows

$$(\tau_{max})_A = \frac{T_A(0.015)}{J_A} = 39.6 \times 10^6 \text{ Pa}, (\tau_{max})_B = \frac{T_B(0.018)}{J_B} = 31.7 \times 10^6 \text{ Pa}$$

Now, let's obtain these solutions using the **Simulation**.

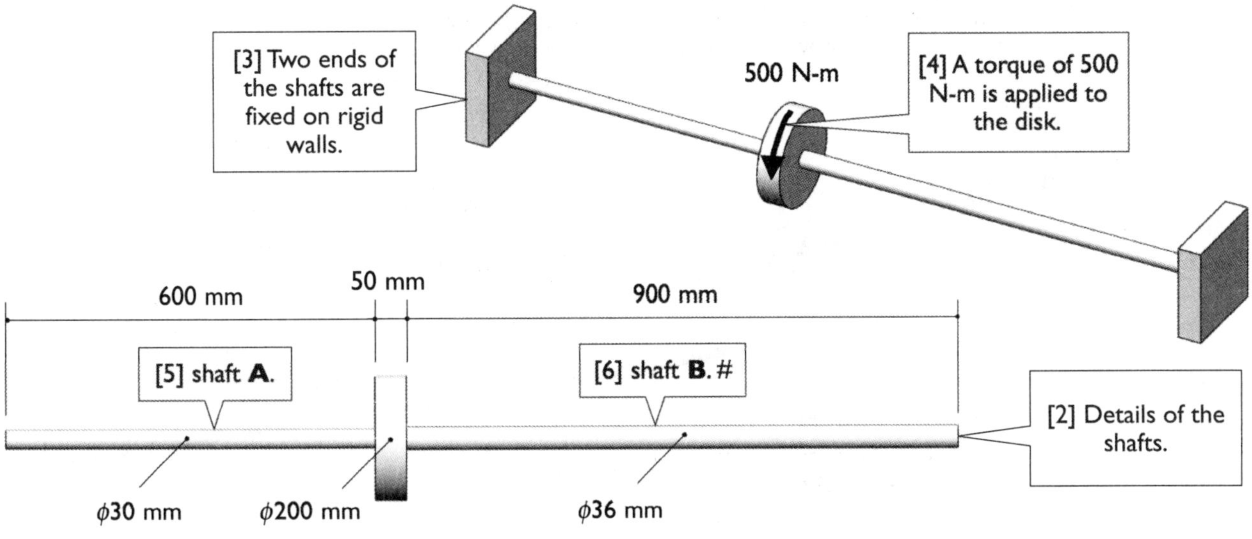

6.3-2 Start Up

[1] Launch **SolidWorks** and create a new part. Set up **MMGS** unit system with zero decimal places for the length unit. #

6.3-3 Create Geometric Model

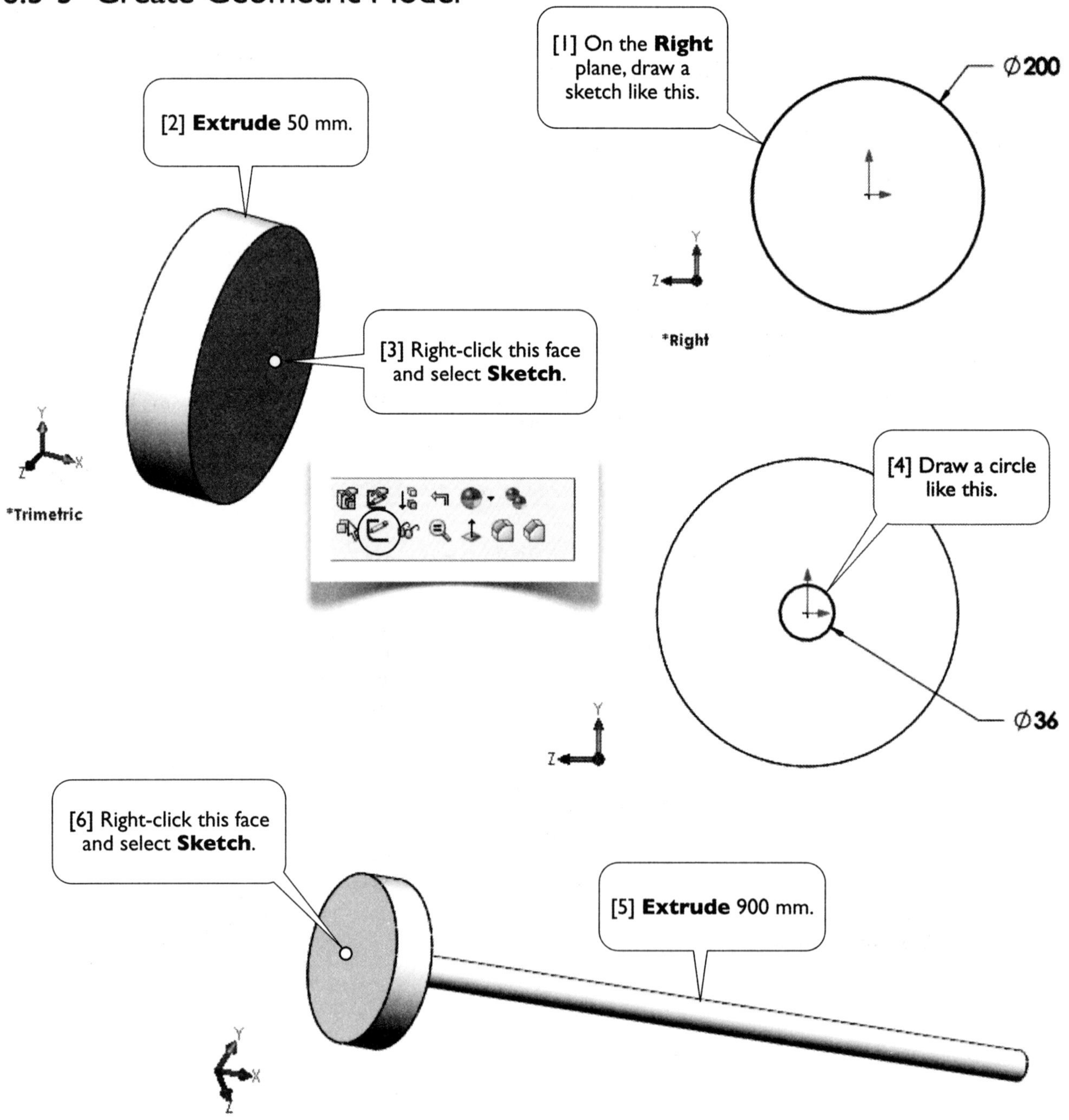

[7] Draw a **circle** like this.

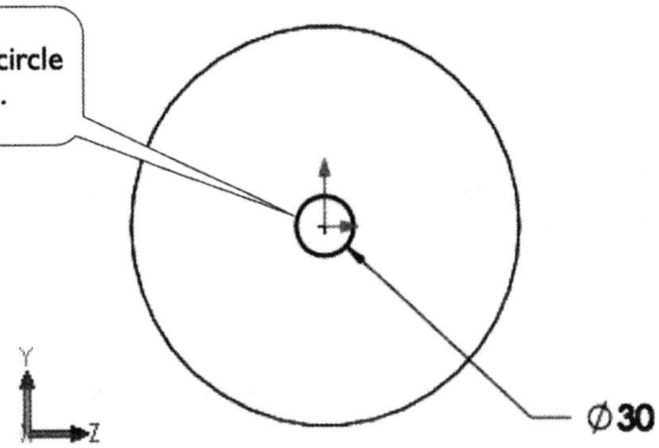

[8] **Extrude** 600 mm.

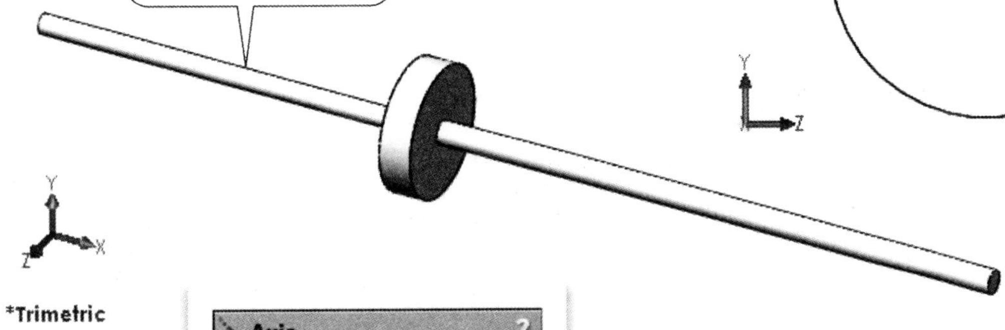

[9] in the **Features Toolbar**, select **Reference Geometry>Axis**.

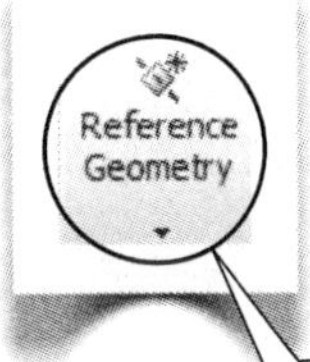

[10] Select **Front** and **Top** planes from the **Part Tree**.

[11] Click **OK**.

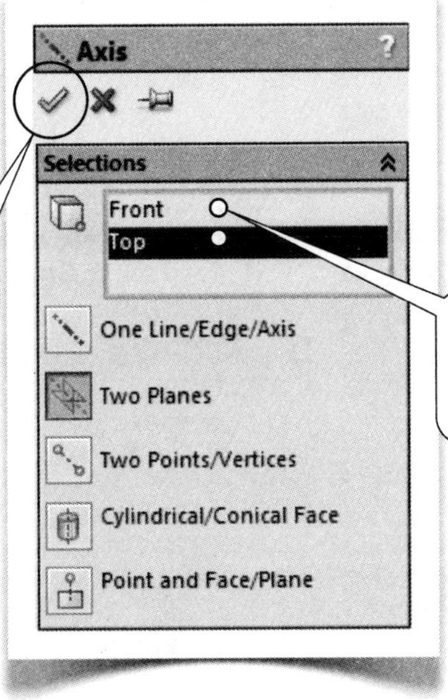

[12] The new axis will be used to define a cylindrical coordinate system.

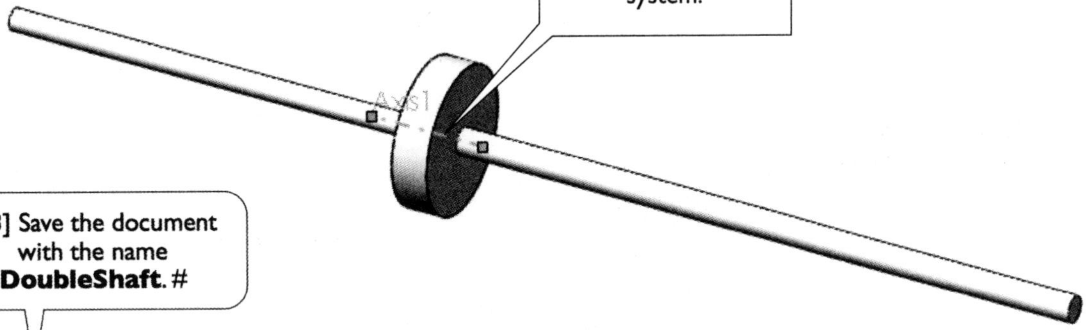

[13] Save the document with the name **DoubleShaft**. #

6.3-4 Create a Study and Apply Material

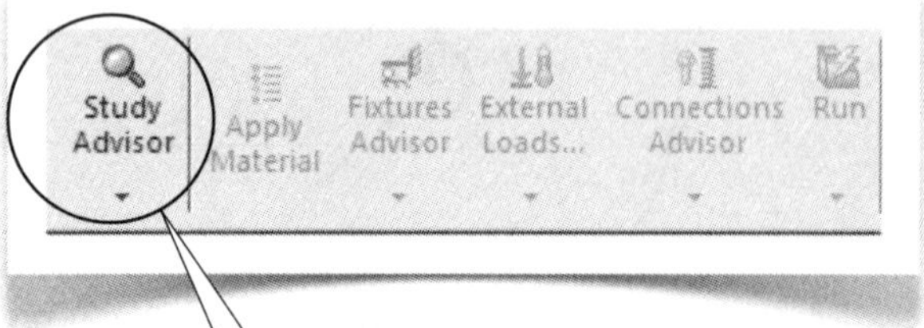

[1] In the **Simulation Toolbar**, select **Study Advisor>New Study**. Name the new study **Torsion**. Leave **Static** as default **Study Type**.

[2] Right-click **DoubleShaft** and select **Apply/Edit Material...**

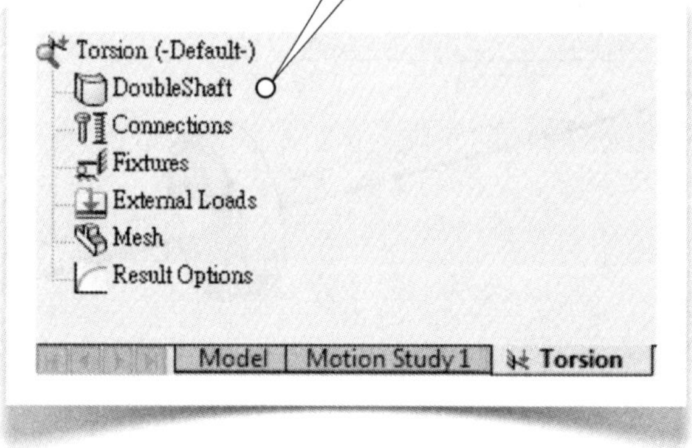

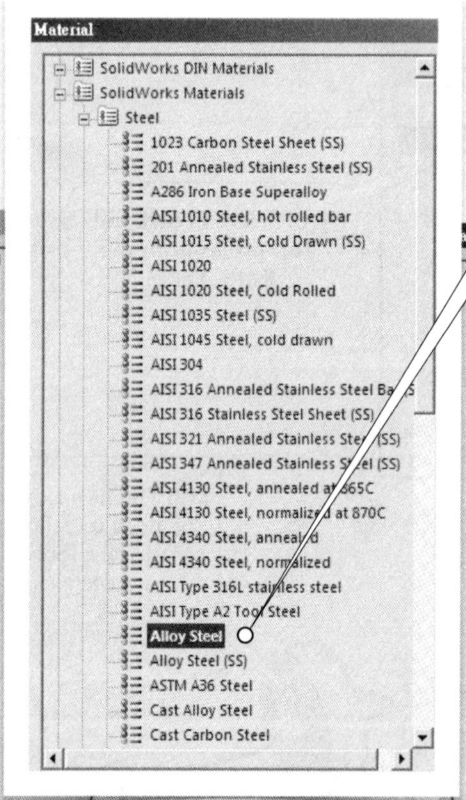

[4] Scroll up to the top. Right-click Alloy Steel and select **Copy**.

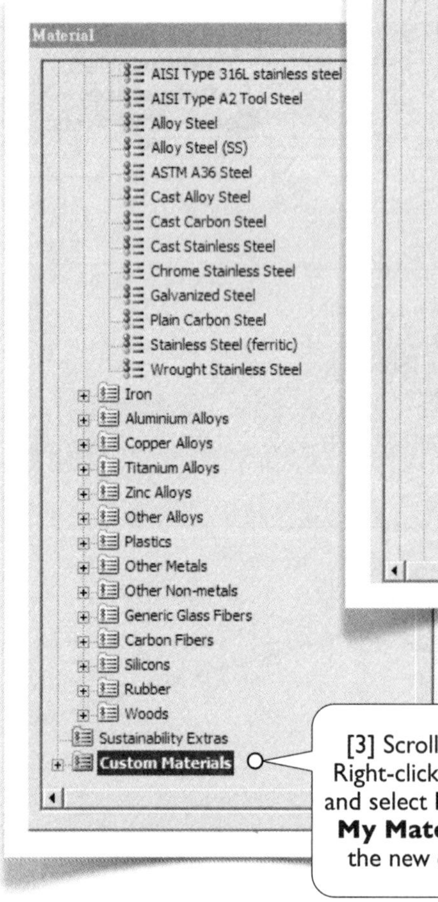

[3] Scroll down to the bottom. Right-click **Custom Materials** and select **New Category**. Type **My Materials** as the name for the new category of materials.

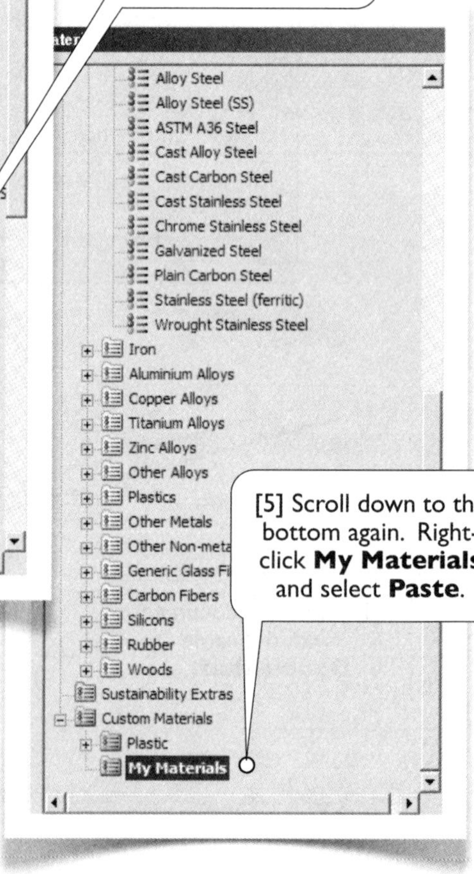

[5] Scroll down to the bottom again. Right-click **My Materials** and select **Paste**.

[7] Type 2e11 (Pa) for **Elastic Modulus**, 0.3 (dimensionless) for **Poisson's Ratio**, and clear the **Shear Modulus** (the shear modulus will be calculated according to Eq. 4.2-1(1), page 80). Except these three, other material parameters are not relevant for this case.

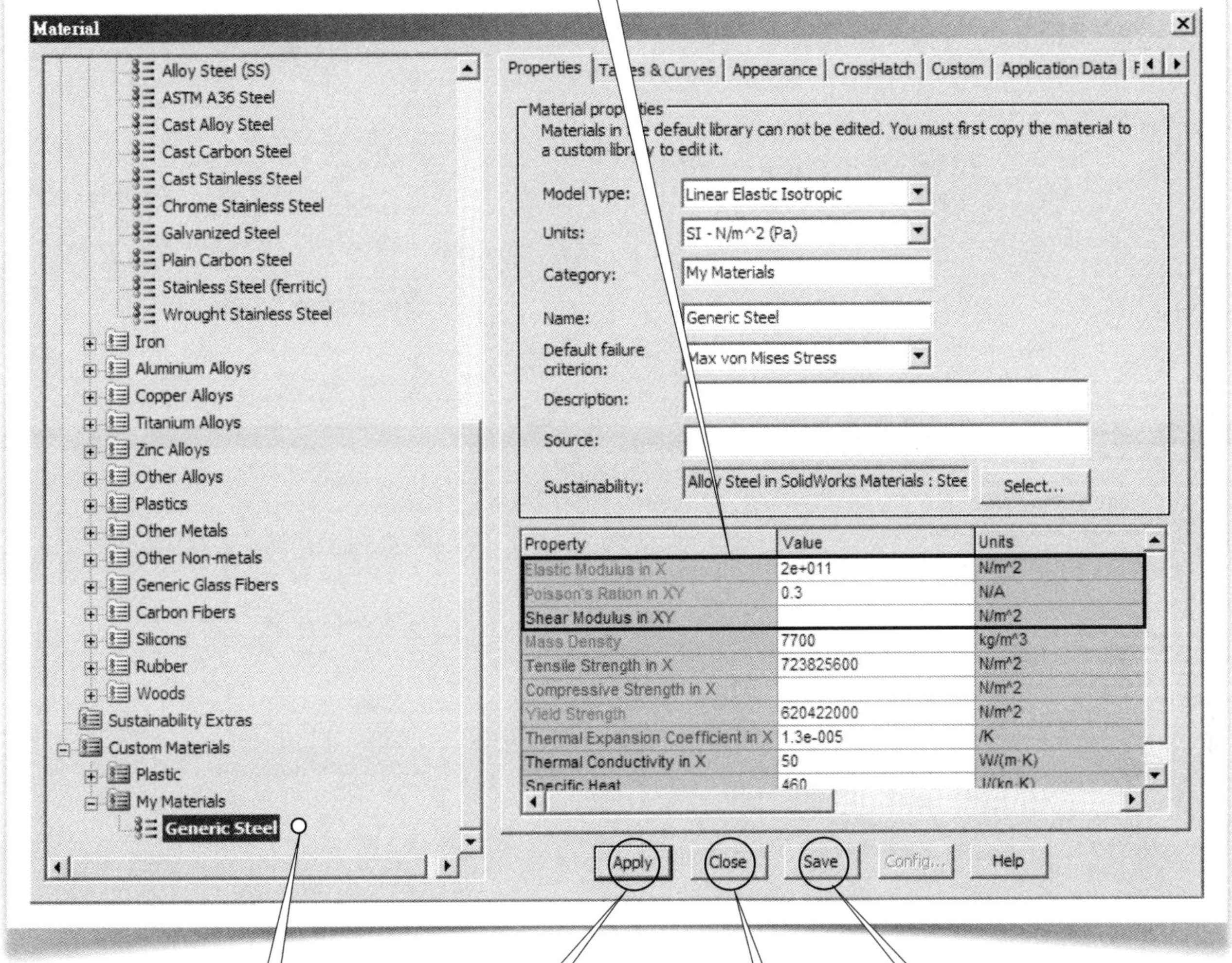

[6] The **Alloy Steel** is duplicated and saved under **My Materials**. Right-click it and rename to **Generic Steel**.

[9] Click **Apply**.

[10] Click **Close**. #

[8] Click **Save**.

6.3-5 Set Up Supports and Loads

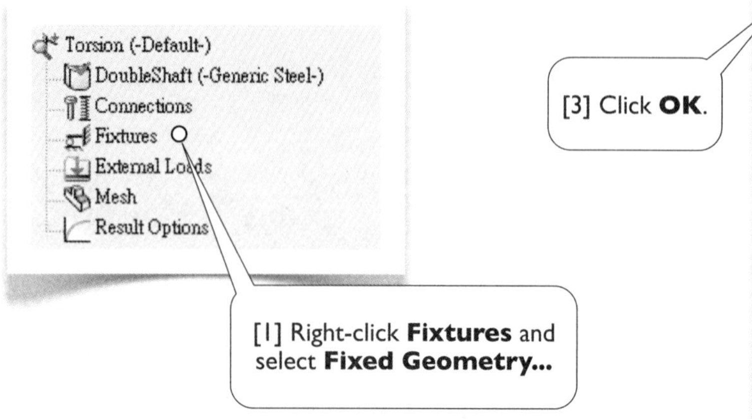

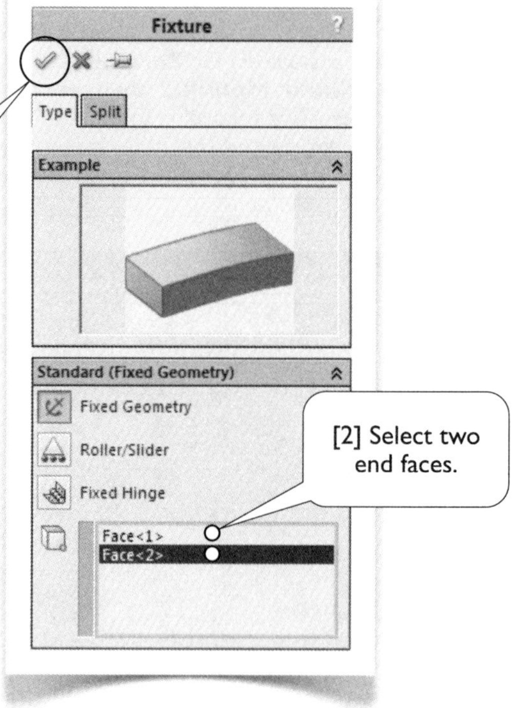

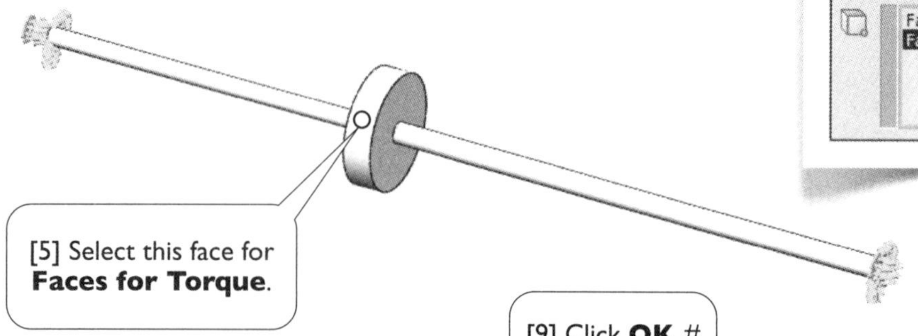

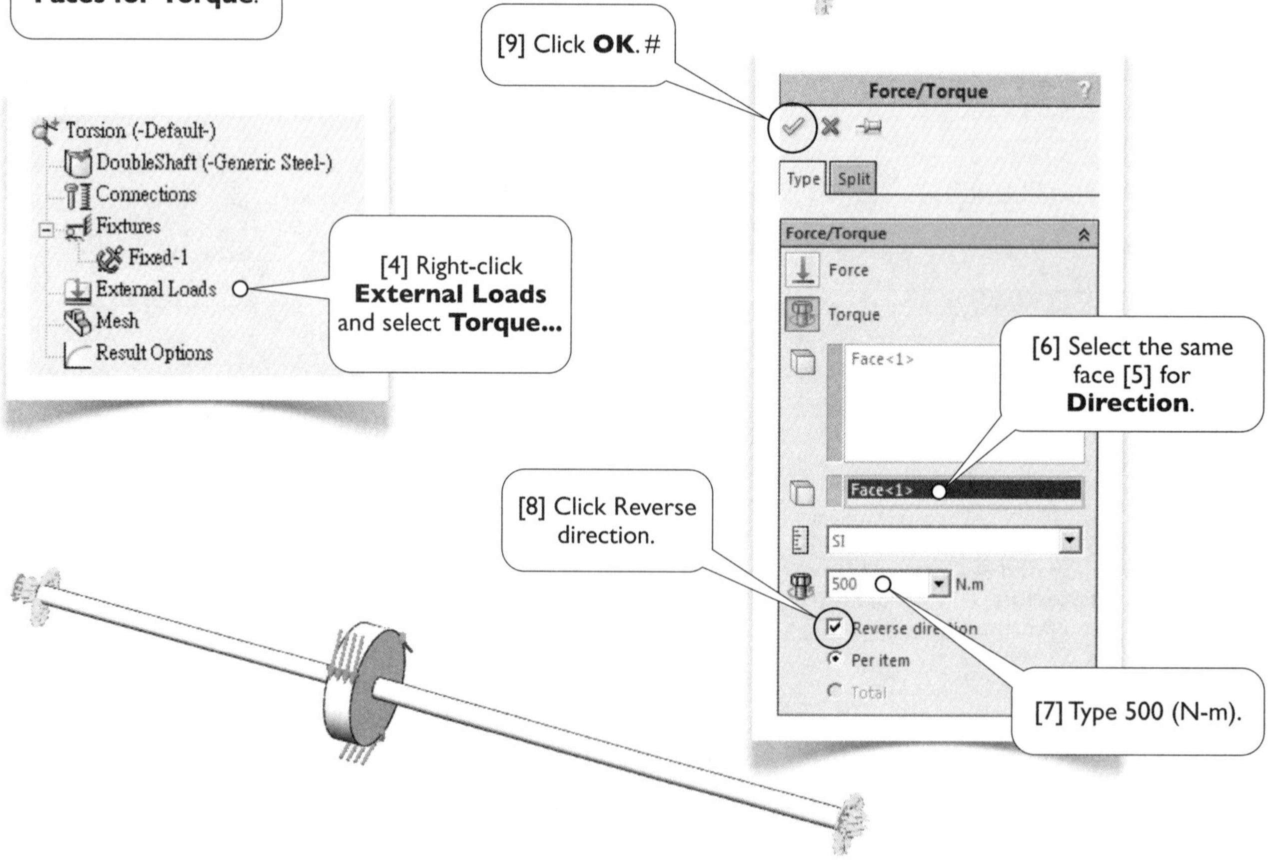

6.3-6 Create Mesh

[1] Right-click **Fixtures** and select **Hide All**.

[2] Right-click **External Loads** and select **Hide All**.

[3] Right-click **Mesh** and select **Create mesh...**

[4] Click **Mesh Parameters**.

[5] Click **Curvature based mesh**.

[6] Type 3 (mm) for **Minimum element size**.

[7] Type 32 for **Minimum number of elements in a circle**.

[8] Click **OK**.

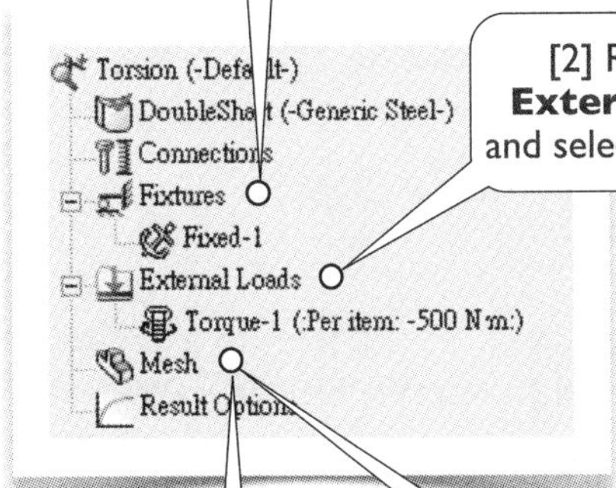

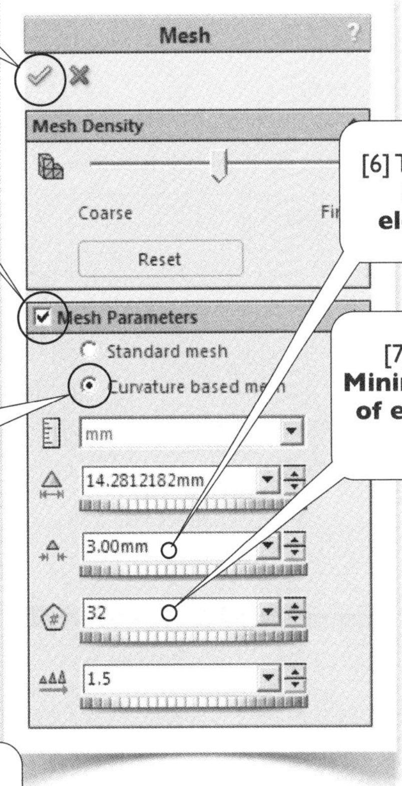

[10] Right-click **Mesh** and select **Details...**

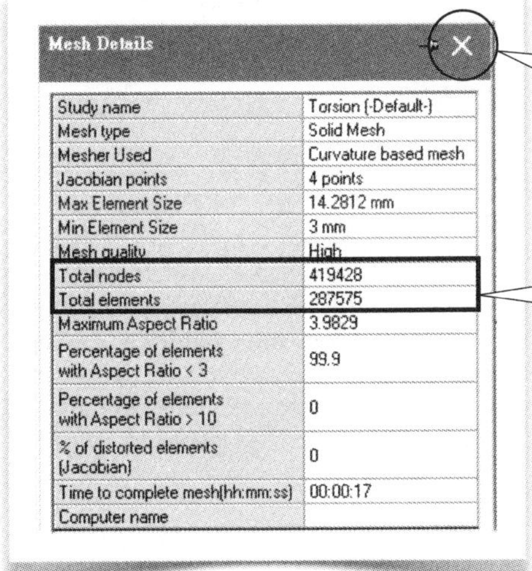

Study name	Torsion (-Default-)
Mesh type	Solid Mesh
Mesher Used	Curvature based mesh
Jacobian points	4 points
Max Element Size	14.2812 mm
Min Element Size	3 mm
Mesh quality	High
Total nodes	419428
Total elements	287575
Maximum Aspect Ratio	3.9829
Percentage of elements with Aspect Ratio < 3	99.9
Percentage of elements with Aspect Ratio > 10	0
% of distorted elements (Jacobian)	0
Time to complete mesh(hh:mm:ss)	00:00:17
Computer name	

[12] Close the **Mesh Details**. #

[11] The mesh consists of about 300,000 elements and 400,000 nodes.

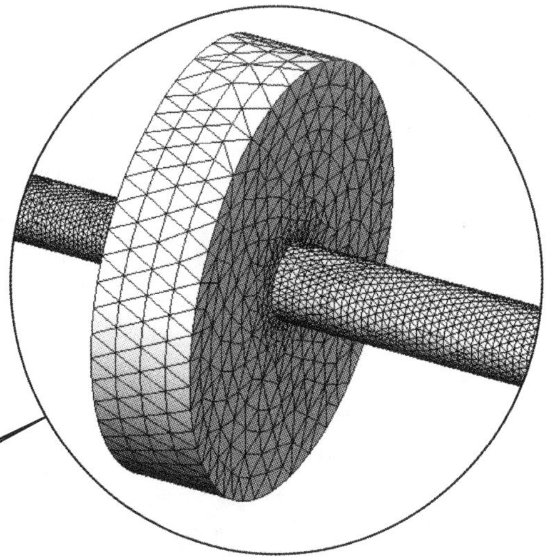

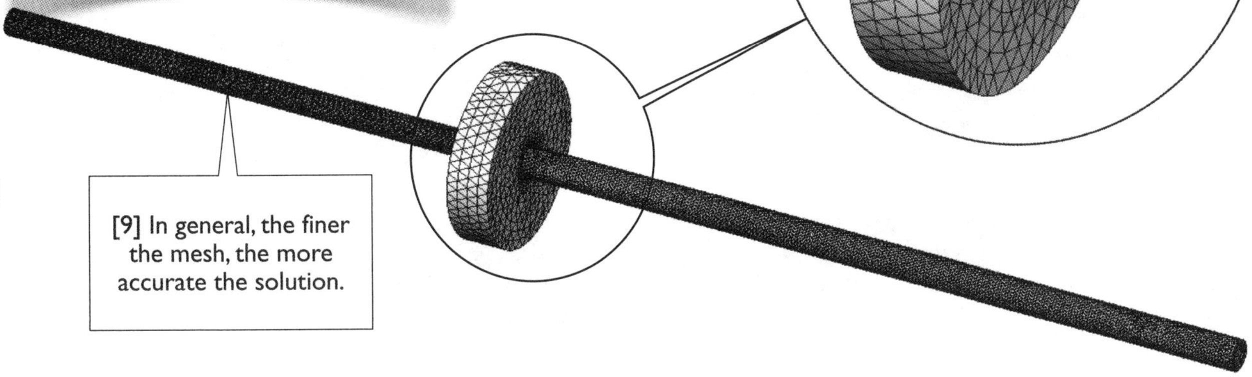

[9] In general, the finer the mesh, the more accurate the solution.

6.3-7 Obtain Maximum Shear Stresses

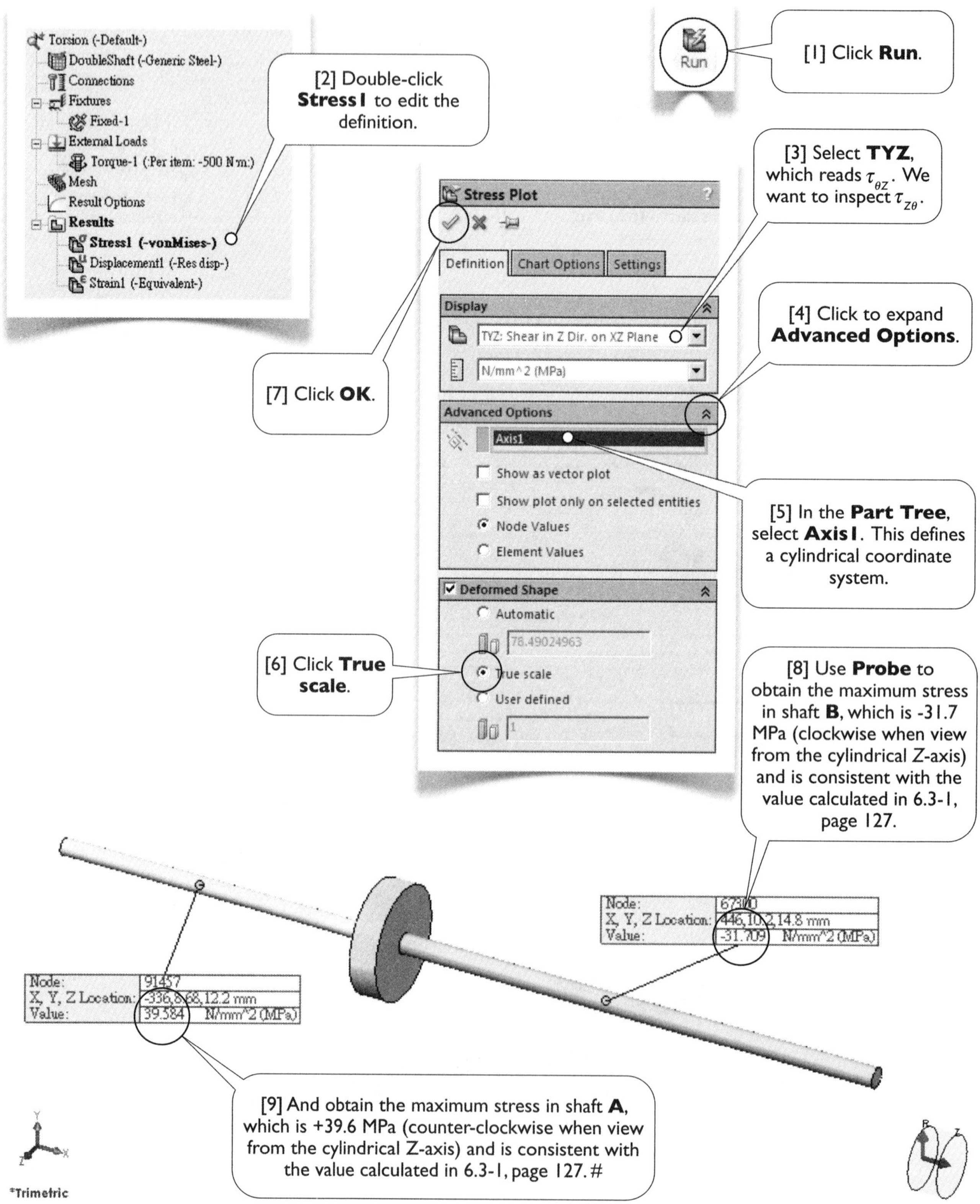

6.3-8 Obtain the Twist Angle

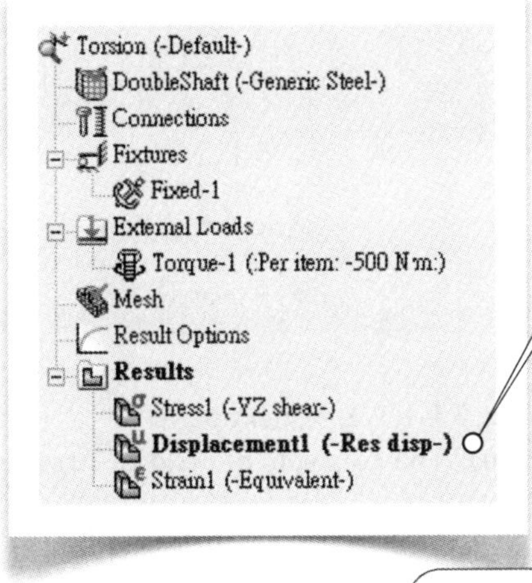

[1] Double-click **Displacement1** to activate it. Double-click **Displacement1** again to edit the definition.

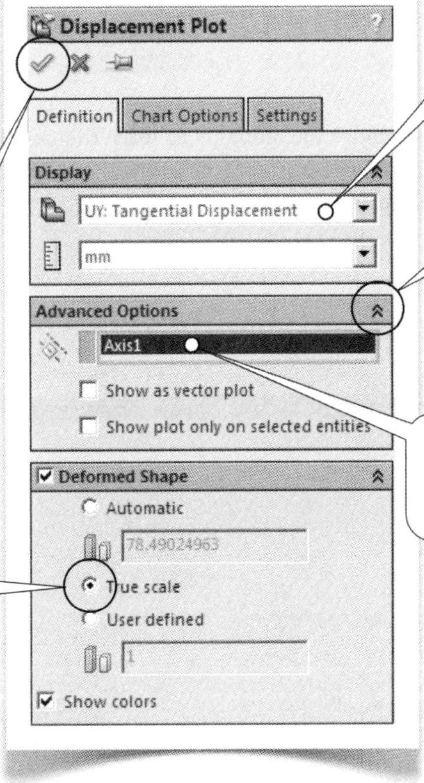

[2] Select **UY**, which reads u_θ. We want to inspect tangential displacement.

[3] Click to expand **Advanced Options**.

[4] In the **Features Tree**, select **Axis1**.

[5] Click **True scale**.

[6] Click **OK**.

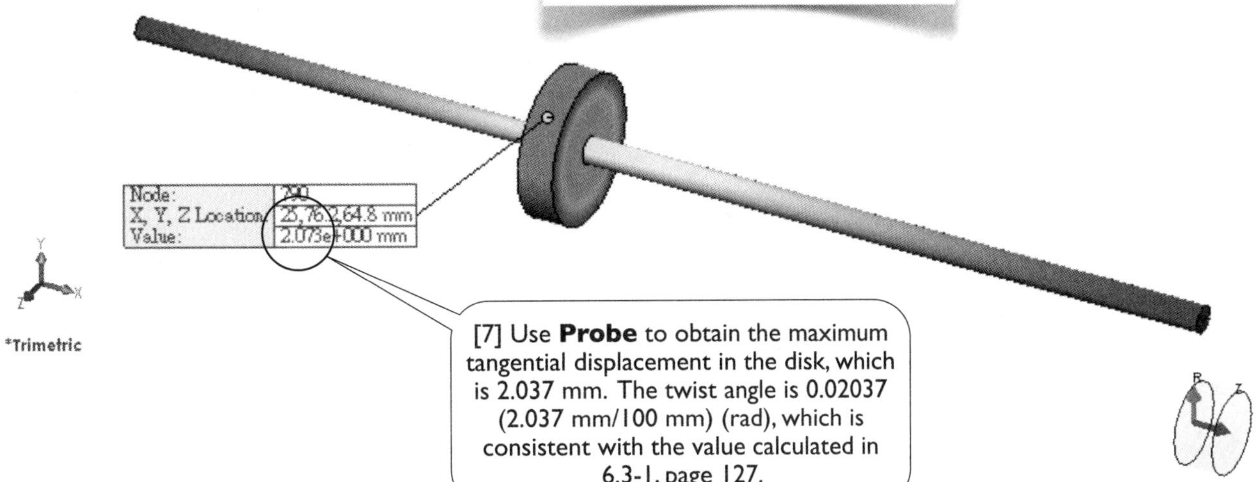

[7] Use **Probe** to obtain the maximum tangential displacement in the disk, which is 2.037 mm. The twist angle is 0.02037 (2.037 mm/100 mm) (rad), which is consistent with the value calculated in 6.3-1, page 127.

[8] Save the document and exit **SolidWorks**. #

Chapter 7

Bending

The first section of this chapter guides the students to learn the bending formula, Eqs. 7.1-1(1, 2, 4), next page.

The second section introduces the elastoplastic analysis of a beam under bending. The concepts of residual stresses are also introduced in this section.

Section 7.1

Pure Bending

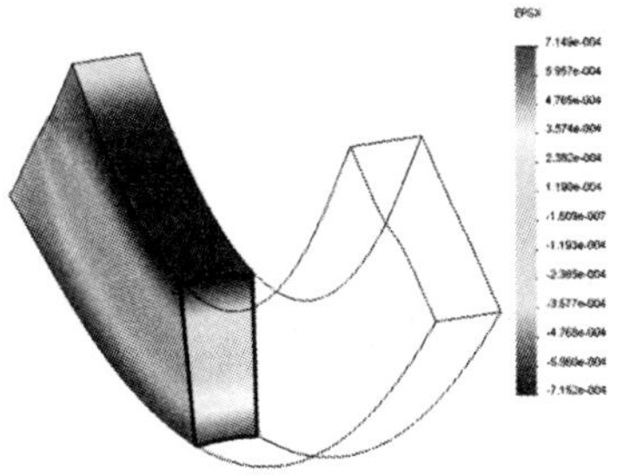

7.1-1 Introduction

[1] Consider a beam subject to a pure bending moment M. The beam has a **Young's modulus** E, a **Poisson's ratio** ν, and a rectangular cross section of width b and depth h [2]. Since the moment is constant along the length, the beam will be bent uniformly; i.e., the curvature k is constant over the length. And the only nonzero stress component is σ_X. At $Y = y$,

$$\sigma_X = -\frac{My}{I} \tag{1}$$

Where $I = bh^3/12$ is the **moment of inertia** of the cross section. The maximum/minimum **bending stress** occurs at $Y = c = \pm h/2$,

$$\sigma_{\text{max/min}} = \pm\frac{Mc}{I} \tag{2}$$

By **Hooke's Law**, Eqs. 4.3-1(1, 2) (page 87), the strain components are

$$\varepsilon_X = \frac{\sigma_X}{E},\ \varepsilon_Y = \varepsilon_Z = -\nu\frac{\sigma_X}{E},\ \gamma_{XY} = \gamma_{YZ} = \gamma_{ZX} = 0 \tag{3}$$

The **curvature** ($k = 1/\rho$) of the **neutral surface** (defined as the surface where $\sigma_X = 0$) [3] is given by

$$k = \frac{1}{\rho} = \frac{M}{EI} \tag{4}$$

The purpose of this section is to guide the students familiarize these formula.

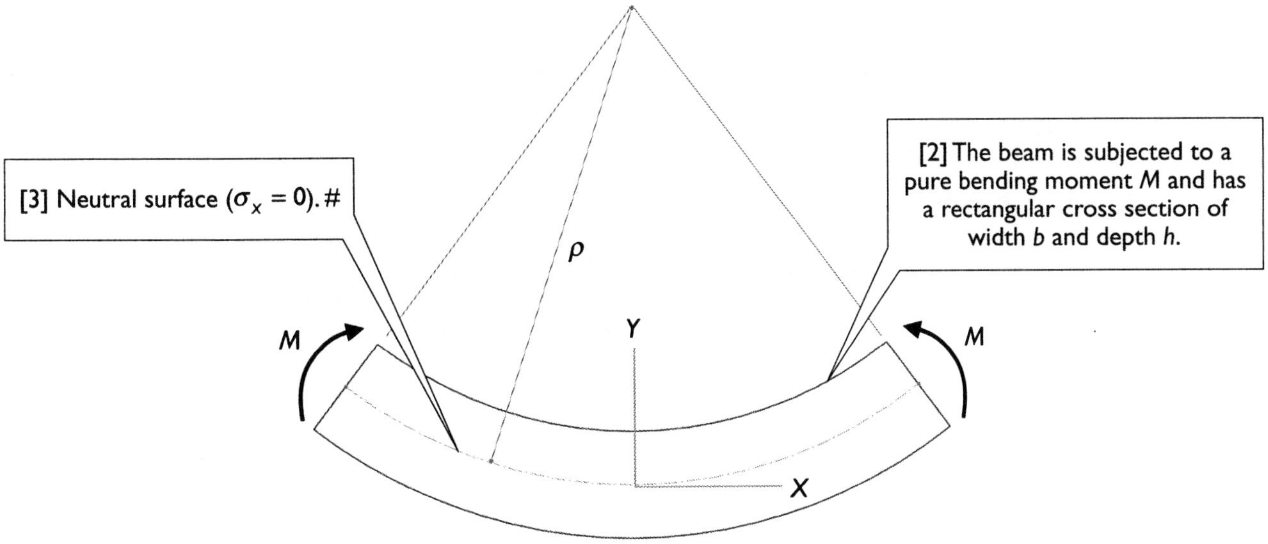

7.1-2 Start Up

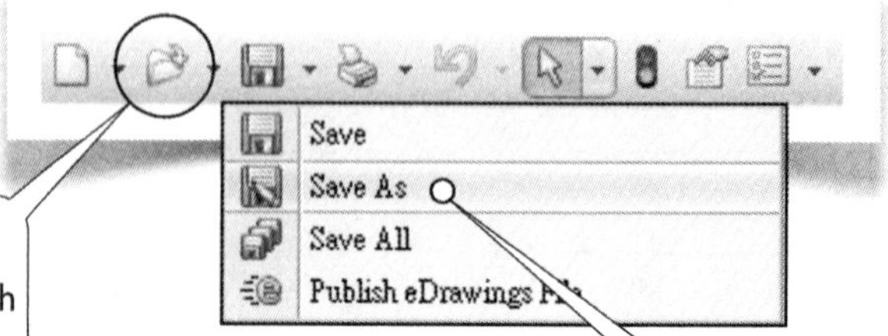

[1] Launch **SolidWorks** and open the file **Cantilever** which was saved in Section 3.1.

[2] Save the document as **SimpleBeam**. Click **NO** for the warning message.

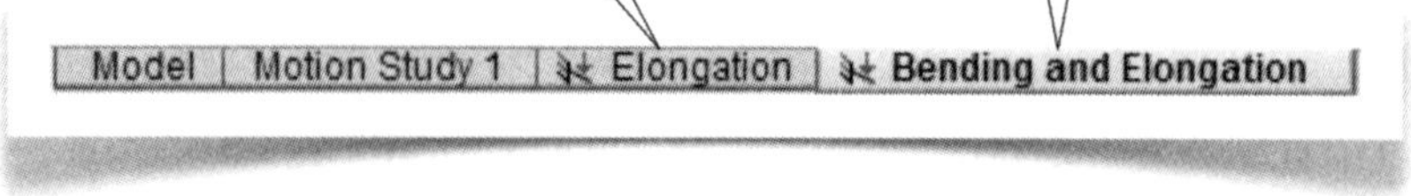

[3] Right-click **Bending and Elongation** and select **Delete**.

[4] Right-click **Elongation** and select **Delete**.

[5] The new document contains a beam of 10 mm x 20 mm x 100 mm. #

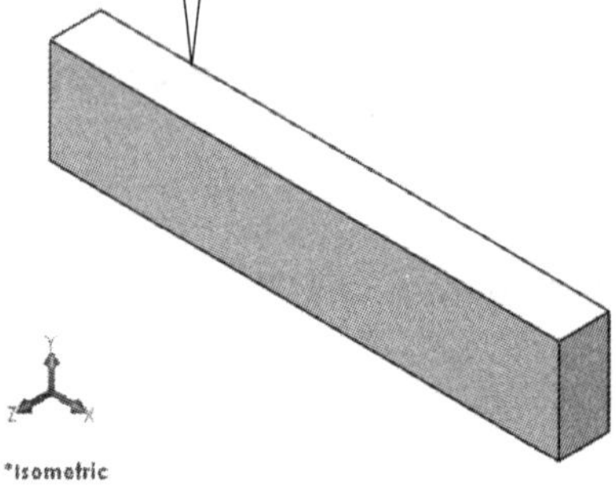

7.1-3 Create Axes

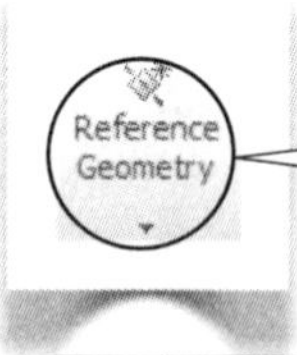

[1] In **Features Toolbar**, select **Reference Geometry>Axis**.

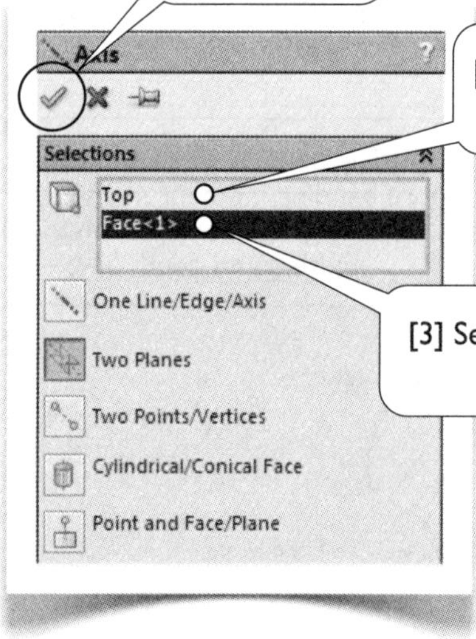

[2] Select **Top** plane from the **Part Tree**.

[3] Select left-end face of the model.

[4] Click **OK**.

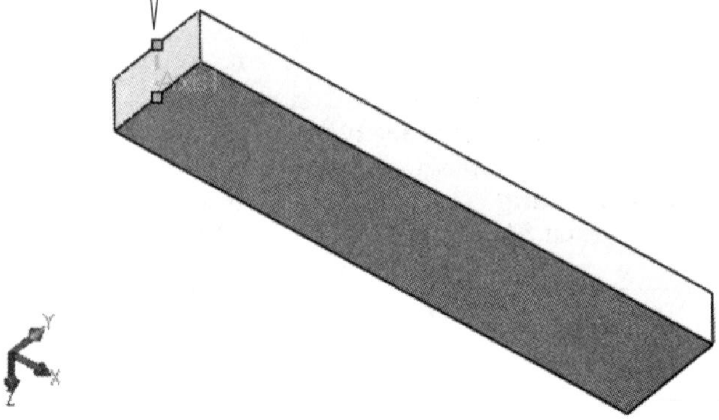

[5] This axis (**Axis1**) will be used to specify the direction of the moment on the left-end face.

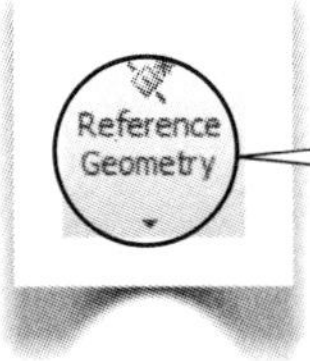

[6] In the **Features Toolbar**, select **Reference Geometry>Axis**.

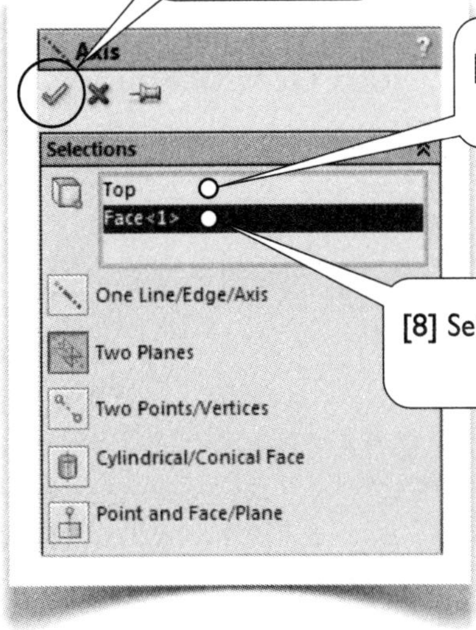

[9] Click **OK**.

[7] Select **Top** plane from the **Part Tree**.

[8] Select right-end face of the model.

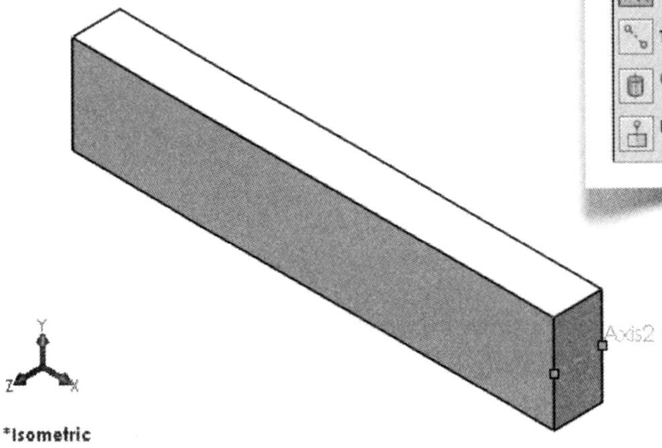

[10] This axis (**Axis2**) will be used to specify the direction of the moment on the right-end face. #

7.1-4 Create a Study and Apply Material

[1] In the **Simulation Toolbar**, select **Study Advisor>New Study**. Name the new study **Pure Bending**. Leave **Static** as default **Study Type**.

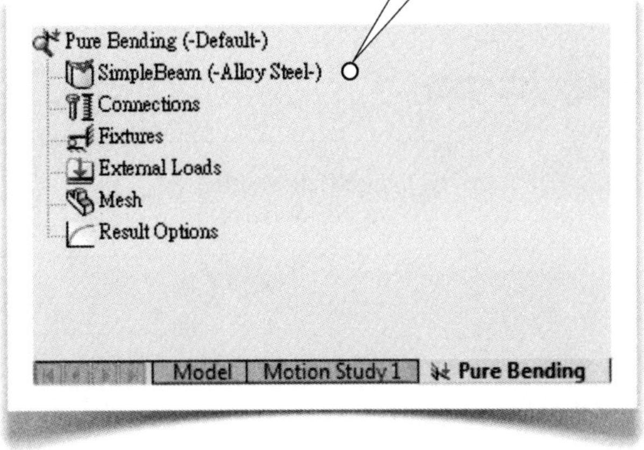

[2] Right-click **SimpleBeam** and select **Apply/Edit Material...** and apply **Alloy Steel** for the model. #

7.1-5 Set Up Supports

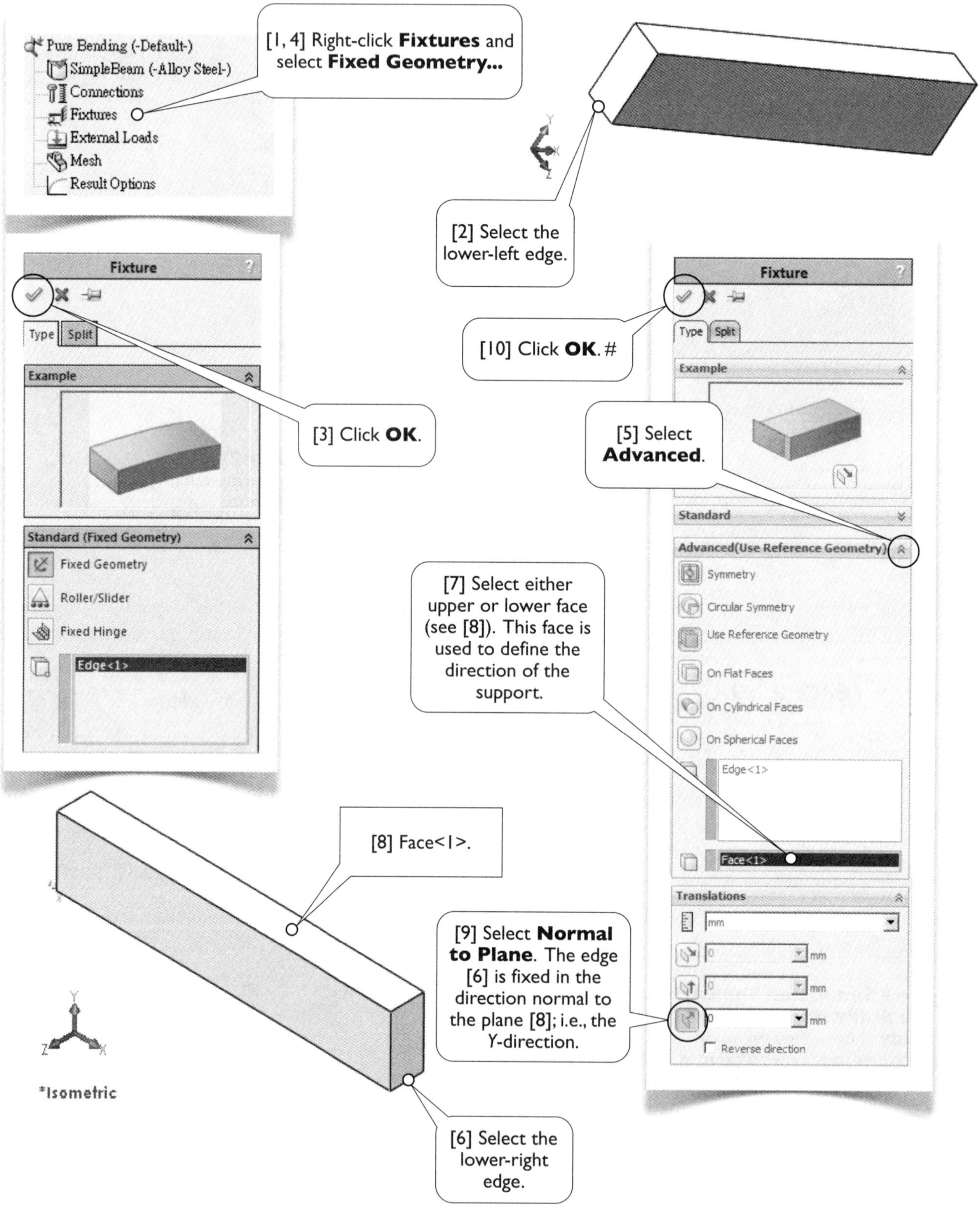

7.1-6 Set Up Loads

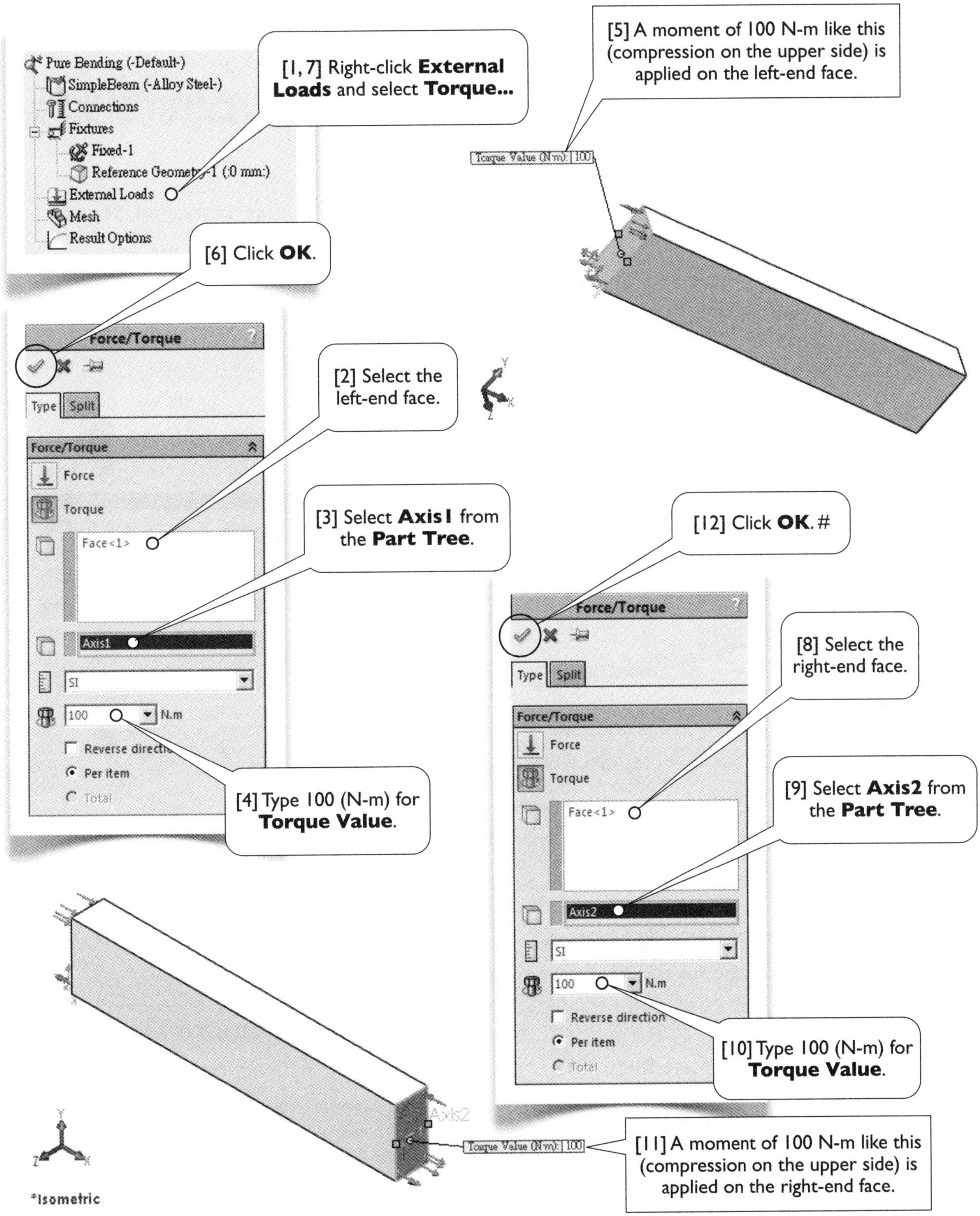

7.1-7 Obtain Solution and View Bending Stresses

[1] Click **Run**.

[2] Right-click **Fixture** and select **Hide All**.

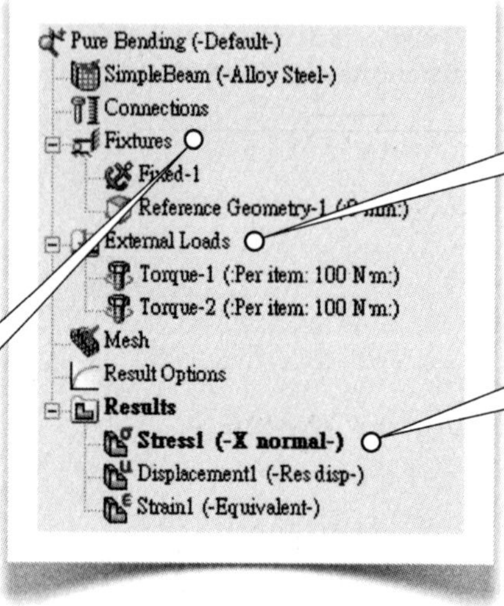

[3] Right-click **External Loads** and select **Hide All**.

[4] Double-click **Stress1** to edit the definition and select **SX** (σ_x) for **Component**.

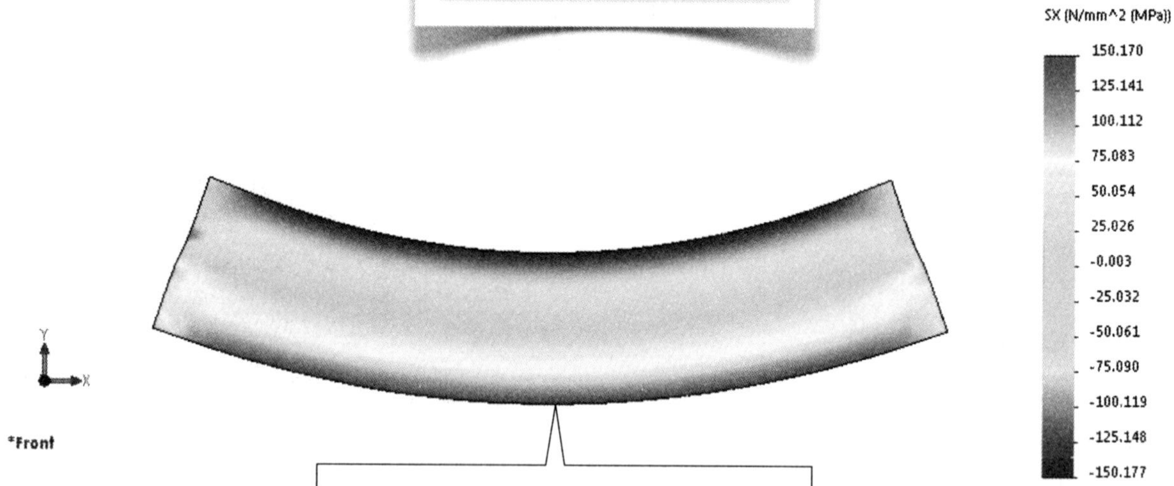

[5] The maximum bending stress (on the bottom) is 150 MPa, and the minimum (on the top) bending stress is -150 MPa.

[6] Hand-Calculation of Bending Stresses

From Eq. 7.1-1(2) (page 137), the maximum/minimum bending stresses

$$\sigma_{max/min} = \pm \frac{Mc}{I}$$

Where $M = 100$ N-m, $c = \pm 0.01$ m, $I = (0.01)(0.02)^3/12 = 2/3 \times 10^{-8}$ m^4. Substituting, we have

$$\sigma_{max/min} = \pm 150 \times 10^6 \text{ Pa}$$

which are consistent with the results in [5].

[7] Bending Stresses Distribution along *Y*-direction

According to Eq. 7.1-1(1) (page 137), The bending stresses change linearly along *Y*-direction. Let's verify this in 7.1-8, next page.
#

7.1-8 Changes of Bending Stresses along Y-direction

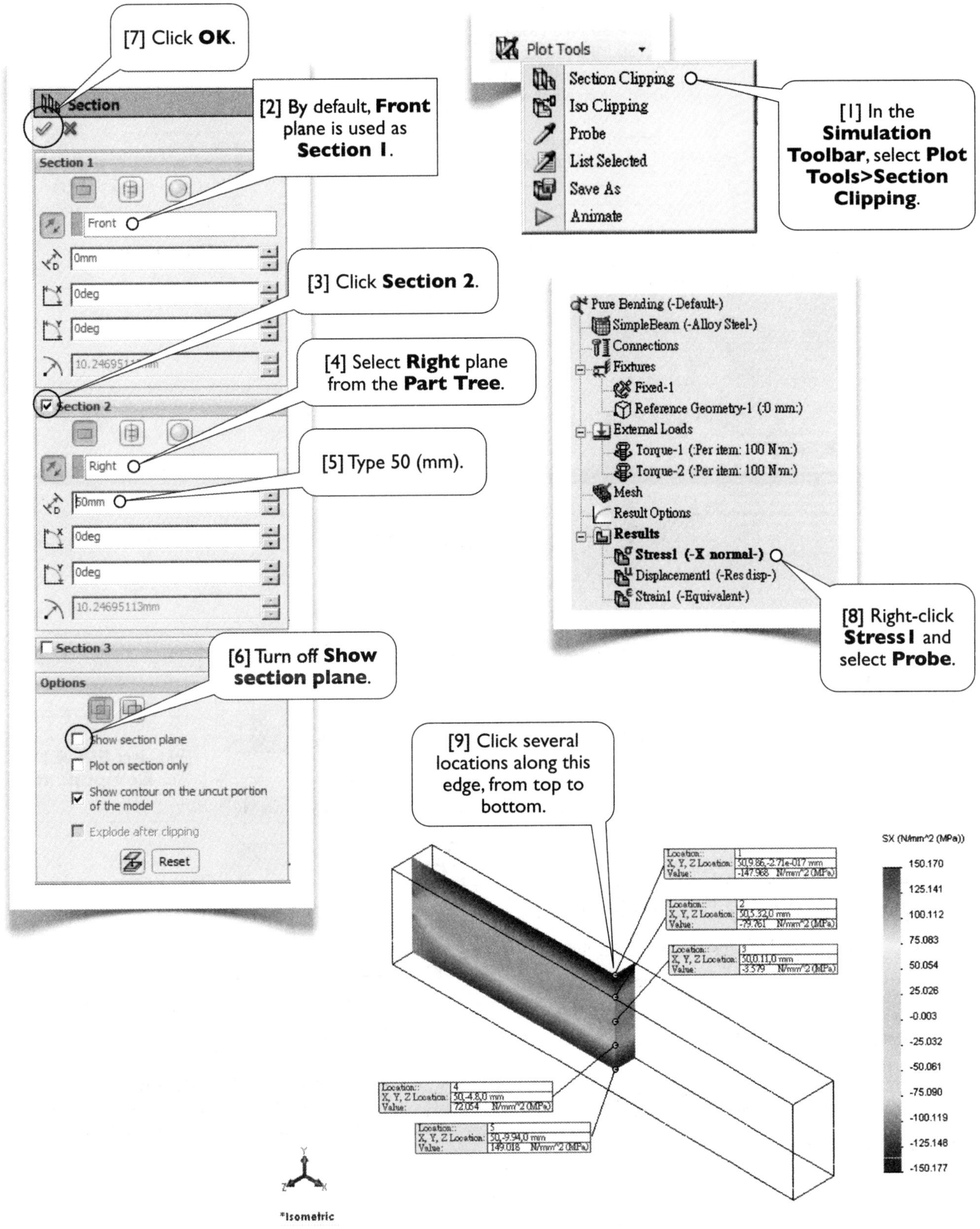

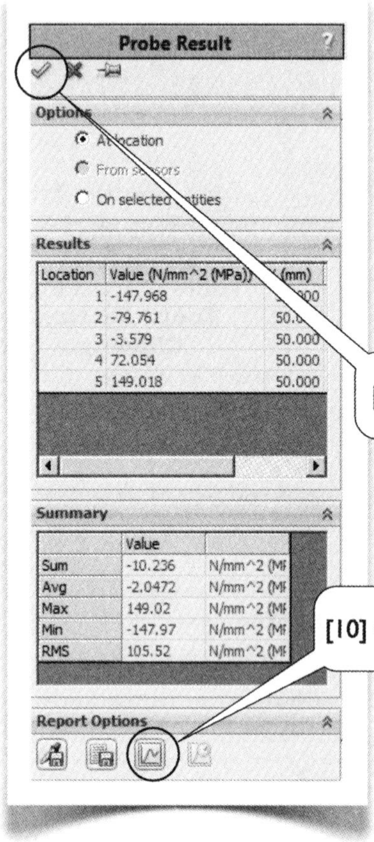

[10] Click **Plot**.

[11] The bending stresses indeed change linearly in Y-direction, from -150 MPa (top) to +150 MPa (bottom). On the neutral surface (mid-surface between the top and the bottom), the bending stress is zero.

[12] Click **OK**. #

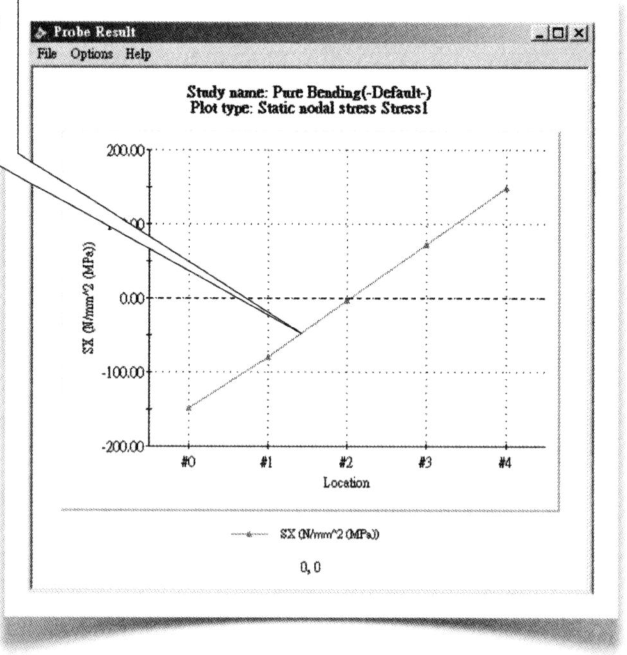

7.1-9 Strains and Poisson's Effects

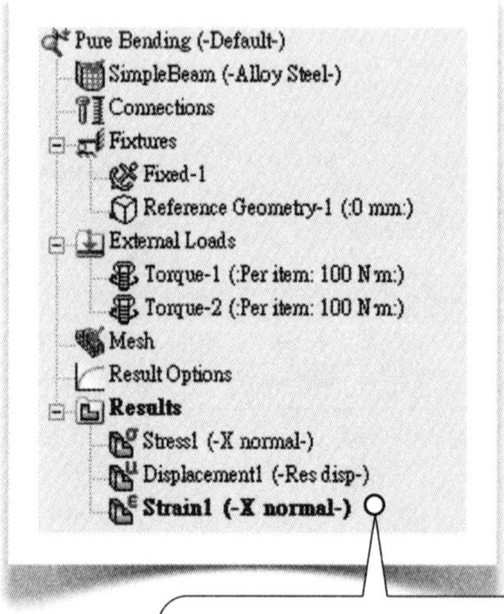

[1] Double-click **Strain1** to activate it. Double-click it again to edit the definition.

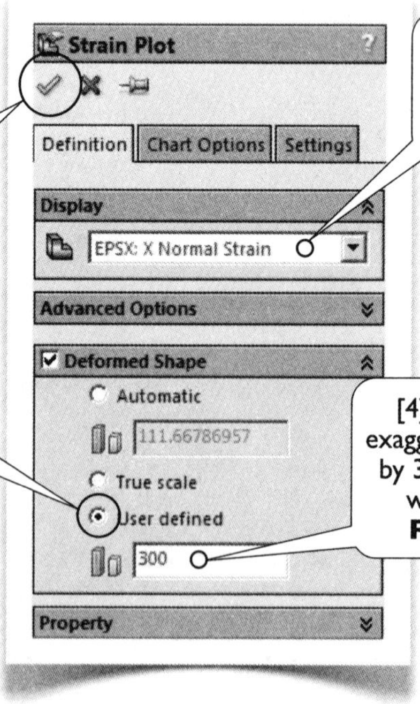

[2] Select **EPSX** (ε_x) for **Component**.

[3] Select **User defined**.

[4] Type 300. We now exaggerate the deformation by 300 times, because we want to observe the **Poisson's effect**.

[5] Click **OK**.

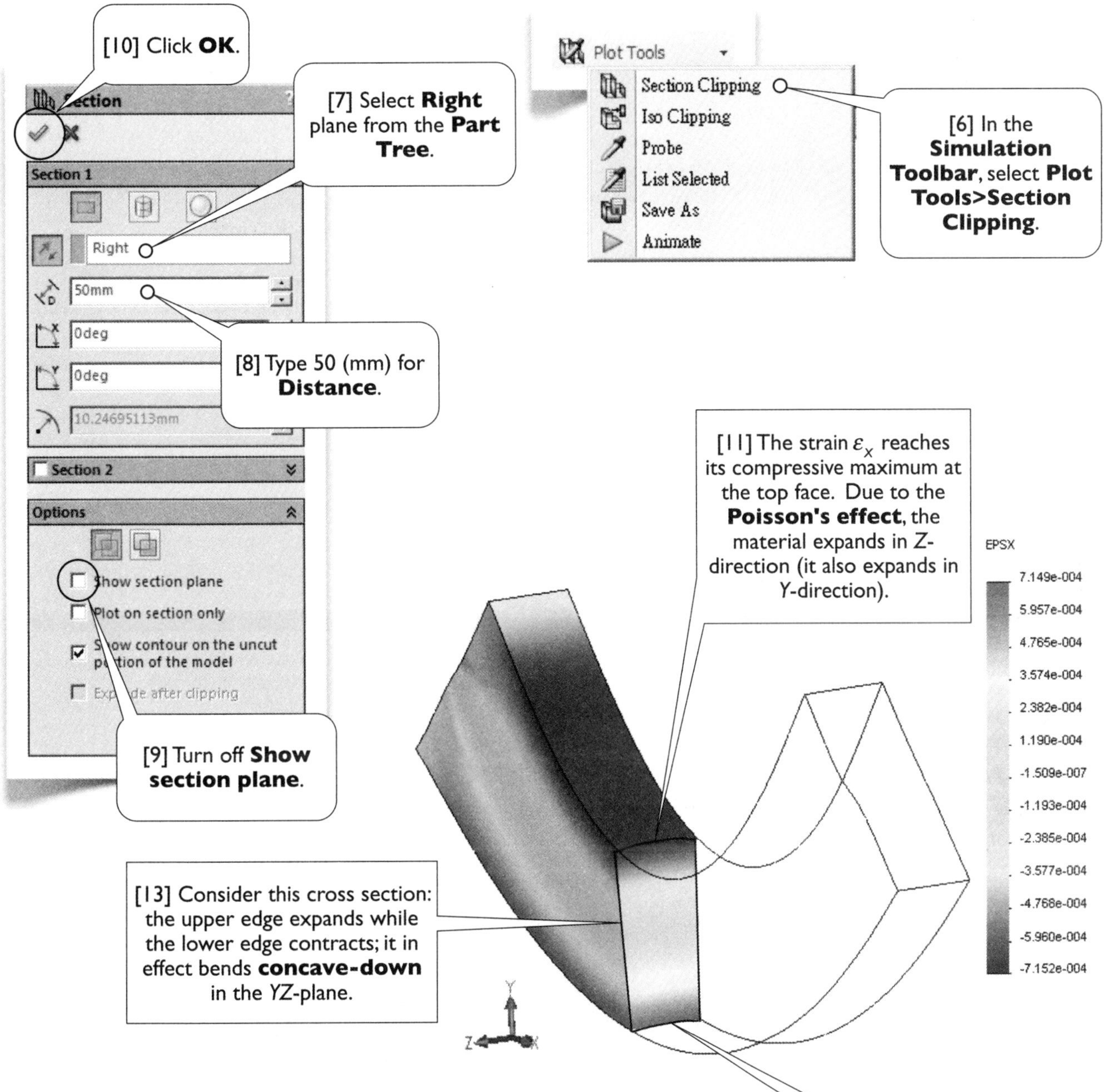

[14] **Hand-Calculation of Strains**

The maximum/minimum strains occur at the upper/lower edges. According to Eq. 7.1-1(3) (page 137),

$$(\varepsilon_X)_{\text{max/min}} = \frac{\sigma_{\text{max/min}}}{E} = \pm\frac{150\times10^6\ \text{Pa}}{210\times10^9\ \text{Pa}} = \pm7.143\times10^{-4}$$

$$(\varepsilon_Y)_{\text{max/min}} = (\varepsilon_Z)_{\text{max/min}} = \nu(\varepsilon_X)_{\text{max/min}} = \pm0.28(7.143\times10^{-4}) = \pm2.00\times10^{-4}$$

Note that, for the **Alloy Steel**, $E = 210$ GPa, $\nu = 0.28$ (see 4.1-4[6], page 75). It leaves for you to verify these strain values with the **Simulation**. #

7.1-10 Radius of Curvature

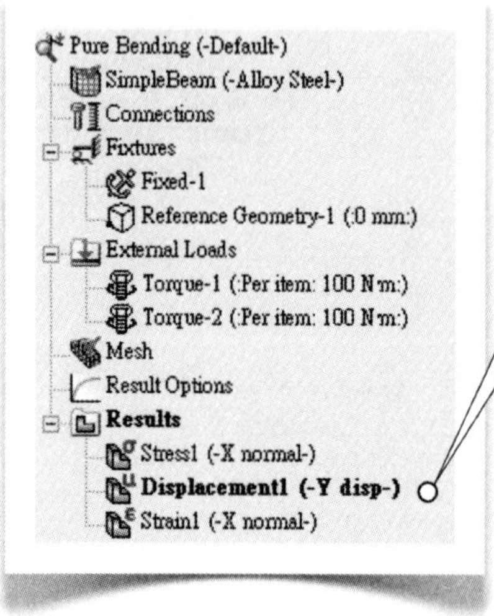

[1] Double-click **Displacement1** to activate it. Double-click it again to edit the definition. Select **UY** (u_Y) for **Component**.

[2] The maximum *Y*-deflection (downward) is $(u_Y)_{max} = 8.955 \times 10^{-2}$ mm, which occurs near the neutral surface. (use **Probe** to explore this fact.)

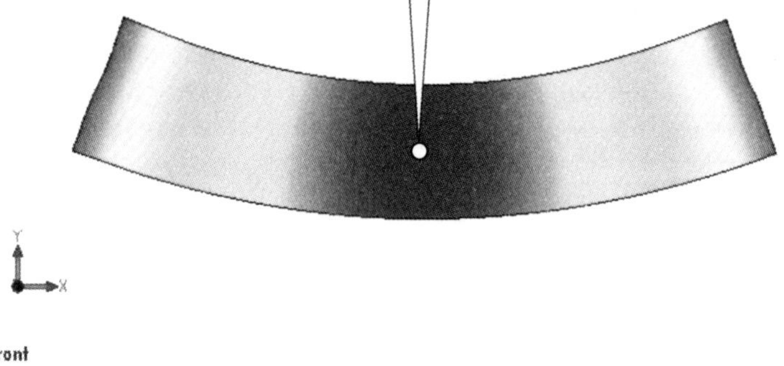

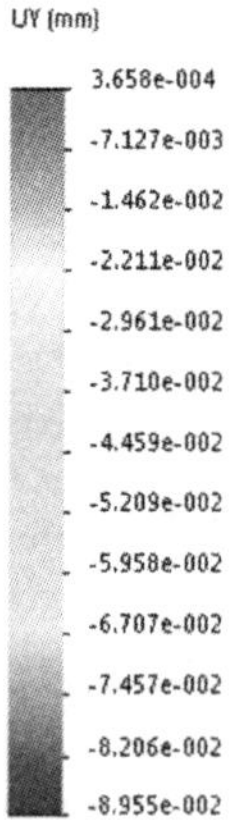

[3] Assume the deformation is infinitesimally small, then $\rho^2 = (L/2)^2 + \left[\rho - (u_Y)_{max}\right]^2$, where $L = 0.1$ m. Solving, we have $\rho \approx 14$ m.

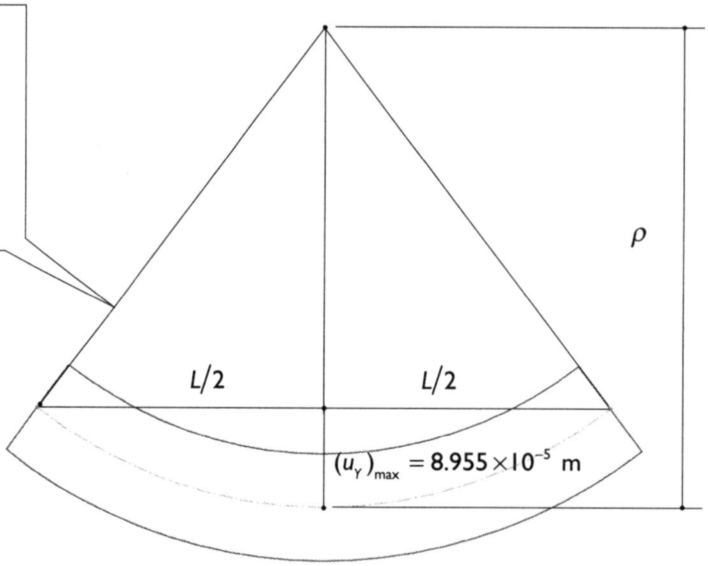

[4] Hand-Calculation of Radius of Curvature

The radius of curvature, according to Eq. 7.1-1(4) (page 137),

$$\rho = \frac{EI}{M} = \frac{(210 \times 10^9 \text{ Pa})(2/3 \times 10^{-8} \text{ m}^4)}{100 \text{ N-m}} = 14 \text{ m}$$

which is consistent with the value in [3].

[5] Save the document and exit **SolidWorks**. #

Section 7.2

Elastoplastic Bending

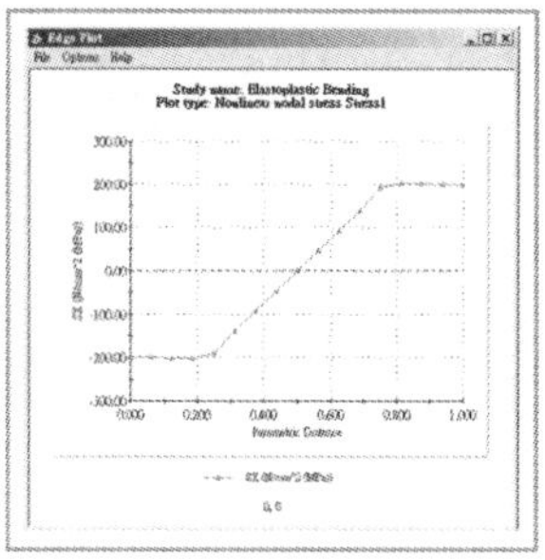

7.2-1 Introduction

[1] In this section, we'll continue the study of the simply supported beam (Section 7.1). We'll change the material model to an **elastic perfectly plastic material**, or simply **elastoplastic material**. In addition to the **Young's Modulus** E and the **Poisson's Ratio** ν, a **Yield Strength** σ_y is needed to define an elastoplastic material [2]. To compare the results with those in Section 7.1, we'll assume $E = 210$ GPa and $\nu = 0.28$, which are used in Section 7.1. And the **Yield Strength** σ_y is assumed to be 200 MPa.

First, we'll apply the same moments (M = 100 N-m) on both end faces of the beam, then release the moments. From the previous study, the maximum stress (150 MPa) doesn't exceed the yield strength (200 MPa); no plastic deformation occurs in the beam. Therefore, after releasing the moments, the stresses and the strains will also be released (return to zeros). No residual stresses or residual strains remain. It is an **elastic deformation**.

Next, we'll increase the moments up to M = 180 N-m. As the moments increase, the stresses at regions closer to the outer surfaces will eventually reach the yield strength (200 MPa) and do not increase anymore. The regions are called **plastic regions**. As the moments continue to increase, the plastic regions will enlarge to balance the external moments. We'll show how the stresses distribute along the depth of the beam when the moments reach 180 N-m.

When the moments are completely released, due to the **plastic deformation** (**permanent deformation**), the stresses and strains are not completely released (do not return to zeros). There exist some **residual stresses** and **residual strains**. We'll show how the residual stresses distribute along the depth of the beam when the moments are completely released.

[2] An elastoplastic material model has a stress-strain curve like this. It can be defined by a **Young's Modulus** E, a **Poisson's Ratio** ν, and a **Yield Strength** σ_y. The **Tangent Modulus** is zero for this material model. #

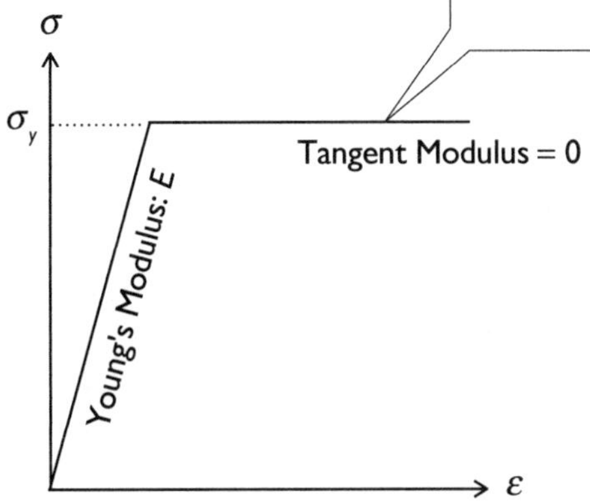

7.2-2 Start Up

[1] Launch **SolidWorks** and open the file **SimpleBeam**, which was saved in Section 7.1.

[2] Make sure **Model** tab is active. #

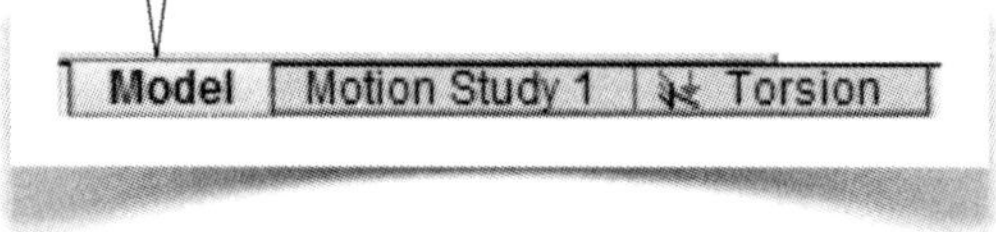

7.2-3 Create a Split Line

[1] Right-click this face and select **Sketch**.

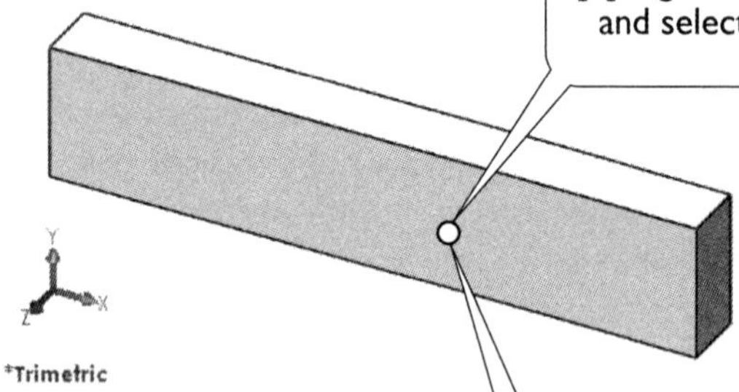

[2] Draw a single line like this. Click **Exit Sketch**.

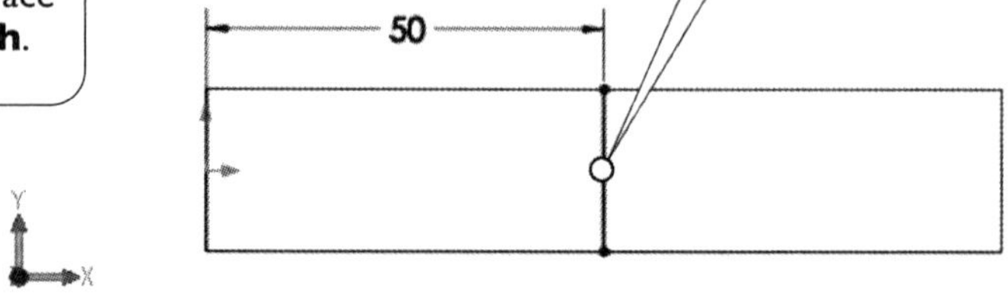

[3] in the **Features Toolbar**, select **Curves>Split Line**.

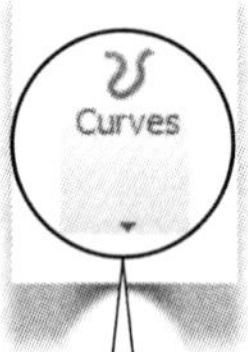

[4] Select the newly created sketch from the **Part Tree**.

[5] Select this face for **Faces to Split**. This face is split into two faces. The reason we create the **Split Line** is that we want to **Probe** the stresses along this **Split Line**.

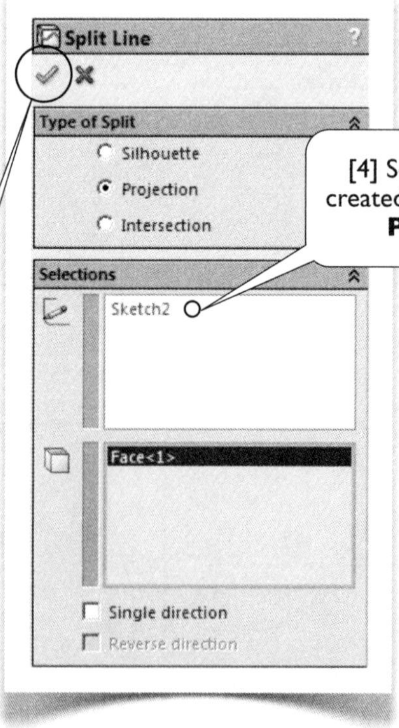

[6] Click **OK**. #

7.2-4 Create a **Nonlinear** Study and Apply Material

[1] In the **Simulation Toolbar**, select **Study Advisor>New Study**.

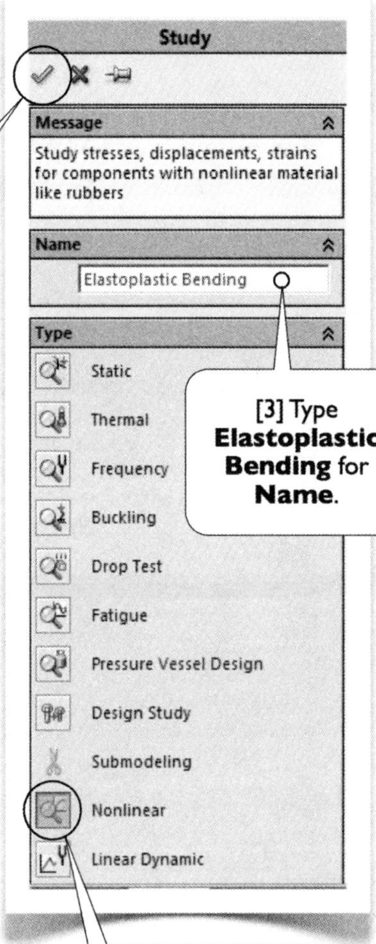

[2] Select **Nonlinear**, which has full capability of nonlinearities. On the other hand, **Static** study has limited capability of nonlinearities.

[3] Type **Elastoplastic Bending** for **Name**.

[4] Click **OK**.

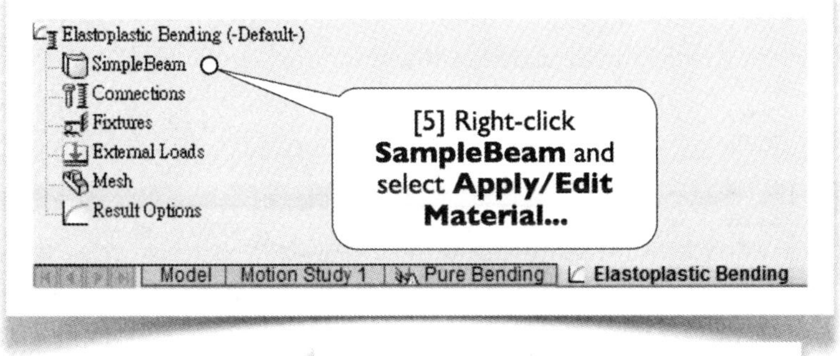

[5] Right-click **SampleBeam** and select **Apply/Edit Material...**

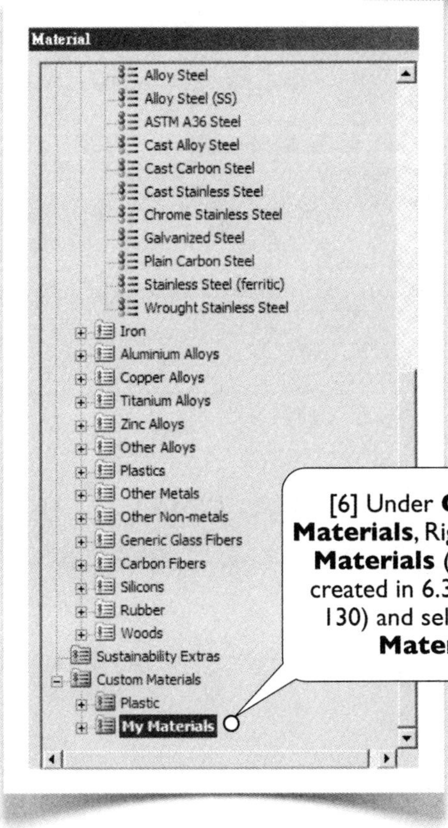

[6] Under **Custom Materials**, Right-click **My Materials** (which was created in 6.3-4[3], page 130) and select **New Material**.

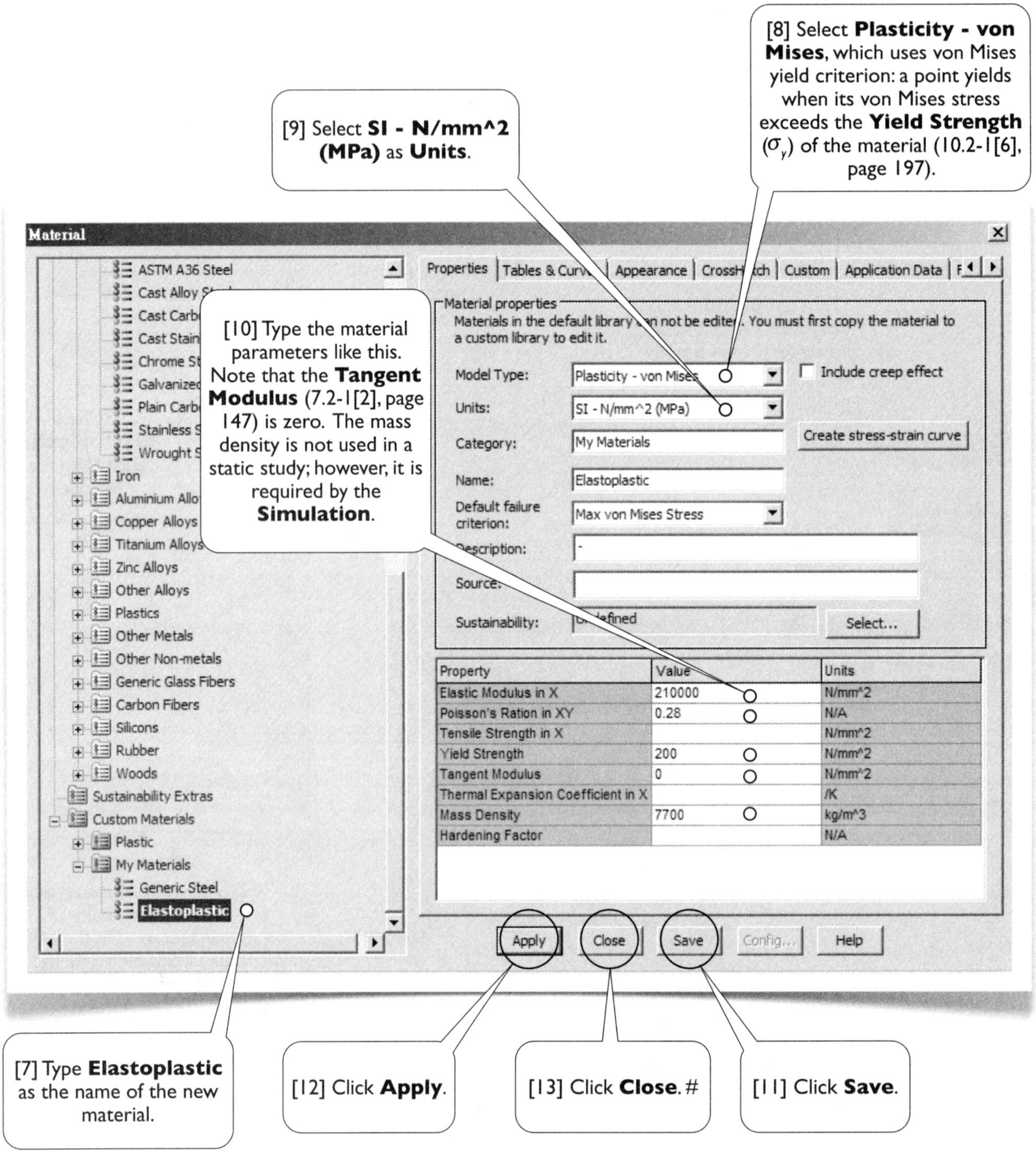
[8] Select **Plasticity - von Mises**, which uses von Mises yield criterion: a point yields when its von Mises stress exceeds the **Yield Strength** (σ_y) of the material (10.2-1[6], page 197).
[9] Select **SI - N/mm^2 (MPa)** as **Units**.
[10] Type the material parameters like this. Note that the **Tangent Modulus** (7.2-1[2], page 147) is zero. The mass density is not used in a static study; however, it is required by the **Simulation**.
[7] Type **Elastoplastic** as the name of the new material.
[12] Click **Apply**.
[13] Click **Close**. #
[11] Click **Save**.
Material
Model Type: Plasticity - von Mises
Units: SI - N/mm^2 (MPa)
Category: My Materials
Name: Elastoplastic
Default failure criterion: Max von Mises Stress
Elastic Modulus in X 210000 N/mm^2
Poisson's Ration in XY 0.28 N/A
Yield Strength 200 N/mm^2
Tangent Modulus 0 N/mm^2
Mass Density 7700 kg/m^3
Apply
Close
Save

7.2-5 Set Up Boundary Conditions

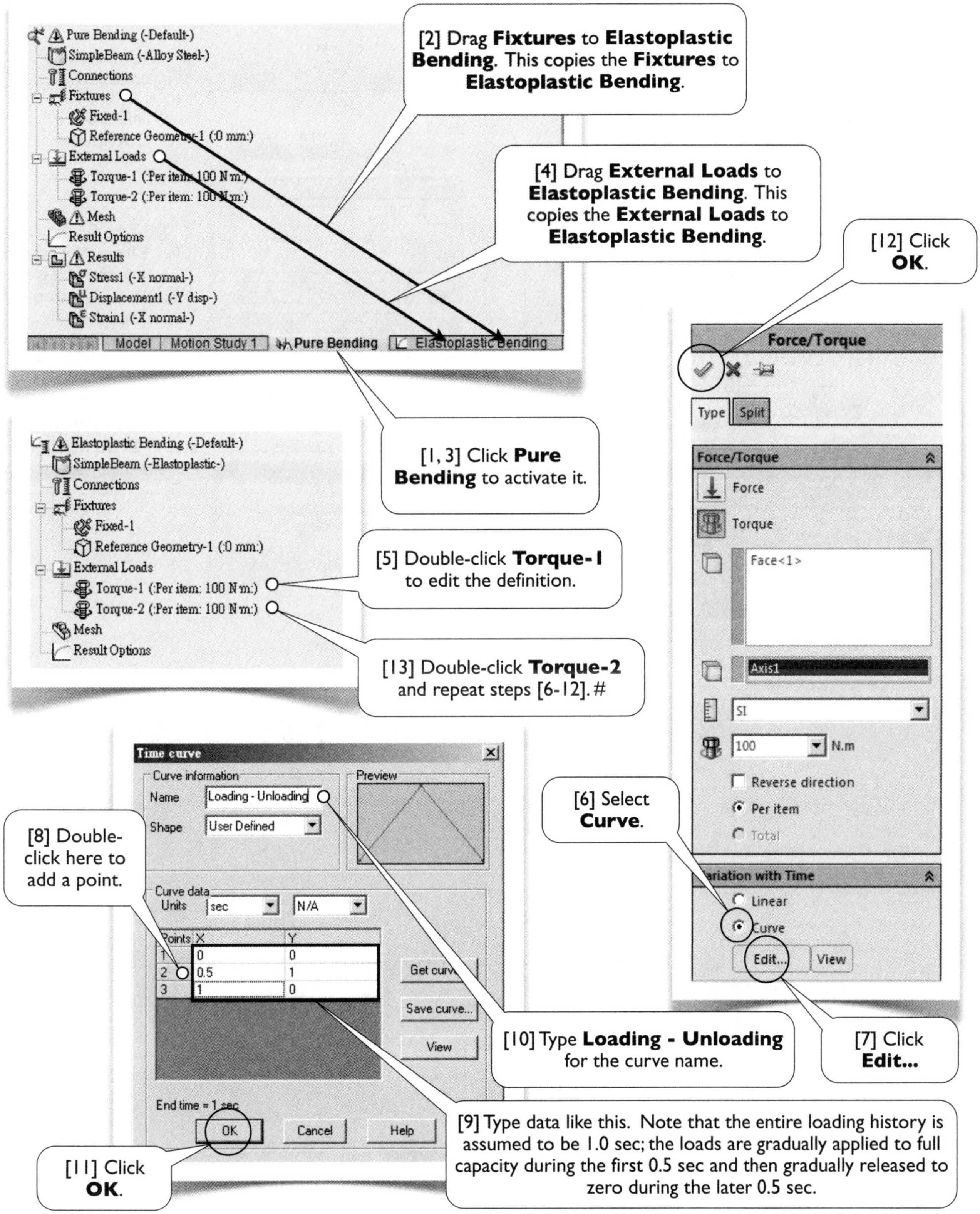

7.2-6 Obtain Solutions and View Stresses

[1] In the **Simulation Toolbar**, click **Run**.

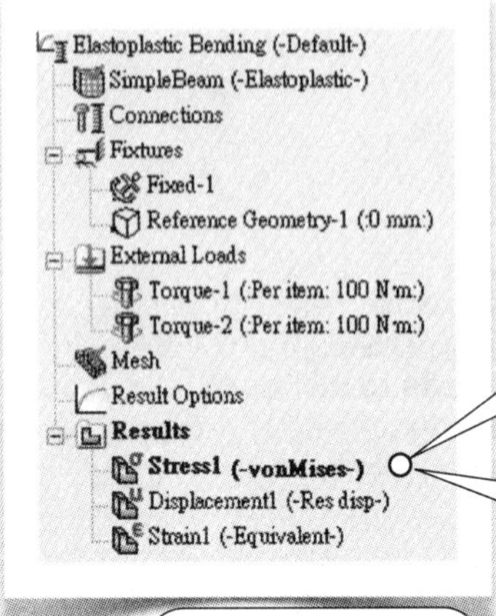

[2] Double-click **Stress1** to edit the definition.

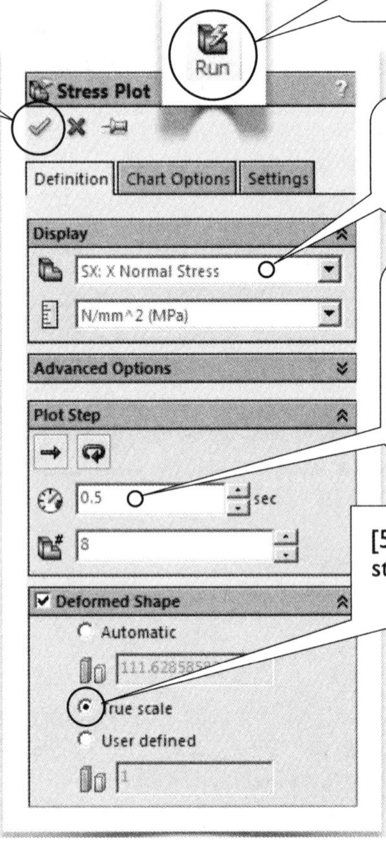

[3] Select **SX** (σ_x) for **Component**.

[4] Type 0.5 (sec) for **Time**. We want to view the stresses at 0.5 sec, when the loads are fully applied.

[5] For a **Nonlinear** study, **True scale** is the default setting.

[6] Click **OK**.

[7] Right-click **Stress1** and select **Probe**.

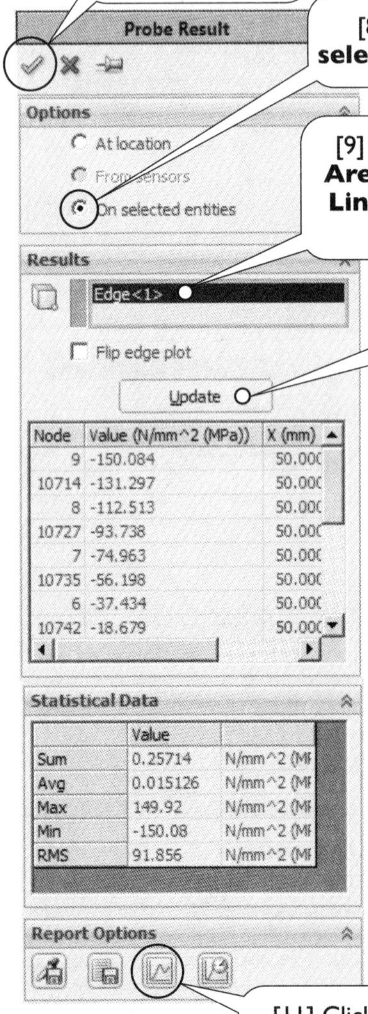

[8] Select **On selected entities**.

[9] In the **Graphics Area**, select the **Split Line**, created in 7.2-3, page 148.

[10] Click **Update**

[11] Click **Plot**.

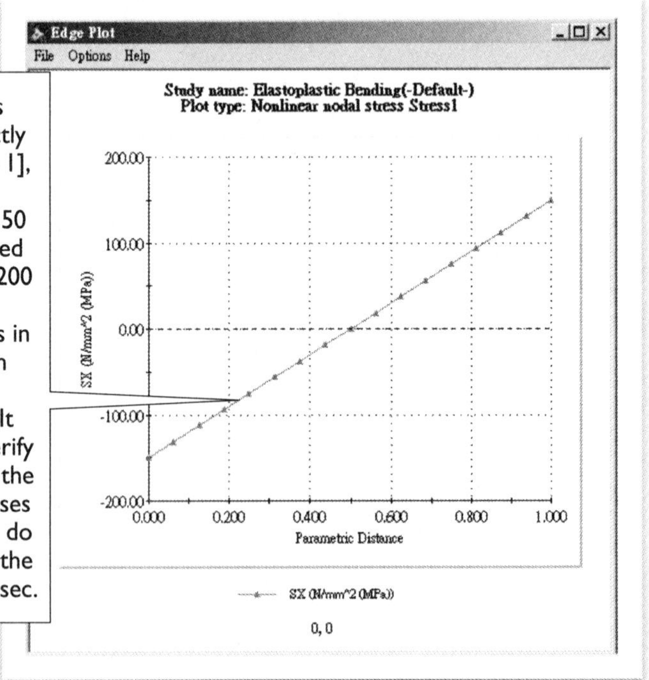

[12] The stresses distribution is exactly the same as 7.1-8[11], page 144. The maximum stress (150 MPa) doesn't exceed the yield strength (200 MPa); no plastic deformation occurs in the beam. It is an **elastic deformation**. It leaves for you to verify that, after releasing the moments, the stresses return to zeros. To do that, simply change the **Time** in [4] to 1.0 sec.

[13] Click **OK**. #

7.2-7 Increase the Moments to 180 N-m

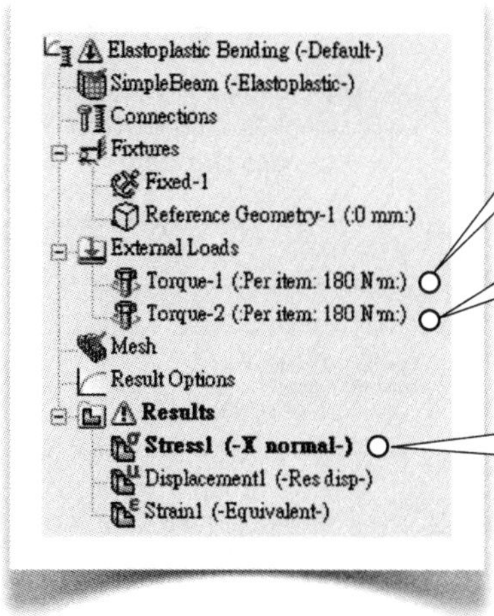

[1] Double-click **Torque-1** to edit the definition. Change the **Torque Value** to 180 (N-m).

[2] Repeat step [1] for **Torque-2**.

[3] In the **Simulation Toolbar**, click **Run**.

[4] Make sure the time is set to 0.5 sec (7.2-6[4], last page). Repeat steps 7.2-6[7-11], last page.

[5] This is the stress distribution across the depth. In some regions, the stresses reach the **Yield Strength** (200 MPa) and become plastic.

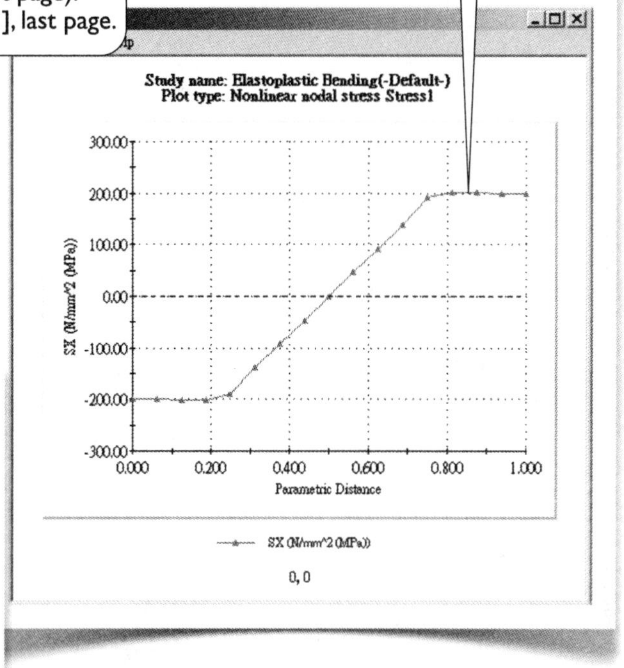

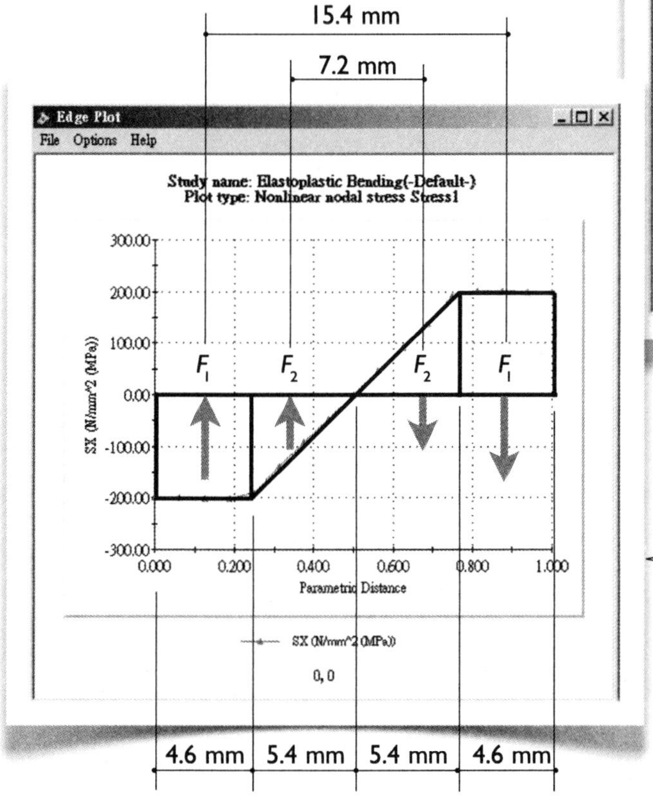

[6] The stresses are so distributed that they balance the external moment (180 N-m). Let's verify this.

$$F_1 = 200 \text{ MPa} \times 4.6 \text{ mm} \times 10 \text{ mm} = 9200 \text{ N}$$

$$F_2 = 200 \text{ MPa} \times 5.4 \text{ mm} \times 10 \text{ mm} \div 2 = 5400 \text{ N}$$

$$\begin{aligned} M &= F_1 \times 15.4 \text{ mm} + F_2 \times 7.2 \text{ mm} \\ &= 9200 \text{ N} \times 0.0154 \text{ m} + 5400 \text{ N} \times 0.0072 \text{ m} \\ &\approx 180 \text{ N-m} \end{aligned}$$

which is equal to the external moment. #

7.2-8 Residual Stresses

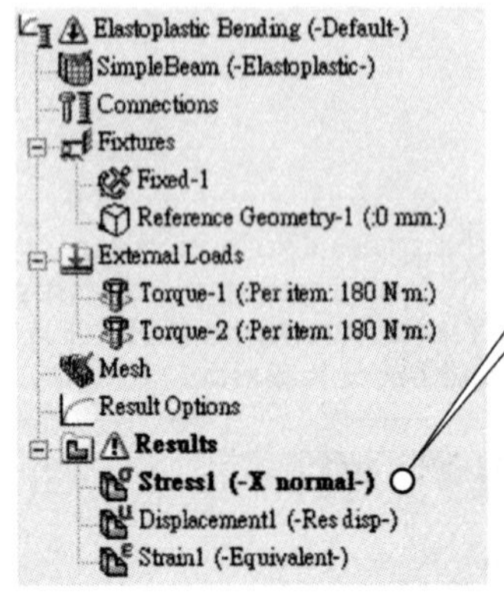

[1] Double-click **Stress1** and set the **Time** to 1.0 (sec) (7.2-6[4], page 152). Repeat steps 7.2-6[7-11], page 152.

[2] This is the residual stresses distribution across the depth.

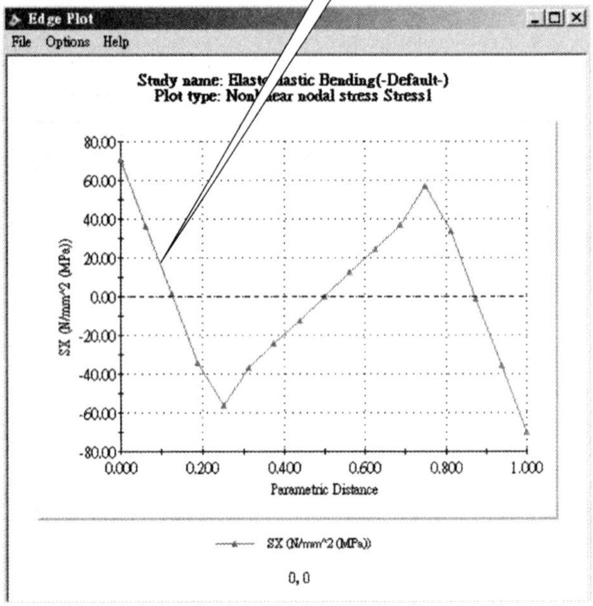

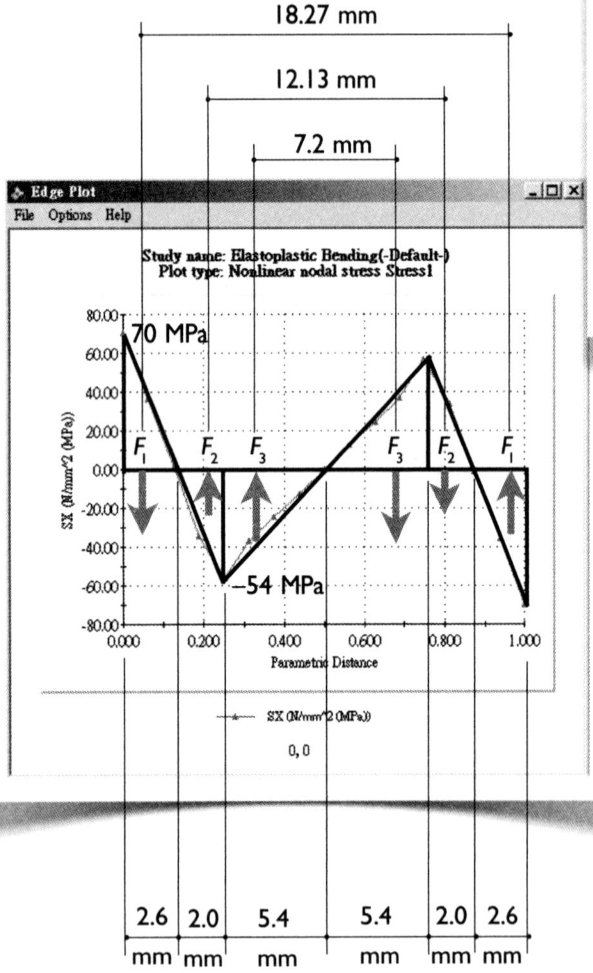

[3] The stresses are so distributed that they balance the external moment (i.e, zero). Let's verify this.

$$F_1 = 70\text{ MPa} \times 2.6\text{ mm} \times 10\text{ mm} \div 2 = 910\text{ N}$$

$$F_2 = 54\text{ MPa} \times 2.0\text{ mm} \times 10\text{ mm} \div 2 = 540\text{ N}$$

$$F_3 = 54\text{ MPa} \times 5.4\text{ mm} \times 10\text{ mm} \div 2 = 1458\text{ N}$$

$$\begin{aligned} M &= F_1 \times 18.27\text{ mm} - F_2 \times 12.13\text{ mm} - F_3 \times 7.2\text{ mm} \\ &= 910\text{ N} \times 0.01827\text{ m} - 540\text{ N} \times 0.01213\text{ m} \\ &\quad -1458\text{ N} \times 0.0072\text{ m} \\ &\approx 0 \end{aligned}$$

which is equal to the external moment.

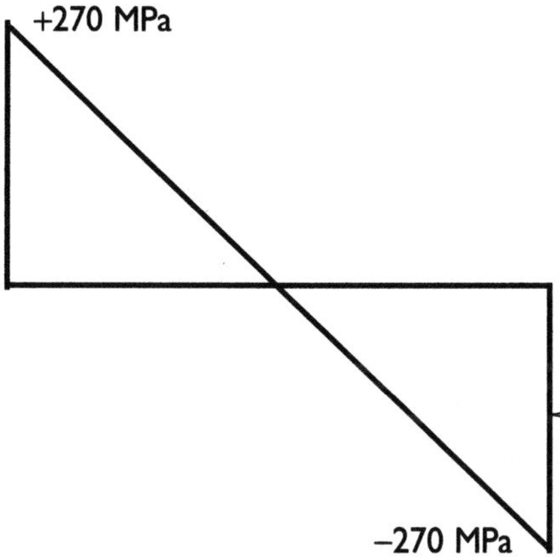

[4] Final Remark

The releasing of the moments of 180 N-m can be thought of applying a pair of moments of 180 N-m in a reversed directions and the process is elastic. Thus, the residual stresses in [3] can be obtained by adding this distribution to 7.2-7[6] (page 153); i.e., [3] = (7.2-7[6]) + [4].

[5] Save the document and exit **SolidWorks**. #

Chapter 8

Shear Stresses in Beams

The first section of this chapter guides the students to learn the shear formula, Eq. 8.1-1(1) (next page), using a rectangular section beam as an example.

Eq. 8.1-1(1) can be used for non-rectangular section beam. The second section reinforces the students' understanding of this shear formula by using a box section beam. The concepts of **shear flow** are also illustrated.

In the third section, the concepts of **shear center** are introduced using a channel section beam.

Section 8.1

Shear Formula

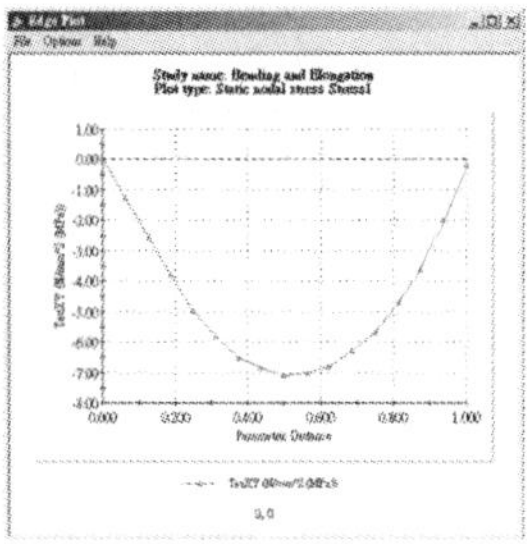

8.1-1 Introduction

[1] Consider a rectangular beam cross section with a width b and a depth h [2], subjected to a shear force V. Across the Z-direction, the shear stresses are relatively uniform. However, across the Y-direction, the shear stresses (or, more precisely, average shear stress across Z-direction) vary with y [3],

$$\tau_{XY} = \frac{VQ}{Ib} \tag{1}$$

where I is the moment of inertia (for rectangle, $I = bh^3/12 = 2bc^3/3$, where $c = h/2$), and Q, a function of y, is the **first moment** of the area beyond y with respect to the neutral axis. Thus,

$$Q(y) = b(c-y)\left[\frac{c+y}{2}\right] = \frac{1}{2}b(c^2 - y^2) \tag{2}$$

Eqs. (1, 2) show that the shear stresses have a parabolic distribution along Y-axis. Substitute I and Q into Eq. (1),

$$\tau_{XY} = \frac{VQ}{Ib} = \frac{V\left[b(c^2 - y^2)/2\right]}{(2bc^3/3)b} = \frac{3}{2}\frac{V}{A}(1 - \frac{y^2}{c^2}) \tag{3}$$

where $A = bh$ is the area of the cross-section. Let $(\tau_{XY})_{ave} = V/A$, then the maximum shear stress (which is at y = 0) is

$$(\tau_{XY})_{max} = \frac{3}{2}\frac{V}{A} = \frac{3}{2}(\tau_{XY})_{ave} \tag{4}$$

We'll verify the results in 1.2-8[3] (page 35) with these formula.

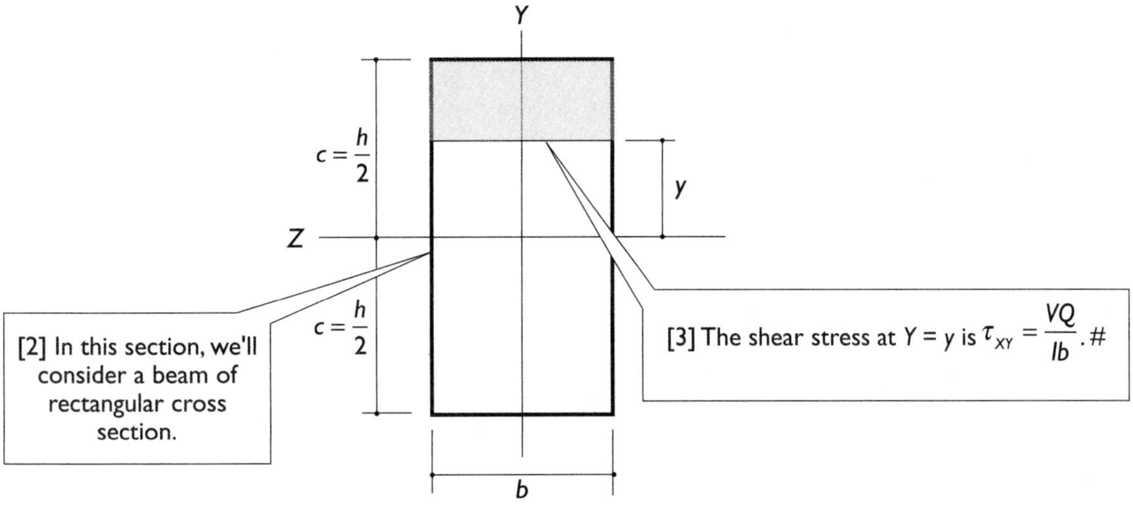

8.1-2 Revisit **Bending and Elongation** Study

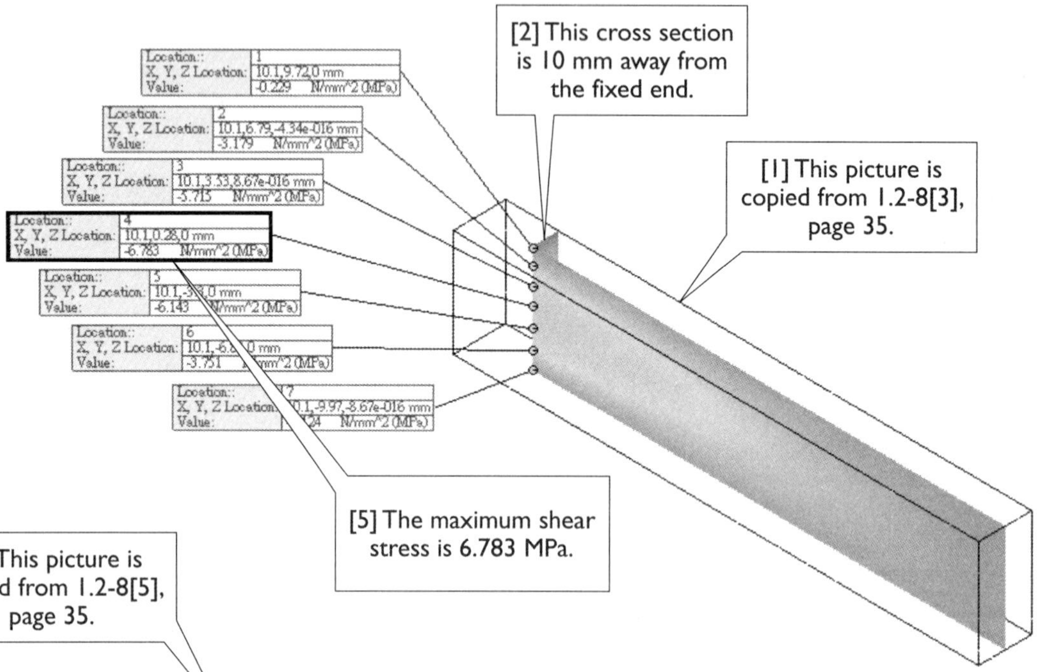

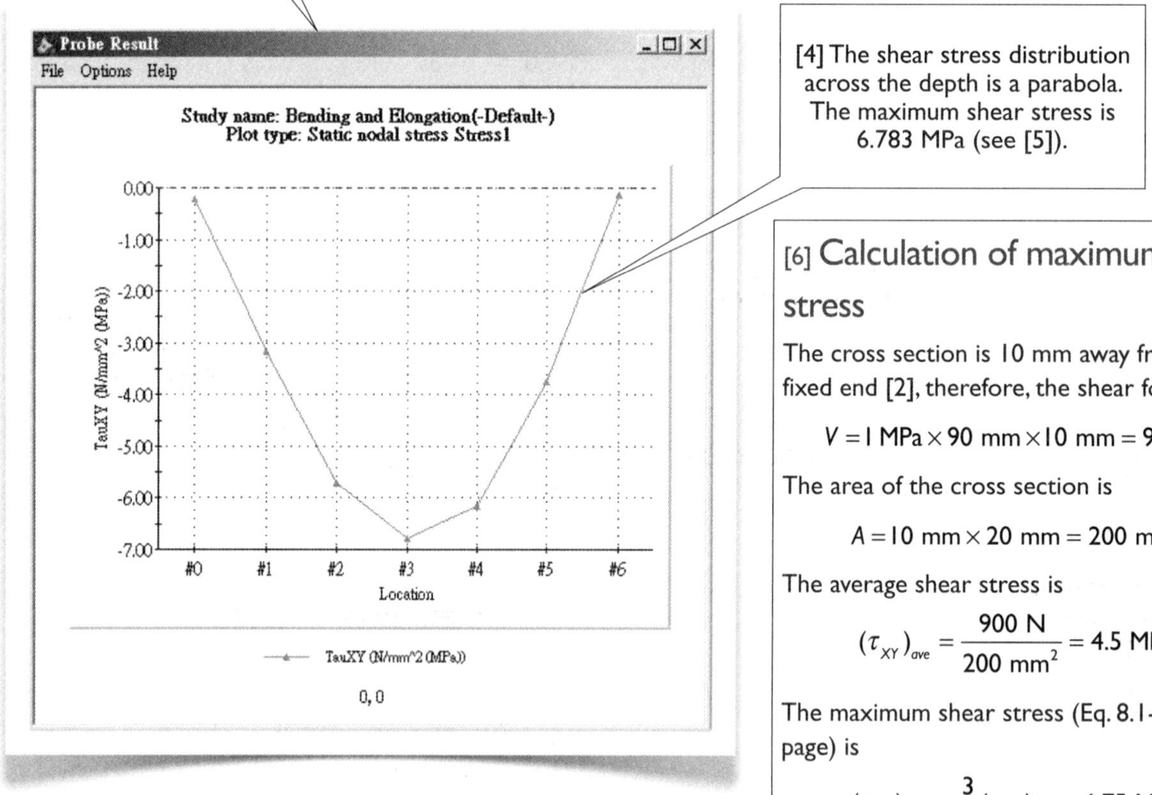

[6] Calculation of maximum shear stress

The cross section is 10 mm away from the fixed end [2], therefore, the shear force is

$$V = 1 \text{ MPa} \times 90 \text{ mm} \times 10 \text{ mm} = 900 \text{ N}$$

The area of the cross section is

$$A = 10 \text{ mm} \times 20 \text{ mm} = 200 \text{ mm}^2$$

The average shear stress is

$$(\tau_{XY})_{ave} = \frac{900 \text{ N}}{200 \text{ mm}^2} = 4.5 \text{ MPa}$$

The maximum shear stress (Eq. 8.1-1(4), last page) is

$$(\tau_{XY})_{max} = \frac{3}{2}(\tau_{XY})_{ave} = 6.75 \text{ MPa}$$

which is consistent with the value in [4, 5]. #

8.1-3 Start Up

[1] Launch **SolidWorks** and open the file **Cantilever**, which was saved in Section 3.1.

[2] Make sure **Model** tab is active. #

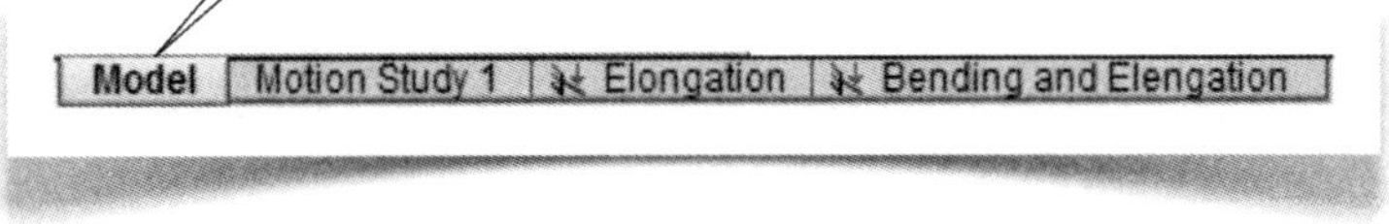

8.1-4 Create a Split Line

[1] Right-click this face and select **Sketch**.

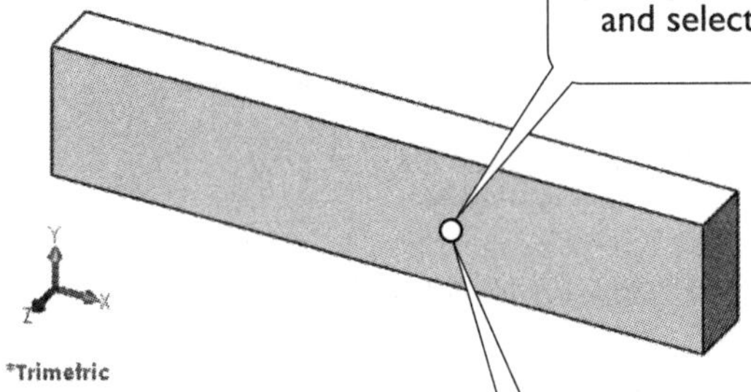

[2] Draw a line like this. Click **Exit Sketch**.

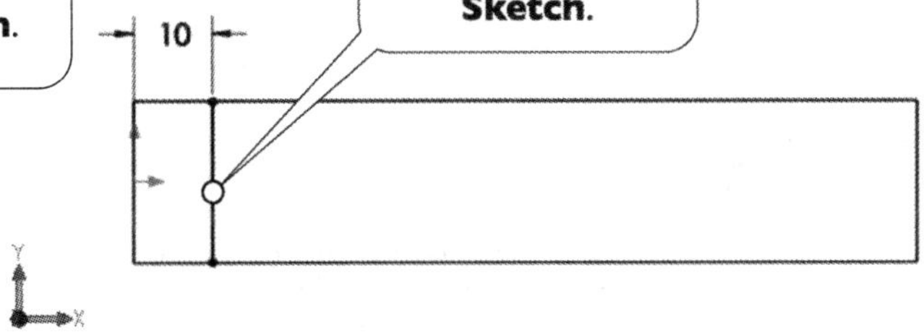

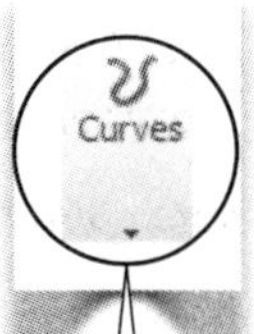

[3] in the **Features Toolbar**, select **Curves>Split Line**.

[4] Select the newly created sketch from the **Part Tree**.

[5] Select this face for **Faces to Split**.

[6] Click **OK**. #

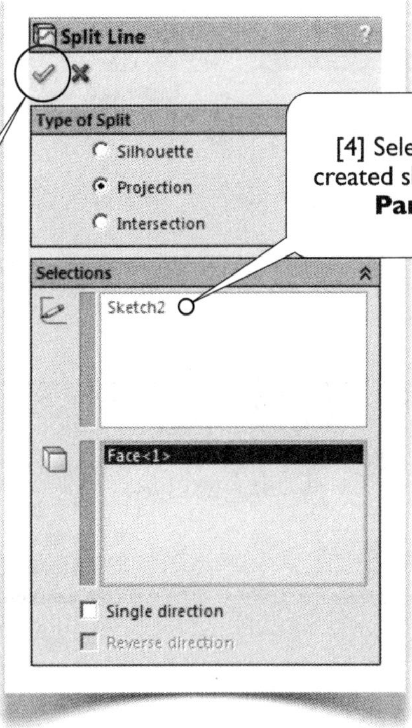

8.1-5 View Shear Stresses Along the **Split Line**

[1] Click **Bending and Elongation** to activate it.

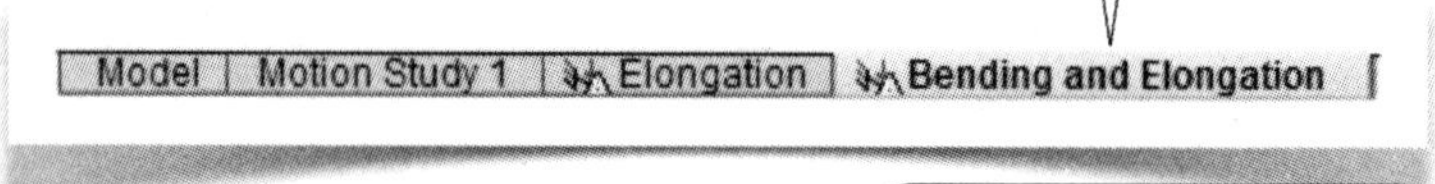

[2] In the **Simulation Toolbar**, click **Run**. Whenever you modified the model, you need to re-generate the results.

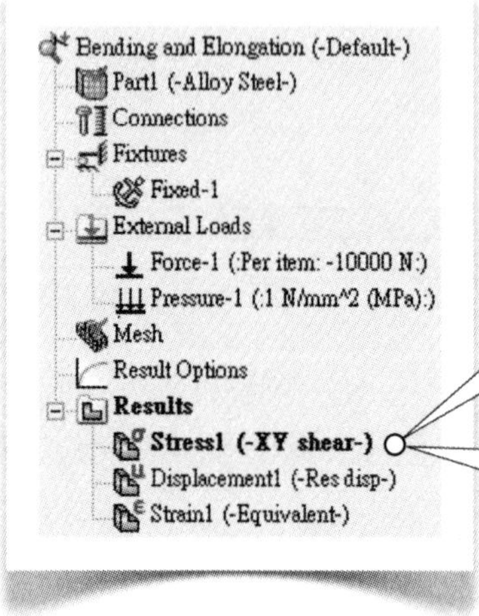

[3] Double-click **Stress1** to edit the definition. Select **TXY** (τ_{XY}) for **Component**.

[6] Right-click **Stress1** and select **Probe**.

[5] At the bottom of the **Property Box**, click to turn **Clipping** off.

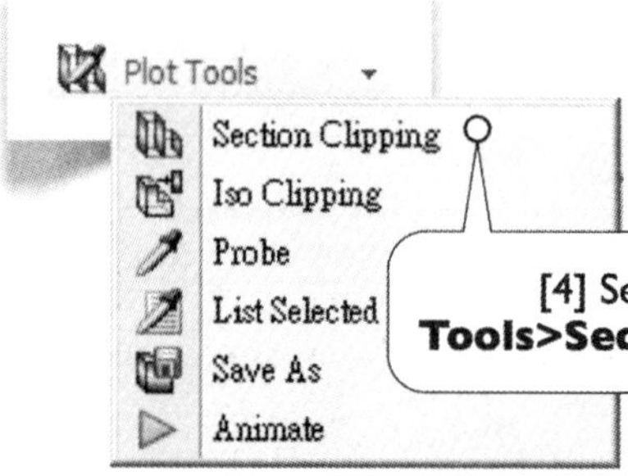

[4] Select **Plot Tools>Section Clipping**.

[12] Click **OK**.

[7] Select **On selected entities**.

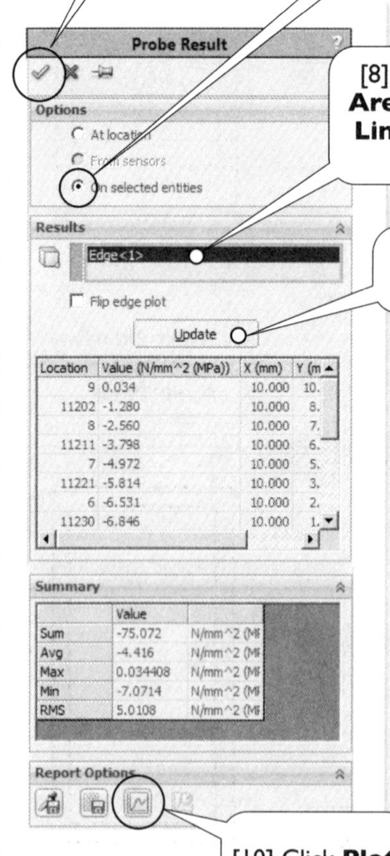

[8] In the **Graphics Area**, select the **Split Line** created in 8.1-4, last page.

[9] Click **Update**.

[10] Click **Plot**.

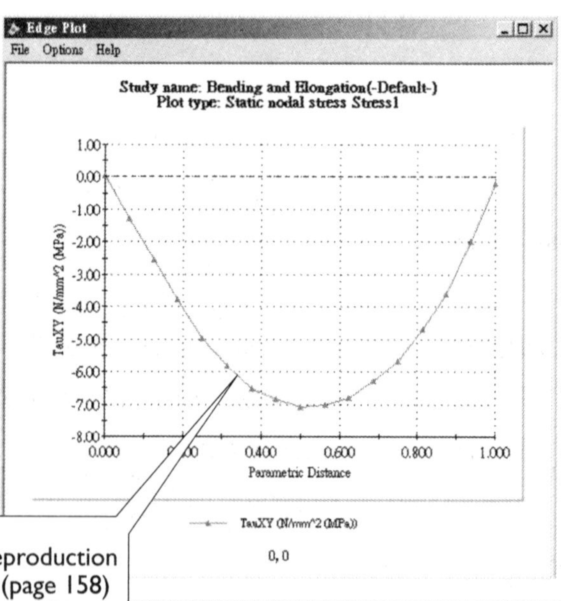

[11] This is simply a reproduction of the graph 8.1-2[4] (page 158) in a more accurate way. This is more convincing that the curve is indeed a parabola.

[13] Save the document and exit **SolidWorks**. #

Section 8.2

Shear Stresses in a Box Beam

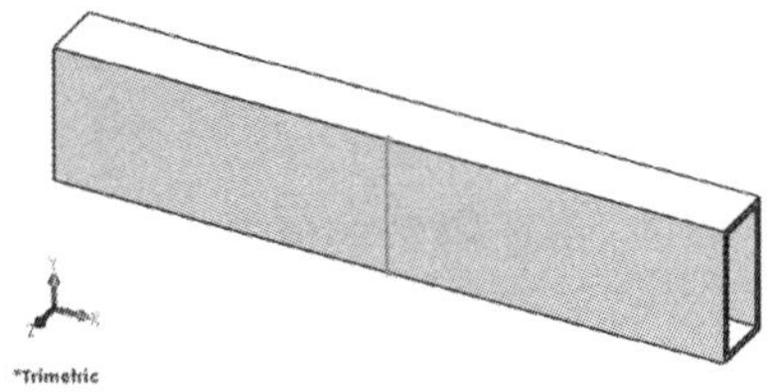

8.2-1 Introduction

[1] In this section, we'll examine the shear stresses in a cantilever beam with a box cross section [2]. The beam is made of **Alloy Steel** (E = 210 GPa, ν = 0.28) and has a length of 100 mm. A force of 1000 N is applied downward on the upper edge of the free end. The shear force is uniform along the beam length. We'll examine the shear stresses across the beam depth. And the average shear stresses at **AB** and **CD** [3] will be verified with Eq. 8.1-1(1), page 157.

[2] This is the cross section of the box beam.

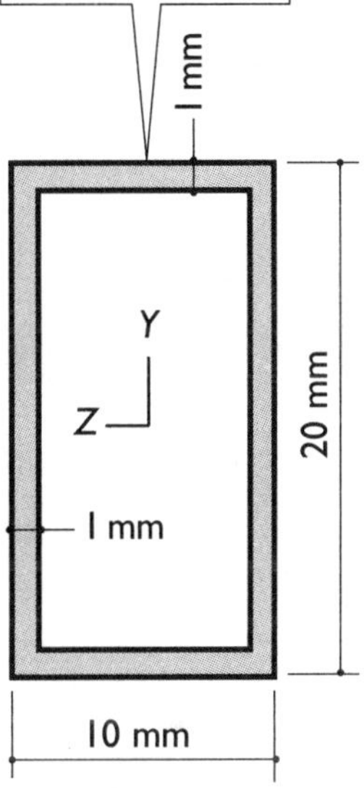

[3] We'll explore the shear stresses on **AB** and **CD**.

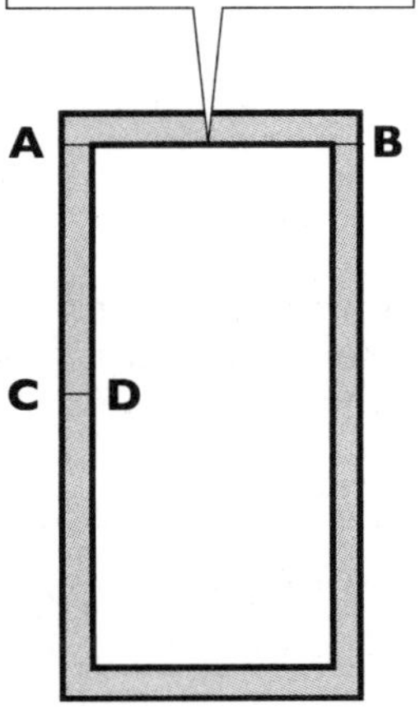

[4] Hand-Calculation of Shear Stresses

Eq. 8.1-1(1) (page 157) can be used to calculate the **average shear stress** across a horizontal line, such as **AB** or **CD**, of a cross section.

$$\tau_{XY} = \frac{VQ}{Ib} \qquad \text{Copy of 8.1-1(1)}$$

The shear force V = 1000 N. The moment of inertia is

$$I = \frac{10 \times 20^3}{12} - \frac{8 \times 18^3}{12} = 2778 \text{ mm}^4$$

At **AB**, b = 10 mm and the first moment is

$$Q = (10 \times 1) \times 9.5 = 95 \text{ mm}^3$$

The average shear stress across **AB** is

$$\tau_{XY}^{\mathbf{AB}} = \frac{VQ}{Ib} = \frac{1000 \times 95}{2778 \times 10} = 3.42 \text{ MPa} \qquad (2)$$

At **CD**, b = 2 mm (for both vertical plates) and the first moment is

$$Q = 95 + (9 \times 1) \times 4.5 \times 2 = 176 \text{ mm}^3$$

The average shear stress across **CD** is

$$\tau_{XY}^{\mathbf{CD}} = \frac{VQ}{Ib} = \frac{1000 \times 176}{2778 \times 2} = 31.7 \text{ MPa} \qquad (3)$$

#

8.2-2 Start Up

[1] Launch **SolidWorks** and create a new part. Set up **MMGS** unit system with zero decimal places for the length unit. Save the document as **BoxBeam**. #

8.2-3 Create Geometric Model

[1] On the **Right** plane, draw a sketch like this.

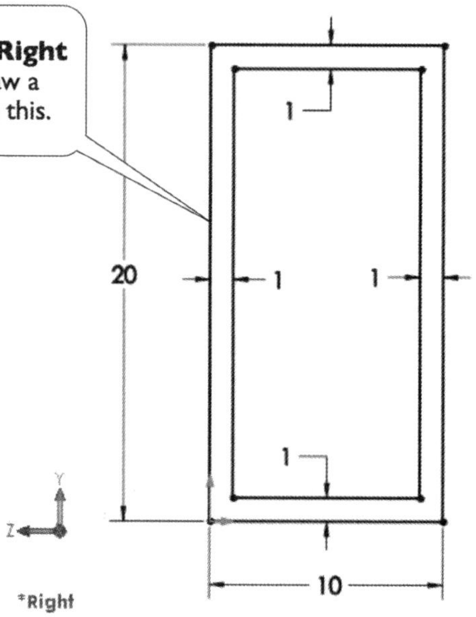

[2] **Extrude** 100 mm.

[3] Follow the steps in 7.2-3 (page 148) to create this **Split Line**.

[4] Create a new sketch on this face.

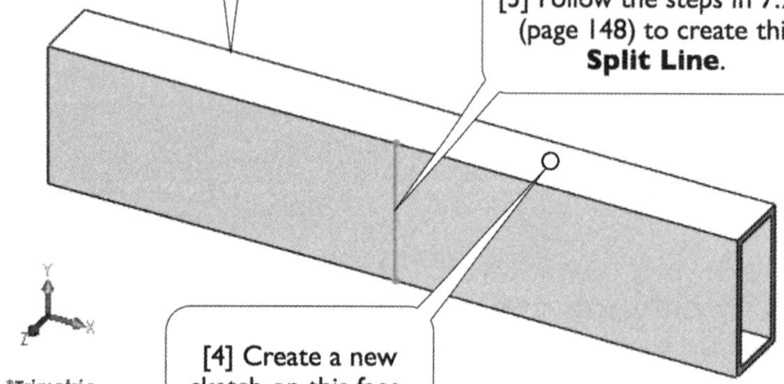

[5] Draw a line connecting the first **Split Line** like this. Click **Exit Sketch**.

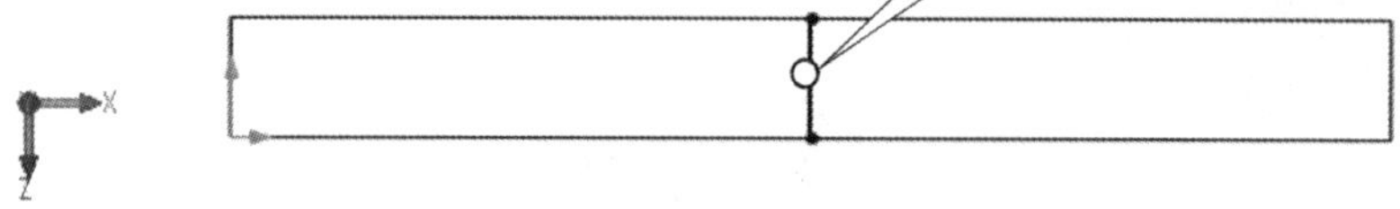

[6] in the **Features Toolbar**, select **Curves>Split Line**.

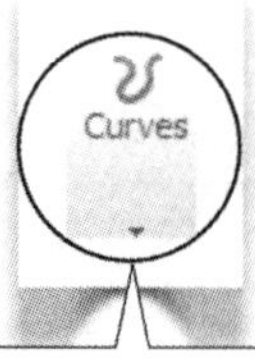

[7] Select the newly created sketch from the **Part Tree**.

[8] Select this face (the inner face of the upper plate) for **Faces to Split**.

[9] Click **OK**.

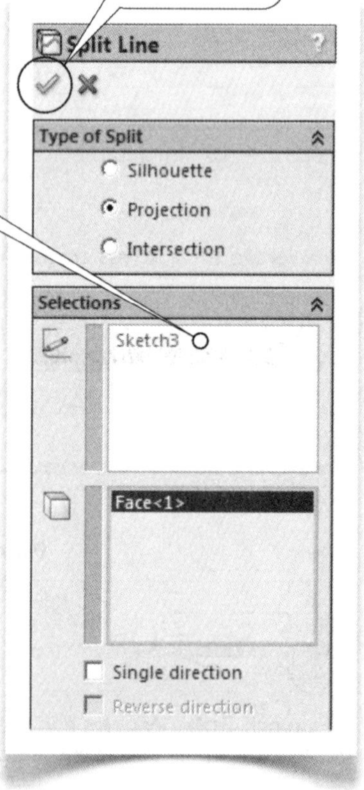

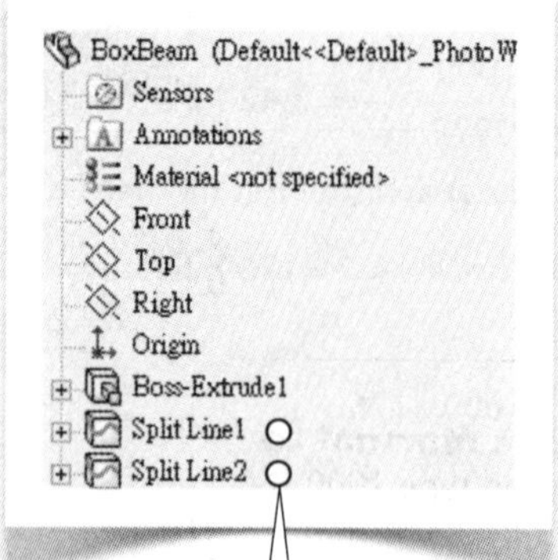

[10] The model includes two **Split Lines**. We'll explore the shear stresses on these two lines. #

8.2-4 Create a New Study

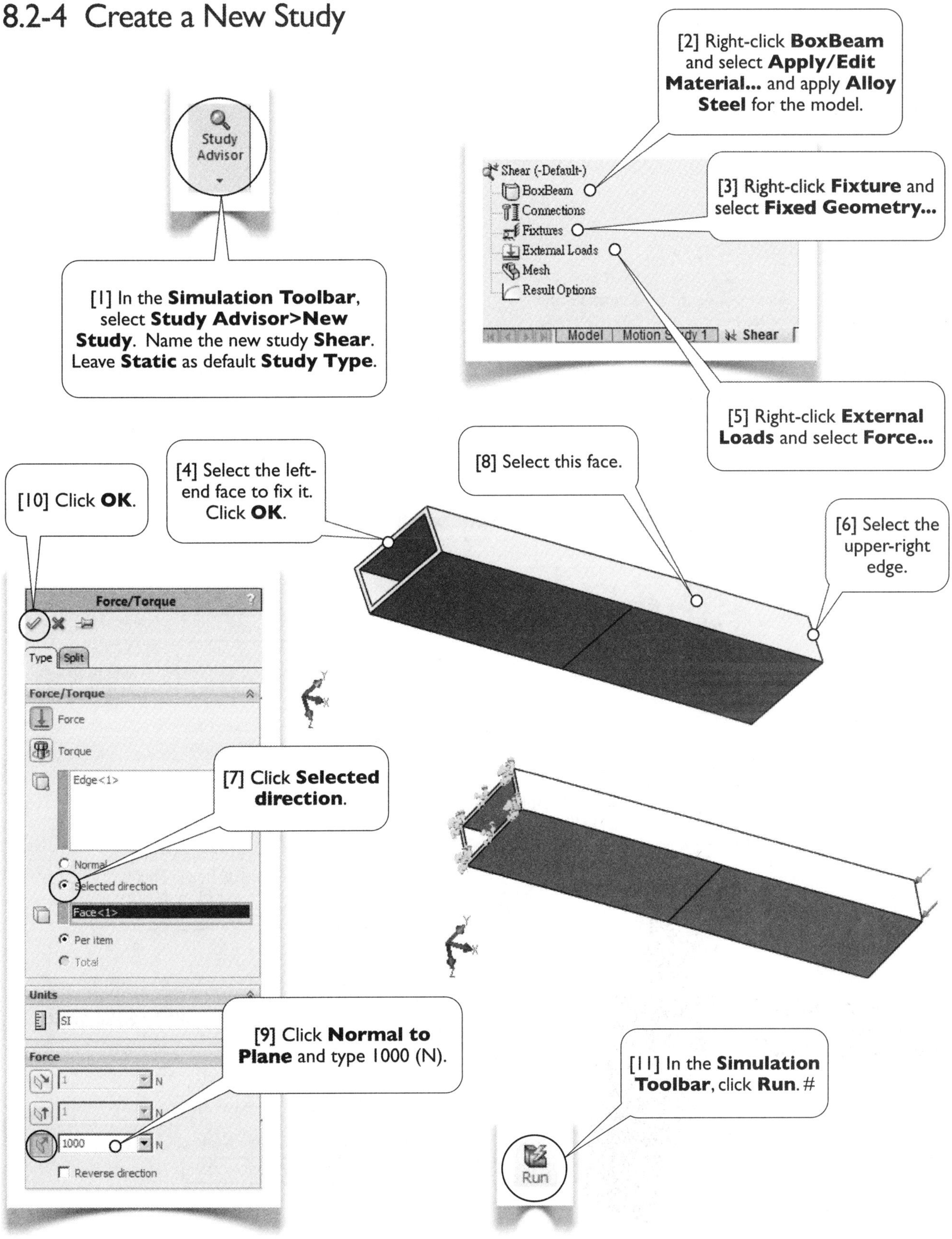

8.2-5 View Shear Stresses on the Vertical **Split Line**

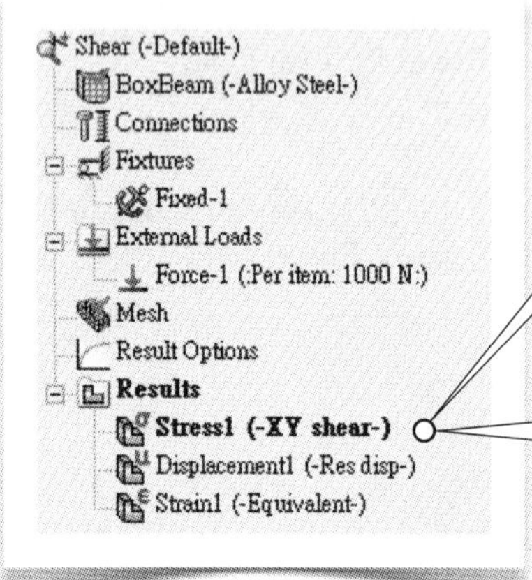

[1] Double-click **Stress1** to edit the definition. Select **TXY** (τ_{XY}) for **Component**.

[2] Right-click **Stress1** and select **Probe**.

[3] Select **On selected entities**.

[4] In the **Graphics Area**, select the vertical **Split Line** (**Split Line1**).

[5] Click **Update**

[6] Click **Plot**.

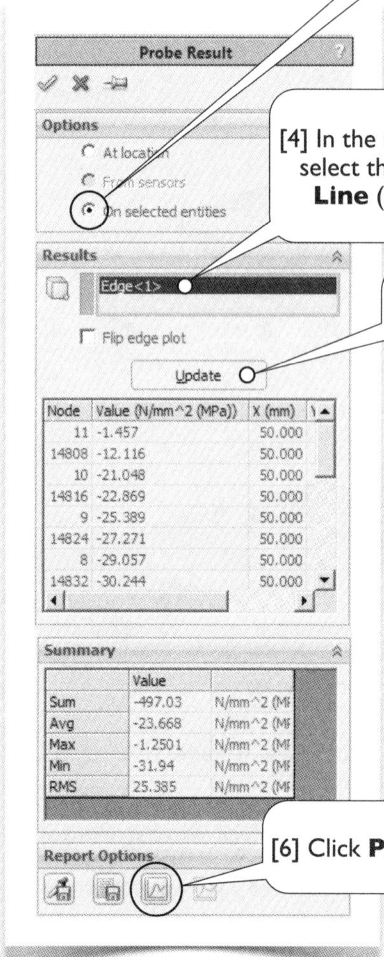

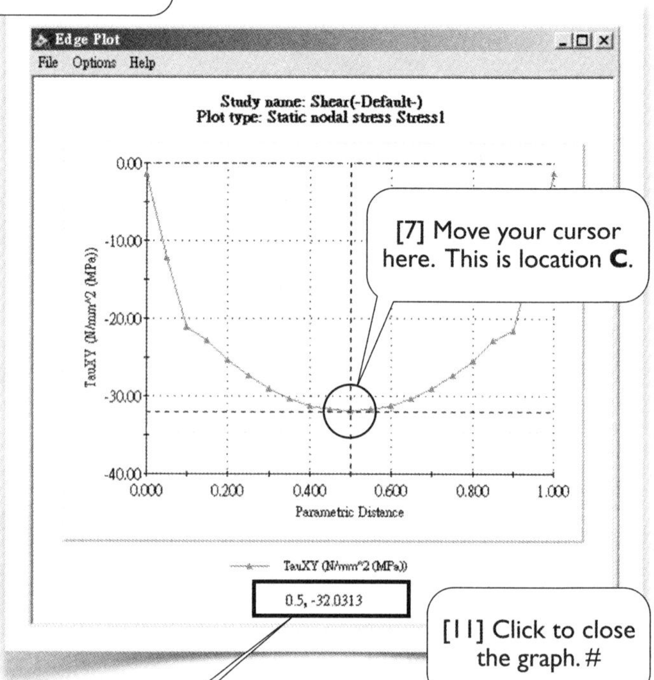

[7] Move your cursor here. This is location **C**.

[8] The distance/stress display here. The shear stress τ_{XY} at location **C** is -32 MPa, which is close to the average stress calculated in 8.2-1(3), page 161.

[9] Move your cursor here. This is location **A**.

[10] The shear stress at location **A** is -12 MPa. We need this value in 8.2-6[6], next page.

[11] Click to close the graph. #

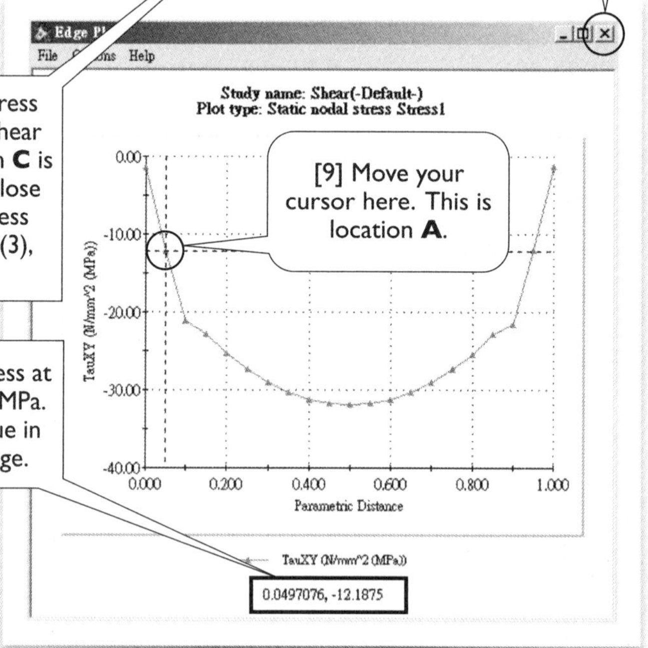

8.2-6 View Shear Stresses on the Horizontal **Split Line**

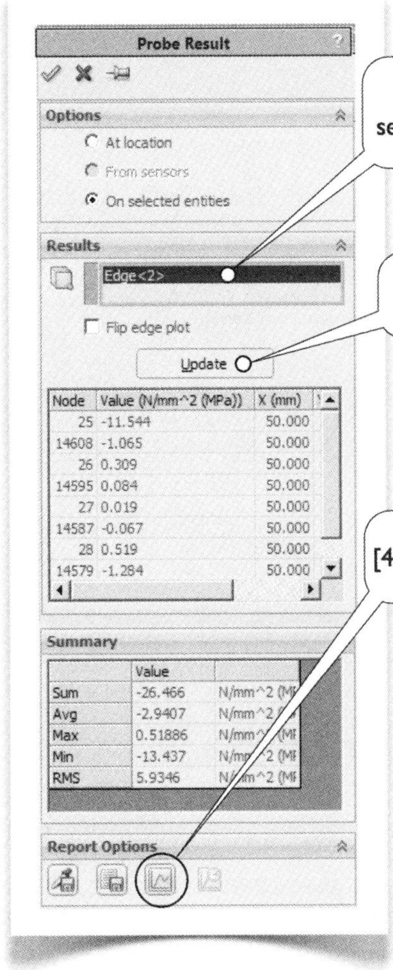

[1] Right-click here and select **Clear Selections**.

[2] Select the horizontal **Split Line** (**Split Line2**). Note that the length of **Split Line2** is 8 mm.

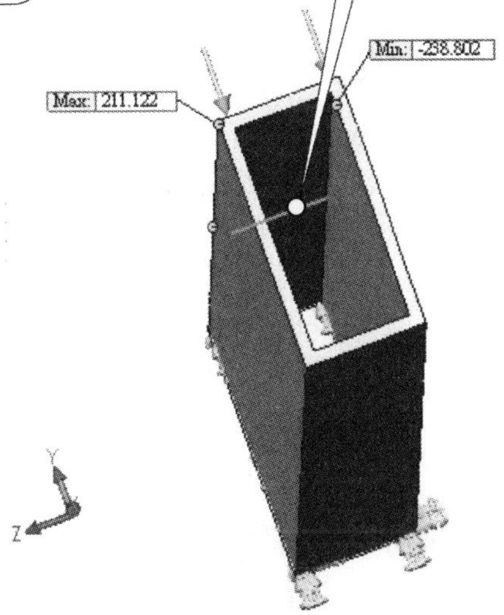

[3] Click **Update**.

[4] Click **Plot**.

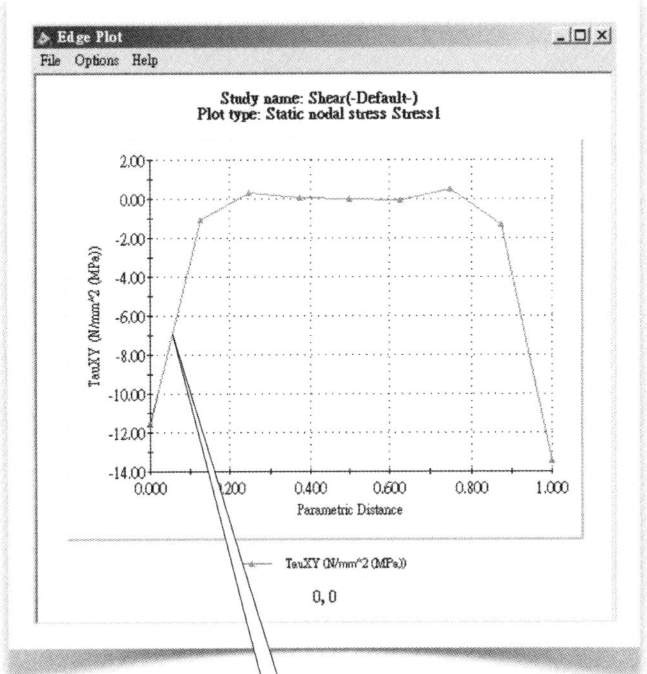

[5] The shear stresses along the horizontal **Split Line**, which has a length of 8 mm.

[6] Combining the results in 8.2-5[10] (last page) and [5], we may conclude that the shear stresses τ_{XY} along **AB** is like this. The average τ_{XY} is 3.6 MPa (shaped area divided by 10 mm), which is close to the calculated value in 8.2-1(2), page 161.#

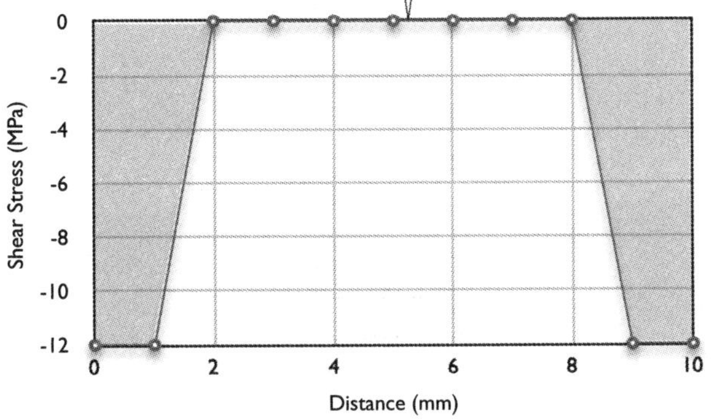

8.2-7 Do It Yourself: **Shear Flow**

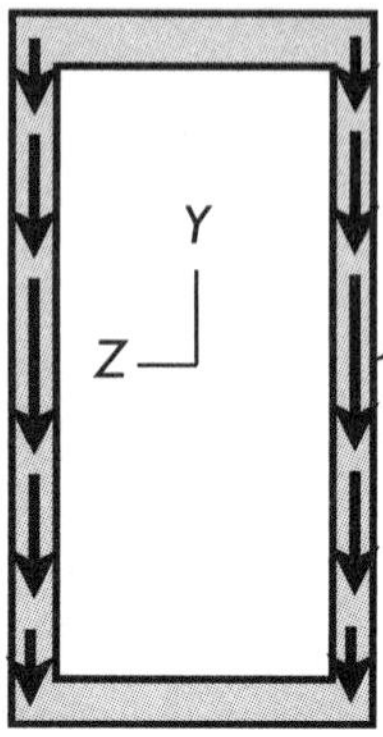

[1] The foregoing exercises show that in the vertical plates, shear stress τ_{XY} distributes like this (a more details are shown in 8.2-5, page 164), while in the horizontal plate, τ_{XY} is negligible.

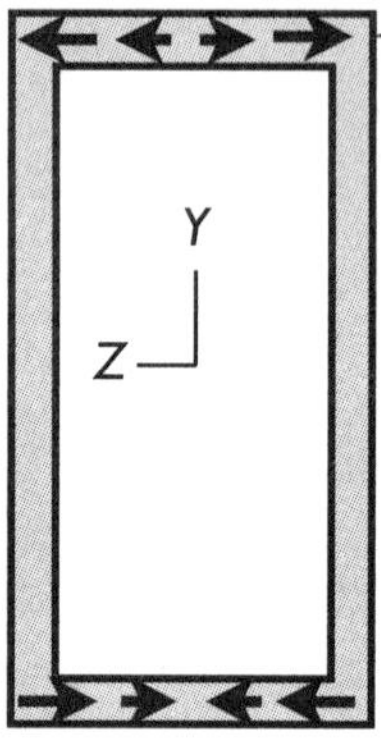

[2] A similar procedure will show that the in the horizontal plates, shear stress τ_{XZ} distributes like this (details are shown in [3, 4]), while in the vertical plate, τ_{XZ} is negligible. Make sure you understand the directions of the stresses.

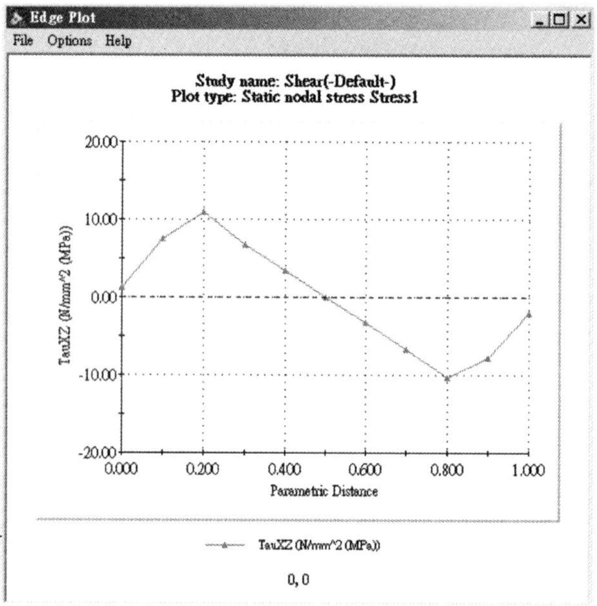

[3] The shear stress τ_{XZ} at the upper horizontal plate.

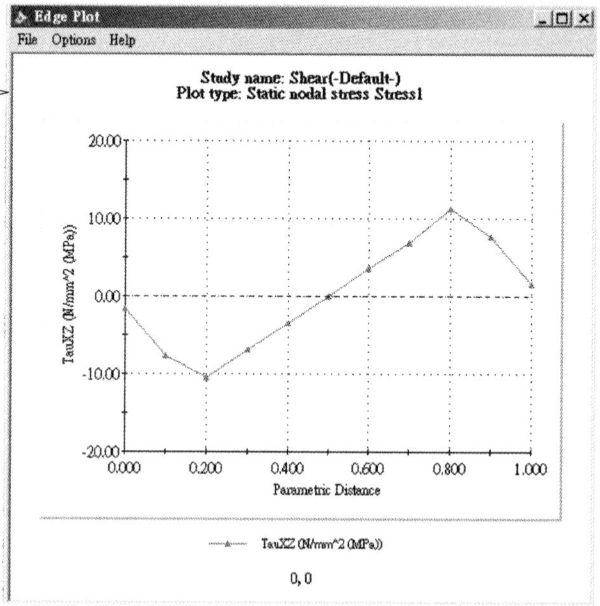

[4] The shear stress τ_{XZ} at the lower horizontal plate.

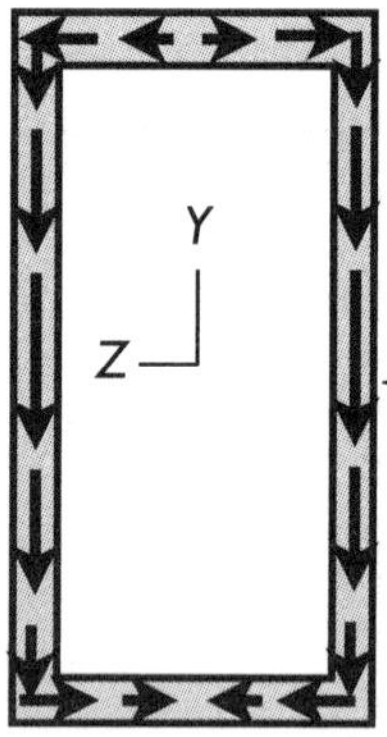

[5] Combining [1] and [2], we have a total shear ($\tau_{XY} + \tau_{XZ}$) distribution like this. It looks like the shear "flows" along the cross section.

[6] Save the document and exit **SolidWorks**. #

Section 8.3

Shear Center

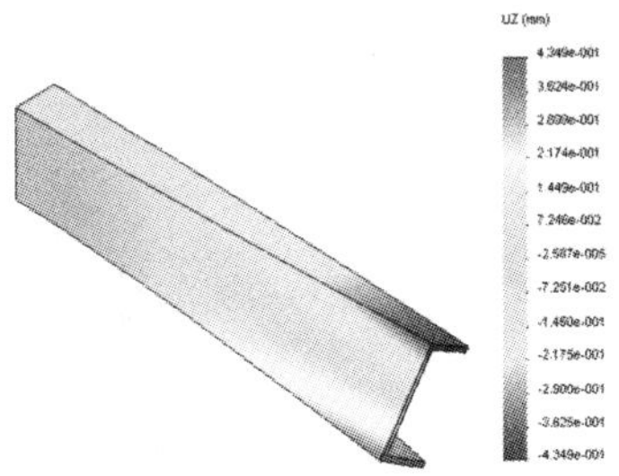

8.3-1 Introduction

[1] In this section, we'll examine the deformation of a cantilever beam with a channel section [2]. The beam is made of **Alloy Steel** (E = 210 GPa, ν = 0.28) and has a length of 100 mm. A force of 200 N is applied downward at the free end. We'll apply the force at different locations of the free end. There exists a unique location where the beam doesn't twist and warp. This location is called the **shear center**. We'll show that it is possible to find the precise location of the shear center, using the **Simulation**.

[2] This is the cross section of the beam.

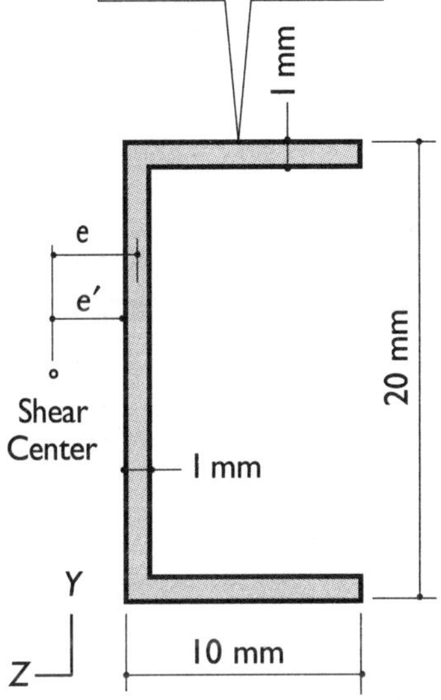

[3] Estimation of the Location of the Shear Center

The formula to estimate the location of the shear center of a channel section can be found in any Mechanics of Materials textbook,

$$e = \frac{b^2}{2b + \frac{h}{3}} = \frac{10^2}{2(10) + \frac{20}{3}} = 3.75 \text{ mm}, \quad e' = 3.25 \text{ mm} \qquad (1)$$

Note that the above formula assumes the section's walls are infinitesimally thin. We'll show, in 8.3-6 (page 171), that a more precise estimation is $e' = 2.755$ mm. #

8.3-2 Start Up and Create Geometric Model

[1] Launch **SolidWorks** and create a new part. Set up **MMGS** unit system with zero decimal places for the length unit. Save the document as **Channel**.

[2] On the **Right** plane, draw a sketch like this.

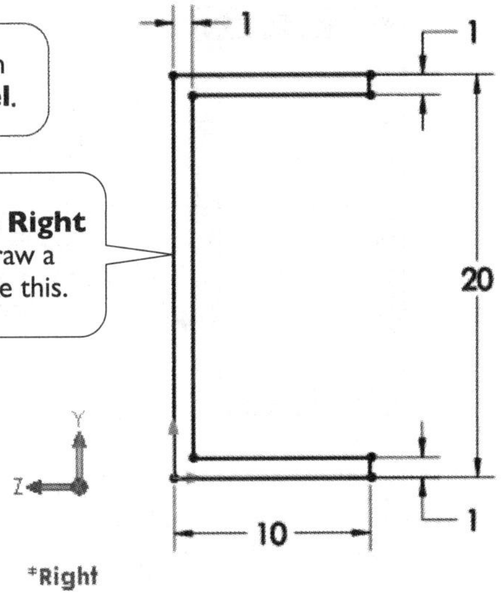

[3] **Extrude** 100 mm. #

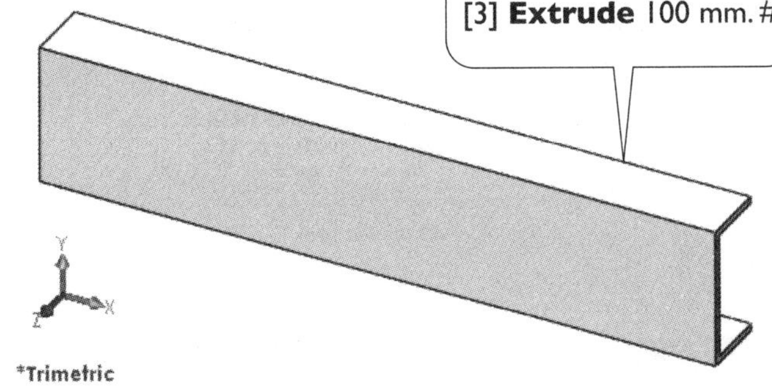

8.3-3 Create a New Study

[1] In the **Simulation Toolbar**, select **Study Advisor>New Study**. Name the new study **Shear Center**. Leave **Static** as default **Study Type**.

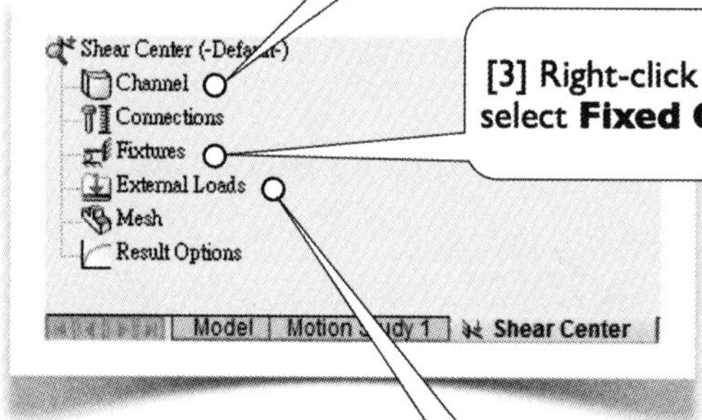

[2] Right-click **Channel** and select **Apply/Edit Material...** and apply **Alloy Steel** for the model.

[3] Right-click **Fixture** and select **Fixed Geometry...**

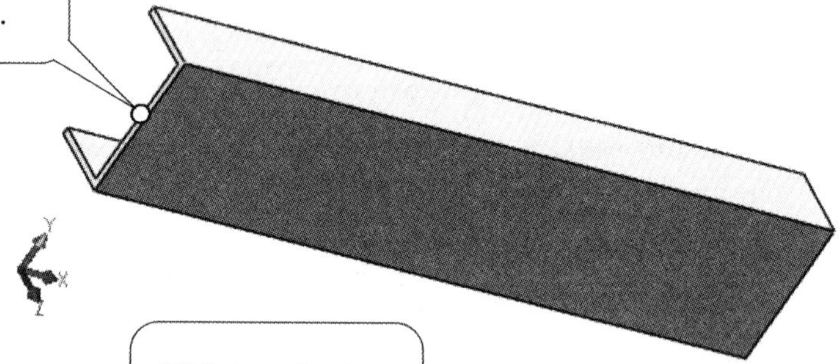

[4] Select the left-end face to fix it. Click **OK**.

[5] Right-click **External Loads** and select **Force...**

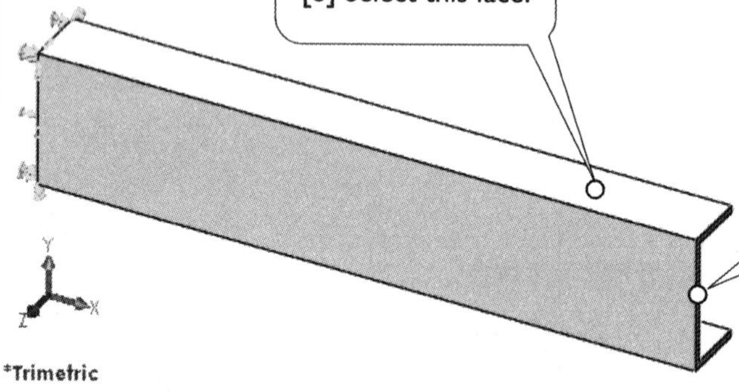

[6] Select the right-end face.

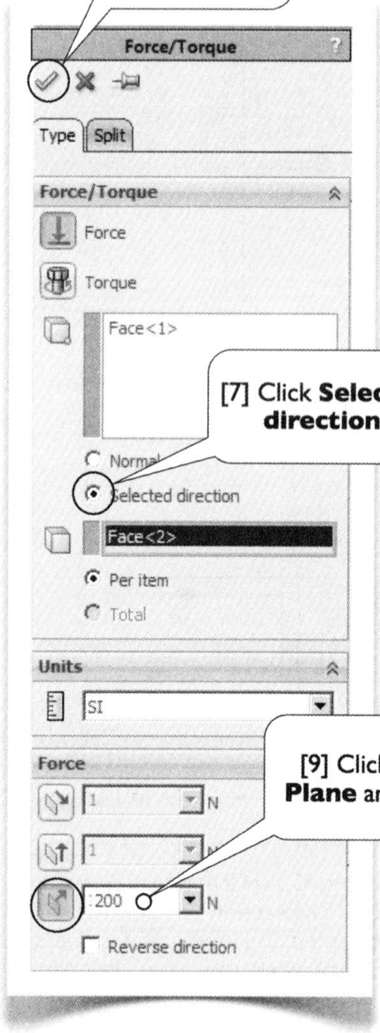

[7] Click **Selected direction**.

[8] Select this face.

[9] Click **Normal to Plane** and type 200 (N).

[10] Click **OK**.

[11] In the **Simulation Toolbar**, click **Run**. #

8.3-4 View the Deformation

[1] Right-click **Fixtures** and select **Hide All.**

[2] Right-click **External Force** and select **Hide All.**

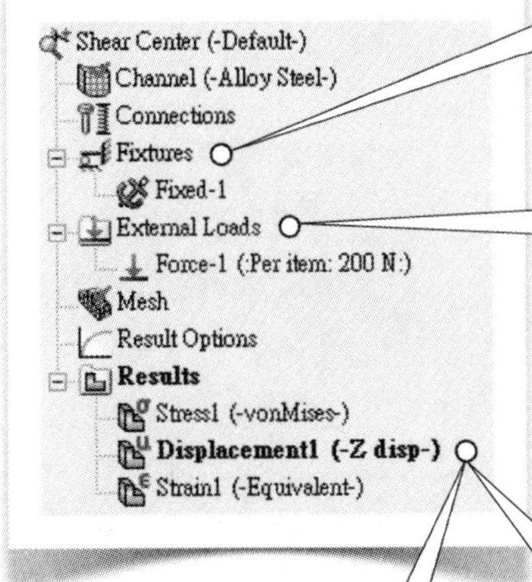

[3] Double-click **Displacement1** to activate it. Double-click it again to edit the definition and select **UZ** (u_Z) for **Component**.

[6] Double-click **Displacement1** to edit the definition and select **UX** (u_X) for **Component**.

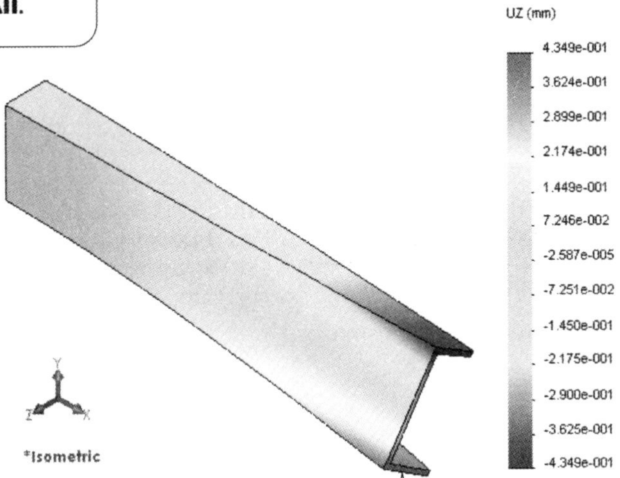

[4] The beam is twisted, rotating clockwise when viewed from the free end.

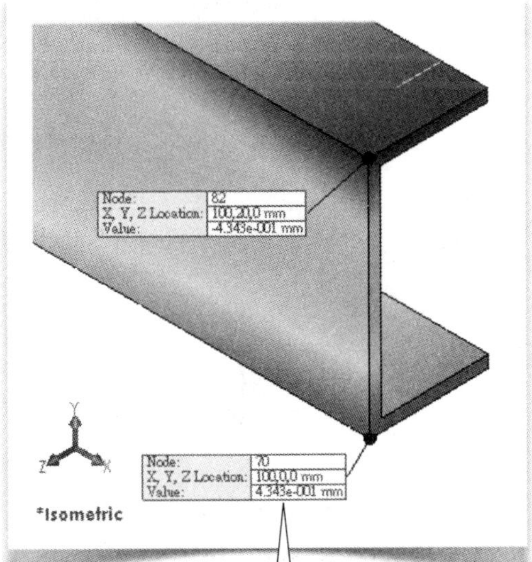

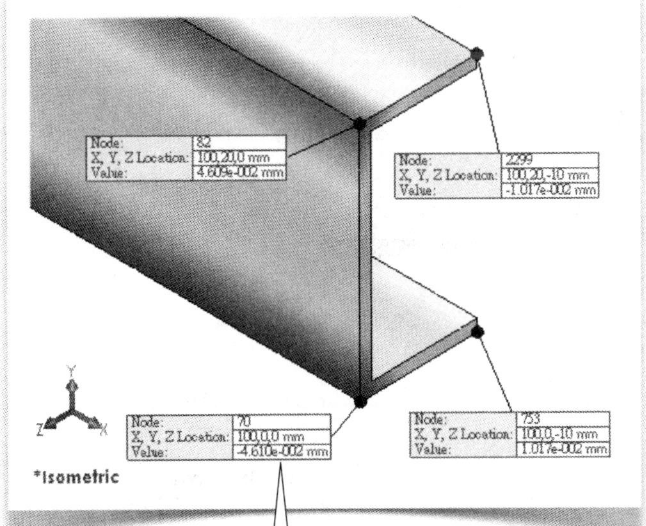

[5] Use **Probe** to obtain the Z-displacement (u_Z) at the top (-0.4343) and bottom (+0.4343) of the section. The rotation angle can be calculated as follows: 0.4343 mm ÷ 10 mm = 0.04343 (rad), which is clockwise when viewed from the free end.

[7] Use **Probe** to obtain the X-displacement (u_X) at the four corners of the section. The section not only rotates [5] but also warps: the upper-left and lower-right corners move out of the section plane, while the upper-right and lower-left corners move inward of the section plane. #

8.3-5 Apply the Force at the Estimated Shear Center

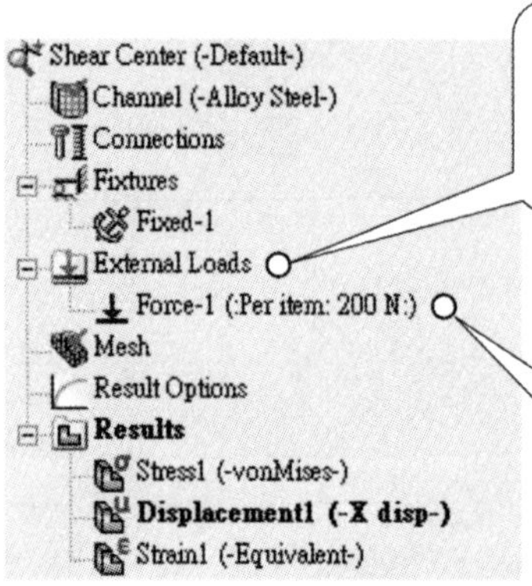

[1] Right-click **Force-1** and select **Suppress**. In effect, the load is deleted.

[2] Right-click **External Force** and select **Remote Load/Mass...**

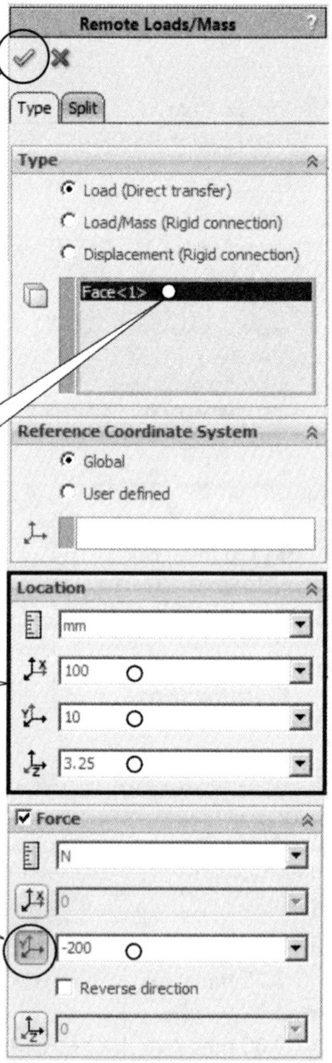

[3] Select the right-end face (8.3-3[6], page 168).

[4] Type the coordinates (100, 10, 3.25) of the estimated shear center.

[5] Click **Y-Direction** and type **-200** (N).

[6] Click **OK**.

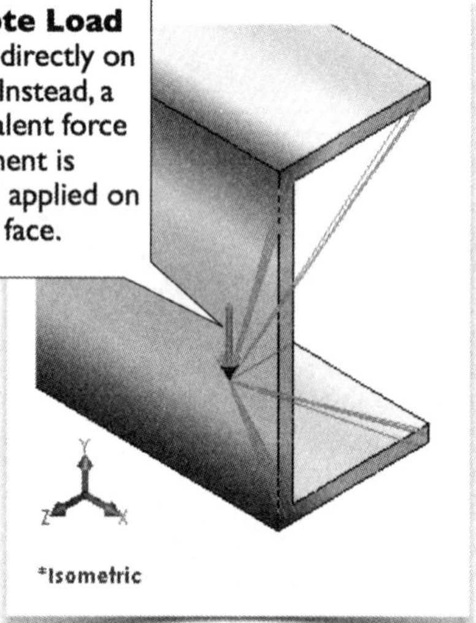

[7] A **Remote Load** doesn't apply directly on the model. Instead, a pair of equivalent force and moment is calculated and applied on the end face.

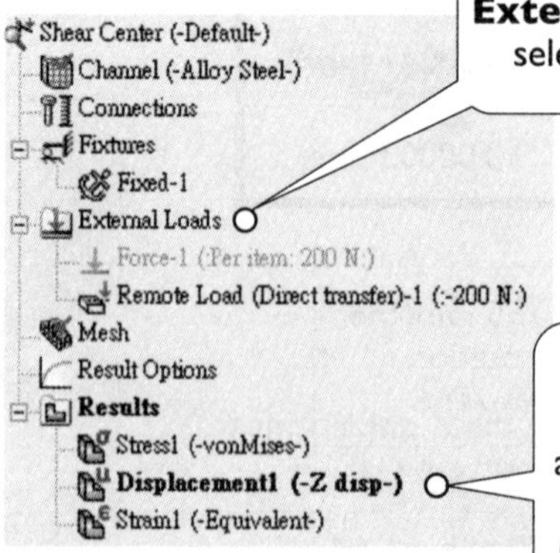

[8] Right-click **External Force** and select **Hide All**.

[9] In the **Simulation Toolbar**, click **Run**.

[10] Double-click **Displacement1** to activate it. Double-click it again and select **UZ** (u_Z) for **Component**.

[11] Use **Probe** to obtain the *Z*-displacement (u_Z) at the top and bottom of the section. Now the section rotates counterclockwise slightly (the top moves 0.03824 mm leftward while the bottom moves rightward). #

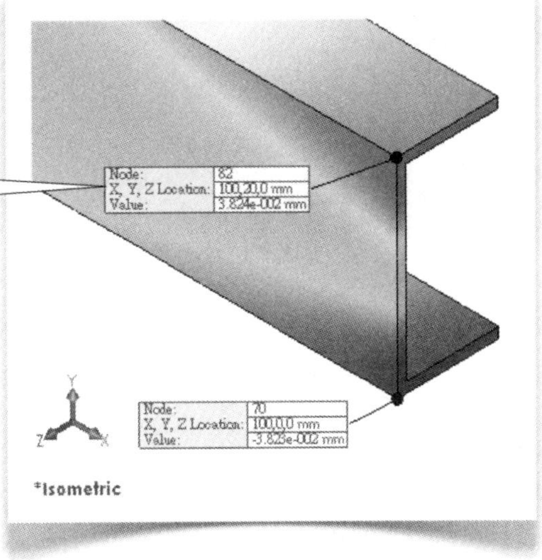

8.3-6 Fine-Tune the Location of the Remote Load

[1] Change the *Z*-coordinate of the Remote Load (8.3-5[4], last page), rerun the model, and use **Probe** to obtain the *Z*-displacement (u_Z) of the top edge (8.3-5[11], this page). You'll eventually locate the shear center with the desired precision.

Z-Coordinate of the Remote Load (see 8.3-5[4])	Z-Displacement of the Top Edge (see 8.3-5[11])
3.25 mm	+0.03824 mm
3.00 mm	+0.01894 mm
2.75 mm	-0.00036 mm
2.76 mm	+0.00041 mm
2.755 mm	+0.00003 mm

[2] At *Z* = 2.755 mm, the section's rotation approaches zero.

[5] Save the document and exit **SolidWorks**. #

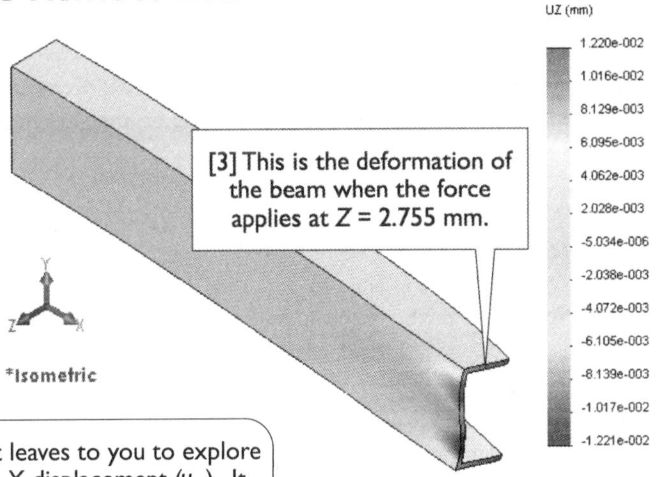

[3] This is the deformation of the beam when the force applies at *Z* = 2.755 mm.

[4] It leaves to you to explore the *X*-displacement (u_X). It doesn't warp now: the top two corners move out of the section plane simultaneously, while the lower two corners move inward simultaneously; it's a bending mode (not a warping mode).

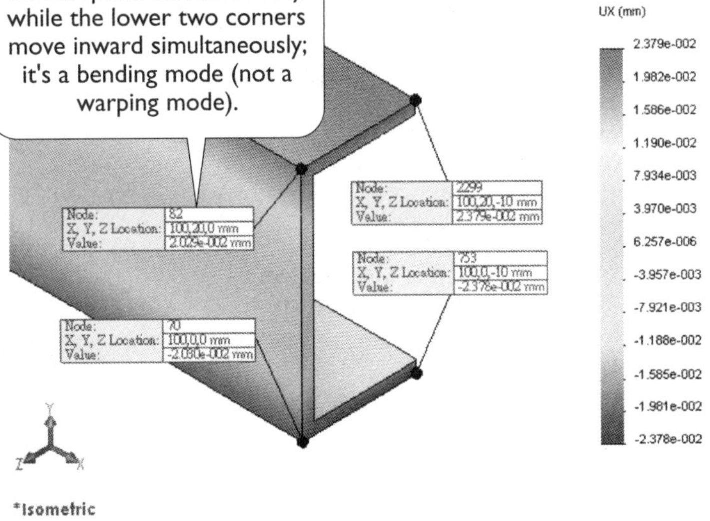

Chapter 9

Strain Energy

Imagine that a force acts on a spring and the spring deforms. The force moves, therefore, it does work. This energy of the work done is transferred and saved in the body of spring. The energy stored in the spring is called a potential energy, as you've learned in high school physics.

Similarly, imagine a set of external forces acts on the surface of a body and the body deforms. The external forces move, therefore, they do work. This energy of the work done is transferred and saved in the body, stored as a potential energy. In a microscopic view, the potential energy is created when the molecules of the material are stretched and twisted. The potential energy stored in a solid body is also called the **strain energy**. In an elastic material, the strain energy can be completely released when the external forces are released.

The **strain energy density** is defined as the strain energy per unit volume. The strain energy density u_0 is related to the stresses and strains by

$$u_0 = \frac{1}{2}\left(\sigma_X \varepsilon_X + \sigma_Y \varepsilon_Y + \sigma_Z \varepsilon_Z + \tau_{XY} \gamma_{XY} + \tau_{YZ} \gamma_{YZ} + \tau_{ZX} \gamma_{ZX}\right) \qquad (1)$$

Concepts of energy are useful. In fact, most of finite element simulation programs, such as **SolidWorks Simulation**, solve problems using energy methods (rather than force-equilibrium methods).

In Chapter 10, we'll introduce several failure criteria. One of them is the **von Mises criterion** (10.2-1[6], page 197), which is often used in ductile materials, especially metals. The von Mises criterion states that when the **von Mises stress** (Eq. 10.2-1(8), page 197) of a point in a body reaches the yield strength of the material, the point would yield. The theory behind the von Mises criterion relies on the notions of strain energy.

Section 9.1

Work Done, Strain Energy, and Strain Energy Density

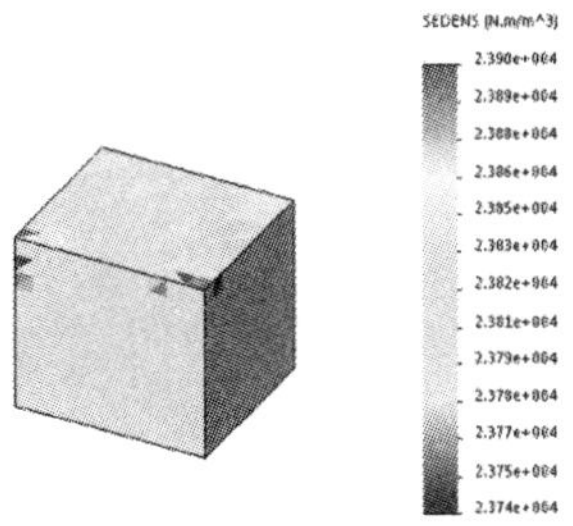

9.1-1 Introduction

In this section, we'll continue the exercises in **Tensile Test** and **Shear Test** (Section 4.2). After deformation, the work done by the forces can be calculated. This amount of energy is then stored as strain energy in the cube. The strain energy density can be calculated by dividing the work done by the block's volume. It also can be calculated using Eq. 9(1), last page. We'll verify these manually calculated strain energy density values with the values reported from the **Simulation**. The purpose of this section is that, through the exercises, the students have clear concepts of work done, strain energy, and strain energy density.

9.1-2 Start Up

[1] Launch **SolidWorks** and open the file **Cube** which was saved in Section 5.3.#

9.1-3 Revisit **Tensile Test**

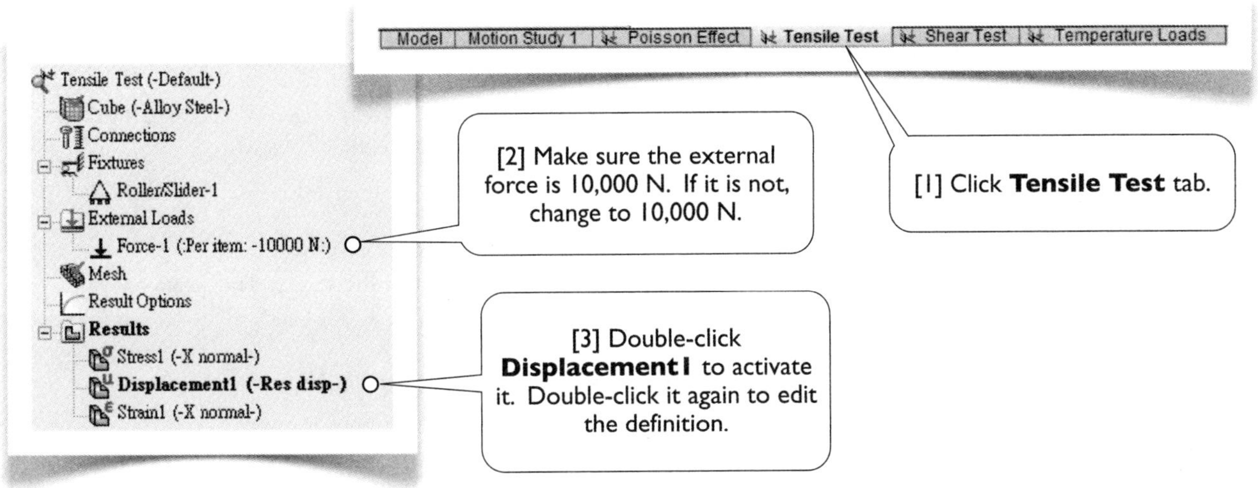

[1] Click **Tensile Test** tab.

[2] Make sure the external force is 10,000 N. If it is not, change to 10,000 N.

[3] Double-click **Displacement1** to activate it. Double-click it again to edit the definition.

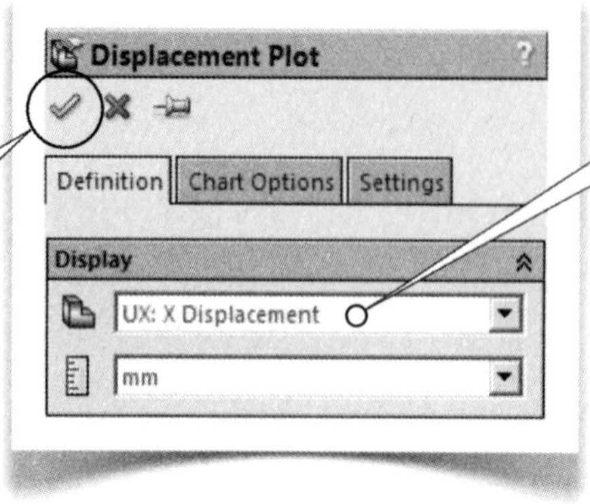

[4] Select **UX: X Displacement**.

[5] Click **OK**.

[6] The displacement at the face where the force is applied is 4.763×10^{-3} mm.

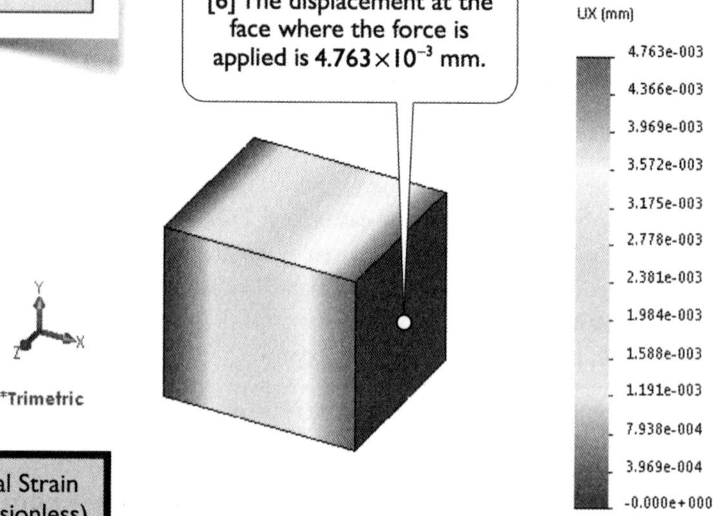

[7] These stress and strain are directly taken from 4.2-3[9], page 82.

Applied Force (N)	Normal Stress (MPa)	Normal Strain (Dimensionless)
10000	100	0.0004761

[8] Calculate Work Done, Strain Energy, and Strain Energy Density

In a static simulation, all external forces are assumed to be applied slowly from zero to their specified values. In our case, the external force is applied slowly from zero to 10,000 N. Accordingly, the displacements are also increasing slowly from zero to 4.763×10^{-3} mm ([6]). Similarly, the stresses and strains are also increasing slowly from zero to their values.

Therefore, the work done by the external force is

$$W = \frac{1}{2} \mathit{Force} \cdot \mathit{Displacement} = \frac{1}{2}(10{,}000 \text{ N}) \cdot (4.763 \times 10^{-6} \text{ m}) = 2.3815 \times 10^{-2} \text{ J}$$

This amount of energy is stored in the block as strain energy; i.e., the total strain energy is $U = W = 2.3815 \times 10^{-2}$ J. Since the cube is uniformly stretched, the strain energy density is uniform over the cube,

$$u_0 = \frac{U}{\mathit{Volume}} = \frac{2.3815 \times 10^{-2} \text{ J}}{(0.01 \text{ m})^3} = 2.3815 \times 10^4 \text{ J/m}^3$$

Note that the unit of the strain energy density is dimensionally equivalent to that of the stress. The strain energy density can also be calculated using Eq. 9(1) (page 172) and the data in [7],

$$u_0 = \frac{1}{2}\sigma_X \varepsilon_X = \frac{1}{2}(100 \times 10^6 \text{ Pa})(0.0004761) = 2.3805 \times 10^4 \text{ J/m}^3$$

Note that, in this case, σ_X is the only non-zero stress component.

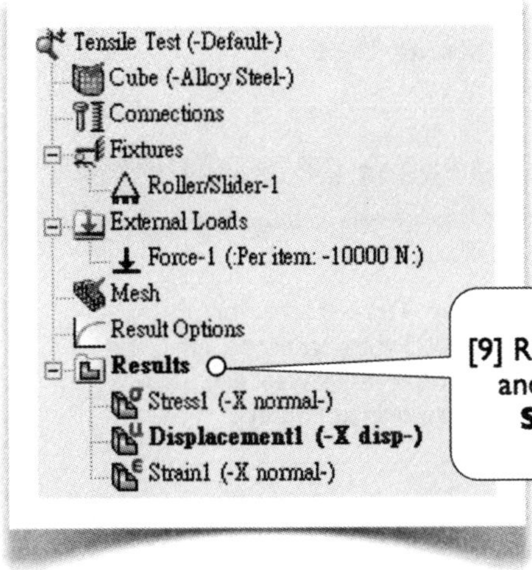

[9] Right-click **Results** and select **Define Strain Plot...**

[11] Click **OK**.

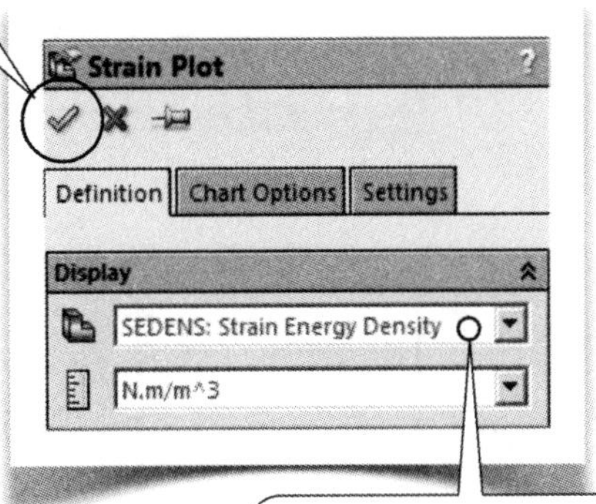

[10] Select **SEDENS: Strain Energy Density**.

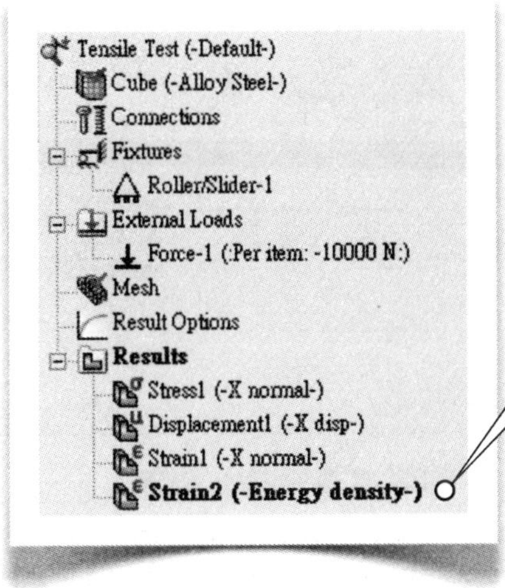

[12] A plot of **Energy density** is added under the **Results**.

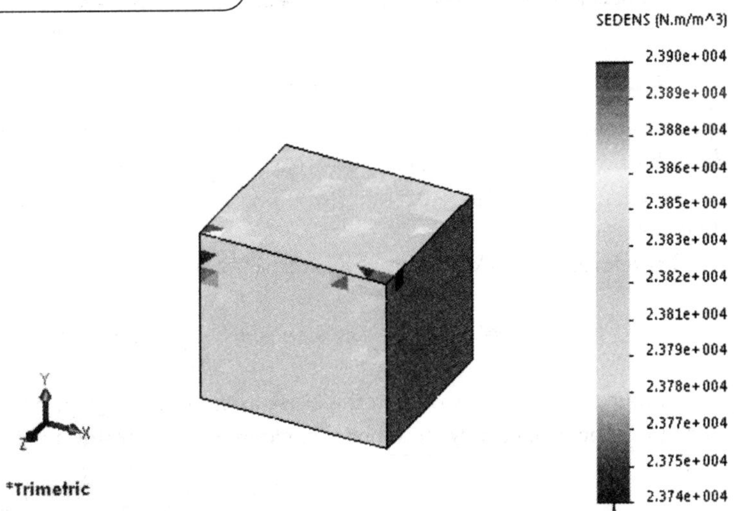

[13] Due to small numerical errors, the strain energy density ranges from 2.374×10^4 J/m^3 to 2.390×10^4 J/m^3. the average strain energy density is 2.382×10^4 J/m^3, which is consistent with the values calculated in [8] (last page). #

9.1-4 Revisit **Shear Test**

[1] Click **Shear Test** tab.

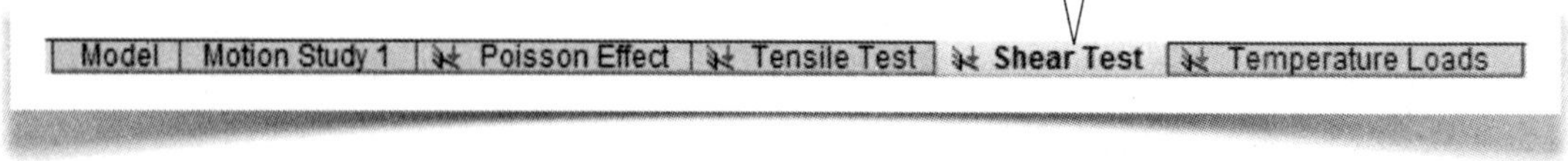

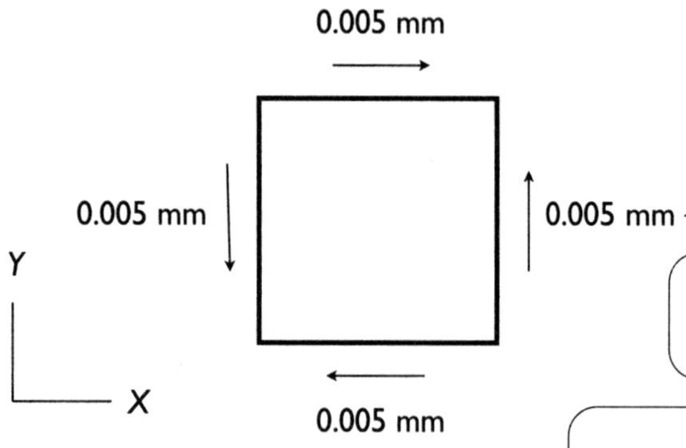

[2] Recall that, in the **Shear Test** study, we applied displacements of 0.005 mm on these four faces. In the next few steps [3-7], we'll list the required forces for these displacements.

[8] Click **OK**.

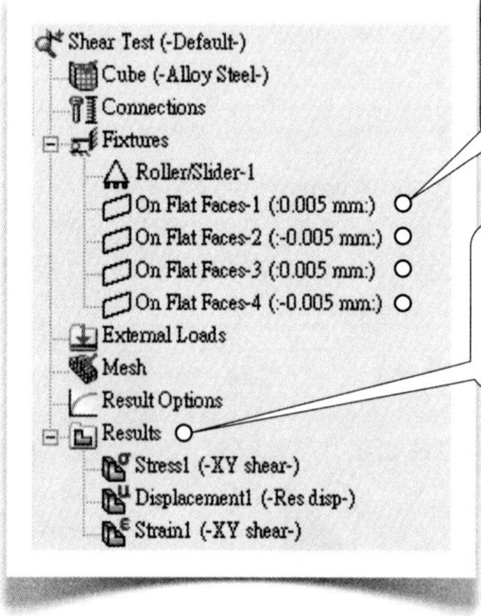

[3] Make sure the applied displacements are 0.005 mm. If they are not, change to 0.005 mm.

[4] Right-click **Results** and select **List Result Force...**

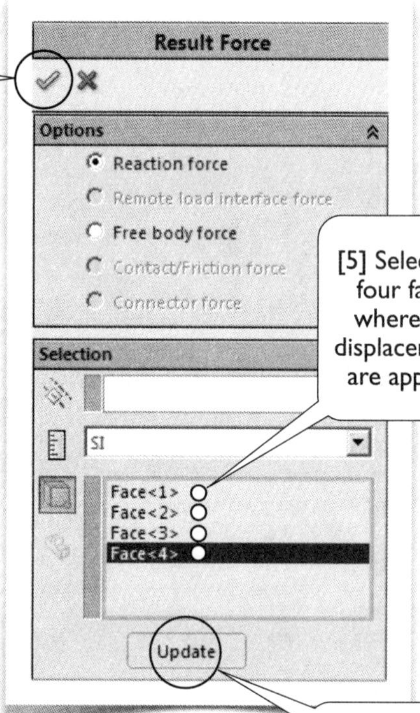

[5] Select the four faces where the displacements are applied.

[6] Click Update.

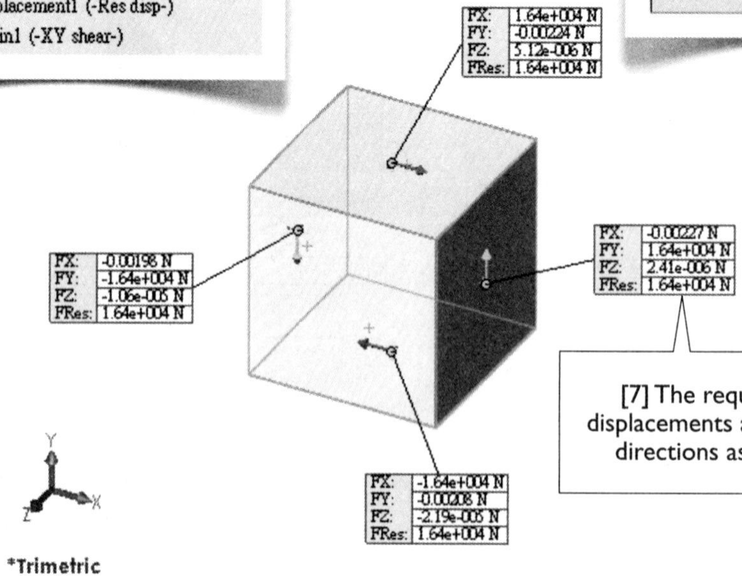

[7] The required forces for the applied displacements are 1.64×10^4 N with the same directions as the applied displacements.

Applied Displacement (mm)	Shear Stress (MPa)	Shear Strain (Dimensionless)
0.005	164.062	0.0020

[9] These stress and strain are directly taken from 4.2-4[23], page 86.

[10] Calculate Work Done, Strain Energy, and Strain Energy Density

The work done by the four applied displacements is

$$W = (\frac{1}{2} Force \cdot Displacement) \times 4 = \frac{1}{2}(1.64 \times 10^4 \text{ N}) \cdot (5 \times 10^{-6} \text{ m}) \times 4 = 0.164 \text{ J}$$

The total strain energy is $U = W = 0.164$ J. Since the cube is uniformly distorted, the strain energy density is uniform over the cube,

$$u_0 = \frac{U}{Volume} = \frac{0.164 \text{ J}}{(0.01 \text{ m})^3} = 1.64 \times 10^5 \text{ J/m}^3$$

The strain energy density can also be calculated using Eq. 9(1) (page 172) and the data in [9],

$$u_0 = \frac{1}{2}\tau_{XY}\gamma_{XY} = \frac{1}{2}(164.062 \times 10^6 \text{ Pa})(0.002) = 1.64 \times 10^5 \text{ J/m}^3$$

Note that, in this case, τ_{XY} is the only non-zero stress component, and γ_{XY} is the only non-zero strain component.

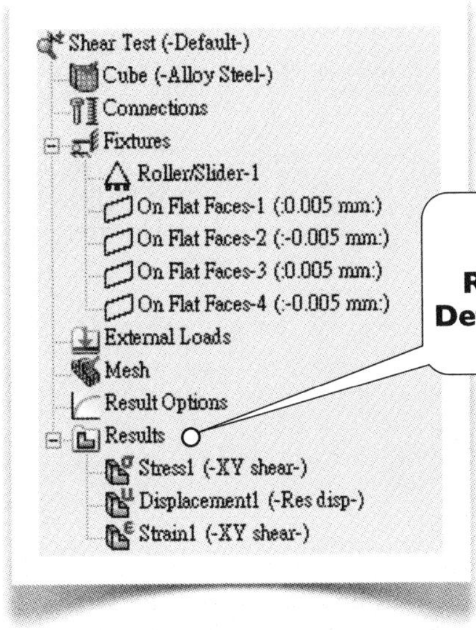

[11] Right-click **Results** and select **Define Strain Plot...**

[13] Click **OK**.

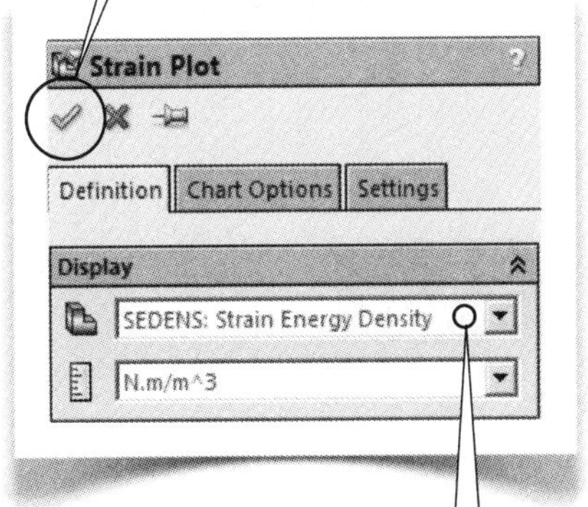

[12] Select **SEDENS: Strain Energy Density**.

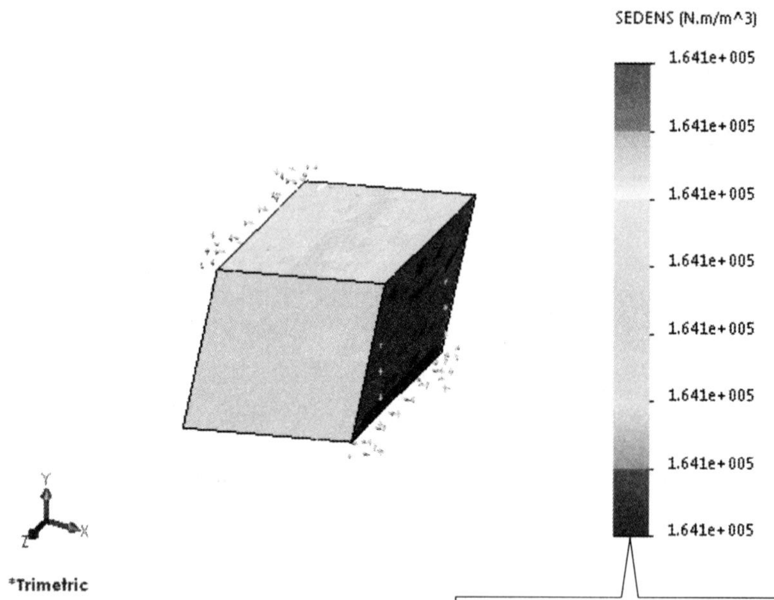

[14] The strain energy density is 1.641×10^5 J/m^3 uniformly distributed over the cube, consistent with the values calculated in [10].

[15] Save the document and exit **SolidWorks**. #

Section 9.2

Strain Energy in the C-Bar

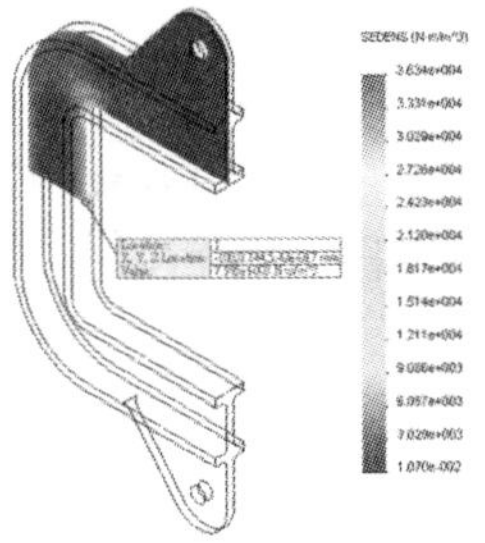

9.2-1 Introduction

In this section, we'll continue the exercises in Section 3.2. We'll verify the manually calculated strain energy density using Eq. 9(1) (page 172) with the values reported from the **Simulation**. The purpose of this section is that, through the exercises, the students have clear concepts of strain energy density in a more general case than in Section 9.1.

9.2-2 Calculate Strain Energy Density

Stress Component	Location **A**	Location **B**
σ_X	0	10.7111 Mpa
σ_Y	59.2488 MPa	23.2952 MPa
σ_Z	0	0
τ_{XY}	0	-20.2619 MPa
τ_{XZ}	0	0
τ_{YZ}	0	0

[1] This table of stress components is duplicated from 4.3-3[1], page 89.

Strain Component	Location **A**	Location **B**
ε_X	-0.00007902	0.00001996
ε_Y	0.0002821	0.00009667
ε_Z	-0.00007881	-0.00004541
γ_{XY}	0	-0.0002470
γ_{XZ}	0	0
γ_{YZ}	0	0

[2] This table of strain components is duplicated from 4.3-3[5], page 89.

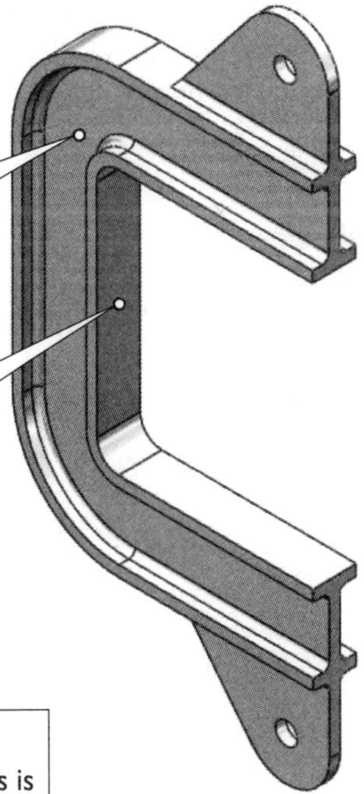

[4] This is location **B**.

[3] This is location **A**.

[5] Calculate Strain Energy Density at Location **A**

Using Eq. 9(1) (page 172) and the data in [1, 2], the strain energy density at location **A** (where the only non-zero stress component is σ_Y) is

$$u_0 = \frac{1}{2}\sigma_Y \varepsilon_Y = \frac{1}{2}(59.2488 \times 10^6 \text{ Pa})(0.0002821) = 8.357 \times 10^3 \text{ J/m}^3$$

[6] Calculate Strain Energy Density at Location **B**

Using Eq. 9(1) (page 172) and the data in [1, 2], the strain energy density at location **B** is

$$\begin{aligned} u_0 &= \frac{1}{2}\left(\sigma_X \varepsilon_X + \sigma_Y \varepsilon_Y + \tau_{XY}\gamma_{XY}\right) \\ &= \frac{1}{2}\left(10.7111 \times 0.00001996 + 23.2952 \times 0.00009667 + 20.2619 \times 0.0002470\right) \times 10^6 \\ &= 3.735 \times 10^3 \text{ J/m}^3 \end{aligned}$$

#

9.2-3 Obtain Strain Energy Density Using the **Simulation**

[1] Launch **SolidWorks** and open the file **Cbar**, which was saved in Section 3.2.

[2] Click **Static Force 2000 N**.

[3] The **Strain Energy Density** is not available with **Sensors**. We'll use **Section Clipping** method to obtain the **Strain Energy Density** at locations **A** and **B**.

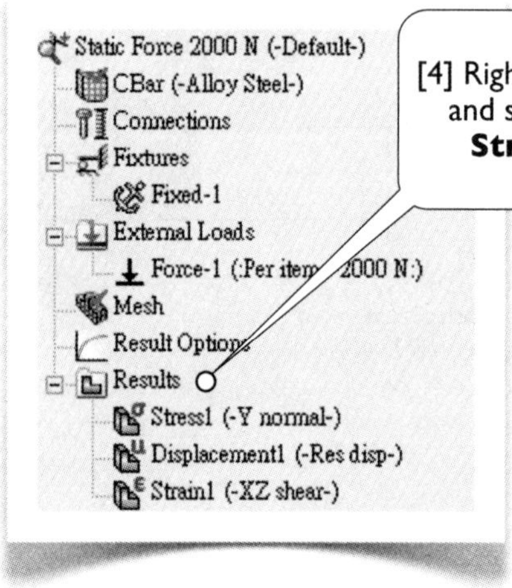

[4] Right-click **Results** and select **Define Strain Plot...**

[5] Select **SEDENS: Strain Energy Density**.

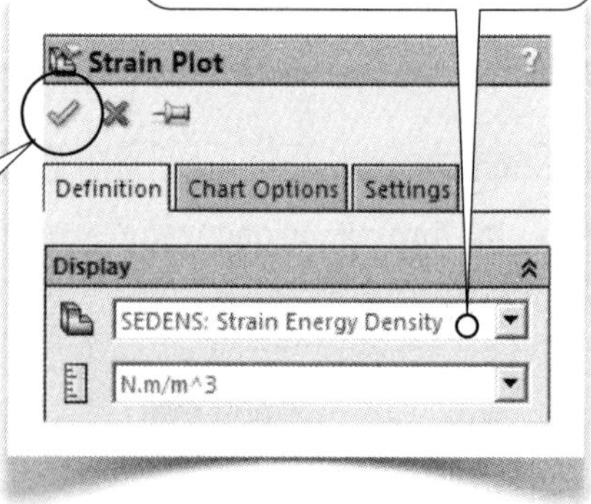

[6] Click **OK**.

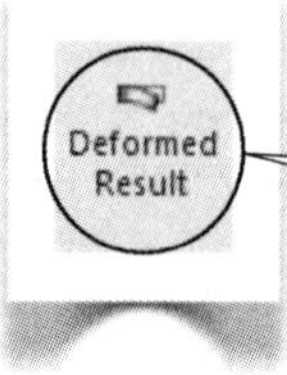

[7] Turn off **Deformed Results**. #

9.2-4 Strain Energy Density at Location **A**

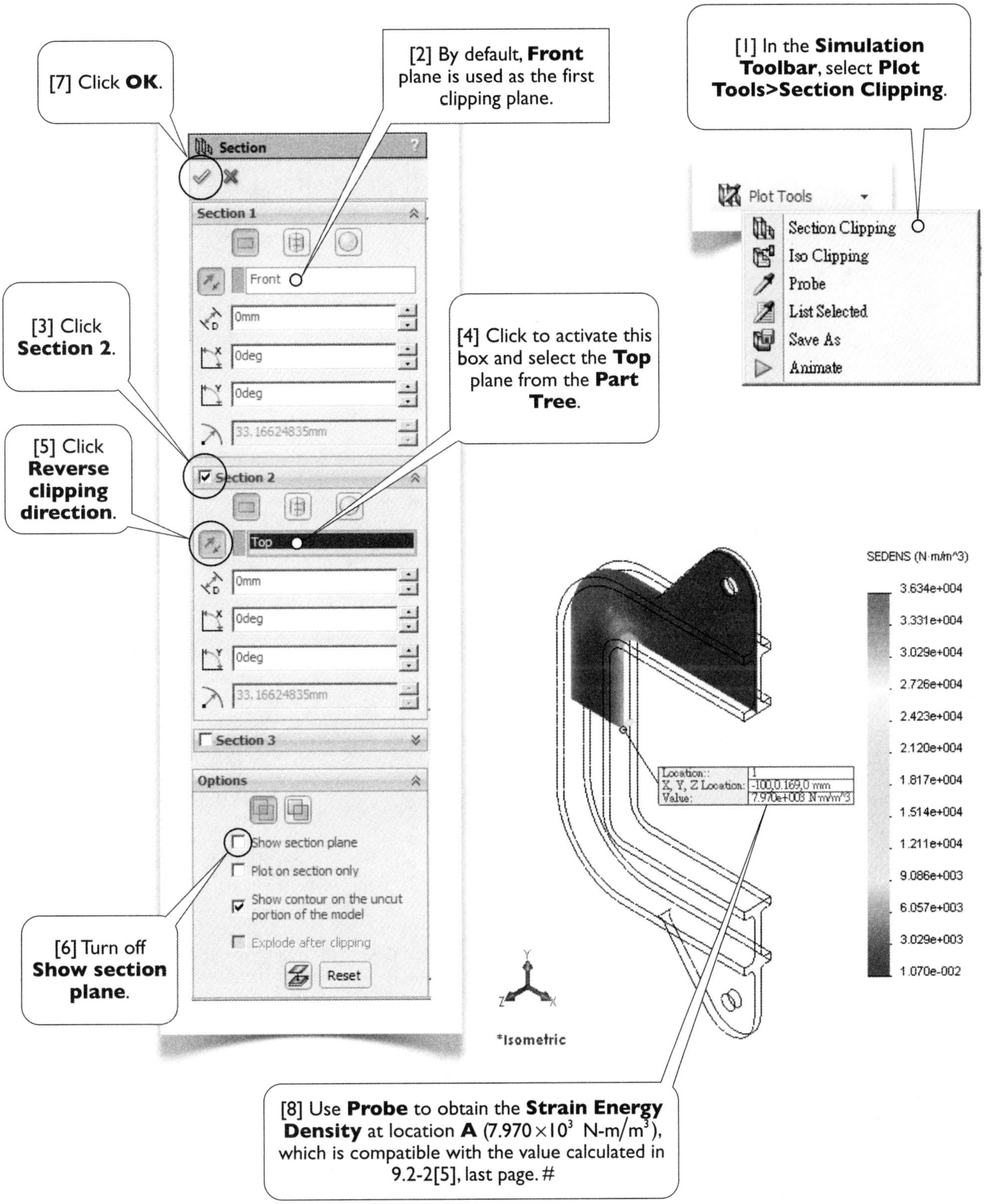

9.2-5 Strain Energy Density at Location **B**

[1] In the **Simulation Toolbar**, select **Plot Tools>Section Clipping**.

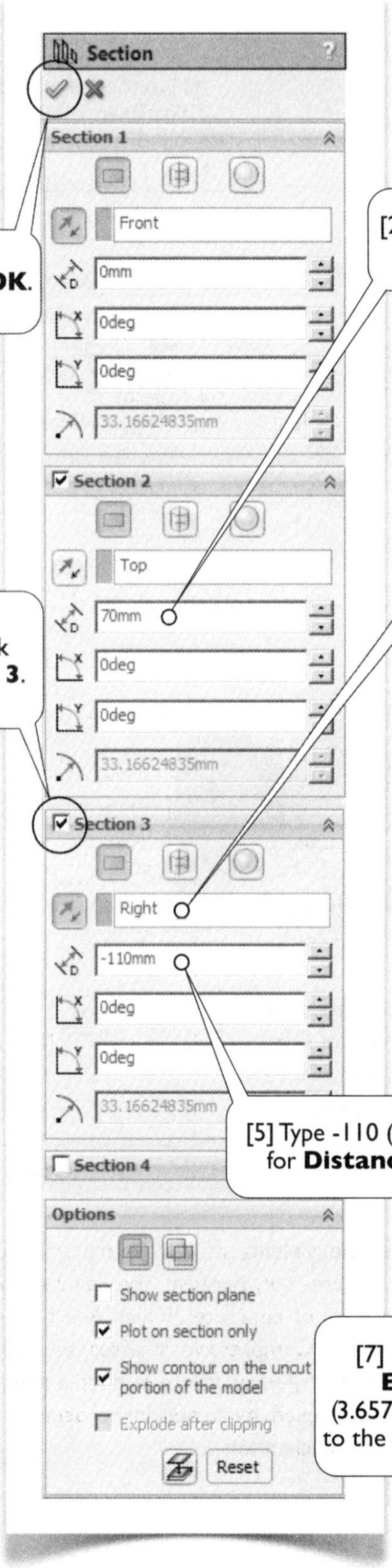

[2] Type 70 (mm) for **Distance**.

[3] Click **Section 3**.

[4] Click to activate this box and select the **Right** plane from the **Part Tree**.

[5] Type -110 (mm) for **Distance**.

[6] Click **OK**.

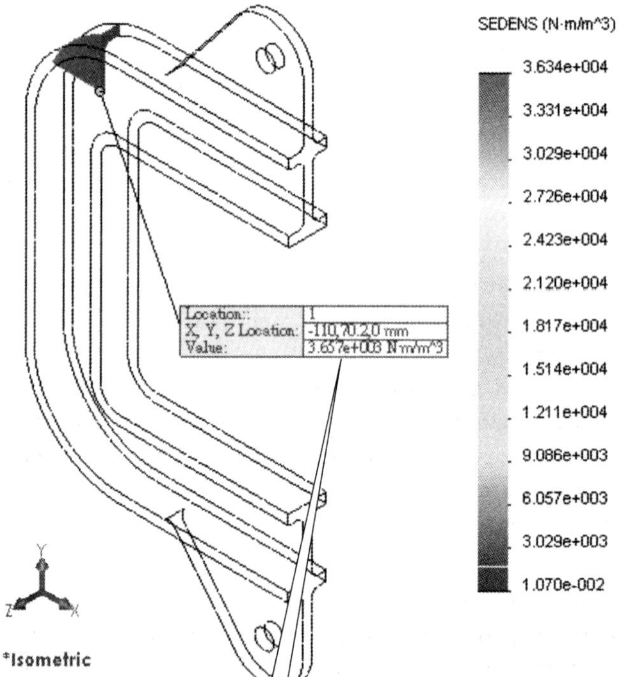

[7] Use **Probe** to obtain the **Strain Energy Density** at location **B** (3.657×10^3 N-m/m^3), which is compatible to the value calculated in 9.2-2[6], page 180.

[8] Save the document and exit **SolidWorks**. #

Chapter 10

Failure Criteria

After solving a model, we usually examine the stresses. Why are we interested in stresses? Why are stresses important? An obvious reason is that the material may fail when its stress reaches a certain critical stress value. The questions are: (a) What does it mean by **fail**? (b) What is the **critical** stress we want to compare with? (c) What **stress** do we need to examine? σ_X? σ_Y? σ_Z? τ_{XY}? τ_{YZ}? τ_{ZX}? or something else?

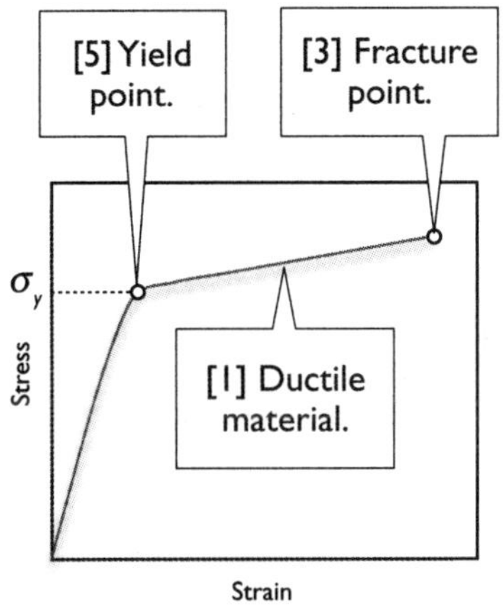

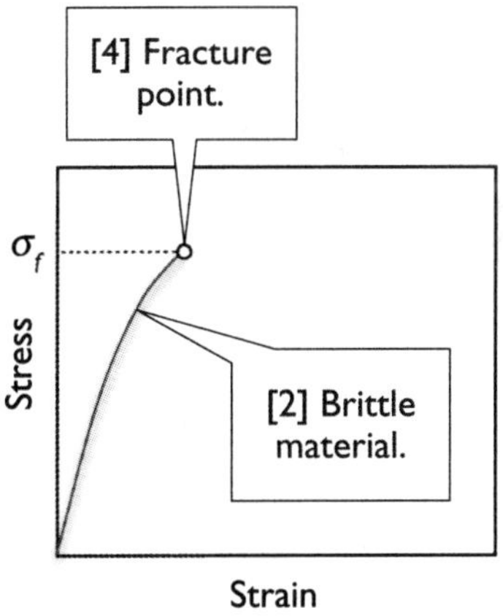

What does it mean by **fail**? What is the **critical** stress?

The stress-strain curve obtained from a uniaxial tensile test such as [1, 2] can determine the critical stress value. According to stress-strain curves, we may roughly classify materials into two categories: ductile materials and brittle materials. For a **ductile material** [1], the material exhibits a large amount of strain before it fractures [3] while, for a **brittle material** [2], the material's fracture strain is relatively small [4]. Fracture strain is a measure of **ductility**.

Mild steel is a typical ductile material. For ductile materials, there usually exists an obvious yield point [5], beyond which the deformation would be too large so that the material is no longer reliable or functional; the failure is accompanied by excess deformation. Therefore, a ductile material is regarded as failure when the stress (which'll be addressed further) reaches its yield point σ_y [5], which is the critical stress we want to compare with.

Glass and ceramics are examples of brittle materials. For brittle materials, there usually doesn't exist any obvious yield point. It fractures (breaks) before large deformation develops. Therefore, a brittle material fails when the stress (which'll be addressed further) reaches its fracture point σ_f [4], which is the critical stress we want to compare with.

What **stress** do we need to examine?

The fracture of brittle materials is mostly due to **tensile failure**; the yielding of ductile materials is mostly due to **shear failure**. The tensile failure of brittle material is easy to figure out, because the failure always occurs after cracking, which is due to tensile stresses. Note that, in a compressive test of concretes, which is a brittle material, the cracking of concrete is due to tensile stresses, not compressive stresses. Compressive stresses seldom directly cause materials failure; compression may cause structures buckle (see Chapter 14). The shear failure of ductile materials can be justified in a standard uniaxial tensile test, in which the failure is accompanied by a necking process and a cone-shape breaking surface. Also note that many materials fail due to a mix-up of both mechanisms.

From here, we may derive failure criteria for materials.

Section 10.1

Mohr's Circles and Stress Extrema

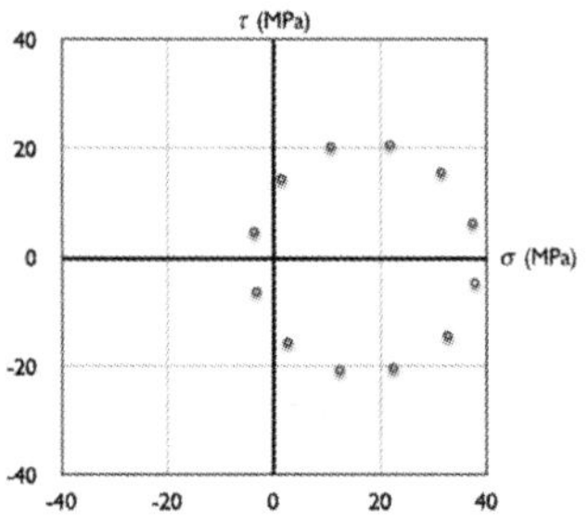

10.1-1 Introduction

[1] Mohr's circle, named after a German engineer Otto Mohr (1835-1918), is a graphical representation of a stress state. It is a useful concept in the study of Mechanics of Materials.

In this section, we'll revisit the C-Bar and arbitrarily select the location **B** [2] to study its stress state. In 1.3-16[5, 7] (page 50), we've listed the stress components [3, 4]. These stress components represent the stress state at that location, referring to a specific coordinate system. You shouldn't be surprised that if the reference coordinate system changes, the stress component values in turn change [5]. Keep in mind that, even the values change, they still represent the same **stress state** at that location. Thus, the numerical values of the stress components (σ_X, σ_Y, σ_Z, τ_{XY}, τ_{YZ}, τ_{ZX}) are coordinate system dependent. Now, you may raise a question: Can we rotate the coordinate system such that a normal stress, or a shear stress reaches its extrema (maximum or minimum)? The answer is yes. This section guide students to fully appreciate **Mohr's circles** and find these **stress extrema** from a Mohr's circle.

Stress Component	Stress Value
σ_X	10.7111 Mpa
σ_Y	23.2952 MPa
σ_Z	0
τ_{XY}	-20.2619 MPa
τ_{YZ}	0
τ_{ZX}	0

[3] This is duplicated from 1.3-16[5], page 50.

[5] If the reference coordinate system rotates, the stress component values also change. #

[4] This is duplicated from 1.3-16[7], page 50.

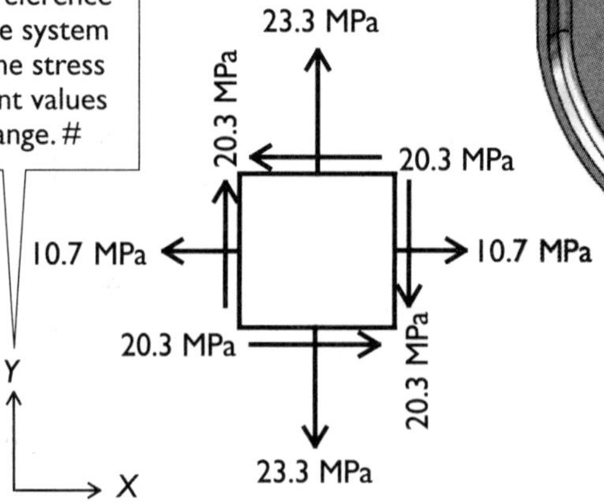

[2] This is location **B**.

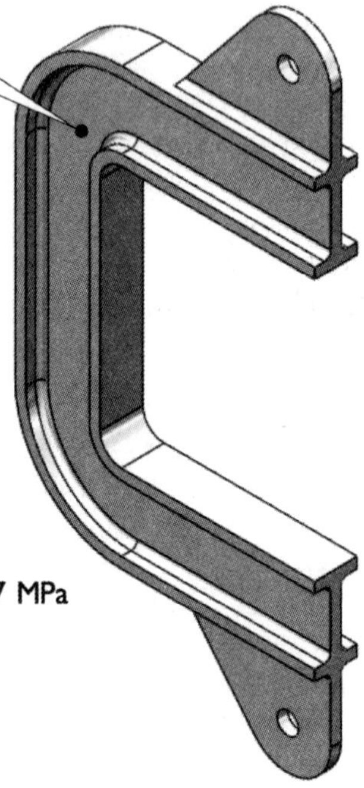

10.1-2 Plot the First Two Points in $\sigma - \tau$ Plane

[1] Constructing a Mohr's Circle

A Mohr's circle is constructed by plotting all possible stress pair (σ, τ) in a σ-τ space; each stress pair (σ, τ) is obtained by rotating the coordinate system a certain angle. Let's denote the original (global) X-direction as $\theta = 0^\circ$ [2]. With the stresses shown in 10.1-1[3, 4] (last page), we may plot two points in the σ-τ space: stress pairs at $\theta = 0^\circ$ and at $\theta = 90^\circ$. Note that θ is the the angle between the direction of the face the stresses acting on and the original X-direction.

Remember that when we represent the stress components (10.1-1[3]) in a cube (10.1-1[4]), we define the sign of stress as follows: For normal stresses, a positive normal stress tends to elongate the material while a negative normal stress tends to compress the material. For shear stresses on a positive face, a positive shear stress points to the positive direction while a negative shear stress points to the negative direction. For shear stresses on a negative face, a positive shear stress points to the negative direction while a negative shear stress points to the positive direction.

When constructing a Mohr's circle, the sign of normal stress is defined as usual. However, the sign of shear stresses is defined differently: a positive shear stress tends to rotate the material **clockwise** while a negative shear stress tends to rotate the material counterclockwise.

Following the above sign convention, we may plot two points in the σ-τ space: (+10.7, +20.3) [3, 4] and (+22.3, -20.3) [5, 6].

[5] At $\theta = 90^\circ, (\sigma, \tau)$ = (+23.3, -20.3)

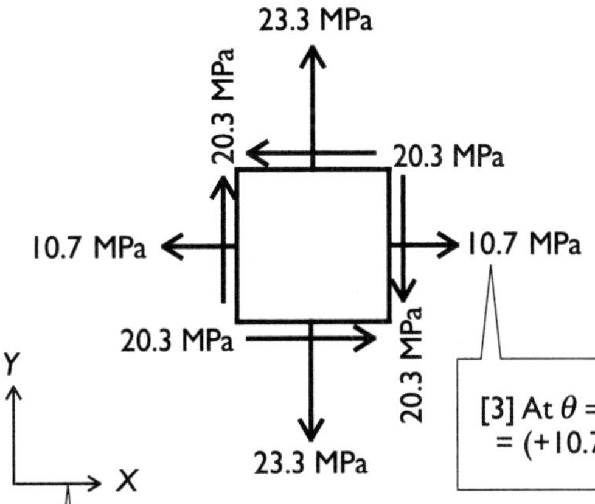

[3] At $\theta = 0^\circ, (\sigma, \tau)$ = (+10.7, +20.3)

[2] Let's denote the original X-direction as $\theta = 0^\circ$.

[4] (σ, τ) = (+10.7, +20.3) at $\theta = 0^\circ$.

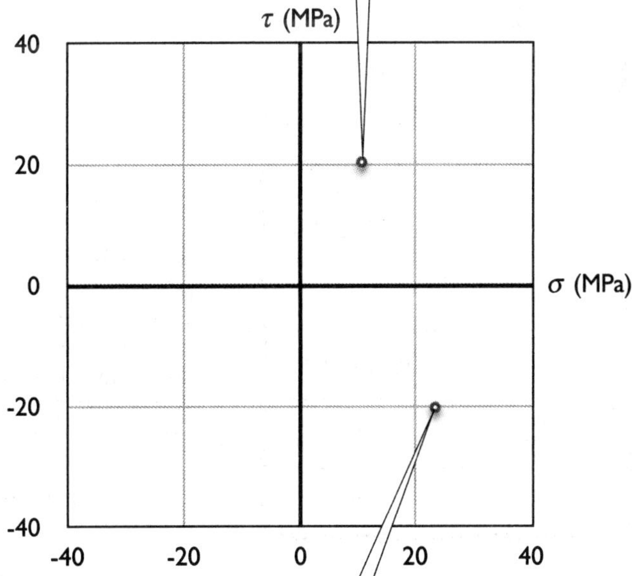

[6] (σ, τ) = (+23.3, -20.3) at $\theta = 90^\circ$. #

10.1-3 Start Up and Create a New Coordinate System

[1] Launch **SolidWorks** and open the file **CBar** which was saved in Section 9.2.

[2] Make sure that **Model** is active.

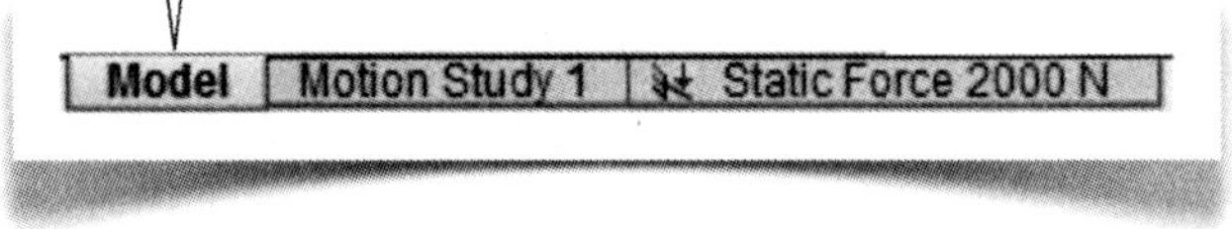

[4] We will use this line to define the X-axis of a local coordinate system.

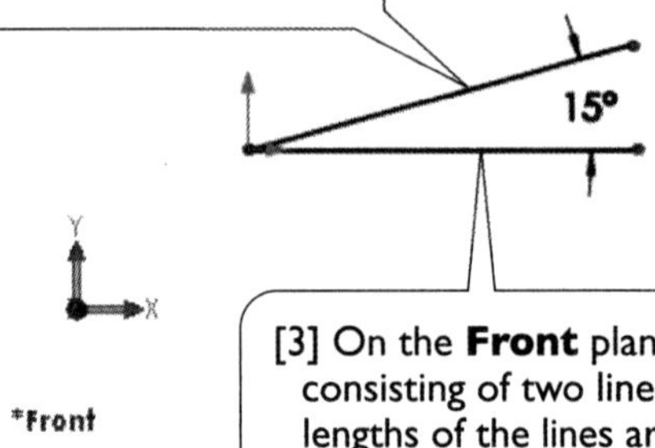

[3] On the **Front** plane, draw a sketch consisting of two lines like this. The lengths of the lines are not relevant. Remember to click **Exit Sketch**.

[5] From the **Head-Up Toolbar**, turn on **View Sketches**, so that the lines is selectable.

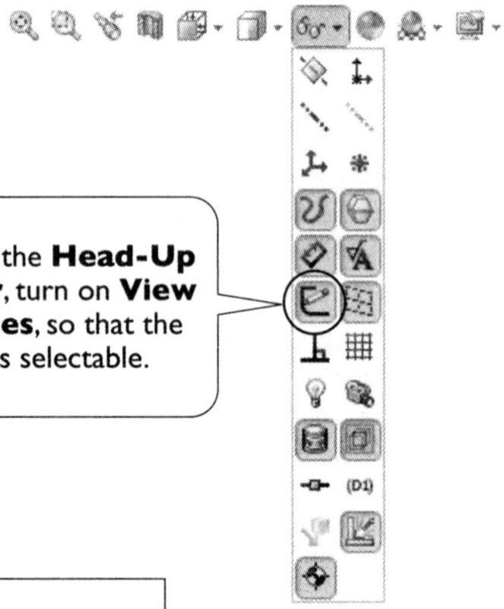

[6] In the **Features Toolbar**, select **Reference Geometry>Coordinate System**.

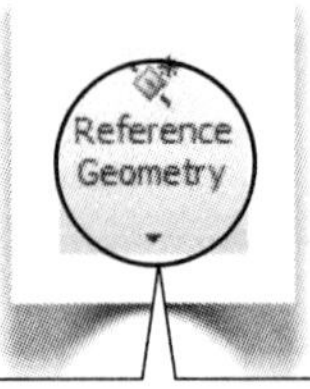

[7] In the **Part Tree**, select **Origin**.

[8] On the **Graphics Area**, select the line shown in [4] as **X axis**.

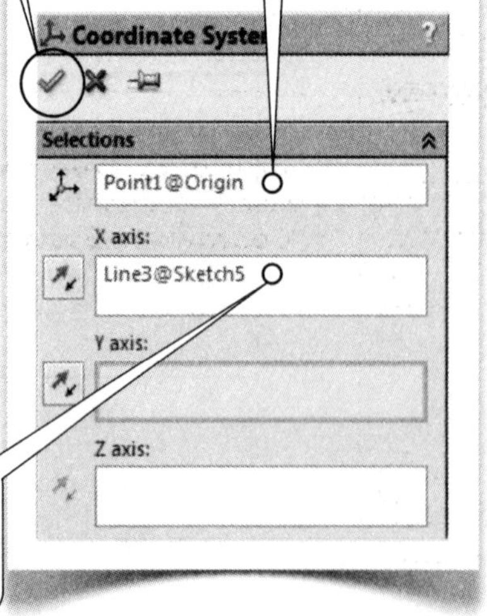

[9] This is the new coordinate system.

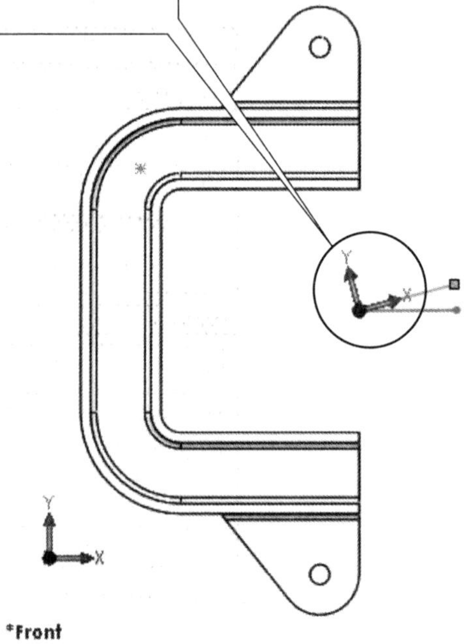

[10] Click **OK**. #

10.1-4 Obtain the Stress Components at $\theta = 15^{\circ}$

[1] Click to activate **Static Force 2000 N**.

[2] In the **Simulation Toolbar**, click **Run**. Since we've modified the model, we need to rerun the model.

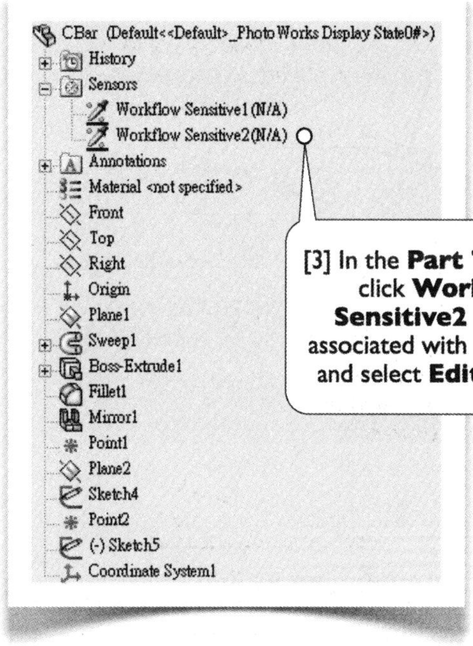

[3] In the **Part Tree**, right-click **Workflow Sensitive2** (which is associated with location **B**) and select **Edit Sensor**.

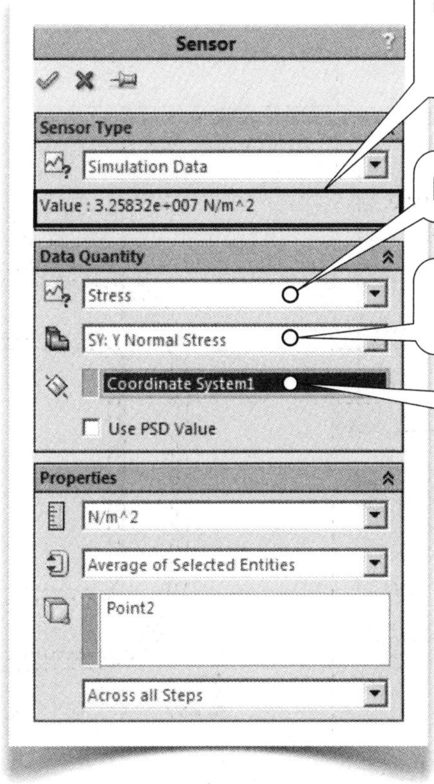

[4] Select **Stress**.

[5] Select a stress component.

[6] In **Part Tree**, select the new coordinate system (**Coordinate System1**).

[7] The sensor reports the stress component value here.

[12] At $\theta = 105^\circ, (\sigma, \tau)$ = (+32.6, -14.4).

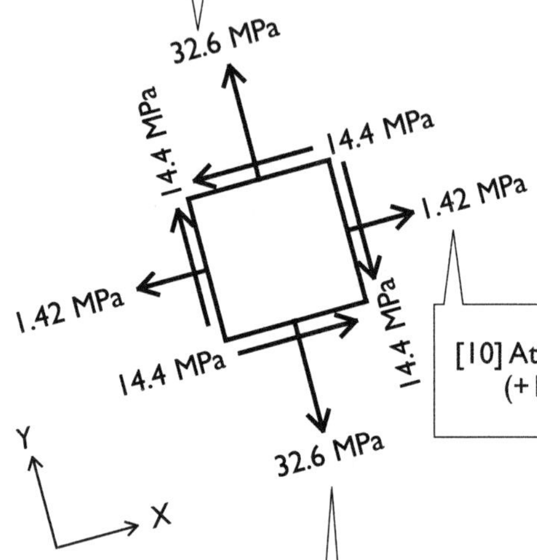

[10] At $\theta = 15^\circ, (\sigma, \tau)$ = (+1.42, +14.4).

[9] These are the stress components when the coordinate system rotates 15°.

Stress Component	Stress Value
σ_X	1.42 Mpa
σ_Y	32.6 MPa
σ_Z	0
τ_{XY}	-14.4 MPa
τ_{YZ}	0
τ_{ZX}	0

[8] Select each stress component [5] and record its value [7].

[11] At $\theta = 15^\circ, (\sigma, \tau)$ = (+1.42, +14.4)

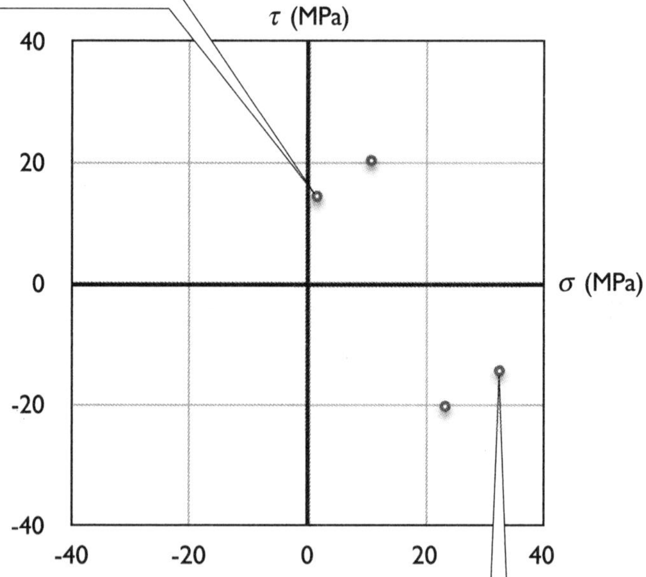

[13] At $\theta = 105^\circ, (\sigma, \tau)$ = (+32.6, -14.4). #

10.1-5 Obtain the Stress Components at $\theta = 30^\circ$

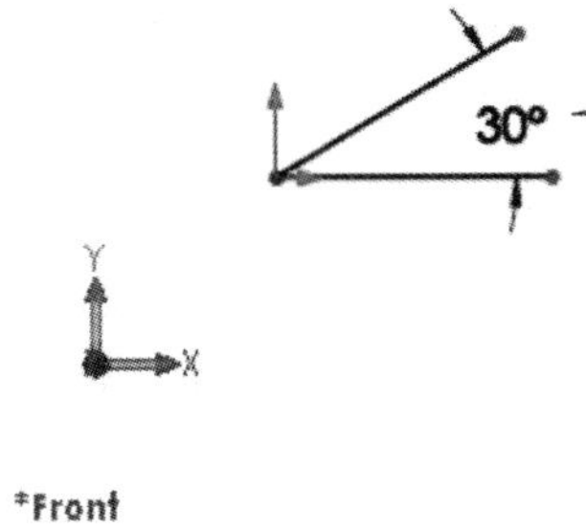

[1] Edit the sketch (**Sketch5**) and change the angle to 30°. Remember to click **Exit Sketch**.

[2] Rerun the model.

[3] Follow the steps in 10.1-4[3-7] (page 187) to obtain the stress components.

Stress Component	Stress Value
σ_X	-3.69 Mpa
σ_Y	37.7 MPa
σ_Z	0
τ_{XY}	-4.68 MPa
τ_{YZ}	0
τ_{ZX}	0

[7] At $\theta = 120^\circ, (\sigma, \tau)$ = (+37.7, -4.68)

[5] At $\theta = 30^\circ, (\sigma, \tau)$ = (-3.69, +4.68)

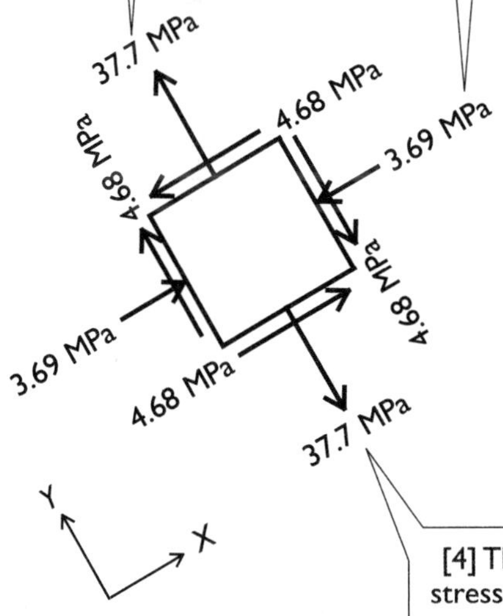

[4] These are the stress components when the coordinate system rotates 30°.

[6] At $\theta = 30^\circ, (\sigma, \tau)$ = (-3.69, +4.68)

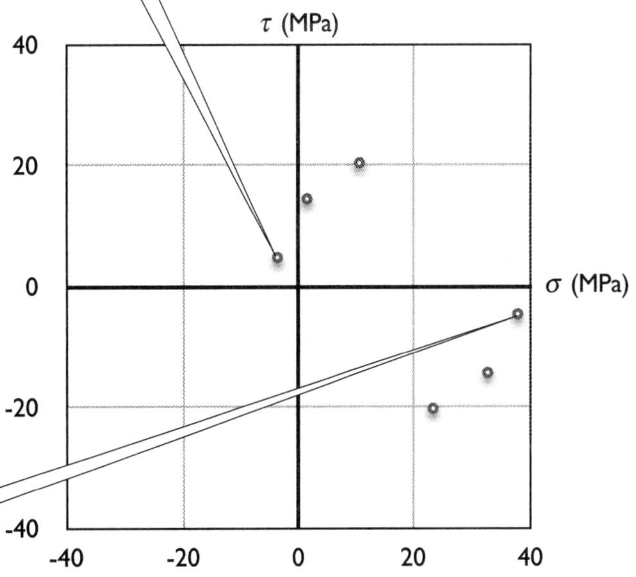

[8] At $\theta = 120^\circ, (\sigma, \tau)$ = (+37.7, -4.68). #

10.1-6 Obtain the Stress Components at $\theta = 45^\circ$

[1] Edit the sketch and change the angle to 45° Remember to click **Exit Sketch**.

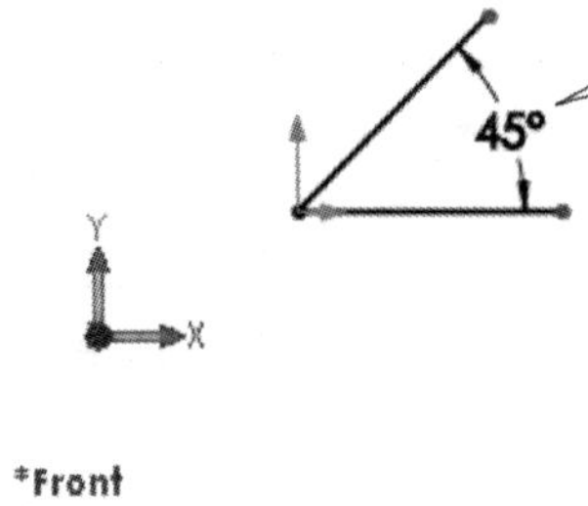

[2] Rerun the model.

[3] Follow the steps in 10.1-4[3-7] (page 187) to obtain the stress components.

Stress Component	Stress Value
σ_X	-3.26 Mpa
σ_Y	37.3 MPa
σ_Z	0
τ_{XY}	6.29 MPa
τ_{YZ}	0
τ_{ZX}	0

[7] At $\theta = 135^\circ, (\sigma, \tau)$ = (+37.3, +6.29)

[5] At $\theta = 45^\circ, (\sigma, \tau)$ = (-3.26, -6.29)

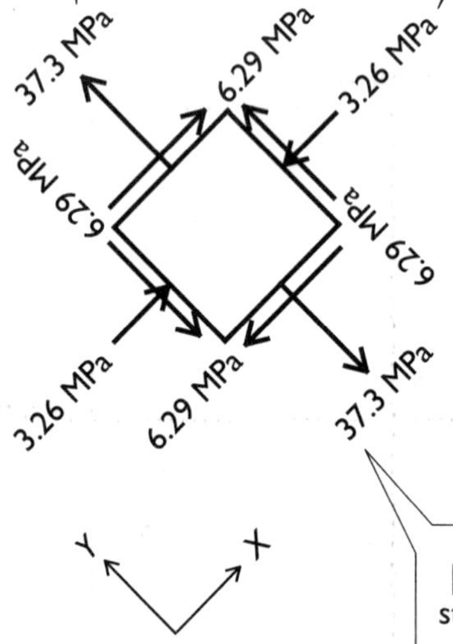

[4] These are the stress components when the coordinate system rotates 45°.

[6] At $\theta = 45^\circ, (\sigma, \tau)$ = (-3.26, -6.29)

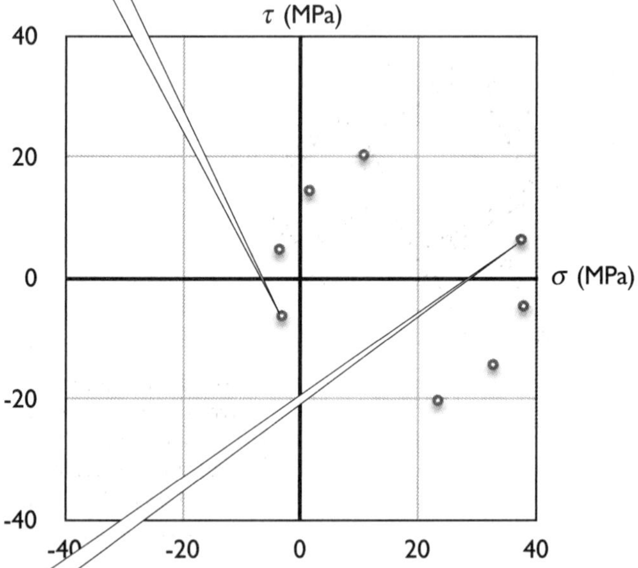

[8] At $\theta = 135^\circ, (\sigma, \tau)$ = (+37.3, +6.29). #

10.1-7 Obtain the Stress Components at $\theta = 60^\circ$

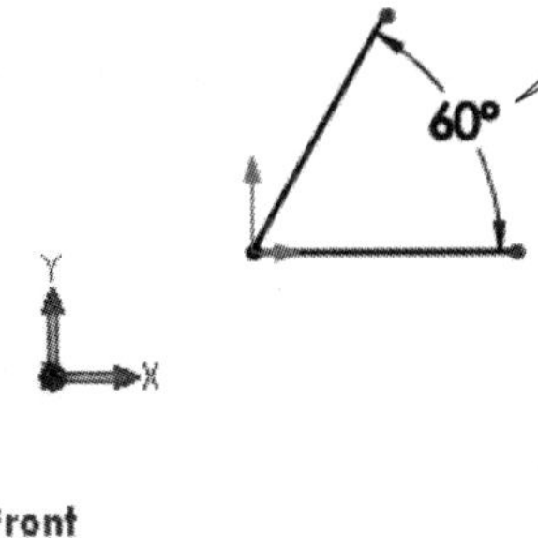

[1] Edit the sketch and change the angle to 60°. Remember to click **Exit Sketch**.

[2] Rerun the model.

[3] Follow the steps in 10.1-4[3-7] (page 187) to obtain the stress components.

Stress Component	Stress Value
σ_X	2.60 Mpa
σ_Y	31.4 MPa
σ_Z	0
τ_{XY}	15.6 MPa
τ_{YZ}	0
τ_{ZX}	0

[7] At $\theta = 150^\circ, (\sigma, \tau)$ = (+31.4, +15.6)

[5] At $\theta = 60^\circ, (\sigma, \tau)$ = (+2.60, -15.6)

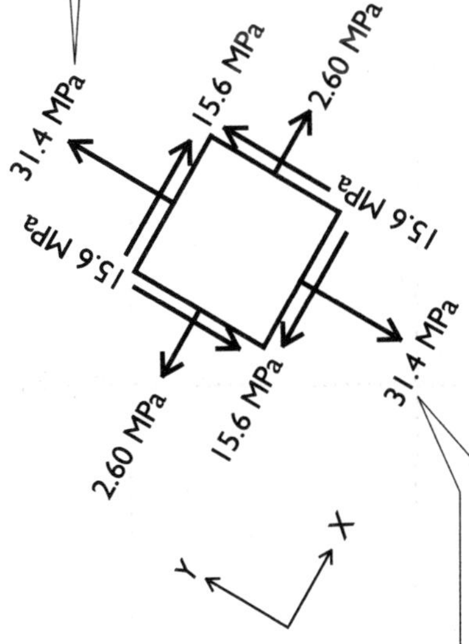

[4] These are the stress components when the coordinate system rotates 60°.

[8] At $\theta = 150^\circ, (\sigma, \tau)$ = (+31.4, +15.6). #

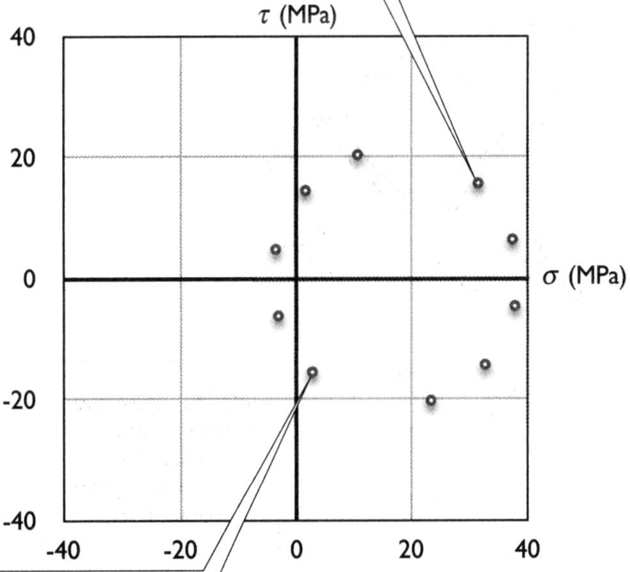

[6] At $\theta = 60^\circ, (\sigma, \tau)$ = (+2.60, -15.6)

10.1-8 Obtain the Stress Components at $\theta = 75^\circ$

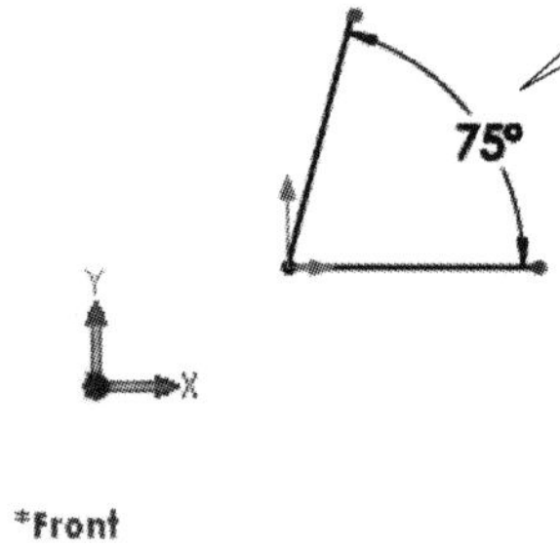

[1] Edit the sketch and change the angle to 75°. Remember to click **Exit Sketch**.

[3] Follow the steps in 10.1-4[3-7] (page 187) to obtain the stress components.

Stress Component	Stress Value
σ_X	12.3 Mpa
σ_Y	21.7 MPa
σ_Z	0
τ_{XY}	-20.7 MPa
τ_{YZ}	0
τ_{ZX}	0

[2] Rerun the model.

[5] At $\theta = 75^\circ, (\sigma, \tau)$ = (+12.3, -20.7)

[7] At $\theta = 165^\circ, (\sigma, \tau)$ = (+21.7, +20.7)

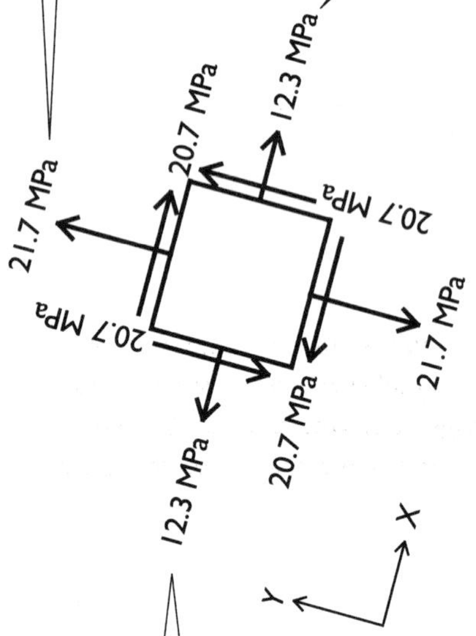

[4] These are the stress components when the coordinate system rotates 75°.

[8] At $\theta = 165^\circ, (\sigma, \tau)$ = (+21.7, +20.7). #

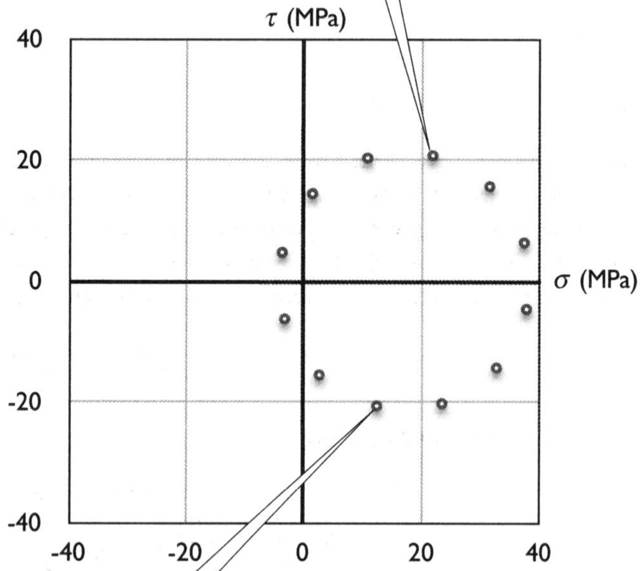

[6] At $\theta = 75^\circ, (\sigma, \tau)$ = (+12.3, -20.7)

10.1-9 Mohr's Circle

[1] Mohr's Circle

If we connect all (σ, τ) points, they form a circle, called a **Mohr's circle** [2]. The foregoing exercises also conclude that as we rotate the coordinate system 15°, the (σ, τ) point rotates 30° along the Mohr's circle with the same direction [3]. In general, as the coordinate system rotates an angle θ, the stress pair (σ, τ) rotates 2θ around the Mohr's circle with the same direction.

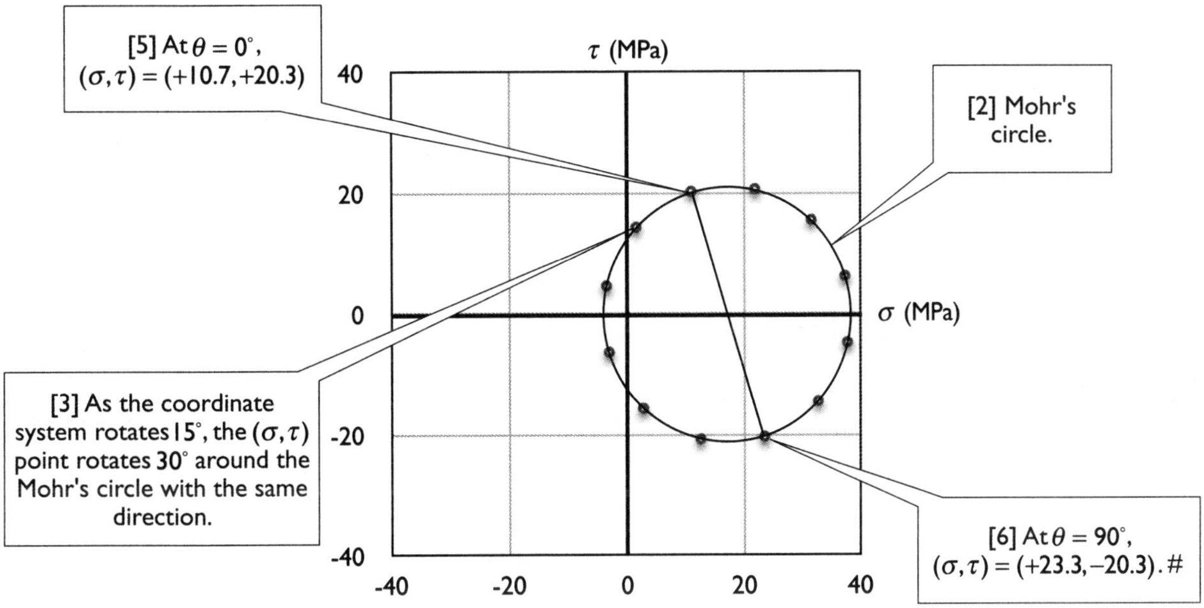

[4] Use of Mohr's Circles

A Mohr's circle represents a stress state at a specific location. The usefulness of the Mohr's circle is that *if we know the stress components in a coordinate system, then we can calculate the stress components in any other coordinate system.* For example, given the stress components in a coordinate system shown in 10.1-1[5] (page 184), where $\sigma_X = 10.7$ MPa, $\sigma_Y = 23.3$ MPa, $\tau_{XY} = -20.3$ MPa and are marked in the σ-τ space as [5, 6], we have enough information to construct a Mohr's circle, as follows. The center of the Mohr's circle is at $(\sigma, \tau) = (\sigma_{ave}, 0)$, where

$$\sigma_{ave} = \frac{\sigma_X + \sigma_Y}{2} = \frac{10.7 + 23.3}{2} = 17.0 \text{ MPa} \tag{1}$$

The radius of the Mohr's circle is

$$R = \sqrt{\left(\frac{\sigma_X - \sigma_Y}{2}\right)^2 + \tau_{XY}^2} = \sqrt{\left(\frac{10.7 - 23.3}{2}\right)^2 + 20.3^2} = 21.3 \text{ MPa} \tag{2}$$

With a center location and a radius, a Mohr's circle can be constructed and stress components in any coordinate system can be calculated.

10.1-10 Stress Extrema

[1] The quadrant points [2-5] of a Mohr's circle are where the stress extrema occur. The maximum/minimum normal stresses are respectively

$$\sigma_{max} = \sigma_{ave} + R = 17.0 + 21.3 = 38.3 \text{ MPa} \quad (1)$$

$$\sigma_{min} = \sigma_{ave} - R = 17.0 - 21.3 = -4.3 \text{ MPa} \quad (2)$$

These extremum normal stresses are called **principal stresses** (Section 10.2). The maximum shear stress is

$$\tau_{max} = R = 21.3 \text{ MPa} \quad (3)$$

The next question is: What is the direction of these extrema? i.e., $\theta = ?$ As mentioned, the rotation in the Mohr's circle is twice as the rotation of the coordinate system. Let θ_p be the angle of rotation of the coordinate system so that the **maximum principal stress** occurs [2], then

$$\sin(2\theta_p) = \frac{\tau_{XY}}{R} \quad (4)$$

In this case,

$$2\theta_p = \sin^{-1}\frac{\tau_{XY}}{R} = \sin^{-1}\frac{20.3}{21.3} = 107.6^\circ,\ \theta_p = 53.8^\circ \quad (5)$$

Note that the rotation is clockwise [6]. The maximum shear stress occurs when the coordinate system rotates

$$2\theta_s = 2\theta_p - 90^\circ = 107.6^\circ - 90^\circ = 17.6^\circ,\ \theta_s = 8.8^\circ \quad (6)$$

The rotation is also clockwise [7].

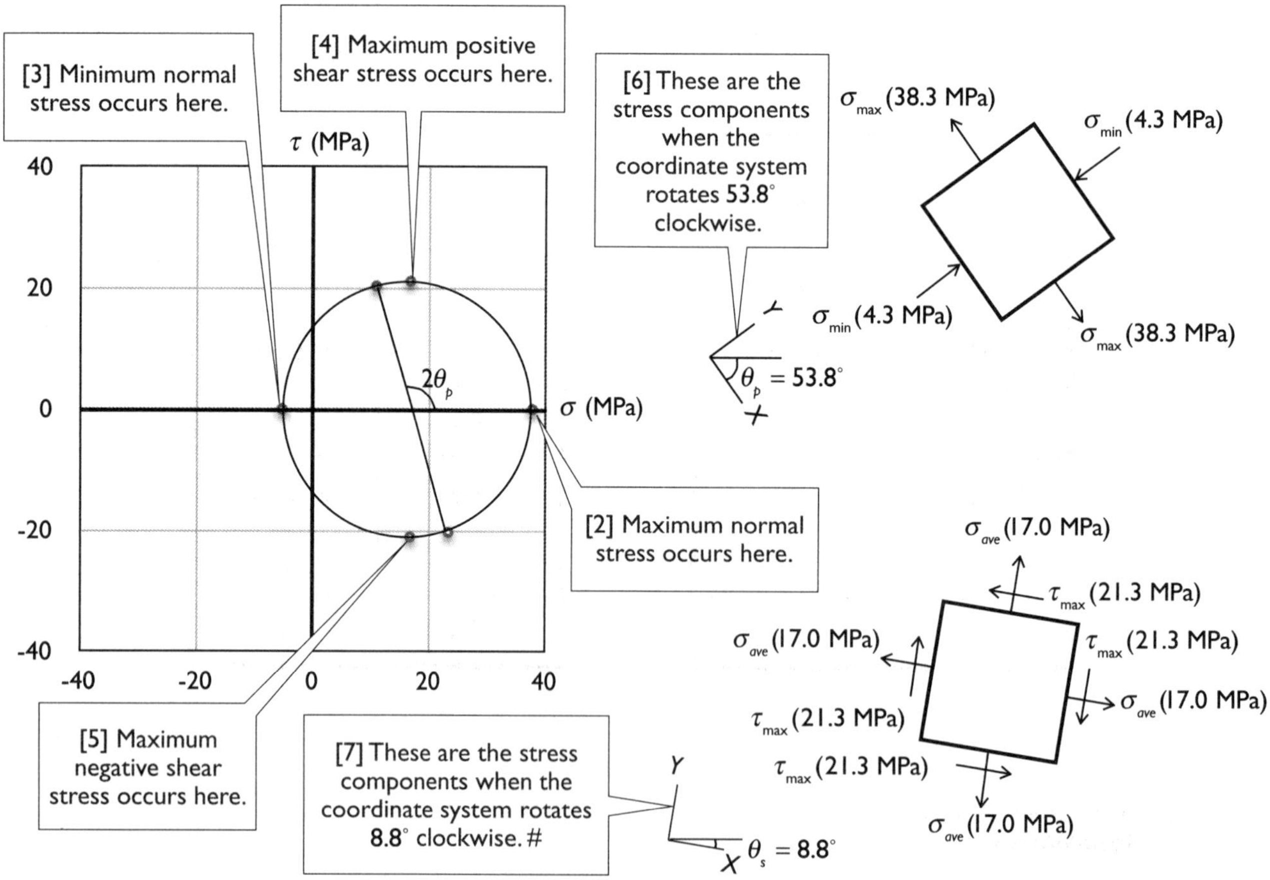

10.1-11 Further Exercises

[1] Do It Yourself

1. Rotate the coordinate system 53.8° clockwise, rerun the model, and obtain all the stress components [2, 3]. Compare the results with those in 10.1-10[6], last page. They are comparable.
2. Rotate the coordinate system 8.8° clockwise, rerun the model, and obtain all the stress components [4, 5]. Compare the results with those in 10.1-10[7], last page. They are comparable.

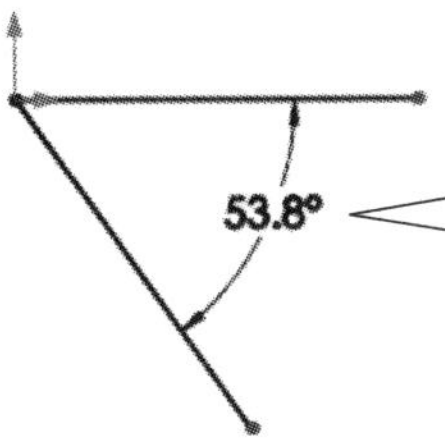

[2] Type -53.8 (deg) for the angle.

[4] Type 8.8 (deg) for the angle.

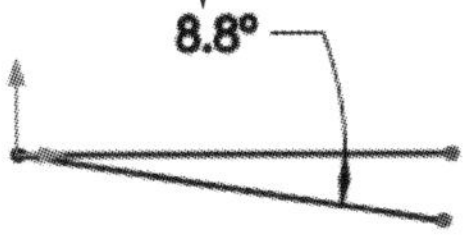

[3] These are the stress components when the coordinate system rotates 53.8 degrees clockwise.

Stress Component	Stress Value
σ_X	38.2 Mpa
σ_Y	-4.2 MPa
σ_Z	0
τ_{XY}	0
τ_{YZ}	0
τ_{ZX}	0

[5] These are the stress components when the coordinate system rotates 8.8 degrees clockwise.

Stress Component	Stress Value
σ_X	17.1 Mpa
σ_Y	16.9 MPa
σ_Z	0
τ_{XY}	-21.2 MPa
τ_{YZ}	0
τ_{ZX}	0

[4] Save the document and exit **SolidWorks**. #

Section 10.2

Principal Stress, Stress Intensity, and von Mises Stress

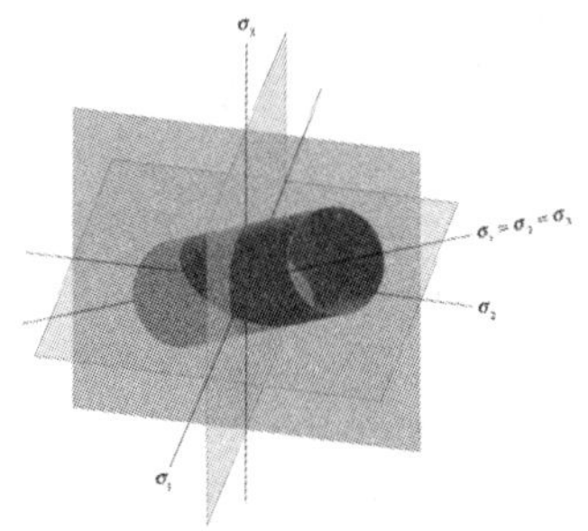

10.2-1 Introduction

[1] Principal Stresses

In 10.1-10[6] (page 194), when we rotate the coordinate system 53.8 degrees clockwise, all shear stress components vanish ($\tau_{XY} = \tau_{YZ} = \tau_{ZX} = 0$), and the three normal stresses reach their extrema. They are called **principal stresses** for that stress state. The maximum principal stress is denoted by σ_1, the middle principal stress by σ_2, and the minimum principal stress by σ_3. The example in Section 10.1 is a special case, called a **plane stress** case, in which one of the principal stress is zero ($\sigma_2 = \sigma_Z = 0$). In a general case, it is possible to rotate a coordinate system such that all shear stress components vanish ($\tau_{XY} = \tau_{YZ} = \tau_{ZX} = 0$) and the three principal stresses are non-zero.

[2] Failure Criterion for Brittle Materials

As mentioned in page 183, the failure of brittle materials is due to fracture (rather than yielding) and the fracture is due to an excessive tensile stress. Therefore, we may establish a failure criterion for brittle materials as follows: At a certain point of a body, if the **maximum principal stress** reaches the **fracture tensile strength** σ_f (which may be obtained from a uniaxial tensile test) of the material, it will fail due to fracture. In short, a point of material fails if

$$\sigma_1 \geq \sigma_f \quad (1)$$

[3] Tresca Criterion for Ductile Materials

Also mentioned in page 183, the failure of ductile materials is initiated by a yielding and the yielding is due to an excessive shear stress. Therefore, we may establish a failure criterion for ductile materials as follows: At a certain point of a body, if the **maximum shear stress** reaches the **yielding shear strength** τ_y of the material, it will fail. In short, a point of material fails if

$$\tau_{max} \geq \tau_y \quad (2)$$

The right-hand-side τ_y can be obtained from a uniaxial tensile test. In a uniaxial tensile test, when the yielding occurs, the stress state is shown in [4], therefore

$$\tau_y = \frac{\sigma_y}{2} \quad (3)$$

and Eq. (2) can be rewritten as

$$\tau_{max} \geq \frac{\sigma_y}{2} \quad (4)$$

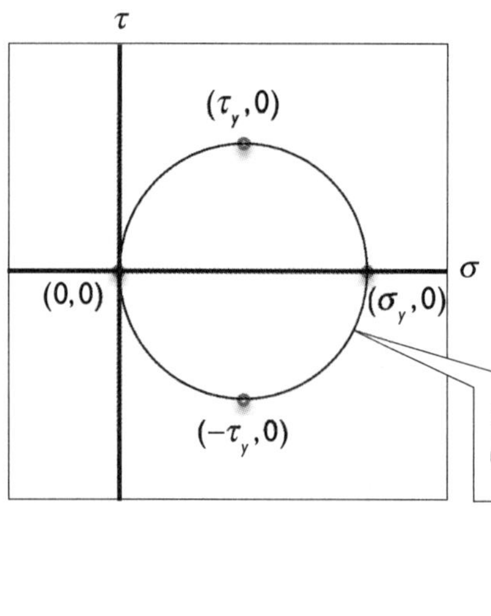

[4] This is the Mohr's circle (stress state) in a uniaxial tensile test when the yielding occurs.

[5] Tresca Criterion for Ductile Materials: Stress Intensity

The left-hand-side of Eq. (4) is related to the maximum principal stress σ_1 and the minimum principal stress σ_3 as

$$\tau_{max} = \frac{\sigma_1 - \sigma_3}{2} \tag{5}$$

Substitution of (5) into (4) yields

$$\frac{\sigma_1 - \sigma_3}{2} \geq \frac{\sigma_y}{2}$$

or

$$\sigma_1 - \sigma_3 \geq \sigma_y \tag{6}$$

The quantity on the left-hand-side $(\sigma_1 - \sigma_3)$ is called the **stress intensity**. The criterion (6) is called the **Tresca criterion**, first proposed by Henri Tresca (1814-1885), a French mechanical engineer, in 1864.

[6] Von Mises Criterion for Ductile Materials

A more sophisticated theory, called **von Mises criterion**, often predicts yielding of metals more accurately than Tresca criteria, Eq. (6). The von Mises theory is also based on shear failure, but derived from an energy consideration. The von Mises criterion states that a point of material yields (fails) if its **distortion energy** reaches the material's **yielding distortion energy**. A detailed account of the theory is presented at the end of this section as an Appendix (10.2-3, pages 200-203). Here, we simply summarize the criterion as follows: a point of material yields if

$$\sqrt{\frac{1}{2}\left[(\sigma_1 - \sigma_2)^2 + (\sigma_2 - \sigma_3)^2 + (\sigma_3 - \sigma_1)^2\right]} \geq \sigma_y \tag{7}$$

The quantity on the left-hand-side is called **von Mises stress**, or **equivalent stress** (also called **effective stress** in some books),

$$\sigma_e = \sqrt{\frac{1}{2}\left[(\sigma_1 - \sigma_2)^2 + (\sigma_2 - \sigma_3)^2 + (\sigma_3 - \sigma_1)^2\right]} \tag{8}$$

[7] Purpose of This Section

We'll continue the exercises of Section 10.1 and obtain the **principal stresses** $(\sigma_1, \sigma_2, \sigma_3)$, **stress intensity**, and **von Mises stress** (these are **coordinate system independent stresses**), which will be verified with the following values. The principal stresses, from Eqs. 10.1-10(1, 2), page 194,

$$\sigma_1 = 38.3 \text{ MPa}, \ \sigma_2 = 0, \ \sigma_3 = -4.3 \text{ MPa} \tag{9}$$

The stress intensity,

$$\sigma_{SI} = \sigma_1 - \sigma_3 = 38.3 - (-4.3) = 42.6 \text{ MPa} \tag{10}$$

The von Mises stress,

$$\begin{aligned}\sigma_e &= \sqrt{\frac{1}{2}\left[(\sigma_1 - \sigma_2)^2 + (\sigma_2 - \sigma_3)^2 + (\sigma_3 - \sigma_1)^2\right]} \\ &= \sqrt{\frac{1}{2}\left[(38.3 - 0)^2 + (0 + 4.3)^2 + (-4.3 - 38.3)^2\right]} \\ &= 40.6 \text{ MPa}\end{aligned} \tag{11}$$

#

10.2-2 Open CBar and Obtain Stresses

[1] Launch **SolidWorks** and open the file **CBar** which was saved in Section 10.1.

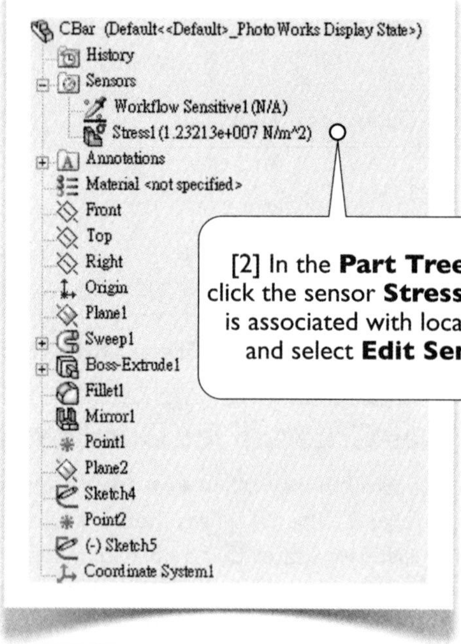

[2] In the **Part Tree**, right-click the sensor **Stress1** (which is associated with location **B**) and select **Edit Sensor**.

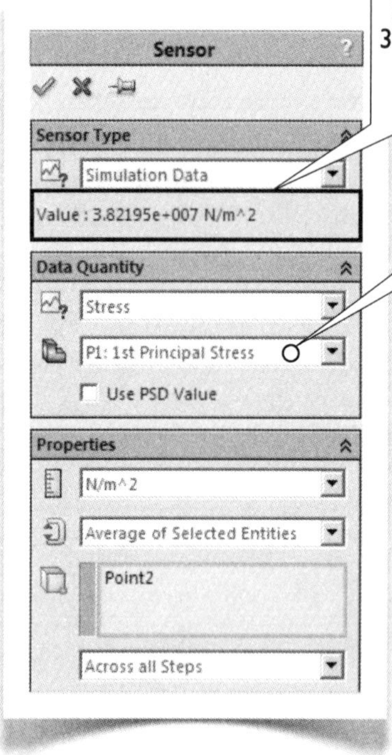

[3] Select **P1: 1st Principal Stress**.

[4] The reported value is 38.2 MPa, which is close to the value (38.3 MPa) in 10.2-1(9), last page.

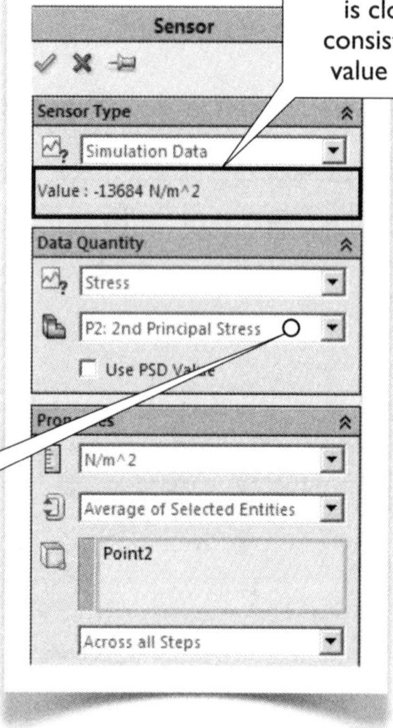

[5] Select **P2: 2nd Principal Stress**.

[6] The reported value is close to zero, consistent with the value in 10.2-1(9).

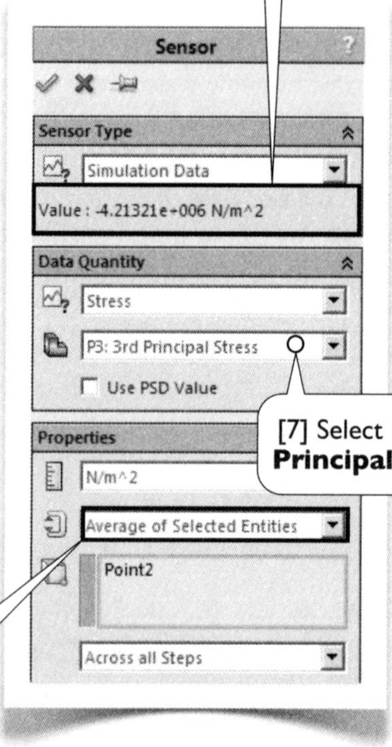

[7] Select **P3: 3rd Principal Stress**.

[8] Make sure **Average of Selected Entities** is selected. Sometimes it changes to other settings.

[9] The reported value is -4.2 MPa, which is close to the value (-4.3 MPa) in 10.2-1(9).

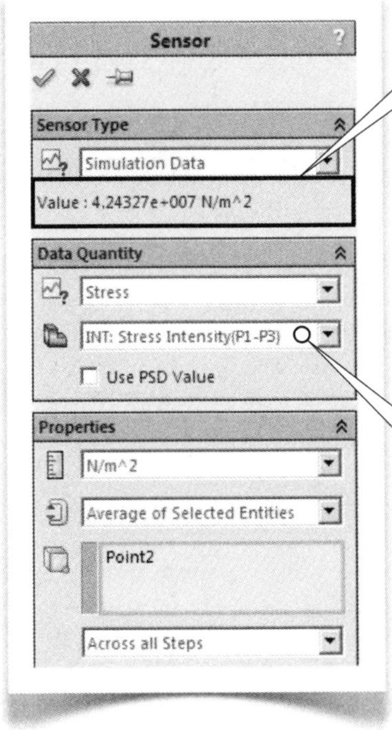

[10] Select **INT: Stress Intensity(P1-P3)**.

[11] The reported value is 42.4 MPa, which is close to the value (42.6 MPa) in 10.2-1(10), page 197.

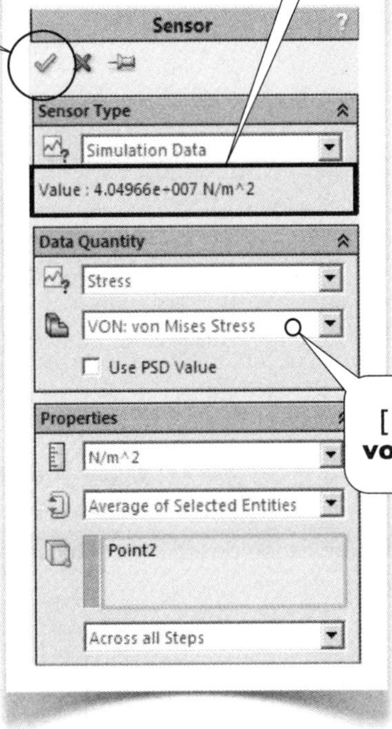

[12] Select **VON: von Mises Stress**.

[13] The reported value is 40.5 MPa, which is close to the value (40.6 MPa) in 10.2-1(11).

[14] Click **OK**.

[15] Save the document and exit **SolidWorks**. #

10.2-3 Appendix: Derivation of von Mises Yield Criterion

Hydrostatic Stress and Deviatoric Stress

Without loss of generality, a stress state

$$\{\sigma\} = \begin{Bmatrix} \sigma_X & \tau_{XY} & \tau_{XZ} \\ \tau_{YX} & \sigma_Y & \tau_{YZ} \\ \tau_{ZX} & \tau_{ZY} & \sigma_Z \end{Bmatrix}$$

can be expressed in principal stresses after appropriate choice of the coordinate system,

$$\{\sigma\} = \begin{Bmatrix} \sigma_1 & 0 & 0 \\ 0 & \sigma_2 & 0 \\ 0 & 0 & \sigma_3 \end{Bmatrix} \tag{1}$$

The **hydrostatic stress** is defined as the average of the normal stresses

$$p = \frac{\sigma_1 + \sigma_2 + \sigma_3}{3} \tag{2}$$

The stress state (1) can be decomposed into two parts

$$\{\sigma\} = \begin{Bmatrix} \sigma_1 & 0 & 0 \\ 0 & \sigma_2 & 0 \\ 0 & 0 & \sigma_3 \end{Bmatrix} = \begin{Bmatrix} p & 0 & 0 \\ 0 & p & 0 \\ 0 & 0 & p \end{Bmatrix} + \begin{Bmatrix} \sigma_1 - p & 0 & 0 \\ 0 & \sigma_2 - p & 0 \\ 0 & 0 & \sigma_3 - p \end{Bmatrix} \tag{3}$$

or, written in a more compact form,

$$\{\sigma\} = \{\sigma^p\} + \{\sigma^d\} \tag{4}$$

The first part is the hydrostatic stress, and the second part is called the **deviatoric stress**, the stress deviating from the hydrostatic stress.

Similarly, the material deformation also can be decomposed into two parts: a dilation (volumetric change) and a distortion. The hydrostatic stress contributes exclusively to the dilation, while the deviatoric stress contributes exclusively to the distortion. The dilation plays no role in shear failure; it is the distortion that causes shear failure. In short, the deviatoric stress

$$\{\sigma^d\} = \begin{Bmatrix} \sigma_1 - p & 0 & 0 \\ 0 & \sigma_2 - p & 0 \\ 0 & 0 & \sigma_3 - p \end{Bmatrix} \tag{5}$$

can be used to establish a shear failure criterion. However, it is not a scalar value. How can we use it to compare with a uniaxial yield stress σ_y? We need more elaborate theory to derive a useful criterion.

Von Mises Yielding Criterion

In 1913, Richard von Mises, an Austria-Hungary born scientist, proposed a theory for predicting the yielding of ductile materials. The theory states that the yielding occurs when the **deviatoric strain energy density** (or **deviatoric energy** for short, and also called **distortion energy**) reaches a critical value.

For linearly elastic materials with a stress state expressed in the form of Eq. (1), the **total strain energy density** is (see Eq. 9(1), page 172),

$$w = \frac{1}{2}\{\sigma\}\cdot\{\varepsilon\} \tag{6}$$

This total strain energy can be decomposed into two parts: energy w^p caused by the hydrostatic stress and energy w^d caused by the deviatoric stress,

$$w = w^p + w^d \tag{7}$$

or

$$w^d = w - w^p \tag{8}$$

The von Mises criterion can be stated as follows: the yielding occurs when

$$w^d \geq w^{yd} \tag{9}$$

where w^{yd} is the deviatoric energy when the material yields in its uniaxial tension test. In the following discussion, we will express w^p and w^d in terms of stresses.

Deviatoric Energy in Uniaxial Test

In a uniaxial tensile test, when yielding occurs, the stress state is (see 10.2-1[4], page 196)

$$\begin{Bmatrix} \sigma_y & 0 & 0 \\ 0 & 0 & 0 \\ 0 & 0 & 0 \end{Bmatrix} = \begin{Bmatrix} \sigma_y/3 & 0 & 0 \\ 0 & \sigma_y/3 & 0 \\ 0 & 0 & \sigma_y/3 \end{Bmatrix} + \begin{Bmatrix} 2\sigma_y/3 & 0 & 0 \\ 0 & -\sigma_y/3 & 0 \\ 0 & 0 & -\sigma_y/3 \end{Bmatrix}$$

or, written in a more compact form,

$$\{\sigma^y\} = \{\sigma^{yp}\} + \{\sigma^{yd}\}$$

The first part of the right-hand-side is the hydrostatic stress and the second part is the deviatoric stress. The Hooke's law, Eqs. 4.3-1(1, 2) (page 87), can be used to obtain the strains. The strains corresponding to the total stress and the hydrostatic stress are respectively

$$\{\varepsilon^y\} = \frac{\sigma_y}{E}\begin{Bmatrix} 1 & 0 & 0 \\ 0 & -\nu & 0 \\ 0 & 0 & -\nu \end{Bmatrix} \text{ and } \{\varepsilon^{yp}\} = \frac{(1-2\nu)\sigma_y}{3E}\begin{Bmatrix} 1 & 0 & 0 \\ 0 & 1 & 0 \\ 0 & 0 & 1 \end{Bmatrix}$$

Using Eq. (6), the energies corresponding to the total stress and the hydrostatic stress are respectively

$$w^y = \frac{1}{2}\{\sigma^y\}\cdot\{\varepsilon^y\} = \frac{\sigma_y^2}{2E} \text{ and } w^{yp} = \frac{1}{2}\{\sigma^{yp}\}\cdot\{\varepsilon^{yp}\} = \frac{(1-2\nu)\sigma_y^2}{6E}$$

From Eq. (8), the deviatoric energy is

$$w^{yd} = w^y - w^{yp} = \frac{(1+\nu)\sigma_y^2}{3E} \tag{10}$$

Deviatoric Energy in General 3D Cases

Now, we consider the general 3D stress state, Eqs. (3, 4). The strains corresponding the total stress $\{\sigma\}$ and the hydrostatic stress $\{\sigma^p\}$ are, using Eqs. 4.3-1(1, 2) (page 87), respectively

$$\{\varepsilon\} = \frac{1}{E}\begin{Bmatrix} \sigma_1 - \nu(\sigma_2+\sigma_3) & 0 & 0 \\ 0 & \sigma_2 - \nu(\sigma_3+\sigma_1) & 0 \\ 0 & 0 & \sigma_3 - \nu(\sigma_1+\sigma_2) \end{Bmatrix} \text{ and } \{\varepsilon^p\} = \frac{(1-2\nu)p}{E}\begin{Bmatrix} 1 & 0 & 0 \\ 0 & 1 & 0 \\ 0 & 0 & 1 \end{Bmatrix}$$

Using Eq. (6), the energies corresponding to the total stress and the hydrostatic stress are respectively

$$w = \frac{1}{2}\{\sigma\}\cdot\{\varepsilon\} = \frac{1}{2E}\left[\sigma_1(\sigma_1 - \nu\sigma_2 - \nu\sigma_3) + \sigma_2(\sigma_2 - \nu\sigma_3 - \nu\sigma_1) + \sigma_3(\sigma_3 - \nu\sigma_1 - \nu\sigma_2)\right]$$

and

$$w^p = \frac{1}{2}\{\sigma^p\}\cdot\{\varepsilon^p\} = \frac{3(1-2\nu)p^2}{2E}$$

From Eqs. (8) and (2), the deviatoric energy is

$$\begin{aligned} w^d &= w - w^p \\ &= \frac{1}{2E}\left[\sigma_1(\sigma_1 - \nu\sigma_2 - \nu\sigma_3) + \sigma_2(\sigma_2 - \nu\sigma_3 - \nu\sigma_1) + \sigma_3(\sigma_3 - \nu\sigma_1 - \nu\sigma_2)\right] - \frac{3(1-2\nu)}{2E}\left(\frac{\sigma_1+\sigma_2+\sigma_3}{3}\right)^2 \end{aligned} \quad (11)$$

After some manipulations, it can be simplified as

$$w^d = \frac{1+\nu}{6E}\left[(\sigma_1-\sigma_2)^2 + (\sigma_2-\sigma_3)^2 + (\sigma_3-\sigma_1)^2\right] \quad (12)$$

Derivation of Eq. (12)

$$\begin{aligned} w^d &= \frac{1}{2E}\left[\sigma_1(\sigma_1 - \nu\sigma_2 - \nu\sigma_3) + \sigma_2(\sigma_2 - \nu\sigma_3 - \nu\sigma_1) + \sigma_3(\sigma_3 - \nu\sigma_1 - \nu\sigma_2)\right] - \frac{3(1-2\nu)}{2E}\left(\frac{\sigma_1+\sigma_2+\sigma_3}{3}\right)^2 \\ &= \frac{1}{2E}\left[\sigma_1^2+\sigma_2^2+\sigma_3^2 - 2\nu(\sigma_1\sigma_2+\sigma_2\sigma_3+\sigma_3\sigma_1)\right] - \frac{1-2\nu}{6E}\left[\sigma_1^2+\sigma_2^2+\sigma_3^2 + 2(\sigma_1\sigma_2+\sigma_2\sigma_3+\sigma_3\sigma_1)\right] \\ &= \frac{1}{6E}\left[3(\sigma_1^2+\sigma_2^2+\sigma_3^2) - 6\nu(\sigma_1\sigma_2+\sigma_2\sigma_3+\sigma_3\sigma_1) - (1-2\nu)(\sigma_1^2+\sigma_2^2+\sigma_3^2) - (2-4\nu)(\sigma_1\sigma_2+\sigma_2\sigma_3+\sigma_3\sigma_1)\right] \\ &= \frac{1}{6E}\left[(2+2\nu)(\sigma_1^2+\sigma_2^2+\sigma_3^2) - (2+2\nu)(\sigma_1\sigma_2+\sigma_2\sigma_3+\sigma_3\sigma_1)\right] \\ &= \frac{1+\nu}{3E}\left[\sigma_1^2+\sigma_2^2+\sigma_3^2 - \sigma_1\sigma_2 - \sigma_2\sigma_3 - \sigma_3\sigma_1\right] \\ &= \frac{1+\nu}{6E}\left[(\sigma_1-\sigma_2)^2 + (\sigma_2-\sigma_3)^2 + (\sigma_3-\sigma_1)^2\right] \end{aligned}$$

Von Mises Stress (Equivalent Stress)

Substituting Eqs. (10) and (12) into the von Mises Yield criterion, Eq. (9), we conclude that the material yields when

$$\frac{1+\nu}{6E}\left[(\sigma_1-\sigma_2)^2+(\sigma_2-\sigma_3)^2+(\sigma_3-\sigma_1)^2\right]\geq\frac{1+\nu}{3E}\sigma_y^2 \tag{13}$$

or, in a more concise form

$$\sqrt{\frac{1}{2}\left[(\sigma_1-\sigma_2)^2+(\sigma_2-\sigma_3)^2+(\sigma_3-\sigma_1)^2\right]}\geq\sigma_y \tag{14}$$

The quantity on the left-hand-side is termed **von Mises stress**, also referred to as **equivalent stress** (or **effective stress** in some books) and denoted by σ_e

$$\sigma_e=\sqrt{\frac{1}{2}\left[(\sigma_1-\sigma_2)^2+(\sigma_2-\sigma_3)^2+(\sigma_3-\sigma_1)^2\right]} \tag{15}$$

To get more insight of Eq. (14), let's plot Eq. (14) in σ_1-σ_2-σ_3 space and consider only equal sign. It will be a cylindrical surface aligned with the axis $\sigma_1=\sigma_2=\sigma_3$ and with a radius of $\sqrt{2}\sigma_y$ [1]. It is called the **von Mises yield surface**. Condition of Eq. (14) is equivalent to say that the material fails when the stress state is outside the von Mises yield surface. When $\sigma_1=\sigma_2=\sigma_3$, the material is under hydrostatic pressure. It is the portion of stress that deviates from the axis contributes to the failure of the material.

Equivalent Strain

In **SolidWorks Simulation**, an **equivalent strain** is defined as

$$\varepsilon_e=\sqrt{\frac{2}{3}\left[(\varepsilon_X-\varepsilon^*)^2+(\varepsilon_Y-\varepsilon^*)^2+(\varepsilon_Z-\varepsilon^*)^2+\frac{1}{2}(\gamma_{XY}^2+\gamma_{YZ}^2+\gamma_{ZX}^2)\right]} \tag{16}$$

where

$$\varepsilon^*=\frac{\varepsilon_X+\varepsilon_Y+\varepsilon_Z}{3} \tag{17}$$

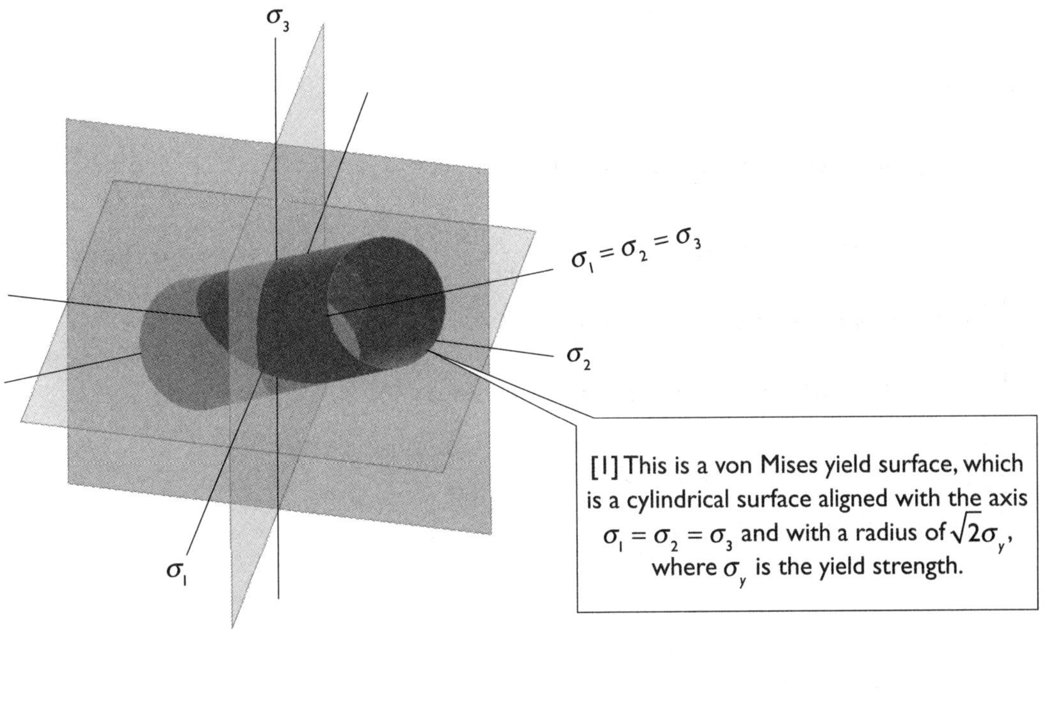

Chapter 11

Trusses and Beams

We've demonstrated that, to study the responses of a body subjected to external forces, we may follow a standard procedure: (1) Create a 3D geometric model; (2) Mesh the model with 3D solid elements, as in 1.3-13[7] (page 46) or 5.1-6[11] (page 95); (3) Apply supports and loads; (4) Solve the model; and (5) Obtain the stresses, strains, and displacements.

When neither the computing efficiency nor the engineer's work hours are your concern, that would be true for most of problems. However, in many cases (which'll be exemplified in Chapters 11, 12, and 13), using specialized elements (rather than 3D solid elements, which have been used so far) may significantly improve the computing efficiency as well as engineers' work hours.

For truss or beam problems, if our concerns are the members' stresses, strains, and displacements (rather than other detail behaviors; for example, the stress concentration near the joints), we may use specialized elements, called **beam elements**, which can be further specialized to **truss elements**.

This chapter will demonstrate how to solve truss and beam problems using these **line elements**.

Section 11.1

Trusses

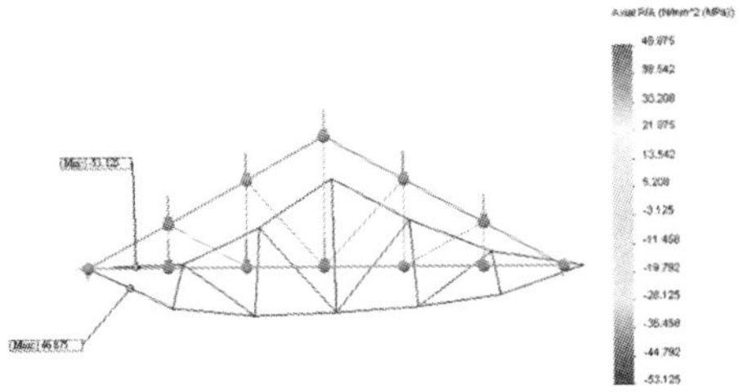

11.1-1 Introduction

[1] In this section, we'll consider a plane truss subject to loads as shown in [2]. This example is taken from Sample Problem 6.3, *Vector Mechanics for Engineers: Statics, 8th ed.*, by F. P. Beer, E. R. Johnston, Jr., and E. R. Eisenberg. The reaction forces and three member forces calculated by the textbook are also shown in [3].

This truss is a **statically determinate structure**, meaning that the member forces can be solved using static equilibrium equations without any information of the cross sections or the material properties, which are needed when solving a statically indeterminate structure. Since the **Simulation** solves either statically determinate structures or statically indeterminate structures using the same methods (finite element methods), these information are required by the program. Here, we assume that all members are made of **Alloy Steel** and have a rectangular cross-section of 10 mm x 50 mm, where the dimension 50 mm is parallel to the truss plane.

[2] This is the plane truss considered.

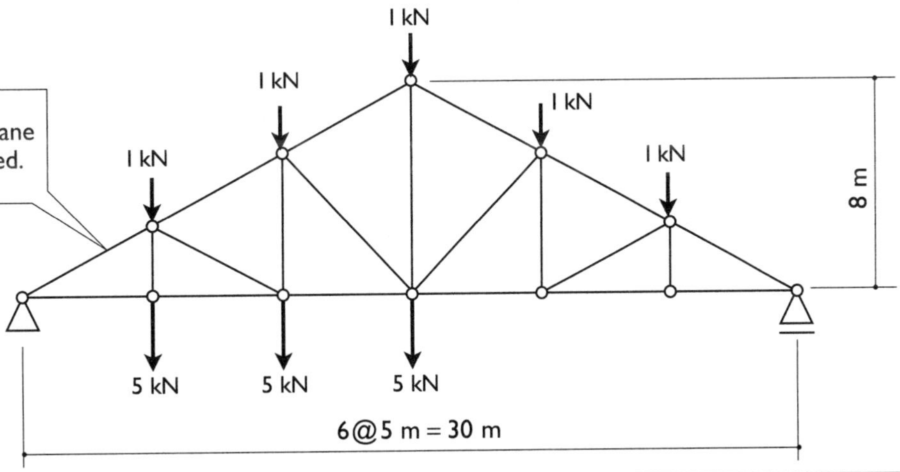

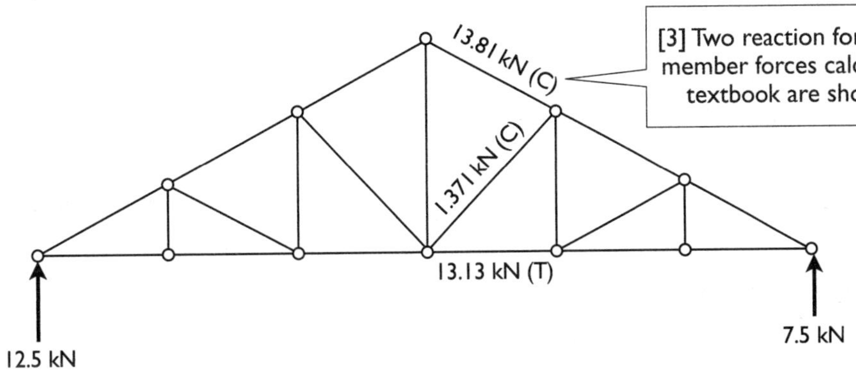

[3] Two reaction forces and three member forces calculated by the textbook are shown here. #

11.1-2 Start Up

[1] Launch **SolidWorks** and create a new part. Set up **MKS** unit system with 3 decimal places for the length unit. #

11.1-3 Sketch the Truss

[1] On the **Front** plane, draw a sketch like this. Note that there are totally 21 line segments. Remember to click **Exit Sketch**.

[4] These 3 line segments on the roof have a **Collinear** relation.

[3] These 3 line segments on the roof have a **Collinear** relation.

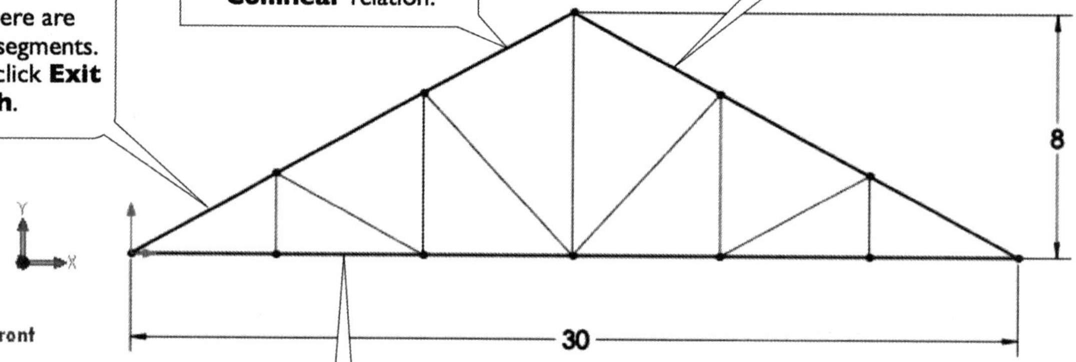

[2] The 6 horizontal line segments have an **Equal** relation.

[5] Save the document with the name **Truss**. #

11.1-4 Create Structural Members

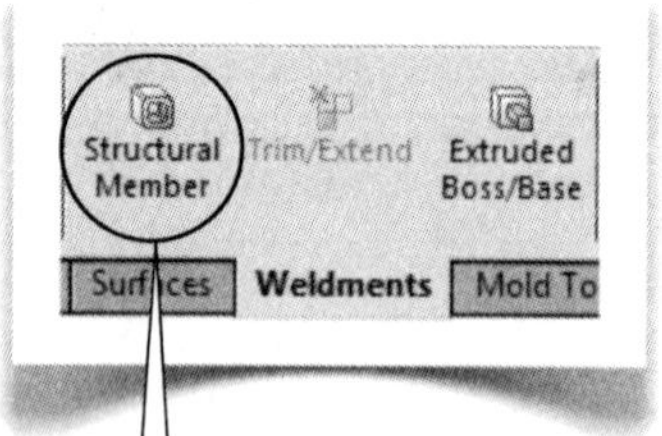

[2] **Structural Member** command is also available in the **Weldments Toolbar**.

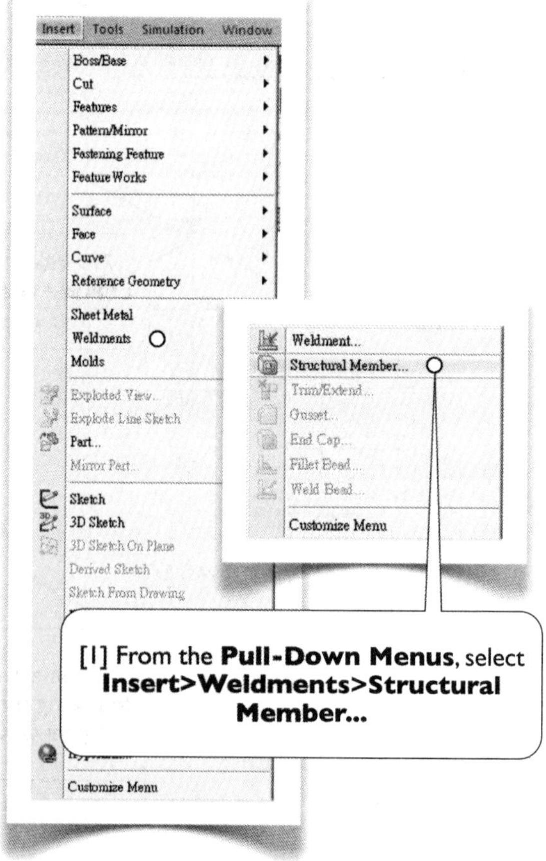

[1] From the **Pull-Down Menus**, select **Insert>Weldments>Structural Member...**

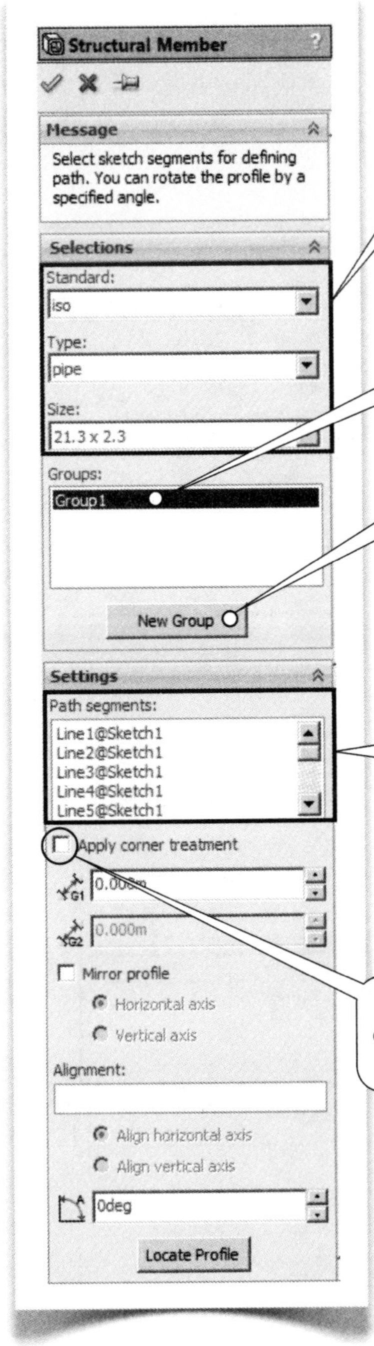

[3] In many other cases, we may select a cross section by specify **Standard**, **Type**, and **Size**. In this case, however, we need to create one. Leave these default settings for now and later we'll modify the cross section for our need.

[6] The group's name shows here.

[8] Click to create a new **Group**.

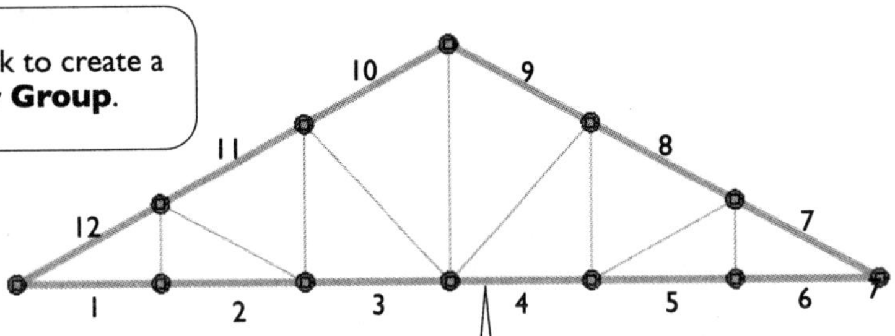

[5] The selected 12 segments show here.

[4] Select these 12 line segments, following the order shown. These 12 segments form a **Group**, sharing the same properties (see [17], next page).

[7] Make sure **Apply corner treatment** is unchecked.

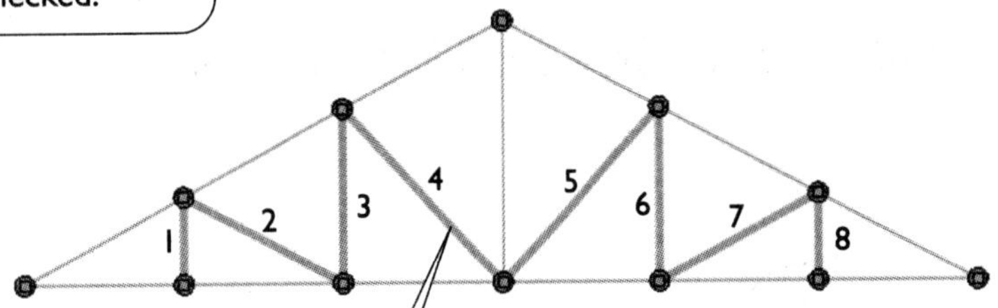

[9] Select these 8 line segments, following the order shown. These 8 segments form a second **Group**.

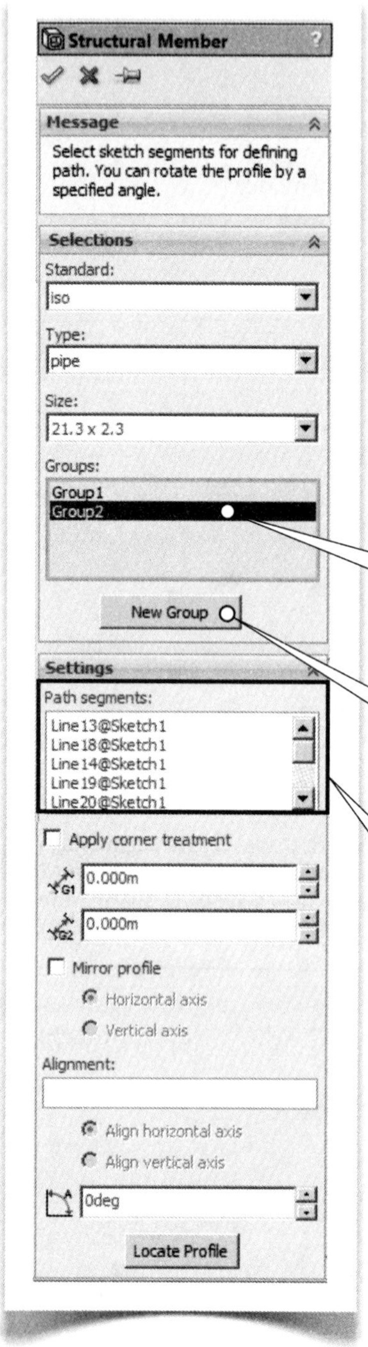

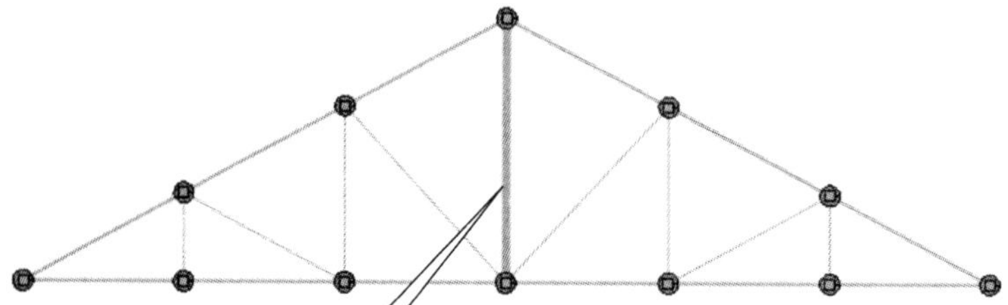

[13] Select this vertical segments. This **Group** has only one segment.

[11] The group's name shows here.

[12] Click to create a new **Group**.

[10] The selected 8 segments show here.

[16] Click **OK**.

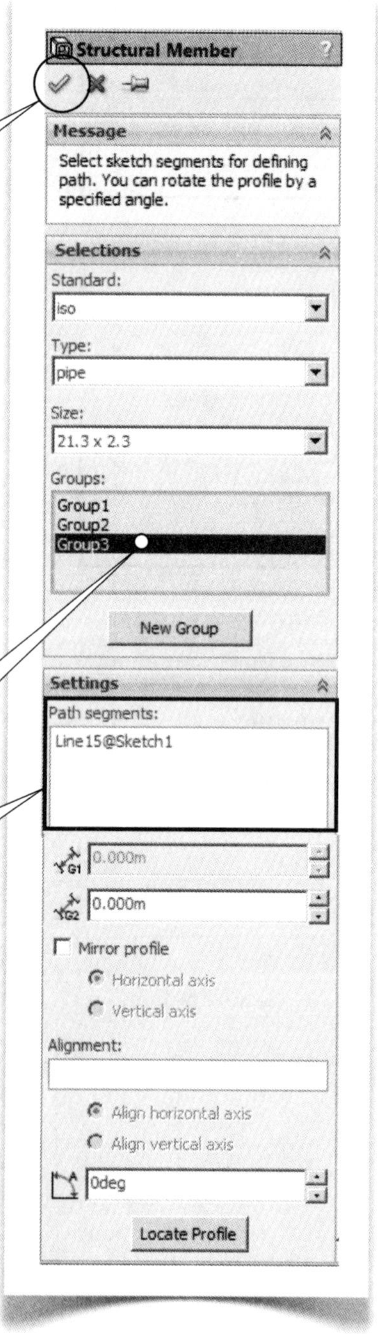

[15] The group's name shows here.

[14] The selected segment shows here.

[17] **Grouping of Structural Members**

Each **Group** of structural members contains either **connected** members or **parallel** members. The members in a **Group** share the same properties, such as **cross section** and sectional **orientations** (see 11.1-5[9], page 210). #

11.1-5 Modify the Cross Section

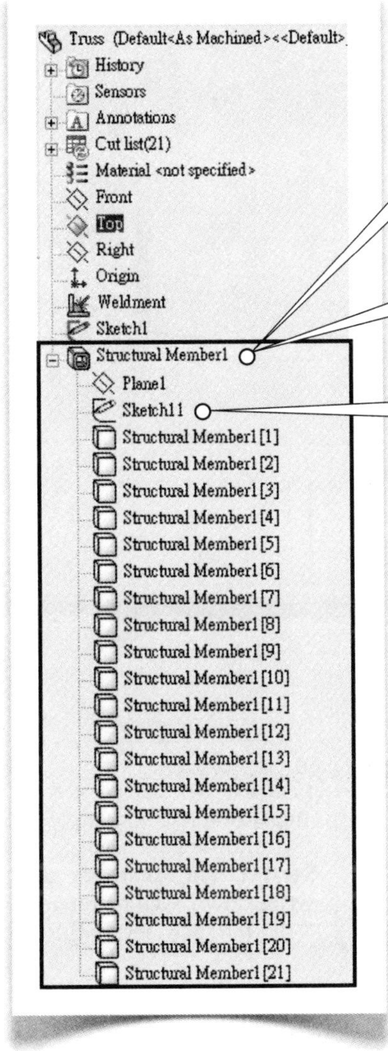

[1] Information about the 21 members are under **Structural Member1**.

[7] Right-click **Structural Member1** and select **Edit Feature**.

[2] The cross section is in **Sketch11**. Double-click to edit it.

[3] Click **Normal To** to rotate the view.

[4] Use **Zoom to Area** to enlarge the cross section. Delete all existing sketch entities.

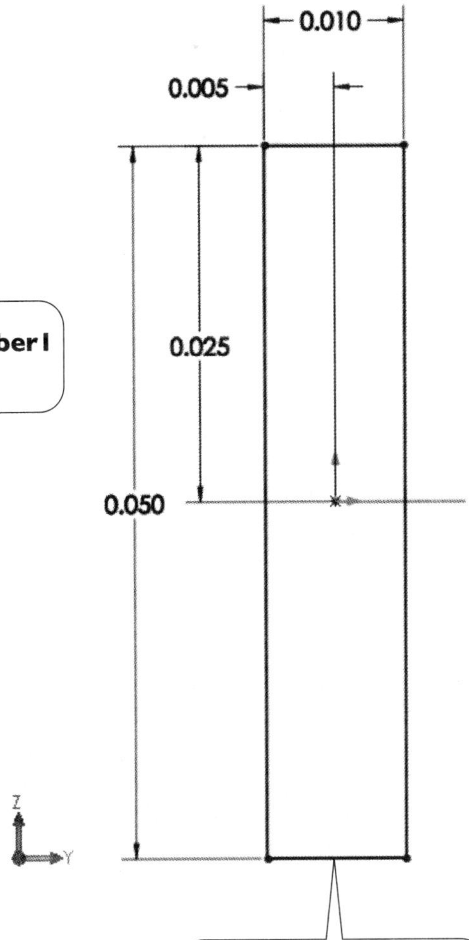

[5] Draw a rectangle like this. Remember to click **Exit Sketch**.

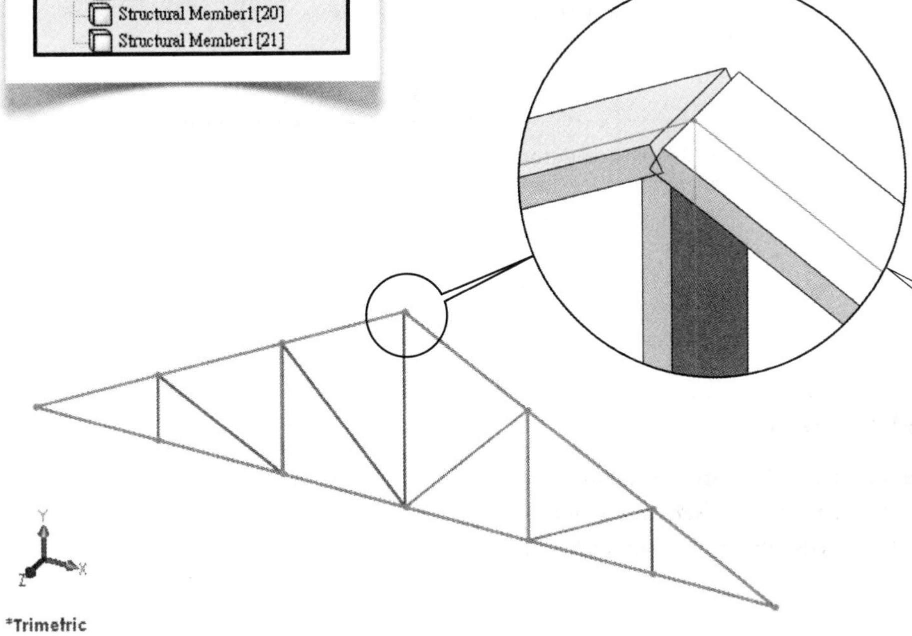

[6] If you enlarge the model, you will see that the section's orientations are not correct. They need to be rotated 90 degrees (as shown in [15], next page).

[14] Click **OK**.

[8] Select **Group1**.

[10] Select **Group2**.

[12] Select **Group3**.

[9, 11, 13] Type 90 (deg) for **Rotation Angle**.

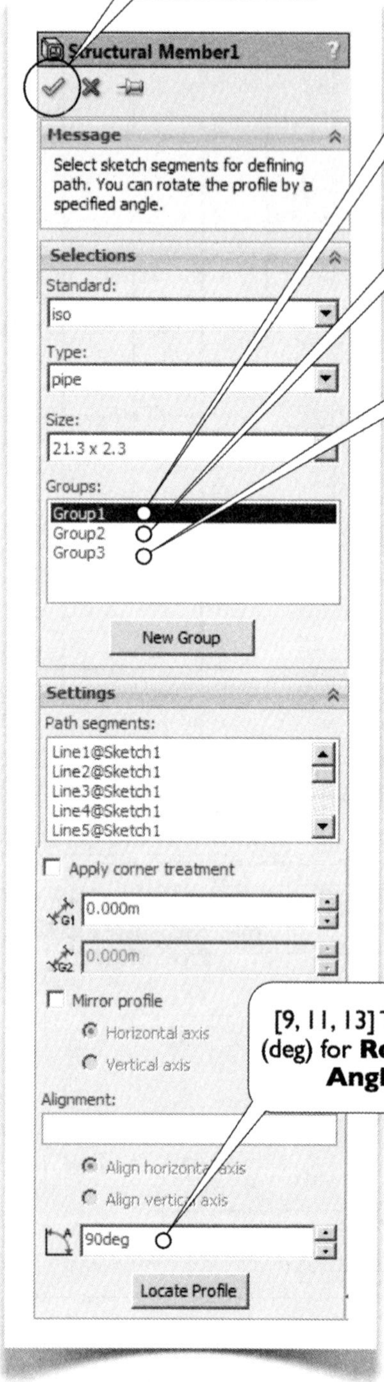

[15] Now the section's orientations are correct.

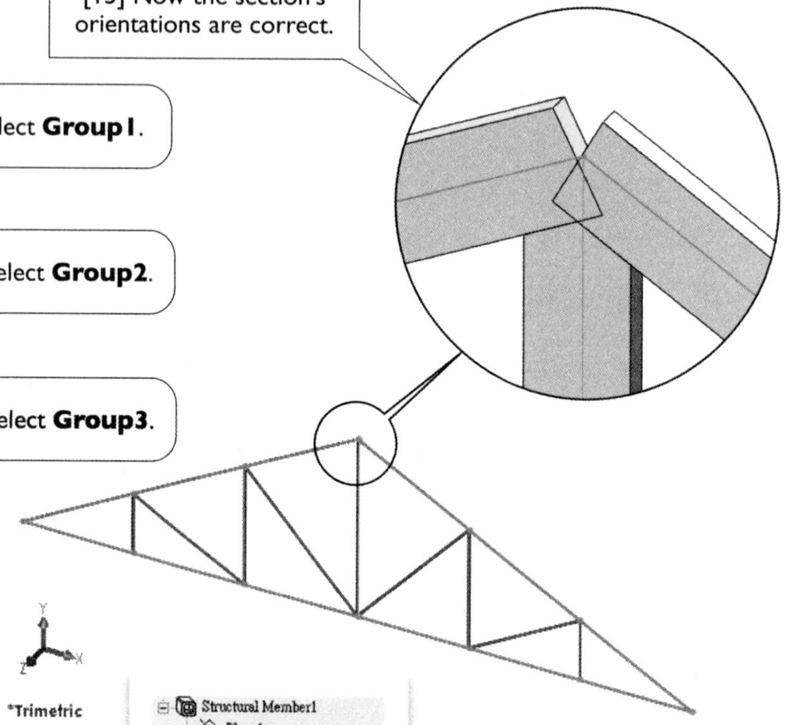

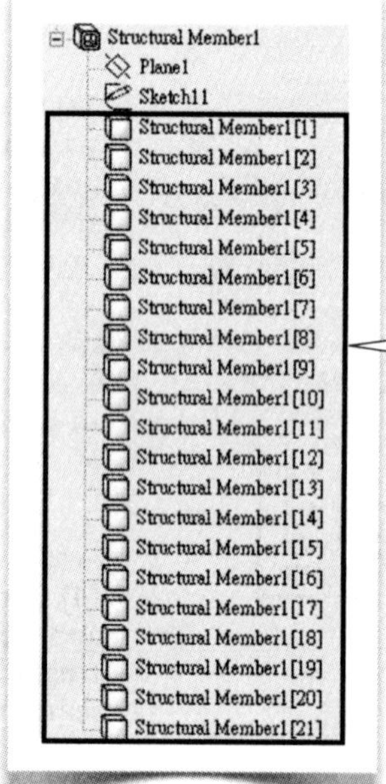

[16] Each member is assigned an ID number. Move your mouse over each **Structural Member** and write down each member's ID number (see [17]).

[17] This shows each member's ID number. Specifically, we are interested in **Structural Members** 4, 9, and 16. Your numbers may not be the same as here. #

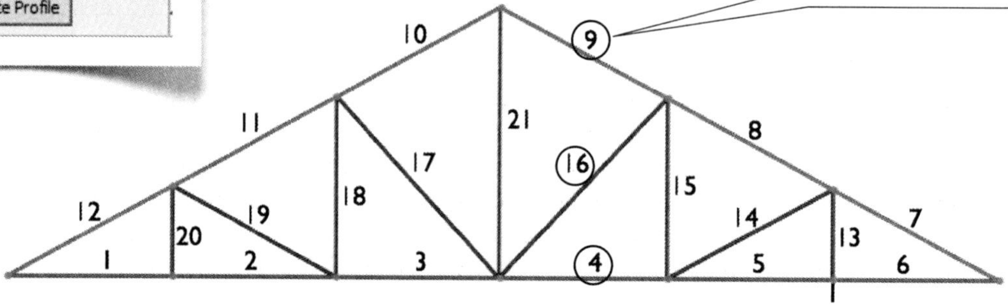

11.1-6 Create a Study and Apply Material

[1] In the **Simulation Toolbar**, select **Study Advisor>New Study**. Leave **Static** as default **Study Type**. Leave **Static 1** as default **Study Name**.

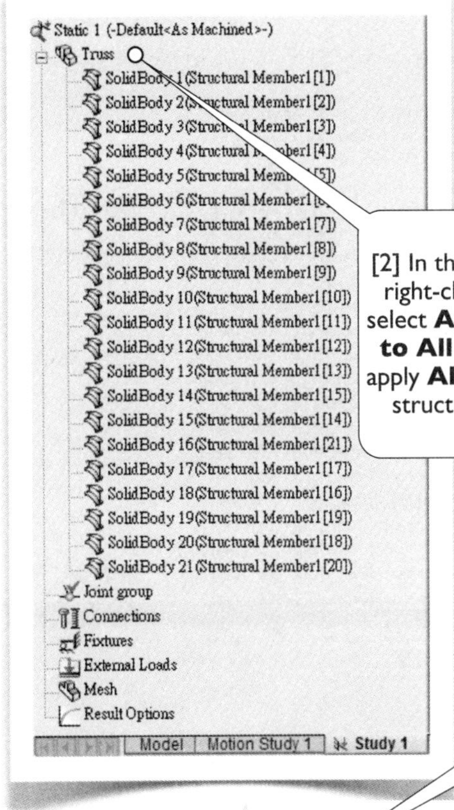

[2] In the **Study Tree**, right-click **Truss** and select **Apply Material to All Bodies...** and apply **Alloy Steel** to all structural members.

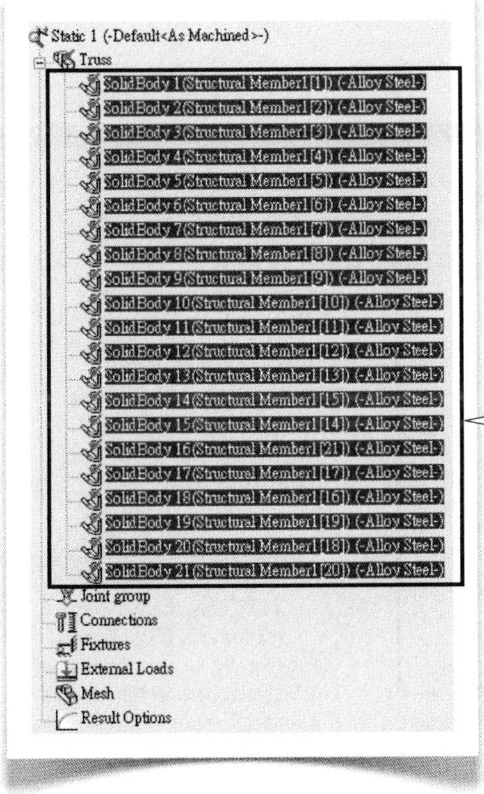

[3] Select all structural members and right-click-select **Edit Definition...**

[4] Click **Truss**. This turns all members into truss members; i.e., all members are pin-joined.

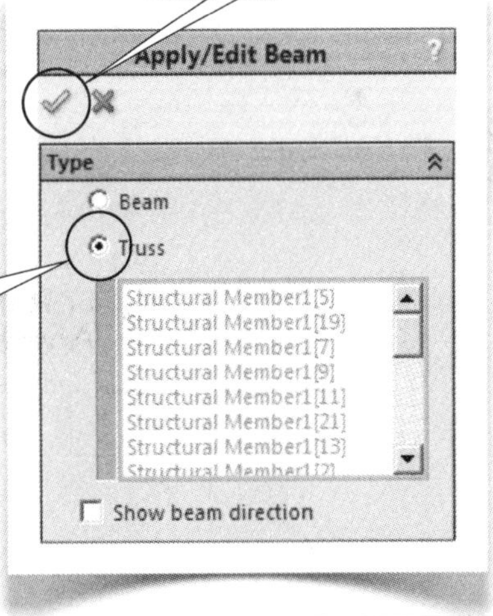

[5] Click **OK**.

[6] **Truss** vs. **Beam**

Truss members are **pin-joined** one another. The external loads can apply at joints only. Under these conditions, truss members are subjected to only axial deformation (either tension or compression); therefore, they are also called two-force members. In the **Simulation**, each truss member is meshed with one **truss element**.

Beam members are **rigid-joined** one another. The external loads can apply at joints or on the members axially or transversally. Therefore, beam members are subjected to axial deformation as well as bending, torsion, and transversal shearing. In the **Simulation**, each beam member is meshed with multiple **beam elements**. #

11.1-7 Set Up Supports

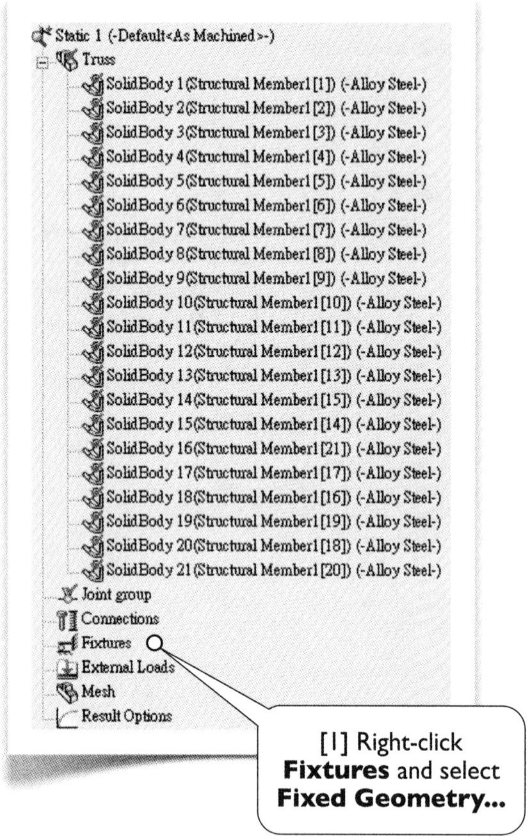

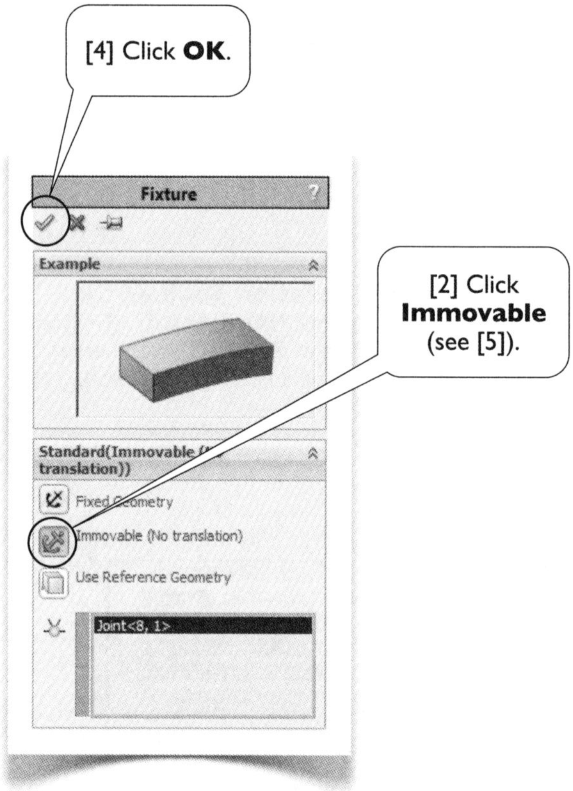

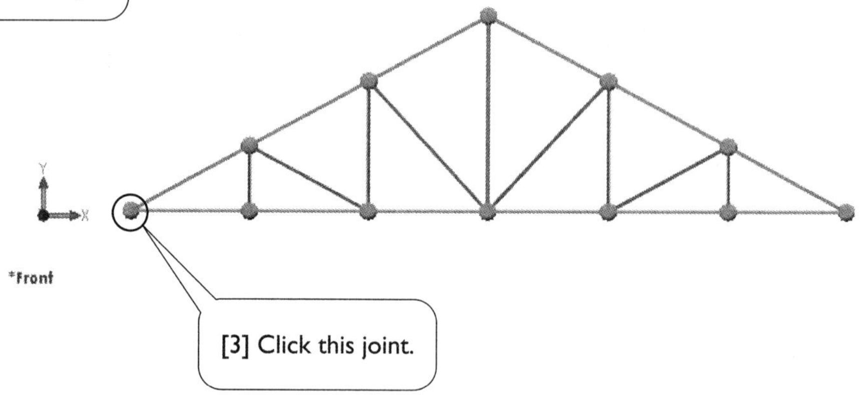

[5] Immovable vs. Fixed Geometry

Immovable prohibits translations in all three directions (*X*, *Y*, and *Z*). **Fixed Geometry** prohibits not only translations but also rotations in all directions. In a truss problem, a member is always free to rotate about its joints, therefore, **Immovable** and **Fixed Geometry** are in effect equivalent.

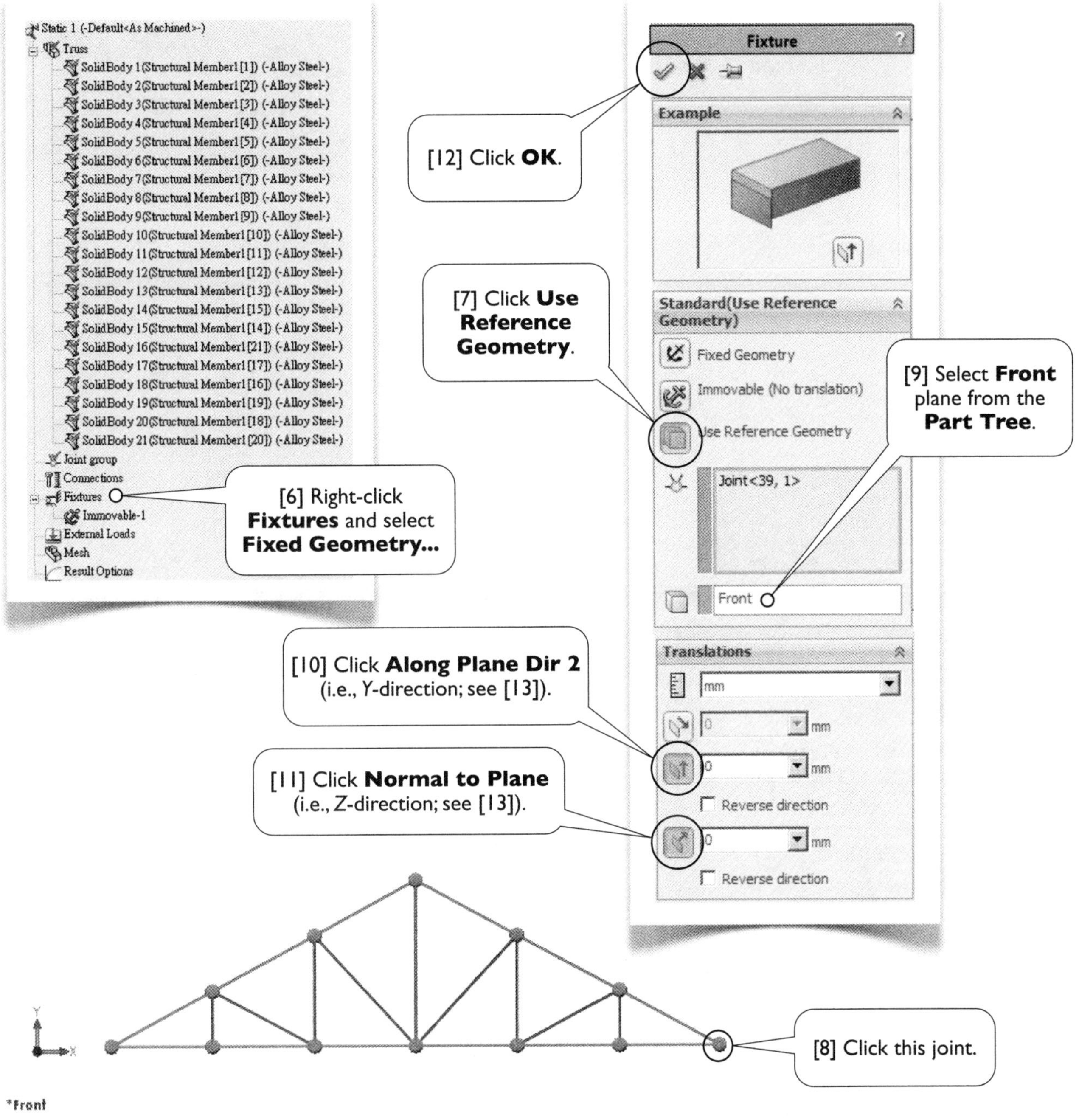

[13] **Direction 1** and **Direction 2** of a Plane

The **Front** plane is the same as the *XY*-plane, the *X*-direction is referred to as its **Direction 1** and the *Y*-direction is referred to as its **Direction 2**. For the **Top** plane (*XZ*-plane), the *X*-direction is referred to as its **Direction 1** and the *Z*-direction is referred to as its **Direction 2**. For the **Right** plane (*ZY*-plane), the *Z*-direction is referred to as its **Direction 1** and the *Y*-direction is referred to as its **Direction 2**.

A simple rule to memorize is: *X*-direction is referred to as **Direction 1** if a plane parallels to the *X*-direction. Otherwise, *Z*-direction is referred to as **Direction 1**.

If a face (instead of a plane) is used, the **longer** direction is always referred to as **Direction 1**.

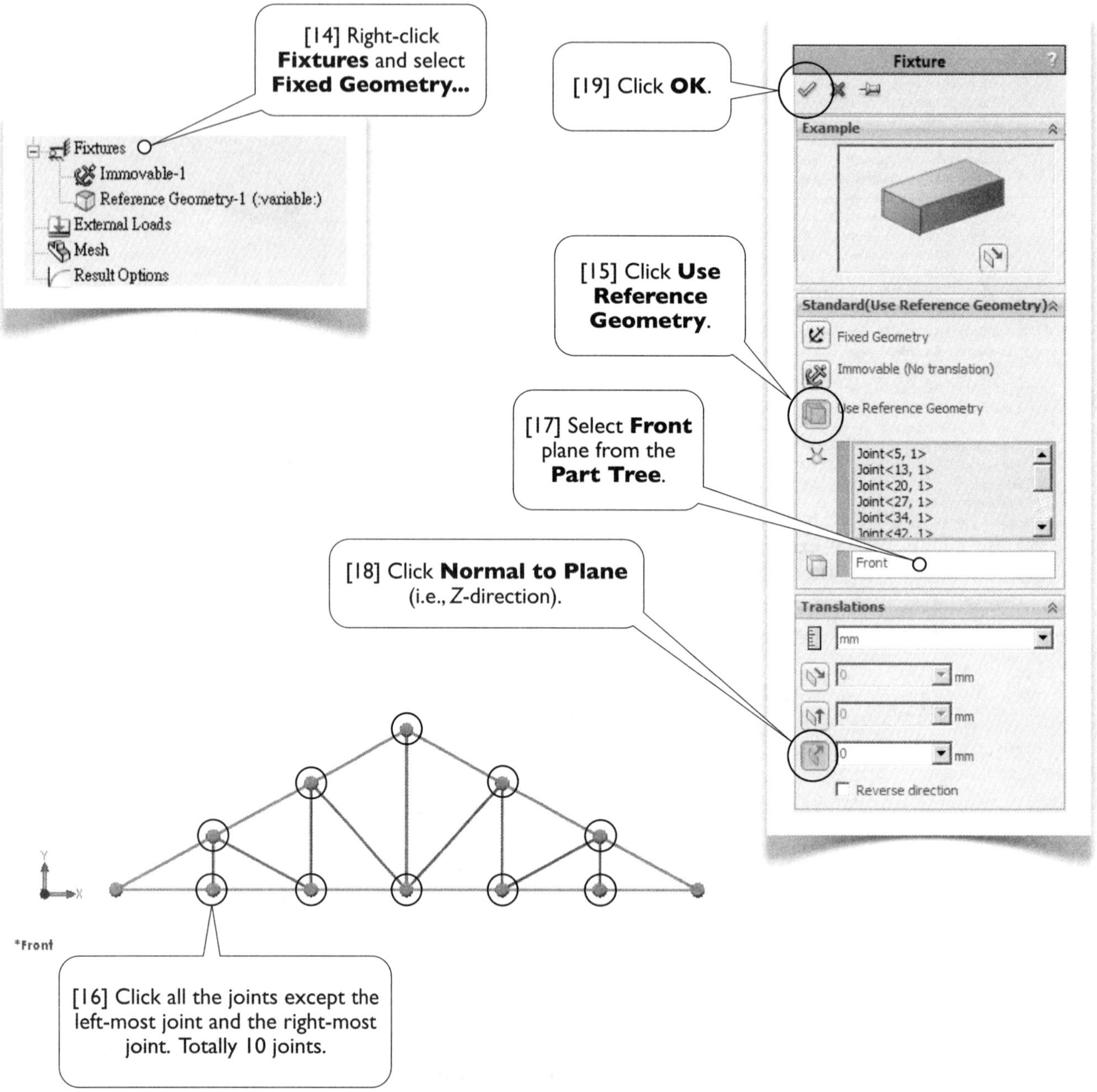

[20] For a **Static** analysis, a structure must be stable.

In a **Static** analysis, a structure must have enough supports so that the structure doesn't collapse under any external loads. In our case, if we didn't restrict the movement in Z-direction ([2, 11, 18]), then the structure would collapse under any (even small) loads in Z-direction, since all truss joints allow members to rotate freely in all direction. Remember that, to analyze a plane truss in a 3D space, always restrict the movements of all joints in the direction normal to the truss plane.

If you don't provide enough supports to stabilize the structure, the **SolidWorks Simulation** simply gives you an error message unless you turn on the **Use soft spring to stabilize model** option (5.1-5[7, 8], page 94).

For a **Dynamic** analysis, an unstable structure is allowed. The **Simulation** would simulate the collapse of the structure. #

11.1-8 Set Up **External Loads**

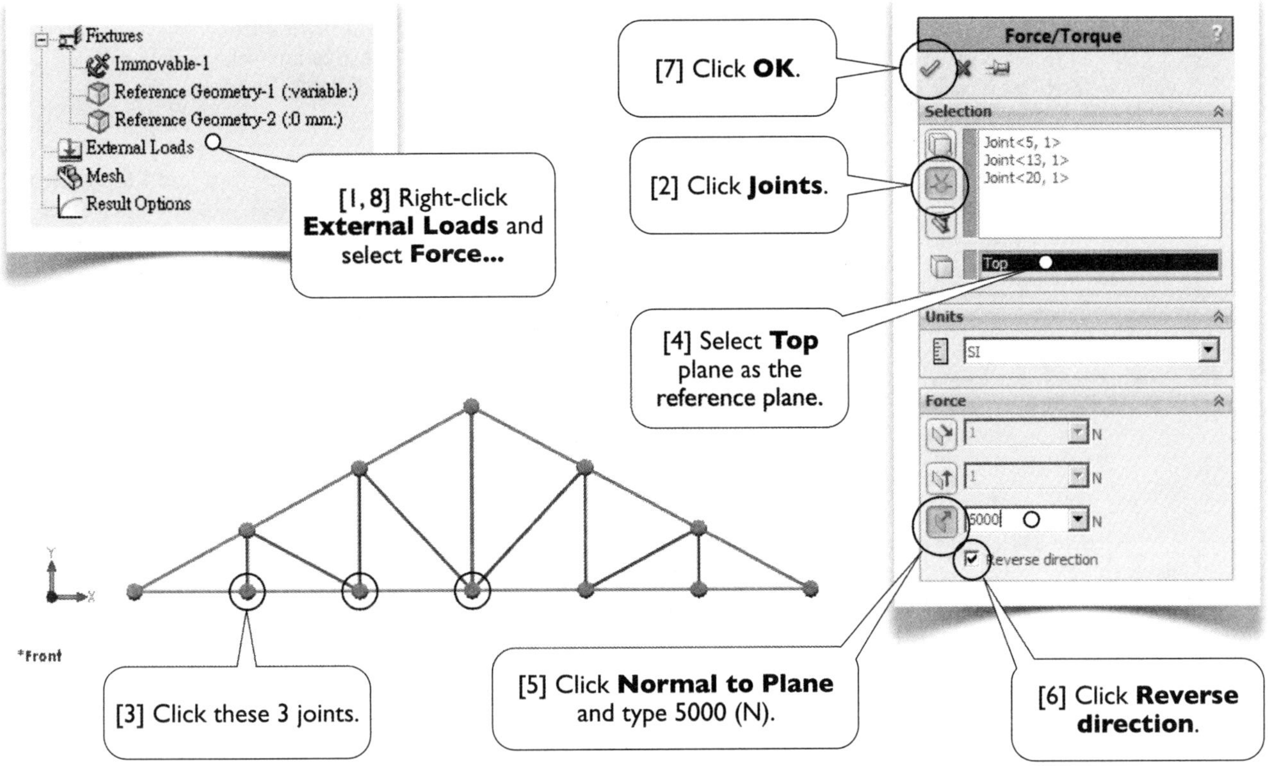

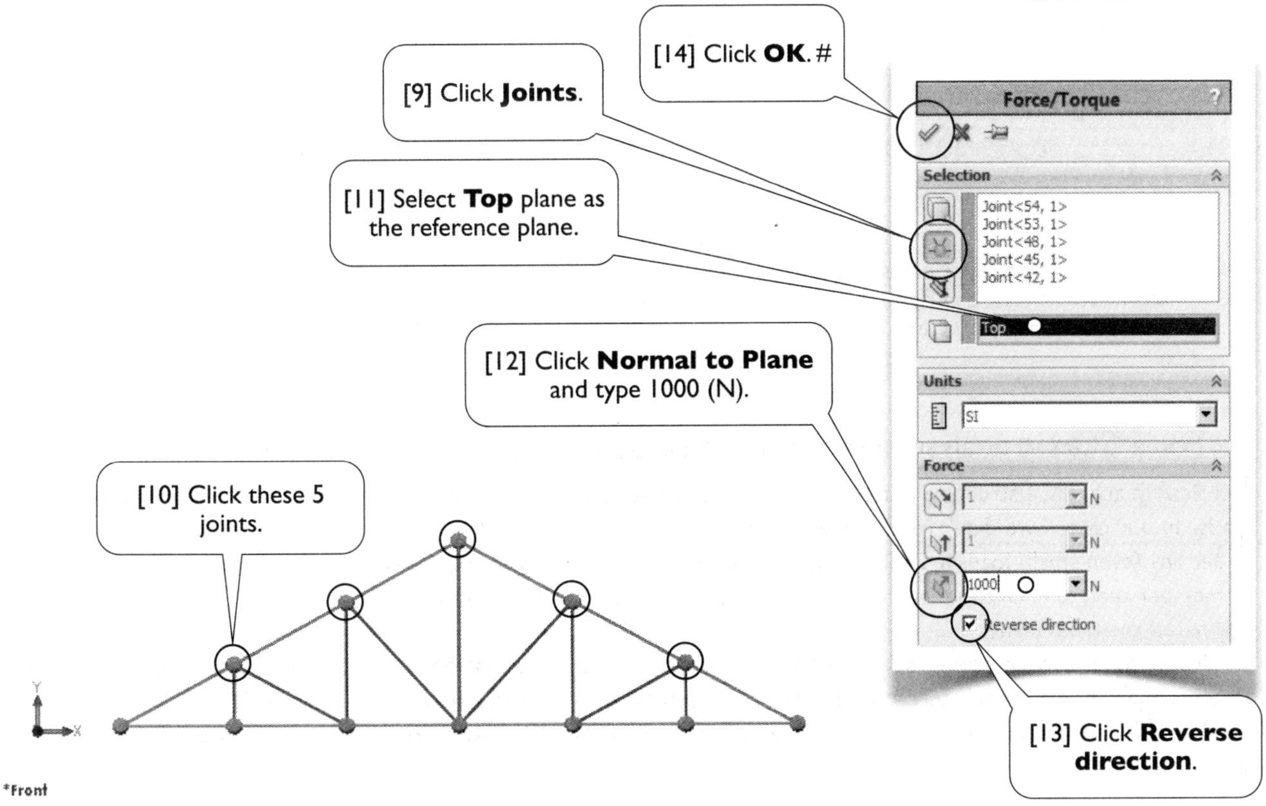

11.1-9 Obtain Solutions

[1] In the **Simulation Toolbar**, click **Run**.

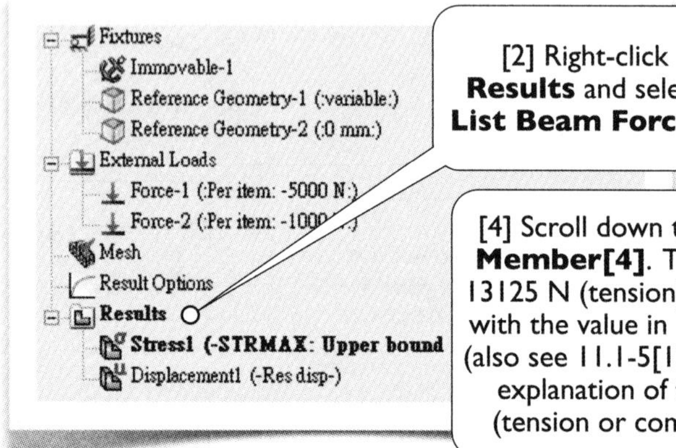

[2] Right-click **Results** and select **List Beam Force...**

[3] Click **OK**.

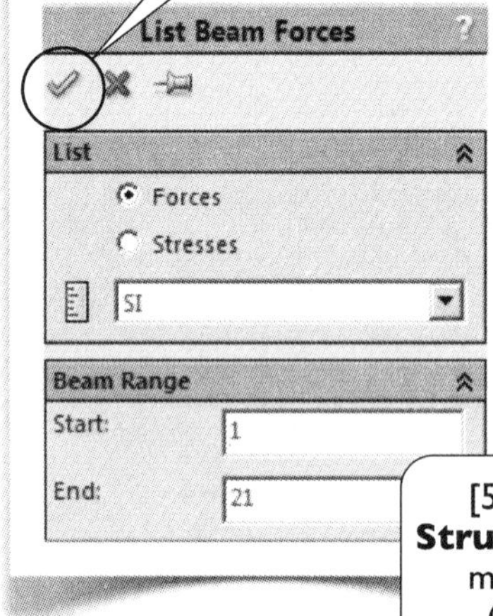

[4] Scroll down to find **Structural Member[4]**. The member force is 13125 N (tension), which is consistent with the value in 11.1-1[3] (page 205) (also see 11.1-5[17], page 210). For an explanation of the signs of forces (tension or compression), see [8].

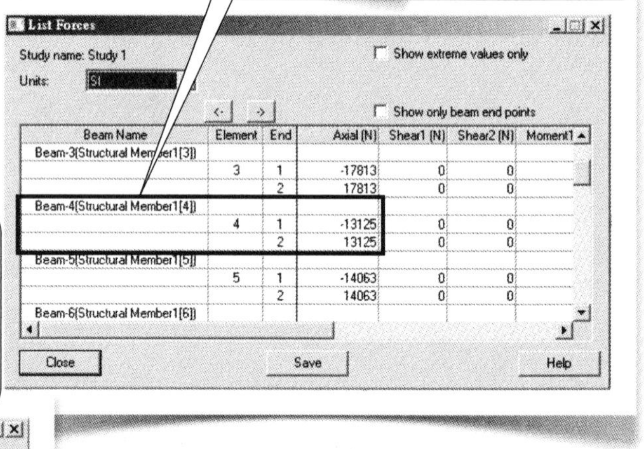

[5] Scroll down/up to find **Structural Member[9]**. The member force is 13813 N (compression), which is consistent with the value in 11.1-1[3].

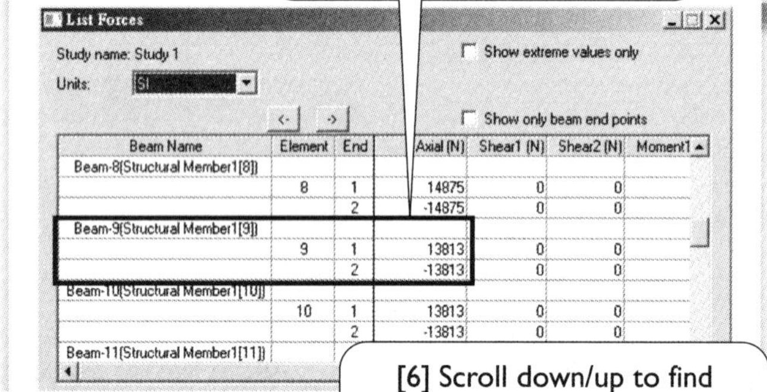

[6] Scroll down/up to find **Structural Member[16]**. The member force is 1370.7 N (compression), which is consistent with the value in 11.1-1[3].

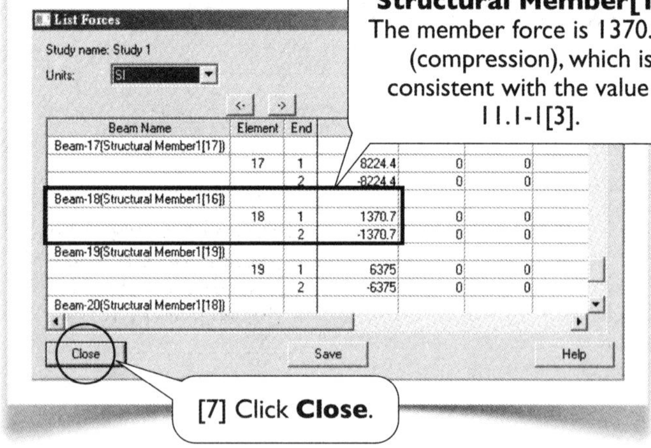

[7] Click **Close**.

[8] Tension or Compression?

The forces reported in [4-6] are the forces acting at the ends of the members.

For each member, there is a coordinate system attached at **End 1** and pointing to **End 2** [9]. The forces refer to this coordinate system. Therefore, the force at **End 1** and the force at **End 2** must be equal in magnitudes but opposite in signs. A positive force at **End 2** means the force pulls away from the member; i.e., a tension. A negative force at **End 2** means the force pushes into the member; i.e., a compression.

[9] Member's coordinate system.

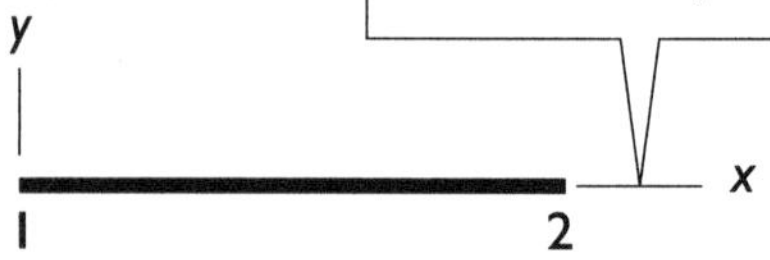

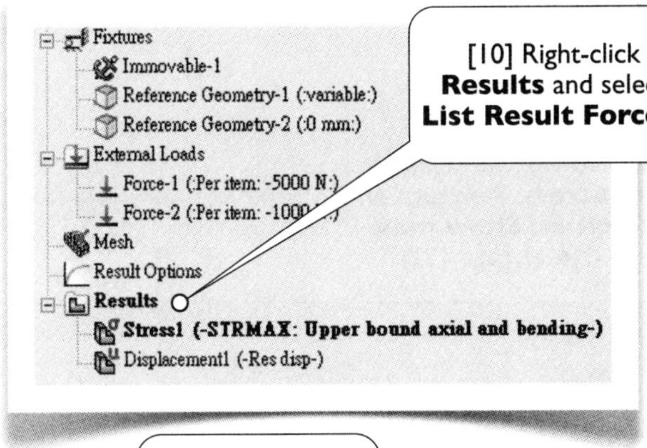

[10] Right-click **Results** and select **List Result Force...**

[15] Click **OK**. #

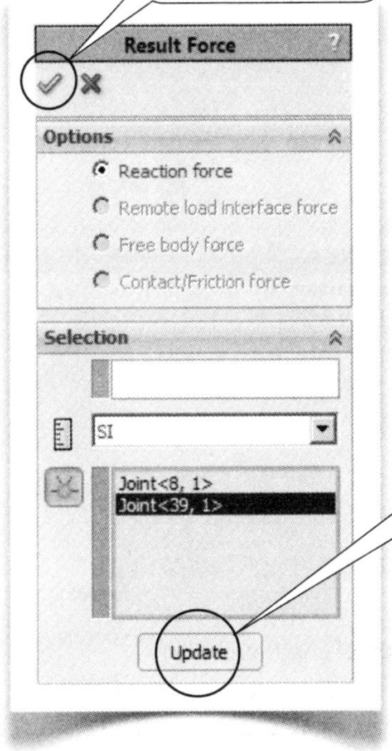

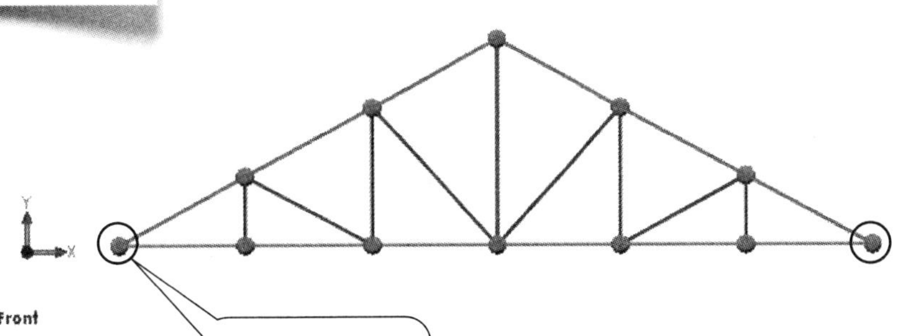

[11] Click these 2 joints.

[12] Click **Update**.

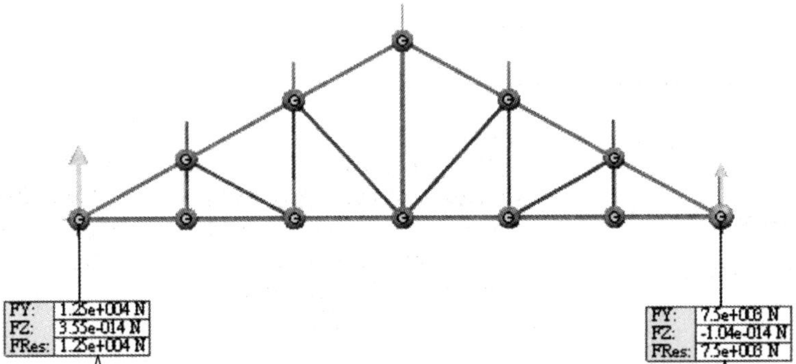

[13] The left support has a reaction force of 12500 N (upward), consistent with the value in 11.1-1[3], page 205.

[14] The right support has a reaction force of 7500 N (upward), consistent with the value in 11.1-1[3].

11.1-10 View Stresses and Displacements

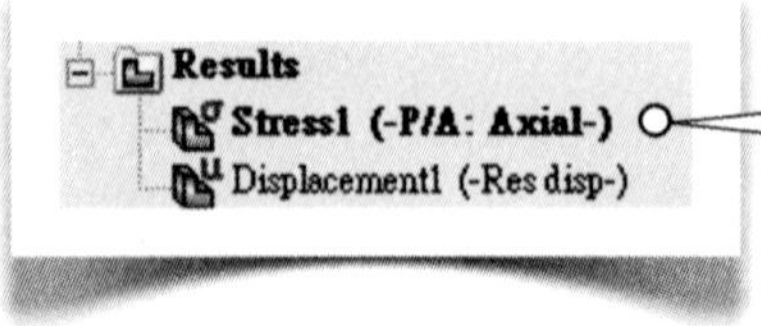

[1] Double-click **Stress1** to edit the definition. Select **Axial** for **Beam Stress**. Also turn on **Show min annotation** and **Show max annotation** (see 6.1-9[4, 5], page 122)

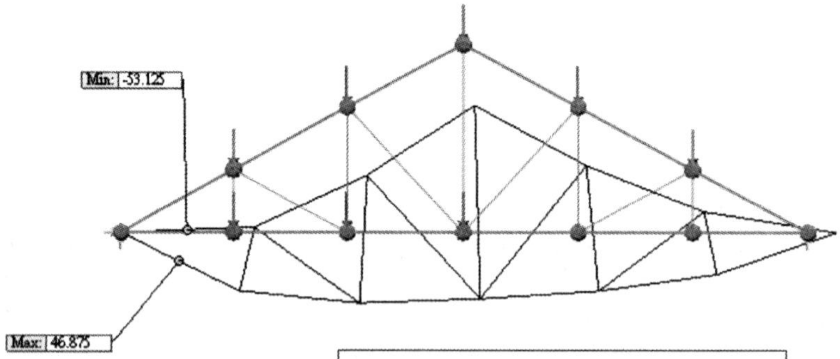

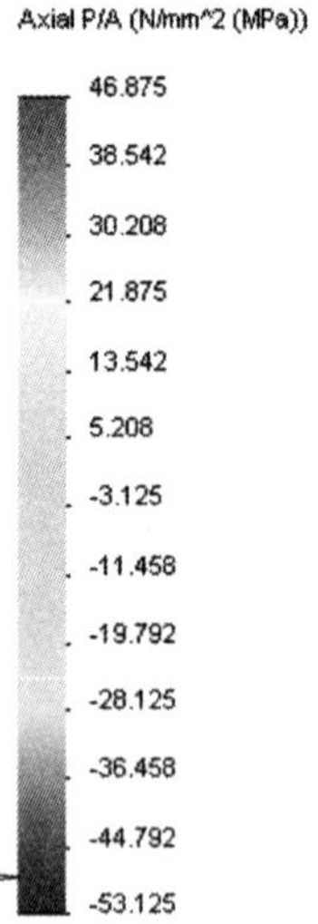

[2] The **Axial** stress is simply a member force divided by its cross sectional area. Note that, for truss members, the axial stress equals to the **principal stress**, which also equals to the **von Mises stress**.

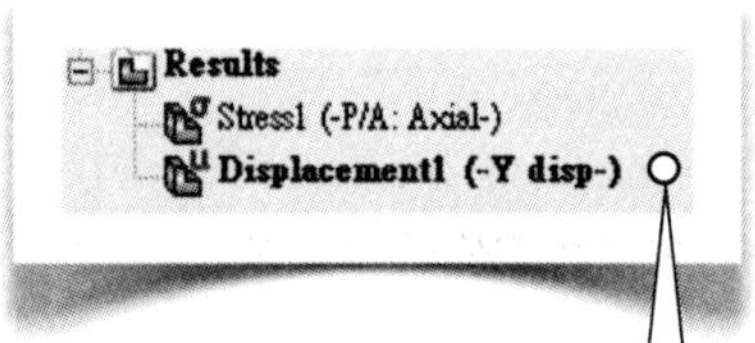

[3] Double-click **Displacement1** to activate it. Double-click again to edit the definition. Select **UY** for **Component**. Also turn on **Show min annotation** and **Show max annotation**.

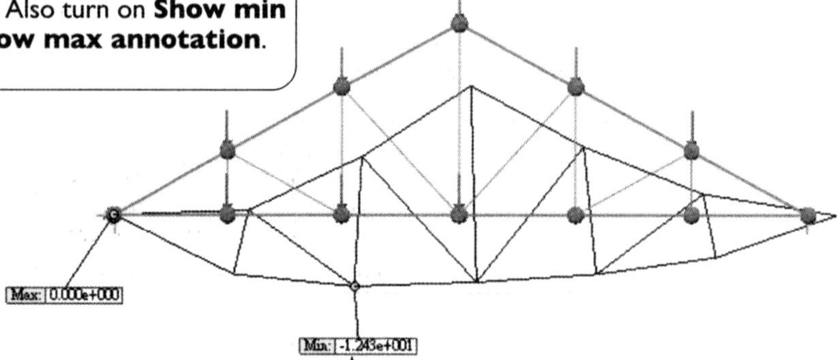

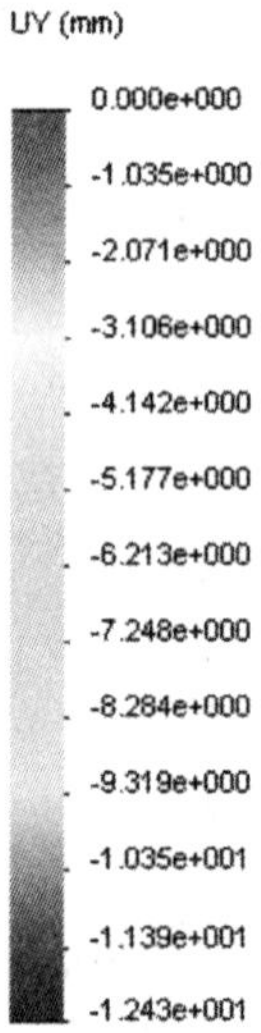

[4] The maximum vertical displacement is 12.43 mm, occurring at this joint.

[5] Save the document and exit **SolidWorks**. #

Section 11.2

Beams

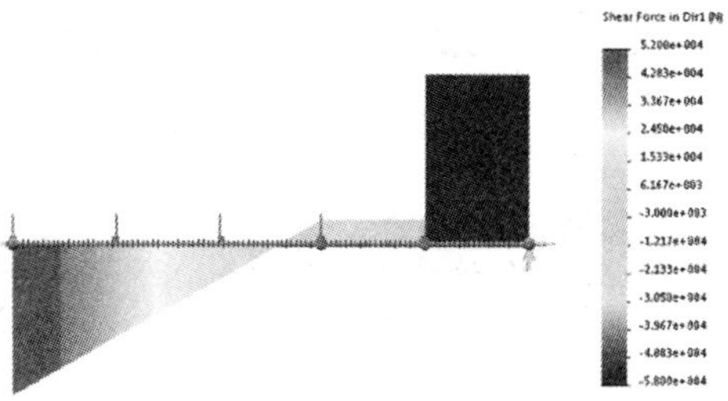

11.2-1 Introduction

[1] Consider a steel beam, which has a cross section of **W360x33**, subject to transversal loads as shown [2, 3]. This example is taken from Sample Problem 5.8, *Mechanics of Materials, 3rd ed.*, by F. P. Beer, E. R. Johnston, Jr., and J. T. DeWolf. The reaction forces and the shear diagram are shown in [4]. The maximum bending moment occurs at 2.6 m to the right of the left end [5], where the shear force is zero. The maximum bending moment is equal to the area under the shear curve, which is 67.6 kN-m [6]. The W360x33 cross section has a moment of inertia of 82.6×10^6 mm^4 in the bending direction (see 11.2-3[19], page 222), the maximum bending stress is (Eq. 7.1-1(2), page 137)

$$\sigma_{max} = \frac{Mc}{I} = \pm\frac{(67.6\times 10^6)\times(349/2)}{82.6\times 10^6} = \pm 142.8 \text{ MPa} \quad (1)$$

In this section, we'll analyze the beam using the **Simulation** and verify the results with the hand-calculated values (Eq. (1) and [4]). Since the structure is statically determinate, these results are independent of material used, however, we assume the beam is made of an ASTM A36 steel.

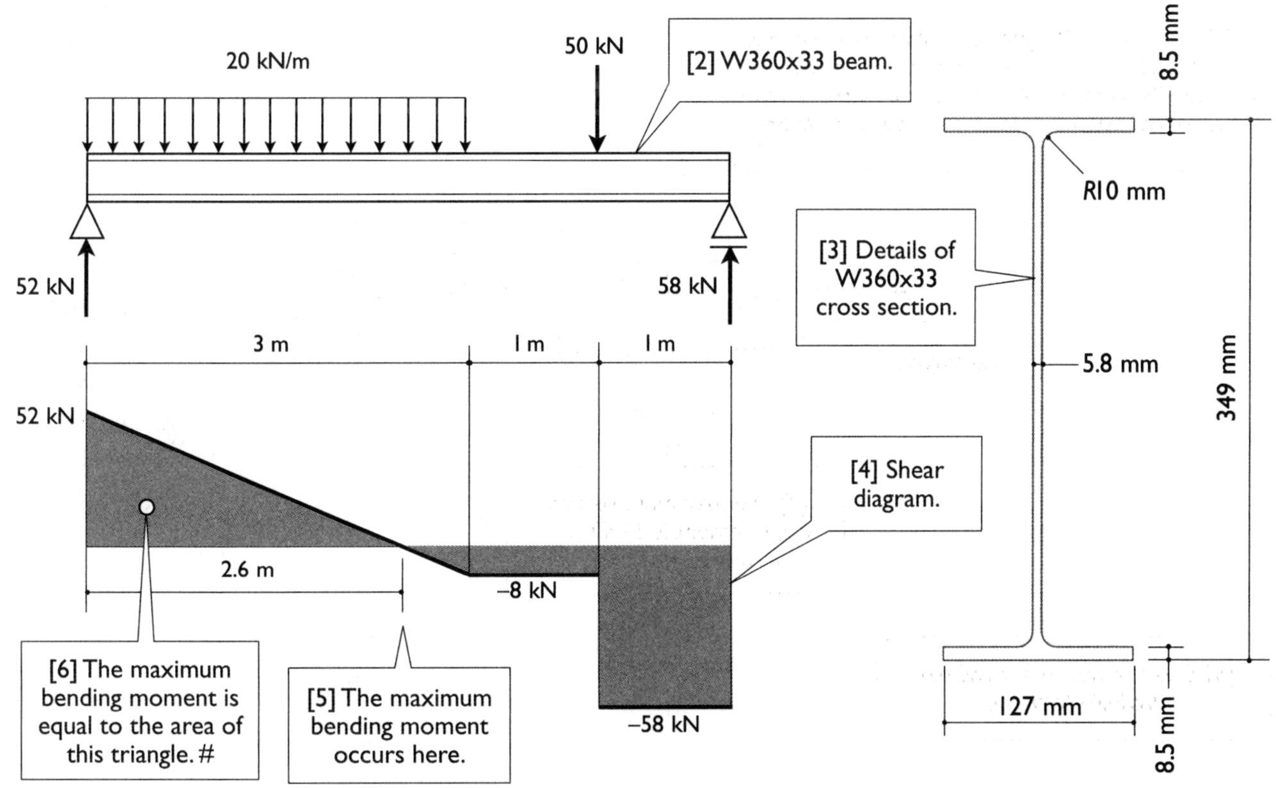

11.2-2 Start Up

[1] Launch **SolidWorks** and create a new part. Set up **MMGS** unit system with one decimal place for the length unit. Save the document with the name **W360x33**.#

11.2-3 Create Geometric Model

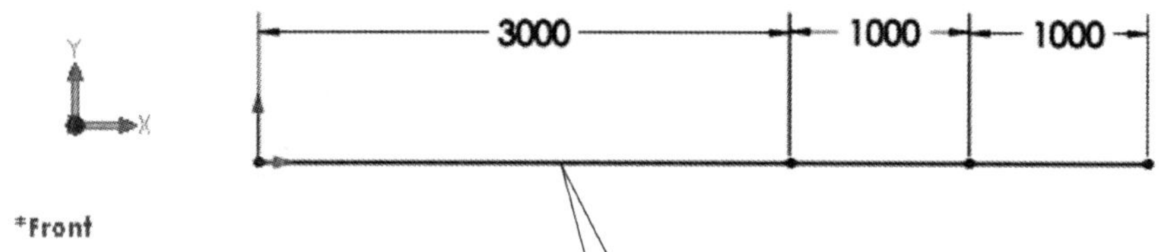

[1] On the **Front** plane, draw a sketch consisting of 3 line segments like this. Remember to click **Exit Sketch**.

[2] Specify Beam Loads

There are many ways to specify loads on a beam. The easiest way is to divide the beam into several segments, such that a distributed load can apply on a beam segment, and a concentrated force can apply at a joint. That's why we sketched 3 line segments [1].

[6] Click **OK**.

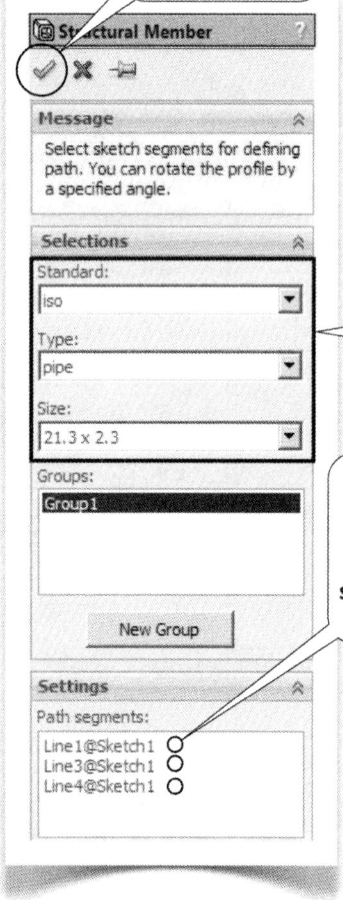

[3] From the **Pull-Down Menus** select **Insert>Weldments>Structural Member...** Or, from the **Weldments Toolbar**, click **Structural Member**.

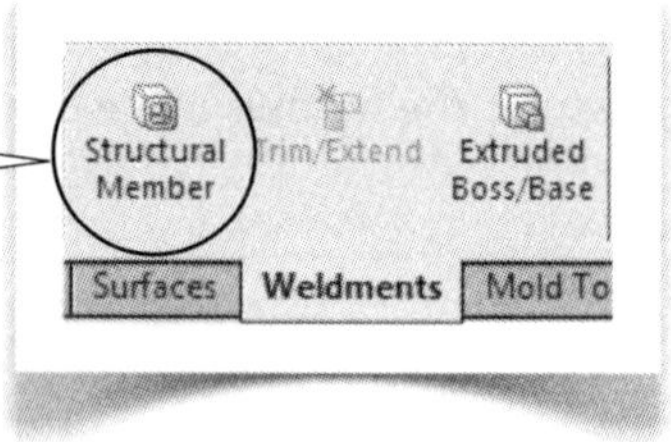

[4] Leave these settings their default values for now and later we'll modify the cross section for our need (11.1-4[3], page 207).

[5] Select the 3 line segments [1]. They'll share the same cross section and orientation.

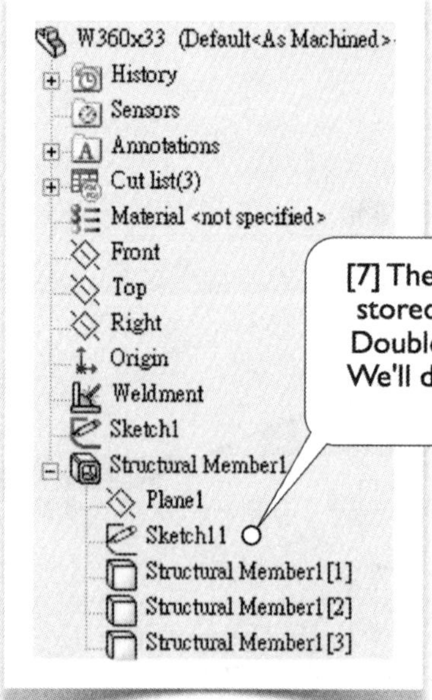

[7] The cross section is stored in **Sketch11**. Double-click to edit it. We'll draw a W360x33 section.

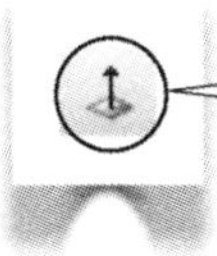

[8] Click **Normal To** to rotate the view.

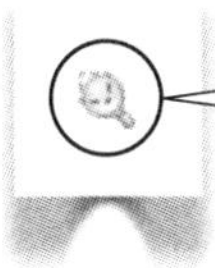

[9] Use **Zoom to Area** to enlarge the cross section. Delete all existing sketch entities.

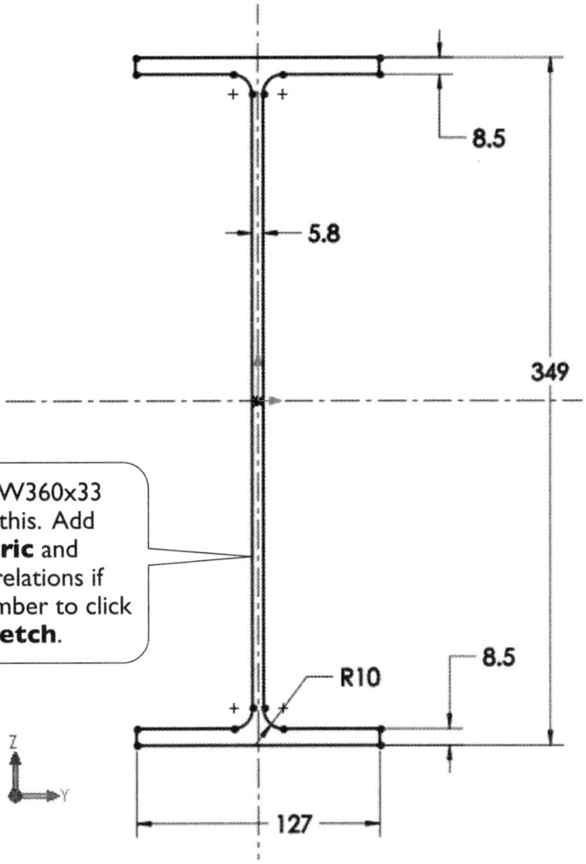

[10] Draw a W360x33 section like this. Add **Symmetric** and **Collinear** relations if needed. Remember to click **Exit Sketch**.

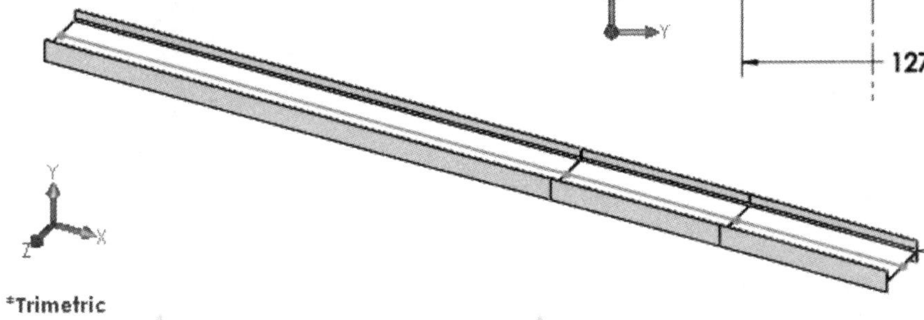

[11] The section's orientations are not correct. They need to be rotated 90 degrees (see [15], next page).

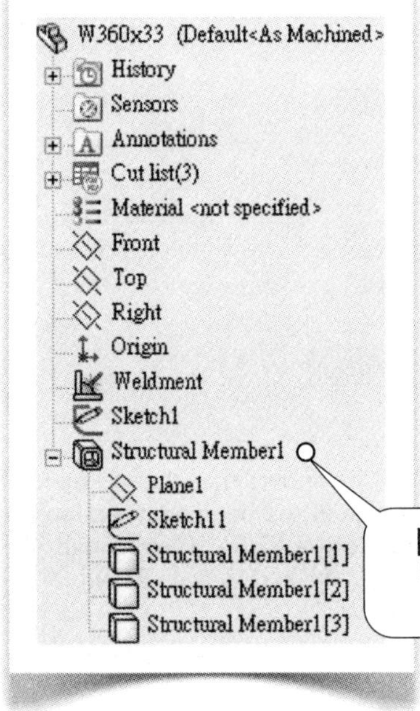

[12] Right-click **Structural Member1** and select **Edit Feature**.

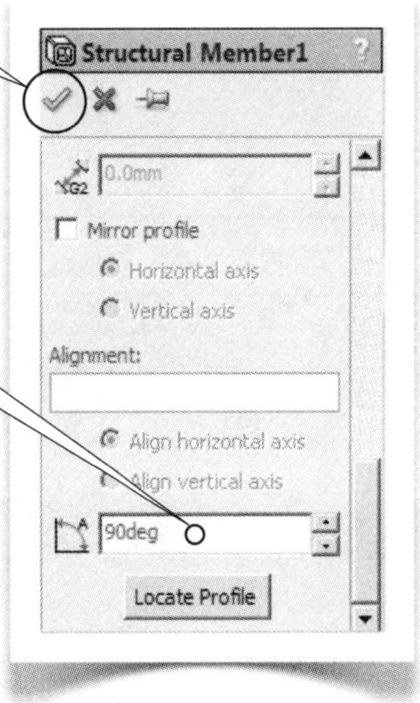

[13] Scroll all the way to the bottom and type 90 (deg) for **Rotation Angle**.

[14] Click **OK**.

[15] Now the section's orientations are correct.

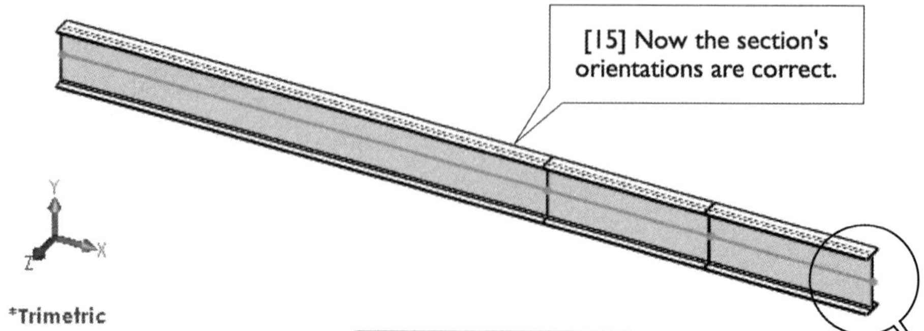

[16] From the **Pull-Down Menus** select **Tools>Section Properties...** The **Section Properties** command is also available in the **Evaluate Toolbar**.

[18] Click **Recalculate**.

[20] Close the window. #

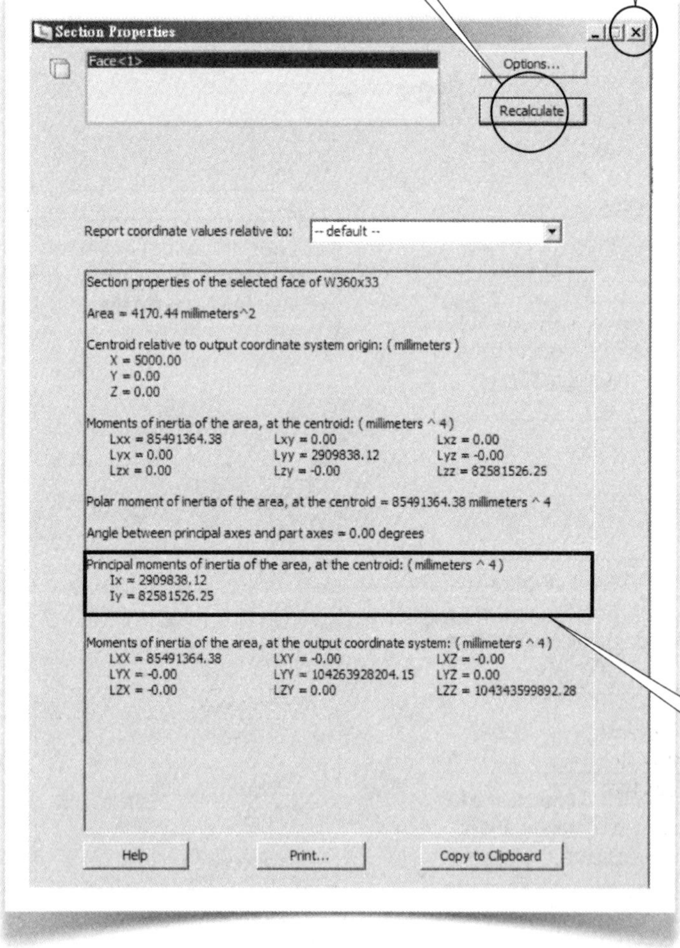

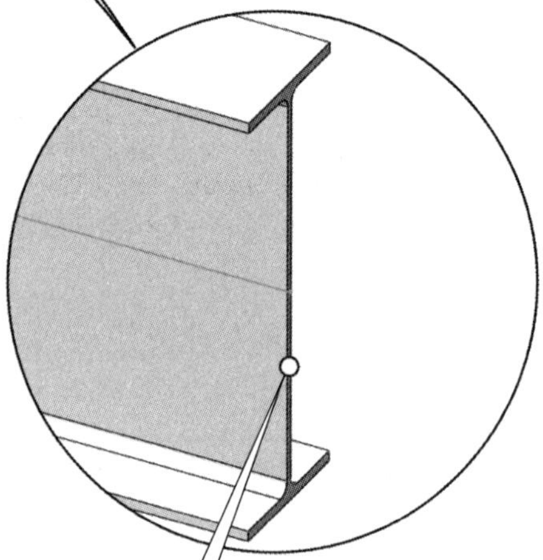

[17] Select the end face.

[19] It reports that the moment of inertia in the bending direction (Y-direction) is 82.6×10^6 mm^4 (also see 11.2-1[1], page 219).

11.2-4 Create a Study and Apply Material

[1] In the **Simulation Toolbar**, select **Study Advisor>New Study**. Leave **Static** as default **Study Type**. Leave **Static 1** as default **Study Name**.

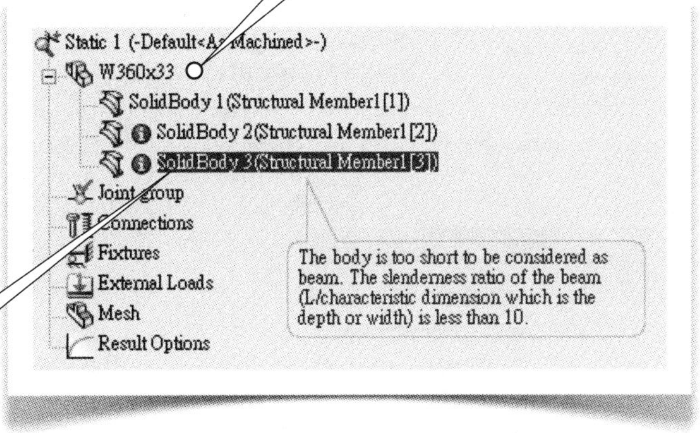

[2] There are warning messages for two of the structural members. Move your mouse over any one of the structural member to read the messages. It warns you that the beam, which is one meter in length and 349 mm in depth, is too short to be considered as beam. Ignore the warning.

[3] Right-click **W360x33** and select **Apply Material to All Bodies...** and apply **ASTM A36 Steel** (which is two materials below the default **Alloy Steel**) to all the structural members.

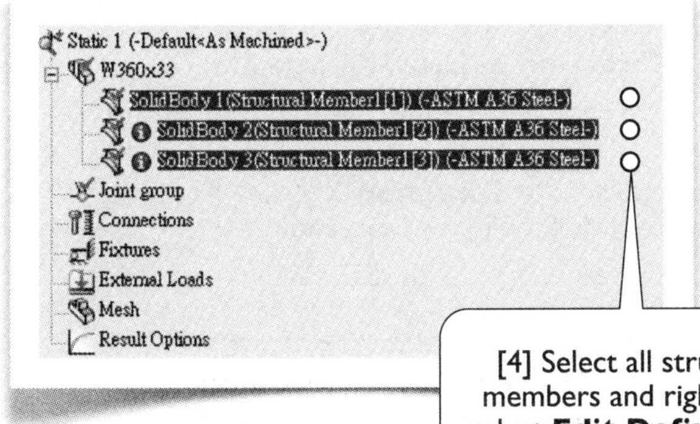

[4] Select all structural members and right-click-select **Edit Definition...**

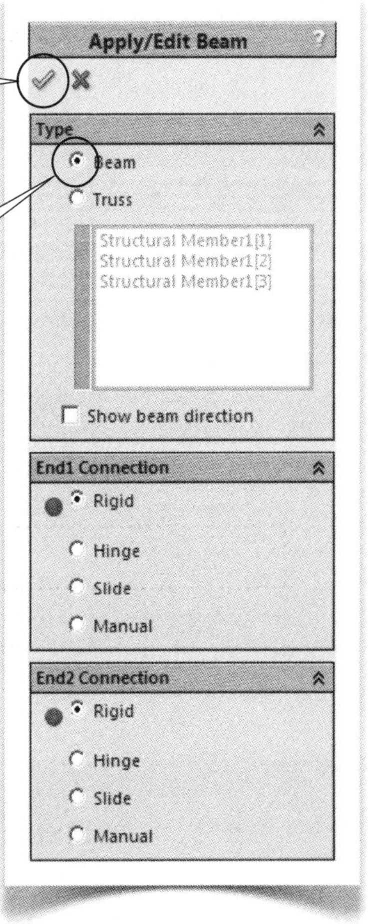

[5] **Beam** is the default **Type** of the structural members.

[6] Click **OK**. #

11.2-5 Set Up Supports

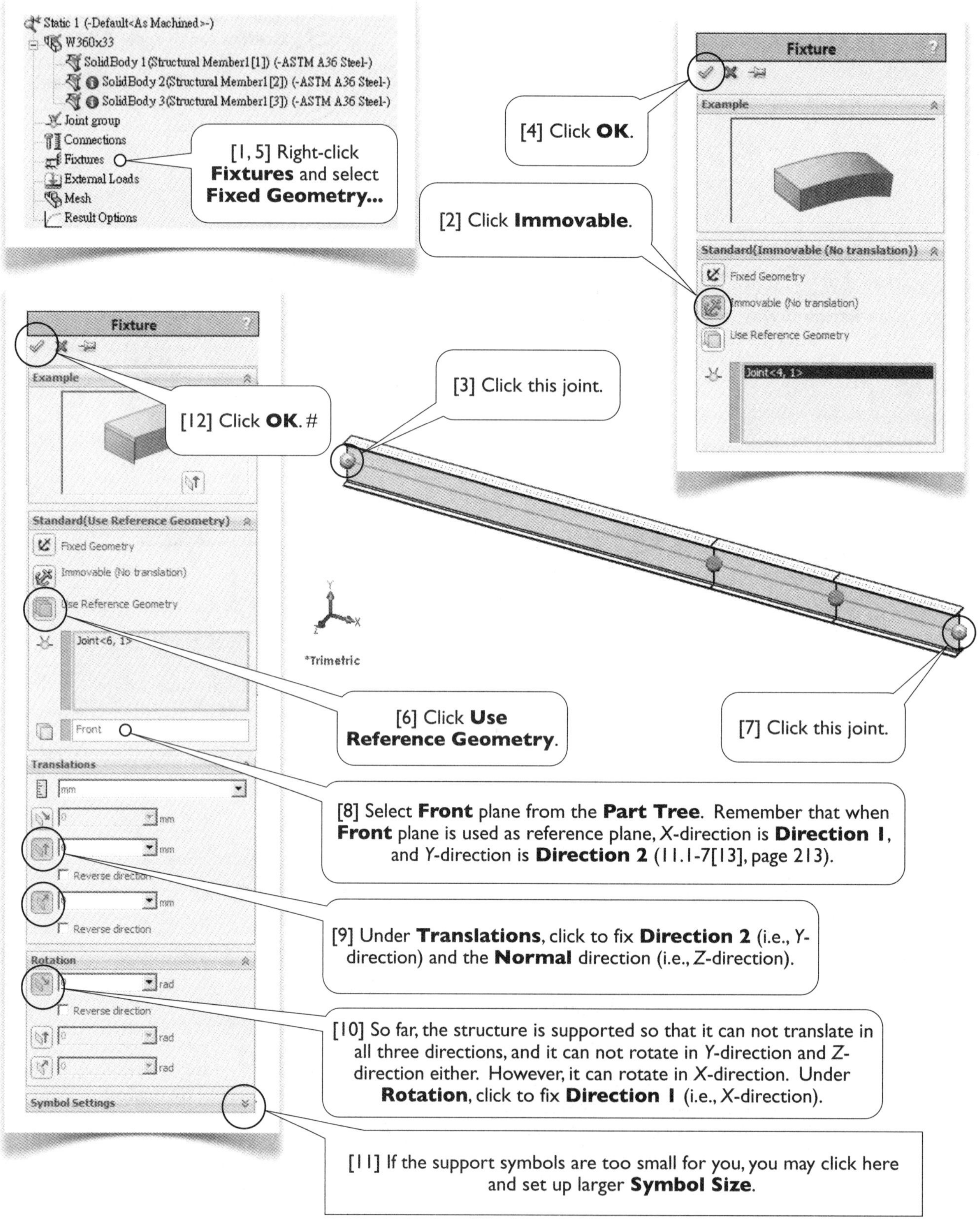

11.2-6 Set Up **External Loads**

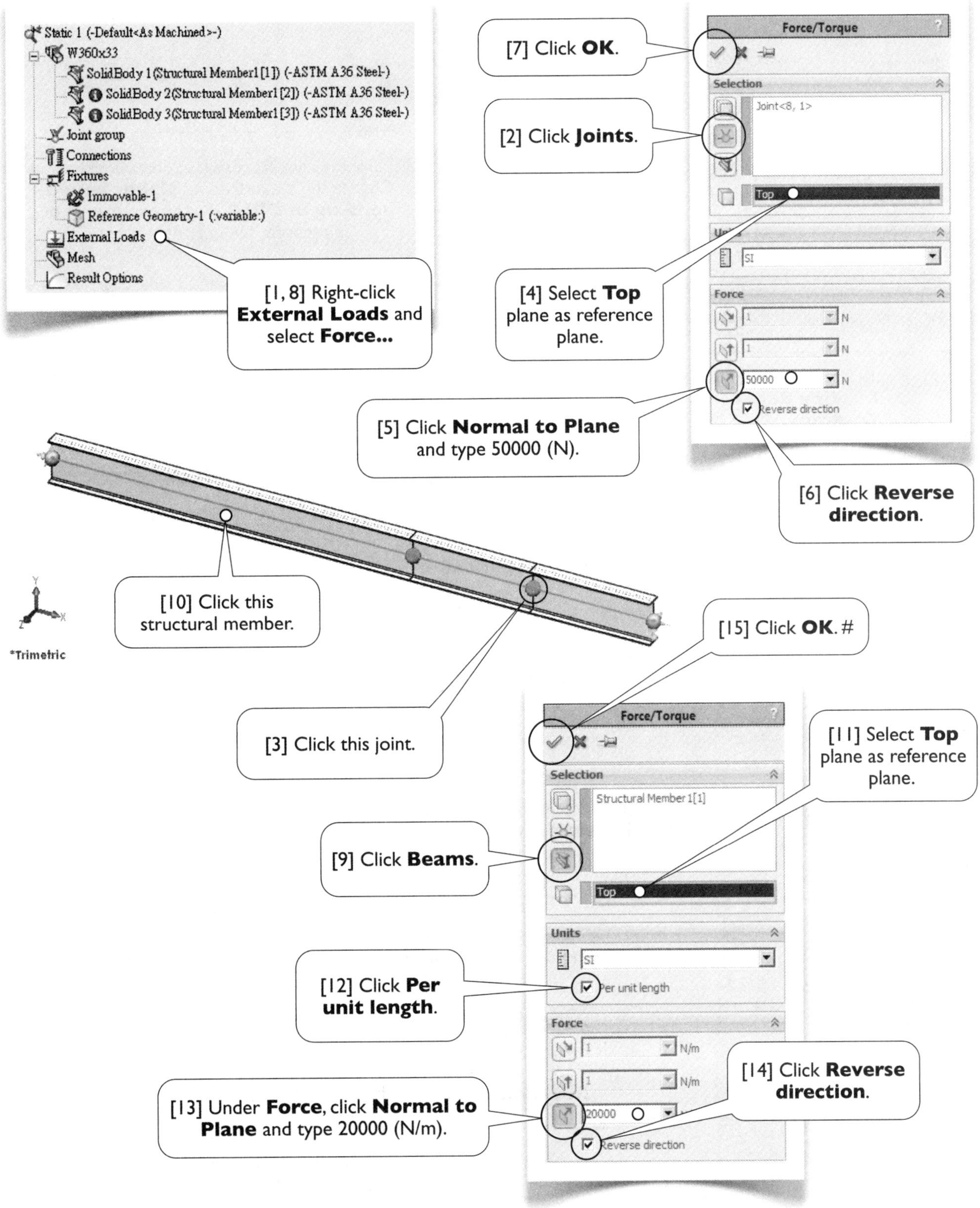

11.2-7 Obtain Solutions

[1] In the **Simulation Toolbar**, click **Run**.

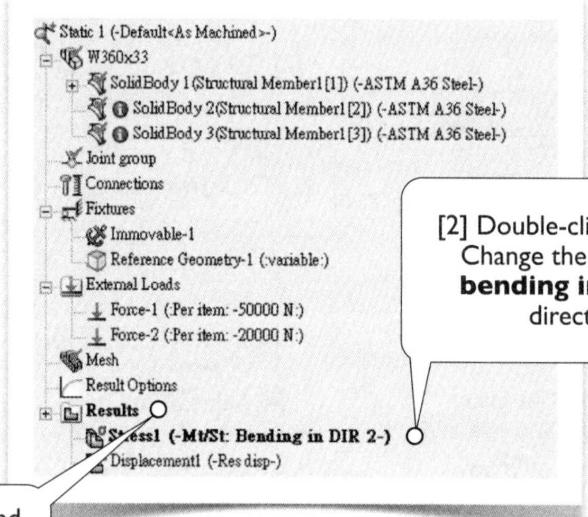

[2] Double-click **Stress1** to edit the definition. Change the Beam tress to **Upper bound bending in DIR 2** (For an explanation of directions, see [13], next page).

[4] Right-click **Results** and select **Define Beam Diagram...**

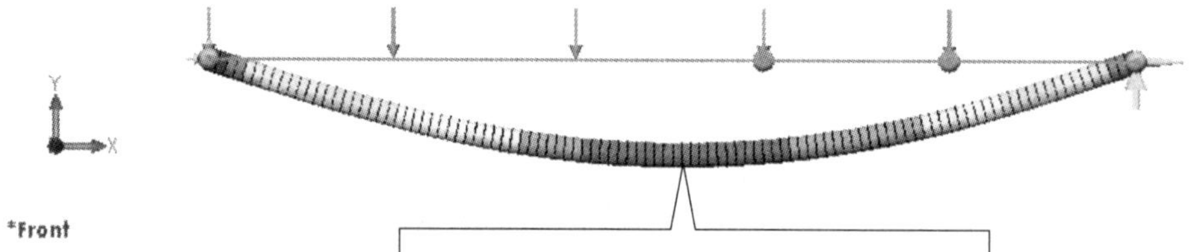

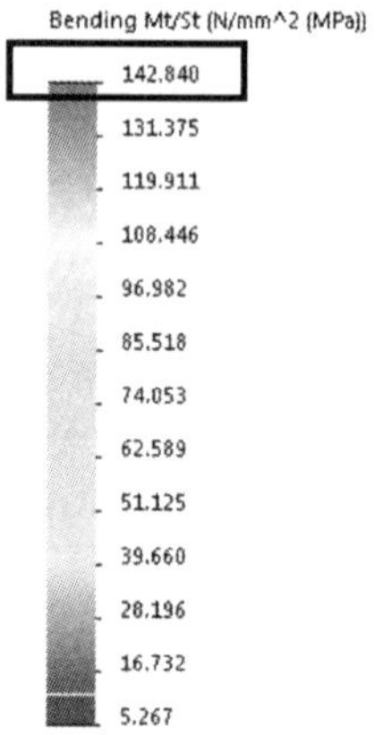

[3] The maximum bending stress is 142.840 MPa, which is consistent with the calculated value (Eq. 11.2-1(1), page 219).

[6] Click **OK**.

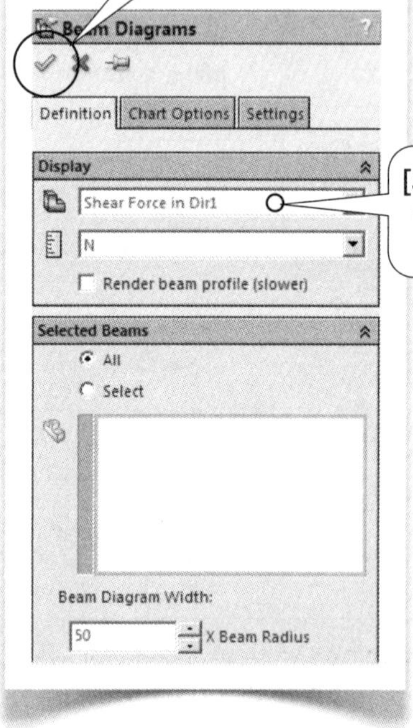

[5] Select **Shear Force in Dir 1**, which is the default setting. (For an explanation of directions, see [13], next page.)

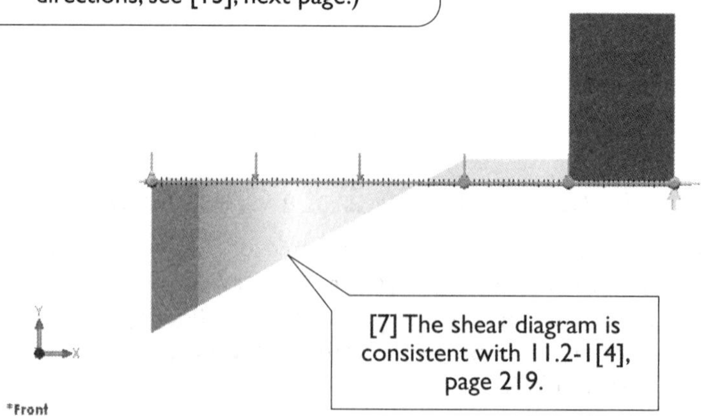

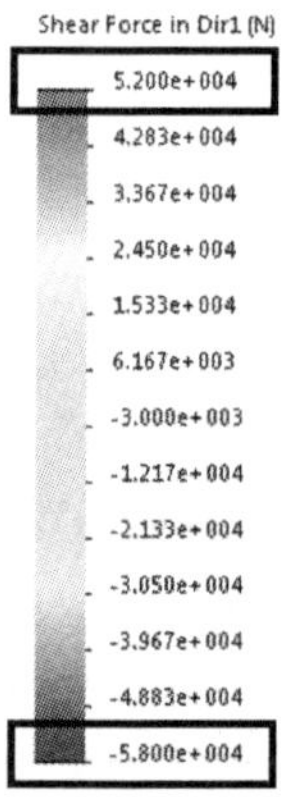

[7] The shear diagram is consistent with 11.2-1[4], page 219.

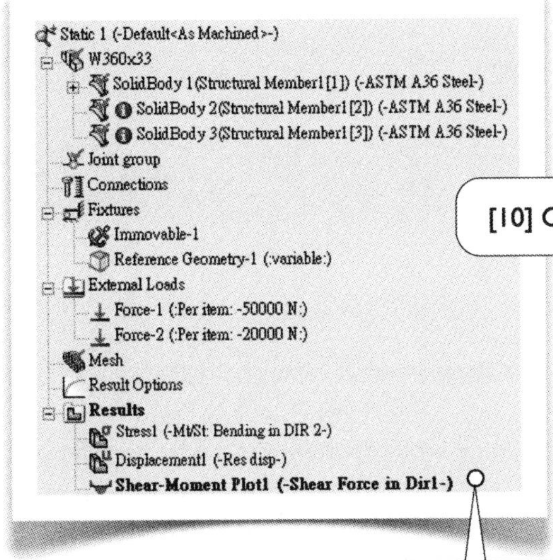

[10] Click **OK**.

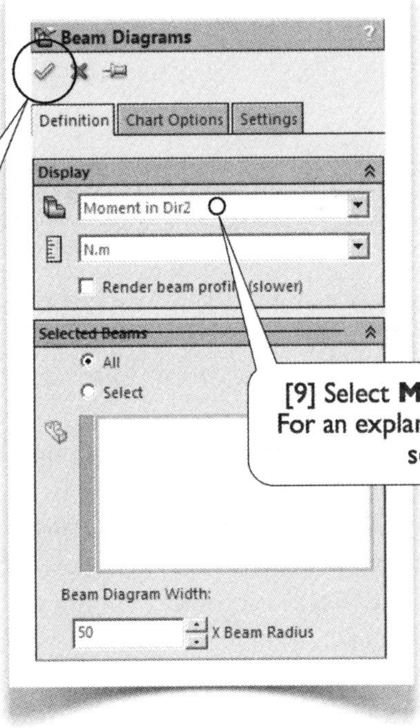

[9] Select **Moment in Dir 2** For an explanation of directions, see [13].

[8] Double-click **Shear-Moment Plot1** to edit the definition.

[11] Rotate to the **Top** view to show the moment diagram in **Direction 2**.

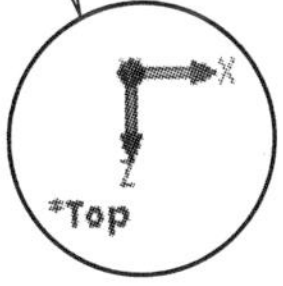

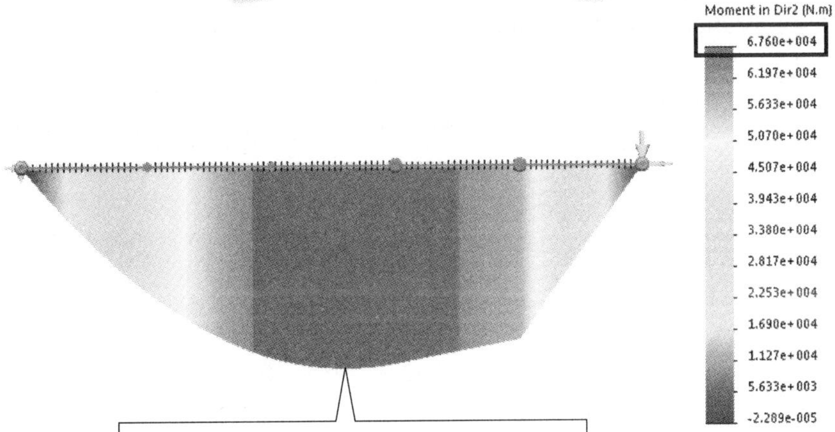

[12] The maximum moment is 67,600 N-m, which is consistent with the calculated value in 11.2-1[1], page 219.

[13] **Direction 1** and **Direction 2** of a Cross Section

There is a coordinate system attached on each cross section. The longer direction is called **Direction 1** and the short direction is called **Direction 2**. In a typical beam, where the loads apply along the longer direction, we usually plot the shear diagram in **Direction 1** and plot the moment diagram in **Direction 2**.

[14] Save the document and exit **SolidWorks**. #

Chapter 12

Plane Problems

In the real-world, everything is 3D; there are no such things as 2D bodies. Some problems, however, can be simplified and treated as plane problems.

For examples, consider the cantilever beam (1.1 and 1.2), the C-bar (1.3), the plate (5.1), and the simple beam (7.1). They all share the following properties: their stresses in Z-face and Z-direction are zeros everywhere (neglect the stresses near the fixed supports); i.e., $\sigma_Z = \tau_{XZ} = \tau_{ZX} = \tau_{YZ} = \tau_{ZY} = 0$. They are called **plane stress problems** and can be solved in 2D space.

Reducing a problem to 2D has many advantages over the 3D approach, and you should always do it whenever possible. These advantages include (a) simpler to build geometry; (b) better mesh quality; (c) less computing time; and (d) easier interpretation of the results. In short, the model becomes smaller and easier to handle. Furthermore, if a problem's nature is indeed a plane problem, it doesn't introduce inaccuracy for the solutions due to the simplification from 3D to 2D.

This chapter will demonstrate how to solve plane problems using specialized elements, called **plane elements**.

Section 12.1

Plane Stress Problems

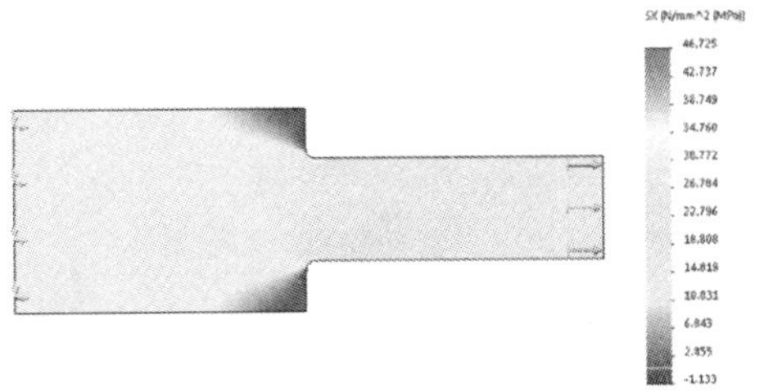

12.1-1 Introduction

Plane Stress Condition

Consider the stress states shown in 1.1-13[5] (page 23), 1.2-6[5, 6] (page 30), 1.3-15[7] (page 49), and 1.3-16[7] (page 50). They all share the following properties: they don't have stresses in Z-face and Z-direction; i.e.,

$$\sigma_Z = 0, \quad \tau_{XZ} = \tau_{ZX} = 0 \quad \tau_{YZ} = \tau_{ZY} = 0 \tag{1}$$

Eq. (1) is termed the **plane stress condition**. If a body has the plane stress condition everywhere, it is called a **plane stress problem**, such as the cantilever beam (1.1 and 1.2), the C-bar (1.3), the plate (5.1), and the simple beam (7.1) (neglecting the stresses near the fixed supports).

A problem may be treated as a plane stress problem if its thickness direction (assuming the *Z*-direction) is not restrained and thus free to expand or contract (due to **Poisson's effects**), and if its loads lie on the structural plane (*XY*-plane) such that no out-of-plane deformation (warping) occurs. All of the examples mention above satisfy this criteria (neglecting the behavior near the fixed supports).

Reducing Plane-Stress Problems to 2D

Substituting the plane-stress condition (1) into Eqs. 4.3-1(1, 2) (page 87), the Hooke's law becomes

$$\begin{aligned} \varepsilon_X &= \frac{\sigma_X}{E} - \nu\frac{\sigma_Y}{E} \\ \varepsilon_Y &= \frac{\sigma_Y}{E} - \nu\frac{\sigma_X}{E} \\ \varepsilon_Z &= -\nu\frac{\sigma_X}{E} - \nu\frac{\sigma_Y}{E} \\ \gamma_{XY} &= \frac{\tau_{XY}}{G}, \quad \gamma_{YZ} = 0, \quad \gamma_{ZX} = 0 \end{aligned} \tag{2}$$

Eq. (2) shows that the strains in Z-direction, except ε_Z, which we'll discuss later, also vanish. Thus, we can eliminate *Z* coordinate and reduce the problem to a 2D problem, on *XY* space.

Note, in Eq. (2), ε_Z is not zero, however, it can be calculated from σ_X and σ_Y, without introducing *Z*-coordinate. The physics behind the nonzero ε_Z is easy to understand: Z-direction is free to expand or contract.

The Purpose of This Section

The purpose of this section is to demonstrate how to solve the plate problem (Section 5.1) using the **plane stress** option in the **Simulation**, and compare the results with those obtained from a 3D model.

12.1-2 Start Up and Create a Plane Stress Study

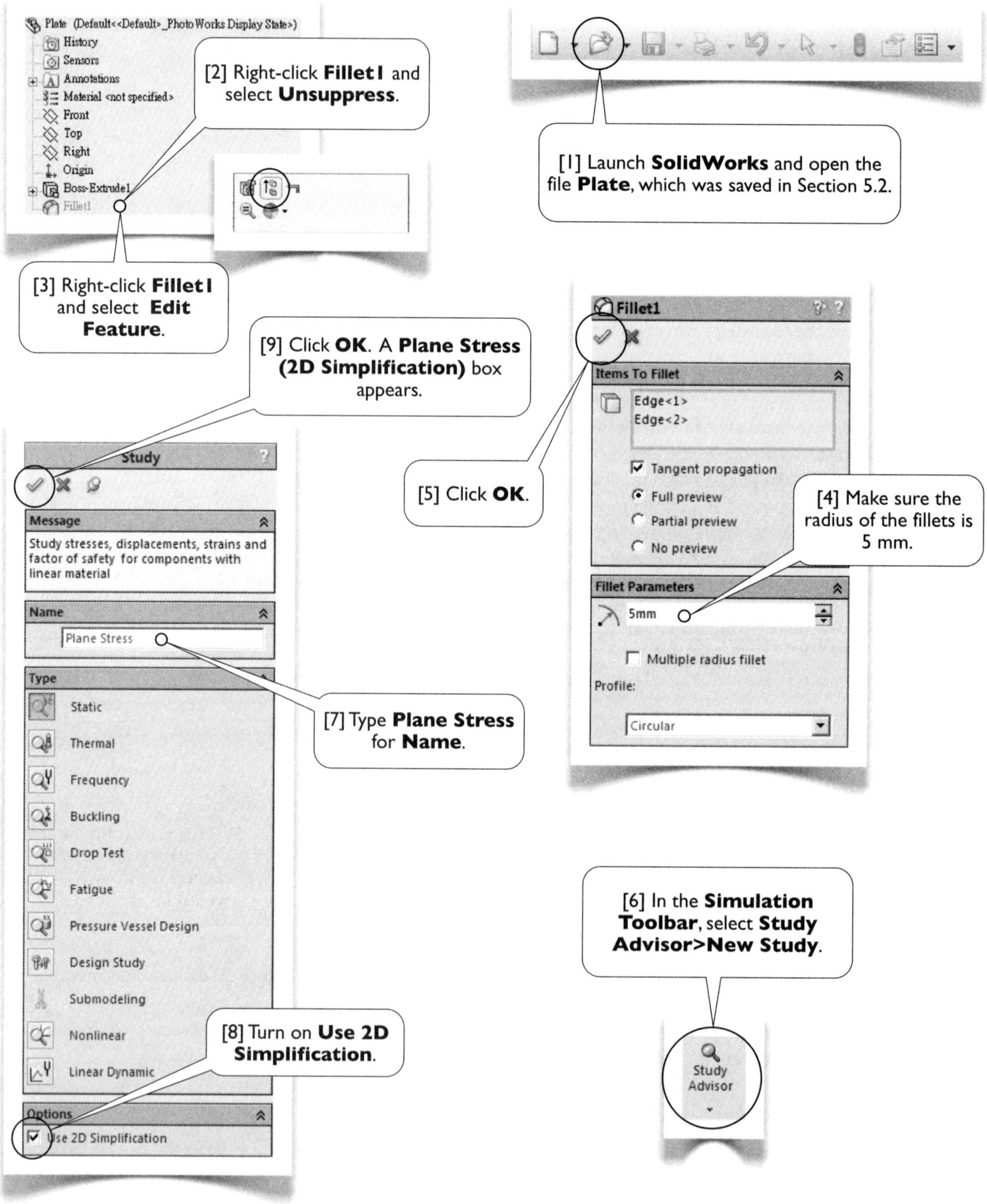

[13] Click **OK**.

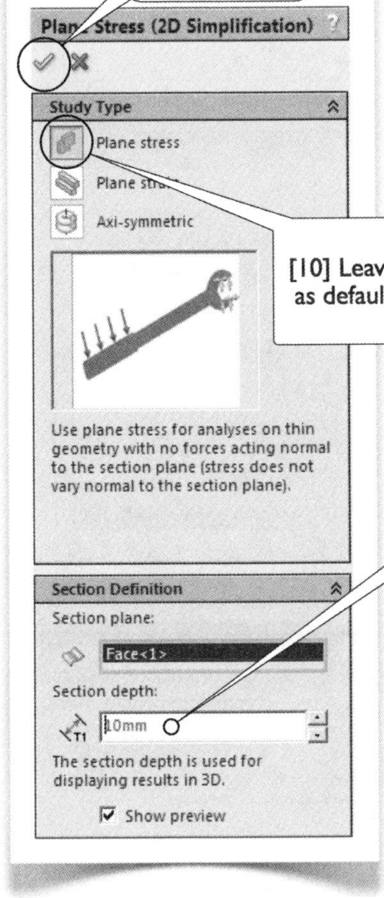

[10] Leave **Plane stress** as default **Study Type**.

[11] Select this face as **Section plane**.

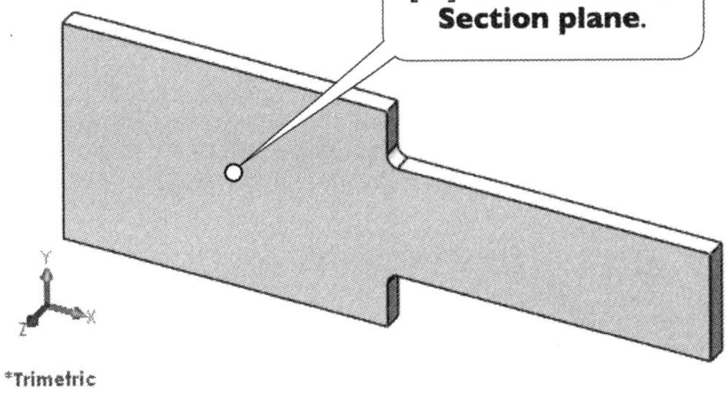

[12] Type 10 (mm) for **Section depth**.

[15] Also note that, due to the change of the model [2], the results of this study become inconsistent with the model.

[14] A new study is created and becomes active.

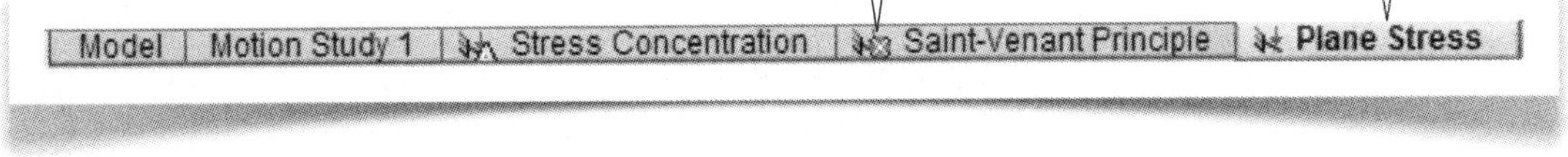

[16] A 2D model is created for the study.

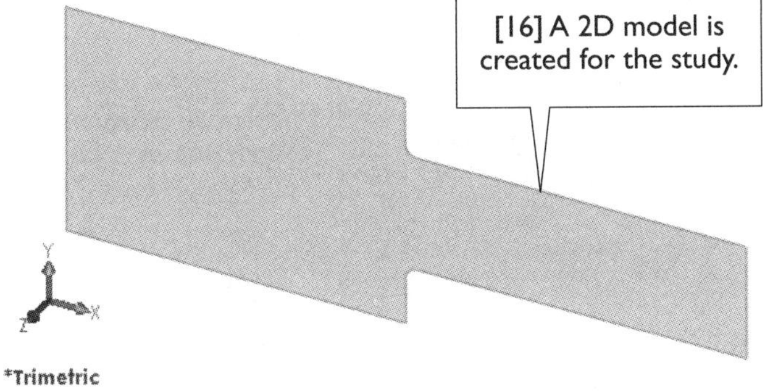

[17] Right-click **Plate** and select **Apply/Edit Material...** and apply **Alloy Steel** for the model. #

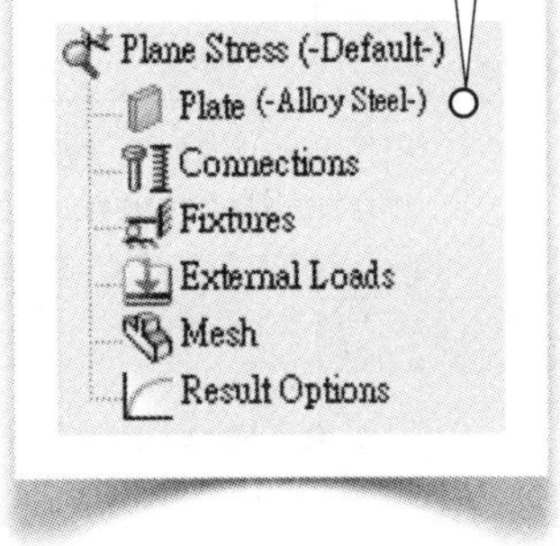

12.1-3 Set Up Boundary Conditions and the Mesh

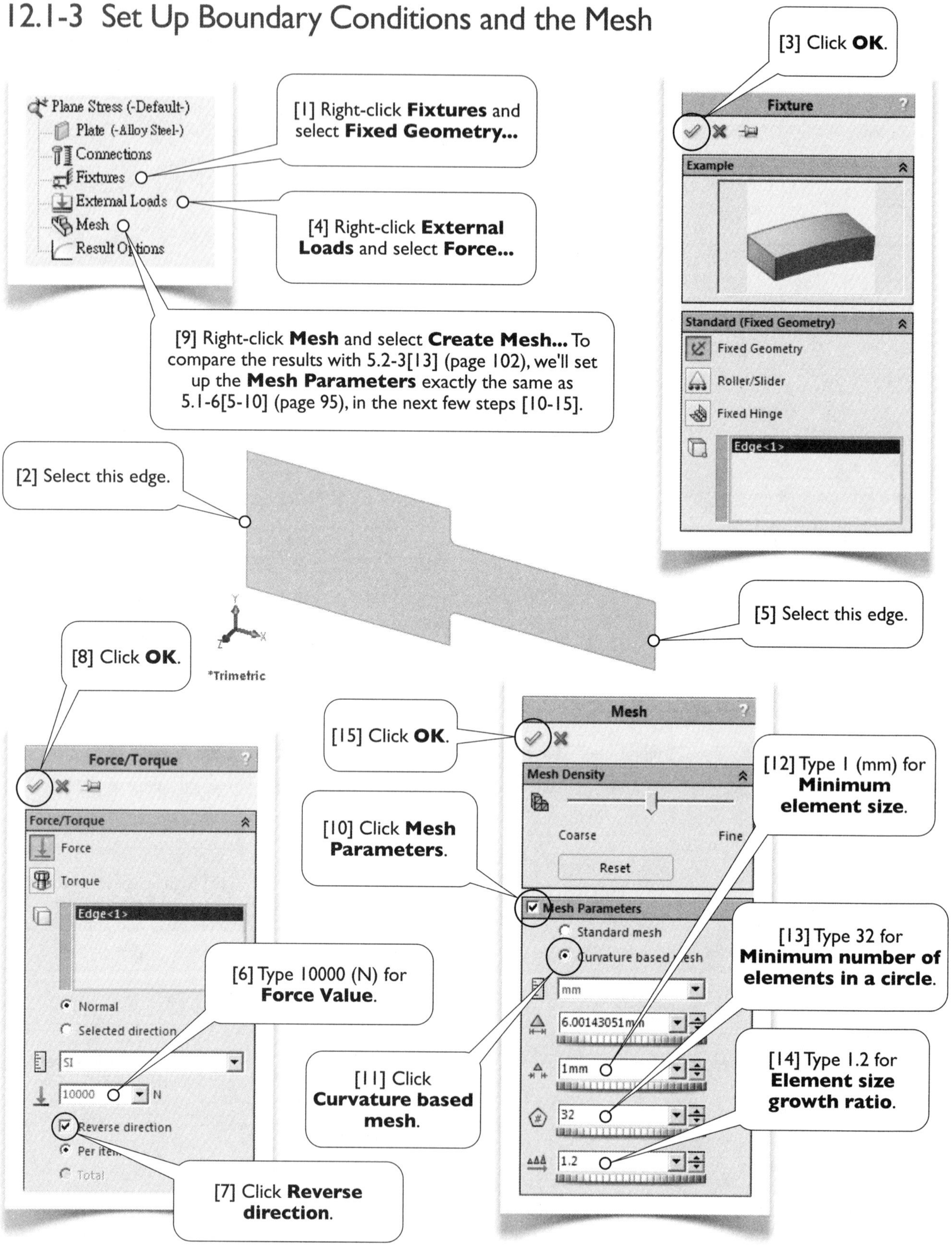

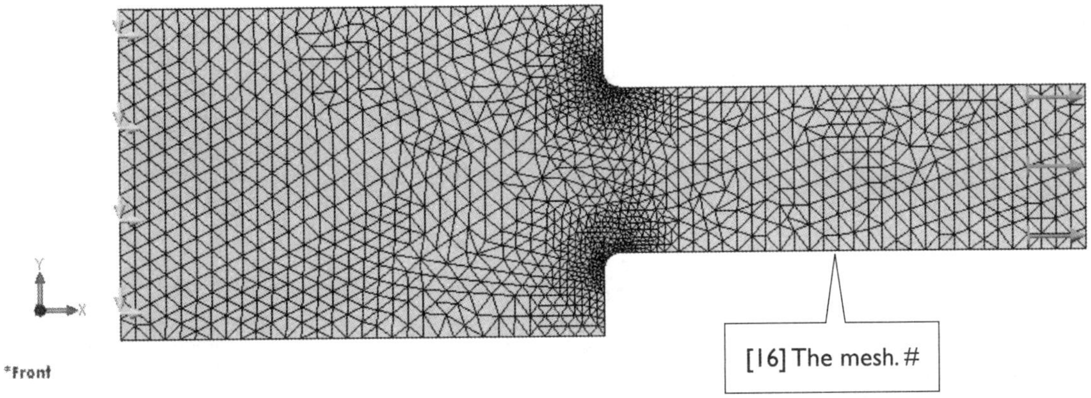

[16] The mesh. #

12.1-4 Obtain Solutions

[1] In the **Simulation Toolbar**, click **Run**.

[2] By default, **von Mises stresses** are displayed after each run.

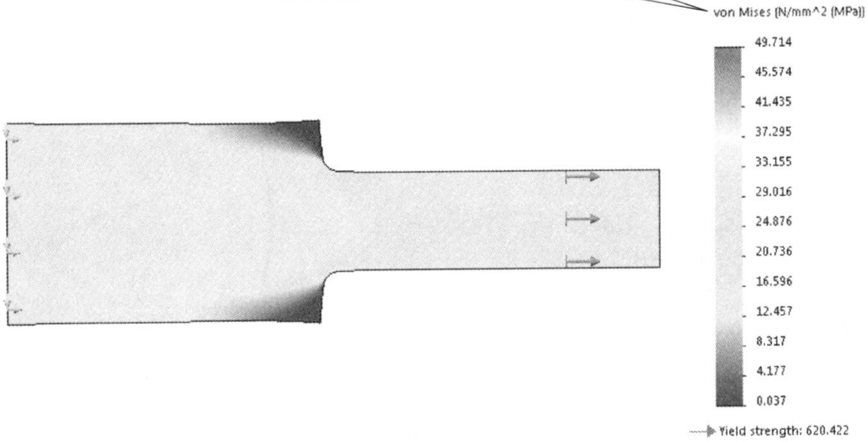

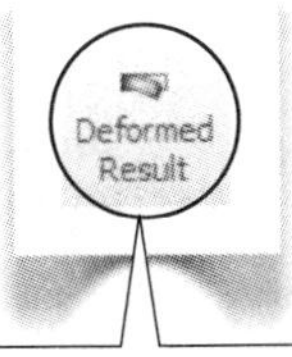

[3] In the **Simulation Toolbar**, click to turn off **Deformed Result**.

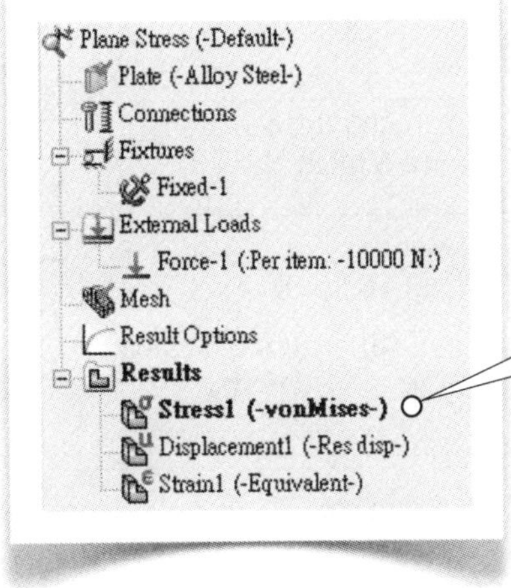

[4] Double-click **Stress1** to edit the definition.

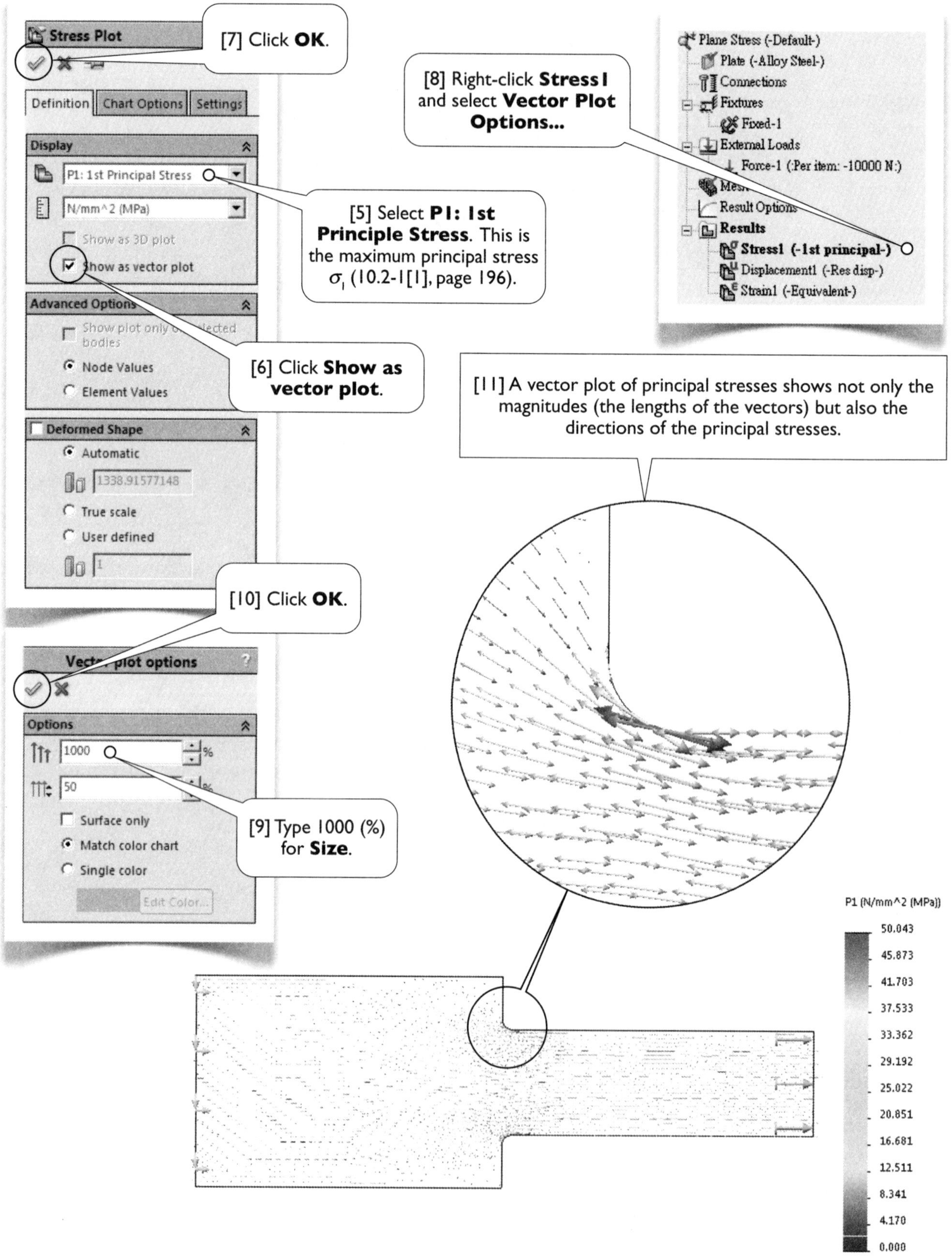
Stress Plot
[7] Click **OK**.
Definition
Chart Options
Settings
Display
P1: 1st Principal Stress
N/mm^2 (MPa)
Show as 3D plot
Show as vector plot
Advanced Options
Show plot only on selected bodies
Node Values
Element Values
Deformed Shape
Automatic
1338.91577148
True scale
User defined
1
[5] Select **P1: 1st Principle Stress**. This is the maximum principal stress σ_1 (10.2-1[1], page 196).
[6] Click **Show as vector plot**.
[8] Right-click **Stress1** and select **Vector Plot Options...**
Plane Stress (-Default-)
Plate (-Alloy Steel-)
Connections
Fixtures
Fixed-1
External Loads
Force-1 (:Per item: -10000 N:)
Result Options
Results
Stress1 (-1st principal-)
Displacement1 (-Res disp-)
Strain1 (-Equivalent-)
[11] A vector plot of principal stresses shows not only the magnitudes (the lengths of the vectors) but also the directions of the principal stresses.
[10] Click **OK**.
Vector plot options
Options
1000
%
50
Surface only
Match color chart
Single color
Edit Color...
[9] Type 1000 (%) for **Size**.
P1 (N/mm^2 (MPa))
50.043
45.873
41.703
37.533
33.362
29.192
25.022
20.851
16.681
12.511
8.341
4.170
0.000

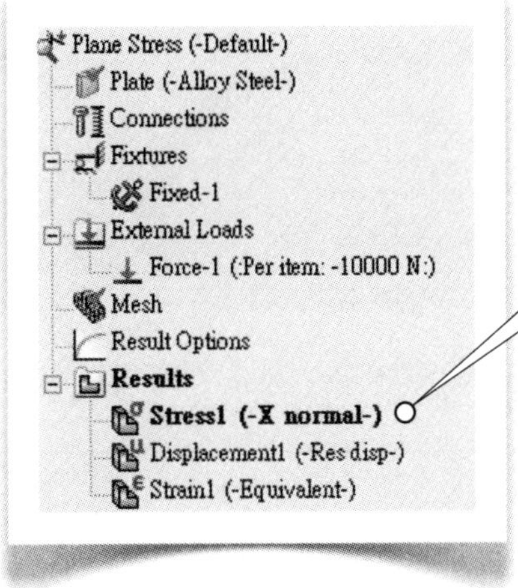

[12] Double-click **Stress1** to edit the definition. Select **SX: X Normal Stress** for **Component** and turn off **Show as vector plot** [6].

[13] The results are comparable with those obtain from a 3D model (5.2-3[13], page 102). #

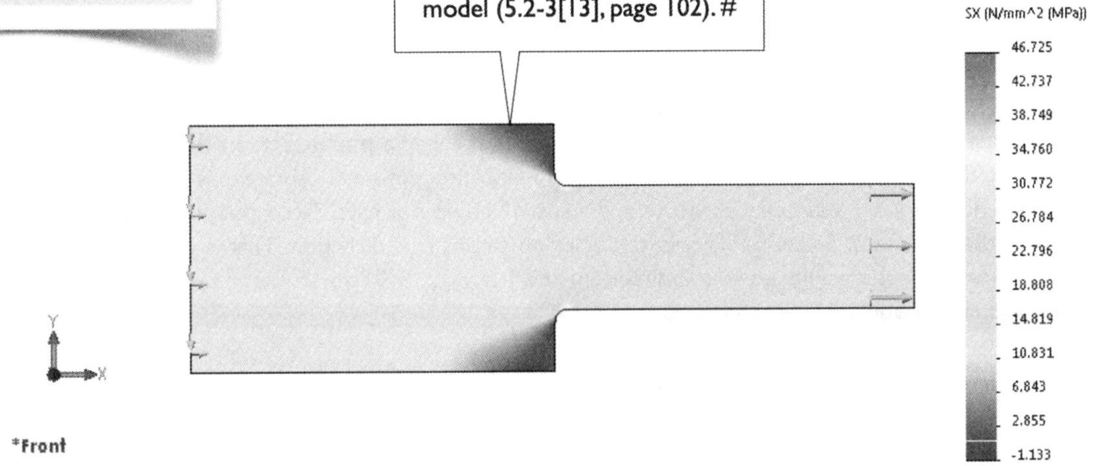

12.1-5 Further Study

[1] Choose a certain point in the model (either 3D or 2D model) and verify the third equation in 12.1-1(2) (page 229),

$$\varepsilon_Z = -\nu\frac{\sigma_X}{E} - \nu\frac{\sigma_Y}{E}$$

[2] Save the document and exit **SolidWorks**. #

Section 12.2

Plane Strain Problems

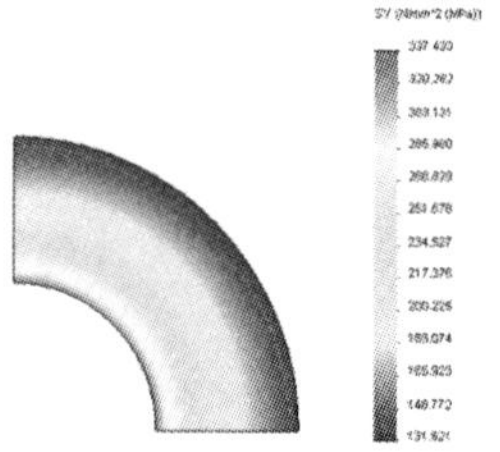

12.2-1 Introduction

Plane Strain Condition

A point in a body is said to be in a **plane strain condition** if there is no strains in Z-face and Z-direction, i.e.,

$$\varepsilon_Z = 0, \quad \gamma_{XZ} = \gamma_{ZX} = 0, \quad \gamma_{YZ} = \gamma_{ZY} = 0 \qquad (1)$$

If a problem has the plane strain condition everywhere, it is called a **plane strain problem**.

If a body is constrained so that it can not deform in Z-direction, and if each cross-section perpendicular to the Z-direction has the same geometry, supports, and loads which do not have Z-components, the problem can be treated as a plane strain problem. Since, in this case, there are no strains in Z-direction. That is, $\varepsilon_Z = 0$ (otherwise particle on the Z-face of a small cube would move in Z-direction) and $\gamma_{XZ} = \gamma_{YZ} = 0$ (otherwise the particles on the X-face and Y-face of a small cube would move in Z-direction).

Reducing Plane-Strain Problems to 2D

Eqs. 4.3-1(1, 2) (page 87), the Hooke's law, can be inverted and rewritten as

$$\begin{aligned}
\sigma_X &= \frac{E}{(1+\nu)(1-2\nu)}\left[(1-\nu)\varepsilon_X + \nu\varepsilon_Y + \nu\varepsilon_Z\right] \\
\sigma_Y &= \frac{E}{(1+\nu)(1-2\nu)}\left[(1-\nu)\varepsilon_Y + \nu\varepsilon_Z + \nu\varepsilon_X\right] \\
\sigma_Z &= \frac{E}{(1+\nu)(1-2\nu)}\left[(1-\nu)\varepsilon_Z + \nu\varepsilon_X + \nu\varepsilon_Y\right] \\
\tau_{XY} &= G\gamma_{XY}, \quad \tau_{YZ} = G\gamma_{YZ}, \quad \tau_{ZX} = G\gamma_{ZX}
\end{aligned} \qquad (2)$$

Eq. (2) is proved at the end of this section (see 12.2-12, page 245).

Substitute the plane-strain condition (1) into Eq. (2), the Hooke's law becomes

$$\begin{aligned}
\sigma_X &= \frac{E}{(1+\nu)(1-2\nu)}\left[(1-\nu)\varepsilon_X + \nu\varepsilon_Y\right] \\
\sigma_Y &= \frac{E}{(1+\nu)(1-2\nu)}\left[(1-\nu)\varepsilon_Y + \nu\varepsilon_X\right] \\
\sigma_Z &= \frac{E}{(1+\nu)(1-2\nu)}\left[\nu\varepsilon_X + \nu\varepsilon_Y\right] \\
\tau_{XY} &= G\gamma_{XY}, \quad \tau_{YZ} = 0, \quad \tau_{ZX} = 0
\end{aligned} \qquad (3)$$

Eq. (3) shows that the stresses in Z-direction, except σ_Z, which we'll discuss later, also vanish. Thus, we can eliminate Z coordinate and reduce the problem to a 2D problem, on XY space.

Note that, in Eq. (3), σ_Z is not zero, however, it can be calculated from ε_X and ε_Y, without introducing Z-coordinate. The physics behind the nonzero σ_Z is easy to understand: Z-direction is restricted to expand or contract.

12.2-2 Problem Description

[1] Consider a pipe that is made of **Alloy Steel** and has an outer diameter of 200 mm and an inner diameter of 100 mm [2, 3]. The pipe is used to transport high-pressure fluid and is supported every several meters [4]. The pipe is designed to withstand an internal pressure of 200 MPa. The lengthwise deformation is prohibited due to the supports [5]. In this section, we'll first conduct a 3D simulation and point out that the plane strain condition

$$\varepsilon_Z = \gamma_{XZ} = \gamma_{ZX} = \gamma_{YZ} = \gamma_{ZY} = 0 \qquad (1)$$

holds. Secondly, we'll perform a 2D simulation using a **plane strain** model. We'll verify the results of 2D simulation with those of 3D simulation, and justify the use of the plane strain model.

In the 2D plane strain model, the length (in Z-direction) is not relevant. In the 3D model, we'll take an arbitrary length of 50 mm, and constrain the body from deformation in lengthwise direction. We'll also demonstrate the use of **symmetry boundary conditions** (using **Roller/Slider**) on both models.

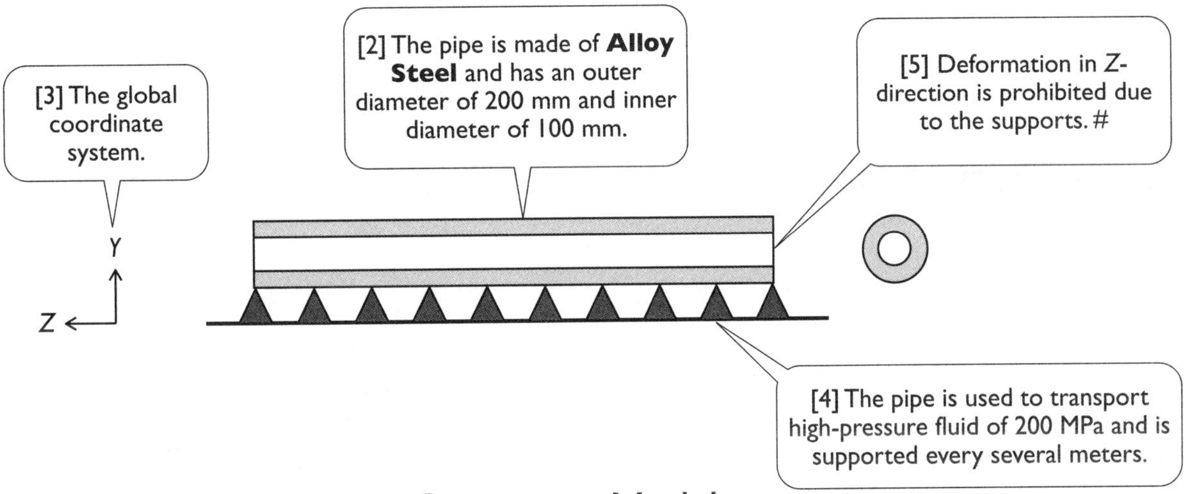

12.2-3 Start Up and Create Geometric Model

[1] Launch **SolidWorks** and create a new part. Set up **MMGS** unit system with zero decimal places for the length unit. Save the document with the name **Pipe**.

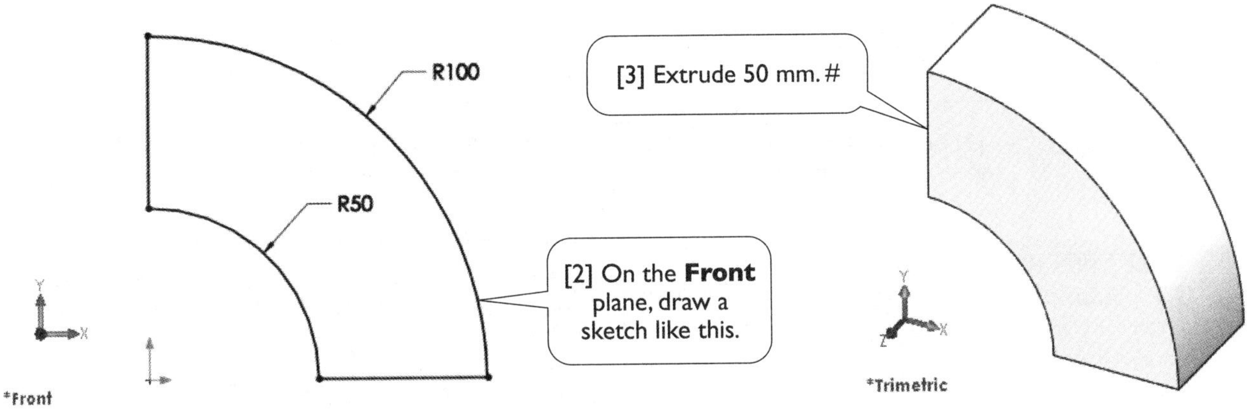

12.2-4 Create an Axis

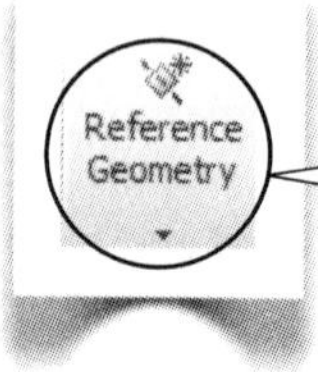

[1] in the **Features Toolbar**, select **Reference Geometry>Axis**.

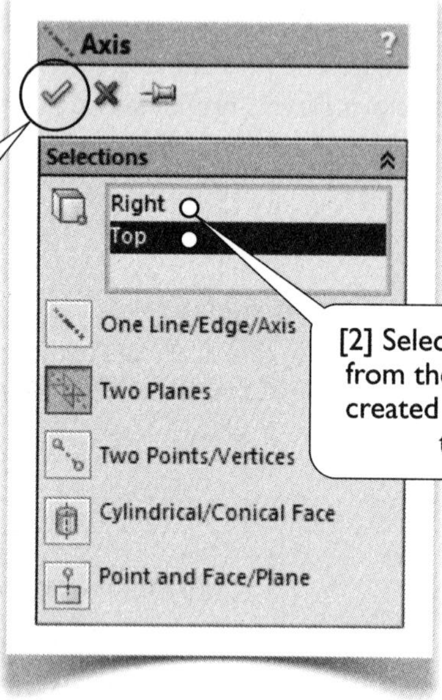

[2] Select **Right** and **Top** planes from the **Part Tree**. An axis is created using the intersection of these two planes.

[3] Click **OK**.#

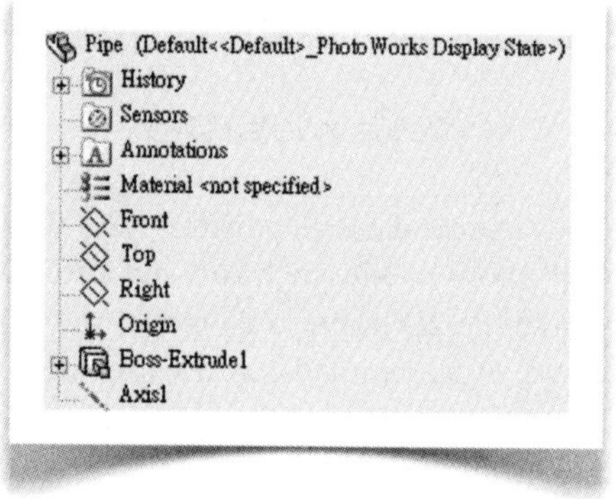

12.2-5 Create a 3D Study

[1] In the **Simulation Toolbar**, select **Study Advisor>New Study**. Name the new study **3D Study**. Leave **Static** as default **Study Type**.

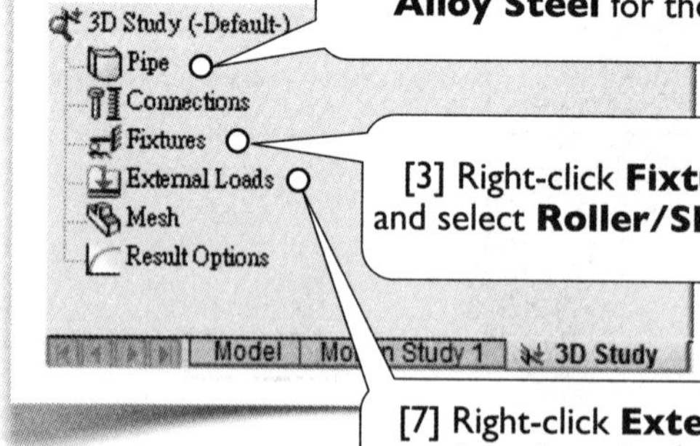

[2] Right-click **Pipe** and select **Apply/Edit Material...** and apply **Alloy Steel** for the model.

[3] Right-click **Fixtures** and select **Roller/Slider...**

[7] Right-click **External Loads** and select **Pressure...**

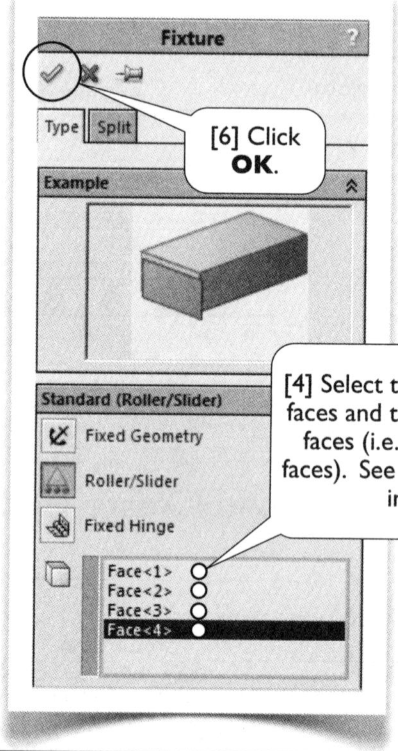

[6] Click **OK**.

[4] Select two rectangular faces and two annual ring faces (i.e., the four flat faces). See an explanation in [5].

[5] The two rectangular faces are faces of symmetry. A face of symmetry should not move along its normal direction, therefore, for **solid elements** (either 3D or 2D), a **symmetry boundary condition** is equivalent to a **Roller/Slider** condition.

Due to the plane strain conditions, the two annual ring faces should not move in their normal directions, therefore, we set up **Roller/Slider** conditions on these two faces. If you view the pipe as infinitely long, the two annual ring faces can be thought of as faces of symmetry.

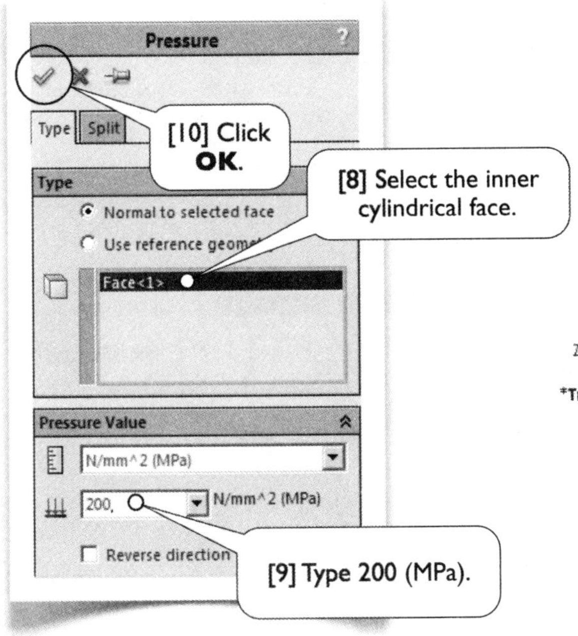

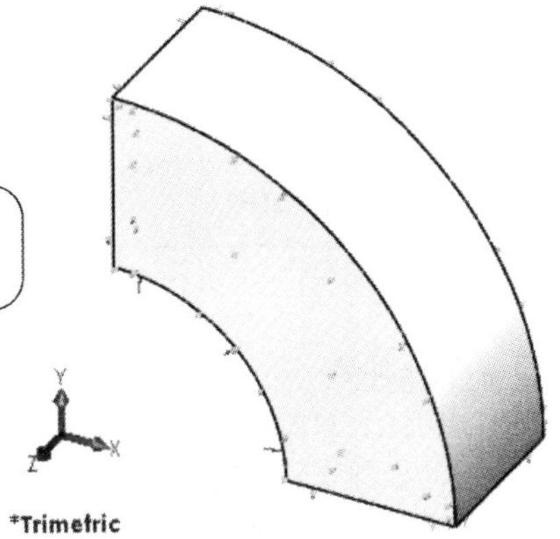

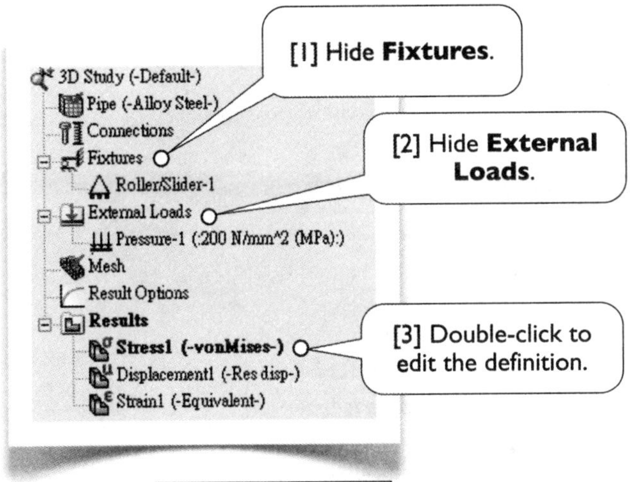

12.2-6 View Radial Stresses

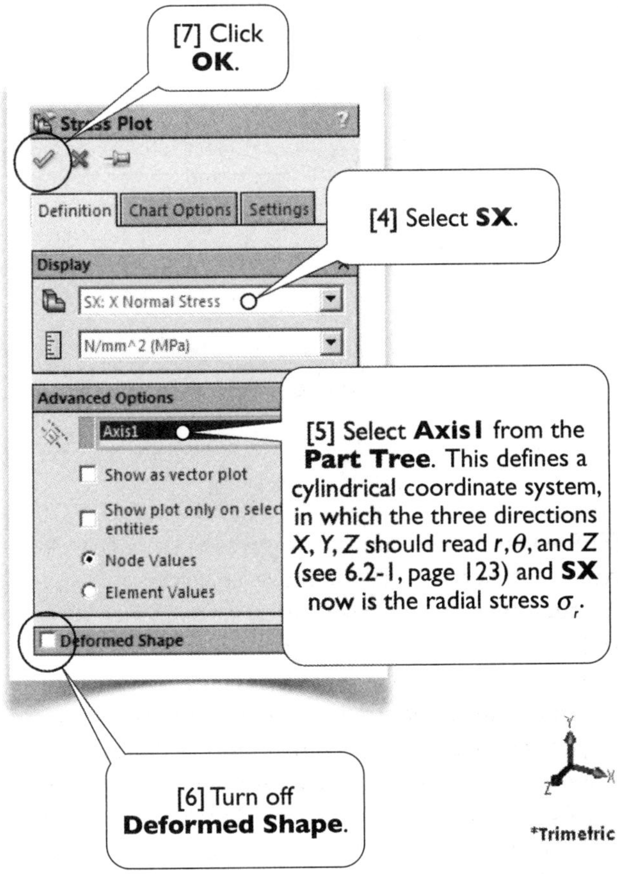

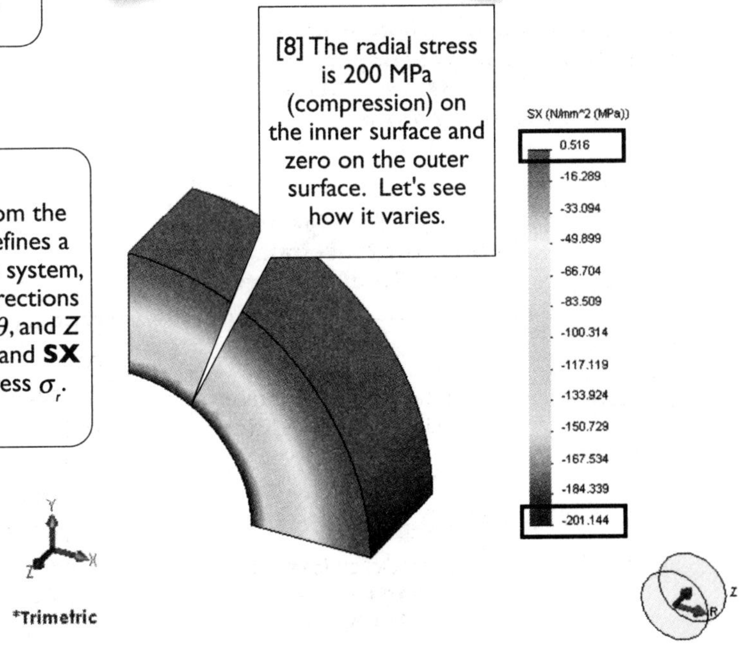

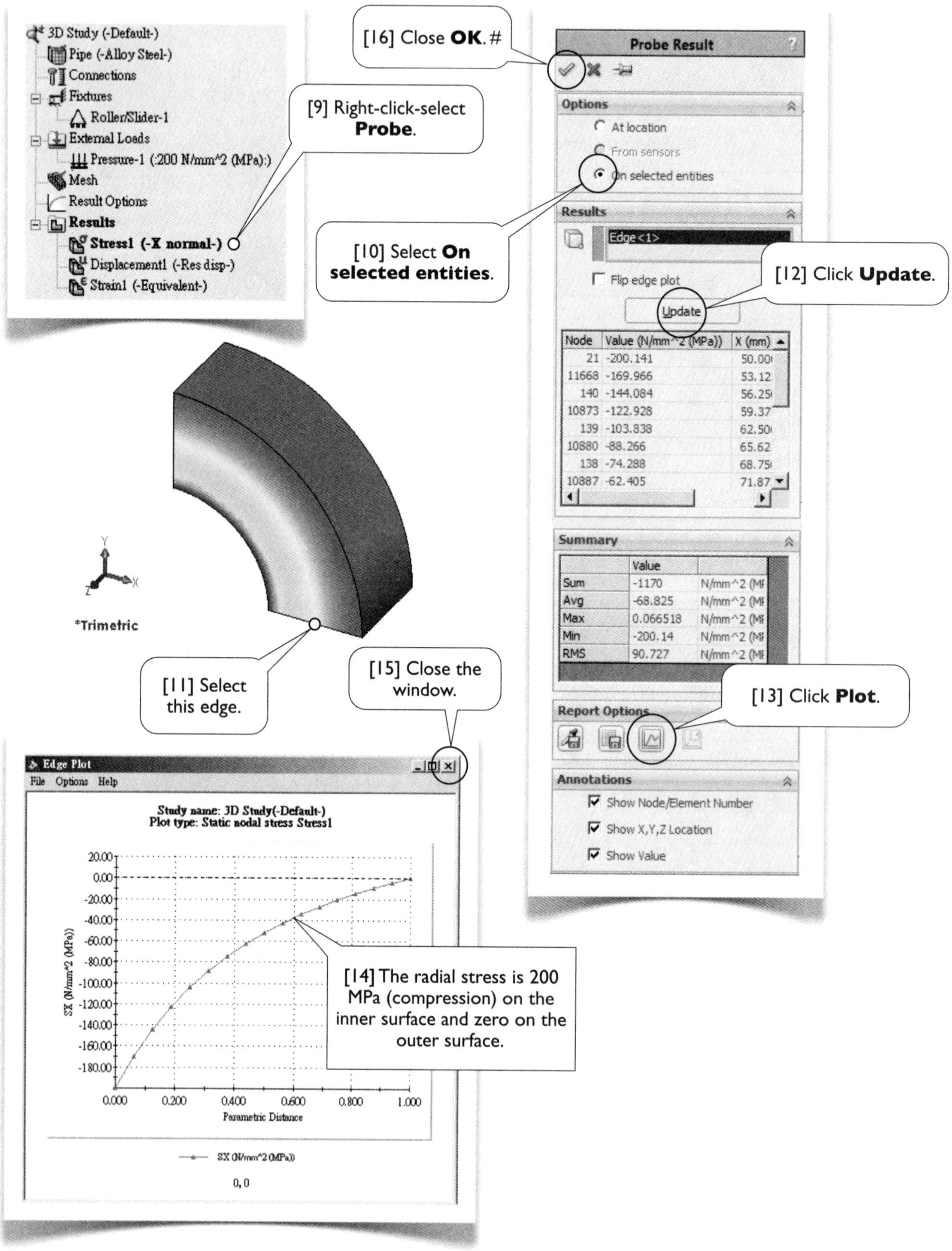
3D Study (-Default-)
Pipe (-Alloy Steel-)
Connections
Fixtures
Roller/Slider-1
External Loads
Pressure-1 (:200 N/mm^2 (MPa):)
Mesh
Result Options
Results
Stress1 (-X normal-)
Displacement1 (-Res disp-)
Strain1 (-Equivalent-)
[9] Right-click-select **Probe**.
[16] Close **OK**. #
Probe Result
Options
At location
From sensors
On selected entities
[10] Select **On selected entities**.
Results
Edge<1>
Flip edge plot
Update
[12] Click **Update**.
Node | Value (N/mm^2 (MPa)) | X (mm)
21 | -200.141 | 50.00
11668 | -169.966 | 53.12
140 | -144.084 | 56.25
10873 | -122.928 | 59.37
139 | -103.838 | 62.50
10880 | -88.266 | 65.62
138 | -74.288 | 68.75
10887 | -62.405 | 71.87
Summary
Value
Sum | -1170 | N/mm^2 (MF
Avg | -68.825 | N/mm^2 (MF
Max | 0.066518 | N/mm^2 (MF
Min | -200.14 | N/mm^2 (MF
RMS | 90.727 | N/mm^2 (MF
Report Options
[13] Click **Plot**.
Annotations
Show Node/Element Number
Show X,Y,Z Location
Show Value
*Trimetric
[11] Select this edge.
[15] Close the window.
Edge Plot
File Options Help
Study name: 3D Study(-Default-)
Plot type: Static nodal stress Stress1
SX (N/mm^2 (MPa))
Parametric Distance
0.000 0.200 0.400 0.600 0.800 1.000
20.00 0.00 -20.00 -40.00 -60.00 -80.00 -100.00 -120.00 -140.00 -160.00 -180.00
0, 0
[14] The radial stress is 200 MPa (compression) on the inner surface and zero on the outer surface.

12.2-7 View Hoop Stresses

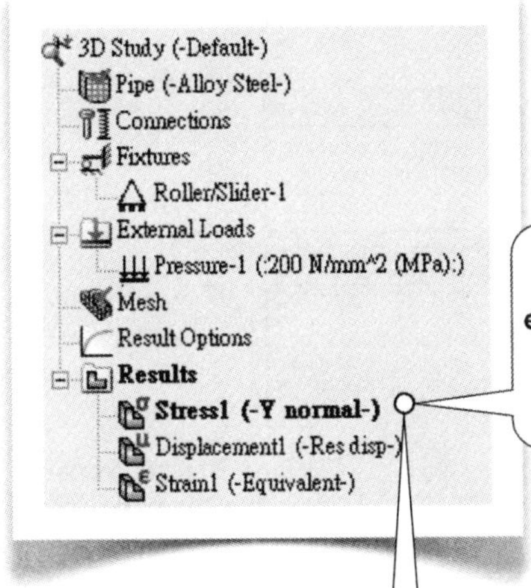

[1] Double-click to edit the definition and select **SY**, which is the hoop stress σ_θ.

[2] The hoop stress is 336 MPa (tension) on the inner surface and 133 MPa (tension) on the outer surface. Let's see how it varies.

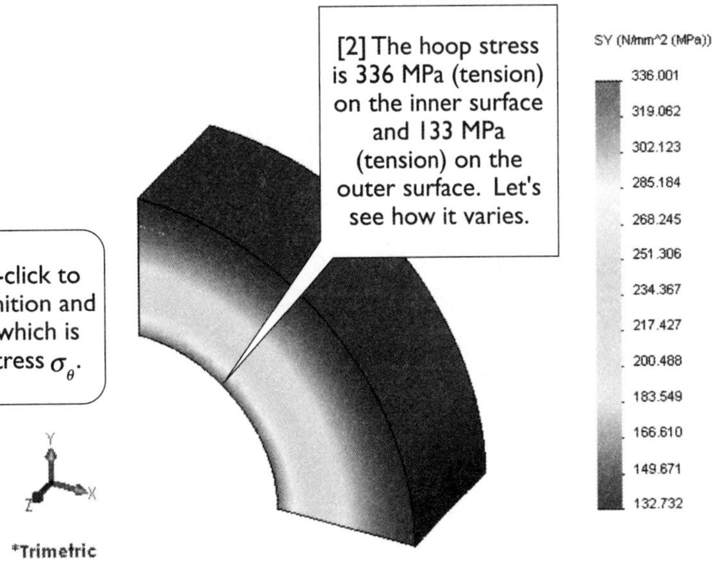

[3] Repeat the steps in 12.2-6[9-13], last page.

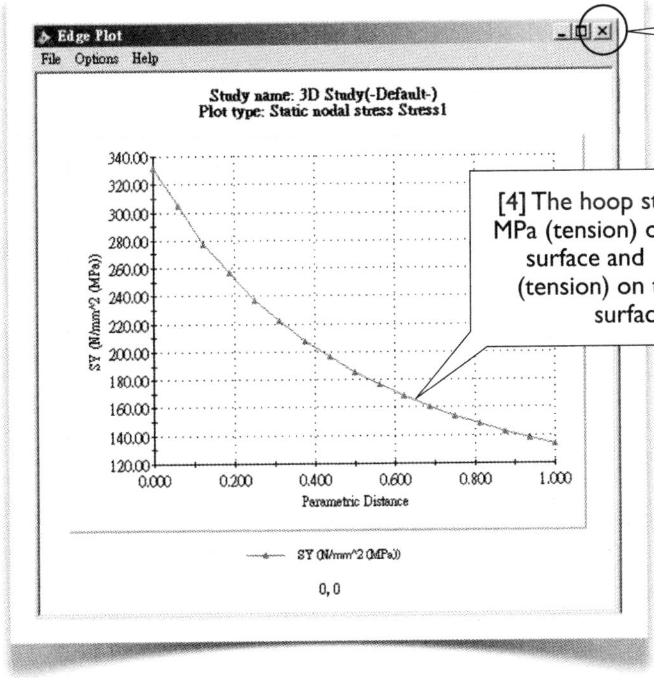

[4] The hoop stress is 336 MPa (tension) on the inner surface and 133 MPa (tension) on the outer surface.

[5] Close the window and click **OK** in the **Probe Result** box. #

12.2-8 Create a Plane Strain Study

[1] In the **Simulation Toolbar**, select **Study Advisor>New Study**.

[2] Type **Plane Strain** for **Name**.

[3] Click **Use 2D Simplification**.

[4] Click **OK**.

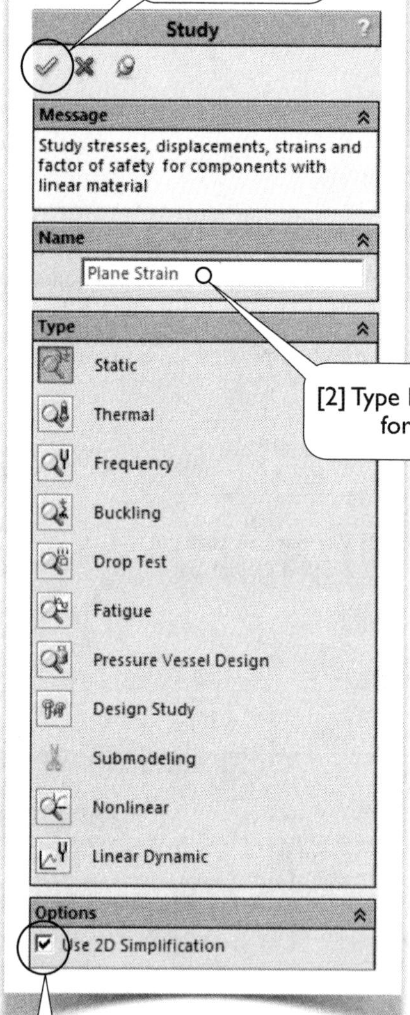

[5] Select **Plane strain**.

[6] Select this face as **Section plane**.

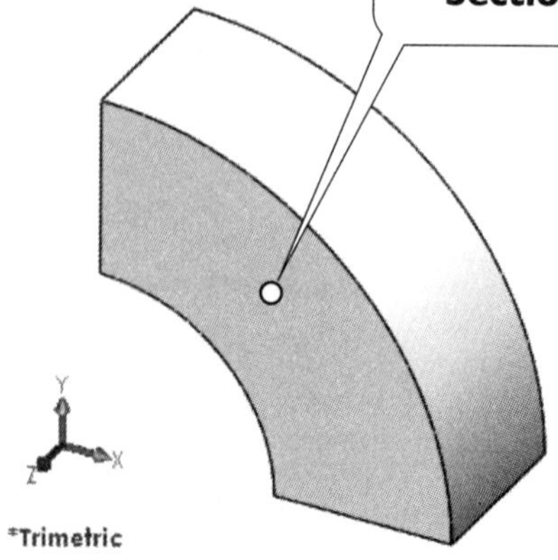

[7] Type 50 (mm) for **Section depth** (see 12.2-2, page 237).

[8] Click **OK**.

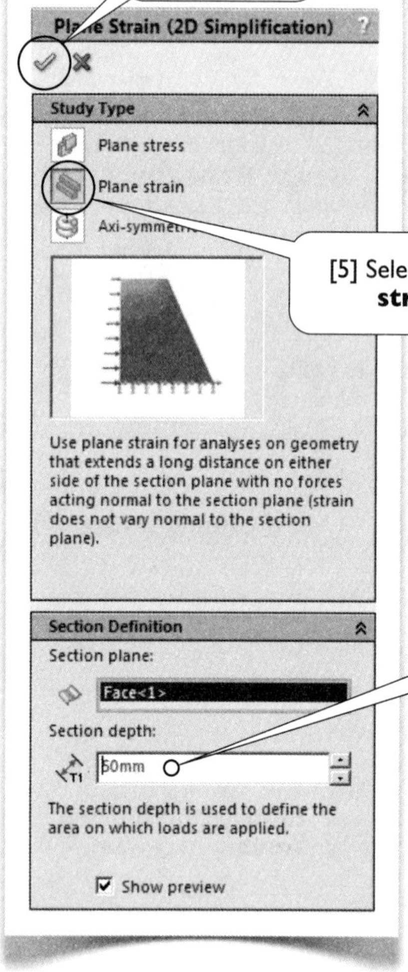

[9] A new study is created and becomes active.

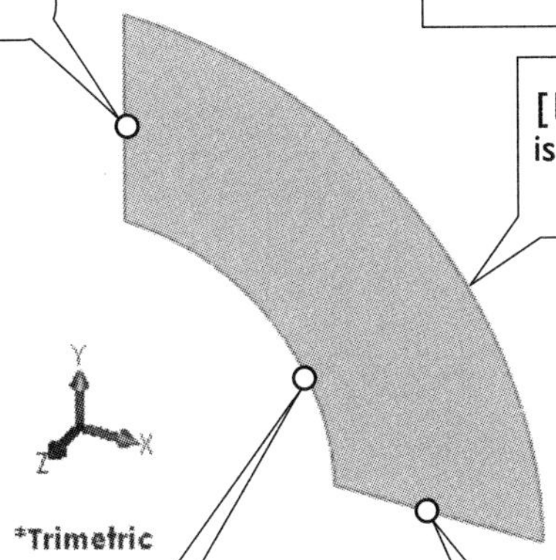

[10] A 2D model is created for the study.

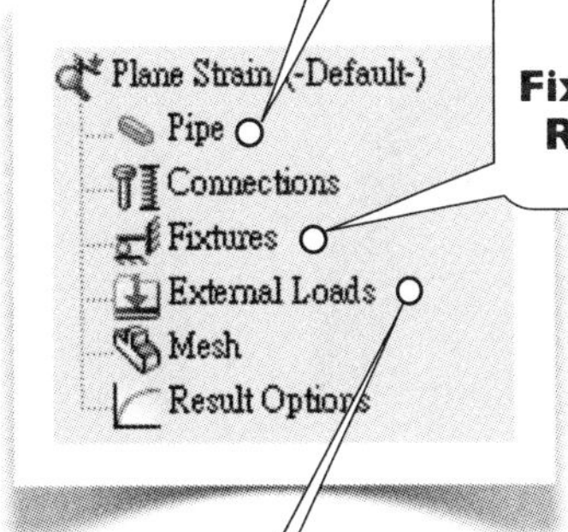

[11] Right-click **Pipe** and select **Apply/Edit Material...** and apply **Alloy Steel** for the model.

[12] Right-click **Fixtures** and select **Roller/Slider...**

[13] Select this edge...

[14] And this edge.

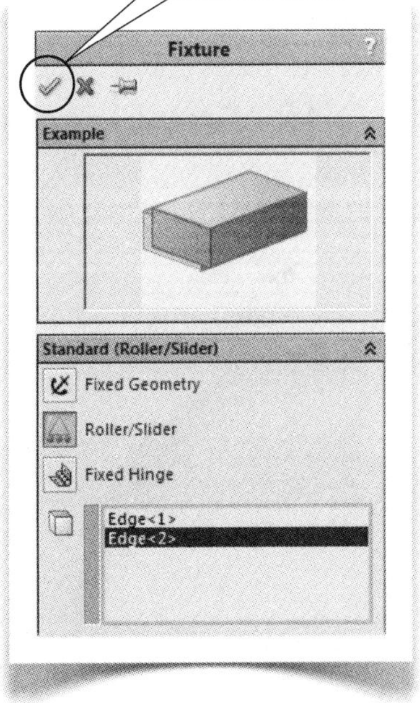

[15] Click **OK**.

[16] Right-click **External Loads** and select **Pressure...**

[17] Select this edge.

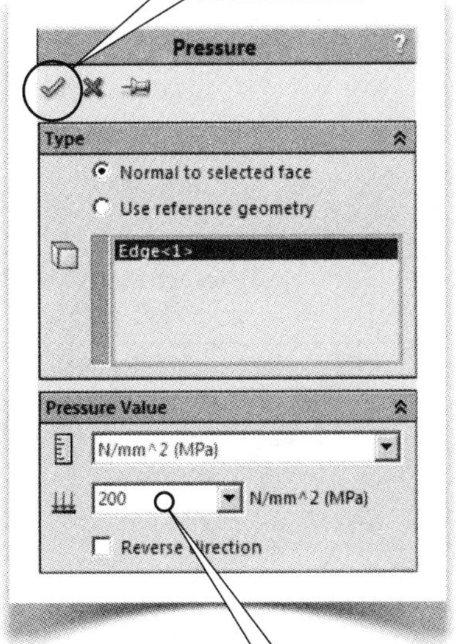

[18] Type 200 (MPa).

[19] Click **OK**.

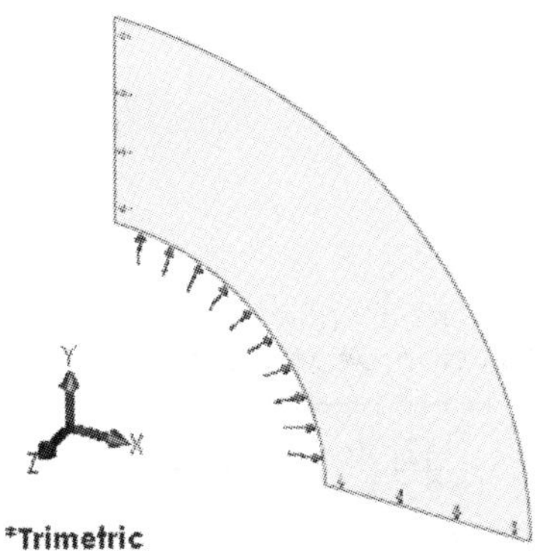

[20] In the **Simulation Toolbar**, click **Run**. #

12.2-9 View Radial Stresses

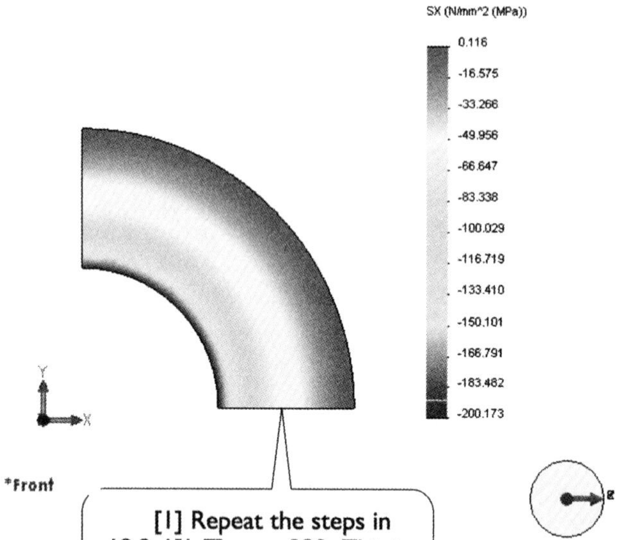

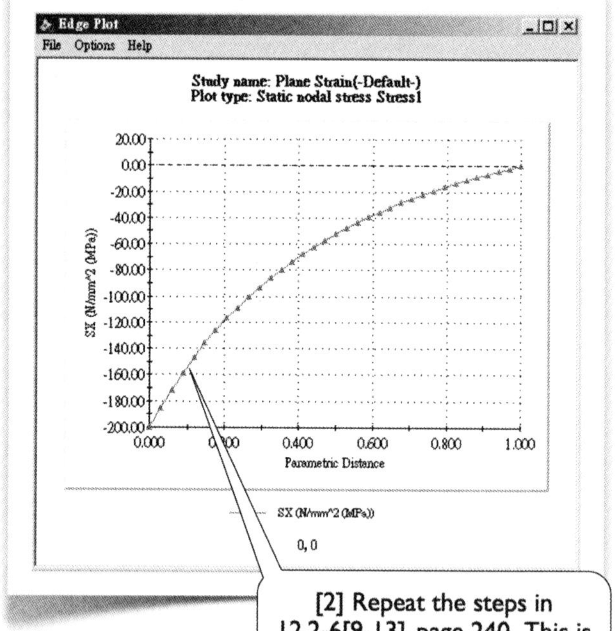

[1] Repeat the steps in 12.2-6[1-7], page 239. This is consistent with the plot in 12.2-6[8], page 239.

[2] Repeat the steps in 12.2-6[9-13], page 240. This is consistent with the plot in 12.2-6[14], page 240. #

12.2-10 View Hoop Stresses

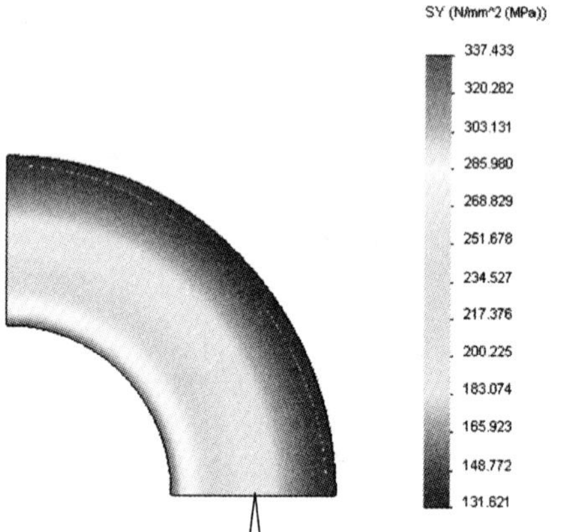

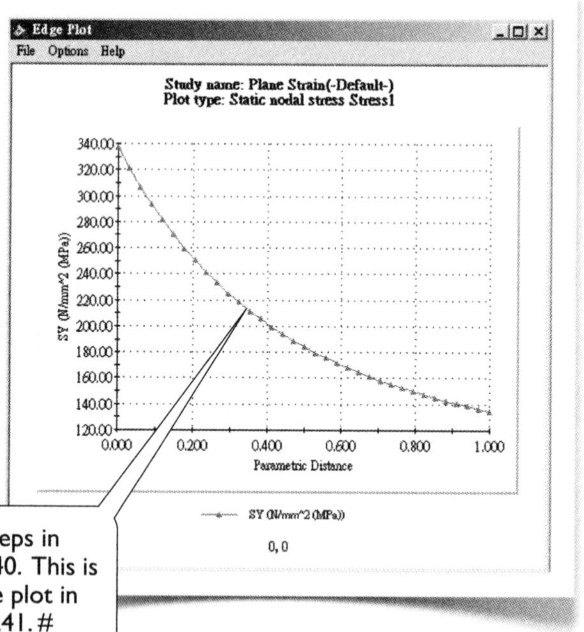

[1] Repeat step 12.2-7[1], page 241. This is consistent with the plot in 12.2-7[2], page 241.

[2] Repeat the steps in 12.2-6[9-13], page 240. This is consistent with the plot in 12.2-7[4], page 241. #

12.2-11 Further Study

[1] Choose a certain point in the model (either 3D or 2D model) and verify the third equation in Eq. 12.2-1(3) (page 236),

$$\sigma_Z = \frac{E}{(1+\nu)(1-2\nu)}\left[\nu\varepsilon_X + \nu\varepsilon_Y\right]$$

Also explore the principal stresses using the 2D model; obtain a plot similar to 12.1-4[11], page 234.

[2] Save the document and exit **SolidWorks**. #

12.2-12 Appendix: Proof of Eq. 12.2-1(2)

The last 3 equations of Eq. 12.2-1(2) (page 236) can be derived directly from Eq. 4.3-1(2) (page 87). We now prove the first 3 equations of Eq. 12.2-1(2), which can be written in the following matrix form

$$\begin{Bmatrix} \sigma_X \\ \sigma_Y \\ \sigma_Z \end{Bmatrix} = \frac{E}{(1+\nu)(1-2\nu)} \begin{bmatrix} 1-\nu & \nu & \nu \\ \nu & 1-\nu & \nu \\ \nu & \nu & 1-\nu \end{bmatrix} \begin{Bmatrix} \varepsilon_X \\ \varepsilon_Y \\ \varepsilon_Z \end{Bmatrix} \text{ or } \{\sigma\} = [F]\{\varepsilon\} \qquad \text{(a)}$$

Similarly, the first 3 equations in Eq. 4.3-1(2) can be written in the following matrix form

$$\begin{Bmatrix} \varepsilon_X \\ \varepsilon_Y \\ \varepsilon_Z \end{Bmatrix} = \frac{1}{E} \begin{bmatrix} 1 & -\nu & -\nu \\ -\nu & 1 & -\nu \\ -\nu & -\nu & 1 \end{bmatrix} \begin{Bmatrix} \sigma_X \\ \sigma_Y \\ \sigma_Z \end{Bmatrix} \text{ or } \{\varepsilon\} = [D]\{\sigma\} \qquad \text{(b)}$$

To prove that Eq. (a) is derived from Eq. (b), we need to prove $[D]\{E\} = [I]$, where $[I]$ is an identity matrix.

$$[D][F] = \frac{1}{E} \cdot \frac{E}{(1+\nu)(1-2\nu)} \begin{bmatrix} 1 & -\nu & -\nu \\ -\nu & 1 & -\nu \\ -\nu & -\nu & 1 \end{bmatrix} \begin{bmatrix} 1-\nu & \nu & \nu \\ \nu & 1-\nu & \nu \\ \nu & \nu & 1-\nu \end{bmatrix} = \begin{bmatrix} 1 & 0 & 0 \\ 0 & 1 & 0 \\ 0 & 0 & 1 \end{bmatrix}$$

This completes the proof.

Section 12.3

Axisymmetric Problems

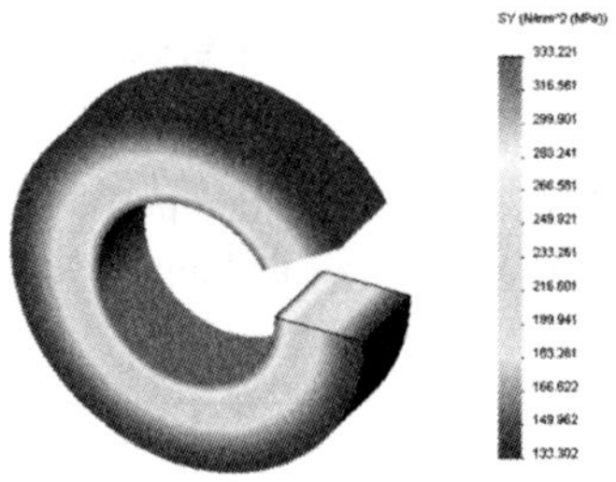

12.3-1 Introduction

Consider a structure of which the geometry as well as the boundary conditions (supports, and loads) are axisymmetric about an axis, say *Z*-axis. In such a case, all quantities are independent of θ coordinate, where a cylindrical coordinate system like the one in 6.2-1 (page 123) is used. That is, all particles having the same *R* and *Z* coordinates have the same stresses, strains, and displacements, regardless of their θ coordinates. Thus, we can eliminate θ coordinate and reduce the problem to a two-dimensional, on *R-Z* space.

Note that, in an **axisymmetric problem**, there are no shear strains in θ-direction, i.e.,

$$\gamma_{R\theta} = \gamma_{\theta R} = 0, \quad \gamma_{Z\theta} = \gamma_{\theta Z} = 0 \qquad (1)$$

(otherwise the *Z*-face and the *R*-face would twist and the problem is no longer axisymmetric). Eq. (1) implies

$$\tau_{R\theta} = \tau_{\theta R} = 0, \quad \tau_{Z\theta} = \tau_{\theta Z} = 0 \qquad (2)$$

Eqs. (1, 2) can be regarded as the **axisymmetric conditions**. Note that both σ_θ (hoop stress) and ε_θ (hoop strain) are generally not zero.

In this section, we'll solve the **Pipe** problem (Section 12.2) again using an axisymmetric 2D model. The results will be compared with those in Section 12.2.

12.3-2 Start Up and Create an Axisymmetric Study

[1] Launch **SolidWorks** and open the file **Pipe**, which was saved in Section 12.2.

[2] In the **Simulation Toolbar**, select **Study Advisor>New Study**.

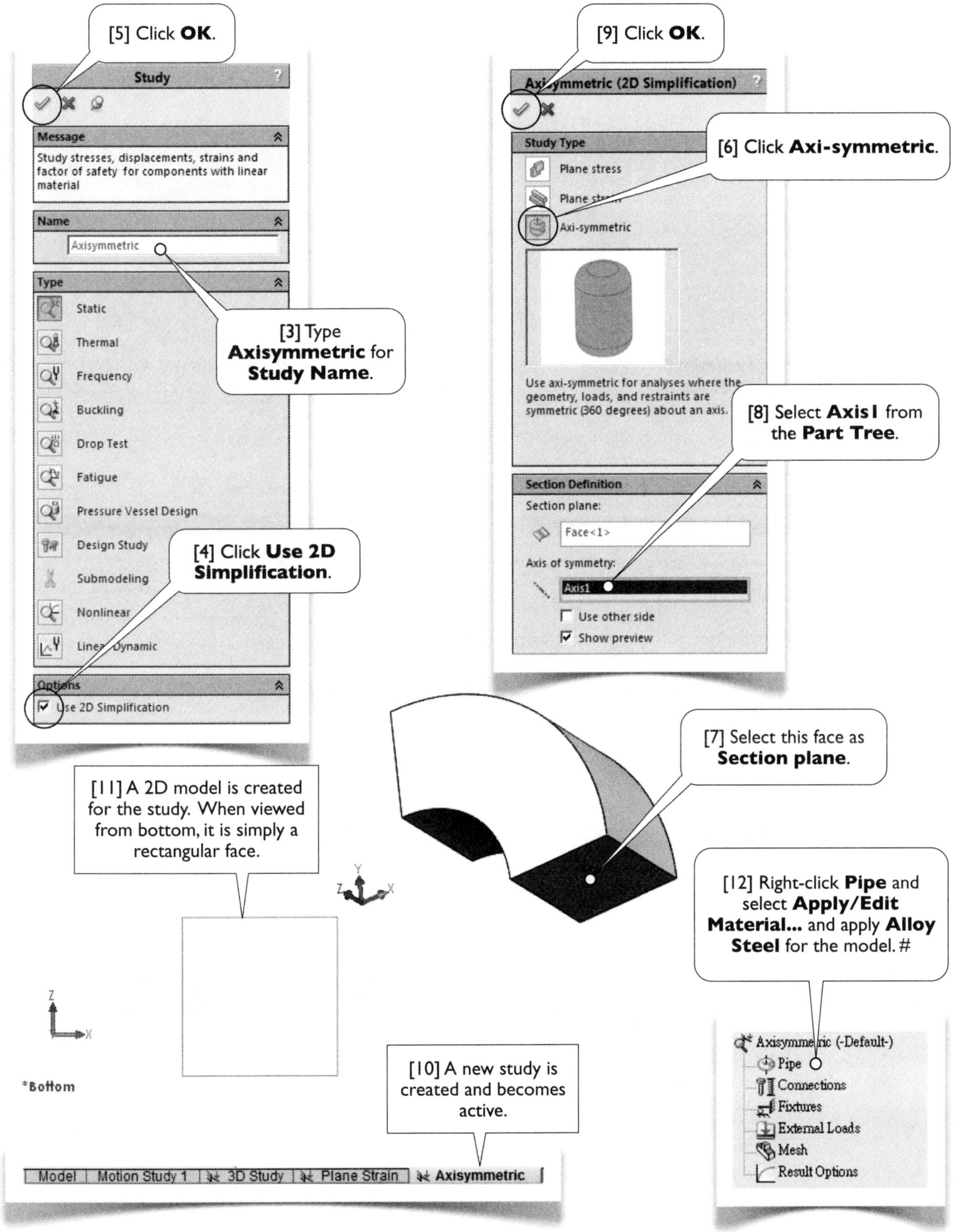
[3] Type **Axisymmetric** for **Study Name**.
[4] Click **Use 2D Simplification**.
[5] Click **OK**.
[6] Click **Axi-symmetric**.
[7] Select this face as **Section plane**.
[8] Select **Axis1** from the **Part Tree**.
[9] Click **OK**.
[10] A new study is created and becomes active.
[11] A 2D model is created for the study. When viewed from bottom, it is simply a rectangular face.
[12] Right-click **Pipe** and select **Apply/Edit Material...** and apply **Alloy Steel** for the model. #
Study
Message
Study stresses, displacements, strains and factor of safety for components with linear material
Name
Axisymmetric
Type
Static
Thermal
Frequency
Buckling
Drop Test
Fatigue
Pressure Vessel Design
Design Study
Submodeling
Nonlinear
Linear Dynamic
Options
Use 2D Simplification
Axisymmetric (2D Simplification)
Study Type
Plane stress
Axi-symmetric
Use axi-symmetric for analyses where the geometry, loads, and restraints are symmetric (360 degrees) about an axis.
Section Definition
Section plane:
Face<1>
Axis of symmetry:
Axis1
Use other side
Show preview
*Bottom
Model
Motion Study 1
3D Study
Plane Strain
Axisymmetric
Axisymmetric (-Default-)
Pipe
Connections
Fixtures
External Loads
Mesh
Result Options

12.3-3 Set Up Boundary Conditions

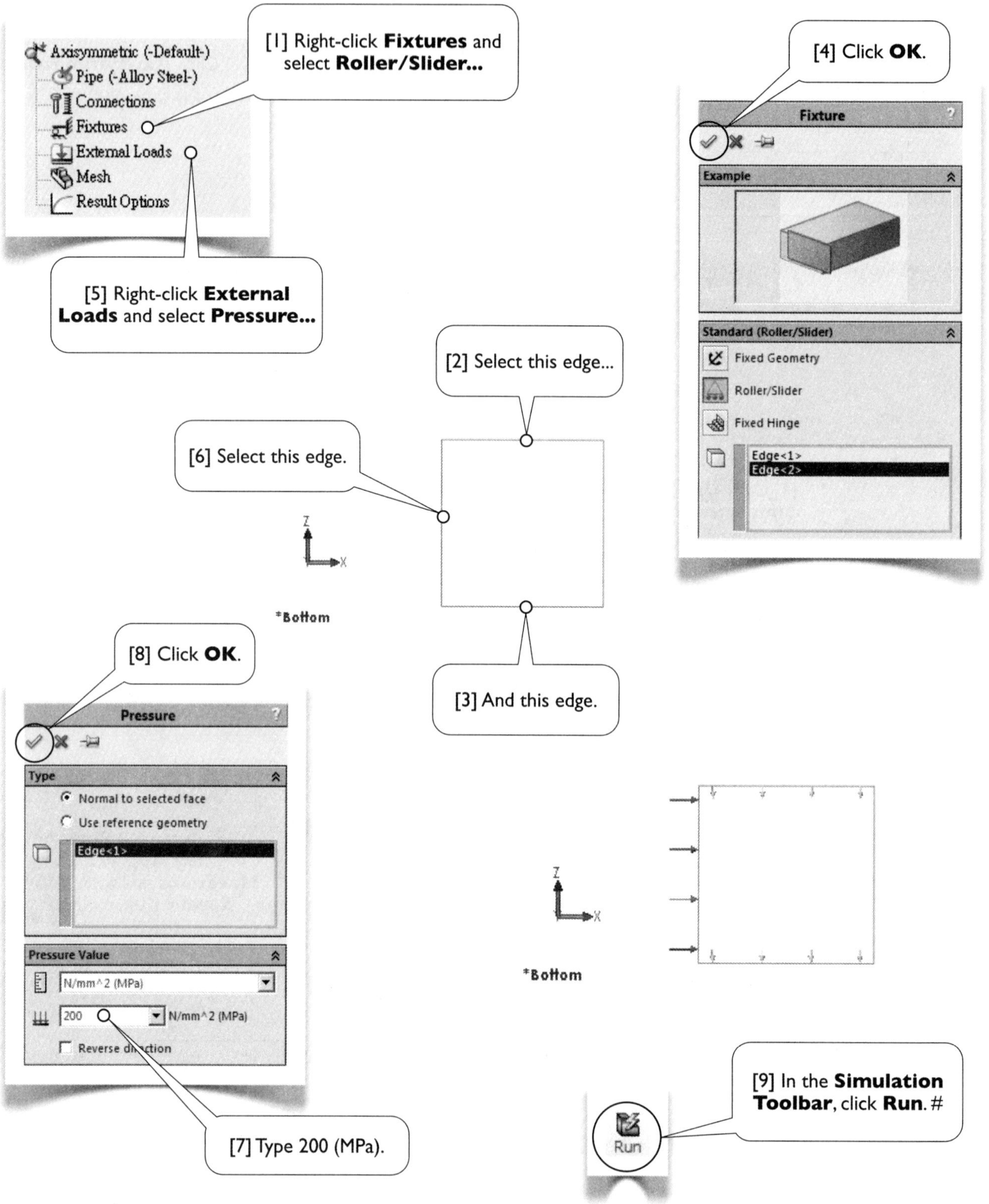

12.3-4 View Radial Stresses

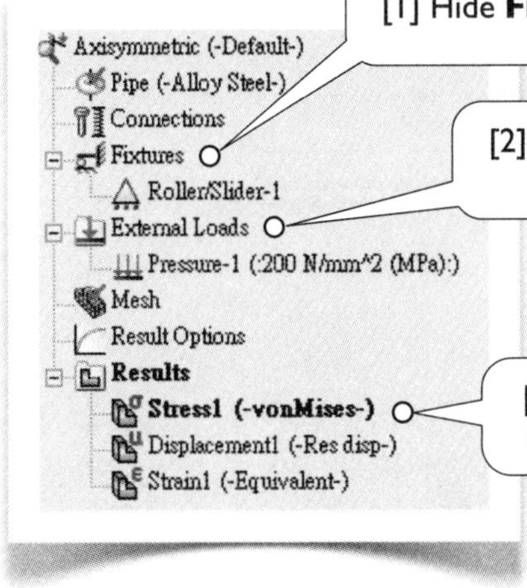

[1] Hide **Fixtures**.

[2] Hide **External Loads**.

[3] Double-click to edit the definition.

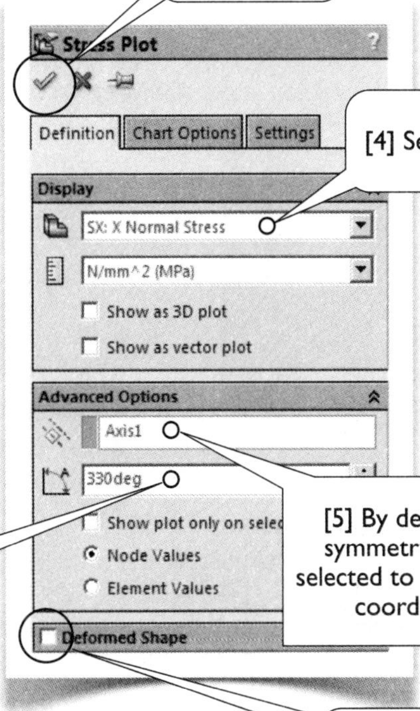

[4] Select **SX** (σ_r).

[5] By default, the axis of symmetry **Axis1** is pre-selected to define a cylindrical coordinate system.

[6] Turn off **Deformed Shape**.

[7] When **Show as 3D plot** is turned on (12.3-5[3, 4], next page), the model will revolve 330° (by default).

[8] Click **OK**.

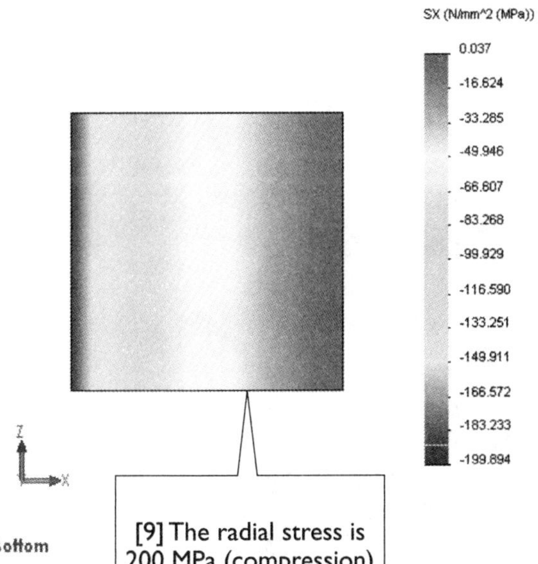

[9] The radial stress is 200 MPa (compression) on the inner (left) edge and zero on the outer (right) edge (see [10]).

[10] Repeat the steps in 12.2-6[9-13], page 240. This is consistent with the plot in 12.2-6[14], page 240. #

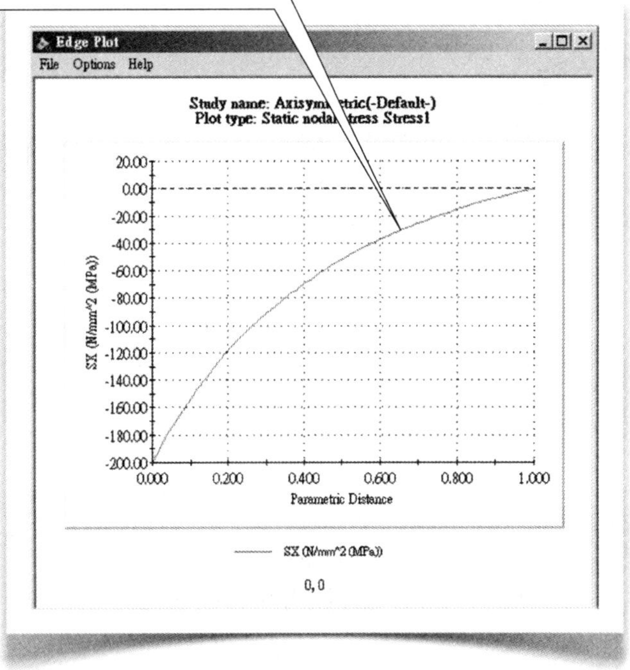

12.3-5 View Hoop Stresses

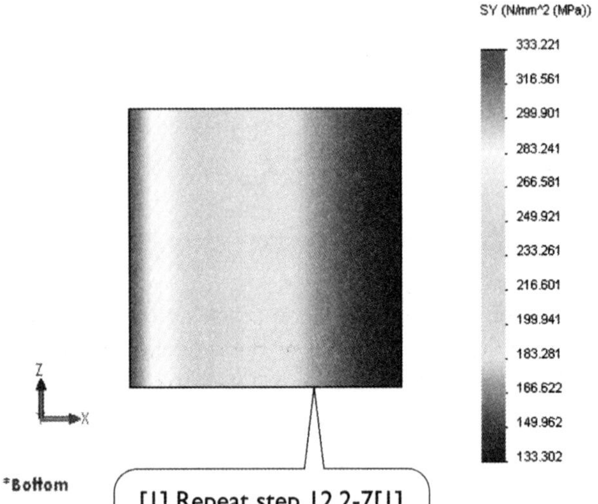

[1] Repeat step 12.2-7[1], page 241. This is consistent with the plot in 12.2-7[2], page 241.

[2] Repeat the steps in 12.2-6[9-13], page 240. This is consistent with the plot in 12.2-7[4], page 241.

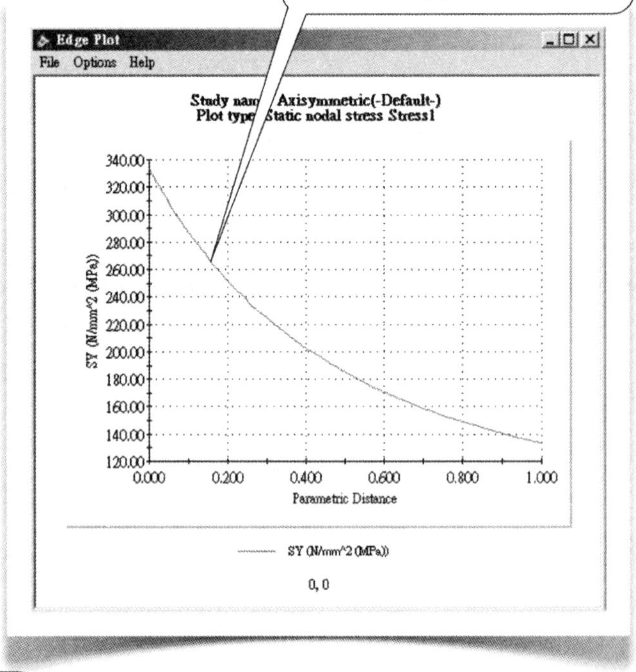

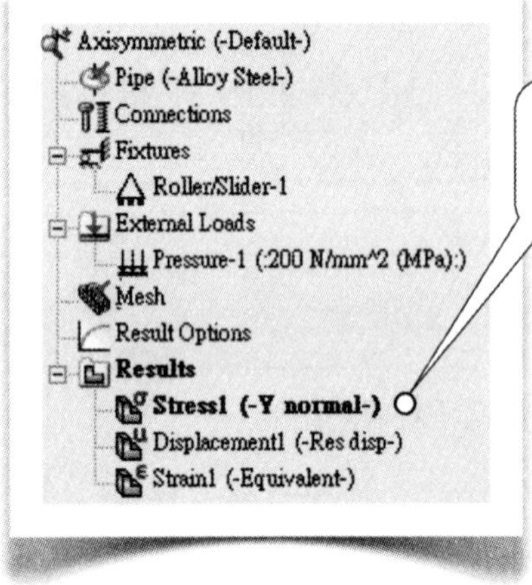

[3] Right-click-select **Show as 3D plot**.

[4] The 2D model is expanded to 3D (also see 12.3-4[7], last page).

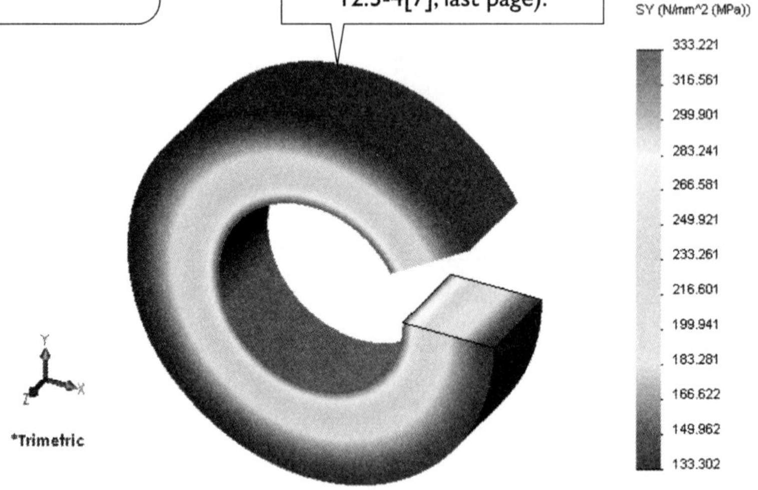

[5] Save the document and exit **SolidWorks**. #

Chapter 13

Plates and Shells

Many structures consist of thin shells or thin plates components. These components can be simplified using **surface models** and meshed with **shell elements**. Using surface models has many advantages over the solid models, and you should always do it whenever possible. These advantages include (a) simpler to build geometry; (b) better mesh quality; (c) much less computing time; and (d) easier display and analysis of the results.

Section 13.1

Channel Beam

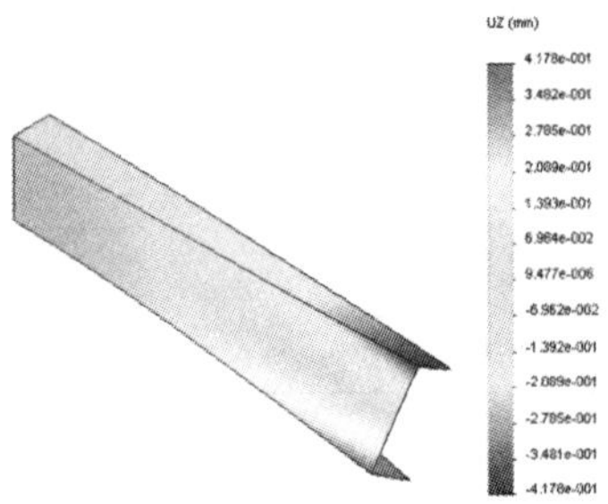

13.1-1 Introduction

In this section, we'll re-analyze the channel beam introduced in Section 8.3, using a **surface model**. The results will be compared with those in 8.3-4, page 169. This section also demonstrates the creation of a surface model by extracting the "mid-surfaces" from a 3D model.

13.1-2 Start Up and Extract Mid-Surface from the 3D Model

[1] Launch **SolidWorks** and open the file **Channel** which was saved in Section 8.3.

[2] From **Pull-Down Menus**, select **Insert>Surface>Mid Surface...**

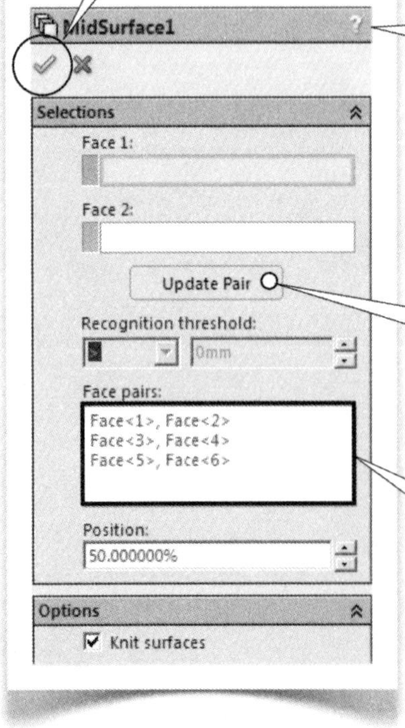

[3] Click **Find Face Pairs**.

[4] Three **Face Pairs** are found in the model. The **Mid Surface** of each **Face Pair** is extracted.

[5] Click **OK**.

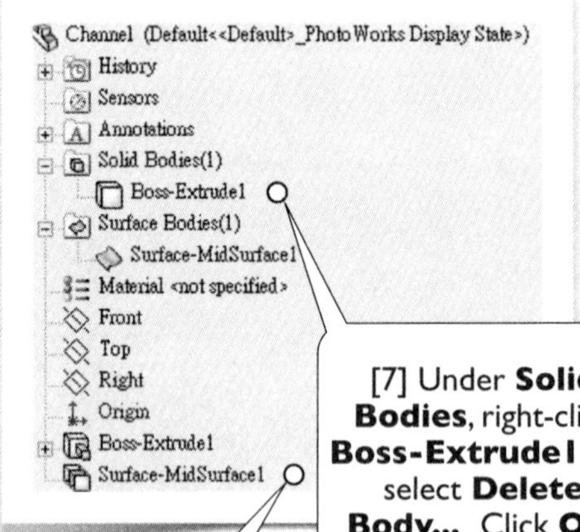

[6] The surface body is added to the model.

[7] Under **Solid Bodies**, right-click **Boss-Extrude1** and select **Delete Body...** Click **OK**.

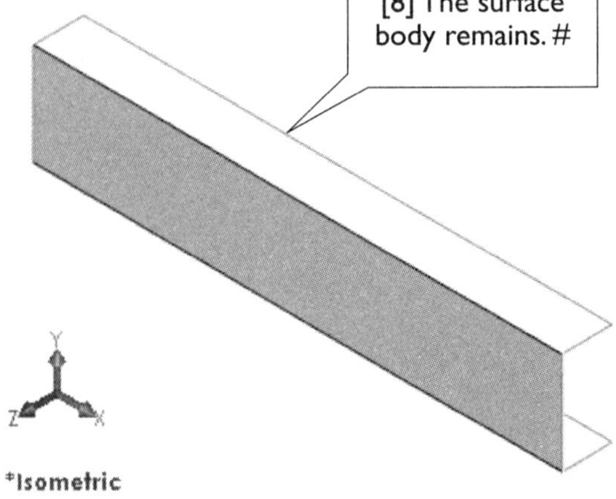

[8] The surface body remains. #

13.1-3 Create a New Study and Set Up Boundary Conditions

[1] In the **Simulation Toolbar**, select **Study Advisor>New Study**. Name the new study **Thin Plate**. Leave **Static** as default **Study Type**.

[2] Right-click **Channel** and select **Apply/Edit Material...** and apply **Alloy Steel** for the model.

[3] Right-click **Channel** and select **Edit Definition...**

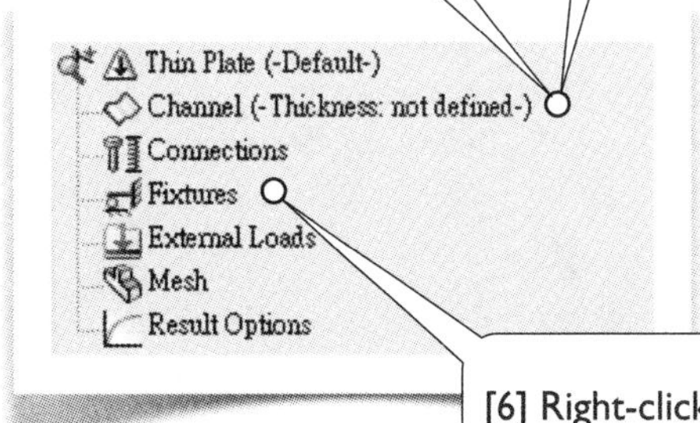

[6] Right-click **Fixture** and select **Fixed Geometry...**

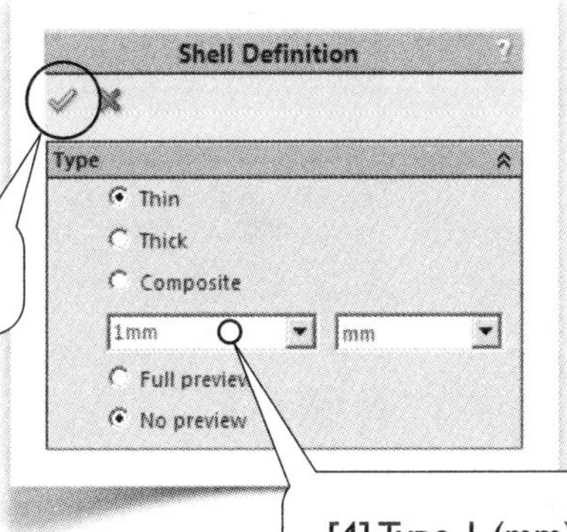

[5] Click **OK**.

[4] Type 1 (mm).

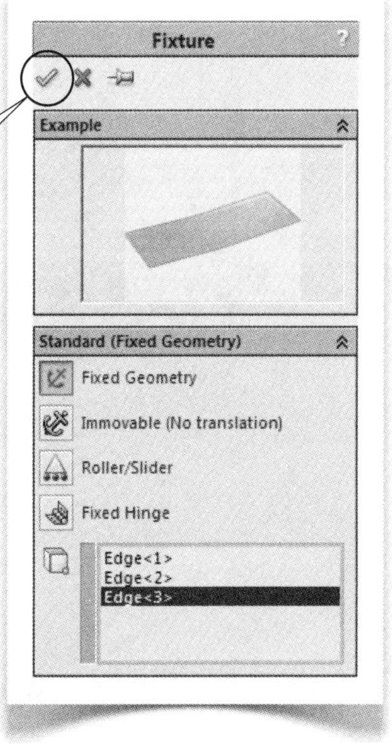

[8] Click **OK**.

[7] Select the three edges at the left-end.

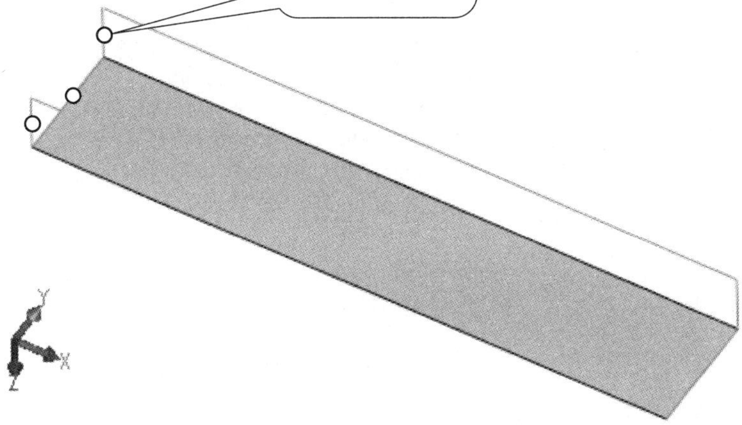

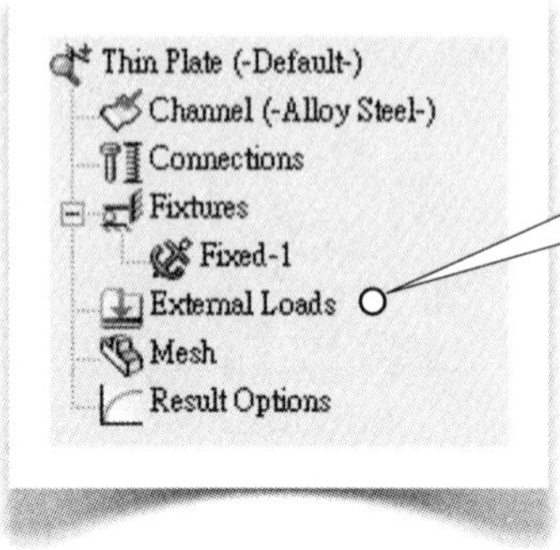

[9] Right-click **External Loads** and select **Force...**

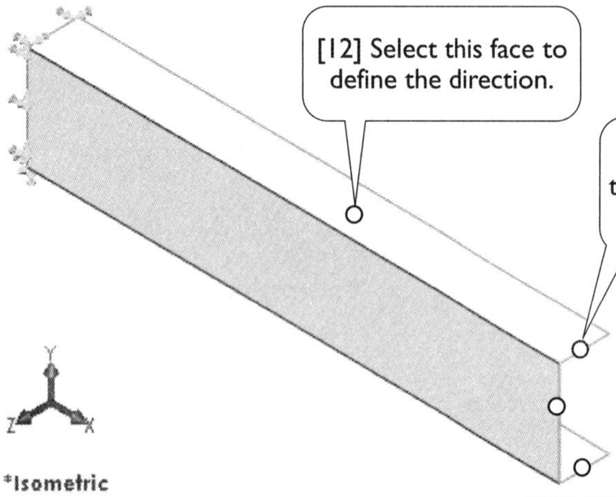

[12] Select this face to define the direction.

[10] Select the three edges at the right-end.

[16] In the **Simulation Toolbar**, click **Run**. #

[15] Click **OK**.

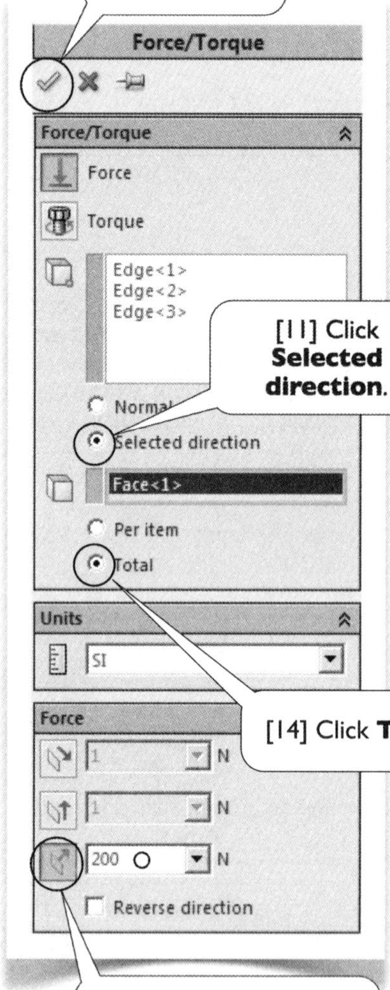

[11] Click **Selected direction**.

[14] Click **Total**.

[13] Click **Normal to Plane** and type 200 (N).

13.1-4 View the Results

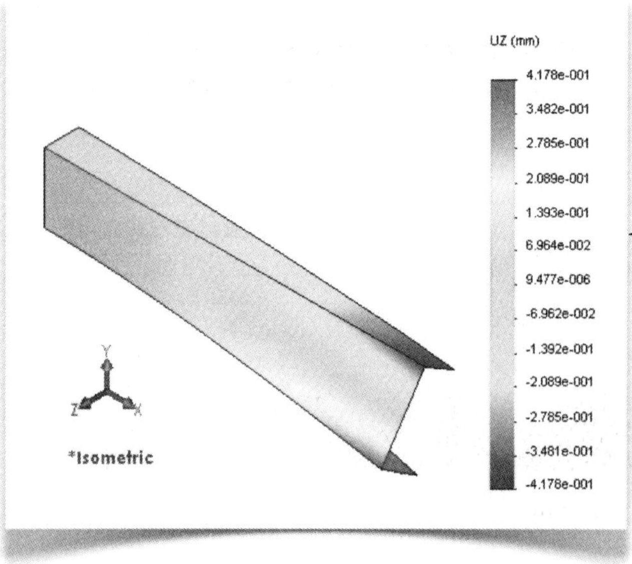

[1] Follow the steps in 8.3-4[1-3] (page 169) to examine the deformation. The results should be comparable to those in 8.3-4[4].

[2] Save the document and exit **SolidWorks**. #

Section 13.2

Storage Tank

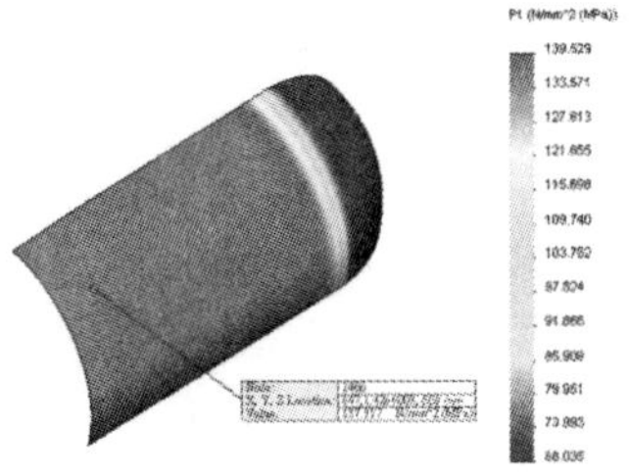

13.2-1 Introduction

[1] Consider a storage tank made of **Alloy Steel** [2]. For an internal gauge pressure of 1.5 MPa, we want to determine the maximum normal stress and the maximum shear stress in the tank. (The **gauge pressure** is the pressure exceeding that of the atmosphere.)

According to the theory of thin-walled pressure vessels, at a typical point around the middle of the cylinder, the maximum principle stress σ_1 is in the hoop (tangential) direction,

$$\sigma_1 = \frac{pr}{t} = \frac{1.5(1650)}{18} = 137.5 \text{ MPa} \tag{1}$$

The middle principle stress σ_2 is in the longitudinal (axial) direction,

$$\sigma_2 = \frac{pr}{2t} = \frac{1.5(1650)}{2(18)} = 68.75 \text{ MPa} \tag{2}$$

The minimum principle stress σ_3 is in the thickness (radial) direction,

$$\sigma_3 = 0 \tag{3}$$

The maximum shear stress τ_{max} (Eq. 10.2-1(5), page 197) is

$$\tau_{max} = \frac{\sigma_1 - \sigma_3}{2} = 68.75 \text{ MPa} \tag{4}$$

Due to symmetries, we'll model only 1/8 of the tank and specify **symmetry boundary conditions** on the boundaries. Note that, for shell elements, a symmetry boundary condition is NOT equivalent to a **Roller/Slider** condition (also see 12.2-5[5], page 238).

[2] The storage tank is fabricated from an **Alloy Steel** plate of thickness 18 mm and is designed to hold a pressure of 1.5 MPa. #

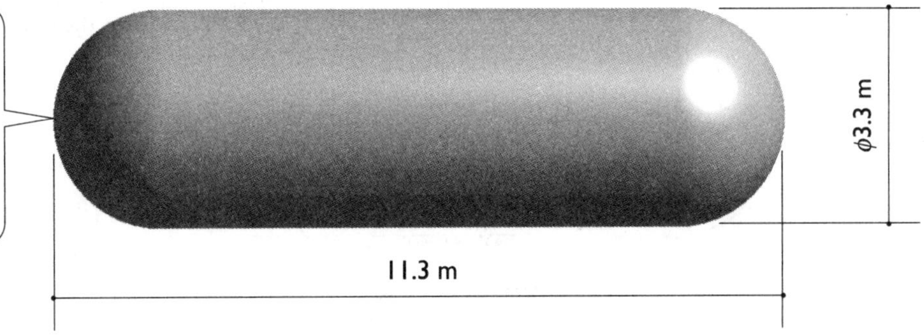

13.2-2 Start Up and Create Geometric Model

[1] Launch **SolidWorks** and create a new part. Set up **MMGS** unit system with zero decimal places for the length unit. Save the document as **Tank**.

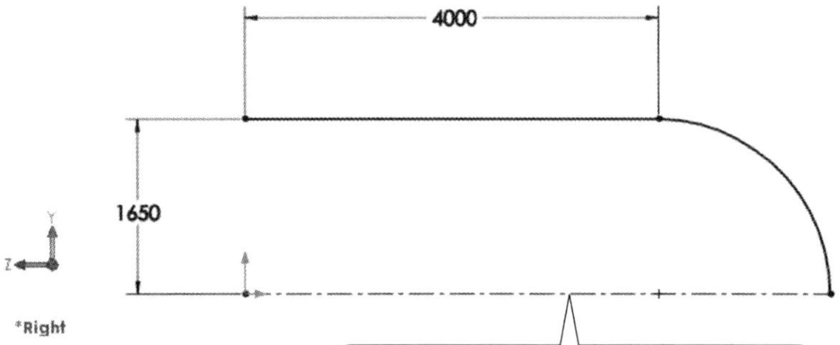

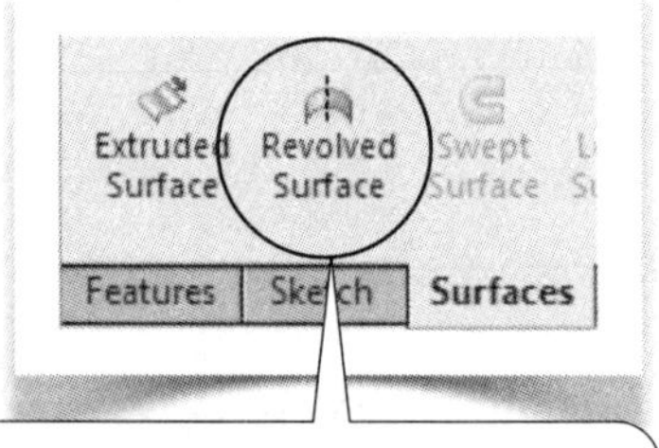

[3] From **Pull-Down Menus**, select **Insert>Surface>Revolve...** The **Revolved Surface** command is also available in the **Surfaces Toolbar**.

[2] On the **Right** plane, draw a sketch like this. Remember to include the **Centerline**. Click **Exit Sketch**.

[7] Due to symmetries, we've created only 1/8 of the tank and will use symmetry boundary conditions. #

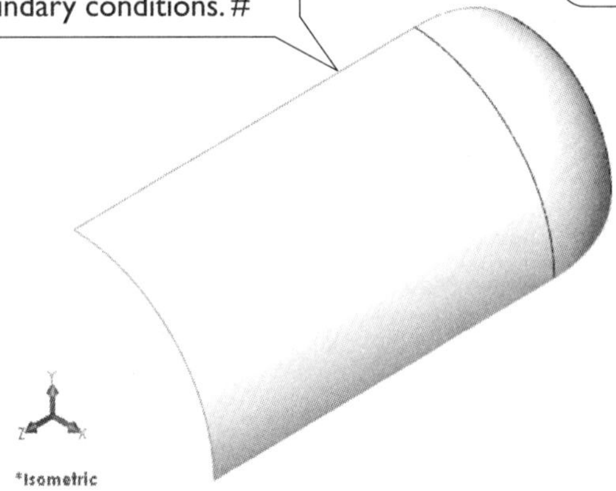

[6] Click **OK**.

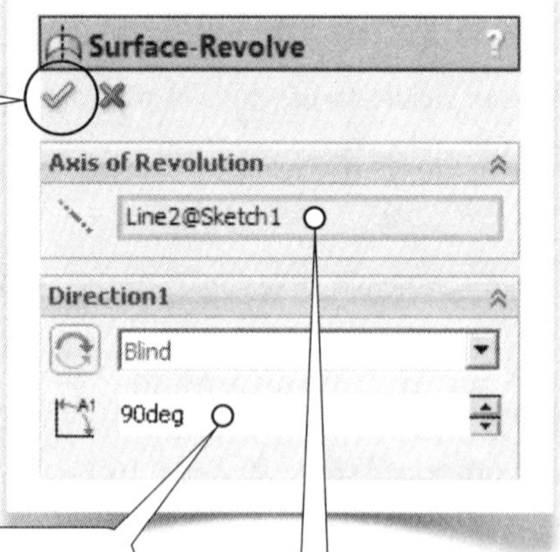

[5] Type 90 (deg).

[4] The **Centerline** is pre-selected as the **Axis of Revolution**.

13.2-3 Create a New Study and Set Up Boundary Conditions

[1] In the **Simulation Toolbar**, select **Study Advisor>New Study**. Name the new study **Thin Shell**. Leave **Static** as default **Study Type**.

[2] Right-click **Tank** and select **Apply/Edit Material...** and apply **Alloy Steel** for the model.

[3] Right-click **Tank** and select **Edit Definition...**

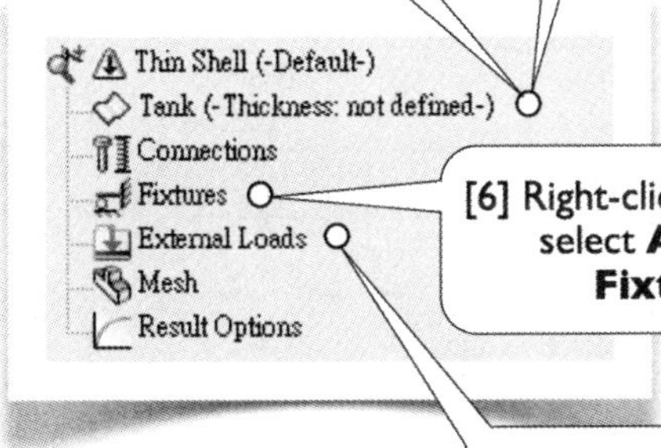

[4] Type 18 (mm).

[5] Click **OK**.

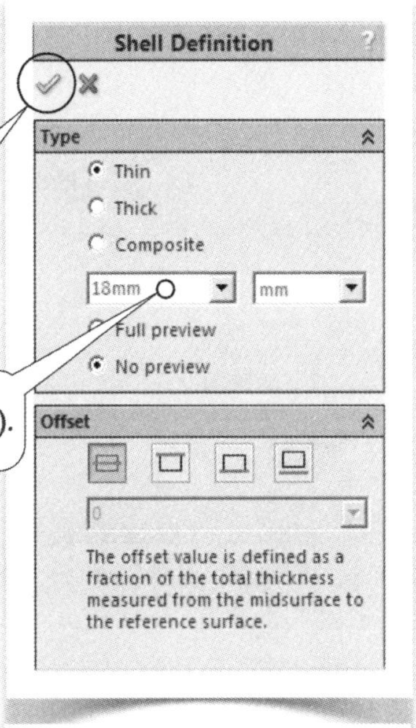

[6] Right-click **Fixture** and select **Advanced Fixtures...**

[7] Click **Symmetry**.

[8] Select all the boundary edges (totally 5 edges).

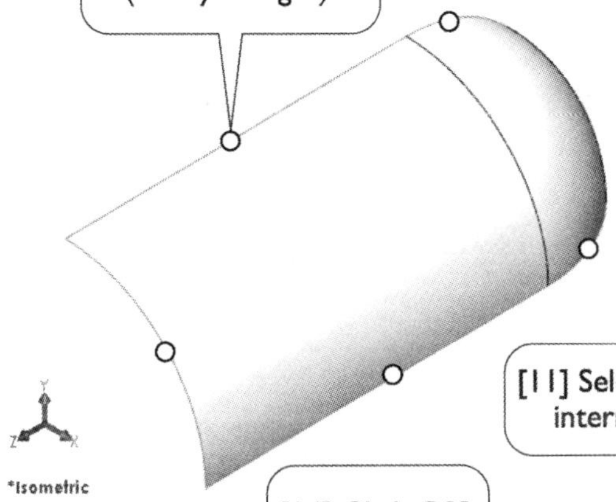

[9] Click **OK**.

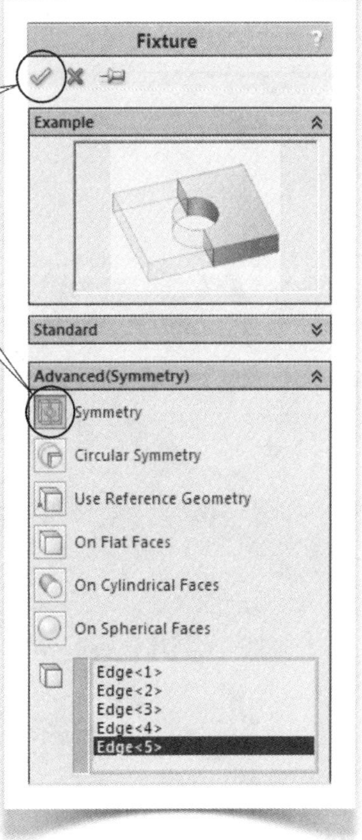

[10] Right-click **External Loads** and select **Pressure...**

[11] Select the two internal faces.

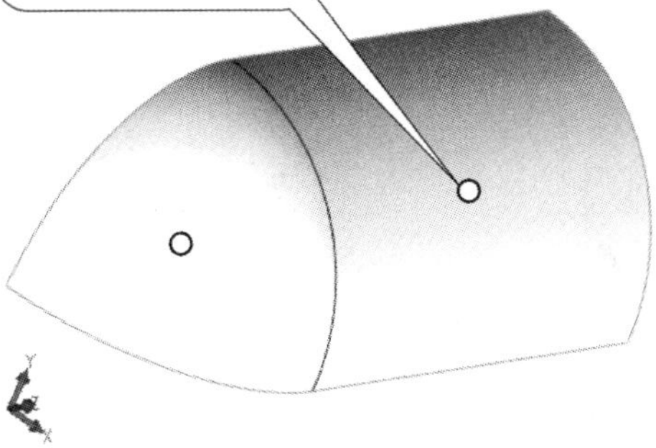

[12] If the direction of the pressure is not toward the outside, click **Reverse direction**.

[13] Type 1.5 (MPa).

[14] Click **OK**.

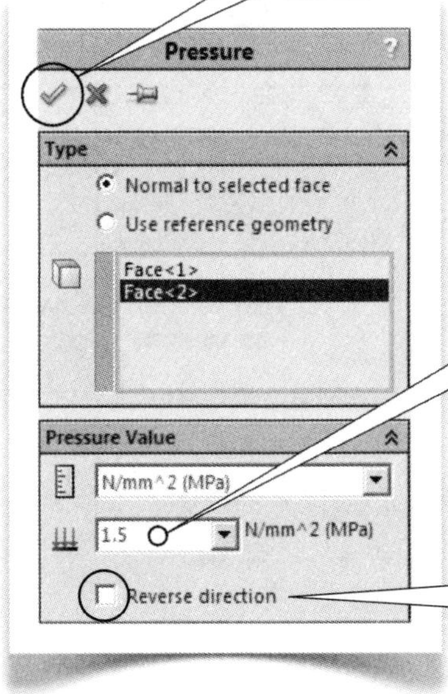

[15] In the **Simulation Toolbar**, click **Run**. #

13.2-4 The Maximum Principal Stresses

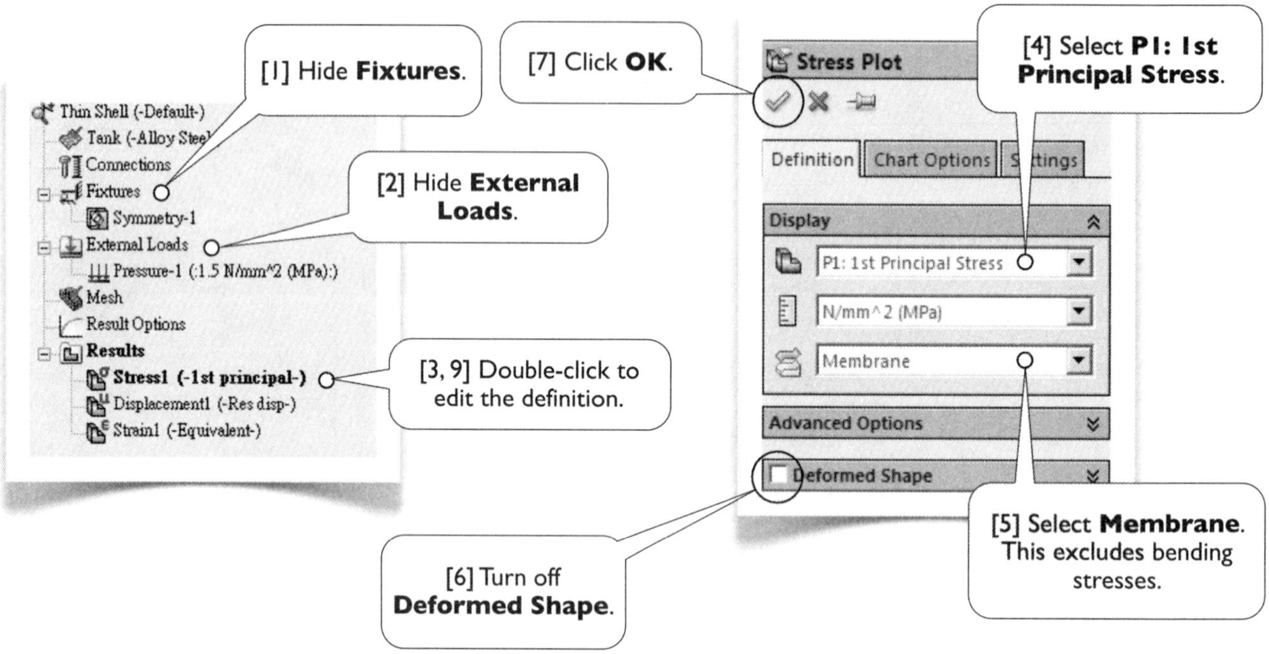

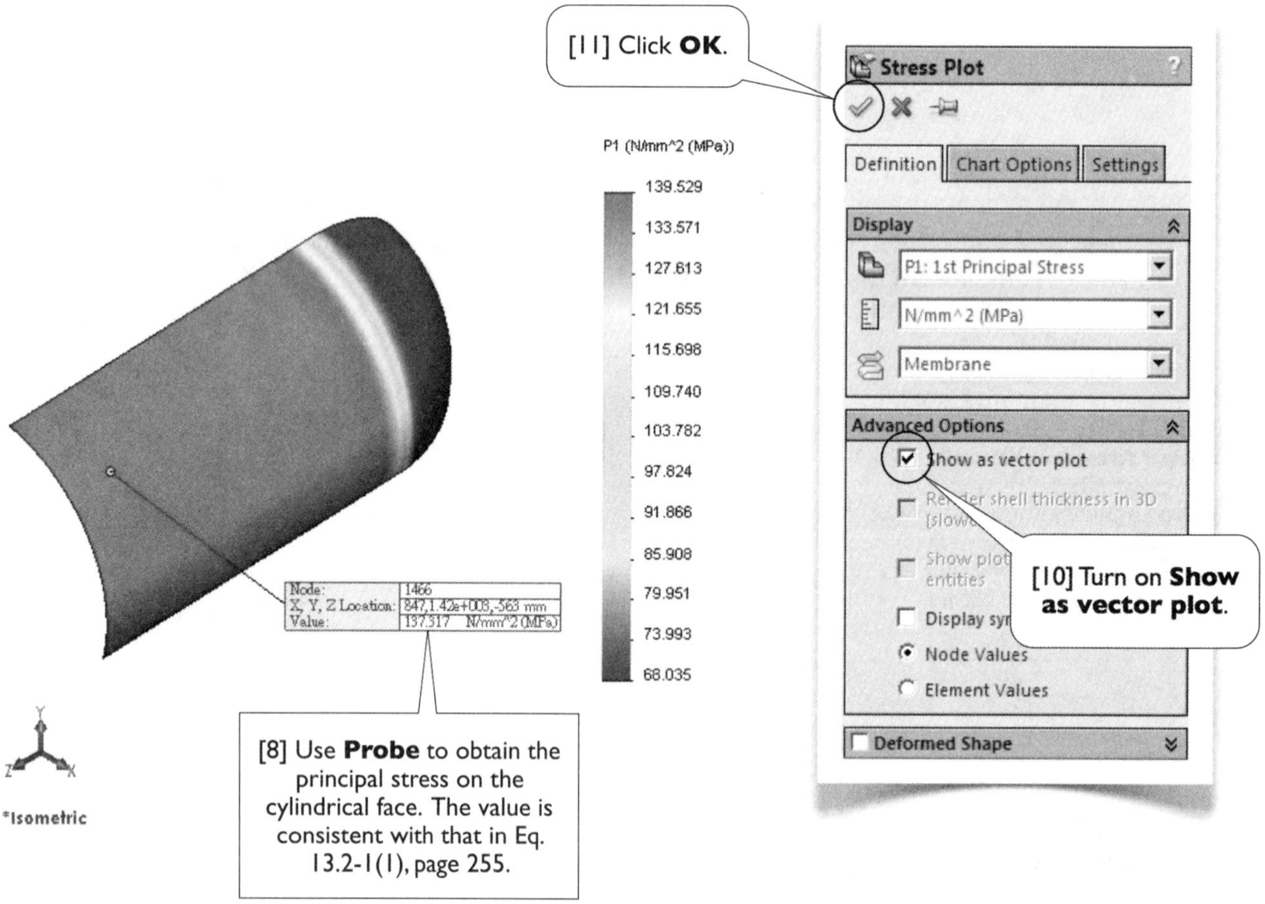

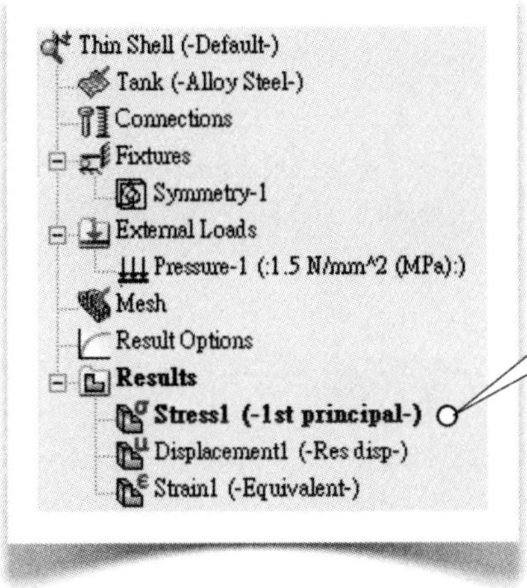

[12] Right-click-select **Vector Plot Options...** and set arrow size to 500%.

[13] The maximum principal stresses align with the hoop direction. #

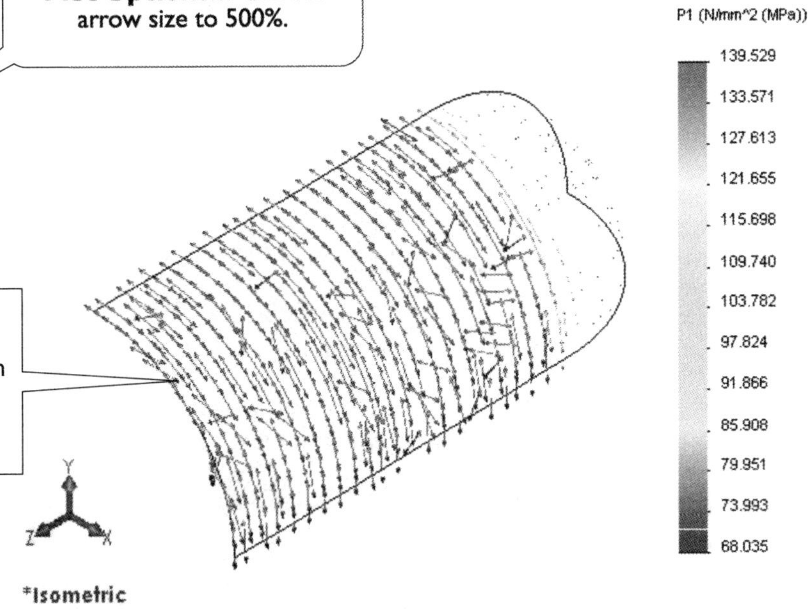

13.2-5 The Middle Principal Stresses

[1] Follow the steps in 13.2-4[3, 4, 7] (last page) to explore the middle principal stresses, which align with the longitudinal direction. Use **Probe** to obtain the stress on the cylindrical face. The value is consistent with the value in Eq. 13.2-1(2) (page 255).

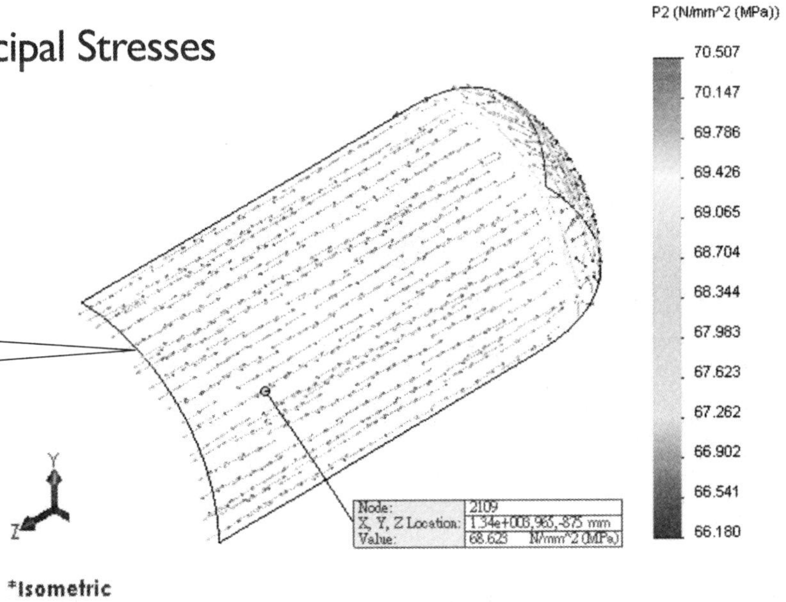

[2] Save the document and exit **SolidWorks**. #

Chapter 14

Buckling

In the truss example (Section 11.1), the roof member (**Structural Member 9** in 11.1-5[17], page 210) is subjected to a compressive force of 13.81 kN (see 11.1-1[3], page 205) under the design loads. The compressive stress is

$$\frac{13810 \text{ N}}{10 \text{ mm} \times 50 \text{ mm}} = 27.6 \text{ MPa}$$

which is well below the material's yield strength. Can we conclude that the design of that member is safe? Not yet. The stress is only one of many design requirements that must be satisfied. For any structural members (particularly slender or thin members) subject to compressive stresses, we need to check their stability. This chapter deals with **stability analysis**, or **buckling analysis**.

Buckling can be viewed as an ultimate case of a more general effect, called **stress stiffening**: a slender or thin structure member's bending stiffness increases with increasing axial tensile stress, and, on the opposite side, the member's bending stiffness decreases with the increasing compressive stress. Buckling occurs when the compressive stress reaches a level such that the decreasing bending stiffness reaches zero; the structure becomes unstable and buckled. At that point, the applying load is called a **buckling load** and the corresponding deformation is called a **buckling mode**. The purpose of buckling analyses is to find the buckling loads and the corresponding buckling modes.

Section 14.1

Buckling of a Truss Member

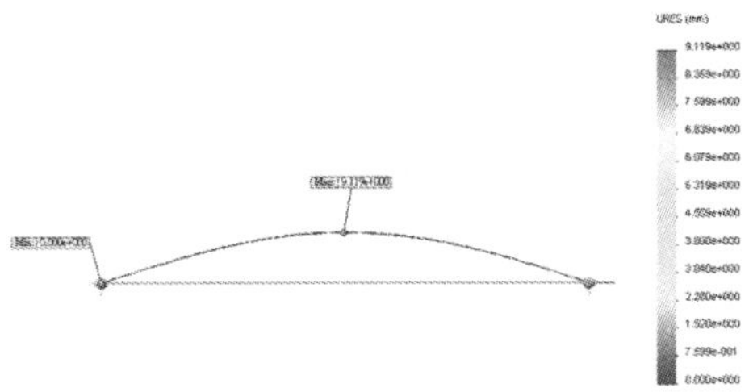

14.1-1 Introduction

[1] In the truss example (Section 11.1), the roof member is subjected to a compressive force of 13.81 kN [2, 3]. It appears safe because the compressive stress is

$$\sigma = \frac{F}{A} = \frac{13810}{10 \times 50} = 27.6 \text{ MPa} \qquad (1)$$

which is well below the material's yielding strength. However, according to the buckling theory, the member will buckle when the compressive force is

$$P = \frac{\pi^2 EI}{L^2} \qquad (2)$$

where the Young's modulus E = 210 GPa, the moment of inertia $I = 50 \times 10^3/12 = \underline{4167 \text{ mm}^4}$ in the weaker direction and $I = 10 \times 50^3/12 = 104167 \text{ mm}^4$ in the stronger direction, and the length $L = \sqrt{5^2 + (8/3)^2} = 5.667$ m. Therefore, in the weaker direction, the buckling load is

$$P = \frac{\pi^2 EI}{L^2} = \frac{\pi^2 (210 \times 10^9)(4.167 \times 10^{-9})}{(5.667)^2} = 268.9 \text{ N} \qquad (3)$$

In the stronger direction, the buckling load is

$$P = \frac{\pi^2 EI}{L^2} = \frac{\pi^2 (210 \times 10^9)(104.167 \times 10^{-9})}{(5.667)^2} = 6723 \text{ N} \qquad (4)$$

Accordingly, the roof member will buckle under the design loads. In this section, we'll perform a buckling study using the **Simulation** and verify the buckling loads with the values calculated in Eqs. (3, 4).

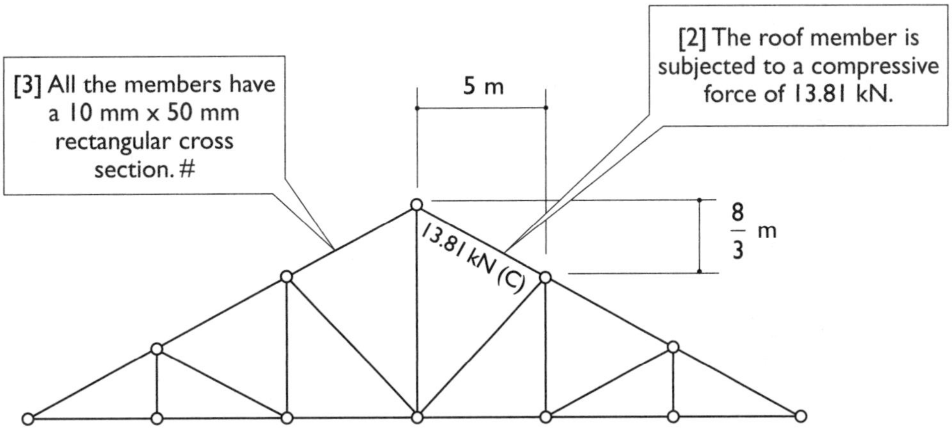

14.1-2 Start Up and Create Geometric Model

[1] Launch **SolidWorks** and create a new part. Set up **MMGS** unit system with zero decimal places for the length unit. Save the document as **Member**.

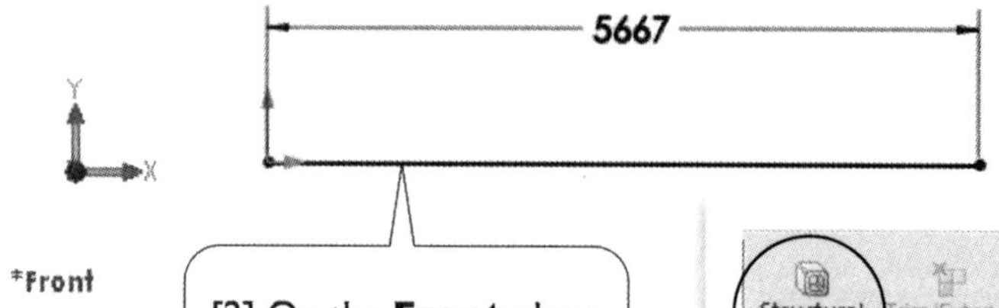

[2] On the **Front** plane, draw a sketch like this. Click **Exit Sketch**.

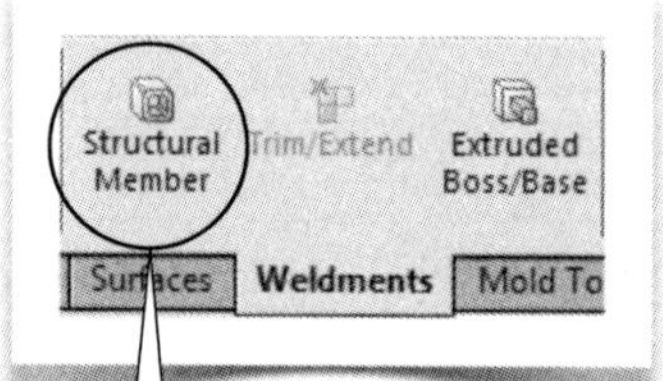

[3] From the **Pull-Down Menus** select **Insert>Weldments>Structural Member...** Or, from the **Weldments Toolbar**, click **Structural Member**.

[4] Leave these settings their default values for now and later we'll modify the cross section for our need.

[5] Select the line segments [2].

[6] Click **OK**.

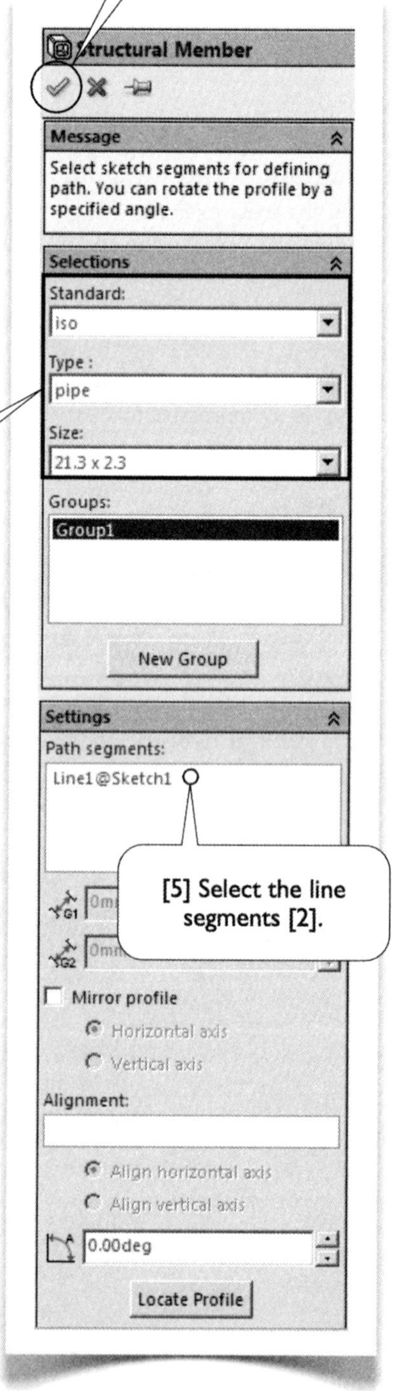

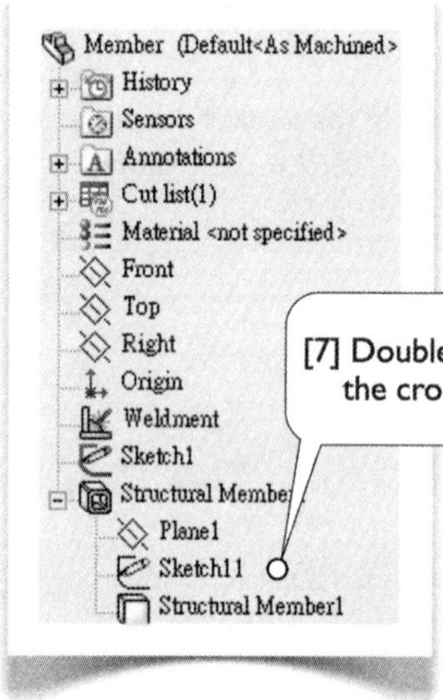

[7] Double-click to edit the cross section.

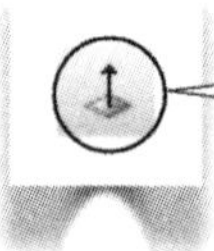

[8] Click **Normal To** to rotate the view.

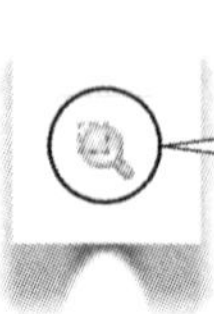

[9] Use **Zoom to Area** to enlarge the cross section. Delete all existing sketch entities.

[10] Draw a 10x50 section like this, using **Center Rectangle** command. Remember to click **Exit Sketch**.

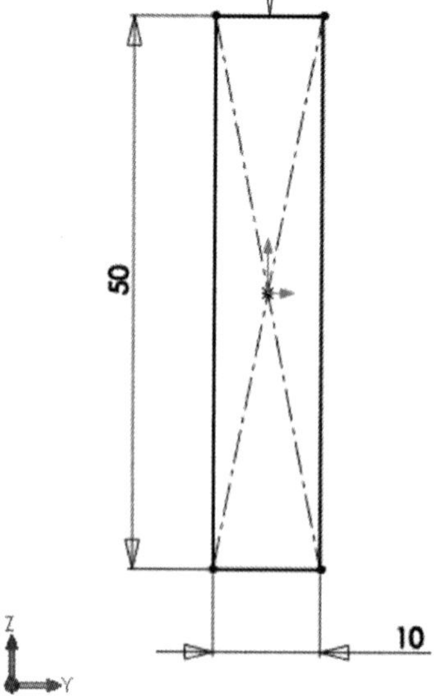

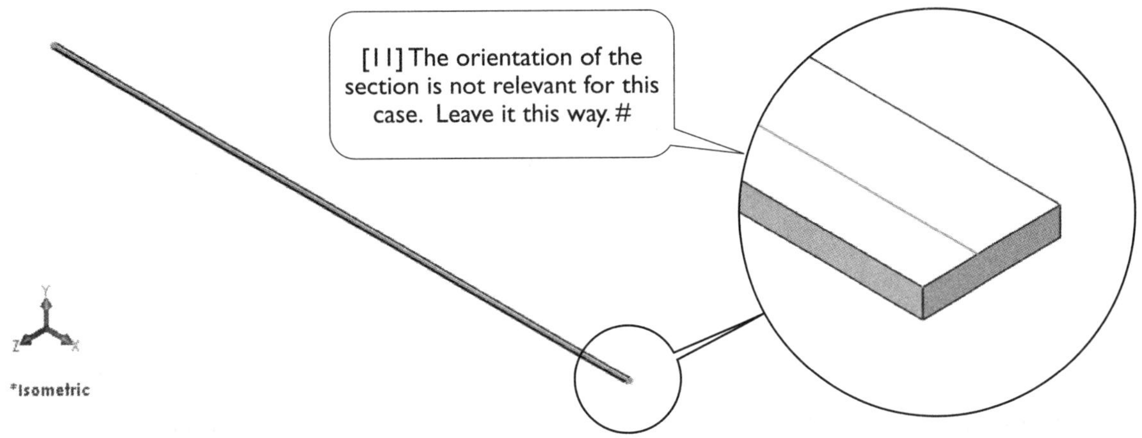

14.1-3 Create a Study and Apply Material

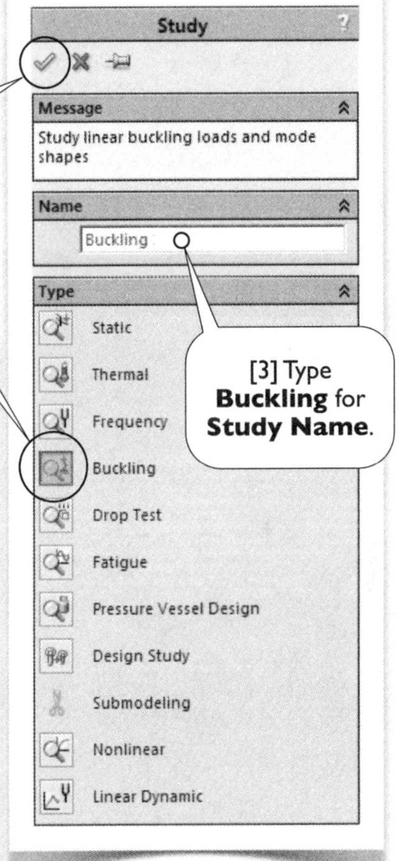

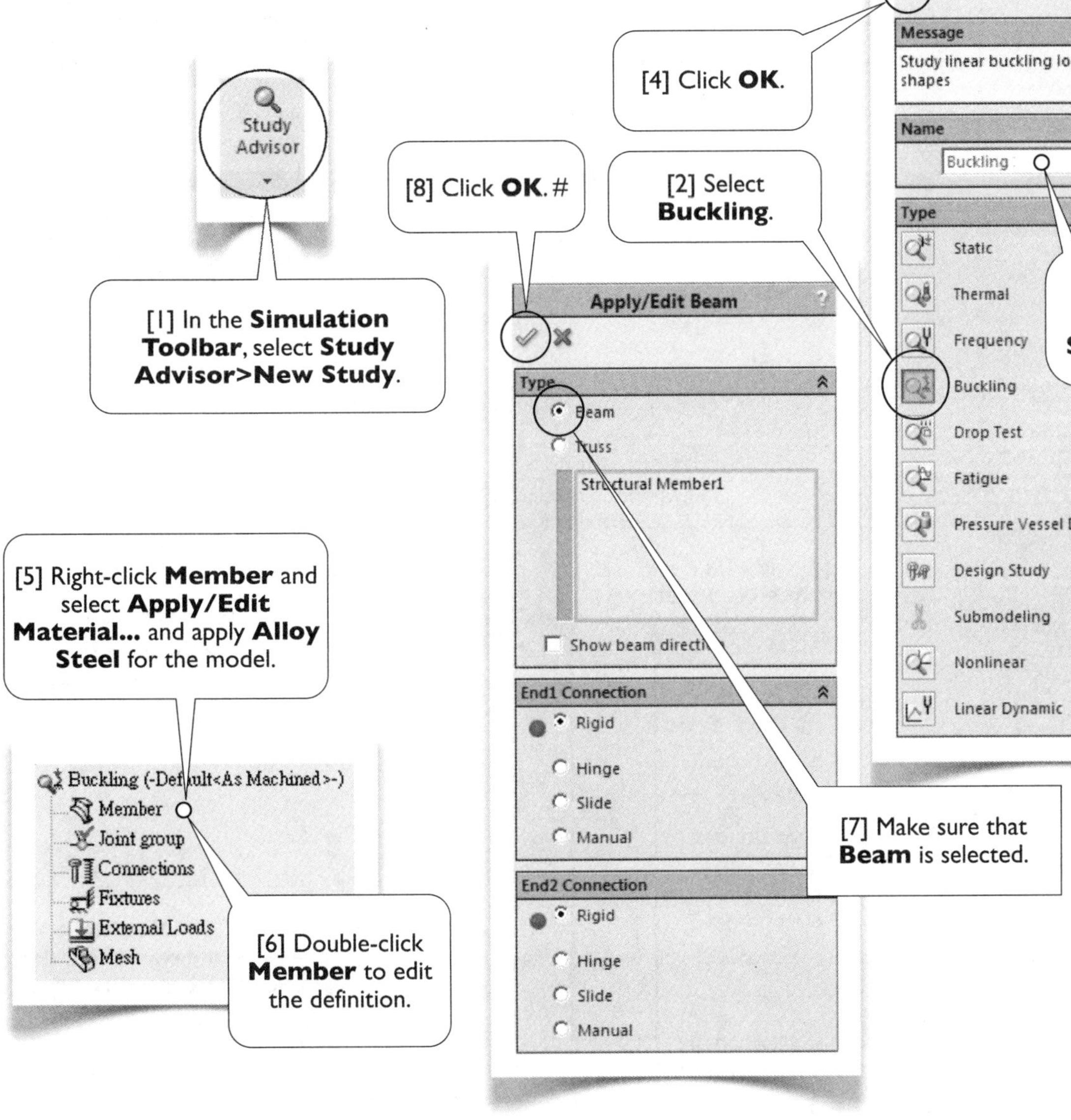

14.1-4 Set Up Supports and External Loads

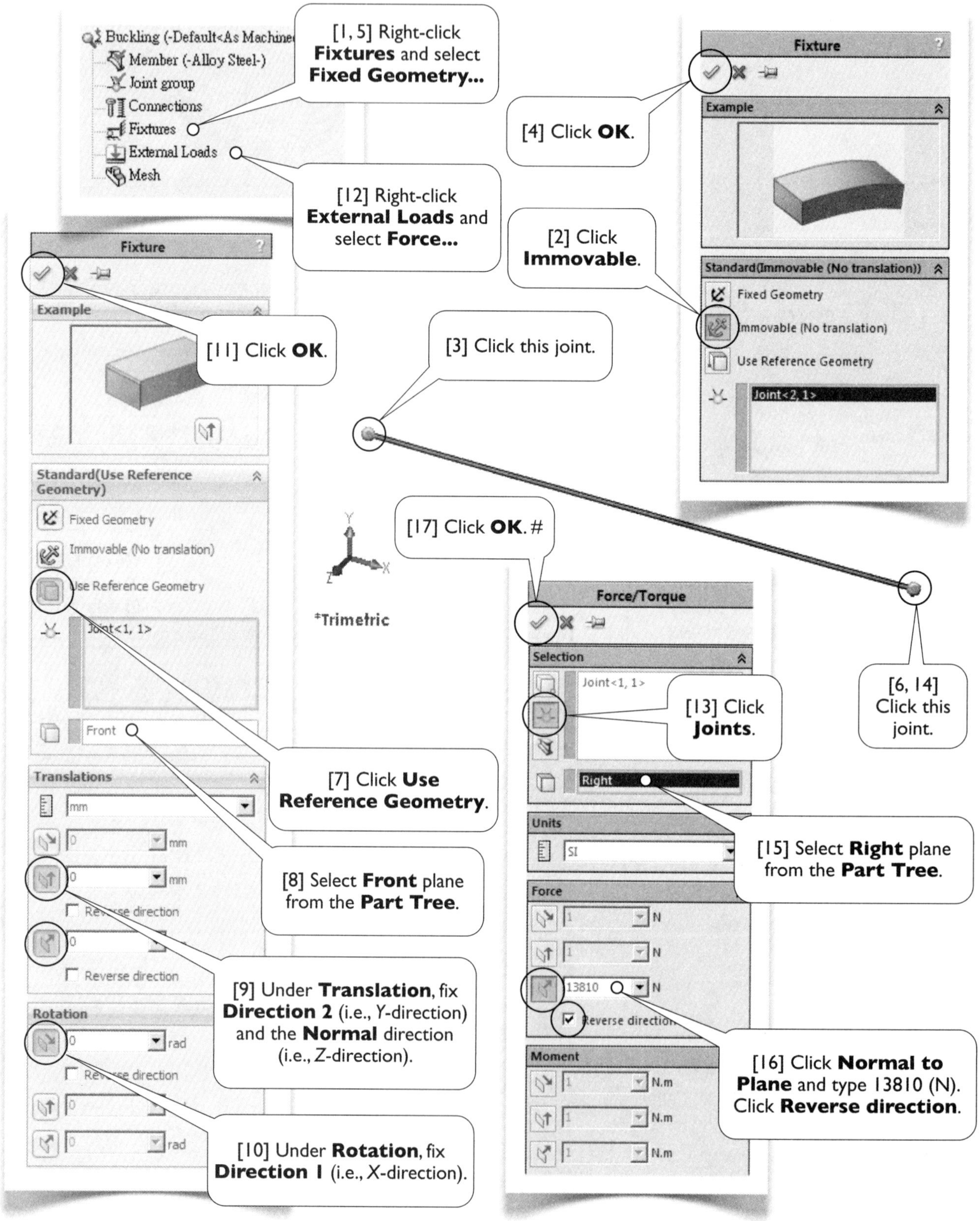

14.1-5 Obtain Buckling Loads and Buckling Modes

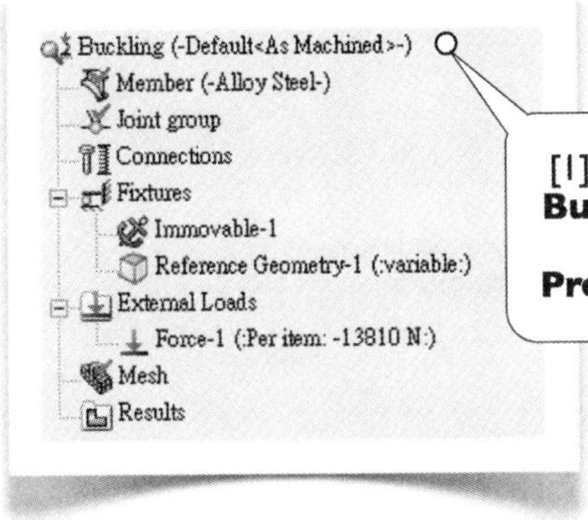

[1] Right-click **Buckling** and select **Properties...**

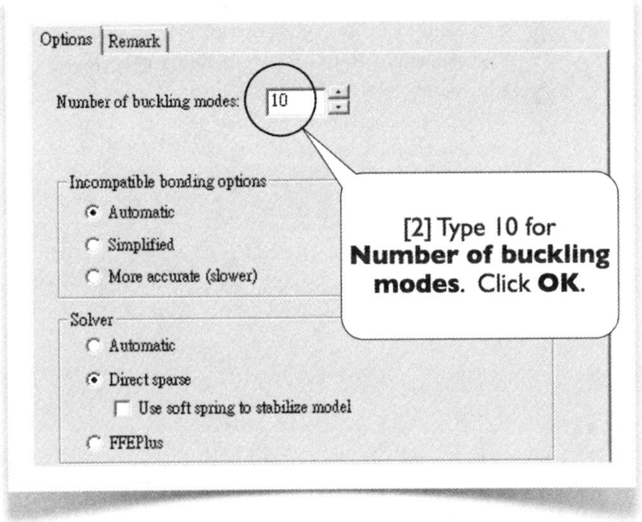

[2] Type 10 for **Number of buckling modes.** Click **OK**.

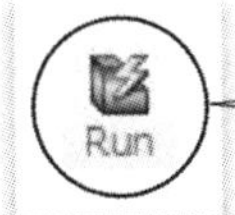

[3] In the **Simulation Toolbar**, click **Run**.

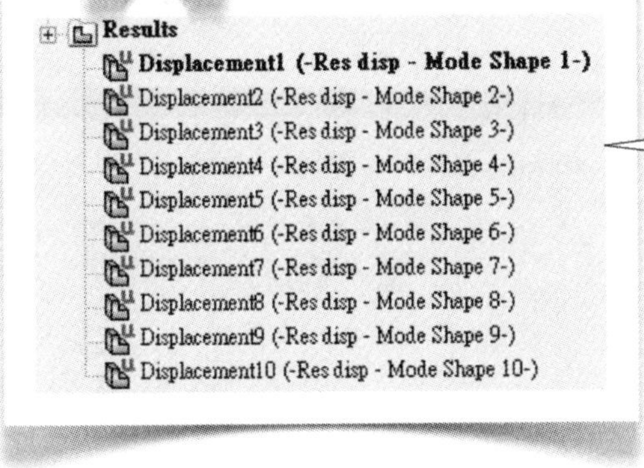

[4] The buckling modes are reported under **Results**.

[5] This is the shape of the buckling mode corresponding to the lowest buckling load, which buckles in the weaker direction of the cross section. Note that the displacement values have no physical significance.

[6] The **Load Factor** is 0.019472, which can be viewed as a safety factor (see [7]).

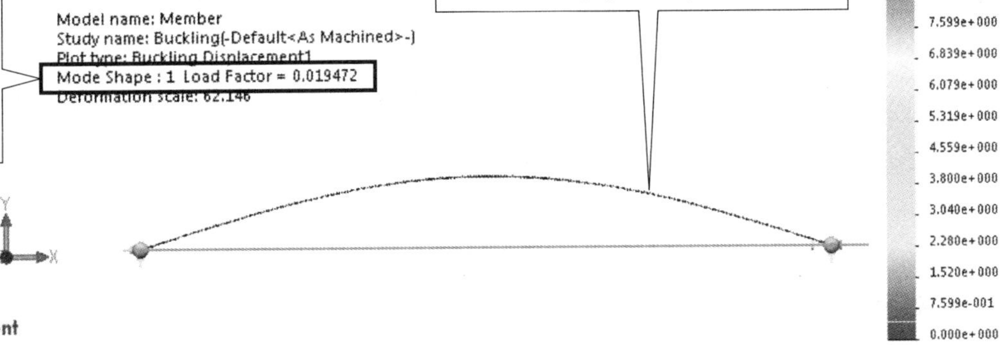

[7] Calculation of the Buckling Load

The buckling load can be calculated by multiplying the **Load Factor** [6] to the applied load (13810 N). In this case,

$$P = 13810 \text{ N} \times 0.019472 = 268.9 \text{ N}$$

which is consistent with the value in Eq. 14.1-1(3), page 261.

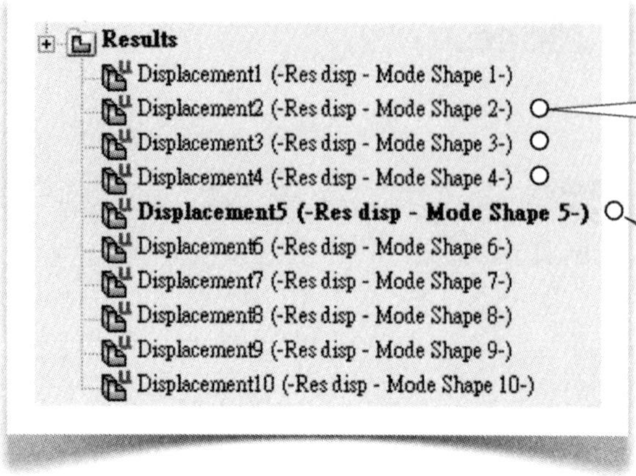

[8] Buckling modes 2-4 have little physical significance. You may view these modes on your own.

[9] Double-click Displacement5 to view 5th buckling mode.

[11] This is the shape of the 5th buckling mode, which buckles in the stronger direction of the cross section. Remember that the displacement values have no physical significance.

[12] The **Load Factor** is 0.4867.

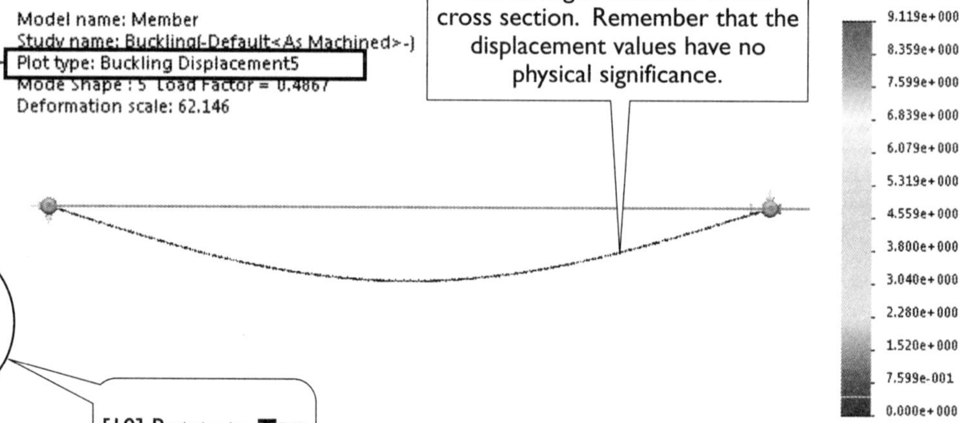

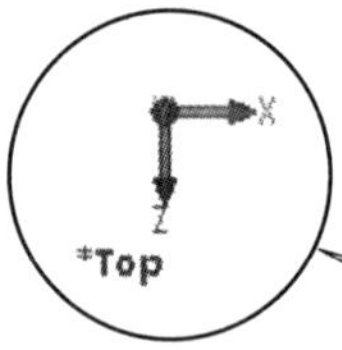

[10] Rotate to **Top** view.

[13] Calculation of the Buckling Load in the Stronger Direction

The buckling load can be calculated by multiplying the **Load Factor** [12] to the applied load (13810 N). In this case,

$$P = 13810 \text{ N} \times 0.4867 = 6721 \text{ N}$$

which is consistent with the value in Eq. 14.1-1(4), page 261. This buckling load is meaningful only when the buckling is prevented in the weaker direction; i.e., the member is fully supported in the weaker direction.

[14] Save the document and exit **SolidWorks**. #

Section 14.2

Buckling of an Aluminum Beverage Can

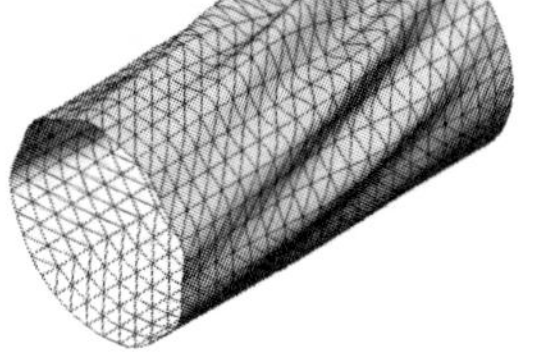

14.2-1 Introduction

[1] It is important to remember that the buckling must be studied for any slender or thin structure subjected to large compression. As an example, an aluminum beverage can [2] may buckle under sufficiently large twist [3]. We'll explore this phenomenon in this section.

A typical aluminum beverage can is made of AA3004 and has a diameter of 64 mm, a depth of 122 mm, and a thickness of 0.1 mm. In this exercise, a beverage can is simplified to a cylindrical surface with one end fixed [2]. We'll show that, under a twist, the maximum and minimum principal stresses (σ_1 and σ_3) have the same magnitudes but opposite directions. The minimum principal stresses (σ_3) are compressive, which would cause the skin to buckle if the compressive stresses are sufficiently large.

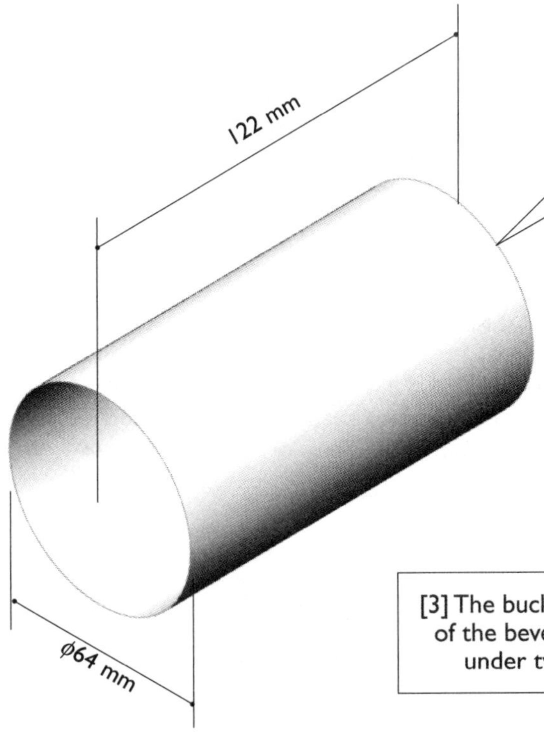

[2] In this exercise, a beverage can is simplified to a cylindrical surface with this end fixed.

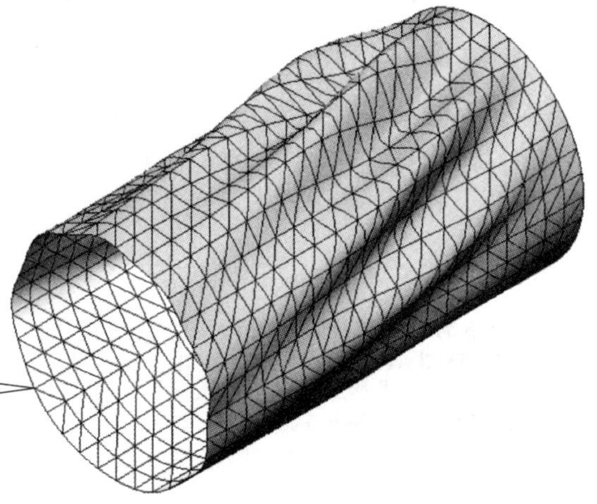

[3] The buckling shape of the beverage can under twist. #

14.2-2 Start Up and Create Geometric Model

[1] Launch **SolidWorks** and create a new part. Set up **MMGS** unit system with zero decimal places for the length unit. Save the document as **Can**.

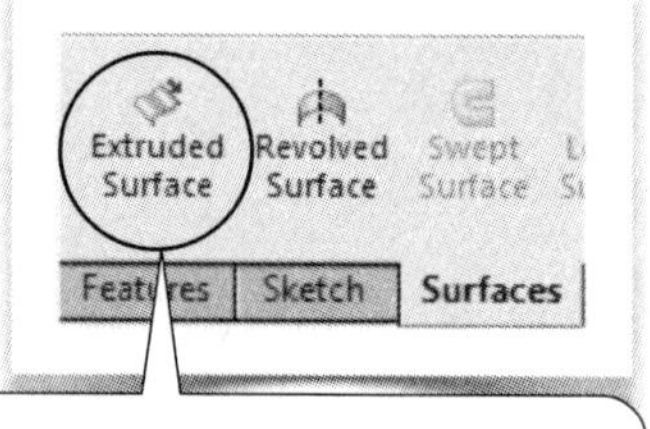

[3] From **Pull-Down Menus**, select **Insert>Surface>Extrude...** The **Extruded Surface** command is also available in the **Surfaces Toolbar**.

[2] On the **Front** plane, draw a circle like this.

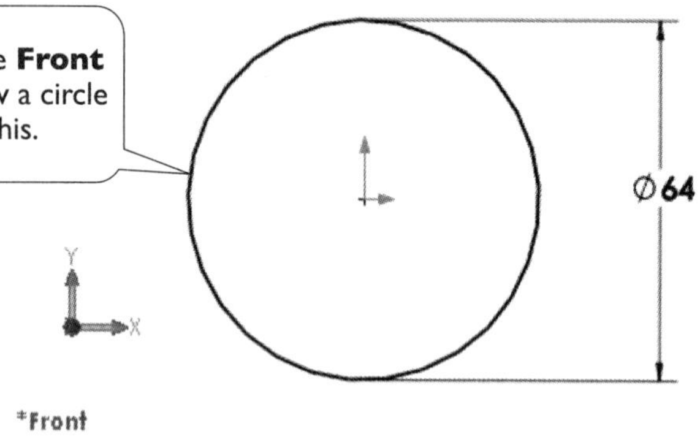

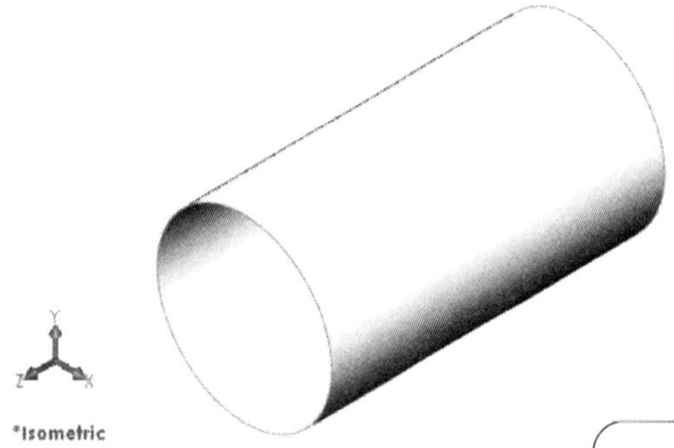

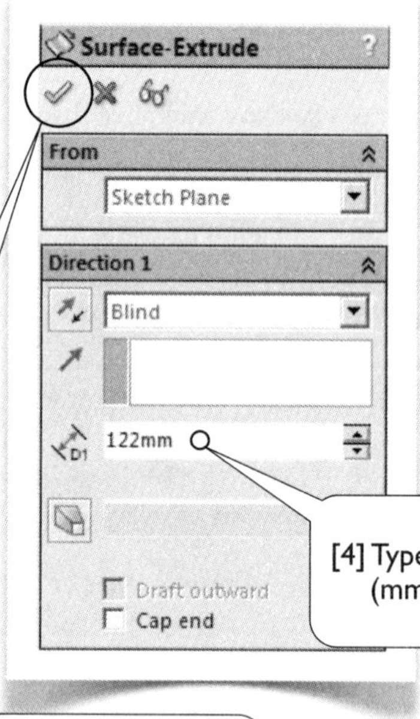

[4] Type 122 (mm).

[5] Click **OK**. #

14.2-3 Create a Static Study

[1] In the **Simulation Toolbar**, select **Study Advisor>New Study**. Leave **Static** as default **Study Type**. Leave **Static 1** as default **Study Name**.

[2] Right-click **Can** and select **Apply/Edit Material...** and apply **3004-O Rod (SS)** (see [3]), which can be found under **Aluminum Alloys**, for the model.

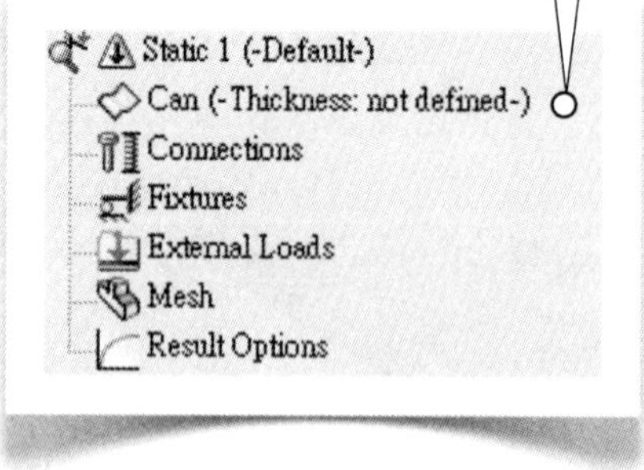

[3] The material **3004-O Rod (SS)** has a Young's modulus of 68.9 GPa and a Poisson's ratio of 0.35.

Property	Value	Units
Elastic Modulus in X	68900	N/mm^2
Poisson's Ration in XY	0.35	N/A

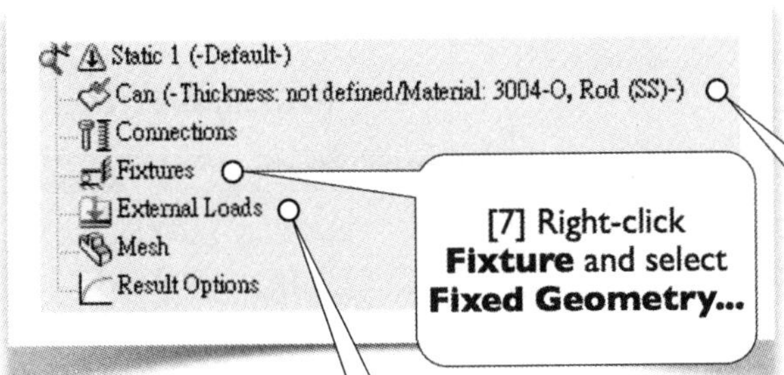

[4] Right-click **Can** and select **Edit Definition...**

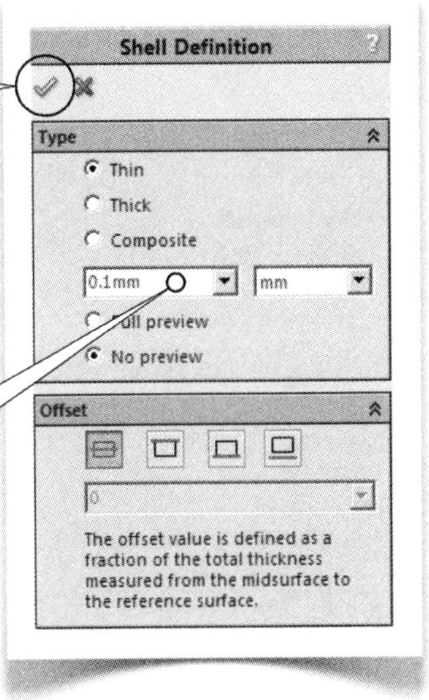

[5] Type 0.1 (mm).

[6] Click **OK**.

[7] Right-click **Fixture** and select **Fixed Geometry...**

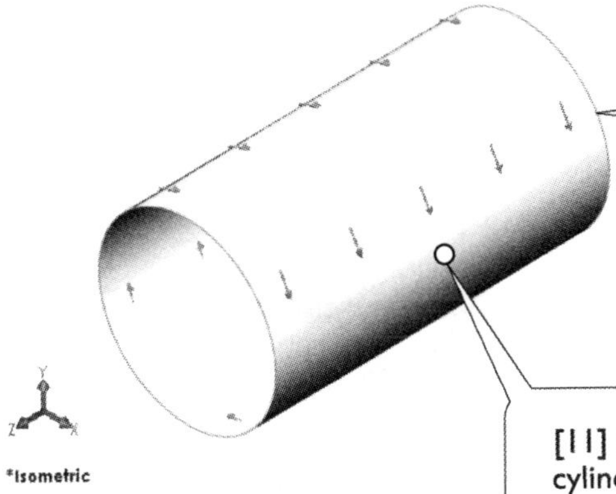

[8] Select this circular edge.

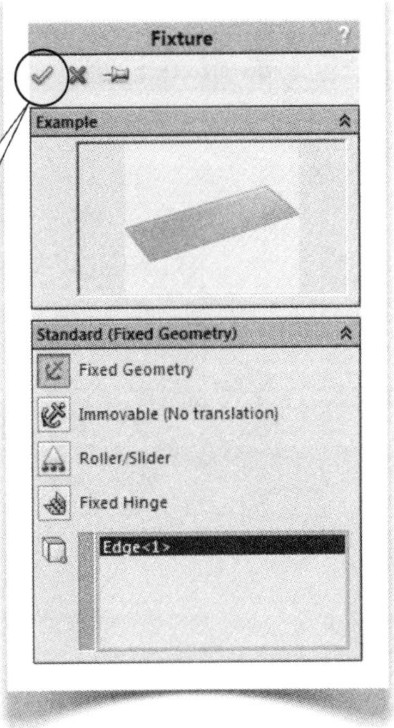

[9] Click **OK**.

[10] Right-click **External Loads** and select **Torque...**

[11] Select this cylindrical face.

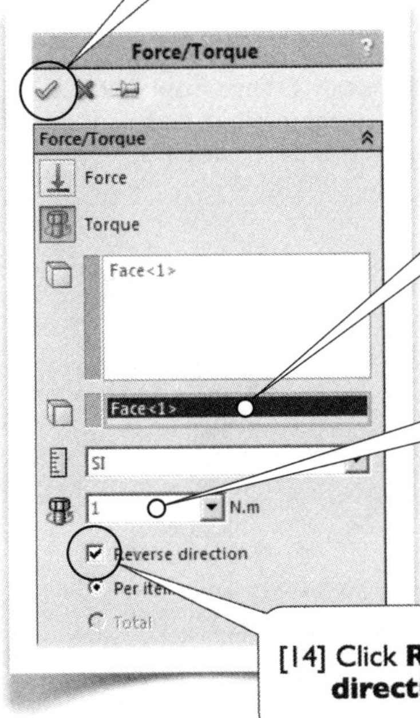

[12] Select the cylindrical face [11] again to define the direction of the torque.

[13] Leave 1 (N-m) as default **Torque Value**.

[14] Click **Reverse direction**.

[15] Click **OK**.

[16] In the **Simulation Toolbar**, click **Run**. #

14.2-4 Examine Principal Stresses

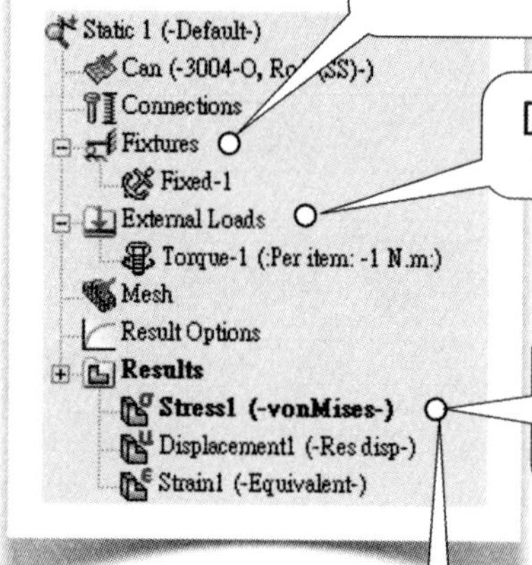

[1] Hide **Fixtures**.

[2] Hide **External Loads**.

[3] Double-click to edit the definition.

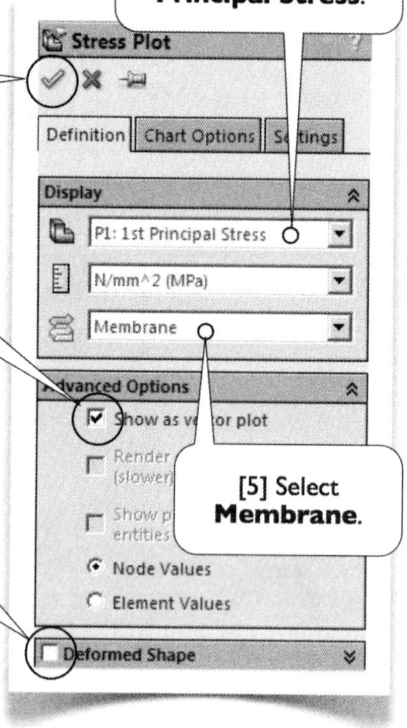

[4] Select **P1: 1st Principal Stress**.

[5] Select **Membrane**.

[6] Click **Show as vector plot**.

[7] Turn off **Deformed Shape**.

[8] Click **OK**.

[9] Right-click-select **Vector Plot Options...** and set arrow size to 500%.

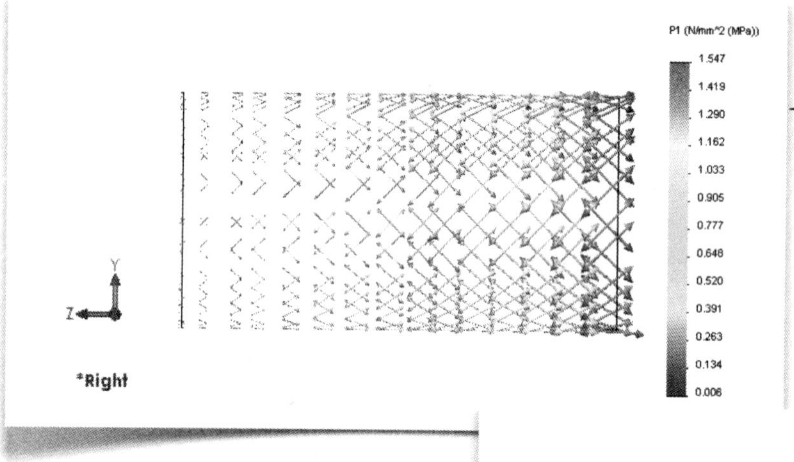

[10] The maximum principal stresses (σ_1) range from 0 to 1.547 MPa (tension), 45° diagonally.

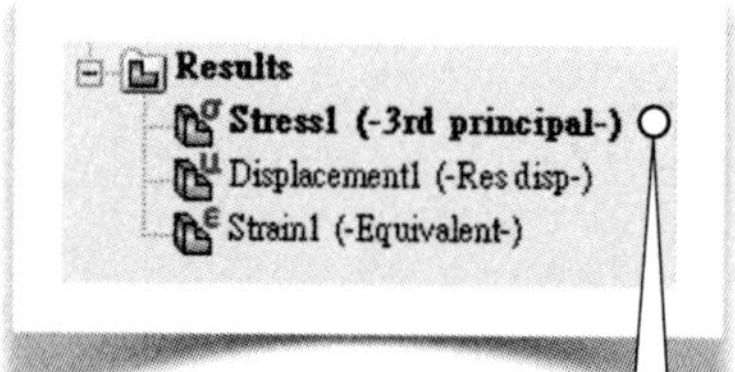

[11] Double-click to edit the definition. Select **P3: 3rd Principal Stress**.

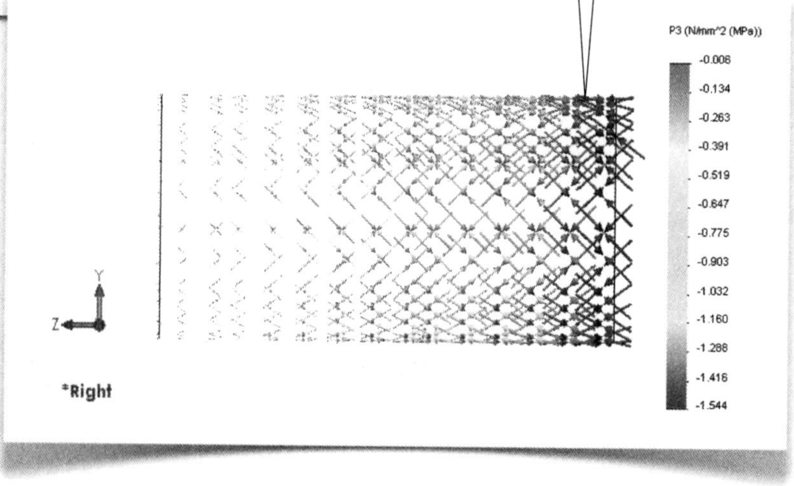

[12] The minimum principal stresses (σ_3) range from 0 to 1.544 MPa (compression), orthogonal to the maximum principal stresses. #

14.2-5 Create a Buckling Study

[1] In the **Simulation Toolbar**, select **Study Advisor>New Study**.

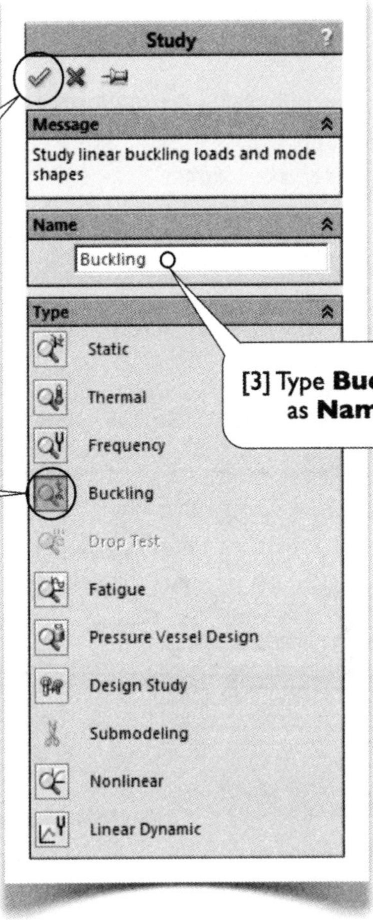

[2] Click **Buckling**.

[3] Type **Buckling** as **Name**.

[4] Click **OK**.

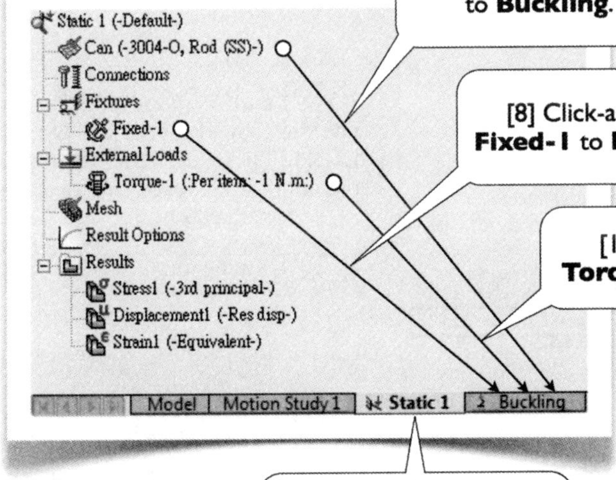

[5, 7, 9] Click **Static 1** tab.

[6] Click-and-drag **Can** to **Buckling**.

[8] Click-and-drag **Fixed-1** to **Buckling**.

[10] Click-and-drag **Torque-1** to **Buckling**.

[11] Material, thickness, and boundary conditions are copied to the new study.

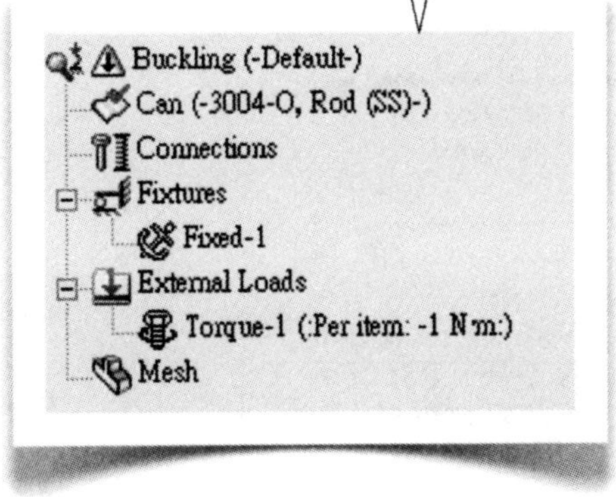

[12] In the **Simulation Toolbar**, click **Run**. #

14.2-6 View the Buckling Shpae

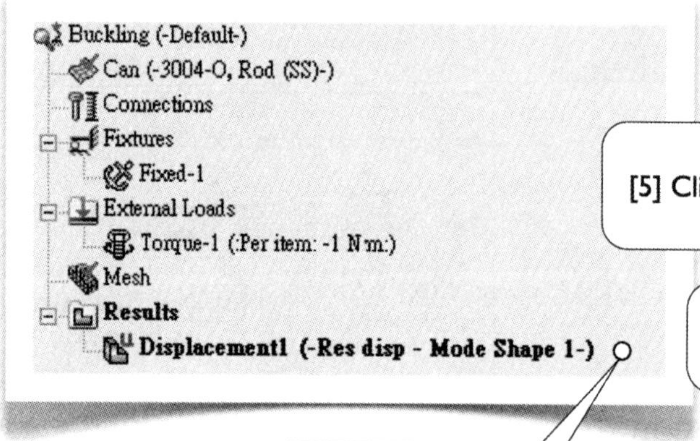

[1] Double-click to edit the definition.

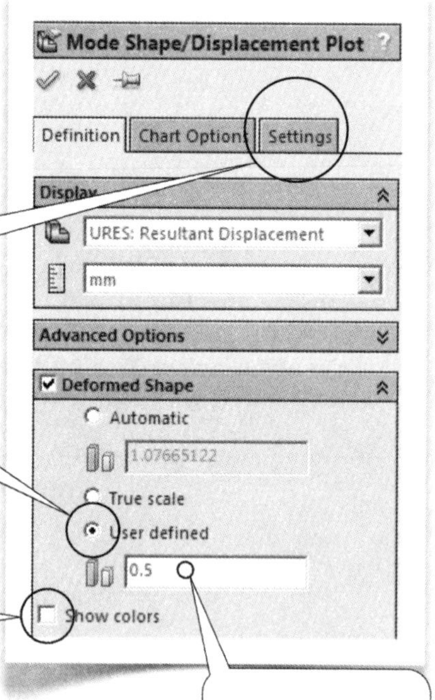

[2] Click **User defined**.

[3] Type 0.5.

[4] Turn off **Show color**.

[5] Click **Settings** tab.

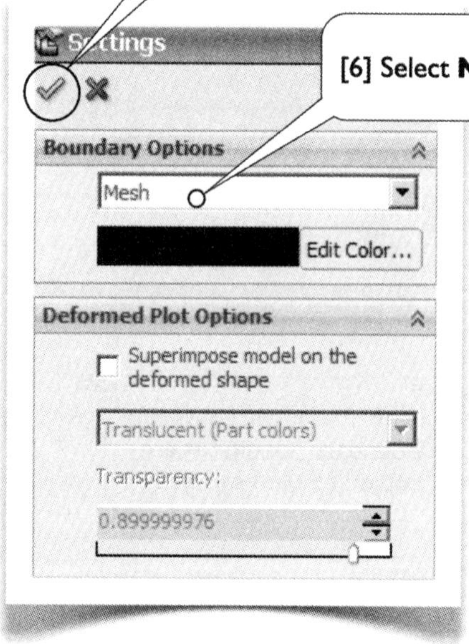

[6] Select **Mesh**.

[7] Click **OK**.

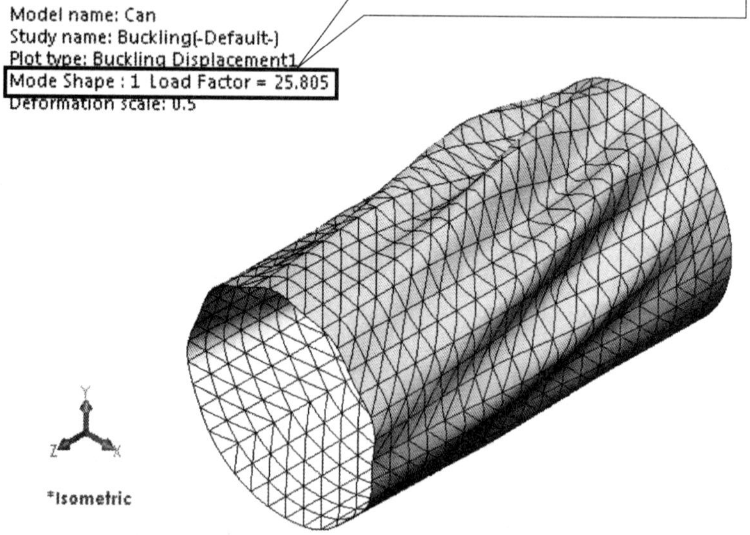

[8] The **Load Factor** is 25.805. Since the applied torque is 1 N-m (14.2-3[13], page 269), the beverage can would buckle when the torque is 25.805 N-m.

[9] Save the document and exit **SolidWorks**. #

Index